WATERLOO HIGH SCHOOL
1464
ATWA1

W9-ACU-143

WATERLOO HIGH SCHOOL LIBRARY
1464 INDUSTRY RD.
ATWATER, OHIO 44201

THE
ENCYCLOPEDIA OF
ALCOHOLISM

Second Edition

WATERLOO HIGH SCHOOL LIBRARY
1464 INDUSTRY RD.
ATWATER, OHIO 44201

THE
ENCYCLOPEDIA OF
ALCOHOLISM

Second Edition

Robert O'Brien
and Morris Chafetz, M.D.

Edited by Glen Evans

Contributing Editors:
Marion C. Chafetz, Lynne M. Constantine

Facts On File
New York • Oxford

362.29
ENC
REF

THE ENCYCLOPEDIA OF ALCOHOLISM, Second Edition

Copyright © 1982 Greenspring, Inc.
Copyright © 1991 Facts On File and Greenspring, Inc.

All rights reserved. No part of this book may be reproduced or utilized in any form or by any means, electronic or mechanical, including photocopying, recording, or by any information storage and retrieval systems, without permission in writing from the publisher. For information contact:

Facts On File, Inc.
460 Park Avenue South
New York NY 10016
USA

Facts On File Limited
Collins Street
Oxford OX4 1XJ
United Kingdom

Library of Congress Cataloging-in-Publication Data

The Encyclopedia of alcoholism / [edited] by Glen Evans, Robert O'Brien, and Morris Chafetz. — 2nd ed.
    p. cm.
      Includes bibliographical references.
      ISBN 0-8160-1955-X   1. Alcoholism—Dictionaries. 2. Alcoholism—United States—Dictionaries. I. Evans, Glen. II. O'Brien, Robert, 1932-
    III. Chafetz, Morris E.
    HV5017.E5 1990
    362.29'2'03—dc20   89-23333

Facts On File books are available at special discounts when purchased in bulk quantities for businesses, associations, institutions or sales promotion. Please contact the Special Sales Department of our New York office at 212/683-2244 (dial 800/322-8755 except in NY, AK, or HI).

Composition by Facts On File, Inc.
Manufactured by Hamilton Printing Company
Printed in the United States of America

10 9 8 7 6 5 4 3 2 1

This book is printed on acid-free paper.

CONTENTS

PREFACE vii

PREFACE TO FIRST EDITION ix

INTRODUCTION: HISTORY OF ALCOHOL AND MAN xi

ENTRIES A-Z 1

APPENDIXES 231

BIBLIOGRAPHY 307

INDEX 339

PREFACE

Almost a decade has passed since we struggled to put out, to our knowledge, the first encyclopedia of alcoholism. As I perused the current literature on alcoholism to revise the first edition, I was struck by the dramatic change in attitude which reflects the recurring historical phenomenon of all efforts in alcoholism: the shift of focus from the study of alcoholism to an attack on the substance, alcohol.

When I became the founding director of the National Institute on Alcohol Abuse and Alcoholism in 1971, my goal was simple and direct: to lower the incidence of alcohol problems. To accomplish this goal, the Institute set out to educate society and its caretakers in the knowledge that alcoholic people were ill people and that quality treatment programs would become available to them. The Institute stressed early intervention, promoted the benefits of prevention and fostered the growth of employee assistance programs at the workplace.

Interest in research on prevention and treatment mushroomed as did the willingness of people—prominent and ordinary—to talk about their alcohol-related illness.

This attention brought many benefits to the plight of alcoholic people; however, the tenor of the times was preparing for its cyclical shift in position from treating the problem to blaming the substance.

The major thrust of this change came from advocacy groups that focused on specific incidents of abuse such as drunk driving victims and fetal damage. Their passion and emotionalism ofttimes masked the facts. For example, some advocacy groups generally present as fact the item that 25,000 innocents are slaughtered each year in drunk driving accidents. However, according to the U.S. Fatal Accident Reporting Service (FARS), this claim is erroneous. FARS reports that 52 percent of the people killed annually in drunk driving accidents are the drunk drivers themselves; another 20 percent of the deaths are passengers who choose to ride with a drunk driver; and 11 percent are drunk pedestrians who walk in front of a car. The statistics show that 17%—not 100%—are innocent victims of drunk driving. Albeit understandable, the powerful emotional current that is unleashed upon hearing news of a drunk driving injury or death causes a lapse in objectivity.

Another area where the facts do not support the unbridled emotions is the Fetal Alcohol Syndrome (FAS). FAS has become an acronym that frightens and bewilders pregnant women about the use of alcohol during pregnancy. The manipulation of research findings obfuscates the facts and erodes one's natural defenses. Not all pregnant women who drink abusively during pregnancy deliver babies with FAS or with alcohol-related defects. For example, in a study of 12,000 pregnant women, 204 were considered abusive drinkers. Yet only five babies from among the 204 abusive drinkers had FAS. Other factors had to be operating during pregnancy that either protected the babies or failed to protect them. According to the government's *Seventh Report on Alcohol and Health*, hardship, deprivation and low socioeconomic status play an important role in FAS.

Some FAS researchers theorized that because alcoholic women did not always have impaired babies, impairment might not be readily observable. A Seattle study showed that mothers who had taken an occasional drink during pregnancy had babies showing mild signs of impairment. Even though the study included a caveat stating that it was impossible to trace these signs to an occasional drink, policy makers and advocacy groups recommended women not take *any* alcohol during pregnancy.

Let me hasten to remind the reader, lest we forget one of the lessons of Prohibition, that alcoholics were neglected or languished in jails and mental hospitals. No one has shown that attacks on alcohol lower the incidence of alcoholism or alcohol problems.

An encyclopedia is like a snapshot; it captures knowledge at a point in time. Thus, some of the information appearing in the second edition reflects America's current puritanical ambivalence toward drinking.

Morris E. Chafetz, M.D.
Washington, D.C.

PREFACE
TO FIRST EDITION

A staff member of a major government agency suggested that *The Encyclopedia of Alcoholism* be published in 100 volumes—one volume of basic information and 99 volumes of caveats, disclaimers, qualifications, special cases and contradictory material. Despite his advice (only partly in jest), we have designed *The Encyclopedia of Alcoholism* as a concise desk reference in dictionary format covering a myriad of topics relating to alcoholism. The more than 500 entries provide extensive information on the substance alcohol itself, on the social institutions, customs, and socioeconomic interrelations that have an impact on alcoholism, and on the physical and psychological manifestations of alcoholism.

The *Encyclopedia* can be of great use to the lay person and the professional alike. For the lay person we have tried to describe the subject as clearly and simply as possible, without resorting to jargon or other unfamiliar language. At the same time we have tried to avoid being simplistic. When a technical term appears repeatedly in the literature of alcoholism and has a precise meaning that must be understood to ensure accurate comprehension, we have taken the time to define and explain it.

For the professional we have tried to provide concise and clear statements of familiar material as well as a handy reference in which he or she can quickly find an elusive fact, date or statistic. Obviously, no article in a volume this concise will always fit the needs of the professional working in that particular area. The usefulness of the book will increase, however, as the professional moves beyond the immediate area of his or her expertise. To assist both the professionals and the lay people who may need more information than we can provide in our limited space, we have appended a short list of references to each of the major articles as well as a substantial bibliography.

To our knowledge this volume is the first A to Z encyclopedia to appear in the field of alcoholism. This distinction has both advantages and disadvantages. On the one hand, it has allowed us to approach the subject with a fresh eye and to select topics for articles because we felt that they should be included and not because they had been traditionally dealt with in volumes of this kind. On the other hand, since the guidelines are largely of our own creation, we may have omitted articles that should have been included or given some subjects insufficient treatment. We expect that some readers will disagree with us (and among themselves) about what should or should not have been included in *The Encyclopedia of Alcoholism* and about the amount of space devoted to individual topics.

Some of the volume's limitations are inherent in its concise format. In the interest of saving words, unfortunate impressions can sometimes be created. Where "alcoholic" is used as a noun, for example, it ideally should read "alcoholic person," lest anyone assume that we are reducing those who suffer from the condition of alcoholism to that single part of their life experience.

Similarly, where the pronoun "he" appears (unless the context clearly suggests the male of the species), we intend the reader to understand that women are being spoken of as well.

In a book of this length and scope, it is inevitable that minor errors have crept in during successive steps in the editorial process. We have taken great pains, however, to avoid significant errors of fact or interpretation, though we cannot guarantee that some egregious flaw has not escaped our notice.

Undoubtedly as communication continues to improve within the alcoholism field, we shall be able to fill gaps and clarify cloudy areas in the present volume in future editions of *The Encyclopedia of Alcoholism*. This volume is a beginning in a field in which the end is still nowhere in sight.

Robert O'Brien
Sharon, Conn.

Morris E. Chafetz, M.D.
Washington, D.C.

INTRODUCTION
HISTORY OF ALCOHOL
AND MAN

There is no period in recorded history free from references to production and consumption of alcoholic beverages. Even in prehistoric times it seems likely that Stone Age cultures made fermented meads by using honey as a base. Since fermentation can occur naturally, with airborne yeasts converting any sugary mash into ethyl alcohol and carbon dioxide, man's first discovery of an alcoholic brew was probably accidental. Thereafter prehistoric man probably began to attempt deliberate production of alcoholic beverages, and such beverages have retained an important and problematic role in most human societies since that time.

When the earliest literate societies sought to explain the origins of the alcoholic beverages they inherited from their ancestors, they recorded these legends on stone tablets and papyrus scrolls. One of the earliest of such mythologies is the pre-Christian epic of Gilgamesh, recorded by the Babylonian civilization. According to this creation myth, the powers of evil fought the powers of good in bloody combat for control of the earth. The powers of good were ultimately victorious, but these gods suffered many casualties in the struggle. Where the benevolent gods fell, their bodies were consumed by the earth to produce vines that memorialized their sacrifice. This myth is one example of the age-old association between wine and sacrificial blood that has been preserved as a symbol by a variety of religious cultures.

In Biblical legends the discovery of wine is also related to creation stories. Many have equated the tree of knowledge in Genesis with a grape vine. Eating the fruit of this tree led to Adam and Eve's awareness of their nakedness and their subsequent expulsion from the Garden of Eden. In Genesis, after the human race was nearly obliterated by the flood, Noah fell victim to the same sin. Having landed the Ark following the recession of the flood waters, "Noah began to be a husbandman, and he planted a vineyard. And he drank of the wine, and was drunken." Noah was discovered naked in his tent by his sons, an incident that was treated as a very serious matter. The Bible is full of similar incidences of drunkenness, involving warnings, denial and remorse.

Not all accounts of the discovery of wine stress the dangers of consumption. In the ancient Persian tale of King Jamshid, the king was so fond of grapes that he stored them in large earthenware containers to maintain a supply beyond the harvest season. Discovering that one batch had spoiled and fearing that it might be dangerous, he set the jar aside and labeled it "poison." One of the king's concubines, suffering from headaches, decided to kill herself by eating from this "poisonous" batch of grapes. Delighted that the juice relieved her malady, she induced the king to sample it. After tasting it, Jamshid too was delighted, and he immediately ordered production of the beverage in years to come, naming it *zeher- e-hoosh* ("the delightful poison").

In addition to such legends, there exist many records of actual consumption of alcoholic beverages in early societies. The oldest are Mesopotamian, dating from 4000 B.C., although actual production may have begun 2,000 years earlier. Clay tablets from this culture contain recipes for using wine as a solvent in medicines, a practice that would continue in other cultures for many centuries. The importance of wine for the Mesopotamians is suggested by the fact that a personal drinking cup accompanied most of their wealthy citizens to the funeral pyre. In the nearly contemporary Egyptian societies, however, the predominant alcoholic beverage was a beer fermented from barley. Called *hek*, the drink was important enough to early Egyptian commerce that, according to papyrus documents unearthed since, government officials were appointed to supervise and control its production. In addition to these early medicinal and commercial roles, alcoholic beverages also became important in religious rituals. Records of early Hebrew society define eight different types of wine to be used for distinct ceremonial occasions. Although the records are less precise, there are indications that fermented beverages also had well-established medicinal and religious functions in early civilizations further east, especially in China and India.

Not surprisingly the history of alcohol is inseparable from the history of alcohol abuse. Legislative codes intended to limit consumption of alcoholic beverages were required as soon as production of such beverages became efficient and widespread. The Code of Hammurabi of Babylonia, which dates from 1700 B.C., contains a variety of restrictions on the sale and consumption of alcohol. The code also documents the early existence of public drinking houses, which it regulated with laws that sometimes called for the execution of offenders. Equally old records from the reign of the Chinese Emperor Chung K'iang note the execution of drunkards as a demonstration to the public of governmental disapproval of alcohol, and one of his successors, Emperor Tei-Tsung, is known to have established, or "licensed," the number of places where the sale of alcohol was permitted.

Perhaps the most dramatic example of governmental restrictions on alcohol consumption was in ancient Persia. Possibly because of the unofficial approbation of alcohol implicit in the legend of King Jamshid, the aristocratic classes in ancient Persia habitually consumed alarming quantities of wine. In response the rising Islamic culture there adopted a complete prohibition of alcohol to combat widespread health problems, now known to be the result of nutritional deficiencies. Like all bans on alcohol consumption, this first known example had only limited success. The aristrocratic classes in Persia continued to drink to excess, an aspect of the culture that inspired the hedonistic attitudes associated with the poet Omar Khayyám. Nevertheless, to this day fundamental Islamic religions have maintained a total ban on alcoholic beverages. Similarly, Buddhist sects originating in India in the fifth century B.C. have maintained to this day a complete prohibition on consumption of alcohol.

The original temperance movements also date from pre-Christian times. The dynastic Egyptian tract called *Wisdom of Ani* opens with the command, "Take not upon thyself to drink a jug of beer." The consequences of excess are then listed in this document as advice for coping with a substance that the prevailing government was unwilling to ban entirely. A similar attitude is found in the Chinese *Canon of History*, written around 650 B.C. Noting that "men will not do without beer," and that "to prohibit it and secure total abstinence from it is beyond the power even of sages," the *Canon of History* provides a series of warnings about alcohol with the intention of fostering moderation.

The single most successful temperance document in history is the Bible, with its more than 150 references to alcohol. Although alcohol is deeply rooted in Jewish culture and granted an important role in religious celebrations, the Hebrew people have enjoyed a relative freedom from alcoholism that must in part be attributed to the many warnings about excess found in the Old Testament. The specifically cultural controls on alcohol consumption are suggested by Proverbs: "Wine is a mocker, strong drink is raging: and whosoever is deceived thereby is not wise." While the "strong drink" mentioned is simply undiluted wine, the warnings against abuse of it in Proverbs are sterner than those found in the writings of most cultures troubled by abuse of distilled alcoholic beverages; as evidenced in the 23rd Chapter.

> Who hath woe? who hath sorrow?
> who hath contentions? who hath babbling?
> who hath wounds without cause?
> who hath redness of eyes?
>> They that tarry long at the wine;
>> They that go to seek mixed wine.
>> Look not thou upon the wine when
>> it is red, when it giveth its color in
>> the cup, when it moveth itself aright.
>> At the last it biteth like a serpent,
>> and stingeth like an adder.

These sorts of warnings about the dangers of excess, deeply ingrained in the society's behavior patterns, created such effective cultural controls that carefully regulated consumption could be condoned and even encouraged without great danger of alcohol abuse.

European and, hence, American cultural attitudes, including those toward consumption of alcohol, derive more from the classical Greco-Roman civilizations than from the older cultures of the Middle East. The history of alcoholic beverage consumption in these classical ages can be described as a shift from the relatively formal and ceremonial use of libations associated with the Greek symposium toward the more excessive and self-indulgent feasts and drunken orgies common under the later Roman emperors. This same shift can be seen on the level of cultural archetypes in the transformation of Dionysus into Bacchus.

The Greek god Dionysus, identified with both wine and natural fertility, is a benevolent presence in the Homeric Hymns, dating from about 800 B.C. Expelled from Greece by Lycurgus, Dionysus embarked on travels to Thrace and India, spreading the cult of the vine as a potent blend of good in moderation and evil in excess. Greek society was notable for both temperance and thorough knowledge of wine-making techniques. Governmental regulations provided for wine inspectors, fines for drunkenness and specific dilutions of wine with water. In Greek culture undiluted wine was considered barbarous. Greek histories retell many stories of military confrontations won because of the drunkenness of the enemy, and moderation was also stressed in the medical tracts of the time. Even Plato, sternly ascetic in many matters, approved of festival libations and the designation of limited farmlands for the growing of wine grapes only.

The symposium was at the heart of Greek culture, and during it wine drinking was both essential and carefully regulated. Two courses were served, one of meats and one of fruits, followed by the drinking of diluted wine out of vessels with regulated capacities. The philosophical discussions at the symposium were thought to have been enriched by this shared and uniform libation.

In Roman society, however, Dionysus gave way to Bacchus and the intellectual symposium became a gluttonous feast. In the Ovidian *Metamorphoses* of the first century A.D., Bacchus is associated less with wine than with excessive consumption of it. In these poems, for example, Midas and Silenus, "filthy drunken good old friends," drink competitively for 10 days and 10 nights. Bacchus is so pleased by this display that he offered the winner the wish that results in the Midas touch. The social reflection of this literary reference was public feasting of gross proportions at which drinking ceremonies overwhelmed conversation. Life for the upper class was more leisurely in Rome than in Greece, and the Romans enjoyed better agricultural conditions for vine propagation, factors that abetted the general social permissiveness in regard to wine consumption. Intellectual support for this attitude was also abundant; Pliny the Elder, for example, devoted an entire volume of his *Historia Naturalis* to wines and wine making and the poet Martial made wine drinking an exception to his otherwise stern philosophy. The Roman culture, of course, gave us the adage *in vino veritas* and the term "bacchanalia."

As a result of the consequences of their excesses, the ancient Romans also instituted some historically important controls on drinking. The symposiums eventually degenerated to the point that the Roman Senate felt constrained to ban them entirely for a period beginning in 186 B.C. In A.D. 81 the Emperor Domitian ordered half the nation's vineyards destroyed and the Senate prohibited planting of new vines until A.D. 276. Having long witnessed the evidence of alcoholism that abounded in Rome a jurist named Domitius Ulpinus was the first to suggest the possibility that habitual drunkenness might be a disease. This cultural ambivalence, this coexisting excess and concern, was the primary characteristic of Roman attitudes toward alcohol and an important aspect of the legacy handed down to western European cultures.

The Middle Ages were a time when enormous improvements were made in the production of wine in Europe. The single greatest contribution was made possible by the Crusades, for when the Europeans returned from battling with the Moslems for control of the Holy Land, they brought with them the sirah grape from Persia. This was the beginning of a series of successful plantings of foreign grapes along the river valleys of France which has made that country world famous for its vineyards and its wine.

An even more important development in the production of alcoholic beverages in general during this period was the introduction of the distillation process, which was imported. While distillation of seawater had been practiced in Europe since pre-Christian times, it was not until the eighth century A.D. that an Arabian alchemist known as Geber perfected a method of purifying the essence of wine.

Distillation of spirits is possible because alcohol boils at a lower temperature than water. As vapors rise from a heated alcoholic beverage, they can be drawn off, and after cooling, the vapors condense into liquid again. While naturally fermented beverages can attain a strength of only 14% alcohol, distillation of purified, or rectified, alcohol enables production of beverages with a much higher alcohol content. Because of the consequences of more potent alcoholic drinks, the first widespread distillation of potable alcohol in Europe during the Middle Ages brought about new attempts to control consumption of the substance.

Since rectified alcohol was considered to be of great medicinal value, distillation processes gained widespread acceptance in Europe. Belief in the value of alcohol as medicine emanated from Montpellier, Switzerland at the end of the 13th century, when the chemists Arnaldus de Villanova and Raymond Lully, both of whom reached the unheard-of age of 70, published testimonials to the powers of this apparent cure-all: "We call it *aqua vitae*, and this name is remarkably suitable, since it is really a water of immortality." Two hundred years later the German physician Hieronymus Brunschwig was proclaiming that distilled alcohol could cure everything, including jaundice, colds, deafness, baldness and much more. "It gives also young courage in a person," Brunschwig declared, "and causes him to have a good memory." This faith in alcohol as a panacea for all ills led the European religious orders of the Middle Ages to begin dispensing drinks to weary travelers. The practice survives in the image of the St. Bernard dog rescuing a snowbound traveler from certain death with a flask of brandy.

Brandy, a fortified beverage made by distilling wine, was in fact a rather late invention. The first distilled alcoholic beverage was whiskey, the "water of life," or *uisce beathadh*, of the Gaelic-speaking natives of Ireland. The origins of this distillation of alcohol by fermenting a mash of grain are obscure, but it seems certain that whiskey production was widespread in Ireland by the 12th century. In Scotland the mash used was slightly different, primarily malted barley rather than a mixture of grains. The reason why distillation processes proliferated in these countries was that the climate would not permit cultivation of vines. Hence, for a time in the British Isles, whiskey was even used for the religious functions that in other cultures traditionally called for wine. At the Battle of Culloden in 1746 "John Maitland, a Presbyter of the Episcopal Church of Scotland, administered the Holy Eucharist to the mortally wounded Lord Strathallan with oatcake and whiskey."

These new and more potent alcoholic beverages made society's susceptibility to drunkenness even more obvious, and as a result temperance regulations were instituted. In 1226 Switzerland introduced the first closing-time laws and in 1285 England followed suit. By 1436 such laws had been adopted in even relatively lenient Scotland. Germany in 1496 banned the sale of alcoholic beverages on Sundays and holy days. Norway decided in 1586 to forbid the sale of liquor during the hours of church services only.

Around this time a variety of often conflicting local regulations on alcohol sale and consumption began to proliferate, and organizations devoted to combating the problem of increasing public drunkenness emerged. The first formal temperance societies started in Germany. The order of St. Christopher was formed in Dietrichstein in 1517 with the aim of reducing excessive drinking, and it was followed in 1524 by a similar organization in Heidelberg. Temperance societies stressing moderation rather than complete abstinence soon began to spring up in other countries, particularly in those areas where the popularity of distilled liquors over wines and beers increased the dangers of relatively limited consumption.

In the years leading to the industrial revolution the patterns of increasing availability of alcoholic beverages and increasing concern about the ensuing alcohol-related problems established during the Middle Ages continued, with Britain becoming the leader in both respects. A typical example of the intertwining of political history with the history of alcohol use in Britain was the defeat of Bonnie Prince Charlie, pretender to the throne, at Culloden in 1756. During his flight after the battle the prince was hidden by a family named MacKinnon. In return he gave them a recipe for his favorite liquor, a blend of brandy and Scotch whisky. The drink, called *an dram budheach* by the Gaelic-speaking Scots, was then produced in huge quantities and its name corrupted into the present "Drambuie."

A similar series of coincidences resulted in the introduction of that most English of all alcohols: gin. In the 17th century a Dutch chemist named Franciscus Sylvius succeeded in producing a competitor for Arnaldus de Villanova's alcoholic aqua vitae. As enthusiasm for extramedicinal imbibing of the liquor grew, the new drink was flavored with juniper to disguise the taste of raw spirit. In France the flavoring ingredient gave rise to the generic name *genievre*, but the ready availability of wine there restricted its commercial possibilities. In England in 1690 Parliament passed the historically important Act for Encouraging the Distillation of Brandy and Spirits from Corn to appease its business community. Since Sylvius' aqua vitae was the most profitable distillation procedure available, the English adopted it and corrupted the French name for the flavoring ingredient into the term "gin." In its spread to the east, Sylvius' process was subject to a similar adoption and received another name, the Russian term "vodka."

Because of the English government's decision to encourage distillation, however, improved methods of production of alcoholic beverages had their most disastrous results in that country. The act of 1690 resulted in the production of a million gallons of gin by 1694, and that figure doubled within 20 years. Later restrictions had little effect, for by 1742 production had reached 20 million gallons a year. Despairing of finding a way to control the flow of gin through the nation, the English government then introduced the measure since imitated by almost all governments: in 1743 it began to levy high and unprecedented taxes on specifically potable alcohols. Henceforth all alcohols not intended for consumption could escape this tax only by being "denatured," or rendered unfit for consumption.

By the beginning of the 19th century, improved technology was conspiring against the government's delayed reaction to the proliferation of alcoholic beverages. Aeneas Coffey of Dublin invented the "continuous still," which was to be instrumental in the mass production of Scotch whisky. Although economically efficient, the continuous still seemed innocuous at first because it produced a distilled alcohol with a raw taste that resisted aging. After some years of mediocre success as a rectifier of gin, however, the still was discovered to work wonders with a malt mash fermented in small amounts in the Scottish Highlands, and Scotch whisky for the first time eclipsed Irish whiskey as the favorite alcoholic beverage of the British Isles.

The rise of British concern about alcohol abuse parallels the country's sudden growth in the availability of alcoholic beverages. In the Age of Enlightenment philosophical warnings about the dangers of excess, like those in ancient Greek society, appeared. "A man may choose," Boswell was told by Johnson, a famous abstainer, "whether he will have abstemiousness and knowledge, or claret and ignorance." Even more important was the growing awareness by London's leading social critics of the dangers of widespread alcoholism among the lower classes. The two most influential spokesmen for this new concern were William Hogarth, illustrator of such horrific images as Gin Lane and Beer Street, and Charles Dickens, whose novels are full of warnings about the dangers of habitual intoxication. These two men also represented different sides in a basic disagreement among social reformers on the issue of alcoholism: in Hogarth's illustrations it is liquor that brings poverty and misery but in Dickens' novels it is poverty and misery that drive people to drink. However disparate these views on the country's alcohol problem may have been, they combined to provoke the British government's carefully engineered and ultimately successful shift of national drinking habits from distilled alcohols to beer and ale.

At this time even more important changes of attitudes toward alcohol were occurring on the Continent, although they would go largely unheeded until modern times. In 1786 a town physician in Bratislava became the first medical doctor to call for government action against alcohol abuse. An even greater symbolic breakthrough came in 1849, when a Swedish physician named Magnus Huss wrote a tract called *Alcoholismus Chronicus*, which introduced the word "alcoholism" to the world. The prevailing climate of alcohol abuse and concern about it was such that only 20 years after the publication of this rather obscure medical essay newspapers in England were attributing deaths to "alcoholism." A precise definition of alcoholism as a disease syndrome, however, was formulated by another physician 3,000 miles away, in America.

Given its prominence in Europe, alcohol quickly found a place in the New World. In 1609, only two years after they had established the first English settlement in America, the inhabitants of Jamestown, Virginia ran an advertisement in London for brewers. By 1640 the first distillery, designed to manufacture gin, was erected by the Dutch settlers of New York. It was soon converted to produce rum, however, for it was that drink that dominated early American commerce in alcohol. "Rumbullion," as it was called, was a rectified alcohol produced from fermented molasses. The rum distillers, located mostly in New England, imported molasses from the West Indies, the best source of this raw material. They shipped some of their product to Africa, where it was bartered for slaves. The slaves were then brought to the West Indies to be traded for molasses, which in turn was shipped to New England. Thus a "triangle trade" was established. Since taxation could not be enforced in such distant lands, the trade remained lucrative and the price of rum was low enough to make it the favorite alcoholic beverage in America until the Revolutionary period, after which an abundance of grain supplies increased the availability of whiskey. In 1808 Congress outlawed slave trading and the rum industry was demolished.

The ban on slave trading was the final step in the rise of the indigenous American whiskeys: rye, bourbon and corn whiskey. These alcoholic beverages no doubt first came into use as substitutes for rum in isolated areas, perhaps as a result of the presence of Irish and Scottish settlers familiar with the whiskey-distilling techniques of the home countries. Because it was easier and more profitable to produce rye whiskey from grain than to transport the grain to market, Pennsylvania farmers, in particular, found rye a convenient medium for exchange, and thus production of the drink increased. A government tax on whiskey resulted in the Whiskey Rebellion of 1794, which was an attempt by distillers in Pennsylvania to resist the tax. Although short-lived, the revolt strengthened local insistence on the right to distill whiskey. A similar attitude prevailed farther south, in what is now Kentucky. Revenue inspectors there eventually despaired of ever adequately taxing local distilleries, thought to number more than 2,000 as early as 1810.

Against this background of burgeoning production and consumption of alcohol, Dr. Benjamin Rush of Philadelphia began his pioneer work on the pathological processes of alcoholism in 1785. His particular innovation was a scientific assumption that alcoholism was a disease and the subsequent study of it in terms of disease complexes like those that had resulted in the formulation of useful therapy for other disorders. Rush was open to the alternative positions on alcohol stressed by temperance societies, however, and these attitudes combined with public outrage over the increasing incidence of drunkenness caused his ideas to be abandoned for the "moral" approach that dominated America's attempts to curb alcoholism in the 19th century.

Early temperance organizations in the United States were closely aligned with religious groups and enjoyed great popularity in rural regions. By 1830 there were over 1,000 local groups affiliated with the American Temperance Society, whose philosophy had progressed from avoidance of alcoholic beverages to total abstinence. In the process, the organization also changed its focus from assisting habitual drunkards to petitioning state governments to prohibit the sale of alcohol in any form. Assisted by popular songs, plays and novels, such as T.S. Arthur's *Ten Nights in a Bar-Room*, the temperance societies had great success during the late 1800s. By 1912 seven states had enacted prohibition laws, others were close to ratifying similar legislation and agitation for a national ban on alcoholic beverages had begun.

In 1919 a national prohibition on beverages with an alcohol content of more than 0.5% went into effect and lasted until 1933. However well-intended, the Eighteenth Amendment to the Constitution and the Volstead Act, which provided for the amendment's enforcement, are now considered to have failed in their attempt to outlaw the use of alcoholic beverages. Heavy drinkers were unaffected, for an enormous illegal production of alcohol immediately replaced the regulated and taxed trade. Moderate drinkers were denied the social outlet of the saloons and then encouraged into general disregard for the law when speakeasies became a fashionable substitute for those meeting places. Teetotalers became even more entrenched in their belief that alcoholism was a sin and undeserving of professional medical treatment. The failure of Prohibition, however, discredited the moral approach to alcohol problems and so allowed the introduction of an alternative approach—a serious study of the issues, in the form of scientific investigation, surrounding alcohol consumption.

This "serious study of the issues" became the modern study of alcoholism. Still in its infancy before World War II, it progressed enormously in both scope and depth during the postwar years. It is to the wealth and variety of approaches and information gained during this most recent period that the bulk of this volume is devoted.

INTRODUCTION TO ALCOHOL

The term "alcohol" dates back at least to the first millennium B.C., and the current use of the word results from a long history of figurative usages and changing chemical definitions. The etymological source of the word has nothing to do with liquids for "alcohol" is derived from the Arabic term *al-kol' l*, meaning a fine cosmetic powder made by pulverizing iron ore and worn as a mascara. The term did not enter European languages until the 16th century, when chemists applied it to any fine, impalpable powder produced by crushing a rougher crystalline substance.

In a series of etymological extensions that have become obscure, the word "alcohol" was eventually used to describe fluids as well as powders produced by a pulverizing process. Hence distilled, or rectified, fluids thought to be the essence, quintessence or "spirit" of another liquid were generally termed alcohols. However, there is a long history in the English language, in particular, of use of the term to describe the essential spirit of anything, including abstract qualities. It was in this sense that Samuel Taylor Coleridge, in his *Lectures on Shakespeare*, for example, described "intense selfishness" as "the alcohol of egotism."

Rectified alcohols were first produced by distilling wine, and when potable alcohols were eventually produced by distilling the fermented mash of other substances, they were called "alcohol" because they shared the essential property of being able to induce intoxication. In the early days of organic chemistry, "alcohol" was the name given to the entire class of compounds sharing the same chemical structure as the "spirit" of wine, even if such compounds were not intended for consumption or could not be consumed without fatal consequences. In popular usage the term "alcohol" has for the past 300 years been synonomous with spirituous liquids.

Alcohols are a remarkably diverse family of organic compounds. Potable alcohols appear relatively insignificant when compared with immensely valuable industrial alcohol compounds, most of which are produced synthetically. The single distinct chemical feature that all alcohols have in common is the presence of an oxygen atom and a hydrogen atom bonded together to form a single unit known as a hydroxyl group, denoted by the symbol OH. An alcohol molecule occurs when this hydroxyl group appears in combination with a carbon atom or hydrocarbon chain. Alcohols therefore differ according to the number of carbon or hydrocarbon units present in their molecular structure, but all alcohols remain distinct from the hydrocarbon family because of the presence of the hydroxyl group. In fact the molecular polarity created by the presence of the hydroxyl group gives alcohol its most important chemical properties, extreme solubility and a low boiling point. The degree to which alcohols of various sorts possess these important properties is determined by the number of hydrocarbon units occurring in combination with the single, all-important hydroxyl group.

Since the hydroxyl group defines the alcohol molecule and determines its behavior in any chemical reaction, alcohols are usually classified according to the number of hydrocarbon units attached to the hydroxyl group. Hence, according to one standard classification, alcohols are primary if the hydroxyl is attached to a single carbon chain, secondary if the hydroxyl is attached to a carbon chain bearing two others and tertiary if the hydroxyl is attached to a carbon chain bearing three others. A more precise classification names alcohols according to the number of carbon units attached to the hydroxyl group; a hydroxyl group with one carbon unit is called a methyl alcohol; with two carbon units, an ethyl alcohol; with three carbon units, a propyl alcohol; and with four carbon units, a butyl alcohol. The most important propyl alcohol is known as isopropyl alcohol because of the position of the hydroxyl group in the molecule, but with that single exception these categories may be considered to include most common alcohols. Although in 1957 an even more specific and sophisticated system of classification was adopted at a congress of the International Union of Pure and Applied Chemistry in Paris, the classifications of methyl, ethyl, isopropyl and butyl alcohols are sufficient for a general discussion of the basic properties of simple alcohols.

Methyl Alcohol (Methanol)

Methyl alcohol is commonly termed "wood alcohol" because it was once produced by destructive distillation of hard woods. A primary alcohol, it is highly soluble because of its low carbon content, and it has a low boiling point, about 65° C. Consumption of this highly toxic alcohol, which is sometimes produced by moonshiners in remote areas of the southern United States, often results in blindness or death. Commercially its primary use is in the production of formaldehyde and other organic chemicals. Other commercial products made from methyl alcohol include antifreeze and industrial solvents. Because distillation processes can produce only limited amounts of varying purity, methyl alcohol is now synthetically manufactured by combining carbon monoxide and hydrogen at high temperatures with oxides of zinc or chromium as a catalytic agent.

Ethyl Alcohol (Ethanol)

Commonly called "grain alcohol" for the material from which it has traditionally been distilled, ethyl alcohol is highly soluble and has a boiling point of about 78° C. This type of alcohol is produced commercially by fermentation and used to make alcoholic beverages. Since potable alcohol is heavily taxed, ethyl alcohol intended for other purposes is denatured, or rendered unfit for consumption, by treatment with a variety of toxic or nauseous chemical substances that cannot be removed. In denatured form ethyl alcohol is used as an industrial solvent and as raw material for acetaldehyde and a variety of other important chemical compounds and tinctures. Some ethyl alcohol intended for industrial use is produced by fermentation of sugars and starches, but most commercial denatured alcohol of this variety is manufactured by combining the petroleum by-product ethene with sulfuric acid.

Isopropyl Alcohol (Propanol)

Known as "rubbing alcohol" because of its popular uses, isopropyl alcohol is a tertiary alcohol that has less solubility than either methyl alcohol or ethyl alcohol and a boiling point of about 82° C. In addition to its use as a rubbing compound, isopropyl alcohol is an ingredient in many hand and shaving lotions. Industrially it is an important additive in antifreeze, shellac and lacquer. Like ethyl alcohol isopropyl alcohol is manufactured mostly from a petroleum by-product, in this case propene.

Butyl Alcohol (Butanol)

Butyl alcohol has limited solubility and a relatively high boiling point, about 117° C. Nevertheless, of all classes of alcohols the butyl class has perhaps the broadest range of commercial uses. In various forms it is an essential ingredient in many types of lacquer, photographic film and dye. Butyl alcohol is also used in the manufacture of plastic, artificial leather and safety glass. It is produced by both fermentation and synthesis. When fermented, butyl alcohol is often made from sterilized molasses and the active enzymes found in certain soil bacteria. It is also produced by synthesizing the petroleum by-product butene in a similar procedure to those employed in the manufacture of ethyl and isopropyl alcohols.

Beyond these basic types there exists a variety of high-carbon alcohols produced in smaller quantities for more specialized uses. A range of alcohols possessing six to 10 carbon units in varying structures is essential to the manufacture of many synthetic plastics. Some complex alcohols with more than 10 carbon units are used to produce biodegradable detergents. Polyester cords for automobile tires, jet fuels, nitroglycerin explosives, inks and numerous other products are all manufactured by exploiting the properties of specific alcohols. In addition glycerol is a sweet-tasting, easily digestible alcohol sometimes used in medicinal syrups, and sterol is a chemically complex crystalline alcohol that exists in some plant tissues without known function.

Common Alcohols   +

Common Name	Chemical Name	Formula	Carbon Atoms	Melting Point C°	Boiling Point C°
methyl alcohol	methanol	CH_3OH	1	-93.9	64.96
ethyl alcohol	ethanol	CH_3CH_3OH	2	-117.3	78.5
isopropyl alcohol	2-propanol	$(CH_3)_2CHOH$	3	-89.5	82.4
butyl alcohol	butanol	$CH_2(CH_2)_2CH_3OH$	4	-89.53	117.25

THE
ENCYCLOPEDIA OF
ALCOHOLISM

Second Edition

A

absenteeism   Absenteeism is a major problem among employed alcoholics. One study reported that male alcoholics had three times the number of sick absences as a matched control group (Maxwell). In addition to normal off-the-job absences, alcoholics often report to work but later disappear from the work place. Another problem is "on-the-job" absenteeism, which occurs when a worker is physically present but not mentally alert. In 1983, the economic cost to the nation resulting from alcoholism and related problems was $116.7 billion; nearly $71 billion of this is attributed to lost employment and reduced productivity and $15 billion to health care costs. The economic cost of alcohol abuse was projected to rise to $136.3 billion in 1990.

EMPLOYEE ASSISTANCE PROGRAMS have been developed to help workers with alcohol problems.

Henrick J. Harwood, D.M. Napolitano and P.L. Kristiansan, *Economic Costs to Society of Alcohol and Drug Abuse and Mental Illness, 1980*, Pub. No. RT1/2734/00-00 FR (Research Triangle Park, N.C.: Research Triangle Institute, June 1984), pp. G-16 and 7.

Observer and M. A. Maxwell, "A Study of Absenteeism, Accidents, and Sickness Payments in Problem Drinkers in One Industry," *Quarterly Journal of Studies on Alcohol* 20 (1959):302-307.

Harrison M. Trice, *Alcoholism in America* (New York: Robert E. Krieger Publishing Co., 1978), pp. 70-72.

absinthe   A flavored spirit with a dry, bitter taste, absinthe is too potent to be drunk straight. It is usually diluted with water, which changes its yellowish-green color to milky white. The name "absinthe" comes from the botanical designation of the plant *Artemisia absinthium,* more commonly known as worm-wood, the basic flavoring ingredient in this beverage.

In addition to wormwood, absinthe is flavored with angelica root, star anise, dittany leaves, licorice, hyssop, sweet flag and other aromatics. These ingredients are macerated and steeped in alcohol. The final product is between 60% and 80% (usually 68%) alcohol.

The effects of absinthe are worse than those associated with excessive use of other forms of alcohol. Not only is it habit forming, but it has a harmful effect on the nerves, causing delirium and, sometimes, a permanent mental deterioration known as absinthism.

Absinthe was invented by a Dr. Ordinaire, a Frenchman living in Switzerland. His recipe was later bought by Henri-Louis Pernod (see PERNOD), who in 1797 became the first to produce absinthe commercially. Because of its severe health hazards, absinthe was banned in most Western countries during the early years of the 20th century. It was outlawed in Switzerland in 1908 and in the United States in 1912. In France, where absinthe houses had been very popular in Paris during the late 19th century, it was banned in 1915.

Although these prohibitions have remained in effect, absinthe may still be consumed legally in some countries, including Spain.

absolute alcohol   The pure alcohol in a beverage, obtained by brewing followed by fractional distillation. (There is always a slight amount of water in alcohol; commercial absolute alcohol, used only for medical or industrial purposes, contains up to 1% of water.)

The term "absolute alcohol" is used to refer to the amount of pure alcohol in a substance. For example, three 1-oz drinks of 100-proof whiskey, four 8-oz glasses of beer and a half bottle of wine all contain approximately the same amount of pure alcohol, about 1-1/2 ounces.

abstainer   Strictly defined, one who abstains completely from the consumption of alcoholic beverages. The application of the term or concept depends on the context in which it is being used and the philosophy of the person or organization using it. For example, many agencies reporting on alcohol abuse group abstainers with moderate or social drinkers, since all are considered nonabusers of alcohol. ALCOHOLICS ANONYMOUS, using a strict interpretation, insists upon complete abstinence. In cultures where the use of alcohol is proscribed or barely tolerated, such as in INDIA, abstention is the norm of social behavior and any use of alcohol is considered abuse.

abstinence   A complete refraining from the use of alcoholic beverages; also called total abstinence. (See also ABSTAINER.)

abuse   Alcohol abuse is a general term applied to the misuse of alcohol, resulting in one or more problems for the drinker. These problems can be psychological, such as loss of control over drinking or depressive states (see DEPRESSION); medical, involving either an acute or chronic illness (see DISEASES); or social, such as problems with family or work. Alcohol abuse does not necessarily involve alcoholism; for example, a person may go on drinking binges and become destructive without necessarily developing the kind of dependency usually associated with alcoholism. The act of getting drunk is itself a form of alcohol abuse.

Since alcohol is itself a drug, alcohol abuse can be classified under drug abuse (see DRUGS). In fact alcohol abuse is the major form of drug abuse in the United States. Both alcohol abuse and drug abuse are types of substance abuse. Food, for example, is a substance that is abused by many people, leading to the establishment of such groups as Overeaters Anonymous.

Substance abuse is subject to individual patterns. Some people may abuse more than one drug, such as those who use both alcohol and marijuana. In addition the amount of a substance that might constitute abuse for one person might be a safe level for another. A large man might be able to consume several

drinks in a sitting with no ill effect, while a small woman consuming the same amount might become very drunk. Some countries, such as Sweden, have a low per capita intake of alcohol but a high incidence of alcoholism. Certain drinkers can consume large quantities of liquor day after day without ever developing social problems, yet they may gradually become victims of CIRRHOSIS or ALCOHOLIC HEPATITIS because of the amount they consume. This too is a form of alcohol abuse, although not one that is noticeable on a daily or even a yearly basis. (See also ADDICTION, ALCOHOLISM, COMPULSION, PROBLEM DRINKER.)

accidents   The role of alcohol consumption in the occurrence of accidents is receiving increasing attention today. In a national survey in the United States, 36% of those who said they drank regularly, compared with 8% of nondrinkers, reported two or more accidental injuries in the previous year (Brenner et al.). Alcohol is a contributing factor in at least 15,000 fatal and six million non-fatal injuries in non-highway settings alone (NIAAA). In 1987, 30,205 Americans died of unintentional injuries related to alcohol. In a national survey of trauma centers (Soderstrom and Cowley) two-thirds of the centers estimated that the majority of their patients had consumed alcohol.

Apart from automobile accidents, the majority of accidents occur in the home or in public places, and of these, falls are the most prevalent.

Occupational accidents affect a significant portion of the working population. The role of alcohol in such accidents has not been well documented to date. Drinking-related industrial accidents may be lower than expected because of a high rate of absenteeism among those who might otherwise be involved (Trice). However, in simulated industrial work, alcohol was shown to inhibit coordination and judgment, lengthen reaction time, and decrease motor performance and sensory skill. Experiments demonstrated that alcohol intoxication could alter a normal person's performance up to 18 hours after the ingestion of alcohol (Wolkenberg et al.). A study of railroad workers by T. A. Mannello and F. J. Seaman estimated that 30,000 workers drank on duty on 90,000 occasions during one year. Between 1975 and 1984, alcohol- or drug-impaired employees were implicated in 48 train accidents/incidents that resulted in 37 deaths, 80 non-fatal injuries and $34.2 million in damage (see RAILROAD ACCIDENTS).

Use of alcohol appears to be significantly involved in fires and BURNS, with alcoholics particularly vulnerable to fire. In a study that compared fire deaths with other deaths, it was found that alcohol was involved in 52% of adult fire deaths (Halpen et al.). Alcohol lowers oxidation in the cells, increasing an individual's risk of being overcome by smoke inhalation. The incidence of alcohol involvement is nearly three times greater in deaths from cigarette-caused fires than in deaths from fires resulting from other causes.

Alcohol is reported to play a significant contributory role in DROWNINGS. During such recreational activities as boating (see BOATING ACCIDENTS) and swimming, alcohol may be consumed frequently and in quantity. Higher consumption can lead to poor judgment, faulty coordination and lack of attention. Alcohol may also depress the swallowing and breathing reflexes and turn a normal situation into a dangerous one. After drinking swimmers may take more risks, and the "warming" effect of alcohol may cause people to stay in cold water too long.

In pilots alcohol may encourage risk taking and daredevil stunts as well as inhibit psychomotor performance. A large percentage of pilots involved in general aviation crashes were found to have a high BLOOD ALCOHOL CONCENTRATION (Lacefield). (See also AUTOMOBILE ACCIDENTS, BICYCLE ACCIDENTS, DRIVING WHILE INTOXICATED, FALLS, MOTORCYCLE ACCIDENTS and PEDESTRIAN ACCIDENTS.)

B. Brenner, I. H. Cisin and C. Newcomb, "Drinking Practices and Accidental Injuries" (paper presented at a session on Alcohol Use and Accidents of the Society for the Study of Social Problems, Miami, Fl., 1966).

Enoch Gordis, ed., *Seventh Special Report to the U.S. Congress on Alcohol and Health* (Rockville, Md.: National Institute on Alcohol Abuse and Alcoholism, 1990), chapter VII.

B. M. Halpen, et al., "A Fire Fatality Study," *Fire Journal* 5 (1975): 11–13.

D. J. Lacefield, "Alcohol Continues to Play a Big Part in Plane Crashes," *Journal of the American Medical Association* 233 (1975): 405.

T. A. Mannello and F. J. Seaman, *Prevalence, Costs and Handling of Drinking Problems on Seven Railroads,* U.S. Department of Transportation, Federal Railroad Administration (Washington, D.C.: University Research Corporation, 1979), passim.

Joy Moser, *Prevention of Alcohol-Related Problems,* (Toronto: World Health Organization, 1980), pp. 45-46.

NIAAA, *Alcohol Health and Research World,* Summer 1985 (9:4) p. 25.

New York Times, "Alcohol Tied to the Deaths of 105,095 in U.S. in '87," March 27, 1990.

C. A. Soderstrom and R. A. Cowley, "A National Alcohol and Trauma Center Survey," *Archives of Orthopedic and Traumatic Surgery* 122 (1987): 1067-1071

Harrison M. Trice. "Work Accidents and the Problem Drinker," *I. L. R. Res,* 3, p.2

R. C. Wolkenberg, C. Gold and E. R. Tichauer, "Delayed Effects of Acute Alcoholic Intoxication on Performance with Reference to Work Safety," *Journal of Research Safety* 7 (1975): 104.

acetaldehyde The first step in the METABOLISM of alcohol results in its conversion to acetaldehyde. Acetaldehyde is even more toxic to the body than ethyl alcohol, although in the second step of metabolism acetaldehyde is converted into acetate, most of which is oxidized to carbon dioxide by the MITOCHONDRIA. Nevertheless some escapes into the bloodstream, especially at high levels of consumption, and is thought to play a central role in the toxicity of alcohol. Alcoholics have been found to have significantly higher levels of acetaldehyde in the blood than nonalcoholics, even when both groups received the same amounts of alcohol and the BLOOD ALCOHOL CONCENTRATION of both was the same. Apparently alcoholics metabolize acetaldehyde less effectively, probably because of LIVER damage caused by excessive consumption of alcohol. Dr. Charles Lieber of the Mount Sinai School of Medicine in New York postulates that the alcoholic may be the victim of a vicious circle: mitochondrial function in the liver is impaired by acetaldehyde, which leads to diminished acetaldehyde metabolism, an accumulation of acetaldehyde and, consequently, further liver damage.

Acetaldehyde has been shown to affect the HEART muscle adversely and may affect other muscles as well. It may also be a contributing factor in ADDICTION to alcohol, by combining with amine neurotransmitters in the brain, which send nerve impulses from one cell to another, to form psychoactive compounds similar to certain morphine derivatives and known for their ability to promote DEPENDENCE. This theory has yet to be confirmed.

Acetaldehyde also plays an important part in ANTABUSE (disulfiram) reactions. Normally acetaldehyde, produced as a result of the initial oxidation of ethanol by the alcohol dehydrogenase of the liver, does not accumulate in the tissues because it is oxidized almost as soon as it is formed, "most likely primarily by the enzyme aldehyde dehydrogenase. In the presence of disulfiram, however, the concentration of acetaldehyde rises because disulfiram seems to compete with NAD [co-factor nicotinamide adenine dinucleotide] for the active centers of the enzyme aldehyde dehydrogenase and thereby reduces the rate of oxidation of the aldehyde" [Ritchie]. When someone taking Antabuse consumes alcohol, his or her blood acetaldehyde concentrations increase five to 10 times higher than normal, resulting in a toxic reaction. The degree of intensity of the reaction depends on the concentration of disulfiram in the body, the quantity of alcohol ingested and the patient's degree of sensitivity to acetaldehyde. The consumption of only 7 milligrams of alcohol (0.24 ounces) has produced a mild reaction in some people and even such products as rubbing alcohol have caused reactions. The Antabuse reaction is sometimes referred to as the acetaldehyde syndrome.

Charles S. Lieber, "The Metabolism of Alcohol," *Scientific American* 234, no. 3 (March 1976): 25-33.

J. M. Ritchie, "The Aliphatic Alcohols," in L. S. Goodman and A. Gilman, *The Pharmacological Basis of Therapeutics,* 5th ed. (New York: Macmillan Publishing Co., 1975), pp. 148-149.

Ackoff's model   The assignment of alcoholic patients to treatment facilities is often determined on the basis of where vacancies exist rather than where particular patients would receive the most effective type of treatment. Such assignments are made under "uncertainty conditions," in which the action leads to any one of a number of possible outcomes but the probability of success of the outcome is unknown.

Ackoff's model describes a method of problem solution for an "evaluative" problem (such as that of placing patients in treatment) where there are alternative courses of action, all of which are specified before the research begins. The problem is to select the best of the alternatives. When Ackoff's model is used, "uncertainty conditions" of assigning patients to the most effective treatment facilities can be changed to "risk conditions," in which the probable outcome of treatment can be determined for specific types of patients.

acne rosacea   (From the Greek *achne* efflorescence via New Latin + the New Latin *rosacea* rosy, reddish.) A facial skin condition usually characterized by a flushed appearance and often accompanied by puffiness and a "spider-web" effect of broken capillaries. Acne rosacea is frequently caused by excessive consumption of alcohol over a prolonged period. (See also RHINOPHYMA.)

acute   A term used to describe a disease or condition that develops quickly into a crisis, as distinguished from a CHRONIC disease or condition.

acute alcohol intoxication   Severe alcohol intoxication or poisoning. The term is also used to refer to a circumscribed episode of alcohol intoxication as distinguished from a chronic, or prolonged, state of intoxication.

acute alcoholic state   A physical or mental disorder of an alcoholic that is associated with and immediately follows a prolonged bout of drinking. This condition can take such forms as acute KORSAKOFF'S PSYCHOSIS or DELIRIUM TREMENS. The term "acute alcoholic state" is also used, more generally, to refer to alcohol intoxication.

acute alcoholism   This term may refer to alcohol intoxication or poisoning, to the state of intoxication of an alcoholic or to a temporary disturbance caused by excessive drinking. Because alcoholism is generally recognized as a CHRONIC disease, the term is considered ambiguous and is thus seldom used.

adaptive cell metabolism   After a prolonged period of steady drinking, the tissue cells of an alcoholic adapt to the constant large quantity of alcohol consumed. This conditioning leads to increased tissue TOLERANCE, with the consequent onset of WITHDRAWAL. If a person's cells have adapted to high quantities of alcohol and alcohol is not supplied, a CRAVING may develop resulting in LOSS OF CONTROL or the INABILITY TO ABSTAIN. Adaptive cell metabolism is one factor in GAMMA ALCOHOLISM. (See also METABOLISM.)

addiction   The use of the term "addiction" has changed over the years, and even today there is considerable variation in (and often confusion about) its usage. In the early 20th century the term "drug addiction" simply referred to the illicit use of drugs, without any distinction between different patterns of drug use and the effects of various drugs. Beginning in 1931 drug HABITUATION was distinguished from drug addiction (Tatum and Seevers). Drug addiction came to mean physical dependence on the effects of a drug, with illness, or WITHDRAWAL, occurring if the intake of the drug was severely reduced or stopped completely. Habituation was viewed as psychological dependence on a drug after repeated use; withdrawal from a habituating drug might involve emotional distress but not physiological illness.

In 1957 the Expert Committee on Addiction-Producing Drugs of the World Health Organization defined drug addiction as

> a state of periodic or chronic intoxication, detrimental to the individual and society, produced by the repeated consumption of a drug (natural or synthetic). Its characteristics include: 1. An overpowering desire or need (compulsion) to continue taking the drug and to obtain it by any means; 2. A tendency to increase the dose; 3. A psychic (psychological) and generally a physical dependence on the effects of the drug.

Drug habituation was defined as

> a condition resulting from the repeated consumption of a drug. Its characteristics include: 1. A desire (but not a compulsion) to continue taking the drug for the sense of improved well-being which it engenders; 2. Little or no tendency to increase the dose; 3. Some degree of psychic dependence on the effect of the drug, but absence of physical dependence and hence of an abstinence syndrome; 4. Detrimental effects, if any, primarily on the individual.

The definitions did not clear up all the confusion surrounding these terms; for example, someone who took a large quantity of a stimulant drug might assault others, thereby invalidating the fourth part of the definition of habituation. The word "addicted" (or "addiction" or "addict") was used both benignly, as in "He's addicted to jazz," and pejoratively, as in "He's been addicted to drugs for years."

In 1965 the World Health Organization abandoned these terms and adopted the more neutral term "drug dependence." This term was defined in a very general way:

A state, psychic and sometimes also physical, resulting from the interaction between a living organism and a drug, characterized by behavioral and other responses that always include a compulsion to take the drug on a continuous or periodic basis in order to experience its psychic effects, and sometimes to avoid the discomfort of its absence. Tolerance may or may not be present. A person may be dependent on more than one drug.

Still used frequently today, the term "addiction" is generally employed to refer to a known physical dependence on the effects of a drug. JELLINEK, for example, uses the following terms in describing an addiction to alcohol: an increased tissue TOLERANCE, ADAPTIVE CELL METABOLISM, WITHDRAWAL SYMPTOMS, CRAVING, and LOSS OF CONTROL or INABILITY TO ABSTAIN.

Physical dependence, or the adaptive consequences of taking certain chemicals repeatedly, is clearly not the only aspect of addiction, however. As Dr. Vincent P. Dole has pointed out, physical dependence does not explain the drug-seeking behavior characteristic of addiction. People can be physically dependent on drugs without being addicted to them. For example, drugs prescribed for medicinal purposes, such as steroids, can give rise to physical dependence without causing a desire for the substance. When intake is optional, most users stop or reduce consumption. On the other hand, addicts who have been freed of their dependence through DETOXIFICATION usually relapse. Unfortunately those definitions that include some concept of psychological dependence are unable to explain such behavior.

Dole, who has worked extensively as a physician and an administrator in the metha-

done program in New York and in addiction research, found that former heroin addicts stabilized on methadone did not have the pleasure-seeking, reality-escaping traits generally associated with addicts. Addicts with a history of two or more years of addiction to heroin seemed to be quite willing to sacrifice the occasional euphoria produced by the drug for a continued feeling of normality. For Dole this finding suggested that the addictive behavior of chronic users of narcotics stemmed less from pleasure seeking than from a need to relieve a recurring discomfort. The same need may also be true for people who are unable to stop smoking or excessive drinking.

Vincent P. Dole, "Addictive Behavior," *Scientific American* 243, no. 6 (December 1980):138-154.

Frederick G. Hofmann, *A Handbook on Drug and Alcohol Abuse: The Biomedical Aspects* (New York: Oxford University Press, 1975), pp. 21-27.

Jerome Jaffe, Robert Petersen and Ray Hodgson, *Addictions: Issues and Answers* (London: Harper and Row, 1980), pp. 7-9.

E. M. Jellinek, *The Disease Concept of Alcoholism* (New Jersey: Hillhouse Press, 1979), pp. 69-77.

A. L. Tatum and M. H. Seevers, "Theories of Drug Addiction," *The Physiological Review* 11 (1931):187.

addictive drinker   See ADDICTION.

addictive drinking   See ADDICTION.

additive effect   See SYNERGY.

advertising   In many countries advertising of alcoholic beverages is considered at least partially responsible for increases in alcohol consumption levels. There are wide differences in opinion on the effect of such advertising, from the belief that a free-enterprise system should impose no restrictions on advertising to the view that government (in the public interest) should ban all alcohol advertising, as Sweden has done. The middle position holds that trade associations should impose their own restrictions to ward off government regulation. The Wine Institute, the Distilled Spirits Council of the United States and the United States Brewers Association have adopted codes for advertising. The middle viewpoint is also reflected by bills in the Michigan legislature and the U.S. Congress that favor allocation of a set percentage of commercial time to explain the dangers of alcohol abuse.

In the United States, advertising of distilled spirits on radio and television is prohibited. Beer and wine advertisements must be "presented in the best of good taste and discretion" and are subject to federal, state and local laws. One generally accepted restriction on television advertising is that all beer and wine commercials avoid any representation of drinking on the screen. Although frowned upon, sexual appeals, appeals to youth etc. are common in much alcohol advertising, but the alcohol industry and television producers appear, reluctantly, responsive to tightening up self-imposed regulations.

Beer, wine and liquor advertisements, including prices, are allowed in all print media. Each state has its own regulations on the type and size of storefront and billboard signs advertising alcoholic beverages. State regulations may be further restricted by local ordinances (Moser).

Advertising expenditures and liquor sales volume rose proportionally from the 1950s through the late 1970s, even when consumption is adjusted for increases in the total U.S. population or the legal-age drinking population *(The Liquor Handbook)*. However, distilled spirits consumption has been declining since 1979 and wine since 1986. Whether increased advertising caused increased sales or increased sales cause increased advertising or both is open to debate. Many factors besides advertising may account for the rising consumption of alcohol, and these may interact with whatever effects advertising has on consumption behavior. Such factors include the decreasing relative price of alcohol, growing affluence, a youth market created by the postwar baby boom, women's liberation, an increasing trend in communities from DRY to WET and the lowering of legal minimum-age requirements.

Advertising aims at achieving higher sales by attracting three types of purchasers: completely new buyers, new-to-the-brand buyers and brand-loyal buyers. There are also attempts to increase the level of purchasing among brand-loyal buyers and to decrease the number of buyers who switch to other products.

Most advertising is directed at drinkers, especially heavy drinkers, rather than nondrinkers. Heavy drinkers are the most important consumers of alcoholic beverages and account for a disproportionate share of product purchases and usage.

From 1974 to 1982 advertising expenditures for alcohol beverages (including wine, beer and distilled spirits) rose from $310 million to $1,108.7 billion. According to the group Leading National Advertisers, advertising spending on alcoholic beverages was $1,153.5 billion in 1988. In 1988, American brewers spent $170 million on sports sponsorships, second only to that of the tobacco industry, which spent $230 million.

Following a precedent set by the anti-smoking campaign, such groups as the National Safety Council and the National Council on Alcoholism have sponsored some counteradvertising. Studies by the Federal Trade Commission have shown that counteradvertising has had a significant impact both on reducing the number of people who started smoking and those who quit. For countercommercials to be effective they must be aired during prime time—frequently and repeatedly— either through revision of regulations now governing public service announcements or through purchase of airtime. As with regular commercials segmentation of the market according to drinking patterns, behavioral tendencies, value patterns and media behavior is essential for the creation of messages with maximum impact (Blane and Hewitt). When messages are not aired properly or targeted at specific populations, the results may backfire. A recent San Francisco countercommercial attempt failed because a high proportion of the audience thought the ads were promoting consumption.

The liquor industry has been fairly active in public education campaigns that stress moderate and responsible use of alcohol. In 1980 Sam D. Chilcote, president of the Distilled Spirits Council of the United States, testifying before a Senate Subcommittee on Alcoholism and Drug Abuse on the issue of consumer warning labels, stated that in 1980 distilling companies would spend $50 million on advertising a message of moderation. Starting in November 1989, the alcohol beverage industry was required to use containers that carry warnings that pregnant women shouldn't drink and that alcohol impairs driving.

See also PUBLICITY.

Howard T. Blane and Linda E. Hewitt, "Alcohol, Public Education, and Mass Media: An Overview," *Alcohol Health and Research World* 5, no. 1 (Fall 1980): 2-13.

The Liquor Handbook, 1975 (New York: Gavin-Jobson Associates, 1975).

Michael Jacobson, Robert Atkins, and George Hacker, *The Booze Merchants: The Inebriating of America*, A Report from the Center for Science in the Public Interest (Washington, D.C.: CSPS Books, 1983).

Joy Moser, *Prevention of Alcohol Related Problems* (Toronto: World Health Organization, 1980), p. 123.

Bonnie Orr, "The Unselling of Alcohol," *Alcoholism* 2, no. 1, (September/October 1981): 36-38.

AIDS   It is not yet established that alcohol is involved in the progression of disease in persons who have been infected with the virus responsible for acquired immunodeficiency syndrome (AIDS). However, acute and chronic doses of alcohol have been shown to suppress all arms of the immune defense system, and it seems likely that these effects are involved in the susceptibility of alcoholics to infectious diseases. The AIDS virus, also known as human immunodeficiency virus

(HIV), human T-lymphocyte virus (HTLV-III), or lymphadenopathy-associated virus (LAV), produces a catastrophic infection of the T-lymphocytes and failure of immune function.

National Institute on Alcohol Abuse and Alcoholism, *The Effects of Alcohol on the Immune System*, Alcohol Research Utilization System Working Document No. 85-02 Rockville, MD: NIAAA, 1986).

aging   See ELDERLY.

Al-Anon   Al-Anon, officially known as the Al-Anon Family Groups, is an organization designed to help the relatives and friends of alcoholics. Its philosophy, program and structure correspond to the related organization ALCOHOLICS ANONYMOUS, although the two operate independently.

History

During the early days of Alcoholics Anonymous, family members of alcoholics used to attend the regular AA meetings. In 1951 relatives of AA members in and near New York City formed a Clearing House Committee; one of the founders was Lois Wilson, wife of Bill Wilson, who started AA. The original staff members were volunteers. The committee adopted the name Al-Anon Family Groups and slightly modified the Twelve Steps and Twelve Traditions of AA as principles for Al-Anon members (see "The Twelve Steps" and "The Twelve Traditions" under ALCOHOLICS ANONYMOUS). By 1954 Al-Anon had grown enormously; it was publishing a monthly newsletter, *The Forum,* and had affiliated groups abroad. It was incorporated as a nonprofit unit under the title The Al-Anon Family Group Headquarters, Inc.

In 1967 delegates from Al-Anon groups across North America attended the first World Service Conference, which has become an annual event. In 1970 Twelve Concepts of Service, explaining the structure of Al-Anon, were adopted. Today the headquarters' office is known as the World Service Office (WSO), which assists more than 30,000 registered Al-Anon and ALATEEN groups. Over 7,800 of these groups are in other countries. Al-Anon literature is available in 25 languages and there are some 5,500 Spanish-speaking Al-Anon groups worldwide.

Organization

The only requirement for membership in Al-Anon is to have a relative or friend who is an alcoholic. The alcoholic may belong to AA, may still be drinking, or may be no longer drinking and not in AA. (Alcoholics may be members of Al-Anon if they have friends or relatives who are alcoholic.) Some members of Al-Anon may have stopped living with the alcoholic but may feel that their lives have been so strongly affected by their former association that Al-Anon can help them. Both men and women attend Al-Anon meetings, but in some cities there are special groups: some composed solely of women, others of homosexuals.

Al-Anon meetings are structured in the same way as AA meetings. A chairman or leader opens and closes the meeting and generally leads discussion on a central theme. There are no dues; groups are self-supporting through voluntary contributions.

Philosophy

Al-Anon members are taught that they are responsible only for their own reactions and responses to what the alcoholic does and not for the actions of the alcoholic. The primary purpose of the organization is not to stop the alcoholic from drinking but to help his or her family or friends. Members are taught neither to interfere actively with the alcoholic's drinking nor to protect the alcoholic from the consequences of drinking. The assumption is that the alcoholic will be forced to a point where the effects of his or her drinking have become so severe that he or she will be motivated to stop voluntarily. Meanwhile Al-Anon mem-

bers focus on their own needs in their relationships with other family members.

Comments and Criticisms

Al-Anon may not be acceptable to those who object to its implicitly spiritual orientation or those who are not willing to attend many meetings and participate in a formal group discussion. While Al-Anon does provide peer counseling and support and an opportunity to see that others share the same problems, GROUP THERAPY can also provide similar support and may be more suited to some people. Critics have complained about the rigidity of the concepts taught at Al-Anon meetings. Members have been severely chastised because they mentioned interfering directly with a spouse's drinking or undergoing professional counseling (Lavino and Kay). Al-Anon teaches a program of "detachment with love," which can sometimes serve as an excuse for walking away from a situation rather than effectively dealing with it.

The almost complete separation of Al-Anon from AA can sometimes create isolated approaches to family problems. It has also been pointed out that Al-Anon and Alateen have not adequately met the needs of people aged 18 to 25 who are single or recently married with no children. Another source of criticism is that over the years most Al-Anon groups have been primarily composed of women and little has been done to attract the husbands of alcoholic women.

Al-Anon Family Group Headquarters, *Al-Anon Faces Alcoholism* (New York, 1977).
Al-Anon Family Group Headquarters, *Living with an Alcoholic with the Help of Al-Anon* (New York, 1978).
John Lavino and Mary Ellen Kay, "The Kemper/Al-Anon Program," *Alcoholism* 1, no. 3 (January/February 1981):46-47.

Alaskan Natives   In 1985 the age-adjusted alcoholism mortality rate for American Indians and Alaskan Natives was 26.1 deaths per 100,000 population, a significant decrease from the 1973 high of 66.1 but still four times higher than the general U.S. rate. From 1973 to 1983, the alcoholism death rate for Alaskan Natives remained fairly constant at 30 to 36 per 100,000, compared with 7 to 8 per 100,000 for white Alaskans. From 1974 to 1983, Alaskan Natives accounted for more than half of the deaths from alcoholism in Alaska, although they constituted only about 15% of the state's population. Between 1975 and 1981, the suicide rate among Alaskan Natives dropped from 43% to 18% of all Alaskan suicides (an estimated 80% of all American Indian suicide deaths are alcohol-related). Alcohol patterns and problems among this Alaskan population appear to have a strong correlation with economic factors, such as unemployment and low income, and with marital and family instability.

See AMERICAN INDIANS.

Indian Health Service, *Indian Health Service Chart Series Book*, DHHHHS Pub no. 1988 0-218-547: QL3 (Washington, D.C.: U.S. Government Printing Office, 1988).

D. Kelso and W. DuBay, "W. Alaskan Natives and Alcohol: A Sociocultural and Epidemiological Review," in *Alcohol Use Among U.S. Ethnic Minorities*, Research Monograph no. 18, DHHS Pub. no. ADM787-1435 (Washington, D.C.: U.S. Govt. Printing Office, in press).

Alateen   Alateen was started in 1957 by a boy in California whose father was an alcoholic in ALCOHOLICS ANONYMOUS (AA) and whose mother was in AL-ANON. Alateen was patterned after Al-Anon and shares with it the same Twelve Steps and Twelve Traditions, but it is designed for teenagers from 12 to 20 who have been affected by someone, usually a parent, with a drinking problem. It is not necessary that the drinker be in AA.

Alateen meetings are conducted by teenagers, although an active adult member of Al-Anon acts as a sponsor. The sponsor, who is generally not a parent of any of the Alateen members, guides the group and shares knowledge of the Twelve Steps and Twelve Tradi-

tions. Emotional detachment is stressed—the teenager is taught to suspend emotional involvement with the alcoholic's problems. When older, Alateen members are encouraged to join Al-Anon.

There are now over 3,000 Alateen groups. They have their own bimonthly newsletter, *Alateen: Hope for Children of Alcoholics*. They also have conventions and Alateen Loner's Service for teens who live where there are no groups.

Alateen Membership

- Is predominantly white, although since 1984 there has been an increase in the number of blacks and other ethnic groups.
- The ratio of females to males is 3 to 2.
- The average age of the member is 14 years.
- Members report an average of 1.7 relationships with alcoholics, mostly an alcoholic parent; however, there has been a decrease in Alateens who report relationships with alcoholic parents and an increase in those who report relationships with alcoholic relatives.
- Two-thirds of Alateens have at least one family member in A.A., and three-quarters have at least one family member in Al-Anon.
- Two-thirds of Alateens attend one meeting a week.
- *Alateen Group Sponsors*
- Most sponsors are female; average age of the sponsor is 42 years.
- One-third of the Alateen groups have at least one sponsor who is a member of A.A.

alcohol abuse   See ABUSE.

alcohol addict   A person addicted to alcohol (see ADDICTION).

alcohol addiction   See ADDICTION.

alcohol amblyopia   (From   Greek *amblys* dim + *ops* eye.) A rare disorder of the eye, alcohol amblyopia usually occurs in alcoholics with a lengthy history of severe drinking problems. The disease begins slowly with a slight vision impairment that becomes progressively worse. The visual failure is not caused by lesions of the eye or refractive error but is believed to be due to a toxic reaction in the orbital portion of the optic nerve. The typical complaint is a painless blurring of vision over a period of several weeks with reduced sharpness for both near and distant objects. Generally changes are relatively symmetrical in both eyes and, if not treated adequately, may be followed by optic nerve degeneration. Treatment consists of administration of VITAMINS AND MINERALS. With proper care and NUTRITION the symptoms are usually reversible. The disease is most common in male alcoholics who are also smokers.

alcohol as medicine   See   MEDICATION.

alcohol concentration   The proportion of alcohol in a tissue or fluid expressed as volume or weight of alcohol per volume or weight of fluid or tissue. (See also BLOOD ALCOHOL CONCENTRATION.)

Alcohol Dependence Scale   A model for alcohol-related diagnoses that analyzes multiple factors was developed by psychiatrist-researcher H.A. Skinner based on Horn and Wanberg's Alcohol Use Inventory. Four scales from the earlier inventory are used: (1) loss of behavioral control; (2) psychophysical withdrawal symptoms; (3) psychoperceptual withdrawal symptoms; and (4) obsessive-compulsive drinking style. Skinner identified general factors that measure, in part, the alcohol dependence syndrome as outlined by Edwards and Gross (1976).

Enoch Gordis, M.D., ed., *Sixth Special Report to the U.S. Congress on Alcohol and Health* (Rock-

ville, Md.: National Institute on Alcohol Abuse and Alcoholism, 1987), p. 122.

J.L. Horn, K.W. Wanberg and F.M. Forster, *The Alcohol Use Inventory—AUI* (Denver: Center for Alcohol-Abuse Research and Evaluation, 1974).

G. Edwards and M.M. Gross, "Alcohol Dependence: Provisional Description of a Clinical Syndrome," *British Medical Journal*, 1(1976): 1058-1061.

alcohol dependence syndrome (ADS)
Researchers and clinicians have long recognized the limitations of using the blanket-term "alcoholism" to describe the range of alcohol-related disabilities and the varying degrees, as well as different types, of alcohol dependence. A new trend in classification of alcohol-related pathology is to focus on the number and types of symptoms that are evident, as opposed to viewing alcoholism as a unitary phenomenon. In fact, in the most recent of the World Health Organization's International Classification of Diseases, ICD-9, the use of the term "alcoholism" was dropped altogether as a recommended diagnosis and the ADS concept was substituted (see INTERNATIONAL CLASSIFICATION OF DISEASES).

Hodgson was among the first to elaborate on this concept, and he defined the alcohol dependence syndrome according to the following factors: (1) loss of behavioral control, (2) psychosocial withdrawal symptoms, (3) increased tolerance to alcohol, (4) repeated withdrawal symptoms, (5) relief drinking, (6) compulsion to drink and (7) readdiction liability (Hodgson et al., 1978).

Advances in the sophistication of the construct have led to such diagnostic tools as the ALCOHOL DEPENDENCE SCALE developed by Skinner. As the concept is further refined, it is thought that clinicians will be able to plan individual treatment with a greater degree of appropriateness and success. (See also CLASSIFICATION OF ALCOHOLICS.)

R. Hodgson et al., "Alcohol Dependence: The Concept, Its Utility and Measurement," *British Journal of Addiction* 73 (1978): 339-342.

alcohol discharge rate   For a given hospital subpopulation or category, the alcohol discharge rate is the number of alcohol-related discharges divided by the total number of discharges multiplied by 100,000. (Discharge is the formal release of a patient from a hospital.) An alcohol discharge is classified by the National Center for Health Statistics as a discharge given to a person who has at least one of the following diseases: a type of alcoholic psychosis, such as DELIRIUM TREMENS, KORSAKOFF'S PSYCHOSIS, or other alcoholic hallucinosis, alcoholic paranoia or other, unspecified psychosis; CIRRHOSIS of the LIVER (alcohol); ALCOHOLISM manifested by episodic excessive drinking, habit-

Alcohol Discharge Rate by Age: United States, 1985

SOURCE: U.S. Department of Health and Human Services, National Institute on Alcohol Abuse and Alcoholism, *Hospital Discharges with Alcohol-Related Conditions* (Rockville, Md., 1989).

Alcohol Discharge Rate by Sex: United States, 1985

SOURCE: U.S. Department of Health and Human Services, National Institute on Alcohol Abuse and Alcoholism, *Hospital Discharges with Alcohol-Related Conditions* (Rockville, Md., 1989).

ual excessive drinking or alcoholic ADDIC-
TION or other, unspecified alcoholism; toxic
effect of ethyl alcohol; or acute or chronic
pancreatitis (see PANCREAS).

The alcohol discharge rate is a significant
index of alcohol abuse and alcoholism and,
when used in conjunction with other indices,
can be used to determine the approximate
alcoholic population at any given time. However, it has limitations: only those who have
gone for treatment are counted, and some
patients may go for more than one treatment.
The following graphs, compiled by the National Institute on Alcohol Abuse and Alcoholism, are based upon 223,000 sample
discharges from 511 short-stay nonfederal

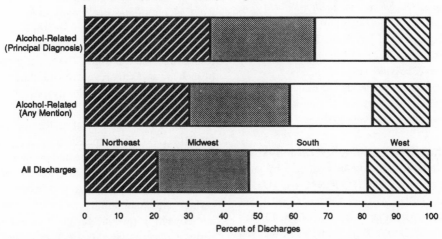

SOURCE: U.S. Department of Health and Human Services, National Institute on Alcohol Abuse
and Alcoholism, *Hospital Discharges with Alcohol-Related Conditions* (Rockville, Md., 1989).

SOURCE: U.S. Department of Health and Human Services, National Institute on Alcohol Abuse
and Alcoholism, *Hospital Discharges with Alcohol-Related Conditions* (Rockville, Md., 1989).

hospitals that mainly serve the civilian noninstitutionalized population.

U.S. Department of Health and Human Services, Utilization of Short-Stay Hospitals by Persons Discharged with Alcohol-Related Diagnoses, United States, 1976 (Hyattsville, Md., 1980), pp. 1-34.

U.S. Department of Health and Human Services, *Hospital Discharges with Alcohol-Related Conditions* (Rockville, Md.; 1989).

U.S. Department of Health and Human Services, *Hospital Discharges with Alcohol-Related Conditions* (Rockville, Md.; 1989).

U.S. Department of Health and Human Services, *Hospital Discharges with Alcohol-Related Conditions* (Rockville, Md.; 1989).

U.S. Department of Health and Human Services, *Hospital Discharges with Alcohol-Related Conditions* (Rockville, Md.; 1989).

Alcohol Epidemiologic Data System (AEDS)   Ongoing surveillance by such organizations as the NATIONAL INSTITUTE ON ALCOHOL ABUSE AND ALCOHOLISM (NIAAA), particularly its ALCOHOL EPIDEMIOLOGIC DATA SYSTEM (AEDS); the NATIONAL CENTER FOR HEALTH STATISTICS (NCHS); the Center for Disease Control (CDC); and the NATIONAL HIGHWAY TRAFFIC SAFETY ADMINISTRATION (NHTSA), provides a broad data base for analysis of patterns and trends in consumption, morbidity and mortality. In-depth, alcohol-related research is performed continually by scientists of various disciplines throughout the United States. Updated reviews also provide comprehensive bibliographies of alcohol-related epidemiologic research.

alcohol impairment   See   IMPAIRMENT.

alcohol intoxication   See INTOXICATION.

alcohol pathology   Any morbid physical damage caused by the direct or indirect effects of alcohol consumption. This term is sometimes used to refer to individual harm caused by the ABUSE of alcohol.

alcohol tolerance   See TOLERANCE.

alcoholic beverage   Any beverage containing alcohol. (See individual entries for WINE, BEER, GIN and other specific beverages.)

alcoholic beverage control laws (ABC laws)   Society's control of the availability of alcohol dates back many thousands of years. The Code of Hammurabi, for example, formulated almost 4,000 years ago, contained four articles on the topic. The usual purpose of such laws was to prevent the fraudulent sale of alcohol, to assure availability and to secure revenue for the state.

In the United States, after the repeal of PROHIBITION, the emphasis was changed to prevention of alcohol abuse and promotion of temperance. But gradually alcoholic beverage control agencies again became primarily concerned with maintaining an orderly market and collecting revenue for government treasuries. Concern over the effects of regulation on consumption gave way to questions about the impact of regulation on the economics of the industry. However, because of the recognition that in the past 40 years there has been an increase in per capita consumption of alcoholic beverages in conjunction with liberalized control laws (although decreases have been noted of late), more attention today is being paid to the possible preventative aspects of ABC laws. A debate has arisen in the field between those who believe that more stringent controls are necessary to curtail alcohol abuse and those who believe that these laws are not very effective and ignore the complex cultural, psychological, biological and social forces involved in problem drinking.

Supporters of increased legislation point to a number of studies that present evidence of a connection between an increase in the overall level of consumption in a population, the prevalence of heavy consumption and the rate of long-term health consequences of drinking, such as CIRRHOSIS. These findings, which show a direct relationship between the per capita consumption for all drinkers and the proportion of heavy users, seem to contradict the DISEASE CONCEPT, which holds that alcoholism affects only people who have some particular underlying physical or psychological problem. Studies in Norway, Finland, Canada and other nations have shown that when consumption of alcohol was suppressed (for instance, during a period of prohibition or a war), the rate of alcohol-related mortality and morbidity sharply decreased. Advocates of regulation feel that vulnerability to alcohol dependence is a widely shared trait. While controls on alcohol are not popular, supporters of regulation believe that it will result in a healthier life for those who might otherwise be addicted and thus promote individual freedom. They cite examples of governments intervening to safeguard public health in such areas as food, drugs and water.

Opponents of stricter restraints claim they will lead to increased costs for the state, resentment of the system by nonproblem drinkers, increased use of toxic substitutes by at least some heavy users of alcohol, and the growth of illicit alcohol trade with attendant criminality, expense and difficulties for law enforcement agencies, loss of revenue by producers, sellers and government, loss of respect for the law through widespread evasion, and loss or substantial reduction of personal benefits derived from alcohol use (Aldoory). Overly restrictive laws, they point out, work in opposition to primary prevention programs based on the promotion of responsible use of alcohol by individuals. Some suggest that educating the public and providing the information needed for responsible decisions about drinking are more effective measures than controlling availability.

A large number of agencies at the federal, state and local levels are responsible for making regulations and enforcing laws relating to drinking. Laws vary a great deal from state to state and from county to county within individual states. To date there has been little data on whether or not restrictions governing alcoholic beverage sales have any significant local effects.

In the United States there are two major types of control system: the monopoly system and the license system. Under the monopoly system the state operates all or part of the wholesale and retail sale of alcohol; under the license system the state creates a partial monopoly for private enterprises by restricting competition. Control is exercised through the threat of license revocation. Comparisons of the two systems have found few significant differences in the area of alcohol consumption and alcohol-related problems, but so far no study has been able to reach significant conclusions about the comparative effects of the two systems.

Outlets

The most frequently employed means of controlling availability throughout history has been regulation of the number of places where alcoholic beverages can be purchased. Particularly targeted have been outlets for on-premise consumption. There are two divergent opinions on the effects of controls on places permitted to sell alcohol: an increase in opportunities to drink results in more drinking and drunkenness; and a widespread availability will promote moderate and civilized drinking. Some studies have concluded that the prevalence of drunkenness is not dependent on the number of outlets, but this conclusion does not hold where there is either extremely low accessibility or where a low accessibility situation changes to one of high accessibility.

States also have regulations that specify the location and kind of outlet which can be operated, that require food to be served with alcohol, that allow only wine and beer to be served and so on. These regulations vary widely from area to area. Limits on closing time, which also vary, have been shown to affect the time when motor vehicle accidents occur, but total consumption and the frequency of consumption generally seem to remain unaffected by closing-hour regulations.

Early closing times may simply make the home a more attractive place in which to drink.

Age

States also regulate age limits. Since 1982, all states plus the District of Columbia have raised drinking ages from 18 to 21. Richard L. Douglass, senior researcher at the University of Michigan, found that after Michigan reduced the legal drinking age to 18 in 1972, alcohol-related casualties increased significantly for 18- to 20-year-olds. Total consumption of alcohol also rose. Michigan's drinking age has since been restored to 21. (See MINIMUM DRINKING AGE.)

Pricing and Taxation

The federal excise tax on liquor in the United States is $12.50 per gallon. Alcohol provides federal, state and local tax funds that totals $13.4 billion in 1987 for spirits, beer and wine combined, with distilled spirits alone accounting for $7.1 billion. Some support a doubling of the excise tax and use of the funds for the prevention and treatment of alcoholism. Regulation through pricing and taxation is unpopular with the public and the liquor industry. The price of alcohol influences alcohol consumption.

Other Controls

Other regulatory controls include laws prohibiting sales to obviously intoxicated persons (known as DRAM SHOP LAWS), laws governing DRIVING WHILE INTOXICATED and PUBLIC DRUNKENNESS and laws protecting the rights of alcoholics. (See also LEGAL ASPECTS OF ALCOHOL ABUSE.)

"Alcohol Controls Unfashionable but Necessary," *The U.S. Journal of Drug and Alcohol Dependence* 5, no. 9 (October 1981):8.

Shirley Aldoory, "ABC Laws: An Overview," *Alcohol Health and Research World* 4, no. 2 (Winter 1979-80):2-10.

Don Cahalan, *Understanding America's Drinking Problem* (San Francisco: Jossey-Bass, 1988), p. 81.

Richard L. Douglass, "The Legal Drinking Age and Traffic Casualties," *Alcohol Health and Research World* 4, no. 2, (Winter 1979-80):19-25.

John R. DeLuca, ed., *Fourth Special Report to the U.S. Congress on Alcohol and Health* (Rockville, Md.: National Institute on Alcohol Abuse and Alcoholism, 1981), pp. 105-107.

Ralph O. Lidman and Jean Shields, "Upping the User Ante," *Alcoholism* 2, no. 3 (January/February 1982):38-39.

David Joshua Pittman, *Primary Prevention of Alcohol Abuse and Alcoholism: An Evaluation of the Control of Consumption Policy* (St. Louis, Mo.: Social Science Institute, Washington University, 1980), passim.

Robin Room and James F. Mosher, "Out of the Shadow of Treatment: A Role for Regulatory Agencies in the Prevention of Alcohol Problems," *Alcohol Health and Research World* 4, no. 2 (Winter 1979-80):11-18.

alcoholic cirrhosis   See CIRRHOSIS.

alcoholic disease   Any disease, mental or physical, caused by the effects of excessive alcohol consumption, including CIRRHOSIS, DELIRIUM TREMENS, KORSAKOFF'S PSYCHOSIS. (See also DISEASES.)

alcoholic hepatitis   A disease of the liver characterized by inflammation and necrosis (cell death), alcoholic hepatitis can develop abruptly in alcoholics after a severe drinking bout. Its appearance may be accompanied by fever, jaundice and abnormal accumulation of fluid in the abdominal cavity. Fatty infiltration and increased FIBROSIS of the liver are frequent but not constant symptoms of this disease.

The mortality rate for those with severe alcoholic hepatitis is high, ranging from 10% to 30%. Some pass rapidly from alcoholic hepatitis to CIRRHOSIS and others recover normal liver function. Most in danger are alcoholics with few or no symptoms who continue to drink. Treatment of alcoholic hepatitis consists of bed rest, a high-protein diet and a multivitamin regimen.

Alcoholic hyaline, a clear glassy substance, is often found in the livers of patients with alcoholic hepatitis. Hyaline deposits may be a result of the degenerative effects of alcohol on subcellular structures called microtubules, which are important to the secretory activity of the liver cells.

alcoholic liver disease   A general category that encompasses a number of alcohol-induced liver diseases. The *Merck Manual* defines alcoholic liver disease as "a variety of syndromes and pathologic changes of the liver caused by alcohol." There is still some debate on exactly how alcohol damages the liver, but both nutritional factors (see NUTRITION) and direct toxicity are known to play a role. The development of alcoholic liver disease has been directly related to the quantity and duration of drinking, although there is a variation in the susceptibility of different individuals.

In its initial and milder form, alcoholic liver disease is characterized by an accumulation of excess fat on the liver, called, appropriately, FATTY LIVER. This is the most common disease of the liver found in hospitalized alcoholics. A more serious form of liver disease, which may or may not be linked with a fatty liver, is known as ALCOHOLIC HEPATITIS, which has a mortality rate ranging from 10% to 30%. This disease occurs when a number of liver cells die and cause inflammation.

The most severe form of liver injury is CIRRHOSIS, which is irreversible (though not always fatal). It is characterized by scarring of the liver with fibrous tissue and breakdown of the liver structure. While the progression from hepatitis to cirrhosis is generally accepted, the relationship between alcoholic fatty liver and alcoholic hepatitis and cirrhosis is still under debate. Not all alcoholics with fatty liver develop cirrhosis, and fat buildup is not always present with cirrhosis. However, fatty infiltration is frequently seen in association with more advanced alcoholic liver diseases, and

the ultrastructural changes found in the early stages of alcoholic fatty liver are identical to those evident in more severe alcoholic liver diseases.

There are a number of misconceptions concerning alcoholic liver disease. One is that liver damage must be accompanied by symptoms of illness after drinking. Another is that drinking is safe provided an individual does not have a physical DEPENDENCY on alcohol. Development of liver disease is directly related to the abuse of alcohol as measured by duration and dosage. Social drinking, particularly heavy drinking short of alcoholism (see HEAVY DRINKER), can result in damage to the liver. A third misconception is that cheap wine and liquor are more harmful to the liver than beer. The important factor is the amount of alcohol consumed. The toxic impurities that may be present in cheap alcoholic beverages are minute in relation to the ethanol content. The belief that an adequate diet will protect a heavy drinker from liver injury is also fallacious. While malnutrition may contribute to liver damage, many individuals with more than adequate diets have had severe liver disease.

It is essential that the diseased patient stop drinking alcohol. Much of alcoholic liver disease is completely reversible, and patients with a more advanced form of the disease who stop drinking have a better chance of survival than those who continue. This may be particularly true for women. A study conducted in 1977 in Britain showed that after five years 72% of male patients with alcoholic hepatitis or cirrhosis who continued to drink were alive but only 30% of female patients with those diseases who continued to drink were still alive.

In 1981 a team of researchers funded by the Addiction Research Foundation and headed by Dr. Yedy Israel found that when large amounts of alcohol are consumed over a long period of time, the individual liver cells expand, squeezing the fine blood vessels that form a network throughout the liver. This squeezing can block the flow of blood, causing stress on these vessels and can sometimes lead to rupture and internal bleeding. The researchers also suspect that the pressure of the swollen liver cells may trigger the formation of fibrous tissue around the blood vessels, which would prevent the exchange of materials between the bloodstream and liver cells. This presents a whole new concept of the cause of mortality from liver disease, because it suggests that it is the size of the liver cells and condition of the blood vessels that indicate the health of the organ, not the presence or absence of a diagnosed liver disease, such as cirrhosis or alcoholic hepatitis. This theory also offers some hope, for while cirrhosis is not reversible, the swelling of the cells and blood vessels is, provided the alcoholic stops drinking. Researchers are continuing their studies to determine why liver cells enlarge.

alcoholic muscle disease   See ALCO-HOLIC MYOPATHY.

alcoholic myopathy (alcoholic muscle disease)   A condition recognized only in the past 25 years, alcoholic myopathy is associated with changes in muscle tissue. Although the cause of the disease, which occurs in several forms, is unknown, it is clear that alcohol is the primary factor in its development. Generally, if the patient stops drinking, the prognosis for all forms of alcoholic myopathy is good, and improvement occurs even in the most severe cases.

Subclinical Myopathy

It has been estimated that subclinical myopathy affects more than one-third of the alcoholic population. Because patients with this disease may not complain of muscular symptoms, it is difficult to detect. Subclinical myopathy is indicated by increased levels of the enzyme creatine phosphokinase (CPK), which is considered to be of muscle cell origin, in the blood. In addition there is frequently a rise in lactic acid. Alcoholic patients may be otherwise asymptomatic, although

some may have a history of muscle cramps. Subclinical myopathy may progress to more severe forms of myopathy.

Acute Alcoholic Myopathy

This disease usually appears abruptly in chronic alcoholics. It is characterized by severe muscle cramps that vary in frequency or by muscle pain and swelling. The cramps usually occur in the arms and legs. Acute alcoholic myopathy is usually localized and relatively benign, and recovery is possible if the patient abstains from alcohol.

Chronic Alcoholic Myopathy

Associated with heavy drinking over many years, chronic alcoholic myopathy is a slowly progressive disease characterized by weakness and muscle atrophy, most often in the legs, although the symptoms may appear anywhere in the body. It can be alleviated if the patient abstains from alcohol.

alcoholic poisoning   An abnormal condition resulting from an extreme state of alcohol INTOXICATION, from which it differs only in degree. Dr. Mark Keller of the Rutgers Center of Alcohol Studies suggests that a BLOOD ALCOHOL CONCENTRATION above 0.4% indicates the occurrence of poisoning.

alcoholic polyneuropathy (peripheral neuritis)   (From *poly-* many + *neuro-* nerve + *-pathy* disease.) A disease of the nervous system, alcoholic polyneuropathy is thought to be caused by a thiamine deficiency, although its origin is still undetermined. It develops slowly, over months and years, affecting first and most severely the lower legs, where numbness and pain may develop. In some cases these symptoms are absent, and diagnosis is made on the basis of muscle wasting, tenderness of the calves of the legs and signs of impaired motor function. In time these symptoms may progress to the upper extremities as well. Partial recovery from this disease may take years and some permanent physical impairment is frequent.

alcoholic psychosis   Any mental disorder caused by the effects of alcohol consumption on the system, including DELIRIUM TREMENS, KORSAKOFF'S PSYCHOSIS and WERNICKE'S ENCEPHALOPATHY. (See also DISEASES.)

Alcoholic Treatment Center   (ATC)

Funded by the National Institute on Alcohol Abuse and Alcoholism, these centers offered treatment in three major settings: hospital, intermediate and outpatient. The system allowed DETOXIFICATION to be followed up by longer outpatient or halfway-house care. Having different modes of treatment in the same place enables a center to fit the type of treatment to the client's needs.

David J. Armor, J. Michael Polich and Harriet B. Stambul of the Rand Corporation Social Science Department divide the types of treatment into 10 major categories, as follows:

Hospital Setting

1. *Inpatient hospital:* traditional 24-hour service based on a medical model but often including psychotherapy.
2. *Partial hospitalization:* partial service that allows the patient to go home or to work at appropriate times.
3. *Detoxification:* a short "drying out" period for patients with serious toxic symptoms.

Intermediate Setting

4. *Halfway house:* living quarters and services, such as job counseling, psychotherapy etc., for patients who need extended care but do not require hospital treatment.
5. *Quarterway house:* similar to a halfway house but offering more intensive, often physical care under more structured conditions.

6. *Residential care:* living quarters but little or no other therapy.

Outpatient Setting

7. *Individual counseling:* treatment sessions given by a paraprofessional (someone without a graduate degree in psychology, medicine, social work or a similar relevant field).
8. *Individual therapy:* treatment sessions given by a professional.
9. *Group counseling:* group sessions given by a paraprofessional.
10. *Group therapy:* group sessions given by a professional.

Most clients at an ATC receive a combination of treatments. Usually hospital care is quite short and intermediate care extends over a much longer period.

David J. Armor, J. Michael Polich and Harriet B. Stambul, *Alcoholism and Treatment* (New York: John Wiley and Sons, 1978), pp. 124-126.

Alcoholics Anonymous (AA)   Alcoholics Anonymous is an international nonprofessional organization of alcoholics devoted to the maintenance of the sobriety of its members through self-help and mutual support; it was founded in the United States in 1935. The organization defines its purpose as follows:

Alcoholics Anonymous is a fellowship of men and women who share their experience, strength and hope with each other that they may solve their common problem and help others to recover from alcoholism.

The only requirement for membership is a desire to stop drinking. There are no dues or fees for AA membership; we are self-supporting through our own contributions. AA is not allied with any sect, denomination, politics, organization or institution; does not wish to engage in any controversy, neither endorses nor opposes any causes. Our primary purpose is to stay sober and help other alcoholics to achieve sobriety.

This "desire to stop drinking" is at the core of the AA program. Membership in a group is voluntary but AA groups, despite their loose organizational structure and concern for anonymity, are remarkably cohesive and able to provide substantial support for (or exert strong pressure on) members in order to maintain their SOBRIETY and ensure continued attendance at meetings. (For this purpose, as in many other areas, AA has a slogan: "Don't drink and go to meetings.")

A new member is asked if he has admitted to himself that he is "powerless over alcohol" and if he is ready to accept his problem. "Surrender" is a word often used in this regard, not in the sense of capitulating to the influence of alcohol or alcoholism but of surrendering to the fact that he cannot cope with alcohol and that he must stop pretending that he can (see DENIAL).

New members are urged to come to 90 meetings in 90 days, a crash program designed to provide maximum support during what is regarded as a dangerous time. They are exhorted to immerse themselves thoroughly in AA participation and are warmly received for having admitted past pride and failure. They are led to recognize their need for AA and to embrace its principles enthusiastically. Skepticism, questioning of AA methods and stories about those who have stayed sober without the help of AA are discouraged.

Each new member is urged to select a "sponsor," an experienced AA member in whom the newly sober beginner can confide on a continuing, individual basis. Members often contact their sponsor on a daily basis, seeking advice or, of even more immediate importance, asking for help when the temptation to drink becomes intense. Another form of AA counseling is known as "twelve-stepping." Two AA members—always two to provide mutual support—will visit someone who is drinking, either a member or nonmember, and try to persuade him to seek help, which may or may not include medical help and professional therapy. The ultimate goal is to bring the individual into, or back into, AA and into sobriety.

Meetings are generally informal sessions. After customary business, announcements and voluntary collections are taken care of, a speaker addresses the group on some aspect of alcoholism, usually from an autobiographical point of view. The talk is followed by a period in which those who wish to be heard have an opportunity to speak. Sometimes all or part of the meeting is run like an "Australian meeting," in which everyone in attendance is called upon to either speak or "pass."

Living "the AA way" includes not only regular attendance at meetings and close contact with one's sponsor but a relationship with the "higher power." In the early days of AA (and in the Twelve Steps), this higher power was identified as God ("as you understand Him"). However, as AA has grown to include those whose religious beliefs range from strict fundamentalism to atheism, the concept of the higher power has been broadened, for some members, to include a rather general sense of spirituality or some spiritual resource within

Estimated Drug Addiction Members of Alcoholics Anonymous
(1986)

	Those 30 Yrs. or Less	Those Coming to A.A. Since Last Survey	Total Sample
Women	n/a	n/a	46%
Men	n/a	n/a	37%
All	n/a	n/a	38%
(1980)			
Women	63%	35%	34%
Men	51%	24%	20%
All	55%	27%	24%
(1977)			
Women	55%	29%	28%
Men	36%	15%	14%
All	43%	19%	18%

SOURCE: General Service Office, Alcoholics Anonymous.

Alcoholics Anonymous Membership

	Reported Membership of U.S. and Canadian Groups	Size of Sample
1968	170,000	11,355
1971	210,000	7,194
1974	331,000	13,467
1977	404,000	15,163
1980	476,000	24,950
1988	916,782	n/a

SOURCE: General Service Office, Alcoholics Anonymous.

the individual. For others this new concept of the higher power has been extended to an entity outside of the normal religious organizations, such as a therapy group or, particularly, AA itself.

The AA member is encouraged to keep his problem as simple as possible and to avoid blowing it up to unmanageable proportions. He does not promise to stop drinking for all time but to "stay away from just one drink for just one day at a time." This stress on simplicity is reflected in the variety of slogans—"easy does it," "first things first," "stick to the program"—designed to help the alcoholic stay out of situations that might hurt him or cause him anxiety or anger. New members are urged not to make serious changes in their lives, except in the case of those aspects that would endanger their sobriety if continued. Major career changes, possibly stressful new relationships with the opposite sex and situations where alcohol is served or even available are to be avoided. The new member is encouraged to focus his social activity on AA and, whenever possible, to place strict limits on his outside social contacts. At the end of each successful day, he is urged to thank his higher power.

AA and Its Critics

Within AA there is mistrust, sometimes considerable, of professionals and others who work with alcoholics outside the organization. It is felt that professionals who are not alcoholics do not know what alcoholism is really about. Even professionals who are themselves alcoholics are sometimes resented for failing to recognize that the only successful cure for alcoholism is AA.

The organization views alcoholism as a permanent state that can only be controlled, not corrected. The heavy emphasis placed upon this philosophy promotes a prolonged, even permanent group dependency. All life situations are recast in terms of a member's sobriety or alcoholism. A preoccupation with nondrinking is substituted for a preoccupation with drinking. For example, *The Grapevine,* AA's monthly publication in the United States, is filled with jokes about the stupidity of people in a drunken state. Simple formulas and slogans, supplemented by an abundant variety of AA literature, are used to combat negative feelings that may lead to a resumption of drinking. Perhaps most important is the emphasis on the AA "program" centered around "doing the steps"—the Twelve Steps (see box). This progress, from one step to another, is the essence of the program and entire meetings are often devoted to the study and analysis of one of the steps. Doing the steps gives the AA member a sense of participation and progress.

Critics have pointed out that this ingrown aspect of AA can lead to conflict in the mind of the member. Alcoholics Anonymous not only helps maintain sobriety—it *is* sobriety and, without it, sobriety is unattainable. The individual may not learn to cope with his disease or gain self-reliance because the program encourages dependency and discourages outside interests that would in any way diminish the central place of AA in the life of the member. Even the name—Alcoholics *Anonymous*—diminishes individual identity. (At meetings, members traditionally identify themselves as follows: "Hello. My name is [first name], and I'm an alcoholic.") The anonymity was originally justified as a way of protecting members against a society hostile to alcoholics and accustomed to discriminating against them. Even with more widespread acceptance of alcoholism as a disease, there is still some hostility and discrimination today. But in the eyes of its critics, AA perpetuates itself by maintaining this gulf; by stripping members of their names and, hence, their identities and leaving them with only the label "alcoholic," AA increases their dependence on the organization. Since there is no known cure for alcoholism and since AA does not consider itself a treatment program with an eventual end, the "fellowship" is therefore permanent and self-perpetuating. Dropping out is, in the eyes of many AA members, almost tantamount to the resumption of drinking. Nevertheless relatively few members remain in AA for 10 years or more.

Alcohol is seen as the alcoholic's "solution" to an uncomfortable state. This discomfort stems from a sense of failure caused by unrealistic goals and expectations and, often, a tendency to fantasize. The inevitable failures lead to a loss of self-esteem and then to uncontrolled drinking. This view is not unique to AA, but others feel that to focus exclusively on this aspect of a problem that is broader oversimplifies it.

There are other criticisms of AA. Meetings have been called exclusionary and their tone conventional and middle class; to some they are offensively inspirational and anti-intellectual.

However, most critics recognize the success that Alcoholics Anonymous has had. While pointing out that neither the achievements nor failures of AA can be proven because there are no membership records to document them, they agree that the organization helps and sustains large numbers of alcoholics who would otherwise be without support or hope.

History

The history of AA begins with the story, raised almost to the level of myth, of its founder, Bill Wilson, or, as he came to be known, Bill W. Born in 1895 and raised in a broken home, Wilson found that alcohol relaxed him socially and gave him a new sense of freedom. After a brief stint in the Army and marriage, Wilson went to work on Wall Street, where he had some success. He gradually became an alcoholic and later described the years from 1930 to 1934 as an "alcoholic hell." In 1934 an old drinking friend who had sobered up introduced him to the Oxford Group, headed by the Episcopal clergyman Dr. Samuel Shoemaker. The nondenominational group stressed the importance of taking stock of oneself, confessing one's defects and a willingness to make up for past wrongs. A member also could choose his own concept of God or a "higher power." It is easy to see in these principles many of the ideas that form the basis of AA.

After attending a meeting, Wilson decided to try to dry out. He went back to his doctor, Dr. Robert Silkworth, who had dried him out several times before. Silkworth, somewhat ahead of his time, believed alcoholism was a disease and a hopeless one. He described it as an "obsession of the mind that condemns one to drink and an allergy of the body that condemns one to die." This idea of alcoholism as a disease became an important concept in AA. Wilson sank into a profound depression during his sobering up process and subsequently had a "conversion" experience. From his experience grew the idea of the hopelessness of the condition of alcoholism, "hitting bottom" as a prerequisite for changing, experiencing a conversion (this is not stressed in AA, though there is a conversion from drinking to sobriety) and realizing the importance of interaction with others, which had first impressed Wilson when his newly sober friend came to talk to him.

Wilson joined the Oxford Group and tried preaching his theories to other alcoholics with no appreciable results. On a business trip to Akron, Wilson met another member of the group, Dr. Bob (Dr. Robert Holbrook Smith), an alcoholic who was still drinking. Wilson told his story, without preaching, and stressed the disease aspect of alcoholism. Dr. Bob sobered up and Alcoholics Anonymous was founded, although not formally under that name. (AA dates its "birth" as June 10, 1935, Dr. Bob's first day of "permanent sobriety.") Wilson and Dr. Bob began talking to alcoholics in Akron. Later Wilson returned to New York and continued work there. He and his followers eventually split from the Oxford Group, rejecting their notions of absolutism and aggressive evangelism. In 1939 a third group was formed in Cleveland. At the time membership was about 100.

In 1938 and 1939 Wilson put together a collection of articles that generally reflected the ideas which formed the basis of the fledgling organization. Published by AA and entitled *Alcoholics Anonymous,* it has been more commonly referred to as "the Big Book." In the process Wilson developed the Twelve Steps for recovery. The book also contained case histories of recovered members. Although it did not do well at first, it gradually gained publicity and sales increased. (As of December 31, 1981 the book had sold 3,171,654 copies.) For some the Big Book has been the basic textbook of AA, for others almost a bible. Different conflicts among the groups, such as those related to religious status, organization, and anonymity, were resolved, and certain practices were formalized in 1946 in the Twelve Traditions (see box). Headquarters were established in New York, and AA began publishing books and a monthly magazine, *The Grapevine.* In 1958 there were 6,000 groups with about 150,000 members; by 1988, there were 85,270 groups worldwide, with 1,734,734 members reported.

Organization

AA is incorporated as a nonprofit organization run by two operating bodies, AA World Services, Inc. and the AA Grapevine, Inc., which are responsible to a board of trustees. Each year there is a conference attended by 91 delegates from AA areas in the United States and Canada; the trustees; the directors of World Services, Inc., and the Grapevine, Inc.; and the staff of the General Service Office and *The Grapevine* in New York.

On the local level, group organization is kept to a minimum, generally a few officers who arrange programs for meetings and maintain contact with the General Service Office. In all AA organizations responsibility for leading groups is rotated.

New groups are started where there is a demand, usually by an experienced member who helps with the initial setting-up process.

Meetings

All AA meetings are open to all alcoholics, whether or not they have ever attended a previous meeting. "Open" meetings are open to everyone, alcoholics and nonalcoholics. "Closed" meetings are limited to alcoholics only so that members will feel more free to discuss particularly difficult or intimate problems. "Step" meetings are conducted like study groups, devoted to one of the Twelve Steps. They are less spontaneous than other meetings and members are encouraged to prepare themselves beforehand.

Leadership of meetings is often self-perpetuating, since leaders are usually chosen from a nucleus of those who have successfully maintained sobriety for a long time and who are willing to serve. (Length of sobriety is of major importance in AA and anniversaries of the date when a member first became sober are important events and are celebrated at appropriate meetings, often accompanied by a small party. Conversely, if a member resumes drinking, he loses all seniority and his sobriety begins from scratch, no matter how many years of previous sobriety he may have achieved.)

Speakers at AA meetings are usually drawn from within the group itself or from other groups—seldom from outside AA. Often members of one group will hold meetings for members of another group.

Membership

The membership of AA is primarily middle aged, middle class, married, white and male. The percentage of women is rising, however, from 22% in 1968, to 31% in 1980, and to 34% in 1986. During the same period the number of members 30 years and younger increased from 11.3% to 21%. Along with the increase in these two populations there was a growth in the number of members addicted to another drug besides alcohol: 18% in 1977 to 24% in 1980 and 34% in 1986.

Only 5% to 10% of the alcoholics in the United States use AA. The organization does not estimate its success rate, but some studies claim success for about 50% to 60% of the alcoholics who use it.

The Twelve Steps

The Twelve Steps stress reliance on a higher power, humility, honest admission of wrongdoing and response to spiritual awakening by sharing with others. The first step involves the idea of despair and a breakdown of denial concerning alcohol. Second is the idea of hope, or seeing the light. Third, acceptance of the incurability of alcoholism is made, and dependence on a higher power is stressed. The next steps involve making amends, continuing confirmation of a new image of oneself and redirecting energy to help others. Much emphasis is put on this 12th step, since in the history of AA it was Bill W.'s carrying of the message to Dr. Bob that saved both of them and made the founding of AA possible. Thus attempts by AA members to help individuals who are drinking are known as "twelve-stepping."

The Twelve Traditions

The Twelve Traditions specify that the unity of AA is paramount, that leaders serve but not govern, that all who desire help be accepted as members, and that groups are autonomous. The AA message is to be spread, but other enterprises are not endorsed and no sides are taken in controversies. Groups are self-supporting and nonprofessional, with as

---

THE TWELVE STEPS
OF
ALCOHOLICS ANONYMOUS

1. We admitted we were powerless over alcohol—that our lives had become unmanageable.

2. Came to believe that a Power greater than ourselves could restore us to sanity.

3. Made a decision to turn our will and our lives over to the care of God *as we understood him.*

4. Made a searching and fearless moral inventory of ourselves.

5. Admitted to God, to ourselves, and to another human being the exact nature of our wrongs.

6. Were entirely ready to have God remove all these defects of character.

7. Humbly asked Him to remove our shortcomings.

8. Made a list of all persons we had harmed, and became willing to make amends to them all.

9. Made direct amends to such people whenever possible, except when to do so would injure them or others.

10. Continued to take personal inventory and when we were wrong promptly admitted it.

11. Sought through prayer and meditation to improve our conscious contact with God *as we understood Him,* praying only for knowledge of His will for us and the power to carry that out.

12. Having had a spiritual awakening as a result of these steps, we tried to carry this message to alcoholics, and to practice these principles in all our affairs.

WATERLOO HIGH SCHOOL LIBRARY
1464 INDUSTRY RD.
ATWATER, OHIO 44201

THE TWELVE TRADITIONS
OF
ALCOHOLICS ANONYMOUS

1. Our common welfare should come first; personal recovery depends upon AA unity.

2. For our group purpose there is but one ultimate authority—a loving God as He may express Himself in our group conscience. Our leaders are but trusted servants; they do not govern.

3. The only requirement for AA membership is a desire to stop drinking.

4. Each group should be autonomous except in matters affecting other groups or AA as a whole.

5. Each group has but one primary purpose—to carry its message to the alcoholic who still suffers.

6. An AA group ought never endorse, finance, or lend the AA name to any related facility or outside enterprise, lest problems of money, property, and prestige divert us from our primary purpose.

7. Every AA group ought to be fully self-supporting, declining outside contributions.

8. Alcoholics Anonymous should remain forever nonprofessional, but our service centers may employ special workers.

9. AA, as such, ought never be organized; but we may create service boards or committees directly responsible to those they serve.

10. Alcoholics Anonymous has no opinions on outside issues; hence the AA name ought never to be drawn into public controversy.

11. Our public relations policy is based on attraction rather than promotion; we need always maintain personal anonymity at the level of press, radio, and films.

12. Anonymity is the spiritual foundation of all our Traditions, ever reminding us to place principles before personalities.

little formal organization as possible. Personal ambition is discouraged and anonymity is protected. However, anonymity is not required on a personal level or in small groups.

Alcoholics Anonymous World Services, *Alcoholics Anonymous,* 3rd ed. (New York, 1978).

General Service Office of Alcoholics Anonymous, *Analysis of the 1988 Survey of the Membership of AA,* 1989.

Margaret Bean, "Alcoholics *Anonymous," Psychiatric Annals* 5, no. 3 (March 1975), pp. 3-64.

Ernest Kurtz, *Not-God: A History of Alcoholics Anonymous,* (Center City, Minn.: Hazelden Educational Services, 1979).

Robert Thomsen, *Bill W.* (New York: Popular Library, 1975).

alcoholism   A chronic disorder associated with excessive consumption of alcohol over a period of time. There has been a continuing discussion over the cause, nature and characteristics of this disorder and, consequently, a variety of definitions. Most authorities recognize alcoholism as a "disease," although this position has been challenged in some medical circles on the ground that a self-inflicted condition cannot properly be designated a disease. Others challenge the assumption that a unitary disease concept can account for the range and variety of alcohol-related problems. (See ALCOHOL DEPENDENCE SYNDROME.)

The earliest known use of the term "alcoholism" was by a Swedish scientist, Magnus Huss of Stockholm. Huss published a treatise, *Chronische Alkohols-Krankheit* ("Chronic Alcohol Disease," Sweden, 1849. Germany, 1852), in which he identified a condition involving abuse of alcohol and labeled it *Alkoholismus chronicus.* However, the disease concept of alcoholism is much older. References to it have been found in the works of the

18th century American physician Benjamin Rush, Chaucer and the Roman philosopher Seneca. Perhaps the first official recognition of alcoholism as a disease was a resolution by the American Medical Association in 1956. This landmark resolution, along with a similar one by the American Bar Association, has had a profound impact upon alcoholism-related state and federal laws, program financing, insurance coverage and hospital admissions policies, and the legal status of alcoholics.

A number of groups oppose the acceptance of alcoholism as a disease. Certain religious groups, particularly fundamentalist Protestants, continue to view alcoholism as drunkenness and, therefore, a "sin." Some social scientists believe the term "alcoholism" inadequately describes a social dysfunction. They claim that to call it a disease is to label it nothing more than a medical-psychiatric problem and that the medical approach is constricted and, often, ineffective. The counter argument is that the solution to the problem, if there is one, is not to reject the medical-psychiatric approach but to supplement it.

There are a variety of other arguments against the disease concept: alcoholism cannot be a disease because there is no anatomic structural abnormality; irresponsible persons will abuse the legal and medical benefits given them as "sick" people; alcoholism is a label that stigmatizes patients; the symptoms of alcoholism vary so widely that they defy definition as a disease; the concept dignifies and excuses drunkenness; the concept does not satisfactorily deal with a wide variety of categories, including heavy drinking nonalcoholics, borderline alcoholics, periodic alcoholics etc.

(Since this entire encyclopedia is devoted to alcoholism, every article in it deals directly or indirectly with the subject. However, there are several articles that may be particularly useful in their coverage of the concepts and aspects of alcoholism: ADDICTION, DEPENDENCY, DISEASES, DISEASE CONCEPT, ETIOLOGICAL THEORIES OF ALCOHOLISM, INABILITY TO ABSTAIN, LOSS OF CONTROL, RELEASE, RELIGION, TOLERANCE.)

alcoholism in industry   See EMPLOYEE ASSISTANCE PROGRAMS.

alcoholist   Although rarely used in the United States, the term is common in some Scandinavian countries, where it is generally employed to refer to a person whose drinking results in abuse of alcohol. The definition of the term varies; it is used to denote both an alcoholic and a person who uses alcoholic beverages but is not an alcoholic.

alcoolisation   A term used by the French to describe a pattern of large daily consumption of alcohol with harmful effects on health and a shortening of the life span but without the development of either physical or psychological DEPENDENCE.

alcoolist   A term used by the French to describe someone who drinks daily and heavily to the extent that his or her life span may be shortened but who is not physically or psychologically dependent upon alcohol.

ale   A beer brewed by TOP FERMENTATION that has a more bitter taste and a slightly higher alcohol content than lager beer. The name is derived from the Old Norwegian *ol* and has been transformed by English dialectical usage. In Britain ale and beer are synonymous; elsewhere ale has a variety of popular usages not strictly related to beers or malt liquors produced by top fermentation.

Fermentation of ale in Britain, the country with which it has been traditionally associated, was a common practice by the time of the Roman invasions during the first century A.D. At that time, however, ale was less popular than fermented meads and ciders, both of which were more easily produced by the predominantly nomadic inhabitants. The Roman influence encouraged permanent settlements, which had the effect of encouraging permanent *tabernae,* or alehouses, where fermented malt liquors were both produced and sold. The Anglo-Saxon invasion in the fifth century brought Britain under the control of a people already familiar with brewing techniques, and it was at this point that ale first became a prominent feature of daily British life.

Thereafter ale became the subject of early legal legislation in Britain. The first alehouses in the country to be licensed were those authorized during the reign of King Edgar, who ruled until 975. By 1100 Henry II had levied the first taxes on malt liquor, the term by which ale was then known, and by 1300 Richard II had required all licensed alehouses to display identifying signs. The first brewery to receive a royal charter was the City Brewing Company of London, which was given its commission in 1437 and retained an official monopoly on ale production for some time. However, most ale brewing remained a cottage industry, one presided over by women, who closely oversaw the drawn-out fermentation process. The product was a beer brewed exclusively from malt barley and commonly mixed with spices to counteract its extremely sweet taste. As one dietary book of 1542 noted, "Ale is made of malt and water; and they the which do put any other thing to ale than rehersed ... doth sofysticate their ale."

A major change in ale brewing came in the late 16th century, when hops were first imported from Bavaria to flavor the sweet brew produced by grains and natural sugars. Hops, or the female flowers of the *Humulus lupus* vine, probably arrived in Britain via Flemish immigrants to Kent during the reign of King Henry VIII. Since that time they have remained an essential ingredient in the mash from which ale is brewed. Their use was first exploited by the large family brewers, such as the Whitbreads, the Barclays and the Courages, who for a time competed with the brewers chartered by the crown and have since replaced them.

Because of top fermentation true ale is generally more bitter and "heavier" to the taste than lager beer, which is made by BOTTOM FERMENTATION. This process employs a dif-ferent yeast than that used in bottom fermentation, and takes place at higher temperatures and for a shorter period of time than the lager-making process. Today three principal types of ale are produced commercially in Britain. Mild ale is generally dark and very "hoppy" in taste; pale ale is lighter in color and drier in taste; and bitter, the most common type, is a compromise between the other two in both appearance and taste.

allergy   The question of whether alcoholism can be due to an allergy to alcohol has been raised at various times in the past, most notably by William D. Silkworth of the Charles B. Towns Hospital, a drying out facility in New York, in 1937. Silkworth's theory that alcoholism was due to an allergy to alcohol was published in ALCOHOLICS ANONYMOUS literature, and AA still uses it as part of the explanation of alcoholism. However, there is no medical evidence to support such a theory. While a person may be allergic to some constituent of an alcoholic beverage, such as a CONGENER, the American Medical Association states, "There is no similarity between the signs and symptoms of alcoholism and those of known allergies."

Alpha alcoholism   The first of five categories of alcoholism defined by JELLINEK. "*Alpha alcoholism* represents a *purely* psychological *continual dependence* or reliance upon the effect of alcohol to relieve bodily or emotional pain." Alpha alcoholism does not lead to LOSS OF CONTROL, and the damage it causes may be limited to a disturbance in the subject's family and/or social relationships. There are no WITHDRAWAL effects and no signs of a progressive process. Alpha alcoholism is not an illness per se, but it signifies some other underlying disturbance. Alpha alcoholism can develop into GAMMA ALCOHOLISM, but it is often seen for years without any signs of progression. Alpha alcoholism is sometimes known as problem drinking, but that term is also used to indicate physical dependence upon alcohol (PROBLEM DRINKER).

American Indians   Alcoholic beverages were unknown in most of North America before the arrival of the European colonists, although some Indians made alcohol from corn and cactus to use for spiritual purposes. White people utilized alcohol to enhance their treaty-making and trading sessions with the Indians and as an item of exchange. The practice of intoxicating the Indians and then cheating them out of their land and goods became so serious that tribal leaders themselves requested the enactment of federal laws to prohibit the sale of alcoholic beverages to Indians. These laws, passed in 1832, not only banned the sale of liquor to the Indians but made it illegal for them to be seen drinking in public; they remained in effect until 1953. Today 408 out of 482 tribes still prohibit the sale of liquor or other alcoholic beverages on their reservations.

It is not known how many Indians drink, since the population is diverse and scattered around the country—on reservations, in cities and in nonreservation rural areas. Therefore figures on Indian drinking are generally estimates and are not precise.

At present alcoholism is probably the number one health problem among Indians and Alaskans. In 1988, accidental injuries, chronic liver disease and CIRRHOSIS, homicide and suicide were the 10 leading causes of death among Indians and Alaskan Natives (Indian Health Services, 1988). These causes of death are almost certainly reflective of wide-ranging alcohol related problems. From 1984 to 1986 the suicide rate for Indians age 15 to 24 was almost twice the national rate for that age group, and in 1985 the homicide rate for Indians age 24 to 44 was nearly twice the national rate. In 1988, 28% of all Indian and Alaskan native arrests were due to drunkenness or driving-while-intoxicated (Indian Health Service). The proportion of convictions for driving-while-intoxicated (DWI) among Indi-

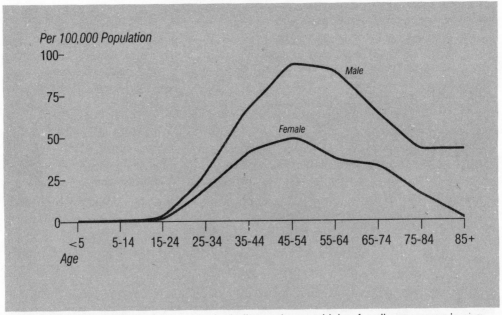

Alcoholism Death Rates by Age and Sex: 1984–86
Indians and Alaska Natives

The age-specific alcoholism death rate for Indian males was higher for all age groups in comparison to Indian females. The Indian male rate ranged from 63.1 to 90.6 deaths per 100,000 population for age groups 35 through 74.
SOURCE: Indian Health Service, *Trends in Indian Health, 1989*, U.S. Department of Health and Human Services.

Alcoholism Mortality Rates by Age and Sex

	Indian & Alaska Native		
	Both Sexes	Male	Female
Under 5 years	—	—	—
5–14 years	—	—	—
15–24 years	0.9	1.2	0.6
25–34 years	22.4	27.4	17.6
35–44 years	52.9	66.6	40.1
45–54 years	68.3	90.6	47.7
55–64 years	61.2	88.5	36.6
65–74 years	46.1	63.1	32.1
75–84 years	25.3	39.9	14.0
85 years +	16.7	42.0	0.0

	U.S. All Races		
	Both Sexes	Male	Female
Under 5 years	—	—	—
5–14 years	—	—	—
15–24 years	0.1	0.2	0.0
25–34 years	2.5	3.4	1.5
35–44 years	8.2	12.4	4.2
45–54 years	16.3	24.6	8.6
55–64 years	21.1	33.7	9.9
65–74 years	17.1	28.4	8.3
75–84 years	8.7	17.7	3.3
85 years +	2.7	6.1	1.3

	U.S. Other than White		
	Both Sexes	Male	Female
Under 5 years	—	—	—
5–14 years	—	—	—
15–24 years	0.2	0.2	0.2
25–34 years	6.9	9.1	4.8
35–44 years	22.8	35.7	11.9
45–54 years	33.8	53.3	17.7
55–64 years	34.9	57.7	16.3
65–74 years	24.6	41.8	11.7
75–84 years	9.5	18.4	3.7
85 years +	7.7	16.9	3.2

NOTE:—represents zero.
American Indians and Alaska Natives, 1984–1986 and U.S. All Races, 1985
Rate per 100,000 Population
SOURCE: Indian Health Service, *Trends in Indian Health 1989,* U.S. Department of Health and Human Services, 1989.

Age-Adjusted Alcoholism Death Rates: 1984–86
Indians and Alaskan Natives

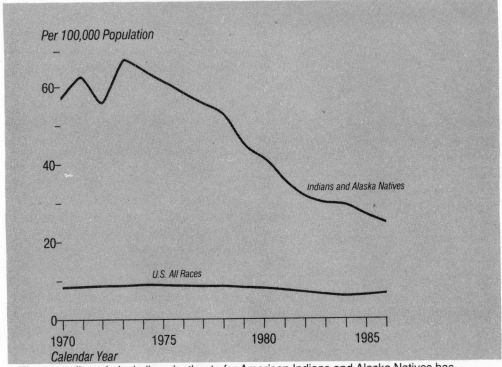

The age-adjusted alcoholism death rate for American Indians and Alaska Natives has decreased 63% since its peak in 1973 of 66.1 deaths per 100,000 population. In 1986, the Indian rate was still 3.8 times the rate for U.S. All Races, 24.6 compared to 6.4.
SOURCE: Indian Health Service, *Trends in Indian Health, 1989*, U.S. Department of Health and Human Services

ans in Los Angeles County was seven times greater than the proportion of Indian drivers in the county. On a reservation in Maine, 47% of all deaths over a 20-year period were alcohol related, and every Indian in the state prison was there for an alcohol-related offense.

The proportion of Indians arrested for drunkenness in 1982 far exceeded the drunkenness arrest rates of all other ethnic groups. The mortality rate from cirrhosis among Indians was nearly three times the national average in 1986 and accidental deaths (often alcohol related) of Indians are more than double the national average. It has been estimated that 30% of the male Indian population and 15% of the female Indian population may be alcoholic (Jones). From 1984 to 1986 Indians

age 25 to 34 experienced alcoholism mortality rates that were nine times the national average; age 35 to 44, six times the national average; and age 45 to 54, four times the national average. These figures show a marked improvement from the late 1970s, when (in 1976 to 1978) the alcoholism mortality rate for Indians age 25 to 34 was 23 times the national average.

For Indians the overall alcohol discharge rate (ADR) from Indian Health Service and contract general hospitals is three times higher than the U.S. all-races ADR and double the U.S. other-than-white ADR.

There have been numerous attempts to explain why the problem of alcoholism is so great among American Indians, and in these

Alcoholism Deaths and Mortality Rates

Calendar Year	Indian & Alaska Native		U.S. All Races		Ratio Indian to U.S. All Races
	Number	Rate	Number	Rate	
1986	272	24.6	15,525	6.4	3.8
1985	281	26.1	15,844	6.2	4.2
1984	316	30.0	15,706	6.2	4.8
1983	293	28.9	15,424	6.1	4.7
1982	298	30.7	15,596	6.4	4.8
1981	338	35.8	16,745	7.0	5.2
1980	382	41.3	17,742	7.5	5.5
1979	398	45.1	17,064	7.4	6.1
1978	437	54.5	18,490	8.1	6.7
1977	429	55.5	18,437	8.3	6.7
1976	425	58.2	18,484	8.6	6.8
1975	403	62.2	18,190	8.6	7.2
1974	417	64.2	18,530	8.6	7.5
1973	399	66.1	17,791	8.6	7.7
1972	315	55.0	17,484	8.6	6.4
1971	334	62.9	16,891	8.4	7.5
1970	272	56.2	16,180	8.1	6.9
1969	267	56.6	15,138	7.7	7.4

NOTE: For 1969–1978 includes deaths due to alcoholism, alcoholic psychoses and cirrhosis of the liver with mention of alcoholism. For 1979 and after includes deaths due to alcohol dependence syndrome, alcoholic psychoses and chronic liver disease and cirrhosis, specified as alcoholic. Population estimation methodology for the American Indian and Alaska Native population revised in 1976. Maine, New York and Pennsylvania included as Reservation States beginning in 1979, Connecticut, Rhode Island and Texas in 1983 and Alabama in 1984. Decennial Census population counts used for 1970 and 1980.
American Indians and Alaska Natives and U.S. All Races, 1969–1986
Age-Adjusted
Rate per 100,000 Population
SOURCE: Indian Health Service, *Trends in Indian Health, 1989,* U.S. Department of Health and Human Services, 1989.

attempts there has been a tendency to ignore the diversity of the population. North American Indians comprise a large number of distinct peoples with unique cultures and world views. There are several myths about Indian drinking, such as that once an Indian has tasted liquor he has an uncontrollable craving for it. No proof exists that the psychological or physiological reactions of Indians to alcohol are different than those of other racial groups. While genetic differences may exist, there is thus far no conclusive evidence of differences in ethanol metabolism by racial group. However, the pattern of drinking among Indians is generally either very heavy or abstinent, and the Indians themselves are concerned about their problems with drinking.

Several reasons have been suggested to explain the high incidence of alcoholism among American Indians. The way in which Indians were introduced to alcohol may have contributed to the way in which they drink, often rapidly and excessively. (Because of variations in the supply of game from hunting and the constraints of frequent intertribal wars, many tribes consumed food in similar ways— at feasts during which large quantities were eaten in one sitting.) In the Passamaquoddy Indian language no words or phrases exist to describe social or moderate drinking. There are only terms to describe someone on a drinking binge—*sputsuwin*—or someone who is habitually drunk—*kotuhsomuin*—(Stevens).

Because alcohol was an entirely new factor in Indian society, with no external controls or socially established norms for its use, its destructive powers were not fully perceived at first. Furthermore drinking was encouraged by the traders. When Indians were later prohibited from drinking, they had to gulp quickly to avoid being seen. The laws against drinking also created a fatalistic attitude towards alcohol—"If it is prohibited to me, it must be because I have no control."

Indians generally do not condemn the drinkers among them, as they believe a drunk person is not himself and, therefore, not responsible for his behavior. Consequently Indians are often unwilling to testify against someone accused of committing a crime while drunk, creating problems for law enforcement officials. There is also heavy peer pressure to drink, and as with food, it is polite to share alcohol and to accept what is offered. Abstainers are sometimes accused of trying to be better than the rest.

The main cause of drinking problems among American Indians is probably sociocultural stress. There is a lack of identification with the ways of white society and a rejection of its goals. Indian traditions have been weakened and family relations have been disturbed; the elderly no longer have the same prestige and guiding role they once held. Indians experience strong feelings of powerlessness and anxiety because of conflicts between their ways and the ways of the white man. They have been placed on reservations, their religions and cultures have been undermined and their children have been placed in schools where they learn non-Indian traditions. Drink tends to loosen tribal social constraints and to blur the differences between Indian and white culture.

Drinking begins early, sometimes as early as age 10. Indian children are often raised on a reservation in one culture until school age, when they are sent to boarding school, where they must give up that style of life. The most problematic age is between 15 and 25, when adolescents are the most conformist and the least occupied. Many drop out of school and are either too young to work or unable to find jobs. The prevalence of drinking among older Indians sets an example for the youth.

Urban Indians have special problems, living in a setting where they are generally economically, educationally and socially disadvantaged and where they do not have the support systems, such as families and familiar customs, found on reservations. The Seattle Indian Health Board estimates that 80% (16,000) of the adult Indian population of Seattle are problem drinkers. The arrest rate for urban Indians was over 40 times higher than that for the nation as a whole in 1980 (38,461 per 100,000 vs. 930 per 100,000).

Another group with special problems is Indian women. Women account for almost half of the total deaths from liver cirrhosis among American Indians, compared with one-third of cirrhosis deaths among both blacks and whites (Indian Health Service, 1988). Indian women were also more likely to die of liver cirrhosis at a younger age than either white or black women; between the ages of 35 and 54 Indian women died of cirrhosis at nine times the rate of white women, and between the ages of 15 and 34 they died at 37 times the rate of white women (Sandmaier).

Recent studies on some reservations in the Plains, the Southwest and Canada have found 5% of children whose mothers drank heavily during pregnancy were affected mentally and physically. Other studies show rates as high as 25%. Worldwide, the rate at which children are born with disabilities caused by alcohol is around 1% or less, experts say.

The Inter-Tribal Alcoholism Center in Sheridan, Wyo. reports that approximately 25% to 35% of its clients are women. The center suspects that because of the family responsibilities held by Indian women, many are afraid to seek help. Indian fathers normally will not do housework or take care of the children, since these tasks are considered to be unmanly and/or counter to Indian tradition. A common fear is that while the Indian mother seeks help, the children are neglected and might be taken by the social welfare department and placed in foster homes.

Indian women with drinking problems can receive help from the North American Indian Women's Council on Chemical Dependencies.

The Indian Health Service (IHS) has been the primary resource for handling alcoholism-related problems of American Indians. IHS provides direct health service through 43 hospitals, 67 health centers, 78 service units and 55 health stations. Currently, the IHS funds over 300 alcohol treatment programs.

The most promising methods of treatment include Indians in the planning and implementation of their own programs on a community basis. It is important for therapists and counselors to be sensitive to tribal cultures and variations from tribe to tribe. Some specifically Indian Alcoholics Anonymous groups have integrated elements of their traditional cultures into the AA setting, and they have achieved more success than standard AA programs.

Enoch Gordis, M.D., ed., *Seventh Special Report to the U.S. Congress on Alcohol and Health* (Rockville, Md.: National Institute on Alcohol Abuse and Alcoholism, 1990), chapter II.

Indian Health Services *Indian Health Service, Chart Series*, DHHS Pub. No. 1988 0-218-547: QL3 (Washington, D.C.: U.S. Government Printing Office, 1986), passim.

Indian Health Service, *Trends in Indian Health, 1989* (Washington, D.C.: U.S. Government Print. Off., 1989), passim.

Bruce Johansen, "The Tepees Are Empty and the Bars Are Full," *Alcoholism* 1, no. 2 (November/December, 1980):33-38.

Gina Kulata, "Alcohol Abuse by Pregnant Indians Is Crippling a Generation of Children," *New York Times*, July 19, 1989.

Marian Sandmaier, *The Invisible Alcoholics* (New York: McGraw-Hill Book Company, 1980), pp. 145-146.

Susan M. Stevens, "Alcohol and World View: A Study of Passamaquoddy Alcohol Use," *Journal of Studies on Alcohol*, supplement no. 9 (January 1981):122-142.

Dale R. Walker, "Treatment Strategies in an Urban Indian Alcoholism Program," *Journal of Studies on Alcohol*, supplement no. 9 (January 1981):171-184.

amethystic (From the Greek *amethystos* not drunken.) The Greeks believed that the gem, amethyst, could prevent intoxication. The term "amethystic" is now used to describe a substance or treatment method that could accelerate the normal sobering process or offset the effects of alcohol on the body. A number of researchers, particularly Ronald L. Alkana and Ernest P. Noble of California, have been looking for an agent that would counteract the effects of alcohol on the CENTRAL NERVOUS SYSTEM, but progress has been slow. Of primary concern to those engaged in research are the possibilities of such an amethystic agent in treating medical emergencies caused by an overdose of alcohol and its potential uses in the prevention of automobile accidents.

Unfortunately there are presently no effective antidotes for acute intoxication. In addition to being effective in combating the effects of alcohol, such an agent would have to be fast acting, free of toxic side effects, inexpensive, and capable of being stored and administered conveniently.

Since it is doubtful that any drug now known could be developed to hasten the METABOLISM of ethanol the 10 to 20 times needed to achieve rapid sobriety in an intoxicated person, research efforts have been focused on finding agents that counteract the effects of ethanol on the central nervous system. Recent findings indicate that chemical stimulation of noradrenalin (a neurotransmitter substance in the brain) can reverse some of alcohol's depressive effects.

amnesia   One of the typical warning signs of alcoholism is a period of temporary amnesia during which a person is conscious but later cannot recall what transpired. Memory is lost temporarily. (See also BLACKOUT, MEMORY.)

amphetamines with alcohol   Some people may take amphetamines in combination with alcohol to try to counter the depressant effects of alcohol or in the mistaken belief that amphetamines will increase the brief high produced by alcohol. While there may in fact be some possible antagonism of the depressant effects of alcohol on the central nervous system, there is no improvement of impaired motor coordination resulting from alcohol consumption, and the combination may pro-

duce a false sense of security. Another danger is that high levels of both alcohol and amphetamines may produce gastrointestinal upset, and if amphetamines are taken with a beverage containing tyramine (a white crystalline base derived from the amino acid tyrosine), such as Chianti wine, an excessive rise in blood pressure may occur. (See also DRUGS.)

amyl alcohol   A colorless liquid with a burning taste, amyl alcohol is the chief constituent of fuel oil and is used as a source of amyl compounds, such as amyl nitrite. This term should not be confused with ETHANOL, the principal chemical in alcoholic beverages.

animal models of alcoholism   Many alcohol-related problems cannot be closely studied in humans. Alcoholics have numerous biomedical and psychosocial problems in addition to their alcoholism that can interfere with studies of the causes and consequences of excessive alcohol consumption. Factors such as poor nutrition, liver damage, psychiatric illness and drug abuse can make it difficult to determine what factors are caused by alcohol consumption and what are the result of these other problems. Animal models may be the only way that the effects of alcohol use can be isolated and examined. Animal models may also be used to study the role of heredity in alcoholism (see GENETICS).

Theodore J. Cicero of the Department of Psychiatry, Washington University School of Medicine in St. Louis has made an extensive review of existing animal models. He states four main objectives of animal studies in the field of alcoholism: to examine the biomedical complexities associated with chronic alcohol consumption, such as LIVER damage and BRAIN dysfunction; to evaluate therapeutic methods that may be useful in the management of the alcohol WITHDRAWAL syndrome; to study the mechanisms underlying TOLERANCE to and physical DEPENDENCE on alcohol; and to investigate the factors that lead to and maintain excessive consumption of alcohol.

To be a true analogue of human alcoholism, an animal must meet a number of criteria. It must self-administer alcohol in pharmacologically significant amounts; TOLERANCE should be demonstrable following a period of continuous consumption; and dependence should develop. Psychological dependence cannot really be examined in an animal. Physical dependence is defined by those responses expressed during withdrawal.

At present no animal meets all the criteria for a true analogue of human alcoholism. For example, there are difficulties in many cases with self-administration. However, for studies of the neurobiological mechanisms underlying tolerance and dependence, forced administration of alcohol is usually sufficient to meet criteria.

Theodore J. Cicero, "A Critique of Animal Analogues of Alcoholism," in *Biochemistry and Pharmacology of Ethanol,* vol. 2, ed. Edward Majchrowicz and Ernest P. Noble, (New York: Plenum Press, 1979), pp. 533-560.

anisette   A liqueur produced from the mixture of aniseed (the seeds of anise) and other herbs, such as cinnamon and coriander, with alcohol. The result is a clear liquid of approximately 60 proof with a sweet, licorice flavor, which comes from the aniseed.

Anisette is primarily a French liqueur; the best known variety originates in Bordeaux.

Anstie's Law   In 1862 Sir Francis Anstie, a British psychiatrist who established the first women's medical school in Britain, made public Anstie's Law of Safe Drinking. Anstie set 1-1/2 ounces of absolute alcohol per day as the upper limit of safe drinking. Today, even after years of research, this law is still viewed as a good general guideline for the average drinker. Of course, it is not applicable to everyone; some individuals cannot tolerate any alcohol. One and a half ounces of absolute alcohol is equivalent to half a bottle of wine, four 8-oz glasses of beer or three 1-oz drinks of 100-proof liquor.

Antabuse   The brand name of the generic drug disulfiram, Antabuse is used to deter consumption of alcohol by persons being treated for alcoholism. By itself Antabuse has little effect in the body. However, if a patient taking Antabuse consumes alcohol, he or she will have a severe reaction to it, exhibiting such symptoms as headache, vomiting, breathing difficulty, and, occasionally, collapse and coma. Reaction to Antabuse begins within five to 10 minutes after ingesting alcohol and may last from 30 minutes to several hours, depending on the amount of alcohol in the body.

Antabuse interferes with the METABOLISM of alcohol in the liver by causing a toxic buildup of ACETALDEHYDE. Its real value is the knowledge of what will occur if a drink is taken. The drug's action often continues to be effective even after treatment is discontinued, and some patients may have had a reaction 14 days after taking their final dosage. Use of Antabuse is far from a complete answer, but it can be a major aid in the treatment of alcoholics. (See PHARMACOTHERAPY.)

Care should be taken when prescribing Antabuse for alcoholics who have such physical conditions as arteriosclerotic heart disease, hypertension, diabetes mellitus, cirrhosis or any other illness that might prevent their ability to tolerate acetaldehyde poisoning. In addition the action of Antabuse may alter the metabolism of some other medicines.

Antabuse is prescribed with the patient's full knowledge and understanding. The dosage is 500 milligrams a day for five to seven days and 250 milligrams a day thereafter. Patients have been treated for 17 years without bad effect (unless they drank). However, some people have experienced certain adverse reactions, including slight drowsiness, headache, and even temporary impotence and psychotic reactions. Since the safe use of this drug during pregnancy has yet to be established, it should not be given to pregnant women.

Anti-Saloon League   The Anti-Saloon League of America was founded in 1895 by a number of men interested in a political approach to what they perceived were the problems of the saloon and of liquor traffic, such as drunkenness, violence and the disintegration of family life. The league worked as a political pressure group, collecting money from church congregations and using it for launching publicity against saloons, for electing political candidates who supported the anti-saloon cause and for running local prohibition campaigns. It gained support in the early 1900s and between 1905 and 1915 the number of churches cooperating with it increased from 19,000 to 40,000. The Anti-Saloon League emphasized the economic advantages of prohibition and argued that alcohol made the working man inefficient and careless.

Larry Engelmann, *Intemperance: The Lost War against Liquor* (New York: The Free Press, 1979), pp. 10-19.

anxiety   One of the primary psychological causes of alcoholism is anxiety. Alcohol is known as a quick tension reducer, and according to some behavioral scientists, the potential alcoholic quickly learns that the immediate effect of drinking is a calming of anxieties. A drinking pattern is then established and alcohol is used as a means of managing disturbing feelings. Of course, many anxious people do not become alcoholics. Social factors and other learned responses to stress may have some effect in determining if an individual turns to alcohol or to some other means of coping. Alcohol's abilities to reduce anxiety may vary from individual to individual, depending on the amount of alcohol consumed and whether or not the subject is an alcoholic. JELLINEK and other researchers have found that drinking to the point of intoxication may increase rather than decrease anxiety. Jellinek concluded that for an alcoholic on a drinking bout, as LOSS OF CONTROL progressed, anxiety increased and was relieved for only very short periods by renewed alcohol intake.

aperitif   (French, *aperitif,* appetizer.) In its broadest sense an aperitif is any drink taken before a meal to stimulate the appetite. Among the more popular alcoholic beverages used for this purpose are champagne, vermouth, gin, sherry, mild whiskey, and cognac and water. These are usually referred to as cocktails.

Certain beverages are manufactured specifically as aperitifs. Such drinks are intended to be drunk slowly, in sips, and are often associated with moderation. They are usually strong in alcoholic content and may have a bitter taste, the degree of bitterness depending on the type of plant used as a flavoring. Among the more bitter of the plants utilized in the making of aperitifs are roots of parsley, fennel, asparagus and butcher's broom. Those with a milder bitter flavor include roots of maidenhair, couch grass, thistle and strawberry plant.

Four well-known French wines manufactured as aperitifs are Dubonnet, St. Raphael, Byrrh (pronounced beer) and Lillet. Although sometimes used in mixed drinks, they are usually drunk by themselves. The flavor of these wines is more pronounced than that of ordinary wines because of the special flavorings (i.e., the roots, barks and flowers of bitter plants) added to them. Dubonnet, for example, is red wine with bitter bark and quinine added. Byrrh and St. Raphael are also flavored with bitter bark and quinine but are fortified with brandy as well.

ABSINTHE, now illegal because of the severe health hazards it poses, was a popular aperitif in France during the late 19th and early 20th centuries. It was flavored with wormwood.

apomorphine   A chemical used in AVERSION THERAPY to produce nausea. Shortly after apomorphine is administered, the patient consumes alcohol; the nausea produced by the apomorphine subsequently becomes associated with the alcohol.

applejack   The American name for apple brandy, applejack is essentially the equivalent of French CALVADOS, although the term is sometimes used loosely to refer to hard cider. It ranges from 80 to 100 proof.

Applejack is usually made by distilling hard or fermented cider or fermented apple pomace. Another method, now rarely used, consists of freezing hard cider, concentrating the alcohol in the center, where it remains unfrozen; removing the ice; and pouring off the alcoholic center.

Applejack was one of the most popular drinks among the early settlers in North America, who sometimes referred to it as "essence of lockjaw." It is still very popular in rural areas and in the South.

It has been suggested that the risk of cancer of the esophagus from daily consumption of alcohol is increased if the beverage has an apple base (Tuyns et al.).

A. J. Tuyns, G. Pequignot and J. S. Abbatucci, "Oesophageal Cancer and Alcohol Consumption," *International Journal of Cancer* 23 (1979):443-447.

Aquavit   An alcoholic beverage distilled in Scandinavia from grain or potatoes and flavored with caraway seeds. The name "aquavit" (also spelled *akuavit, akvavit* and *akavit*) is the Scandinavian form of aqua vitae (WATER OF LIFE), the Latin term that was used in the late Middle Ages to refer to any distilled spirit.

Aquavit is particularly associated with Denmark, where it is also sometimes referred to as *schnaps* (see SCHNAPPS); in Sweden it is also known as *snaps*. *Linie Aquavit* ("equator aquavit") is a Norwegian variety which gets its name from the fact that it is shipped south from Norway and across the equator twice while it is still in casks. The exposure to the high temperatures of the equatorial zone is supposed to improve its flavor, much as the heating process used in the making of MADEIRA wine.

Aquavit is generally between 86 and 90 proof. Since it is usually not aged, it is normally colorless. Aged aquavit has a light brown color.

Aquavit is most often drunk straight as an aperitif. It is customarily gulped from a small glass, sometimes with beer as a chaser.

Argentina   Second to Brazil among South American countries in both size and population, Argentina is a predominantly Catholic, Spanish-speaking country largely peopled by Caucasians of European descent. The majority of this Caucasian population is descended from Spaniards and Italians, and the country as a whole has to some extent adopted the drinking habits of those nationalities.

In 1987, per capita consumption of wine, based on total population was 58.1 liters. This consumption rate placed Argentina fifth in a survey of the consumption rates of 47 countries worldwide. For the same year, per capita consumption of all alcoholic beverages, in liters of ABSOLUTE ALCOHOL, was 8.5 liters, placing the country 14th in the same survey. Beer consumption in Argentina measured 18.54 liters per capita, placing the country 40th in beer consumption.

The overall national drinking pattern is characterized by toleration of daily consumption of alcoholic beverages with effective cultural admonition of public drunkenness. Most drinking takes place in the home, usually in conjunction with meals, and the effective inhibition of drunkenness is thus provided by the family structure. Drinking outside the home generally takes place in family-oriented restaurants, which have the same inhibitory effect on drunkenness. The modern trends affecting this established pattern are heavier drinking among the middle and upper classes, increased acceptance of drinking by females and higher rates of alcohol abuse in rural areas than in urban areas. The country has few legal restrictions on advertising of alcoholic beverages, hours of sale or minimum age for purchase.

The cost of alcoholism to the country has not yet been statistically researched, but authorities acknowledge the presence of rising job absenteeism, family problems and social aberrations related to alcohol abuse.

It was not until 1977 that Argentina formed a national body, known as the Advisory Technical Committee on Alcoholism (CO.TE.SAL.), to study alcohol problems and their effects. Its authority to plan programs for prevention, treatment and rehabilitation, however, has been limited by the country's constitution, which grants virtual autonomy to each of the 22 provinces, and by its recent history of severe economic and political problems. Furthermore the Argentine wine industry, which is completely in private hands, is a powerful opponent of legislative restrictions on alcohol production and distribution. As a result treatment facilities for alcohol problems mostly consist of small general medical and psychiatric centers in the major cities of individual provinces. A major concern is the general lack of cooperation between these facilities and most of the country's non-psychiatric physicians. But an equally important problem is the general reluctance to diagnose maladies as alcohol- related or to seek specific antialcoholism treatment. The principal efforts to combat this attitude are provided by the ALCOHOLICS ANONYMOUS, ALANON and ALATEEN organizations in most of Argentina's largest cities.

Hoeveel alcoholhoude dranken worden er in de wereld gedronken? (How many alcoholic beverages are being consumed throughout the world?) 27th ed. Schiedam, Netherlands: Produktschap Voor Gedistilleerde Dranken, 1987.

Armagnac   The best known French brandy after Cognac, it takes its name from the Armagnac region, located in the *departement* of Gers in southwest France. Armagnac is somewhat stronger and drier in taste than Cognac. It is also distilled by a different method. Whereas Cognac is distilled by a two-part process, the distillation of Armagnac is one continual operation. It comes from the still at approximately 104 proof (Cognac is between 140 and 150 proof at this stage) with less of the raw product distilled out than is the case with Cognac. Armagnac is aged in casks made of black Gascon oak and marketed at around 80 proof.

Asian Americans   Asian Americans comprise a number of diverse groups, making generalizations about them difficult. They are one of the less visible populations in the United States because of their comparatively small numbers (though this is changing as a result of increased immigration), geographic distribution (heavy concentration on the West Coast and in Hawaii), housing pattern (segregated) and low-profile life style.

Traditionally there has been a low incidence of alcohol abuse among Asian Americans, although their use of alcohol may be increasing as a result of assimilation and acculturation. Nonetheless the amount of drinking among them is lower than that among other ethnic groups, and Asian Americans are more likely than other racial groups to be abstainers. Asian Americans have some cultural taboos against drinking, which are reinforced by allergic and toxic reactions to alcohol. Recent studies have indicated that many Orientals develop a skin flush after drinking very small amounts of alcohol. This physiological response, which occurs in a high proportion of Asian people, is characterized by headaches, dizziness, rapid heart rate, itching, or other feelings of discomfort and a strong wish to stop drinking.

While it is believed that Asian Americans display only minor problem behavior when they drink, both Chinese Americans and Japanese Americans (who as groups have minimal arrest records, according to FBI statistics) are most likely to be charged with an alcohol-related violation if arrested. In 1988, arrests for driving under the influence accounted for nearly 12% of the arrests.

Asian Americans have a low rate of use of alcohol treatment facilities mainly because of a philosophy that the family can best take care of its members. Other reasons include a cultural sensitivity to stigma, fear of losing face, unawareness of existing services, and cultural and language problems. Most Asian Americans do not recognize alcoholism as a problem except when it occurs in their own families, and then there is a tendency to hide or deny it.

Enoch Gordis, M.D., ed., *Seventh Special Report to the U.S. Congress on Alcohol and Health* (Rockville, Md.: National Institute on Alcohol Abuse and Alcoholism, 1990), chapter II.
H. L. Kitano, *Asian American Drinking Patterns,* National Institute on Alcohol Abuse and Alcoholism, Special Population Issues, Alcohol and Health Monograph no. 4. (Rockville, Md., in press).
P. H. Wolff, "Ethnic Differences in Alcohol Sensitivity," *Science* 175 (1972):449-50.

Asian skinflush reaction Elevated levels of acetaldehyde, the first metabolic product of alcohol, have been implicated as the cause of the alcohol flush reaction that is common in Asians. The physiological response, which occurs in a high proportion of Asian people, is characterized by headaches, dizziness, rapid heart rate, itching, or other feelings of discomfort.

aspirin and alcohol Aspirin is not a risk-free drug, and the combination of aspirin and alcohol carries an increased risk of gastric bleeding, as discussed in several NIAAA special reports to the U.S. Congress. Randall and Anton (1984) have hypothesized that aspirin might also retard the teratogenic effects of alcohol. They conducted tests involving aspirin and alcohol using pregnant mice. They found that while aspirin reduced the frequency of birth defects (to a level that was still very high), aspirin did not prevent birth defects. The investigators point out that further work is needed to demonstrate conclusively that aspirin prevents alcohol-related birth defects.

Enoch Gordis, M.D., ed., *Sixth Special Report to the U.S. Congress on Alcohol and Health* (Rockville, Md.: National Institute on Alcohol Abuse and Alcoholism, 1987) p. 92.

C.L. Randall and R.F. Anton, "Aspirin Reduces Alcohol-induced Prenatal Mortality and Malformations in Mice," *Alcoholism: Clinical and Experimental Research*, 8(1984): 513-515.

Australia As acknowledged by its Alcohol and Drug Addicts Treatment Act of 1961, Australia is a country with enduring serious problems because of widespread alcohol abuse throughout a diversified population. The single most important cause of the alcohol problem, according to several government reports on the subject, is that excessive consumption of alcoholic beverages, usually in the form of beer, is not only accepted by most of the population but actually expected and encouraged. Although there is significant variation of the drinking pattern in urban and rural areas of the country, the nation as a whole is prone to associate heavy drinking with civil liberty, a pioneer identity, and other images of pride and freedom embedded in the Australian concept of "mateship." While these characteristics are most dominant among the population descended from English and Irish settlers of the country, the condition of the native aboriginal population in regard to alcohol is, in its own respect, even worse because of the poverty and lack of opportunity affecting these people.

However, beer consumption decreased 10% from 1973 to 1985 even as wine consumption more than doubled.

In 1987, Australia ranked fifteenth among reporting nations in apparent per capita consumption of all alcoholic beverages in liters of absolute alcohol. The figure was 8.8. They were tenth in beer consumption (108.2 liters) and eigteenth in wine consumption—21.5 liters. All figures are based on total population.

Treatment of alcoholism in Australia is complicated by the difficulty of operating a centralized program in a country of continental proportions. Establishment of treatment centers is the responsibility of the individual states of the commonwealth, and treatment facilities and philosophies vary considerably throughout the country.

Hoeveel alcoholhoude dranken worden er in de wereld gedronken? (How many alcoholic beverages are being consumed throughout the world?) 25th ed. Schiedam, Netherlands: Produktschap Voor Gedistilleerde Dranken, 1987.

M.M Horgan et al., *International Survey: Alcoholic Beverage Taxation and Control Policies*, 6th ed. (Toronto: Brewers Association of Canada, 1986).

auto accidents   See DRIVING WHILE INTOXICATED.

aversion therapy   A behavior therapy based on the experiments of Ivan Pavlov (1849-1936), a Russian scientist who worked extensively in the field of conditioned reflexes. Typically in aversion therapy, after detoxification a patient might be given a powerful nausea-producing drug, such as emetine or APOMORPHINE, and then a shot of liquor. The liquor must be drunk just before the drug-induced nausea occurs in order for the therapy to be successful. Once a patient undergoes this therapy a few times, he or she grows to associate the nausea with the liquor. Conditioning sessions last 30 to 60 minutes and are given on alternate days for a total of four to six treatments. Reinforcement is given any time a patient develops a desire to drink.

Electric shock may sometimes be applied in the same way, a jolt of electricity given with a shot of liquor. However, this procedure has gradually become discredited and is not much used today. Another variation is the verbally induced aversion, also known as covert sensitization therapy.

It has been stressed that alcoholics treated by aversion therapy must also be provided with alternative ways of securing gratification while sober if abstinence is to be maintained (Bandura).

There is disagreement over whether aversion provides any long lasting cure. It seems to be more effective with some personality types than with others; Robert S. Wallerstein feels that the best results are achieved with depressed patients because the "punishing aspect helps to alleviate guilt and externalize aggressive charge." He suggests that patients who are paranoid, antisocial or hostile passive-aggressive are not helped by aversion therapy. There is also the danger that a patient will have a serious physical reaction if the treatment is not carefully supervised by medical specialists. Many patients drop out of this type of treatment just because it is quite unpleasant. Aversion therapy is popular in some Eastern European countries, but it is not widely used in the United States.

David J. Armor, J. Michael Polich and Harriet B. Stambul, *Alcoholism and Treatment* (New York: John Wiley and Sons, 1978), pp. 33-34.

Albert Bandura, *Principles of Behavior Modification* (New York: Holt, Rinehart and Winston, 1969), passim.

Morris E. Chafetz and Harold W. Demone, Jr., *Alcoholism and Society* (New York: Oxford University Press, 1962), pp. 204-207.

John Langone, *Bombed, Buzzed, Smashed, or ... Sober: A Book About Alcohol* (Boston: Little, Brown and Company, 1976), pp. 132-133.

Robert S. Wallerstein, "Comparative Study of Treatment Methods for Chronic Alcoholism: The Alcoholism Research Project at Winter V.A. Hospital," *American Journal of Psychiatry* 113 (1956):228-233.

aversive conditioning
See AVERSION THERAPY

B

BAC   See BLOOD ALCOHOL CONCENTRATION.

Bacchus   In Greek and Roman mythology the god of wine, identified with the Greek god Dionysus. A "son of Bacchus" is a hard drinker or drunkard.

BAL   Blood alcohol level. See BLOOD ALCOHOL CONCENTRATION.

bar   In its broader usage, a bar is a shop where alcoholic beverages are sold and drunk. Meals are not usually served. In this sense, bar is synonymous with SALOON. More specifically a bar is the counter over which drinks are served. (See also BAR DRINKER.)

bar drinker   One who habitually consumes alcoholic beverages in public establishments rather than at social functions or at home. A pronounced tendency to drink solely in bars, saloons and other public places can be caused by any of a number (or combination) of reasons: because drinking in the home is discouraged or prohibited for religious or other reasons; because the drinker is a minor and does not have parental approval to drink; because the drinker is trying to hide a drinking problem or the nature of his or her behavior while drinking.

Characteristic of bar drinking is the convivial anonymity. Most bar relationships are transient, limited to the confines of the bar and unscheduled (that is confined to chance encounters or "normal" routines of bar socializing). There is little peer pressure beyond the call to continuous or ever greater consumption. Most bar relationships are conducted in an atmosphere of at least mild intoxication and alcohol is therefore central to them. For this reason it has been suggested that recovering alcoholics with past patterns of bar drinking are most receptive to help from support groups, such as ALCOHOLICS ANONYMOUS, which stress anonymity, group support and a preoccupation with alcohol. (See also SOLITARY DRINKER.)

barbiturate   One of a number of generalized central nervous system depressants belonging to a class of drugs that includes alcohol. The most commonly abused barbiturates are short acting agents, such as pentobarbital (Nembutal) and secobarbital (Seconal). Because there is CROSS-TOLERANCE between alcohol and barbiturates, physicians sometimes prescribe them during WITHDRAWAL to achieve a gradual reduction of the physical dependence on alcohol. In such cases barbiturates are given in small quantities and gradually decreasing doses so that the patient does not in turn develop a dependence on them. Physicians also often prescribe barbiturates for alcoholics to help combat nervousness and insomnia stemming from abstinence, but instead of curing alcoholism, this practice can bring about a pattern of multiple drug use.

Alcoholics sometimes use barbiturates with alcohol in order to achieve an enhanced degree of intoxication. The combination increases central nervous system depression, possibly resulting in coma and respiratory arrest (see SYNERGY). (See also SEDATIVE.)

B & B   A dark-colored 86-proof liqueur, B & B consists of one part BENEDICTINE and one part brandy (often Cognac). It is a drier version of straight Benedictine and is often preferred in the United States.

Beaujolais   A French wine that takes its name from the Beaujolais region in southern Burgundy, where it is produced. Although there are several varieties and qualities of Beaujolais wine, 99% of them are red and have a fruity taste. These wines are intended to be drunk when they are young and fresh (i.e., by the time they are three years old). Their alcoholic content is usually 12% or more, although it is sometimes as low as 10%.

beer   An alcoholic beverage produced by fermenting and aging a mash of malted cereal grain and hops (see BREWING). Alterations in the proportion of cereal and hop ingredients and variations in the fermentation process account for the wide variety of different beers. These include lager, ale, stout, porter, malt beer ("malt liquor"), bock beer and pilsner beer.

Beer's origins date back to prehistoric times. It was undoubtedly among the first alcoholic beverages known to man. The first recorded producers of beer were the Egyptians and Mesopotamians, both of whom are known to have fermented some forms of "barley-water" long before 2000 B.C., with one Mesopotamian record dating back to 4000 B.C. The Babylonian Code of Hammurabi in 1800 B.C. included an injunction against drunkenness that in all likelihood was provoked by overconsumption of beer.

From Egypt beer traveled to Greece, where it was produced in substantial quantities as early as 600 B.C., and, later, to Rome. In both the classical Greek and Roman societies, however, beer was considered a rather crude and even barbaric beverage in comparison with wine. It was left to the Gauls, in their colder climates, to pursue the refinement of brewing techniques. They began to do so, according to Tacitus, as early as the first century A.D., and this to a large extent reinforced the association of beer with barbarism and wine with culture, which, in muted forms, survives today.

During the same time span knowledge of beer brewing passed south from Egypt throughout most of Africa and north and east to regions that became part of Russia, where beer was called *quass;* China, where it became known as *samshu;* and Japan, where it was named *sake.* Beer's movement north and west to Europe, however, proved to be the most important. Just as the early history of beer began in regions that were too warm and dry for widespread cultivation of wine grapes, its later evolution occurred in lands too cold and damp for such cultivation, particularly Germany and Britain, where the greatest quantitative and qualitative advances in brewing were achieved. Originally done in homes and monasteries in western Europe, brewing became commercialized during the 16th century. For a short time, before the introduction of coffee and tea, some form of beer was one of the few available and affordable alterna-

tives to water or milk for most of the population. Beer consumption was a habit easily transported to the New World by its western European settlers. With only brief interruptions by enthusiasm for other alcoholic beverages, beer has remained a prominent feature of life in western Europe as well as the United States, Commonwealth nations and a number of other countries.

Today the alcohol content of most beers varies from 3% to 6%, with malt beers ("malt liquors") slightly exceeding that proportion. The caloric value of beer depends on the variety, but in most cases it falls between 12 and 14 calories per ounce. Nutritionally beer is high in carbohydrates and low in fats and has a comparatively low proportion of B vitamins.

behavior modification   In behavior modification, also known as behavior modification therapy, the focus is on the behavior of the individual alcoholic rather than on underlying and perhaps deeply buried causes of the behavior. After it is determined what types of behavior are not useful to the individual, techniques are used to manipulate these in a manner that will benefit the alcoholic and possibly prevent future deviations.

There are two main goals of behavior therapy in the treatment of alcoholism. The first is to eliminate excessive alcohol consumption as a primary response to stress or other uncomfortable situations. The second is to establish alternative methods of coping with stressful situations. Initially the addiction cycle must be broken and then new habits must be established. Since most approaches today concentrate only on the first goal, they constitute only partial treatment.

The best known behavior modification technique is that of AVERSION THERAPY, in which a negative value is associated with the consumption of alcohol. Another technique is blood alcohol discrimination training, based on internal cues, although this type of training is being questioned because of doubts about the ability of alcoholics to estimate their blood alcohol level. Other techniques include assertiveness training and biofeedback.

Some behavior therapies employ a number of techniques. Individualized behavior therapy (Sobell and Sobell) for instance, has four major components: shock avoidance procedures; videotaped self-confrontation with drunken behavior; availability of alcohol as part of the treatment program; and individualized talk therapy focused on training in problem-solving skills. Unfortunately with this program there is no way of knowing which therapy contributes most to the outcome of the treatment.

One of the most recent trends in behavior modification is an attempt to teach controlled drinking as an alternative to alcoholic drinking. This approach is highly controversial since it directly contradicts the traditional LOSS OF CONTROL model of alcoholism. Because excessive consumption is viewed as learned behavior rather than an irreversible process, controlled drinking is seen as a viable alternative for some alcoholics. This is flatly denied by most opponents of CONTROLLED DRINKING.

Advocates of behavior modification point out that it is a much more efficient mode of treatment than psychoanalytic approaches, which often take years or may never be able to uncover the deep-seated causes of alcoholism. Opponents of behavior modification feel that it is a superficial treatment which does not really solve the problem, that its record to date is unimpressive and that symptoms frequently reappear. Moreover, in 1982, the methods and validity of the Sobells' research came under sustained attack. Several psychologists and sociologists (notably G. Marlett and R. Roizen) have concluded that while the Sobells' study contained methodological flaws, it was, in Don Cahalan's words, "legitimate for them to try to find a means of possible improvement of the lot of the many alcoholics who just will not accept the traditional total-abstinence treatment methods."

David J. Armor, J. Michael Polich and Harriet B. Stambul, *Alcoholism and Treatment* (New York: John Wiley and Sons, 1978), passim.

Don Cahalan, *Understanding America's Drinking Problem* (San Francisco: Jossey-Bass, 1987.)

John R. DeLuca, ed., *Fourth Special Report to the U.S. Congress on Alcohol and Health* (Rockville, Md.: National Institute on Alcohol Abuse and Alcoholism, 1981), pp. 152-153.

Cyril M. Franks, "Behavior Modification and the Treatment of the Alcoholic," *Alcoholism: Behavioral Research, Therapeutic Approaches,* ed. Ruth Fox (New York: Springer Publishing Company, 1967), pp. 186-203.

G. Marlett, "The Controlled-Drinking Controversy: A Commentary," *American Psychologist,* October 1983, 38:1097-1110.

M. Pendery, I. Maltzman and L. West, "Controlled Drinking by Alcoholics? New Findings and a Re-evaluation of a Major Affirmative Study," *Science,* 1982, 217:169-175.

R. Roizen, "The Great Controlled Drinking Controversy," in M. Galantes (ed.), *Recent Developments in Alcoholism,* Vol. 5 (New York: Plenum, 1987).

M. B. Sobell and L. C. Sobell, *Behavioral Treatment of Alcohol Problems* (New York: Plenum Press, 1978), passim.

behavioral learning theory   A psychological model of alcoholism that focuses on observable behavior and on the environmental conditions that serve to cause or maintain excessive drinking. It is thought that drinking patterns can be unlearned through modification of environmental stimuli and situations that reinforce negative behavior.

On the most basic level, the cause and continuation of alcoholic behavior are attributed to the association of alcohol consumption with a positive experience. To change such behavior, drinking is lined with aversive consequences, so that alcohol is given a negative rather than a positive value (see AVERSION THERAPY). As more is understood about alcoholism, however, the behavior model has become more complicated. Alcoholic behavior is broken into separate components and each is viewed as subject to modification through a number of different possible techniques.

Albert Bandura asserts that excessive drinking is acquired and maintained by a two-stage conditioning process. The positive value of alcohol derives first from the CENTRAL NERVOUS SYSTEM depressant and anesthetic properties of the drug that provide relief from stress. The behavior of drinking is reinforced by the reduction of unpleasant experience. When excessive use of alcohol becomes a habit, it begins to have consequent aversive effects on the individual, such as guilt or loss of a job, that in turn set up renewed stimulus for drinking. Eventually prolonged heavy alcohol usage produces alterations in the metabolic system creating physiological ADDICTION. Once addiction occurs, the second stage of the conditioning mechanism is reached. In this stage WITHDRAWAL symptoms (such as tremulousness, nausea, vomiting etc.) become the stimuli for alcohol consumption. Drinking is then reinforced automatically and continually through the termination of withdrawal symptoms that it provides.

The assumption behind the behavioral learning theory is that alcoholics drink because alcohol ingestion is followed by a reduction in anxiety, stress and tension. To change this response, either the situation that induces the psychological stress must be altered or the individual's response to the stress must be changed. This theory is now questioned because of contradictory evidence regarding alcohol's role as a tension reducer.

A number of behavior theorists, including Bandura, recognize that factors other than tension reduction, such as social reinforcement (peer approval), imitative learning (family drinking styles) and specific situational cues (bars, cocktail parties), may play a significant role in the development of alcoholism. Careful attention is therefore given to the specifics of each individual case.

David J. Armor, Michael Polich and Harriet B. Stambul, *Alcoholism and Treatment* (New York: John Wiley and Sons, 1978), pp. 22-24.

Albert Bandura, *Principles of Behavior Modification* (New York: Holt, Rinehart and Winston, 1969), passim.

Belgium   Although alcohol retains an important place in the social life of Belgians, the country experiences only limited alcohol abuse problems. One reason is the national preference for beer over all other alcoholic beverages: fully 56% of all alcohol consumed was taken in the form of beer in 1984, followed by smaller amounts of wine and very small amounts of distilled spirits. The established drinking pattern also plays a part in limiting alcohol abuse. Alcohol is seldom drunk before meals, and there is rarely heavy drinking during special family and social occasions. The Flemish northern population and the French southern population, both predominantly Roman Catholic, display a generally controlled acceptance of alcohol. One useful indicator of the national attitude toward alcohol is the law that permits sale of distilled spirits in grocery stores but only in quantities larger than 2 liters, which are not conducive to the casual drinking associated with smaller, cheaper and more portable quantities.

Per capita consumption of ABSOLUTE ALCOHOL in 1987 was 10.7 liters a year, based on total population, ranking Belgium sixth among 47 reporting countries in overall consumption. From 1970 to 1984 (most recent available figures) total alcohol consumption in Belgium increased 1.2%. Consumption of beer dropped slightly (.4%) during this period.

Using the JELLINEK formulation, authorities in Belgium calculated that the number of alcoholics in the country in 1980 was about 1% of the total population of 10 million. Legal regulations on alcohol consumption include a 1939 law against public drunkenness and a 1968 drunk driving law, which was modified in 1975 to lower the permissible level of alcohol in the blood to 0.8 grams of ethanol per 1,000 grams of blood.

The agencies charged with addressing alcohol abuse in Belgium are the National Committee for Study and Prevention of

Alcoholism and Other Drug Addictions, the National Federation of Consulting Bureaux and Institutions for the Care of Alcoholics and Other Drug Addicts and the Volksbond ("People United") Against the Abuse of Alcohol. All are private bodies working in close cooperation with each other. The National Committee, established in 1949, concentrates on statistical records; the National Federation, established in 1972, on hospital care; and the Volksbond, established in 1972, on secondary school prevention programs. In 1980 formation of a new National Committee on Alcohol and Other Drugs was announced. The committee will help coordinate funding and redistribute activities among the three existing agencies.

Hoeveel alcoholhoude dranken worden er in de wereld gedronken? (How many alcoholic beverages are being consumed throughout the world?), 27th ed. Schiedam, Netherlands: Produktschap Voor Gedistilleerde Dranken, 1987.

bender   A drinking spree or bout, as in "on a bender" (on a drunken spree).

Benedictine   Benedictine, an amber-colored French liqueur, was first manufactured by the monks of the Benedictine Order at the Abbey Fecamp in Normandy. It contains approximately 43% alcohol by volume and has a somewhat sweet taste. Like other liqueurs, it is meant to be sipped in a relaxed manner as a digestif. Although the exact recipe is a carefully guarded secret, Benedictine includes among its ingredients at least 30 different aromatic plants, honey, sugar, fruit peels and brandy (generally Cognac). At one time it also contained China tea.

Benedictine is said to have been invented during the early 16th century (possibly 1510) by Dom Bernardo Vincelli, one of the monks at the Abbey Fecamp. The monks at Fecamp continued to manufacture Benedictine until 1793, when the abbey was destroyed in the French Revolution. The recipe was preserved among the monastic documents entrusted to

the *procureur fiscal* ("civil administrator"). Over 70 years later one of the *procureur*'s descendants, Alexandre le Grand, established a distillery on the same grounds where the abbey had been. Benedictine is still manufactured there today, although it is no longer associated with the religious order.

Beta alcoholism   The second of five categories of alcoholism defined by JELLINEK. Victims eventually develop such medical complications as ALCOHOLIC POLYNEUROPATHY or CIRRHOSIS, but Beta alcoholism is not associated with either physical or psychological dependence on alcohol and WITHDRAWAL symptoms do not emerge. This type of alcoholism may result from the customs of a certain social group in conjunction with poor nutritional habits.

Beta alcoholism can develop into GAMMA ALCOHOLISM, but this is less likely to occur than in the case of ALPHA ALCOHOLISM.

bicycle accidents   Alcohol is a significant factor in bicyclist fatalities, as shown by blood alcohol test results obtained for 41% of such victims, according to the National Highway Traffic Safety Administration (1985). In about 42% of the tests, the blood alcohol concentration (BAC) exceeded 0.10%, and in 23% of the tests the BAC was 0.20% or higher. Precise figures for the number of alcohol-related bicyclist fatalities are not available; the United States averages more than 1,000 deaths per year for bicycle riders, with about 1.2 deaths per 100,000 bicycles.

biological models   See PHYSIOLOGICAL ETIOLOGICAL MODELS.

birth defects   See FETAL ALCOHOL SYNDROME (FAS).

black Americans   Blacks are the largest ethnic minority in the United States, but as with other minorities, there is a scarcity of data on drinking problems among them. A 1984 survey focusing on a national sample of blacks found that black and white men had similar drinking patterns, although important differences did exist (Herd). Studies have tended to examine only lower-class black males, from which generalizations have been made about the entire black population.

Alcohol abstention rates for black males are higher than those for white males. Surveys in 1983 showed 42.8% of black men were abstainers compared with 23.8% of white men and 12.4% of black men were heavy drinkers compared with 17% of white men. Of black women 66% were abstainers compared with 43% of white women, and the proportion of heavy drinkers among black women was also lower than that among white women—3% to 5%. There are also important differences within age group categories. Heavy drinking was most prevalent among white men in the 18 to 29 age category and declined in successive age groups (Herd). In contrast, abstention rates were high among black men between 18 and 29, but rates of heavy drinking rose sharply in the thirties.

Alcoholism is a serious problem in the black community, particularly in urban areas, where CIRRHOSIS mortality rates are unusually high. In seven major cities (Baltimore, Chicago, Detroit, Los Angeles, New York, Philadelphia and Washington, D.C.) deaths from cirrhosis among black males aged 25 to 34 are 10 times as high as among white males of the same age group. For all ages the cirrhosis mortality rate for nonwhites is about 1.5 times that for whites (Sixth Special Report to the U.S. Congress). In the period from 1940 to 1973 cirrhosis rates increased rapidly, from 5.8 per 100,000 to 15.0 per 100,000, but by 1986 the rate had declined to 13 per 100,000.

Blacks are more susceptible to CANCER of the upper digestive tract and they suffer from a significantly higher rate of hypertension, further complicated by drinking, than do other groups (see HEART).

Alcohol also plays an important role in influencing a large proportion of crimes in urban and rural black communities. Blacks have a significantly higher incidence of alcohol-related homicide than whites.

Some theorists, such as Frederick O. Harper, professor of psychoeducational studies at Howard University, suggest that black drinking problems may have begun when black slaves were sometimes encouraged to drink on weekends in order to pacify them and keep them from escaping. Drinking was a way for slaves to forget temporarily about the drudgery endured in the fields. Today a pattern of weekend drinking still exists in black communities, so much so that many liquor stores in black areas open on Friday and close on Monday.

Racism and economic frustration no doubt cause many blacks to drink. In ghettos, where blacks are separated and alienated from the rest of society, alcohol may help dull the senses against intolerable living conditions and a sense of powerlessness.

Another contributing factor, as Harper points out, is the location of liquor stores in residential areas of black neighborhoods, in contrast to many white communities, where liquor stores are located in commercially zoned business areas. Thus, with the easy availability of liquor, drinking becomes a major source of recreation and social activity. Status is achieved by drinking certain types of liquor and by buying rounds of drinks for friends. For example, black Americans buy 30% of the nation's scotch, which ranks high on their list of status liquors (Pettigrew, cited in Hornick).

In comparison with white adolescents, adolescent blacks reported a higher abstention rate and a lower heavier-drinking rate—about one-quarter that of whites the same age. As social, familial and economic pressures increase with age, so do drinking problems.

There is a significantly higher rate of nondrinkers among black women than among white women. While black women once had a greater rate of heavy drinking than white women, that trend has recently been reversed, and the most recent statistics show that 5% of white women are heavy drinkers compared to 3% of black women.

Blacks are underrepresented in most treatment programs, partly because the problem of alcoholism has not yet been recognized and accepted in the black community. There is a kind of general DENIAL of the problem and more tolerance of drunks than in white communities. This tolerance is indicated by the much greater dependence black skid row alcoholics have on the black community than their white counterparts have on their community. A lack of culture-specific treatment programs and failure to study the needs of blacks in treatment further undermines the hope of success of treatment for alcohol problems in the black community. Alcoholics Anonymous is often perceived by blacks as white and middle class, although there are some primarily black AA groups. Many blacks are unable to pay for alcoholism treatment and are less likely to have insurance coverage for such treatment. There is also a lack of knowledge about free social services. However, Melvin Porche, Sr., director of the Total Community Action Alcoholism Program in New Orleans, reports that black alcoholics admitted to hospitals and clinics show stronger motivation and cooperation in treatment than do white alcoholics.

In one recent study of drinking patterns of inner-city black American and Puerto Rican alcoholics (Fernandez-Pol et al., 1986), it was found that a significantly higher percentage of alcoholic black females used drinking to "make friends" and there was a definite tendency for black alcoholics to encourage their spouses to drink.

Enoch Gordis, M.D., ed., *Seventh Special Report to the U.S. Congress on Alcohol and Health* (Rockville, Md.: National Institute on Alcohol Abuse and Alcoholism, 1990), chapter II.

B. Fernandez-Pol, H. Bluestone, C. Missouri, G. Morales and M.S. Mizruchi, "Drinking Patterns of Inner-City Black Americans and Puerto Ricans," *Journal of Studies on Alcohol*, 47 (1986):156-160.

Frederick D. Harper, "Research and Treatment with Black Alcoholics," *Alcohol Health and Research World* 4, no. 4 (Summer 1980):10-16.

D. Herd, "The Epidemiology of Drinking Patterns and Alcohol-related Problems Among U.S. Minorities," NIAAA monograph no. 18, DHHS Pub. no. (ADM) 89-1435, Washington, D.C.: U.S. Government Printing Office, 1989.

National Institute on Alcohol Abuse and Alcoholism, Quick Facts Bulletin Board, 1987.

Melvin Porche, Sr., "Report to the 29th Annual Forum of the NCA" (a summary), *U.S. Journal of Drug and Alcohol Dependencies* 5, no. 4 (May 1981):10.

Marian Sandmaier, *The Invisible Alcoholics* (New York: McGraw-Hill Book Company, 1980), passim.

blackout   A temporary loss of memory during and following a period of drinking. Blackout is not a state of unconsciousness; it is rather a condition in which the alcoholic is able to walk and talk but later cannot remember anything. Blackout is a common early warning sign of alcoholism, and as the illness progresses, blackouts may become more frequent and last for longer periods of time. The amount of alcohol needed to produce a blackout is often unpredictable—the ingestion of a relatively small amount may sometimes produce a blackout, while at other times a very large quantity may be necessary to produce the same effect in the same individual. It is not known why some alcoholics are susceptible to blackouts and others are not or have only mild blackouts. The reason why an individual may have a blackout on one occasion and not another is also unknown. Several factors have been associated with blackouts, including drinking large amounts rapidly (gulping), a history of frequent head injuries, fatigue, and concurrent ingestion of hypnotics, tranquilizers or sedatives with alcohol. MARIJUANA WITH ALCOHOL may have a synergistic effect that results in memory loss. Some blackouts are psychologically rather than chemically induced: the individual cannot bear to remember his or her behavior and so represses all memory of a drinking episode. These are not equivalent to true alcoholic blackouts, however, as repressed memories are often retrievable under the influence of hypnosis or such drugs as sodium pentothal. In the case of true alcoholic blackout, no information can be retrieved.

Those who have had one blackout are likely to have subsequent ones. The highest incidence of blackouts occurs in heavy drinkers who have a considerable CRAVING for and a high TOLERANCE to alcohol and who are solitary, gulping drinkers. Blackouts can last for short periods of time or for days. Neither the drinker nor those around him or her are usually aware of the memory loss, which can be explained by an inability to transfer short-term memories to long-term storage sites. The drinker is able to perform because immediate memory is retained and retrieval of information from long-term memory banks is only partially disturbed.

It is not known what causes blackout. It may be that the processing and storage of new information is disturbed when high concentrations of alcohol come in contact with brain cells involved in the transfer process.

Sidney Cohen, "Blackouts," *Drug Abuse and Alcoholism Newsletter* 10, no. 2 (February 1981).

blood alcohol concentration (or content) (BAC)   An individual's degree of intoxication can be measured by the concentration of alcohol in the bloodstream. When a blood sample is tested for alcohol, the findings are reported in the form of blood alcohol concentration (BAC), also called blood alcohol level (BAL), which measures, in percentages, the weight of the alcohol in a fixed volume of blood. In certain countries, including the United States, BAC for 7 parts of alcohol per 10,000 parts of blood, for example, is expressed as .07%. In Canada and some other nations the equivalent would be 70 milligrams per 100 milliliters of blood, expressed as 70 mg%. In Sweden it would be recorded as 0.7

promille. Each system records the same percentage of alcohol.

While medical facilities and alcohol treatment centers use BACs as guides for immediate treatment of a presumably inebriated patient, BAC tests are most often given to motorists suspected of DRIVING WHILE INTOXICATED. In Idaho and Utah any driver with a BAC over .08% is considered legally intoxicated. In other areas of the United States, including the District of Columbia, the figure is .10% (many critics consider this level abnormally high and permissive). In Canada the limit is 80 mg%; in Sweden 0.5 promille is evidence of second-degree drunken driving and 1.5 promille of first degree, a very serious offense.

BAC varies according to a number of factors:

1. *Sex*. Pound for pound of body weight, the increase in BAC per drink is less for men than for women, because men generally have more muscle than women. Women have a larger percentage of fatty tissue, which has a smaller blood supply than muscle tissue. Consequently, given persons of equal weight, the ingestion of equal amounts of alcohol will result in higher blood concentrations in women than in men.

2. *Weight*. In general the larger (and heavier) a person is, the greater the blood supply is and, thus, the more alcohol can be accommodated. But as noted above, in men and women of equal weight, fatty tissue is a major determinant of BAC levels. The same is true for overweight people. Since their excess weight is stored in the form of fat, their blood supply is not increased in proportion to the additional weight. Therefore a fat person of 170 pounds will have a higher BAC from a given amount of alcohol than a lean person of the same weight.

3. *Time of consumption*. On the average, unless consumption is limited to less than one full drink an hour, BAC will continue to rise. The body will slowly

Calculation of Estimated Blood Alcohol Concentration (BAC)

Body Weight: Calculations are for people with a *normal* body weight for their height, free of drugs or other affecting medication and neither unusually thin nor obese.

Drink Equivalents: 1 drink equals:
1½ ounces of rum, rye, scotch, brandy, gin, vodka etc.
1 12-oz bottle of normal-strength beer
3 ounces of fortified wine
5 ounces of table wine

Using the chart: Find the appropriate figure using the proper chart (male or female), body weight and number of drinks consumed. Then subtract the time factor (see Time Factor Table below) from the figure on the chart to obtain the approximate BAC. For example, for a 150-lb man who has had 4 drinks in two hours, take the figure .116 (from the chart for males) and subtract .030 (from the Time Factor Table) to obtain a BAC of .086%.

Time Factor Table

Hours since first drink

	1	2	3	4	5	6
Subtract from BAC	.015	.030	.045	.060	.075	.090

Males

Ideal Body Weight (lbs)	Number of Drinks									
	1	2	3	4	5	6	7	8	9	10
100	.043	.087	.130	.174	.217	.261	.304	.348	.391	.435
125	.034	.069	.103	.139	.173	.209	.242	.278	.312	.346
150	.029	.058	.087	.116	.145	.174	.203	.232	.261	.290
175	.025	.050	.075	.100	.125	.150	.175	.200	.225	.250
200	.022	.043	.065	.087	.108	.130	.152	.174	.195	.217
225	.019	.039	.058	.078	.097	.117	.136	.156	.175	.195
250	.017	.035	.052	.070	.087	.105	.122	.139	.156	.173

Females

Ideal Body Weight (lbs)	Number of Drinks									
	1	2	3	4	5	6	7	8	9	10
100	.050	.101	.152	.203	.253	.304	.355	.406	.456	.507
125	.040	.080	.120	.162	.202	.244	.282	.324	.364	.404
150	.034	.068	.101	.135	.169	.203	.237	.271	.304	.338
175	.029	.058	.087	.117	.146	.175	.204	.233	.262	.292
200	.026	.050	.076	.101	.126	.152	.177	.203	.227	.253
225	.022	.045	.068	.091	.113	.136	.159	.182	.204	.227
250	.020	.041	.061	.082	.101	.122	.142	.162	.182	.202

excrete the alcohol as follows: oxidization by the liver, 95%; breath, 2%; urine, 2%; perspiration, 1%.

4. *Food consumption.* A "full" stomach will retard the absorption of alcohol but much less so than is commonly believed. Furthermore the effect of food on BAC varies according to the individual.

5. *Quantity.* Two to four 1-1/2-oz. shots of 86-proof liquor or an equivalent amount of wine or beer approaches the danger limit for drivers (see tables).

BAC may be determined by testing a person's urine or breath as well as his or her blood. Urine tests are difficult to administer

and are rarely used. Blood tests are both difficult to perform and often unsatisfactory, since
the analysis frequently cannot be made for up
to two hours after the suspect is apprehended.
However, through the use of batmobiles, mobile blood laboratories, the results of blood
tests can often be given within minutes. Despite past legal difficulties and problems of
accuracy, breath analyzers are in common use,
particularly for preliminary, on-the-spot analysis.

For more information, see Appendix 1,
Blood Alcohol Concentration.

blood alcohol level (BAL)   See BLOOD
ALCOHOL CONCENTRATION.

blood clotting   See VASCULAR SYS-
TEM.

blood pressure   See HEART.

blood sugar   Consumption of alcohol
can affect blood sugar levels. The effects vary
depending upon the body's physical state
when alcohol is consumed. If carbohydrate
stores in the LIVER are adequate, ETHANOL
appears to bring about a rise in blood glucose
levels (hyperglycemia). If carbohydrate re-
serves are low, as when the body is fasting, the
opposite effect, low blood sugar (hypoglycemia), occurs. This condition is apparently due
to the interference of alcohol with the normal
conversion of carbohydrates into sugar. Alcohol may also indirectly stimulate the hormone
insulin, which works to lower blood sugar. An
adequate supply of blood sugar from a meal
or a snack is generally protection against the
effects of low blood sugar produced by the
consumption of alcohol. However, when alcohol and sugar are taken together, such as in a
gin and tonic, the combination may increase
stimulation of insulin production and thereby
produce a hypoglycemic effect.

Alcoholics are often hypoglycemic, possibly because the impairment of liver function,
caused by heavy drinking, may interfere with
the ability to metabolize glucose; alcoholics

who have stopped drinking often experience
a craving for sweets. Inadequate food intake
also contributes to hypoglycemia (see NUTRI-
TION). Low blood sugar may be a cause of the
HANGOVER effect. (See also DIABETES.)

boating accidents   Boat operators' peripheral vision, balance and reaction time are
impaired by alcohol consumption, and studies
show ability to safely operate a boat is significantly affected at a BAC of 0.035%. In most
states, it is unlawful to operate a recreational
boat while under the influence of alcohol—
but many states (18)—have not defined the
level of intoxication for operators of vessels
and most states can't perform tests without
consent.

In 1983, the U.S. Coast Guard received
reports of 5,569 recreational boating accidents
that resulted in 1,241 fatalities and 2,913 injuries. In 1988, the death rate had dropped to 5.5
fatalities per 100,000 boats—or 946 people
killed in recreational boating accidents. However, the Coast Guard estimates that it receives reports of only 5% to 10% of all
reportable accidents that do not involve fatalities. Studies by California, Maryland, and
North Carolina indicate that the full extent of
alcohol involvement in boating accidents is
grossly under-reported. The state studies
(NTSB) show that 75% to 80% of boating
accidents and deaths were alcohol-related;
and, in Maryland in 1986–87, 60% of the
fatally injured victims were legally drunk
(with BACs of 1.008% or higher). The Coast
Guard has estimated that 40% of boaters carry
alcohol on their outings. In a review of literature analyzing drownings during boatings,
Howland and Hongson suggested that at least
17% to 31% of boaters who drowned had
consumed alcohol.

National Transportation Safety Board, "Safety
    Study: Recreational Boating and Safety and Al-
    cohol," NTSB No. 55-83-02, NTIS No. PB 83-
    917006 (Washington, D.C.: NTSB, 1983).
J. Howland and R. Hongson, "Alcohol as a Risk
    Factor for Drowning: A Review of the Literature

How State Laws Compare

Thirty-two states have boating laws that declare people intoxicated when they have certain blood concentrations of alcohol. Implied consent signifies that refusal to take a sobriety test can be used in court.

State	Boats registered	Blood alcohol	Implied consent	1988 boat deaths
Alabama	212,406	-	No	23
Alaska	28,945	.10	Yes	34
Arizona	120,500	.10	Yes	4
Arkansas	147,050	-	No	13
California	734,817	.10	No	51
Colorado	82,783	.10	Yes	8
Connecticut	94,819	-	No	12
Delaware	41,563	-	No	1
District of Columbia	4,054	-	No	1
Florida	675,474	.10	Yes	94
Georgia	264,698	.12	Yes	22
Hawaii	14,250	-	No	5
Idaho	61,392	.10	No	16
Illinois	326,483	.10	Yes	19
Indiana	213,585	.10	Yes	12
Iowa	187,279	-	No	8
Kansas	89,664	.10	No	2
Kentucky	114,571	-	No	17
Louisiana	293,390	.10	Yes	60
Maine	123,723	.08	No	11
Maryland	168,763	.10	No	16
Massachusettes	224,115	-	No	18
Michigan	788,453	.10	No	30
Minnesota	692,528	.10	Yes	23
Mississippi	159,413	-	No	19
Missouri	264,652	-	No	21
Montana	34,343	.10	Yes	3
Nebraska	55,525	.10	Yes	4
Nevada	38,279	.10	Yes	4
New Hampshire	14,600	.10	Yes	8

How State Laws Compare   (*continued*)

State	Boats registered	Blood alcohol	Implied consent	'88 boat deaths
New Jersey	173,208	.10	Yes	14
New Mexico	34,549	-	No	3
New York	385,000	.10	No	38
North Carolina	256,264	.10	No	26
North Dakota	40,495	-	No	2
Ohio	375,194	.10	Yes	27
Oklahoma	181,335	-	No	20
Oregon	159,999	-	No	24
Pennsylvania	266,315	.10	Yes	14
Rhode Island	29,855	-	No	2
South Carolina	282,611	-	No	31
*outh Dakota	45,867	-	No	2
Tennessee	224,709	.10	Yes	13
Texas	607,111	.10	No	72
Utah	45,311	.08	Yes	4
Vermont	36,209	.10	Yes	0
Virginia	186,426	.10	Yes	27
Washington	179,066	.10	No	28
West Virginia	45,336	-	No	10
Wisconsin	480,821	.10	Yes	26
Wyoming	21,965	.10	No	2

(1950–1985)," *Public Health Rep* : 475–483, 1987.

Lori Sharn, "States to Boaters: Lakes, Rivers not Watering Holes," *USA Today*, August 15, 1989, p. 5A.

S. J. Wright, "SOS: Alcohol, Drugs, and Boating," *Alcohol Health and Research World* 9(4): 28–33, 1985.

bock beer   A seasonal beer whose name derives from the German *Einbecker Bier* (literally, beer from Einbeck), shortened in the dialect of Bavaria, where it originated, to *Bockbier*. Bock beer, sometimes simply called bock, is brewed in winter from the residue collected from vats before they are cleaned for another year's brewing. Stronger and sweeter in taste than most lagers, of which it is a variety, true bock beer is dark and has a life of about six weeks. The day on which the product is first ready for consumption, Bock Beer Day, is traditionally associated with the coming of spring.

boom towns   In communities that either spring up almost overnight or become prosperous suddenly because of some new industry or the discovery of a valuable resource, the incidence of alcohol and drug abuse usually jumps markedly or, in new communities, establishes itself at a level well above the norm for other communities of similar size. In studies done in the United States during the mid- and late-1970s, the pattern was repeated in community after community, with the increase in alcohol abuse considerably higher than the rise in drug abuse (overwhelmingly marijuana).

The characteristics of these boom towns are very similar. There is an influx of young, often blue-collar males (single or without their wives) into an area where the social fabric is strained by economic and population changes. Wages and prices are high and amenities, including recreational facilities, are scarce or nonexistent. Drinking is the only major social activity and is done in bars. Prostitution often flourishes. Treatment for alcohol-related problems generally rises but the pattern is erratic and hard to measure. Alcohol-related arrests show a marked increase, particularly those for DRIVING WHILE INTOXICATED. (See also DEPRESSED COMMUNITIES.)

booze   (Formerly spelled "boose" but pronounced "booze," from early Germanic sources via the early modern Dutch *buisen* and Middle English *bousen*.) The word "booze" has always been a slang term for drinking excessively, usually to get drunk quickly. As a verb it means to guzzle; to drink to excess. As a noun it is the alcoholic beverage that one "boozes," often whiskey, such as that made around 1840 by a Philadelphia distiller named E. G. Booze. Both the verb and the noun predate Mr. Booze by many centuries. From booze come "boozing it up," "boozer," "boozy" and other such terms.

booze fighter   One for whom BOOZE has become a habit, a compulsion or an addiction and who is determined to "fight" the habit. The term implies an ongoing, and therefore unsuccessful, battle with a continuous stream of good intentions and broken resolutions. It is sometimes used synonymously with BOOZE HOUND.

booze hound   A heavy drinker; one whose life is greatly influenced by, even dedicated to, the consumption of alcoholic beverages. (See also BOOZE FIGHTER.)

bootlegging   A possible derivation of the term "bootlegging," referring to traffic in illegal whiskey, dates back to the post-Revolutionary period, when the government first started imposing taxes on whiskey. Distillers were required to buy tax stamps and display them on their whiskey barrels. To avoid the tax, some distillers had their deliverymen remove the stamps from the barrels after the whiskey was delivered and return them in their bootlegs for use on the next shipment.

In 1880 Kansas incorporated prohibition into its constitution, "bootlegging"—apparently the practice of carrying flasks of whiskey concealed in boot tops—gained widespread popularity. Later other areas of the country established similar laws, resulting in an increase in bootlegging from wet communities to dry ones. During PROHIBITION (1920-1933) bootlegging became a major racket as well as a familiar term across the nation. In the early days of Prohibition a great deal of liquor was smuggled into the United States across the Canadian and Mexican borders and from ships anchored off the coast. As the Coast Guard increased its campaign against those smuggling liquor into the country from ships, bootleggers began to rely more on industrial alcohol, which they washed of noxious chemicals, diluted with water and sometimes flavored with a small amount of real liquor. Liquor was also obtained from government-supervised warehouses, where it was being held for medical use or for export. Bootleggers delivered the liquor to speakeasies, which were mostly controlled by gangsters, although the small-scale bootlegger was usually not a gangster. Bootlegging continued after Prohibition and is still a problem today.

Although bootlegging is generally associated with the United States, other nations have had similar problems. During World War I the Russian government banned the sale of vodka as a war measure. After the war the Communist regime continued the prohibition, but by 1925 bootlegging was so widespread that the government rescinded the ban on vodka. In the late 1980s, the government again restricted the sale of vodka—and bootlegging has once more become a widespread practice among the Russians.

Alice Fleming, *Alcohol: The Delightful Poison* (New York: Dell Publishing Co., 1975), p. 34.
"Bootlegging." *Encyclopedia Britannica* (USA: William Benton, 1972).

Bordeaux   See RED WINE.

bottom fermentation   Fermentation of a hop wort with a yeast that sinks as sediment in the course of brewing lager beer. Beer yeasts are selected strains of bacterial enzymes that flocculate, or separate themselves from the brewing beer, so that they may be drawn off at the end of the process. This process, in conjunction with the different blend of cereal grains employed, accounts for the lighter flavor of lager beers in comparison with that of ales which are brewed by a process called TOP FERMENTATION. Bottom fermentation is typically carried out at temperatures between 38° and 48° F. It ordinarily takes between seven and 11 days for the yeast to convert the soluble sugar of the grains into the desired level of alcohol content.

bourbon   A spirit distilled from a fermented mash of grain that is at least 51% corn (Indian maize). Bourbon is the most distinctly American of all whiskeys. Particularly regional in origin and history, it continues to be produced almost exclusively in north-central Kentucky.

Of the three principal types of American whiskey—rye, corn whiskey and bourbon—both rye and corn whiskey predate bourbon,

which to some extent must be considered a compromise between these earlier spirits. Bourbon is distilled in a process identical to that used to produce RYE WHISKEY, but the mash from which it is distilled contains a high proportion of corn to which other grains, such as rye, have been added. In fact, according to one apocryphal story, bourbon originated when the rye whiskey distillers of Kentucky were faced with a crop failure of their preferred grain.

Most histories date the origin of bourbon as 1789 and the originator as Elijah Craig, a Baptist minister in the village of Georgetown in Bourbon County, then a part of Virginia. The harsh taste of the early bourbons was in keeping with the frontier life style of that region, which was settled from Virginia through the Cumberland Gap after the American Revolution, but it also made bourbon a poor competitor with rye and rum elsewhere in the early United States. Until the Civil War bourbon production remained at a level of about 1,000 barrels per year, most of which came from family distilleries catering to local markets. After the Civil War, however, the highly publicized exposure of a "whiskey ring" with connections to President Ulysses S. Grant's administration brought about sudden government regulation of the bourbon trade. Such regulation tended to reduce the distinct qualities of the various individual brands of bourbon, but it also modernized production of the whiskey and increased its availability in mass markets.

Today production of bourbon begins with the cleaning and milling of the basic corn grain. After the kernels are crushed, the corn is soaked, traditionally in limestone water, and additional grains, such as rye and malted barley, are added. In the "sweet-mash" method an unusually high proportion of malted barley is added to encourage fermentation. In the "sour-mash" method fermentation is encouraged by adding a "slop" of residue from a previous distillation. In both methods the grain mash is then poured into open-topped fermenting vats and yeast is added. Once fermentation has produced enough alcohol to qualify the mash as "distiller's beer," distillation is begun. Originally carried out in pot stills, distillation of bourbons is now almost exclusively done in patent stills. Because of the content of the grain mash, distilled bourbon is considered a "heavy" whiskey and requires two or three years more aging than Scotch whiskey or Irish whiskey.

Most commercially sold bourbon is blended before bottling, a process that involves mixing a single distillate with at least one other distillate and sometimes with flavorless or "neutral," spirits. Less commonly, bourbon is sold as "bottled in bond," a designation that indicates a "straight" bourbon produced by a single distillation.

Bowery   A street and section in lower Manhattan, New York City that was once notorious for its cheap theatres, dance halls, drinking gardens etc. Today the Bowery is an impoverished area populated in large part by derelicts, although it has been partially rehabilitated. The Bowery contains a large SKID ROW area and its inhabitants are the source of the term "Bowery bum."

brain   Alcoholism was first linked to brain damage over 100 years ago, when three patients were described as suffering from delirium, visual problems, imbalance in walking and muscle tremors. Their condition came to be known as WERNICKE'S ENCEPHALOPATHY and there have been hundreds of thousands of such cases since then. In 1887 another form of brain damage was linked to alcoholism—KORSAKOFF'S PSYCHOSIS, characterized by disorientation, memory failure and a tendency to recite imagined occurrences.

Today there is a substantial amount of evidence indicating that prolonged heavy consumption of alcoholic beverages has a negative effect on the brain (and not all forms of brain damage are as extreme as Wernicke's encephalopathy). CAT scanner X rays of heavy drinkers who are not noticeably ill have shown brain atrophy (loss of brain cells). O.

A. Parsons concluded in 1977 that in any given sample of alcoholics from 50% to 100% have brain atrophy. Tests have shown deficits in cognition and perception in alcoholics similar to those in patients with brain damage that is not related to alcohol. However, there seems to be a continuum of alcohol effects on the brain, ranging from little or no effect in light social drinkers to moderate or severe impairment in late-stage alcoholics. Evidence suggests that some brain damage may be partly reversible in abstinent alcoholics.

Medical researchers at the University of California at Irvine have found that in addition to causing atrophy of the brain, excessive drinking led to brainstem abnormalities in 40% of the alcoholic patients they studied. The brainstem connects the brain to the spinal cord and controls such vital functions as respiration, heart rate and blood pressure. Abnormalities of these functions appear to have a strong link to alcohol abuse and are most prevalent in older patients who have already shown neurological complications resulting from extended alcohol use. A correlation between brainstem abnormalities and cerebral atrophy has been found.

New Imaging Techniques

Innovative imaging techniques in alcohol research are being used to study brain structure and function. One such is positron emission tomography (PET). A noninvasive imaging technique, PET measures the localized brain metabolism of substances such as glucose. The images obtained are similar in topography to CT scans (computerized tomography), but they reflect local rates of glucose metabolism instead of anatomical detail and provide information on subcortical as well as on cortical processes. CT scans are limited in this respect. PET scans also allow the measurement of biochemical and metabolic processes in the living brain. This technique has also been used to study brain receptors.

PET and other new noninvasive imaging techniques promise to advance correlation of neurochemical and anatomic changes with behavioral and physiological responses to alcohol. This will aid greatly in researching central nervous system (CNS) deficits associated with alcohol-induced brain damage.

How Alcohol Affects the Brain

Alcohol inhibits the brain's ability to use oxygen and reduces its capacity to utilize glucose. Nerve cell transmission and the transport of ions in and out of brain cells are affected. Insufficient oxygen in the brain may cause the brain cells to die, and excessive alcohol intake can result in permanently impaired brain function, although several studies show that partial reversal of atrophy and impairment can occur in abstinent alcoholics. For very moderate drinkers there is no clear evidence that alcohol harms the brain. Nutritional deficiencies associated with alcoholism may also play a role in brain damage (see NUTRITION).

According to experiments (in mice and in humans) cited in the U.S. Department of Health and Human Services report to Congress in December 1983, the alteration of electrical charges and neurotransmitters—the chemicals crucial for moving messages across the synapses that connect the neurons—is different after chronic exposure to alcohol than after a single acute dose. Mice chronically exposed to alcohol, for example, showed a reduced number of neuronal receptor sites for gamma amino-butyric acid (GABA), the neurotransmitter that helps inhibit convulsions, which are often a symptom of acute alcohol withdrawal.

RNA and protein synthesis in the brain both play important roles in learning and memory. Studies by Drs. Sujata Tewari and Ernest Noble of the University of California at Irvine have shown that alcohol interferes with the manufacture of RNA and protein in the brains of mice. This effect may be partly responsible for alcoholic BLACKOUT.

The ACETALDEHYDE produced when alcohol is metabolized (see METABOLISM) may also affect the brain, and investigators have suggested that acetaldehyde may be responsible for the DEPENDENCY which characterizes alcohol addiction. The mechanisms of this effect are still unclear. (See also CENTRAL NERVOUS SYSTEM.)

Lawrence K. Altman, "Alcohol-Linked Brain Damage Is Subtle, but Deadly," *New York Times,* December 22, 1981.

"Brainstem Abnormalities in 40% of Alcoholic Patients," *U.S. Journal of Drug and Alcohol Dependence* 5, no. 5 (June 1981):14.

John R. DeLuca, ed., *Fourth Special Report to the U.S. Congress on Alcohol and Health* (Rockville, Md.: National Institute on Alcohol Abuse and Alcoholism, 1981), pp. 52-57.

Enoch Gordis, M.D., ed., *Seventh Special Report to the U.S. Congress on Alcohol and Health* (Rockville, Md.: National Institute on Alcohol Abuse and Alcoholism, 1990), chapter II.

Robert G. Niven, M.D., *Fifth Special Report to the U.S. Congress on Alcohol and Health.* (Rockville, Md.: National Institute on Alcohol Abuse and Alcoholism, 1983).

Ernest P. Noble, ed., *Third Special Report to the U.S. Congress on Alcohol and Health* (Rockville, Md.: National Institute on Alcohol Abuse and Alcoholism, 1978), pp. 93-107.

brain damage   See BRAIN.

brandy   An alcoholic beverage distilled from the fermented juice of grapes (i.e., wine) or other fruits. The term "brandy" without further qualification usually refers to grape brandy. When fruits other than grapes are used, the name of the fruit precedes the term "brandy" (e.g., apricot brandy, cherry brandy, orange brandy or apple brandy, particularly the French CALVADOS and the American APPLEJACK). Many of these fruits go through a "wine stage" similar to that of the grape, and several are actually made into wines (e.g., apple wine, elderberry wine).

Sometimes the term "brandy" is extended to include what the French call *marc* (pronounced *mar*) and the Italians refer to as *grappa. Marc* and *grappa* are inexpensive brandies made from the stems, pips and skins of grapes after the juice has been pressed from them to make wine.

Brandies are produced all over the world. The chief producers are France and the United States, but other important sources include Greece, Spain, Portugal, Italy, Peru and South Africa. The name, therefore, is often also qualified by the country or region where it is produced (e.g., French brandy, California brandy). The best known brandy is COGNAC, which is named after the town of Cognac in southwestern France. Another popular French brandy is ARMAGNAC, also named for the region that produces it.

Brandy is thought to be the oldest of the distilled alcoholic beverages; its production can be traced back to the 13th century. The art of distillation itself was originated in the Eastern world. It was first introduced to the Italians, who produced *acqua di vite* or *arzente*. From Italy the technique traveled to France, where its product was called EAU DE VIE, and then to Spain. By the end of the 17th century the production of brandy had spread throughout Europe.

It is not known when the name "brandy" was first applied to distilled wine. However, it was originally a compound term: brandy-wine, brandewine or brandwine, which came from the Dutch *brantewijn* (from *branden* to burn + *wijn* wine).

The first step in the production of grape brandy is to press the grapes in the usual way to make wine. The wine is then stored in casks until it is distilled into brandy. It takes approximately 10 casks of wine to produce one cask of brandy.

In the distillation process the wine is placed in pots constructed to retain the impurities, or CONGENERS, which give brandy its characteristic flavor and aroma. The congeners in brandy include normal propyl alcohol, normal butyl alcohol, amyl alcohol, hexyl alcohol, ethyl acetate and oenanthic ether, which provides one of the main taste characteristics that

distinguishes brandy from other distilled liquors, such as whiskey or rum.

When first distilled, brandy is a colorless liquid with a very high alcoholic content. The exact percentage of alcohol at this stage of production varies among the different brandies. California brandy, for example, is approximately 102 proof, while Cognac is between 140 and 150 proof.

Before being bottled, brandy is aged in wooden casks for at least three years. As it ages, it mellows and acquires a yellow color that grows darker the longer the brandy remains in the casks. However, depth of color is not an accurate indicator of age, for producers often artificially color brandy with caramel. Brandy also loses some of its alcoholic content in the aging process, and, frequently, through the addition of distilled water. Bottled Cognac, for example, is between 68 and 80 proof.

Brandy is usually drunk by itself as an after-dinner drink. It is also sometimes used in mixed drinks, such as cocktails, punches and so-called dessert drinks, and as a flavoring in coffee and foods.

brewing   A process that combines cereal grains, water, hops and yeasts to produce beer or ale.

Records of early brewing processes for creating "barley water" appear on a Mesopotamian clay tablet from 4000 B.C. and on a wooden model of a brewery in Thebes from 2000 B.C. The Egyptians developed the most extensive primitive brewing techniques, which were later adopted by the Greeks and ultimately brought to western Europe by the Romans. Early European brewing was based principally in monasteries and homes until the 16th century, when significant commercial breweries emerged. Gradually there evolved a process of brewing that has remained essential to the production of all commercial beers—lager, ale, stout, porter.

The first stage in the process is the preparation of a cereal mash. The principal grain used is barley, which is malted by milling it, soaking it until it germinates and then drying it. Most beers also contain a blend of other cereal grains, which are soaked separately and then mixed with the malted barley in mash tuns. There the grain content is cooked in water, a process that liquefies the starches present and converts them into soluble sugars, chiefly maltose and dextrin, which are essential to fermentation. The result, once filtered, is a liquid called wort.

In the next stage hops, the ripened cones found on the female hop vine, are combined with the wort in a brew kettle, traditionally a copper one, and boiled for several hours. Technically the term "brewing" refers to just this stage of beer production, but the term is commonly used to describe the entire process. The brew is then strained through a hop separator and the result is known as hop wort.

The third stage is fermentation, a process carried out in a fermenting tank and initiated by adding yeast enzymes to the sugar-rich hop wort. The yeast employed must produce sufficient fermentation to create the desired alcohol content and it must also flocculate, or separate itself from the beer, to enable its removal at the end of the process. Two types of brewing yeast have these properties. The first type rises in the beer during fermentation; the product of this process, known as TOP FERMENTATION, is ale. The second type sinks in the beer during fermentation; the result of this process, called BOTTOM FERMENTATION, is lager. In both cases, fermentation is carried out at temperatures in the range of 40° to 60° F and requires anywhere from five to 11 days to complete. Also during both processes gases emitted by the beer are collected and returned to the liquid for carbonation. "Krausened" beers are entirely carbonated by naturally active yeasts, but most beers are carbonated, at least in part, by the introduction of carbon dioxide.

The final stages of the process are aging and packaging. All beers are kept in chilled aging tanks for the last stages of fermentation. Once aged, beer is filtered to remove most of its yeast content and placed in barrels or in smaller consumer containers, such as cans or bottles. If barreled, usually in aluminum kegs, beer requires no further processing and has a short storage life. To extend their shelf life, bottled and canned beers are usually pasteurized to destroy the remaining yeast enzymes and prevent further fermentation.

British Road Safety Act of 1967   A much-publicized campaign of enforcement for drunk-driving laws called the "Cheshire Blitz" resulted in greatly increased print and electronic media coverage used in 1975 to apply the British Road Safety Act of 1967. The campaign, based on a belief in the perceived certainty of threat, saw a statistically significant decline in serious auto crashes.

Burgundy   See RED WINE.

burns   A 1983 study found 2.4% of the violent deaths of alcoholics were caused by fires; this figure was 26 times the expected rate (Comes-Orme et al.). A review of the medical records of 70 burn patients over 14 showed that 46% had been using alcohol at the time of injury. Fifty-seven percent of burns took place near vehicles. Males who were burned were likely to have been drinking at the time of injury–a rate of 58% was indicated. Thirty-six percent of female victims had been drinking (Voughtsberger and Taylor). Careless smoking is associated with drinking and plays a large role in such deaths.

T. Comes-Orme, R.R. Taylor, E.B. Scott and S.J. Holmes, "Violent Deaths among Alcoholics: A Descriptive Study," *Journal of Studies on Alcohol*, 44(1983): 938-949.

K. Voughtsberger and R. Taylor, "Psychosocial Factors in Burn Injury," *Texas Medicine* 80 (1984): 4346.

business   See EMPLOYEE ASSISTANCE PROGRAMS.

butyl alcohol   A colorless liquid made by the fermentation of glucose, butyl alcohol is used as a solvent. It should not be confused with ETHANOL, the principal chemical in alcoholic beverages. (See INTRODUCTION.)

C

caffeine   Because it is a stimulant, caffeine has been thought to counteract the effects of alcohol, but it is not a sobering agent. Both antagonistic and additive interactions between alcohol and caffeine have been reported, but generally the effects are quite small. When alcohol is acting to reduce inhibition of behavior, caffeine may increase this effect; when alcohol is acting as a depressant, caffeine may act antagonistically. It does not speed up the elimination of alcohol and may provide a false sense of security to those who drink excessively in the belief that they can always sober up quickly with coffee or another source of caffeine.

Since it constricts the blood vessels, caffeine may provide some relief for the headache experienced during a hangover, which is related to overdilation of the blood vessels caused by the consumption of alcohol.

Heavy coffee consumption is often associated with heavy alcohol use and smoking.

calorie   A unit of measure used to express the heat- or energy-producing value of food when it is metabolized in the body. On an average, ABSOLUTE ALCOHOL contains about 150 to 200 calories per ounce. These are so-called empty calories, which may, in some circumstances, provide quick energy but will not serve the body's nutritional needs.

The calories contained in alcohol cannot be stored, so the body burns them before it burns food calories, which are stored and used as fat. Therefore for someone interested in losing weight it is important to reduce alcohol consumption. Continued consumption of a high level of alcohol while cutting down on food may lead to malnutrition.

Calvados   A famous French apple brandy from the Normandy region of the same name. The production of alcohol from apples was first developed by the Vikings who settled in Normandy over a thousand years ago.

Calvados is distilled from apple cider or, sometimes, apple pulp and aged in oak casks for six years. It is bottled at around 80 proof and has a distinct applelike flavor.

Campari   An alcoholic beverage made in Milan, Italy, Campari belongs to the class of drinks known as BITTERS. It is 48 proof, reddish in color and has a somewhat bitter flavor. In Italy, Campari is one of the most popular APERITIFS. It is drunk either neat with soda as a chaser or mixed in cocktails.

Canada   As in most other developed Western countries, attitudes toward alcohol consumption in Canada have undergone many changes since World War II. The proportion of abstainers may have dropped as much as 50% between 1950 and 1980; and holiday sales of liquor indicate a greater popularity of alcoholic beverages at social celebrations. A 1987 Gallup poll shows that 78% of Canadian adults aged 18 years and older have used alcohol in some form. The general pattern of drinking in Canada is one of increased consumption on weekends and holidays throughout the year. Only about one-sixth of the country's alcohol consumption takes place in public places, but the overwhelming amount of drinking in private places has resulted in a higher level of consumption because of the absence of inhibitions associated with public drinking. The legal drinking age in most of Canada is 19 years old. It is 18 years old in four provinces: Prince Edward Island, Quebec, Manitoba and Alberta.

Controls on the sale and consumption of alcoholic beverages are a matter of provincial rather than federal authority in Canada, and statistics on consumption are also gathered on the provincial level. The highest annual rates of per capita consumption are found in the Yukon and Northwest Territories (18.2 liters and 13.34 liters of ABSOLUTE ALCOHOL, respectively in 1985–86). The lowest annual rates of consumption per capita are in New Brunswick and Prince Edward Island (7.87 liters and 8.72 liters of absolute alcohol, respectively, in 1985–86).

In 1985-86, Canadians consumed 205.4 million liters of absolute alcohol. This works out to 10.3 liters per person aged 15 years and older, or 17.6 drinks per week or two drinks per day per consumer. About 50% of what Canadians drink today is in the form of beer. In 1985-86, Canadians spent $8.2 billion for alcohol in retail stores and another $3.1 billion for alcohol consumed in taverns, restaurants and hotels.

In 1985-86, Canadian federal and provincial government revenue derived directly from the control and sale of alcoholic beverages reached $3.8 billion, or 1.9% of all government revenue. Include general retail sales taxes and federal taxes on producers and distributors in the equation and the figure reached roughly $5.1 billion.

In 1984 there were an estimated 503,000 alcoholics in Canada, that is, people whose consumption was sufficiently high to cause them physical damage.

Alcohol is thought to be the cause of 40% of all fatal auto accidents and 62% of all alcohol-related traffic accidents in Canada. An equal proportion of all murders has been attributed to alcohol abuse, by either the victim or the perpetrator of the crime.

In the country as a whole, in 1984 alcohol-related social costs due to excess use of health care, reduced labor productivity, law enforcement and social welfare reached $6.4 billion and $1.8 billion for Ontario.

The agencies responsible for combating alcohol abuse are the federal and provincial ministries of health, whose jurisdictions in this respect overlap. Most provinces maintain research foundations, alcohol and drug abuse programs, health facilities for alcoholics and

Liters of Absolute Alcohol Per Person Aged 15 Years and Over, Canada and Provinces, 1984–85 to 1985–86

Province	1984–85	1985–86
Newfoundland	10.00	8.95
Prince Edward Island	9.05	8.72
Nova Scotia	9.40	9.19
New Brunswick	8.10	7.87
Quebec	9.07	9.45
Ontario	10.59	10.57
Manitoba	10.46	10.09
Saskatchewan	9.43	9.21
Alberta	11.67	11.69
British Columbia	12.00	11.67
Yukon	19.25	18.20
Northwest Territories	13.94	13.34
Canada	10.28	10.27

SOURCES: Statistics Canada, *The Control and Sale of Alcoholic Beverages in Canada 1984* and *1985* (Ottawa: Statistics Canada, Catalog No. 63-202, 1986 and 1987 respectively).

drug addicts, and education programs for both the general and school-age populations. At the same time, however, there is a lack of formal policies aimed at reducing alcohol abuse and few efforts to encourage alterations of environments considered conducive to alcohol abuse.

Canada has acknowledged a need for comprehensive training programs, which are presently limited to the training provided by medical schools and various foundations concerned with the problem. Many of the most successful efforts to address the problem of alcoholism in Canada remain wholly voluntary and charitable, including the work of Alcoholics Anonymous and the Salvation Army in individual provinces.

---

[1]All dollar figures are Canadian. Because of the fluctuations in the value of both Canadian and U.S. currencies, it is difficult to give precise U.S. dollar equivalents.

Dollar Sales of Beverage Alcohol, Canada and Provinces, 1985–86

Province	Total (in thousands)
Newfoundland	$ 198,691
Prince Edward Island	41,019
Nova Scotia	286,402
New Brunswick	187,746
Quebec	1,875,552
Ontario	2,966,885
Manitoba	337,371
Saskatchewan	297,550
Alberta	893,886
British Columbia	1,107,441
Yukon	14,941
Northwest Territories	24,926
Canada	$8,232,410

SOURCES: Statistics Canada, *The Control and Sale of Alcoholic Beverages in Canada 1985* (Ottawa: Statistics Canada, Catalog No. 63-202, 1987).

Manella Adrian, Stats-Facts in *Statistics on Alcohol and Drug Use in Canada and Other Countries*, vols. 1 and 2 (Toronto: Addiction Research Foundation, September 1988), p. 5.

Canadian whisky

An alcoholic beverage produced in Canada by distilling a fermented mash of barley, rye and corn. The distilled alcohol is subjected to secondary extraction and rectification processes that leave it with a very low level of heavy CONGENERS. For that reason it is known as the lightest of all whiskies. Individual Canadian whiskies are aged for four, eight or 12 years and then blended with others before final filtering and bottling. They are sold at 86.6 proof.

The origins of Canadian whisky are not known, but it is assumed that distillation of grains in Canada was begun by Irish and Scottish settlers around the end of the 18th century. Although the whisky was no doubt prized by pioneers, particularly during the harsh Canadian winters, effective temperance movements controlled its distribution throughout the 19th century. There were also several provincial prohibitions on alcohol distillation in Canada, and consequently the Canadian whisky industry developed much later than its American counterpart.

A law banning the distillation of alcohol in Canada was being drafted when Prohibition was enacted in the United States with the passage of the Volstead Act in 1919. Bolstered by the sudden lack of competition from America, distillers in Canada prevailed on the government to abandon its plans for instituting prohibition there. Canadian whisky subsequently became enormously popular in the United States as the cheapest safe alternative to "bathtub gin" and other illegal distillates, and the Canadian liquor industry boomed. When Prohibition ended in the United States in 1933, Canadian distillers were able to extend their syndicates across the border before producers of domestic brands of whiskey could establish themselves.

cancer

Excessive alcohol consumption is known to increase the risk of cancer at various sites in the body. Relative to the rest of the population, alcoholics and heavy drinkers show a high incidence of mortality from cancer of the mouth, pharynx, larynx, esophagus, liver and lung as well as excessive mortality from other causes. In the United States cancer associated with alcohol accounts for 6.1% to 27.9% of the total incidence of all cancer. Alcohol itself has not been shown to act as an independent carcinogen, but it is thought to act as a "co-carcinogen," a substance that promotes cancer in conjunction with a carcinogen. Studies indicate that alcohol and cigarettes together act synergistically to increase carcinogenic potential, particularly in the mouth and throat. So far it has been difficult to separate the effects of drinking from the effects of smoking because most heavy drinkers are also heavy smokers. Smokers risk developing cancer of the mouth and throat and smokers who also drink heavily run an even greater risk of developing such cancers. It has been estimated that when drinking and smoking are combined, the risk of developing cancer of the mouth and throat is 15 times greater than normal, i.e., the risk among the nondrinking and nonsmoking population.

There are a number of theories about why alcohol increases the incidence of cancer. The diets of alcoholics are often poorly balanced and nutritionally inadequate (see NUTRITION). Cancers of the mouth, esophagus and pharynx have been linked to deficiencies of VITAMINS AND MINERALS. Consumption of alcohol may also weaken the body's entire immune defense system, leaving it vulnerable to other cancer-causing agents. Alcohol is known to damage cellular tissue, especially the MITOCHONDRIA, the source of cellular energy. In addition alcohol has an effect on the cell membrane—possibly increasing the ability of carcinogens to affect the cells themselves. All alcoholic beverages consumed by man contain chemicals other than ETHANOL, and these may be carcinogenic, or these plus alcohol may act in SYNERGY to produce cancer.

CONGENERS, pharmacologically active molecules other than ethanol present in alcoholic beverages, may also play a role in the development of cancer. Known carcinogens have been found in many alcoholic beverages. Beer, for example, has been found to contain asbestos fibers from the filters used in its manufacture. Different beers, liquors and wines have varying quantities of contaminants that are by-products of distillation.

Cancer of the Mouth, Tongue, Pharynx and Larynx

Alcohol consumption, usually in combination with smoking, increases the risk of developing most cancers of the upper respiratory and digestive tracts. The mechanisms of the combined action of alcohol and tobacco are complex and vary from site to site. One theory is that tobacco carcinogens have easier access to the mucous membranes if the cells have been saturated in alcohol, with its solvent effects. Another theory is that alcohol and tobacco each independently exert a direct effect on the mucous membranes. Tobacco may contribute to cancer of the roof of the mouth, the nasopharynx (which connects with the nostrils), the larynx and the lung, where it directly contacts the mucous membranes. Alcohol may play more of a role in cancer of the floor of the mouth, the lower pharynx and the esophagus, where contact is most direct.

Esophagus

The cancer-causing role of alcohol among smokers was found to be even greater in cases of cancer of the esophagus than in those of cancer of the mouth and larynx. There is an increased risk of esophageal cancer among all drinkers, although it is apparently greater for whiskey drinkers than for wine or beer drinkers. Between 60% and 80% of patients who develop cancer of the esophagus have a history of alcohol abuse. Alcohol may destroy the chemical barriers in the esophagus, exposing susceptible cells to carcinogens. A study done in France in 1977 showed that the risk of esophageal cancer is 44 times greater for heavy users of both alcohol and tobacco than for abstainers from both drugs, compared with 18 times greater for heavy users of alcohol and five times greater for heavy users of tobacco.

Liver

Primary liver cancer (hepatoma) is very often accompanied by and probably preceded by CIRRHOSIS. In a study cited in the *Sixth Special Report to the U.S. Congress on Alcohol and Health,* the prevalence of cirrhosis in patients with liver cancer was found to be between 55% and 80%. There are possibly two stages involved in liver cancer: liver damage due to alcoholism, followed by intervention of a secondary agent setting off the actual malignancy.

Dr. Nicholas Pace, one of the nation's leading alcoholism treatment specialists and founder of Pace Health Services in Manhattan, recently told reporter Lucinda Franks, a Pulitzer Prize-winner for *The New York Times*, "If we thought yesterday's alcoholic was haunted by internal conflict, we know that today's is primarily haunted by his liver."

There are several risks for alcoholic patients who have cancer, including the development of WITHDRAWAL as a postoperative complication. Such patients have poorer chances of survival and greater chances of developing another primary tumor than other patients with the same type of cancer.

More research on the exact relationship between alcohol and cancer is needed. Cell study tests are currently being conducted to detect precancerous cells at sites associated with alcohol consumption.

American Association for Cancer Research, "Alcohol and Cancer Workshop," *Cancer Research* 39, no. 7 (July 1979).

Lucinda Franks, "A New Attack on Alcoholism," *The New York Times Magazine*, October 20, 1985.

carbohydrate   Alcohol affects carbohydrate metabolism and may increase or decrease blood sugar depending on the state of nutrition in the body. It appears that when hepatic (liver) carbohydrate stores are adequate, ethanol induces hyperglycemia, whereas when they are low, hypoglycemia results (see BLOOD SUGAR). Although it contains calories, alcohol has no nutritional value.

Beer is very high in carbohydrates as well as calories, and wine contains some carbohydrates. Most distilled liquors, such as gin and whiskey, have almost no carbohydrates. This lack of carbohydrates in hard liquor has become the basis for some fad diets, such as "the drinking man's diet." However, hard liquor has a lot of "empty calories" that must be metabolized before food calories, such as those in carbohydrates, which are then stored as fat. Therefore if someone drinks large

amounts of alcohol and eats, he or she is likely to gain rather than lose weight.

carcinogenesis   See CANCER.

cardiac arrhythmia   See HEART.

cardiovascular system   See HEART.

Career Teacher Program (CTP)   Jointly sponsored by the NATIONAL INSTITUTE ON ALCOHOL ABUSE AND ALCOHOLISM (NIAAA) and the NATIONAL INSTITUTE ON DRUG ABUSE (NIDA), this program has been the impetus for many of the new courses or expanded substance abuse curricula at 60 medical education institutions. The problems of alcohol abuse and alcoholism are, at long last, receiving increased emphasis in many medical school curricula, an area of longstanding criticism of medical professionals. The CTP was instituted in 1986-87 and is an ongoing endeavor by NIAAA and NIDA.

Catholicism   See RELIGION.

causes of alcoholism   See ETIOLOGY.

central nervous system (CNS)   The part of the nervous system made up of the brain, the spinal cord and the nerves originating from it. Sensory impulses are transmitted to the CNS and motor impulses pass out of it. When alcohol acts on the CNS, intoxication occurs, affecting emotional and sensory functions, judgment, memory and learning ability. While sight and hearing are not significantly changed, smell and taste are dulled, and the ability to withstand pain increases as BLOOD ALCOHOL CONCENTRATION rises. Alcohol slows reaction time, especially at blood alcohol levels above 0.10%, and disturbs motor control. With increased intoxication there are disturbances of speech and gait. At very high concentrations, alcohol in the blood suppresses the respiratory and cardiac centers in the lower brain, which can lead to shock and then death.

The way in which alcohol acts on the CNS tissue is not completely understood. The most prominent theory is that alcohol has the ability to interfere with the transfer of ions across the nerve cell membranes, reducing transmission of nerve impulses from one nerve cell to the next. It is known that alcohol inhibits the production and propagation of electrical impulses in nerves and disrupts nerve cell membranes.

Alcohol has a depressant effect on the CNS, slowing down the action of the nerves. At first alcohol may seem to have a stimulating effect, because the depression of certain functions of the cerebral cortex caused by alcohol consumption may reduce the inhibitory effects they have on some lower centers. Different parts of the brain appear to be affected by alcohol at different rates. Restlessness, excitement and agitation may all occur during the early part of intoxication. This early-release phenomenon must be distinguished from the hyperexcitability state that occurs as the blood alcohol content begins to drop (see WITHDRAWAL, SEDATIVE).

The long-term effects of alcohol on the central nervous system include TOLERANCE and DEPENDENCY, which show an adaptational process occurring in the brain tissue. When an individual develops a tolerance for alcohol, increasingly larger amounts are required to produce the same effect. After tolerance is established, the alcoholic develops a need for the drug in order to function.

There are a number of disorders of the CNS associated with heavy consumption of alcohol. Some of these, such as impaired judgment, increasing "highs" and "lows" in an individual with normally stable moods, diminished concentration and attention span and poor memory, are reversible if the patient abstains from alcohol, although the recovery process may take several months. These problems can occur in well-nourished individuals and increase in severity with age.

There are several more serious diseases of the CNS caused by excessive consumption of alcohol. After sustained heavy drinking alcoholics eventually develop irreversible brain tissue damage. Deficiencies in NUTRITION probably contribute to this process. Alcohol affects protein and nucleic-acid synthesis in the brain, which may be related to disturbances in learning and memory exhibited by alcoholics and to mental deficiencies and malformation in children with FETAL ALCOHOL SYNDROME. Another disease of the CNS, ALCOHOLIC POLYNEUROPATHY affects first and most severely the lower portions of the legs. ALCOHOL AMBLYOPIA, a relatively infrequent disease that involves a blurring of vision which may be followed by optic nerve degeneration, results from nutritional complications associated with alcoholism. WERNICKE'S ENCEPHALOPATHY, a disorder characterized by ocular abnormalities, uncoordination and mental confusion, is related to thiamine deficiency (see VITAMINS AND MINERALS) and can lead to KORSAKOFF'S PSYCHOSIS, which is distinguished by a severe impairment of memory and learning. Alcoholics also suffer from structural changes in the BRAIN, some of which are due to head injuries incurred while intoxicated and others, such as cerebellar degeneration and cerebral atrophy, are of unknown origin.

central pontine myelinolysis   A rare disease of unknown origin that occurs in a group of brain nerve fibers known as the pons. It is most often found in long-time alcoholics suffering from malnutrition. Difficult to diagnose, the principal symptoms are a progressive weakness in the muscles extending from the lowest part of the brain to the spinal cord, an inability to swallow and an absence of the gag reflex. As the disease progresses, the patient becomes drowsy and, finally, comatose.

cerebral atrophy   Decreased brain size (cerebral and cortical atrophy) has been a rather recent and major finding in studies of alcoholic patients. It has been demonstrated repeatedly by autopsy examination and computerized axialtomography (CT scan). Widespread atrophy has been revealed (along with cell loss) in many brain regions. Damage can result in memory disorders, including Wernicke-Korsakoff syndrome and aggregate signs and symptoms consisting of an acute (Wernicke) and chronic (Korsakoff) stage. The reversibility of alcohol-induced organic brain damage and neuropsychological impairment remains one of the most controversial yet important issues in all of alcohol-related research. (See also BRAIN and BRAIN DAMAGE.)

champagne   See SPARKLING WINE.

chaser   A mild liquid, such as water or beer, taken after a drink of strong liquor. The term and perhaps the custom derive from the French *chasser*. In France a *chasse-cafe* is a liqueur used to "chase" coffee. It is served as a digestif after a meal. The chaser has something of a soothing effect after a jolt of hard liquor, but its major use is to provide a contrast—a distinct, opposite sensation—just as the *chasse-cafe* contrasts with coffee.

Cheshire Blitz   See BRITISH ROAD SAFETY ACT OF 1967.

child abuse   According to the National Committee for Prevention of Child Abuse, 2.4 million cases of child abuse were reported to child welfare agencies in 1989, about 27% of which involved physical abuse. Although it is known that 30% to 40% of cases involve substance abuse of some kind, previous research has shown that alcohol may play a role in as many as one-third of all reported cases of child abuse *(Fourth Special Report to the U.S. Congress on Alcohol and Health)*. However, there has been a great deal of controversy about how strong the link between child abuse and alcoholism really is. To date little research has been done in this area, and a variety of methodological and conceptual problems exist to obscure the real nature of the relationship *(Seventh Special Report)*. In fact the percentage of alcoholics and misusers of alcohol in the general population appears to be almost identical to the percentage of alcoholics among child abusers. Margaret Hindman of the National Clearinghouse for Alcohol Information suggests that alcoholism may be more clearly associated with child neglect, both physical and emotional, than with actual abuse.

While the exact connection between child abuse and alcoholism is not known, there are certain characteristics common to both. One of the most striking is the repetitive cycle from generation to generation of both alcoholism and family violence. Lt. Cdr. Daniel W. Behling of the Naval Regional Medical Center in Long Beach, Calif. and others have reported a "generational" pattern of family violence and alcoholism. Behling found that 63% of abused children had at least one grandparent who was alcoholic or abused alcohol (Sanchez-Dirks). Abuse in the form of incest may also be related to alcoholism. One counselor estimated that half of the women she saw at a treatment center for alcoholics and drug addicts were or had been involved in an incestuous relationship with either a father or a brother (Youcha). Most had alcoholic fathers and those with alcoholic mothers became their replacements in bed. Alcohol dependence plays a role in nearly one-third of all reported cases of father-daughter incest, according to a study by researchers involved in the National Study on Child Neglect and Abuse Reporting in Denver, Colo.

While alcoholics may not personally abuse their children, they may abuse their spouses, who in turn may abuse the children. Alcoholics also may be in a state of withdrawal when they are not drinking, so that their level of irritability is very low. While alcohol misuse may not be a causal factor in child abuse, it can be said that in a family in which child abuse exists, alcohol misuse may aggravate the problem.

Few services aimed at abused children and battered wives focus on the possibility of alcohol involvement. In cases of severe abuse, the usual course of action used to be to remove the children to foster homes and jail the parents. More recently attempts have been made to rehabilitate the parent as well as protect the child. Joseph Mayer and Rebecca Black found that alcoholics in treatment for their drinking problems were likely to recognize their potential for inflicting physical abuse and were thereby often able to avoid it (Hindman). There is a growing awareness of the need to treat all members of the family in cases of family violence. (See also SPOUSE ABUSE.)

D.G. Hassett, "Family Alcoholism and Child Abuse. Where Do You Start?" *Focus on Family and Chemical Dependency*, 8(4) (July–August 1985): 14–15, 31.

Terri C. Orme and John Rimmer, "Alcoholism and Child Abuse: A Review," *Journal of Studies on Alcohol* 42, no. 3, (March 1981): 273-287.

P. Reagans, ABC News/Washington Post Poll, Survey #0190, May 1985.

Ruth Sanchez-Dirks, "Reflections on Family Violence," *Alcohol Health and Research World* 4, no. 1 (Fall 1979): 12-16.

Geraldine Youcha, *A Dangerous Pleasure* (New York: Hawthorn Books, 1978), passim.

children of alcoholics   Recently attention has been focused on the children of alcoholics. There are many negative effects associated with having an alcoholic parent; perhaps the most unfortunate is an increased likelihood that the child will become an alcoholic. Studies have shown that the best prediction of a child's drinking habits is the drinking pattern of his or her parents. Mothers seem to have more influence than fathers (Youcha). Daughters of alcoholics become alcoholics 20% to 50% of the time (Youcha), and daughters of alcoholic mothers are three times more likely to become alcoholics than daughters of non-alcoholic mothers. If they escape becoming alcoholics, they are likely to marry an alcoholic—half of the Al-Anon members (spouses of alcoholics) in a West Coast city had an alcoholic parent. And characteristic brain electrical patterns have been found in subjects who are not alcoholic but are judged to be at high risk for alcoholism if their fathers

or mothers are alcoholics. Fast EEG activity and deficiencies in alpha, theta and delta EEG activity have been reported in the high-risk sons of alcoholics. Also, investigators in the field suggest that electroencephalography may be the most sensitive indicator of fetal alcohol toxicity. It is also possible that the electroencephalographic disturbances noted could be a sign of alcohol withdrawal in the infant rather than toxicity; also the persistence and precise meaning of these EEG changes are not known.

Children of alcoholics generally do not completely understand the problem and are confused about their own responsibility for their parents' behavior. The alcoholic parent often shifts between being overly affectionate to neglectful or abusive. Children cannot understand this treatment in terms of their own behavior and become frightened and anxious. The alcoholic parent is often unavailable to the children because of drinking, and the spouse is unavailable because of his or her concerns about the alcoholic. The children may be used by one parent in maneuvers against the other, or they may blame themselves for their parents' drinking.

Some children may seem to cope with their parents' drinking and not really suffer because of it. However, as Claudia Black, family program coordinator for Raleigh Hills Hospitals in Irvine, Calif., points out, the children of alcoholics run a high risk of developing a variety of problems, and even those who appear to handle the situation well are affected by parental alcoholism. The ways in which such children have learned to adjust may eventually be the source of problems later in life. A child who takes the responsible role, attempting to care for his parents, his siblings and himself, may be unable to depend on others in later life and will always need to feel in control of a situation. A child who adjusts to a drinking parent's mood changes and to the various commotions occurring in the family may later continue to allow himself to be manipulated by others and lose his or her self-esteem. A child who always tries to smooth over conflicts and help others in the family feel at ease may later fear and deny his or her own feelings of anger and be constantly trying to please others. The roles that seemed positive in childhood may have negative consequences in adulthood.

Because even the responsible, independent children are likely to develop problems later in life, it is important that the whole family be involved in treatment. In the past, children who have been neglected by alcoholic parents have often been sent to foster homes. Today it is recognized that this approach is not always the answer. A child who is sent away may feel increased guilt, possibly believing that he or she has failed completely. Furthermore a mother who fears that her child will be taken away is less likely to enter into treatment.

Family life does not immediately get better after an alcoholic parent stops drinking. A child may meet a parent's sobriety with resentment or hostility, having grown accustomed to living without rules and doing what he or she pleases. The child may also be upset that the parent can no longer be used as the scapegoat for misbehavior. A family needs time to adjust to the new situation. (See also ENVIRONMENT AND ALCOHOLISM.)

ALCOHOLICS ANONYMOUS sponsors AL-ATEEN, a group designed primarily to help the children of alcoholics.

Recently, much attention has been paid to the treatment needs of children of alcholics once they've reached adulthood. Meetings of adult children of alcoholics groups, modeled after the 12-step meetings of AA, have proliferated, and a wealth of supportive literature on the subject has been published.

Claudia Black, "Innocent Bystanders at Risk: The Children of Alcoholics," *Alcoholism* 1, no. 3, (January-February 1981): 22-25.

Geraldine Youcha, *A Dangerous Pleasure* (New York: Hawthorn Books, 1978), passim.

Janet G. Woititz, *Adult Children of Alcoholics* (Deerfield Beach, Fl.: Health Communications, 1983).

chronic   A term used to describe a disease or condition that continues for a long time and is characterized by slowly progressing symptoms, as distinguished from an ACUTE disease or condition.

chronic alcohol intoxication   A state of intoxication maintained by repeated consumption of alcohol before or just after previously taken alcohol has been metabolized. The term is sometimes also used generally to refer to ALCOHOLISM, although of course many alcoholics are not continually intoxicated.

chronic alcoholic   See CHRONIC ALCOHOLISM.

chronic alcoholism   A redundant term since alcoholism is itself a chronic disorder. The term "chronic alcoholism" is sometimes used to refer to alcoholism without complications or to a long lasting alcoholic disorder, in order to distinguish it from more severe phases of the disease. (See ACUTE ALCOHOLISM.)

chug-a-lug   A slang term meaning to drink a glassful of a beverage in one gulp or in a series of uninterrupted swallows. The practice is somewhat popular among students, who have "chug-a-lug" contests, usually with beer.

Chug-a-lugging is a drinking fad, along with a number of other similar practices, such as "one-a-minute," in which a drinker consumes a shot of beer a minute for an hour. These contests and styles of drinking are generally part of a tradition in which virility and social acceptance are equated with the ability to consume large amounts of alcohol. Aside from producing rapid intoxication, these contests can be quite dangerous and may result in coma or death, particularly when hard liquor is consumed.

Church of England Temperance Society

The largest British temperance society, it was founded in 1862 and reconstituted in 1873 with the dual goal of promoting total abstinence and general anti-intemperance.

The society supported measures of reform, rather than prohibition, and, in particular, reduction of licenses to sell alcohol and popular control of the alcohol traffic. It had an extensive publication department, educational courses, missions and homes for inebriants. The society's comparative moderation contrasted with the extreme stance of many other temperance societies. In 1909 total membership was 636,233, including 485,888 members of the juvenile division. The numerical strength of several temperance societies at this time was provided by juvenile contingents.

cigarettes   See SMOKING.

cirrhosis   (From the Greek *kirrhos* orange-colored—the color of a cirrhotic liver.) The U.S. Department of Health and Human Services defines cirrhosis as "a chronic inflammatory disease of the liver in which functioning liver cells are replaced by scar tissue." It involves a disruption of the liver structure by fibrous tissue and nodule formation, which results in impaired liver function.

Cirrhosis is the result of the normal reaction of the liver to injury, whatever the cause. The vast majority of cases, particularly in the United States, are secondary to chronic alcohol abuse. Usually it takes from five to seven years of steady drinking to develop cirrhosis. Each time alcohol is abused, the liver is injured only mildly, but continuous abuse has a cumulative effect over the years. The liver cells are slowly replaced by fibrous scar tissue, resulting in irreparable damage and leaving a smaller and smaller fraction of the liver to carry on the organ's normal functions (including the detoxification of alcohol).

Although the majority of cirrhotic deaths are related to alcoholism, no more than approximately 10% of alcoholics develop cirrhosis, so there is reason to believe that genetic and other factors, particularly NUTRITION, play an important role in the contraction of or immunity from cirrhosis.

Malnutrition, from which many alcoholics suffer, can increase the severity and degree of alcoholic fatty liver development. However, studies have shown that even with an adequate diet, high alcohol consumption damages the liver. In one such study, despite receiving a high-protein, nutritionally adequate diet, baboons developed severe liver damage as a result of forced heavy ingestion of alcohol over a prolonged period.

Different racial groups are affected differently—American JEWS tend to have a lower-than-average incidence of cirrhosis, whereas among AMERICAN INDIANS the rate is considerably higher. And according to 1986 figures compiled by the U.S. Department of Health and Human Services, cirrhosis mortality is 1.5 times as high for nonwhites as for whites, the rate for nonwhite males aged 25 to 34 is nearly three times as high as that for white males in the same age group.

Cirrhosis is the final stage of liver injury in alcoholics. Heavy drinking over a period of years can produce a FATTY LIVER, which, as the name indicates, is characterized by a buildup of increased amounts of fat on the liver. However, if the patient abstains from alcohol, the abnormal accumulation of fat will disappear (see LIVER). If drinking continues, fatty liver, in most people, will evolve into more severe liver diseases, such as ALCOHOLIC HEPATITIS and irreversible cirrhosis. Exactly why the liver may lose its ability to adapt to alcohol has not been clearly established. Symptoms of cirrhosis usually become apparent after a person reaches 30 and more severe problems appear after 40.

There are many types of cirrhosis, but one type—portal cirrhosis—is predominant and most frequently affects alcoholics. Portal cirrhosis is named for the portal vein, a large vein that transports blood from the stomach and spleen to the liver, where it is dispersed into the capillaries. This type of cirrhosis is also

Mortality from Cirrhosis of the Liver in 26 Countries with Complete Data for Period 1955–1959 and for 1971 and 1974, Rate per 100,000 Population, by Sex

| | Males | | | | | | Females | | | | | | Male | | Female | |
| | Period 1955–59 | | Year 1971 | | Year 1974 | | Period 1955–59 | | Year 1971 | | Year 1974 | | Around 1987[a] | | Around 1987[a] | |
Country	Rate[1]	Posi-tion	Rate[1]	Posi-tion	Rate[1]	Posi-tion	Rate[1]	Posi-tion	Rate[1]	Posi-tion	Rate[1]	Posi-tion	No.	Rate	No.	Rate
AMERICA																
Canada	8.80	14	14.24	13	16.0	13	5.19	15	7.73	14	7.3	13	1418	11.2	738	5.7
Chile	49.22	1	71.87	1	39.0	5	23.73	1	28.56	1	15.4	6	1688	27.2	683	10.8
United States	15.42	10	22.52	8	21.2	10	8.25	10	11.65	7	10.6	9	17051	14.4	9150	7.3
Venezuela[b]	24.44	5	21.92	10	9.1	17	15.24	4	10.59	8	4.3	20	44604	5.1	34752	4.1
ASIA																
Israel	6.68	16	8.20	18	7.5	19	5.26	14	6.31	16	4.9	18	189	8.8	85	3.9
Japan	18.37	9	22.36	9	19.7	11	12.63	5	10.52	9	7.3	12	11689	19.5	5303	8.5
EUROPE																
Austria	25.13	4	43.26	5	49.3	1	9.92	8	14.26	6	17.9	4	1385	38.3	582	14.6
Belgium	9.96	13	13.09	14	17.8	12	5.87	13	8.18	12	11.2	8	814	16.9	567	11.2
Czechoslovakia	10.25	12	21.53	11	24.6	7	7.47	11	8.84	11	9.7*	10	2239	29.5	809	10.1
Denmark	6.04	17	10.03	16	12.5	15	9.88	9	8.07	13	8.4	11	465	18.4	236	9.1
Finland	5.25	19	6.19	19	8.3	18	3.67	22	3.38	21	2.8	24	283	11.8	140	5.5
France	38.27	3	48.04	3	47.6	2	18.23	3	20.06	3	18.6	2	7919	29.2	3288	11.5
Germany, W.	19.35	8	32.09	6	37.8	6	10.62	6	14.41	5	17.0	5	8998	30.5	5081	15.9
Hungary	11.01	11	16.66	12	21.3	9	7.32	12	9.63	10	11.3	7	3207	62.7	1444	26.3
Ireland	2.76	25	2.90	26	4.8	24	1.82	26	2.21	26	2.6	26	61	3.4	32	1.8
Italy	24.17	6	14.73	4	46.4	3	10.17	7	15.90	4	18.1	3	11680	42.0	5808	19.7
Netherlands	4.66	20	5.47	21	5.7	22	4.07	18	3.75	19	3.4	22	500	6.9	282	5.8
Norway	3.69	23	4.43	22	5.5	23	3.88	20	2.89	23	2.7	25	203	9.8	115	5.4
Portugal	40.03	2	50.64	2	44.7	4	20.08	2	24.94	2	19.9	1	2013	40.5	792	14.9
Sweden	5.42	18	10.28	15	15.1	14	4.13	17	5.46	17	6.0	15	393	9.5	219	5.1
Switzerland	22.00	7	24.29	7	23.0	8	5.07	16	6.86	15	6.9	14	543	16.9	216	6.4
United Kingdom																
England and Wales	2.70	26	3.05	25	3.8	26	2.19	25	2.66	25	3.4	23	1495	6.1	1307	5.1
Northern Ireland	3.01	24	3.50	24	4.2	25	3.15	23	2.88	24	4.5	19	33	4.3	26	3.2
Scotland	4.51	21	4.37	23	7.2	20	3.77	21	3.52	20	5.4	16	242	9.8	187	7.1
OCEANIA																
Australia	7.05	15	8.82	17	11.6	16	3.96	19	4.44	18	4.9	17	863	10.6	319	3.9
New Zealand[c]	4.22	22	5.58	20	7.2	21	2.62	24	3.12	22	3.7	21	72	4.4	41	2.5

[1] Rate per 100,000 population, standardized by the direct method; standard population Switzerland 1971.
*1973.
Figures for 1955–1959 and 1971: WHO (1976).
Figures for 1974: WHO (1977).
[a] WHO. *1989 World Health Statistics Annual.* Geneva, 1989 for most recent year.
[b] PAHO/HST/TIS Technical Information System, for most recent year.
[c] WHO. *1988 World Health Statistics Annual.* Geneva, 1988 for most recent year.

known as Laennec's, nutritional or alcoholic cirrhosis. Portal cirrhosis is characterized by small diffuse nodules and, usually in the alcoholic, extensive fatty infiltration of the liver. Frequently there are also signs of considerable inflammation. Because of the size of the nod-ules, this type of cirrhosis has recently been classified by some as micronodular cirrhosis.

The onset of cirrhosis is associated with such nonspecific complaints as weakness and fatigability. As the disease progresses, some of the associated effects may include:

1. Jaundice, because bilirubin pigment (a reddish-yellow pigment) can no longer be removed by the liver;
2. Fluid accumulation in the legs (edema) or in the abdomen (ascites), because the liver cannot make enough albumin, which normally holds this fluid in the body's vessels;
3. Uncontrolled bleeding due to a decrease in clotting factors in the blood; and
4. Increased sensitivity to drugs because the liver cannot inactivate them.

No successful therapeutic treatment has been developed for cirrhosis. Long-term survival of patients with portal cirrhosis is markedly improved by abstinence from alcohol. In a study the five-year survival rate after diagnosis of portal cirrhosis was 63% for abstainers compared with 40.5% for those who continued to drink.

Research conducted in 1981 by a team under the direction of Yedy Israel and funded by the Addiction Research Foundation in Toronto may lead to significant progress in the understanding of cirrhosis. The researchers found that prolonged heavy drinking causes liver cells to swell, which in turn can block the flow of blood in the organ. They feel that the relative health of the liver is indicated by the size of its cells and the condition of the blood vessels and not by the presence or absence of cirrhosis. Backing up this theory are figures which show that about 10% of the alcoholics seen by the researchers had completely normal liver function and yet had full-grown cirrhosis, yet alcoholics who are free of cirrhosis can die of portal hypertension or hepatic coma (caused by swollen liver cells that squeeze the fine blood vessels and block the flow of blood). Since the swelling of the liver cells is reversible with abstinence—while cirrhosis is not—the finding of the research team indicates some hope for cirrhotic patients.

There are many varieties of cirrhosis that are less common than portal cirrhosis. One kind that may also affect alcoholics is called postnecrotic cirrhosis, which follows liver damage caused by toxic or viral hepatitis. The difference between portal cirrhosis and postnecrotic cirrhosis is that in the latter the nodules are larger and more widely spaced. Because of the larger nodules, postnecrotic cirrhosis is sometimes classified as macronodular cirrhosis.

Among the types of cirrhosis not related to alcoholism are several that affect children and two types of biliary cirrhosis: primary biliary, a rare form of unknown etiology affecting chiefly middle-aged women, and secondary biliary resulting from obstruction or infection of the bile ducts.

"Cirrhosis in Women Is Up," *The Journal,* Toronto, 10, no. 6 (June 1, 1981): 6.

Charles S. Lieber, "The Metabolism of Alcohol," *Scientific American* 234, no. 3 (March 1976): 25-33.

————, L. M. DeCarli and E. Rubin, "Sequential Production of Fatty Liver, Hepatitis, and Cirrhosis in Subhuman Primates Fed with Adequate Diets," *Proceedings of the National Academy of Sciences* 72, no. 2 (February 1975): 437-441.

"Liver Ailments—Part I: Cirrhosis," *The Harvard Medical School Health Letter* 6, no. 3 (January 1981).

Pat Ohlendorf, "Key to Liver Dysfunction Spotted?" *The Journal,* Toronto, 10, no. 3 (March 1, 1981): 1-2.

classification of alcoholics   The *Seventh Special Report to the U.S. Congress on Alcohol and Health* (DHHS, 1990) covered recent developments in both nomenclature and diagnosis of alcoholics. Attention was given to the revised third edition of the *Diagnostic and Statistical Manual of Mental Disorders*—DSM III-R (American Psychiatric Association, 1987) as well as to work on the INTERNATIONAL CLASSIFICATION OF DISEASES sponsored jointly by the U.S. Alcohol, Drug Abuse, and Mental Health Administration and the World Health Organization (WHO). Each concept (e.g., alcoholism, alcohol abuse, alcohol dependence, alcohol-related disabilities) is a useful category for certain purposes and certain populations, but none, it seems, is adequate to represent the full range of problems associated with alcohol consumption. Continuing attention is being paid to the heterogeneity apparent among alcoholics, and ongoing attempts to develop concepts and measurements appropriate to such heterogeneity are apparent. The ALCOHOL DEPENDENCE SYNDROME (ADS) concept has been gaining acceptance. DSM-III-R has incorporated a dimensional model of dependence resembling the ADS construct. The International Classification of Diseases has used such a construct since 1978. Possible applications of this concept involve approaches to individualized treatment planning.

co-alcoholic `   See PARA-ALCOHOLIC.

codeine with alcohol   A dangerous combination the possible effects of which include respiratory arrest and depression of brain activity. The same effects can result from combinations of alcohol with other narcotic analgesics, such as morphine, Demerol and methadone. (See also DRUGS.)

coffee   See CAFFEINE.

Cognac   Under French law, the name "Cognac" may be given only to BRANDY produced in an officially defined region in and around Cognac, a town in the Charente *department* of southwestern France. The Cognac region is divided into seven subregions according to the quality of the brandy produced in each. A Cognac is usually a blend of two or more Cognacs from the different subregions. Blends with the highest proportion of Cognac produced in the Grande Champagne subregion are thought to be the best. The differences in quality are due to differences in the soil in which the grapes used in the production are grown.

Cognac undergoes a double-distillation process known as the *methode charentaise.*

The product of the first distillation is called *brouillis,* which is a liquid between 50 and 60 proof. The *brouillis* is then returned to the still for a second distillation, the product of which is raw Cognac, or *bonne chauffe,* whose proof is between 140 and 150.

The *bonne chauffe* is placed in specially made oaken casks to age. Standard Cognacs are normally aged from five to 20 years; the finest may be aged for as long as 50 or even 100 years. As it ages, Cognac loses some of its alcoholic content, which may be further reduced through the addition of distilled water. Most bottled Cognac is between 68 and 80 proof.

Like other brandies Cognac is usually sipped by itself as an after-dinner drink.

cognitive function   The current state of knowledge concerning neuropsychological deficits as markers of genetic predisposition to alcoholism is still not well developed. There does seem to be a link between alcoholism in a parent and certain neurobehavioral characteristics in offspring, but environmental causes for such a link haven't been ruled out.

cold turkey   The act of being taken off a drug suddenly and completely, without preparation (see WITHDRAWAL).

Commission on Accreditation of Rehabilitation Facilities (CARF)   See JOINT COMMISSION ON ACCREDITATION OF HOSPITALS (JCAH).

compulsion   A term used by psychologists usually to refer to a psychological force that makes an individual act against his or her own will. In that sense compulsion does not cover the type of behavior described in WITHDRAWAL, whereby the need to drink arises from physical sources. The term "compulsion" is often used interchangeably with CRAVING.

congeners   The organic alcohols and salts formed in the manufacture of alcoholic

Monthly Share of Annual Liquor Consumption in the United States

January	6.9%	July	7.8%
February	7.2%	August	7.5%
March	8.1%	September	8.0%
April	7.9%	October	8.0%
May	7.9%	November	9.7%
June	8.6%	December	12.4%

NOTE: Data exclude beer and wine consumption.
SOURCE: Distilled Spirits Council of the United States, Inc., 1987.

beverages are called congeners. They provide the distinctive flavor and pungency of various beverages. Different liquors have different congener contents; vodkas contain the least and bourbons and brandies the most.

Congeners have been suspected of contributing to the HANGOVER effect, but because of the small amounts used, their role is thought to be unimportant. They may compete with ethanol for its metabolizing enzyme, alcohol dehydrogenase, resulting in the buildup of unmetabolized alcohols in the body and a toxic effect (see METABOLISM). However, pure ethanol has been shown to be the major cause of hangovers.

Congeners may play some part in the development of CANCER, but how much is not known. A study published in 1979 showed that the risk of cancer of the esophagus was more pronounced in alcoholics who drank apple brandy, which has a high congener content, and less apparent in those who drank beer and wine (Tuyns et al.).

A. J. Tuyns, G. Pequinot and J. S. Abbatucci, "Oesophageal Cancer and Alcohol Consumption," *International Journal of Cancer* 23 (1979): 443–447.

consumption   There are two principal ways of estimating consumption: apparent consumption, which is derived from official reports of states, tax records and, in some cases, reports of sales by the alcoholic beverage industry; and self-reported consumption, which is derived from responses to surveys of individuals.

Total Per Capita Ethanol Consumption, 1935–1987

Gallons of Ethanol

Note: Vertical axis does not start at zero.

SOURCE: U.S. Department of Health and Human Services, National Institute on Alcohol Abuse and Alcoholism, *Apparent Per Capita Alcohol Consumption National, State and Regional Trends, 1977–1987*, (Rockville, Md., 1989).

Per Capita Ethanol Consumption by Beverage Type, 1977–1987

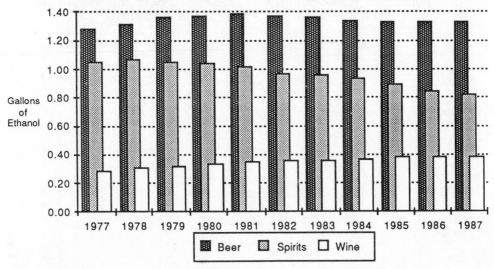

SOURCE: U.S. Department of Health and Human Services, National Institute on Alcohol Abuse and Alcoholism, *Apparent Per Capita Alcohol Consumption National, State and Regional Trends, 1977–1987,* (Rockville, Md., 1989).

In the United States from 1934 to 1978 apparent consumption of beer, wine and distilled spirits increased, with the rate of increase varying for given periods and types of beverages. During the 1960s there was a rapid rise in apparent consumption, as the relatively stable rate of 2 gallons of 100% ethanol (ABSOLUTE ALCOHOL) per person per year of the 1950s grew to 2.5 gallons by 1970, a 25% increase in apparent consumption during one decade. In the 1970s the rate of growth in apparent consumption slowed to 8%.

During the 1980s, a consistent decrease has been witnessed, and consumption declined by about 8% from 1980 to 1987. Alcoholic beverage sales have also been declining since the early 1980s, according to the industry trade publication *Impact.* Sales of distilled products fell 4.2% in 1988, compared to 1987.

Apparent consumption in the United States averaged 2.54 gallons in 1982, slightly less than 1 ounce of 100% ethanol (approximately 2 drinks) per day for each person 14 years of age and older. Since approximately one-third of the United States adult population reported

abstaining (Clark and Midanik), daily average consumption for those who drink is higher, 1.5 ounces of 100% ethanol (3 drinks). This average is still somewhat misleading because a small proportion of adults drink far more than the average and the majority drink less. It has been estimated that more than 16 million adults 18 years and older (approximately 11% of the adult population) consume about half of all beverages sold in the United States (Malin et al.). In 1987, the gallons of alcohol consumed per year per person had dropped back to 2.54 from an estimate of 2.76 gallons in both 1981 and 1982.

Beer consumption has remained relatively level from 1978 to 1987, with the most recent apparent per capita rate for the population age 14 and older (in absolute alcohol) of 1.34 gallons (nearly 30 actual gallons). For the first time in 10 years, at the end of the same period, wine consumption did not increase (.039 gallons in 1987). Consumption of distilled spirits experienced a consistent decline from 1978 to 1987 (from just under 1.1 gallons in 1978 to 0.83 gallons in 1987). An increasingly conservative social climate may have contributed to

Apparent Per Capita Ethanol Consumption for United States, 1850–1987
(gallons of ethanol, based on population age 15 and older prior to 1970 and
on population age 14 and older thereafter)

Year	Beer	Wine	Spirits	Total
1987	1.34	0.38	0.83	2.54
1986	1.34	0.39	0.85	2.58
1985	1.33	0.38	0.90	2.62
1984	1.35	0.37	0.94	2.65
1983	1.37	0.36	0.96	2.69
1982	1.38	0.36	0.98	2.72
1981	1.39	0.35	1.02	2.76
1980	1.38	0.34	1.04	2.76
1979	1.37	0.32	1.06	2.75
1978	1.32	0.31	1.07	2.71
1977	1.29	0.29	1.06	2.64
1976	1.27	0.32	1.10	2.69
1975	1.26	0.32	1.11	2.70
1974	1.25	0.31	1.11	2.67
1973	1.20	0.31	1.10	2.62
1972	1.17	0.30	1.09	2.56
1971	1.15	0.31	1.12	2.59
1970	1.14	0.27	1.11	2.52
1969	1.12	0.26	1.13	2.51
1968	1.09	0.26	1.10	2.45
1967	1.07	0.25	1.05	2.37
1966	1.06	0.24	1.02	2.32
1965	1.04	0.24	0.99	2.27
1964	1.04	0.24	0.95	2.23
1963	1.01	0.23	0.91	2.15
1962	0.99	0.22	0.90	2.11
1961	0.97	0.23	0.86	2.06
1960	0.99	0.22	0.86	2.07
1959	1.00	0.22	0.84	2.06
1958	0.96	0.22	0.80	1.98
1957	0.97	0.22	0.80	1.99
1956	1.00	0.22	0.81	2.03
1955	1.01	0.22	0.77	2.00
1954	1.01	0.21	0.74	1.96
1953	1.04	0.20	0.77	2.01
1952	1.04	0.21	0.73	1.98
1951	1.03	0.20	0.78	2.01
1950	1.04	0.23	0.77	2.04
1949	1.06	0.22	0.70	1.98
1948	1.07	0.20	0.70	1.97
1947	1.11	0.16	0.76	2.03
1946	1.07	0.24	0.99	2.30
1945	1.17	0.20	0.88	2.25
1944	1.13	0.18	0.76	2.07
1943	1.00	0.17	0.66	1.83
1942	0.90	0.22	0.85	1.97

Apparent Per Capita Ethanol Consumption for United States, 1850–1987
(continued)

Year	Beer	Wine	Spirits	Total
1941	0.81	0.18	0.71	1.70
1940	0.73	0.16	0.67	1.56
1939	0.75	0.14	0.62	1.51
1938	0.75	0.13	0.59	1.47
1937	0.82	0.13	0.64	1.59
1936	0.79	0.12	0.59	1.50
1935	0.68	0.09	0.43	1.20
1934	0.61	0.07	0.29	0.91
(PROHIBITION)				
1916–19	1.08	0.12	0.76	1.96
1911–15	1.48	0.14	0.94	2.56
1906–10	1.47	0.17	0.96	2.60
1901–05	1.31	0.13	0.95	2.39
1896–1900	1.19	0.10	0.77	2.06
1891–95	1.17	0.11	0.95	2.23
1881–90	0.90	0.14	0.95	1.99
1871–80	0.56	0.14	1.02	1.72
1870	0.44	0.10	1.53	2.07
1860	0.27	0.10	2.16	2.53
1850	0.14	0.03	1.88	2.05

SOURCES: Steffens, R.A.; Stinson, F.S.; Freel, C.G.; and Clem, D. *Surveillance Report #10: Apparent Per Capita Consumption: National, State, and Regional Trends, 1977–1986.* Rockville, MD: National Institute on Alcohol Abuse and Alcoholism, Division of Biometry and Epidemiology, Alcohol Epidemiologic Data System, October 1988.

Data updated from: Hyman, M.; Zimmerman, M.; Gurioli, C.; and Helrich, A. *Drinkers, Drinking and Alcohol-Related Mortality and Hospitalizations: A Statistical Compendium,* 1980 edition.

this turning away from beverages with a high alcohol content.

In 1988, vodka was the best-selling liquor at 38 million cases, up from 21 million in 1970.

Nevada is the leading state in per capita apparent consumption, just ahead of Washington, D.C., although both have substantial nonresident sales which may inflate values. For the period of 1977 to 1987 Connecticut, Ohio, Delaware and Alaska showed the largest percentage increases in per capita consumption. The greatest decreases in consumption in this period came in Nevada, Wyoming, New Hampshire and Hawaii.

In 1987, the drinking habits of men indicated 14% heavier drinkers, 36% moderate drinkers, 28% light drinkers and 22% abstainers. Among women, the percentage of drinkers ran from 7% listed as heavier, 21% moderate, 40% light and 32% abstainers. (Note: These basic data from NIAAA stipulate that abstainers consume 0-12 drinks per year, light drinkers have 3 drinks per week, moderate drinkers have 4-13 drinks per week, and heavier drinkers have 14 or more drinks per week.)

Per capita consumption of alcohol is lower in the United States than in many countries. In 1987, a report published in the Netherlands ranked the United States 21st out of 47 countries countries surveyed, with a per capita consumption of 7.6 liters of 100% ethanol (see Table 4). The same year the consumption level in France was 13.0 liters.

See tables and figures in Appendix 1 for more recent data on consumption. There has

International Apparent Per Capita Consumption of All Alcoholic Beverages, 1985–1987 (in liters of absolute ethanol based on total population)

Country	1985	1986	1987
France	13.3	13.2	13.0
Luxembourg	13.0	12.7	13.0
Spain	11.8	11.7	12.7
Switzerland	11.2	11.0	11.0
Hungary	11.5	11.4	10.7
Belgium	10.5	10.3	10.7
West Germany	10.8	10.5	10.6
Portugal	13.1	11.2	10.5
East Germany	10.3	10.5	10.5
Italy	11.6	10.2	10.0
Austria	9.9	10.0	9.9
Denmark	9.9	10.0	9.6
Bulgaria	8.8	9.3	8.9
Argentina	8.9	9.0	8.9
Australia	9.0	8.7	8.8
Czechoslovakia	9.4	9.0	8.6
Netherlands	8.5	8.6	8.3
New Zealand	8.2	8.3	8.3
Canada	7.9	7.8	na
Rumania	7.9	7.8	7.6
U.S.A.	8.0	7.6	7.6
Yugoslavia	6.3	7.4	7.6
United Kingdom	7.1	7.1	7.3
Poland	7.0	7.2	7.2
Finland	6.5	6.9	7.1
Japan	5.7	5.9	6.3
Cyprus	5.6	5.9	6.3
Uruguay	5.1	5.0	5.5
Sweden	5.2	5.5	5.4
Ireland	5.6	5.5	5.4
Greece*	6.2	4.6	5.4
Chile*	5.6	5.0	5.2
South Africa	4.2	4.5	4.4
Norway	4.2	4.2	4.4
Iceland	4.0	4.1	4.1
Venezuela*	3.1	3.1	3.7
U.S.S.R.	5.7	3.5	3.2
Colombia**	2.6	2.7	2.8
Peru*	1.6	1.9	2.2
Brazil*	1.4	1.9	1.9
Paraguay*	1.9	1.5	1.9
Mexico*	1.7	1.8	1.8
Cuba**	1.3	1.4	1.5

International Apparent Per Capita Consumption of II Alcoholic Beverages, 1985–1987 (*continued*)

Country	1985	1986	1987
Turkey	1.0	1.0	1.0
Tunisia*	0.7	0.6	0.6
Algeria*	0.3	0.3	0.3
Morocco*	0.2	0.3	0.3

na: Data not available

*Either no reliable or no complete statistical data on the consumption of distilled spirits were available for this country

**Covers only consumption of beer. No figures are known on the consumption of distilled spirits or wine.

NOTE: When calculating the quantity in liters of absolute alcohol in beer, in the absence of precise data, an average of 5% alcohol content was used; wine was calculated with an average of 12% alcohol content. Other alcoholic beverages, such as cider, sake, fruit wines, British wines, and wine coolers, were included in the calculation of the total alcohol consumption above, if consumption figures were known for them.

SOURCE: *Hoeveel alcoholhoude dranken worden er in de wereld gedronken?* (How many alcoholic beverages are being consumed throughout the world?) 27th ed. (Schiedam, Netherlands: Produktschap voor gedistilleerde dranken, 1987).

been a debate in recent years over the relationship between the general level of alcohol consumption in a population and the percentage of heavy drinkers. This issue is still unresolved and while some countries have shown increases in hospital admission rates for patients with a diagnosis of alcoholism or alcoholic psychosis where there have been increases in per capita consumption, there has so far been little evidence of a decrease in rates with decreased consumption.

Laura Z. Chatfield, "Alcoholic Beverage Sales Staggered by Baby Boomers," *USA Today*, August 17, 1989.

W. B. Clark and L. Midanik, "Alcohol Use and Alcohol Problems among U.S. Adults," *Alcohol Consumption and Related Problems,* Alcohol and Health Monograph no. 1 (Rockville, Md.: National Institute on Alcohol Abuse and Alcoholism, in press).

Enoch Gordis, M.D., ed., *Seventh Special Report to the U.S. Congress on Alcohol and Health,* (Rockville, Md.: National Institute on Alcohol Abuse and Alcoholism, 1990), chapter II.

Hoeveel alcoholhoude dranken worden er in de wereld gedronken? (How many alcoholic beverages are being consumed throughout the

world?), 27th ed. Schiedam, Netherlands: Produktschap Voor Gedistilleerde Dranken, 1987.

H. Malin et al. "An Epidemiologic Perspective on Alcohol Use and Abuse in the United States," *Alcohol Consumption and Related Problems,* Alcohol and Health Monograph no. 1 (Rockville, Md.: National Institute on Alcohol Abuse and Alcoholism, in press).

Joy Moser, *Prevention of Alcohol-Related Problems* (Toronto: World Health Organization, 1980), pp. 50-53.

National Institute on Alcohol Abuse and Alcoholism, *Apparent Per Capita Alcohol Consumption National, State and Regional Trends, 1977–1987,* Surveillance Report No. 13, 1989.

controlled drinking   Drinking within a socially acceptable context, well short of intoxication, by a person who deliberately sets a limit on the number of drinks he or she will take and stops drinking when that limit is reached. The concept, as applied to alcoholics, runs directly contrary to the traditional belief that complete ABSTINENCE is the only course to recovery.

Among those who have suggested that alcoholics may resume drinking—as long as it is controlled drinking—are David J. Armor, J.

Michael Polich and Harriet B. Stambul, the authors of the RAND REPORTS. They feel that certain types of patients might successfully exercise controlled drinking under proper circumstances. According to their findings, patients with a relatively short history of problem drinking have a greater likelihood of success with controlled drinking than those with a long history of alcoholism. Those able to control their drinking showed fewer alcoholic symptoms than those who could not, and they were often younger and had generally lower consumption rates than those who were not able to exercise control. The authors point out that today therapists have a wider range of treatment possibilities and can gear the treatment to suit the patient rather than impose a uniform program of abstinence upon all.

Opponents have responded, many quite vehemently, that the studies are faulty. They insist, citing past experience, that the time span of the study was too short and that most, if not all, of the controlled drinkers will eventually begin again to drink alcoholically. They also question whether many of the controlled drinkers in the sample were really alcoholics, pointing out such aspects of the sample as "youth," "short history of problem drinking" and "lower consumption rates." Furthermore they argue that controlled drinking places abnormal pressures on those whose most basic problem is LOSS OF CONTROL. But most importantly opponents see controlled drinking as a tempting illusion presented with scientific authority. They argue that even if some controlled drinking is possible by some alcoholics, the possibility will be most tempting to those least able to cope with it. Supporters of the Rand Reports counter that objective scientific study, with its possible future benefits, should not be suppressed simply because there are some who would distort or misuse it. See BEHAVIOR MODIFICATION.

controlled substance   A psychoactive drug, such as a narcotic, which is strictly controlled by law. Stringent requirements govern the prescribing and dispensing of these sub-stances as well as their manufacture, storage and transport, and an exact inventory of the quantities on hand and dispensed must be maintained at all times.

Although alcoholic beverages are sometimes said to be "controlled," they are not; they are regulated. Most countries and states have laws governing the sale and purchase of alcoholic beverages, but from manufacture through retail sales there is no strict enforcement and the supplier is not held accountable for every ounce of the substance. (For an overview of the articles on regulation of the manufacture and sale of alcoholic beverages, see REGULATION.)

convulsions   When alcoholics who are physically dependent on alcohol do not drink, they go through WITHDRAWAL. This process can be relatively mild, but in severe cases convulsions may occur. These can begin as early as 12 hours after the start of ABSTINENCE, but they more often appear during the second or third day after an alcoholic stops drinking. The number of seizures and their duration vary from individual to individual. (See also DELIRIUM TREMENS.)

cordial   (From the Latin *cor* heart.) Broadly defined, a cordial is any medicine, food or beverage that is believed to steady or stimulate the heart. In the case of alcoholic beverages, "cordial" is simply another name for LIQUEUR. These beverages are made by adding the flavor of fruits, herbs, roots, flowers or juices to an alcohol base. In addition they are sweetened and, in most cases, colored. Most cordials are between 40 and 80 proof. They are sold under the name of their particular flavor preceding the word "cordial" (for example, blackberry cordial, clove cordial, mint cordial).

corn whiskey   A spirit distilled from a fermented mash that is at least 80% corn (Indian maize). Along with rye and bourbon, corn whiskey is a distinctively American spirit. Until the early part of the 19th century, it rivaled the other two types in popularity, but since then a preference for less harsh whiskeys has made it commercially unfeasible. Corn whiskey is a colorless spirit that is bottled without aging. For this reason it has an extremely raw taste, similar to that of neutral grain spirits.

coronary heart disease   See HEART.

Costa Rica   The smallest and one of the least populated countries in Central America, Costa Rica has for some time supported one of the more advanced antialcohol programs in the hemisphere. A state committee on alcoholism has existed since 1954, when alcoholism was declared a disease by presidential decree in order to facilitate treatment in public health centers. Since 1973 there has been a complete ban on consumption of alcoholic beverages in government buildings, and legal penalties for alcohol-related offenses are severe.

Seventy-two percent of the population was considered abstinent in 1982, and although total alcohol consumption in the country remains low, some alcohol abuse is reported among this relatively small drinking population. The preferred beverages are gin, dark rum and *aguardiente,* a distilled alcohol common in Hispanic countries; all are potent, with an average ethanol content of 35.5%.

The government maintains a monopoly on distilled alcohol production; beer and wine production is in private hands. A significant supplement to the amount of spirits legally produced is the substantial amount of illegal alcohol distilled from fermented sugar cane in rural areas. One report estimated annual consumption of this *guaro contrabando* at 4 million liters, and in an isolated area one in three houses were found to be engaged in the production of this illegal liquor.

The government has estimated that there are nearly 100,000 "abnormal drinkers" in Costa Rica, or about one out of every 20 persons. The incidence of alcoholism is higher in rural than in urban areas, and the highest incidence of heavy drinking is among males who began to drink between ages 15 and 19 and have experienced unemployment.

Treatment of alcoholism in Costa Rica comes under the authority of the National Institute on Alcoholism and the Center for Studies on Alcoholism, which are attached to the country's Ministry of Health and operate in cooperation with the Ministry of Public Education. Enforced treatment of alcoholism is made possible by a 1970 addition to the penal code that defines the alcoholic as a patient in need of protection and rehabilitation. The Social Security Institution guarantees financial assistance to alcoholics and their families. Costa Rica's alcoholism prevention measures include mass media campaigns, primary school education sessions, and special training programs for teachers, nurses, police and social workers. These programs and others are currently being expanded, and all are monitored by the National Institute on Alcoholism.

cough medicine   Most cough medicines on the market today, even those designed for children, contain a fairly high percentage of alcohol. Those intended for nighttime use have about 25% alcohol, around 15% less than found in most hard liquor—whiskey, gin, vodka—and more than twice the amount in wine, which is normally about 12%.

Alcoholics using cough medicines containing alcohol may develop a CRAVING for more of the medicine, and those taking ANTABUSE could have a reaction to the alcohol in the

Alcohol Content of Some Common Cough Medicines

Brand	% of Alcohol
ChlorTrimeton Allergy Syrup	7.0
Comtrex Nighttime	25.0
Pertussin Cough Syrup for Children	8.0
Robitussin Cough Formula	3.5
Vick's Formula 44D	10.0
Vick's Nyquil Cold Medicine	25.0

preparation. As with other seemingly harmless products containing alcohol, there is also a potential for abuse of cough medicines.

counseling   Although forms of psychotherapy and counseling are ubiquitous in the modern treatment of alcoholics, little is known with scientific certainty about such procedures. S.R. Valle, for example, has shown that counselors who interact actively with patients rather than take a passive role have patients who show fewer relapses, fewer relapse days and less use of alcohol during the two years after treatment.

Because of the key role played by counselors and therapists in alcoholism treatment, much additional empirical study of what makes counselors effective is needed.

Abstention from alcohol and other psychoactive drugs continues to be the most reasonable treatment goal for diagnosed alcoholics in light of the most recent scientific and clinical information.

Enoch Gordis, M.D., ed., *Sixth Special Report to the U.S. Congress on Alcohol and Health* (Rockville, Md.: NIAAA, 1987).

S.R. Valle, "Interpersonal Functioning of Alcoholism Counselors and Treatment Outcome," *Journal of Studies on Alcohol*, 42(1981): 783-790.

craving   The term "craving" is often used in explanations of alcoholism, but thus far it has not been well defined. There appear to be two types of craving: one physiological, otherwise referred to as physical dependence (see DEPENDENCY), and one psychological. The physical craving occurs in persons who have been drinking over a long period of time, and is manifested by the symptoms of WITHDRAWAL from alcohol. The craving in this case may arise out of a need for relief from the distress of withdrawal rather than from an actual desire for alcohol. The second kind of craving is thought to account for the initial abuse of alcohol and for relapses after the start of abstinence. During a period of abstinence there is a buildup of psychological tension, which provokes a desire for alcohol as a means of relief.

One major question is whether the craving in alcoholics is for the alcohol itself or for its intoxicating effects.

crime   The full extent to which alcohol is responsible for crime is not known, but alcohol use and its subsequent effects have been related to formation of criminal intent, aggravation of the criminal event through excess violence and influence of the outcome of a completed crime *(Fourth Special Report to the U.S. Congress on Alcohol and Health)*. A nationwide interview of 6,000 jail inmates in 1983 by the Department of Justice, intended to provide a representative sampling, indicated that nearly half of convicted inmates were under the influence of alcohol at the time of their criminal offense.

A number of theories have attempted to explain the role of alcohol in criminal and violent behavior. Alcohol may release inhibitions or intensify certain mental states. If anger is released or increased, it may enhance the likelihood of aggression and violence. The relationship between the physiological effects of alcohol and aggressive behavior has not yet been clearly established. Some violent behavior may be explained by a seizure-like reaction to alcohol called PATHOLOGICAL INTOXICATION. The effect of combining alcohol with other DRUGS may result in increased violent behavior (see SYNERGY).

The proportion of alcoholics and problem drinkers with criminal records is far higher than the national average. It is not clear, however, whether drinking alcohol leads to criminal behavior or whether involvement in criminal behavior (and perhaps incarceration) leads to drinking. Statistics on the involvement of alcohol in different types of crime vary widely.

property crime

One study of alcohol and property crime in 1985 found an opposite cause and effect relationship depending on the nature of the crime. Alcohol use appears to deter professional property crime; but people who commit unplanned, unskilled crimes are more likely to drink heavily before the crime, often as part of

Alcohol Use Among Convicted Offenders Just Before Committing Current Offense, by Crime Type, United States, 1983

Current Offense	Number Convicted	Percentage of Convicted Persons Who Use Alcohol
Total	132,620	48%
Violent	32,112	54
Murder/attempted murder	3,345	49
Manslaughter	1,188	68
Rape/sexual assault	4,017	52
Robbery	11,945	48
Assault	9,609	62
Other violent[a]	2,008	49
Property	51,660	40
Burglary	17,335	44
Auto theft	2,960	51
Fraud/forgery/embezzlement	5,976	22
Larceny	18,001	37
Stolen property	3,676	45
Other property[b]	3,712	51
Drugs	13,181	29
Traffic	5,469	26
Possession	6,830	30
Other drugs	882	44
Public order	34,036	64
Weapons	2,769	32
Obstructing justice	6,856	43
Traffic	3,734	36
Driving while intoxicated[c]	13,406	93
Drunkenness/morals offenses[d]	4,894	70
Other public order[e]	2,377	28
Other[f]	1,008	40
Information unavailable	623	—

SOURCE: U.S. Department of Justice, 1985.
[a] Includes kidnapping, purse snatching, hit-and-run driving, and child abuse.
[b] Includes arson, destruction of property, property damage from hit-and-run driving, and trespass.
[c] Includes driving while intoxicated and driving under the influence of drugs.
[d] Also includes vagrancy and commercialized vice.
[e] Includes rioting, habitual offender, family-related offenses such as nonsupport or abandonment, invasion of privacy, and contributing to the delinquency of a minor.
[f] Includes juvenile offenses and unspecified offenses.

a group. Overall, alcohol was involved in property crime among 40% of offenders.

Alcohol use among convicted offenders just before committing property crimes in the United States in 1983 included burglary, auto theft, fraud-forgery-embezzlement, larceny, stolen property and other property (e.g., property damage from hit-and-run driving). According to U.S. Department of Justice data for 1985, there were 51,660 cases of alcohol use among convicted offenders just before they committed property crimes in 1983. In a 1986 survey of prison inmates, 18% of prisoners convicted of property crime reported they were under the influence of alcohol at the time of their crime.

The U.S. Department of Justice reports that in 1985 62% of those convicted of assault and 68% of those convicted of manslaughter used alcohol. In addition, 45% of homicide victims had been drinking. (For alcohol-related crimes, see DRIVING WHILE INTOXICATED, PROPERTY CRIME, PUBLIC DRUNKENNESS. See also SPOUSE ABUSE, CHILD ABUSE.)

John R. DeLuca, ed., *Fourth Special Report to the U.S. Congress on Alcohol and Health* (Rockville, Md.: National Institute on Alcohol Abuse and Alcoholism, 1981), pp. 83-84.

Enoch Gordis, M.D., ed., *Seventh Special Report to the U.S. Congress on Alcohol and Health* (Rockville, Md.: National Institute on Alcohol Abuse and Alcoholism, 1990).

Joy Moser, *Prevention of Alcohol-Related Problems* (Toronto: World Health Organization, 1980), pp. 46-47.

U.S. Department of Justice, Bureau of Justice Statistics, "Jail inmates 1983," *Bureau of Justice Statistics Bulletin*, November 1985.

criminal behavior and alcohol use See CRIME.

cross-addiction A term used to describe a mutual or interchangeable addiction between drugs within the same group. A person addicted to alcohol, which belongs to a group of drugs known as sedatives, will have some degree of addiction to all other sedatives. Therefore an alcoholic could prevent withdrawal symptoms by taking sufficient quantities of another SEDATIVE, such as Librium, and someone addicted to Librium could stem withdrawal by taking alcohol. However, for someone addicted to a sedative no drug from another group, such as a narcotic, would be effective. (See also CROSS-TOLERANCE.)

cross-dependence   A term used to describe a mutual or interchangeable dependence between drugs within the same group, such as sedatives. For example, alcohol and Librium, both sedatives, are cross-dependent.

cross-tolerance   A condition that occurs in alcoholics or heavy drinkers whose TOLERANCE for alcohol produces an equivalent tolerance for other SEDATIVE drugs. Alcoholics, for instance, are more difficult to anesthetize with ether than are nonalcoholics. Cross-tolerance may be caused either by an increased ability to metabolize another drug (metabolic tolerance) or by changes in the tissues of the central nervous system (CNS) that make the system less responsive to another drug (cellular tolerance). Both increased metabolic ability and changes in CNS tissue result from prolonged heavy ingestion of alcohol.

cultural etiological theories   Several studies, while recognizing the importance of physiological and psychological factors, have shown that alcoholism is related more to ethnic and social background (McCord et al.; Cahalan, Cisin and Crossley). Cultural etiological theories, also known as SOCIOCULTURAL ETIOLOGICAL THEORIES, suggest that individual attitudes toward alcohol and alcoholism to a large extent reflect the attitudes of the culture as a whole toward those subjects; customs and codes of behavior regulating drinking practices, environmental support for

drinking and level of "appropriate" intoxication are largely determined by cultural setting. For example, the low rates of alcoholism among Jews and Moslems can be traced to cultural proscriptions against the use or abuse of alcohol, whereas the extremely high rate of alcoholism among the Irish may be attributed to cultural support for excessive consumption of alcohol.

D. Cahalan, I. H. Cisin and H. M. Crossley, *American Drinking Practices: A National Survey of Behavior and Attitudes,* Rutgers Center of Alcohol Studies Monograph, no. 6, 1969.

W. McCord, J. McCord and J. Goodman, *Origins of Alcoholism* (Stanford: Stanford University Press, 1960), passim.

cultural stress etiological theories   Some theorists feel that the incidence of alcoholism in a society may be related to the degree of stress produced by the culture. In 1946 R. F. Bales suggested that if the use of alcohol is accepted under the societal norms, then it will be used to reduce the anxiety and tension produced by that society. Bales listed three major factors affecting the rate of alcoholism in a given society: the degree of stress and inner tension produced by the culture; the attitudes toward drinking held by the culture; and the opportunity for alternative means of satisfaction and coping with anxiety. In 1943, after studying the relation between social stress and alcohol consumption in primitive societies, D. Horton found that where alcohol use was sanctioned, there was a correlation between a high degree of anxiety and a high level of consumption.

David J. Armor, J. Michael Polich and Harriet B. Stambul, *Alcoholism and Treatment* (New York: John Wiley and Sons, 1978), passim.

R. F. Bales, "Cultural Differences in Rates of Alcoholism," *Quarterly Journal of Studies on Alcohol* 6 (1946): 480-499.

D. Horton, "The Functions of Alcohol in Primitive Societies: A Cross-Cultural Study," *Quarterly Journal of Studies on Alcohol* 4 (1943): 199-320.

D

de-alcoholized beverage   A beverage from which most of the alcohol has been removed *after* it has been made into a full-strength alcoholic beverage. Since the alcohol content of de-alcoholized beverages is less than 0.5%, they are not classified as alcoholic beverages for purposes of taxation or for regulation of sale and consumption. There are two principal types of de-alcoholized beverages: malt beverages (formerly known as NEAR BEER) and wines—red, white and sparkling.

Although many alcoholics drink de-alcoholized beverages, there are conflicting opinions on the advisability of this practice. To some in the field the substitution of a nonaddictive beverage is a harmless, even beneficial way for an alcoholic to fill the void left by the elimination of alcohol. But many others view the consumption of substitute "beer" and "wine" as reinforcing old drinking patterns and possibly leading to the resumption of drinking.

debauch   A drinking spree or bout that usually includes excessive sexual activity.

delirium tremens   The D.T.'s. One of the most dramatic and serious conditions associated with alcoholism, delirium tremens is the last and severest stage of WITHDRAWAL, beginning two to three days after abstinence following a long period of heavy drinking. Symptoms of this form of alcoholic psychosis may include vivid and frequently terrifying auditory, visual and tactile hallucinations (alcoholic hallucinosis), profound confusion, disorientation, severe agitation and restlessness, insomnia, fever and abnormally rapid heartbeat. Since there is a 10% mortality rate associated with this stage of withdrawal, it is considered a medical emergency and the patient should be hospitalized. Sedation may be required, but extreme caution should be used to avoid oversedation, for a drug dosage that would suppress all tremors would also seriously depress the patient's respiration. The D.T.'s can last for three to four days. With proper care recovery is usually complete, although a few patients do not recover and remain in a psychotic state. There have been reported cases of delirium tremens occurring after operations, trauma and severe illness in patients who claimed to have abstained from alcohol for several months. More research is needed to determine the exact nature of the condition and the circumstances under which it occurs.

Delta alcoholism   The fourth of five categories of alcoholism defined by JELLINEK. Delta alcoholism, like GAMMA ALCOHOLISM, is characterized by an acquired tissue tolerance for alcohol, adaptive cell METABOLISM and WITHDRAWAL symptoms. However, instead of the LOSS OF CONTROL found in Gamma alcoholism, there is an INABILITY TO ABSTAIN. The Delta alcoholic cannot stop drinking for even a few days without showing some withdrawal symptoms; he can, however, control the amount of intake on any given occasion. His consumption of alcohol, though large, is steady over a long period of time and less "explosive" than that of a person with Gamma alcoholism. Delta alcoholism is the predominant form of alcoholism in FRANCE and some other countries with a significant wine consumption.

dementia   "A syndrome of progressive, irreversible cerebral insufficiency caused by organic factors and characterized by predominant cognitive functional loss" (*Merck Manual,* 10th ed.). One of the many possible causes of dementia is alcoholism. The early symptoms, which vary greatly from patient to patient, include a slow disintegration of personality and intellect. Judgment and insight as well as speech and motor activity are affected. There is an impairment of memory, which becomes progressively worse. Personal habits deteriorate, and in the later stages of the illness the patient requires total nursing care.

denatured alcohol   ETHANOL made unfit for drinking by the addition of a substance such as METHANOL.

denial   This term describes one of the alcoholic's most characteristic psychological defense mechanisms: a refusal to admit the existence of a drinking problem. Denial is one of the main methods alcoholics use to deal with life. They deny their emotional problems and their dependence on alcohol, declaring that they do not have a problem or that they only drink "a little." When confronted with his intoxicated state, the alcoholic is likely to respond that he can stop any time he wishes. One of the first aspects of denial is concealment of the amount of alcohol consumed. This posture distinguishes the alcoholic from the social drinker. Considering society's negative attitude toward alcoholics, denial is understandable; it is hard for any individual to admit publicly that he is an alcoholic when there is such a stigma attached to the problem.

Spouses, relatives and friends will often deny an alcoholic's problem to protect him from friends and neighbors; employers will ignore an uneven work record or fire an alcoholic rather than discuss his drinking problem; physicians will prescribe tranquilizers rather than confront an alcoholic patient with his drinking problem.

In treatment, denial should be dealt with quickly, since otherwise severe physical and psychological damage is likely to occur over time. The recognition of denial allows the alcoholic to be more aware of his problem and his role in its creation.

Denmark   There is a liberal attitude toward alcohol consumption in Denmark and the country experiences few problems with alcohol abuse. The national drinking pattern is one of frequent but temperate consumption of alcoholic beverages, mostly beer. The majority of consumption takes place in the home;

initial drinking by adolescents is usually done in the presence of adults; and there is little increase in the rhythm of drinking on weekends or holidays. Alcoholic beverages, including distilled spirits, are sold in virtually all retail food outlets. There has been little variation in these patterns for years, although authorities now note some increase in preference for distilled spirits over beers.

In 1987 per capita consumption of alcoholic beverages, computed as ABSOLUTE ALCOHOL, was 9.6 liters for the total population. This reflects an increase of less than 1% over 1977, compared with an increase of about 50% in the decade from 1967 to 1977. In fact, consumption has been gradually declining since the mid-1980s. Between 1977 and 1987, per capita consumption of beer declined 8% and spirits declined 17% while consumption of wine increased 77%.

Based on World Health Organization guidelines, the country reported a mortality rate from alcohol abuse of 18.4 men and 9.1 women per 100,000 population in 1987.

The Danish government believes that regulation of alcohol consumption is suitable only if agreeable to the majority of the population. For this reason it limits controls on consumption to taxation of alcoholic beverages and licensing of public drinking places. Further action is left to private health and charitable organizations. There is a National Commission on Alcohol and Narcotics, but its purpose is primarily an advisory one. All public responsibility for prevention and treatment of alcohol-related problems remains in the hands of county-level government. The only government spokesmen for antialcohol causes are appointees with limited advisory status within existing government agencies, such as the Ministry of Education.

Hoeveel alcoholhoude dranken worden er in de wereld gedronken? (How many alcoholic beverages are being consumed throughout the world?), 27th ed. Schiedam, Netherlands: Produktschap Voor Gedistilleerde Dranken, 1987.

dentistry   Dentists should be aware of the possible existence of alcoholism in their patients and the special precautions that must be taken if anesthesia is to be used on such patients.

Dentists can recognize alcoholism in patients who otherwise appear normal through attention to certain details. A routine dental exam will frequently disclose general deficiencies in oral hygiene; there has often been long-term neglect of the teeth, as evidenced by coated tongue, heavy plaque formation, and deposits of calculus. Alcoholics have a rate of permanent tooth loss three times that of the general population. They are more likely to come in for treatment of an emergency, such as a severe toothache, than for a routine checkup. Many alcoholics are heavy smokers and the combination of alcohol and tobacco has a synergistic effect that has been associated with an increased susceptibility to cancer of the head and neck. Alcoholics often have enlarged, but otherwise asymptomatic, parotid glands (the largest salivary glands). Wounds heal more slowly in alcoholics, as alcohol and, to a lesser degree, the congeners in alcoholic beverages interfere with the proper formation and deposition of collagen. Dentists should be on the lookout for such warning signs so that they can aid the patient in getting proper treatment for alcoholism.

Alcoholism may also complicate dental surgery. If such surgery for a known or suspected alcoholic is elective, he or she should be completely detoxified before the operation because the stress of surgery may precipitate WITHDRAWAL. Care must be taken in the use of anesthetics, since both CROSS-TOLER-ANCE and synergistic effects can result from alcohol-anesthetic combinations (see SYN-ERGY). Chronic alcoholics are more resistant to the effects of anesthesia, and cross-toler-ance with both chloroform and ether has long been observed. If the patient has alcohol in his or her system while undergoing surgery, the initial phase of anesthesia will be followed by a synergistic interaction that produces a deeper and possibly more dangerous narcosis

and an increase in sleeping time. After surgery, healing may take longer than normal and there is an increased incidence of infection among alcoholics. During DELIRIUM TRE-MENS any dental surgical procedure should be avoided if possible.

"Alcohol-Drug Interactions," *Anesthesia Progress* (September-October 1979) 26 (5): 129-132.
Charles E. Becker, "Review of Pharmacologic and Toxicologic Effects of Alcohol," *Journal of the American Dental Association* 99 (September 1979): 494-500.
Marc A. Shuckit, "Overview of Alcoholism," *Journal of the American Dental Association* 99 (September 1979): 489-493.

dependency   A person who is an alcoholic has developed a dependency on alcohol. This dependency has two aspects: physical, as exhibited by the WITHDRAWAL symptoms, such as severe anxiety, tremors, and nausea, that occur when drinking stops; and psychological, as exhibited by the "need to have a drink" in order to function or to relieve stress. Some individuals develop a dependency rapidly and others gradually, over a few years. (See also ADDICTION.)

depressant   See SEDATIVE.

depressed communities   Communities that show a decline in economic growth and/or population also tend to experience an increase in alcohol and drug abuse, although less so than BOOM TOWNS. A study of depressed towns during the mid- and late-1970s showed that, as in the case of boom towns, the growth of alcohol abuse was higher than that of drug abuse.

Unlike boom towns depressed communities are usually stable and long-established areas whose economy and population have declined over a period of time. Since young people generally leave such areas in search of employment, the population is older and therefore itself well established. Increases in drug abuse are usually low; alcohol abuse is higher and tends to reflect a variety of factors, such as individual (rather than mass) reaction, ethnic and religious makeup of the community and the social classes affected. Arrests for DRIVING WHILE INTOXICATED are erratically (but often substantially) higher while treatment for alcoholism declines or falls off sharply. Although there is less money to spend, and presumably less to spend on alcohol, liquor provides a ready sedative for problems. In addition drinking is often much cheaper than other forms of recreation and can be indulged in at any time of the day or night.

National Institute of Drug Abuse, *Drug and Alcohol Abuse in Booming and Depressed Communities,* DHEW publication no. (ADM) 80-960, 1980.

depression   One of the disorders often associated with alcoholism is depression which may be a reason for drinking or a result of heavy use of alcohol that could possibly be alleviated by abstinence. Since alcohol can enhance pleasant feelings and raise optimism and self-confidence for a short time, someone with a pre-existing depression may be sensitized to its pleasurable effects. However, the EUPHORIA experienced is quickly followed by a return to the state of depression, and prolonged ingestion nearly always leads to a deterioration of mood. The state of depression following alcohol use may be even less tolerable than the one preceding it. Studies have shown that alcoholics become more depressed and hostile after drinking and that drinking, instead of raising their self-esteem, makes them feel even more worthless than before. Postdrinking depression may lead to suicide attempts. A study conducted at Duke University Medical Center showed that 26 of 29 people who had attempted suicide were intoxicated at the time of their attempt. Various studies have found that from 20% to 37% of suicide victims had either been drinking or had a history of alcohol abuse. Doctors sometimes prescribe tranquilizers in an attempt to calm the patient, but these simply add to the effects of alcohol and worsen the depression (see SEDATIVE.)

John Langone, *Bombed, Buzzed, Smashed, or ... Sober* (Boston: Little, Brown and Company, 1976), pp. 67, 106, 107.

deprivation   One of the major psychological theories of alcoholism posits that alcoholism is the result of disturbance and deprivation in early infantile experience. According to this theory, the alcoholic is deprived of a significant emotional relationship during the early years of his or her life. Because of the lack of a warm relationship with a mother figure in infancy, usually as a result of death or emotional or physical absence, he or she becomes fixated in the oral stage of development (see ORAL FIXATION). The object loss early in life causes the alcoholic to have primitive, excessive and insatiable demands. Interpersonal relationships fail and long-suppressed feelings of loss and rejection in infancy are reawakened. There is so much pain from this experience that an intense rage develops, and rather than destroy another, the alcoholic turns his or her anger inward and consumes it with alcohol.

detoxification   (From the Latin *de* reversing or undoing + *toxicum* poison.) Also known as detoxication, detoxification is a treatment process by which a patient addicted to a drug is withdrawn from that drug under supervision. The symptoms that occur during this WITHDRAWAL reflect the type of drug involved, the length of use and the kind of services provided during withdrawal. After detoxification the patient is able to abstain from the drug without severe physical discomfort and is no longer *physically* dependent upon it.

Decisions concerning where and how a patient should be detoxified depend on a number of factors. The severity of the withdrawal symptoms is a primary consideration; those with severe symptoms require close medical supervision and management, usually in a hospital. Patients who have alcohol- or non-alcohol-related complications, such as cardiac disease or hypertension, also generally require hospitalization. However, those with mild or moderate withdrawal symptoms and no complications may not need the care of a hospital and may be able to go through the detoxification process in a more social setting. As alternatives to hospitalization, some states provide nonhospital social setting detoxification centers and others have nonhospital medical detoxification centers.

There has been some interest in the possibility of limited use of ambulatory detoxification for carefully screened patients. Under this program the patient would return daily to a clinic for medication and counseling. Family and friends are encouraged to participate in the program.

Detoxification is generally accomplished during a short confinement (five to 10 days) in a general hospital. Hospitalization has several advantages: it removes the alcoholic from his or her drinking environment, emphasizes the disease nature of the condition, protects the patient from the sometimes fatal effects of withdrawal and gives him or her an opportunity to commence REHABILITATION. In a hospital an alcoholic patient is usually given an appropriate sedative to control withdrawal symptoms.

Opinions vary among researchers and clinicians on which medications should be used to treat alcohol withdrawal (see PHARMACO-THERAPY). According to the clinical state of the patient, chlordiazepoxide (Librium) or a similar drug may be prescribed on a three-hour basis. Generally 50 to 100 milligrams are administered upon admission and tapered doses are given thereafter. An attempt is made to keep the patient alert but not tremulous. All medications are discontinued before discharge. The patient generally receives instruction about alcoholism from a physician as well as a plan for further rehabilitation, such as ALCOHOLICS ANONYMOUS, psychiatric examination, ANTABUSE therapy or GROUP THERAPY. Frequently the patient is discharged from the hospital to an alcohol reha-

bilitation center. Some such centers have their own detoxification facilities. See also INPATIENT TREATMENT; OUTPATIENT TREATMENT.

diabetes   There has been some controversy about whether or not diabetics should be allowed to have alcoholic beverages in their diets. Proper diet is of primary importance in achieving control of hyperglycemia (high blood sugar), the principal manifestation of diabetes mellitus. While the effects of alcohol vary from individual to individual and depend on kind, dosage and whether taken in the fasting or fed state, small amounts of alcohol consumed close to or with a meal generally produce little change in the blood sugar levels of diabetics whose disease is under control. However, excessive alcohol consumption can cause many problems if taken in a fasting state or if sweet dessert wines, port or liqueurs are consumed. These beverages contain high amounts of sugar (up to 50%). Diabetics should consult their physicians about the advisability of including alcohol in their diets.

On the simplest level, alcohol can disrupt diet control, provide extra calories and stimulate the appetite. Alcohol should not contribute more than 6% of the total calories consumed per day by a diabetic (see CALORIE). For a 70-kg (154-lb) man this standard amounts to approximately 160 kcal (kilogram calories) per day, or two 4-oz glasses of dry wine. Alcohol is considered a "fat exchange," or a food with the nutritive equivalent of fat, in the "food-exchange" terminology used in diabetic diets. To compute the alcohol calories in one serving of a beverage, the following formula can be used:
0.8 X proof X ounces per serving = kcal.
Example: A 2-oz serving of 80-proof whiskey equals 128 kcal. 0.8 X 80 (proof) X 2 (ounces) = 128 kcal.

When the alcohol content is expressed as a percentage, such as in wines and beers, double the percentage and apply the same formula.
0.8 X double the % of alcohol listed on the bottle X ounces per serving = kcal from alcohol.

Example: A 4-oz serving of wine containing 14% alcohol equals 89.6 kcal. 0.8 X 28 (double the % of alcohol) X 4 (ounces) = 89.6 kcal.

Any carbohydrate kcal (in beer, wine, mixers) should be added to the alcohol kcal for total kcal.

If alcohol is taken in a fasting state, it can precipitate hypoglycemia (low blood sugar). Alcohol consumed in this state can enhance the blood sugar-lowering action of insulin and interfere with the body's ability to produce its own glucose. Insulin-dependent diabetics in a fasting state are especially susceptible to hypoglycemia. Because the symptoms are similar to those of intoxication, a hypoglycemic reaction may not be recognized, and necessary treatment may therefore be delayed. If alcohol is consumed, it is essential that it be taken with food or shortly before or after a meal. Alcohol ingestion raises the level of triglyceride (a type of fat) in the blood. Excessive levels of this fat, known as hypertriglyceridemia, are believed to be a major cause of atherosclerosis. Hypertriglyceridemia is more common in diabetics than in nondiabetics, and anyone with high triglyceride levels should be discouraged from drinking.

Alcohol can cause a reaction in diabetics using oral glucose-lowering agents that are sulfonyl derivatives (Orinase, Diabinese). Possible symptoms include dizziness, flushing and nausea.

The sugar content of wine varies a great deal. Information about sugar content can be obtained by writing to the quality control laboratories of wineries. An alternative is to use the reducing sugar tablets, which measure the percentage of glucose and fructose (Clinitest) to determine sugar concentration. Since wine contains sugars other than glucose, tests that measure only glucose (Tes-Tape, Diastix, Clinistix) should not be used.

Janet McDonald, "Alcohol and Diabetes," *Diabetes Care* 3, no. 5 (September-October 1980): 629-637.

———"Whiskey or Water?" *Diabetes Forecast,* November-December 1980, pp. 17-20, 42.

digestion   In small quantities alcohol may aid digestion. Its mild anesthetic effect overcomes the "dry mouth" associated with stress and allows freer salivation, which in turn triggers motility, the gentle motion that empties the stomach and is considered beneficial to digestion. Wine in particular is thought to be good for this purpose because the type of acid in wine is close to that in the gastric juices.

While one or two glasses of wine may stimulate digestion, heavier doses can result in an irritated stomach wall, an increased concentration of alcohol and a stomach too anesthetized to move.

dipsomania   (From the Greek *dipsa* thirst + *mania* madness.) A term, generally in disuse in North America, that refers to an uncontrollable CRAVING for alcohol, often of a periodic nature (see EPSILON ALCOHOLISM). Dipsomania is also improperly used as a synonym for persistent drunkenness or alcoholism. The slang word "dipso" means drunkard.

disease concept   The disease concept provides the basis for most of the current approaches to the treatment of ALCOHOLISM.

According to the *Seventh Special Report to the U.S. Congress on Alcohol and Health*, "Alcohol dependence, like hypertension, diabetes and coronary artery disease, may be characterized as a biologically based disease in which a genetic predisposition is activated by environmental factors." There is a misconception that the disease concept is of recent origin, perhaps because only recently has it gained widespread acceptance. Actually the concept has a long and controversial history. Mark Keller of the Rutgers Center of Alcohol Studies points out that as early as the first century the Roman philosopher Seneca distinguished between "a man who is drunk" and one who "has no control over himself ... who is accustomed to get drunk, and is a slave to the habit." The 18th century American physician Benjamin Rush said of drunkenness that it "resembles certain hereditary, family and contagious diseases." The idea of alcoholism as a disease was accepted in the 19th century by a large part of the medical community. In 1952 JELLINEK distinguished alcohol addiction as a specific diagnostic category and elaborated a developmental course of the addiction process. While his theoretical progression of the major symptoms has been seriously questioned, most authorities still affirm the major elements of the disease concept.

Both the American Medical Association and the World Health Organization regard alcohol dependence as a specific disease entity. Recently, both organizations have been reevaluating their classification of alcohol dependence, and are moving away from using the blanket term "alcoholism." The ALCOHOL DEPENDENCE SYNDROME (ADS) construct has been gaining influence in this regard (see CLASSIFICATION OF ALCOHOLICS).

Perhaps the major advantage of the disease concept is that it shifts the emphasis from the idea of alcoholism as a moral issue requiring punitive measures to the notion that an alcoholic is the victim of an illness that requires medical and psychological treatment. The stigma is thereby lifted from the patient and some of his guilt is relieved, guilt that is often a stimulus to further drinking. The disease concept emphasizes social support rather than punishment of the alcoholic. Making alcoholism a medical category has permitted some of the personal economic costs to be handled by INSURANCE, disability payments and workmen's compensation.

Some arguments against the disease model are that it overemphasizes the medical aspects, leading to the (probably erroneous) assumption that alcoholism is essentially a singular entity, like tuberculosis, and ignores the fact that it may be a symptom of a number of quite separate problems. Some doctors feel that for alcoholism to be classified as a disease there must be some manifest abnormality of the anatomic structure. But this requirement would eliminate all behavioral disorders from the classification of disease.

It is also thought that the disease model takes inadequate account of the sociocultural factors which may play a causal role, and fosters irresponsibility in the patient, allowing him or her to be passive. Another danger with this model is that alcoholism may be considered an all-or-nothing disease entity, with no degrees in between.

Discoveries of anomalous brain waves in children of alcoholic fathers as well as recent research into genetic markers for a predisposition to alcoholism (see GENETICS) are helping to build a stronger case for the disease model. Nonetheless, none of these studies has come close to ruling out a significant role for sociocultural and other environmental factors as contributing to alcoholism.

David J. Armor, J. Michael Polich and Harriet B. Stambul, *Alcoholism and Treatment* (New York: John Wiley and Sons, 1978), pp. 9-11.

R. Williams, "Nature, Nurture, and Family Predisposition." *New England Journal of Medicine* 318(12): 770-771 (1988).

diseases   There are several diseases caused by extended heavy use of alcohol and others in which alcohol abuse may play a role.

In the first category are a number of diseases of the LIVER, such as ALCOHOLIC LIVER DISEASE, CIRRHOSIS, FATTY LIVER and ALCOHOLIC HEPATITIS. Heavy alcohol use can damage the BRAIN and the CENTRAL NERVOUS SYSTEM, resulting in such disorders as DELIRIUM TREMENS, KORSAKOFF'S SYNDROME, WERNICKE'S ENCEPHALOPATHY and ALCOHOLIC POLYNEUROPATHY as well as less common diseases, including MARCHIAFAVA-BIGNAMI DISEASE and CENTRAL PONTINE MYELINOLYSIS. Other diseases caused by excessive alcohol consumption include FETAL ALCOHOL SYNDROME, ALCOHOL AMBLYOPIA, ALCOHOLIC MYOPATHY, HEMOCHROMATOSIS, RHINOPHYMA and ACNE ROSACEA.

Excessive use of alcohol may be a contributing factor in such diseases as CANCER and DIABETES, and in some diseases of the HEART, STOMACH and PANCREAS. It may also be harmful to the fetus during PREGNANCY. In fact, Fetal Alcohol Syndrome (FAS) is the third leading cause of birth defects, with accompanying mental retardation, and the only preventable one among the top three. The incidence of FAS is approximately 1 in 750 live births, or 4,800 babies per year in recent years. Thirty-six-thousand newborns each year may be affected by a range of less severe alcohol-related fetal alcohol effects (FAE).

Hennick J. Harwood, et al., *Economic Costs to Society of Alcohol and Drug Abuse and Mental Illness*, (Research Triangle, N.C., Reaearch Triangle Institute, June 1984), p. B-3.

distillation   The process of separating or purifying liquids by boiling them, collecting the vapors emitted and recondensing the vapors into liquid form. Distillation is used for a variety of purposes, ranging from oil refining to desalinization of seawater. It takes place naturally in the cycle by which groundwater evaporates into clouds and then recondenses to fall as rainwater.

In the production of alcoholic beverages, distillation involves heating a fermented mash, collecting the alcohol content that vaporizes before the water (because it has a lower boiling point) and then collecting the recondensed alcohol as a distillate.

Distillation of alcoholic beverages is generally considered to have been a discovery of Arab cultures, although they never fully refined the technique because of Moslem strictures against consumption of alcohol. Classical Greek and Roman societies used distillation processes to purify water but apparently never distilled their wines into spirits to any great extent. It was not until after 1000 A.D. that distillation of alcohols became common in Europe, with the first spirits probably being crude brandies distilled from wines in

Italy. The procedure also has a long history in Ireland, where the fermented material was a mash of grains rather than wine.

The early motivation for distillation may have been economic: producers of wines or beers could reduce the cost of transport if they shifted to smaller quantities of more potent alcoholic beverages, and distilled spirits are also more stable than wines or beers. Inevitably, however, a new preference for the more potent beverages developed, and continental Europe's early *aqua fortis* ("strong water") and Ireland's *uisce beathadh* ("water of life") were prized for their superior powers as intoxicants before their recorded histories began in the early 16th century.

Today distillation of potable spirits begins with the production of a fermented mash. Grains are the most common material employed, and they are generally malted, or germinated, to make soluble sugars. Once yeast is introduced, these sugars convert into alcohols, creating a fermented "wash," or "wort," from which the alcohol content can be distilled. Two types of apparatus are used for distillation: the traditional pot still or the newer and more efficient patent still, sometimes called the continuous still. In either case the alcohol distillate is the base from which any number of potable spirits can be produced by various flavoring, dilution and aging processes.

Distilled Spirits Council of the U.S. (DISCUS)   The Washington, D.C.-based trade group representing the country's liquor industry, it monitors such things as advertising, marketing, sales, consumption and promotion. In 1975, DISCUS adopted an advertising code for the industry called *The Code of Good Practice*. (See also ADVERTISING.)

DNA   Deoxyribonucleic acid; with RNA, one of the two main types of nucleic acid, an organic substance found in the chromosomes of all living cells. DNA plays an important role in the storage and replication of hereditary information and in protein synthesis. DNA is actually an extremely complex molecule composed of substructures of phosphates, bases and sugars. The particular sequence of these subunits determines the genetic information carried by the chromosomes and regulates all metabolism. (See GENETICS.)

doctor   Slang for a person who sells liquor at higher prices when bars and liquor stores are closed. The term is also used, as a verb, to refer to the addition of alcohol to a drink, often without the drinker's knowledge.

domestic violence   See CHILD ABUSE; SPOUSE ABUSE.

dram   (From the weight of the ancient Greek coin the drachma. In modern fluid measurement, 1 dram = 1/8 ounce.) Although a dram is too small a portion to have ever been used seriously as a measurement of liquor, it was a common measure of medicine (1 teaspoon = 1-1/3 drams), with which it was first associated, and liquor has often been euphemistically referred to as "medicine." "Taking a dram" (like "having a wee nip") is a way of playing down the amount of alcohol consumed. Usually a dram, like a SHOT (which is what the word "dram" most often means today), is downed in a single gulp. As early as the 17th century, "dram-drinking" and "dramming" were terms usually reserved for habitual drinking to the point of mild intoxication. (See also DRAM SHOP LAW.)

dram shop law   A law which provides that a person, usually a tavern keeper, who supplies alcoholic beverages to another person who then becomes intoxicated is responsible for damages done by that other person, as a result or consequence of his intoxification, to the person or property of others and even to himself.

drinker   A person who consumes alcoholic beverages, as opposed to someone who abstains. In popular usage the term "drinker" is also used to refer to an alcoholic or drunk.

drinking   Consuming alcoholic beverages; not abstaining.

drinking patterns   See Appendix 1, Drinking Patterns.

drive reduction   See   HORMONES, MALE SEX.

driving-and-drinking   See DRIVING WHILE INTOXICATED.

driving under the influence (DUI) See DRIVING WHILE INTOXICATED.

driving while intoxicated (DWI)   During the period 1982 through 1987, approximately 142,550 people lost their lives in alcohol-related traffic crashes. This is an average of one alcohol-related fatality every 22 minutes. Fifty-two percent of these deaths are the drivers themselves; another 20% are passengers with the drunk drivers. Eleven percent of alcohol-related deaths are drunk pedestrians. Seventeen percent of the fatalities are innocent bystanders or drivers.

Each year, about 534,000 people suffer injuries in alcohol-related traffic crashes, an average of one person injured every minute; about 40,000 of these are serious injuries.

In 1987, there were:

- 41,435 fatal traffic crashes, compared to 41,090 in 1986, an increase of 0.8%. However, the percentage of fatal crashes which involved at least one driver or pedestrian with a BAC of 0.10 or above remained about the same as in 1986: 40% (16,561).
- 61,434 drivers involved in fatal traffic crashes. Of these, 25% (15,329) were drunk.
- 26,831 drivers killed in traffic crashes. Of these, nearly 38% (10,103) were drunk.

- 17,058 single-vehicle crashes in which at least one occupant was killed. More than 53% of the fatally-injured drivers in these crashes were intoxicated.
- 46,386 people killed overall in traffic crashes. Approximately one-half of these fatalities, taken together, were alcohol related according to the National Highway Traffic Safety Administration (1988).

Each year, motor vehicle accidents in the United States involving alcohol result in more than $1 billion in property damage, insurance costs and medical services, injuries to more than a half million people and several hundred thousand arrests.

Studies have shown that alcohol causes degeneration of driving skills, including reaction time, coordination, attention, visual awareness and judgment. In an average person some degree of impairment can usually be demonstrated at a BLOOD ALCOHOL CONCENTRATION (BAC) of 0.05%; above 0.08% the risk of an accident rises appreciably; and beyond 0.10% there is a definite increase in risk for all drivers. (This is the legal limit for intoxication in most jurisdictions.) At a BAC of 0.15% the risk is 10 times higher than normal and 0.20% it is 20 times greater. The National Highway Traffic Safety Administration (NHTSA) defines a traffic crash or fatality as alcohol-related when a participant (e.g., driver, pedestrian or bicyclist) has registered a BAC of 0.01 percent or above (NHTSA 1988).

In 1987, the National Center for Statistics and Analysis estimated that the risk of a fatal crash, per mile driven, could be at least eight times higher for drunk drivers than sober drivers. Apparently excessive consumption of alcohol also diminishes a driver's ability to avoid the mistakes of others on the road. In a study by Drs. A. Waller and M. W. Perrine of the University of Vermont, 18% of fatally injured drivers not at fault were found to have BAC levels above 0.10% (2% of the population on the road at the time but not involved in accidents were found to have BACs above

0.10%). Of those at fault 50% had BACs at or above the 0.10% level.

Studies by the National Highway Traffic Safety Administration showed that more than one-third of all fatally injured pedestrians had BACs of 0.10% or more. The majority of alcohol-related accidents occur at night, and a larger proportion of men than women are involved, perhaps partly because of different drinking patterns (women tend more to drink at home).

The biggest menace on the highway is the PROBLEM DRINKER who has previous arrests for offenses involving alcohol. Studies indicate that persons with severe drinking problems are disproportionately involved in all kinds of crashes. According to 1975 figures, problem drinkers, who made up 7% of the driving population, were involved in 33% of all fatal crashes. In 1987, there were 46,386 traffic fatalities, of which 18,524, or 39.9%, occurred in crashes in which at least one driver or non-occupant had a blood alcohol concentration (BAC) of 0.10 or higher. This represents a 1.2% decrease from 1986's fatalities where at least one driver or non-occupant had a BAC of 0.10 or higher. Of alcoholics who drive, incidentally, some 24% to 40% have had at least one traffic crash previously on their driving records.

Young people are inexperienced in both drinking and driving and, therefore, at a particularly high risk of being involved in a traffic accident. In addition they are more likely to combine alcohol with other drugs and the simultaneous presence of alcohol and some other drug (or drugs) in the system may have a greater effect on driving than that produced by either alcohol or another drug alone (see SYNERGY).

More than 40% of all teenage (15-19 years old) deaths result from motor vehicle crashes. About half of these motor vehicle fatalities involved drinking. Approximately, 3,259 teenagers died in alcohol-related crashes in 1987. The same year, nearly 27% of the fatally-injured 15-19-year-old teenage drivers were intoxicated. However, the proportion of drivers 15 to 19 years of age who were involved in fatal crashes and were drunk, dropped from 28% in 1982 to 19% in 1987, the largest decrease of any driver age group during this time period (NHTSA, 1988).

Significantly, drivers who have been drinking use safety belts at a substantially lower rate than sober drivers. Of the passenger car drivers who were fatally injured in 1987, safety belts were used by only 8% of the drivers who were drunk (BAC of 0.10% or above), by 9% of the drivers who had some alcohol involvement (.01-.09), but by more than 24% of the sober drivers.

All 50 states have laws against driving under the influence of alcohol (DUI) and impose various penalties for the offense. In most states the determination of whether or not someone is intoxicated is based on blood alcohol concentration, as measured by a breath tester, urinalysis or direct analysis of the blood. The Breathalyzer, used frequently today, is a chemical photometric device that determines BAC by testing a sample of breath from deep inside the lungs. In many states there is an implied consent law that requires a motorist to submit to a BAC test or face fines or suspension of his or her driving privileges.

In the majority of states a BAC level of 0.10% is considered evidence of intoxication. In Idaho and Utah the level is 0.08% and a few states have two levels: 0.10%, with less severe penalties, and 0.15%, with harsher penalties. Most countries have similar legal limits, and a few, such as the USSR and other Communist-block countries, completely prohibit alcohol consumption before and while driving.

Penalties for drunken driving also vary from place to place. The Scandinavian Countries have the strictest laws in the world, some calling for automatic imprisonment and loss of driver's license. Although early studies of these laws found no significant changes in the number or rate of fatal motor vehicle crashes after they went into effect, the laws have not yet been adequately evaluated and are still under study. It has generally been found that strict penalties in themselves do little to prevent drunken driving unless they are enforced and perceived to be enforced. Surveys have shown that severe laws which are highly publicized work well at first, but if drivers learn that the actual level of arrests and convictions is very low, within a few months the laws have little deterrent effect. Maine's 1981 drunk-driving law is considered one of the toughest in the United States. The law introduced a civil charge for DRIVING WHILE INTOXICATED (DWI) so that the state needed to prove only preponderance of evidence rather than guilt beyond a reasonable doubt; a BLOOD ALCOHOL LEVEL (BAL) of 0.10 became per se evidence of driving under the influence of alcohol. Repeating offender alcohol-impaired drivers were denied second jury trials, and minimum mandatory penalties were established (The table on page 94 lists current mandatory minimum jail terms by state).

The first year after the law was passed, DWI conviction rates increased 85%. During the first two years after the law was in force, fatal crashes and single-vehicle nightime crashes declined 35%. Three years after the law's enactment, however, fatal accidents returned to the pre-1981 level. Thus, the law did not achieve a sustained reduction in alcohol-impaired and fatal crashes. Just what effect the authority of police to stop and arrest alcohol-impaired drivers has had on the overall impact of the law is unknown. What is known: The public no longer regards the state's penalties for DWI as severe.

There are many problems related to enforcing drinking-and-driving laws. Only motorists who give evidence of erratic or illegal driving or who become involved in a crash are likely to be apprehended for driving under the influence or while intoxicated. And after an intoxicated motorist is stopped, there are several loopholes through which he or she can escape. A recent study showed that experienced police failed to recognize approximately 40% of the drivers who were over the 0.10% BAC level (Kletta). Roadside breath tests, while not always accurate, improve the probability of detecting drinking drivers. However, even

Mandatory Minimum Jail Term for Drunk-Driving Conviction

	Jail term (in days)	Number of offenses before imprisonment		Jail term (in days)	Number of offenses before imprisonment
Alabama	2	2	Montana	1	1
Alaska	3	1	Nebraska	2	2
Arizona	1	1	Nevada	2	1
Arkansas	0	NA	New Hampshire	10	2
California	2	2	New Jersey	2	2
Colorado	7	2	New Mexico	2	2
Connecticut	2	1	New York	0	NA
Delaware	60	2	North Carolina	7	2
Dist. of Columbia	0	NA	North Dakota	4	2
Florida	10	2	Ohio	10	2
Georgia	2	2	Oklahoma	0	NA
Hawaii	2	1	Oregon	2	1
Idaho	10	2	Pennsylvania	30	2
Illinois	2	2	Rhode Island	2	2
Indiana	5	2	South Carolina	2	1
Iowa	7	2	South Dakota	0	NA
Kansas	2	1	Tennessee	2	1
Kentucky	7	2	Texas	3	2
Lousiana	2	1	Utah	2	1
Maine	2	1	Vermont	2	2
Maryland	2	2	Virginia	2	2
Massachusetts	14	2	Washington	1	1
Michigan	0	NA	West Virginia	1	1
Minnesota	30	2	Wisconsin	0	NA
Mississippi	0	NA	Wyoming	7	2
Missouri	2	2			

NA = Not applicable. Community service or probation can be substituted for imprisonment in some states. Fines may also be levied.
SOURCE: U.S. Dept of Transportation, 1988.

under an implied consent law, drivers can refuse to take the test. And in Connecticut, for example, no one was convicted of refusing to take the test for a period of at least 10 years (Condon). Furthermore revocation of a driver's license often fails to prevent a person from driving.

Robert D. Arnold's report (DOT HS 806 902) for the National Highway Traffic Safety Administration in late 1985 on the effect of raising the legal drinking age on driver involvement in fatal crashes in 13 states, showed a net effect of 13% reduction in fatal accident involvements. During 1975 through 1982, 15 states raised their legal minimum drinking ages. Arnold's report, as noted, covers 13 of those states and shows a reduction in driver involvements in fatal crashes ranging from 29% to an increase of 14%.

It is generally believed that to reduce traffic fatalities and accidents the amount of drinking-and-driving must be reduced. A higher risk of arrest through the use of targeting patrols by day, time and location, breath tests that are easier to administer both legally and physically, simplification of the process for making a DWI arrest and increased motivation for police to make such arrests may help to deter the drinking driver. On the other hand, increasing the severity of penalties might result in fewer arrests, fewer convictions and more plea bargaining as well as lengthier trials and appeals that could cost the taxpayer more. Public education may help reduce the amount of drinking-and-driving, although so far there is no strong evidence that this is the case. Improving the safety of cars and highways might help cut the number of fatalities, although such measures will not solve the problem.

Some states require individuals arrested for driving while intoxicated to attend a drinking driver program. More extensive programs may be needed for drivers recognized to be problem drinkers. In many places there are citizens action groups that work not only to educate drivers but to put pressure on law enforcement agencies to enforce driving laws strictly. Federal efforts have been increased with the establishment, in 1982, of a presidential commission on drunk driving.

Robert D. Arnold, "Effect of Raising the Legal Drinking Age on Driver Involvement in Fatal Crashes: The Experience of Thirteen States," NHTSA Technical Report No. DOS HS 806 902 (Washington, D.C.: National Highway Transportation Safety Administration, 1985).

John R. DeLuca, ed., *Fourth Special Report to the U.S. Congress on Alcohol and Health* (Rockville, Md.: National Institute on Alcohol Abuse and Alcoholism, 1981), pp. 81, 82, 131, 132, 157, 158.

Enoch Gordis, M.D., ed., *Seventh Special Report to the U.S. Congress on Alcohol and Health* (Rockville, Md.: National Institute on Alcohol Abuse and Alcoholism, 1990).

R. Hingson et al., "Effects of Maine's 1981 and Massachusetts' 1982 Driving-Under-the-Influence Legislation," *American Journal of Public Health* 77 (5) (1987): 593-597.

Insurance Institute for Highway Safety, *To Prevent Harm* (Washington, D.C., 1978), passim.

H. Kletta, "On the Possibilities for the Police to Detect Low Blood Alcohol Concentrations," *Alcohol and Highway Safety,* Swedish Government Committee Report, SOU (1970): 61.

Joy Moser, *Prevention of Alcohol-Related Problems* (Toronto: World Health Organization, 1980), pp. 211-218.

National Highway Traffic Safety Administration, National Center for Statistics and Analysis. *Drunk Driving Facts,* Washington, D.C., 1988.

drowning   Drowning is currently the third leading cause of accidental deaths in the United States, with alcohol involved in an estimated 38% of drowning deaths. Of the 946 boating deaths in 1988, 788 or 83% were the result of drowning (USCG, 1989). Research has shown that a person under the influence of alcohol is much more susceptible to drowning than is a person who is sober. Reasons: disorientation, exacerbated thermal responses to water temperature, and impairment of psychomotor skills and breath-holding time (NTSB, 1983). (See BOATING ACCIDENTS.)

Centers for Disease Control, *Morbidity and Mortality Weekly Report,* Vol. 39, No. 11, March 23, 1990.

National Transportation Safety Board, *Safety Study: Recreational Boating Safety and Alcohol,* NTSB No. 55-83-02, NTIS No. PB83-917006 (Washington, D.C.: NTSB, 1983).

U.S. Coast Guard, *Boating Statistics, 1988* (Washington, D.C.: USCG, 1989).

drunk and disorderly   See PUBLIC DRUNKENNESS.

drug addiction   See ADDICTION.

drug interaction   See DRUGS. See also SYNERGY.

drugs   Chemical substances used to diagnose, treat or prevent disease or other abnormal conditions, to relieve pain or to alter the state of body or mind. Alcohol is classified as a drug. Pharmacologically it is a member of a group of compounds generally known as sedatives that act as depressants on the central nervous system (see SEDATIVE). These compounds include barbiturates, "minor tranquilizers," such as Valium, and general anesthetic agents, such as ether. The patterns of misuse of alcohol are similar to those of other drugs.

In the past 30 years the use and abuse of alcohol and other drugs—prescription, illicit and over the counter—have increased greatly. Combining alcohol with drugs has become increasingly popular, often resulting in dual or multiple addiction. A survey conducted by ALCOHOLICS ANONYMOUS (AA) in 1986 showed that 38% of alcoholics in AA were addicted to one or more drugs. This was especially true of women: 46% of women as opposed to 37% of men in the survey reported that they were addicted to drugs as well as alcohol. Eighteen-year-olds had the highest level of drug and alcohol addiction, at 80%.

Another major problem with combined drug and alcohol use is the danger that arises from the interaction of the two within the body. The *Third Special Report to the U.S. Congress on Alcohol and Health* defined an interaction between alcohol and a drug as "any alteration in the pharmacologic properties of either due to the presence of the other." The report classified three different types by interactions:

1. Antagonistic, in which the effects of one or both drugs are blocked or reduced;
2. Additive, in which the effect is the sum of the effects of each;

3. Supra-additive (synergistic or potentiating), in which the effects of the two drugs in combination is greater than it would be if the effects were additive.

The supra-additive effect is the most dangerous, because when combined, even safe levels of both alcohol and drugs can at times prove fatal (see SYNERGY). For example, when alcohol and another drug are present in the system, the alcohol competes for the enzymes that would normally be used to metabolize the drug. The drug then accumulates in the body and has a greater impact than it would normally have. This effect most commonly occurs when alcohol is combined with barbiturates, which, like alcohol, are central nervous system depressants. Although not quite as dangerous, the antagonistic effect can be hazardous when the therapeutic effects of one drug are reduced by the presence of alcohol.

Drugs also have a half-life, which is the amount of time it takes for the body to remove half of the drug from the system. For drugs with a half-life of 24 hours or more, such as Valium, half of the first dose may still be in the body when the next is taken. After several days the buildup in the body can be fairly large, and the result of taking a drink at this point can be devastating.

The chart on page 97 shows the interaction between alcohol and various other drugs.

drunk   Slang for a person who is intoxicated or under the influence of alcohol; also an alcoholic. The state of being intoxicated (see INTOXICATION). A drinking spree is sometimes referred to as a drunk.

drunk driving   See DRIVING WHILE INTOXICATED.

dry   A person who is against drinking or the sale of liquor, a prohibitionist; opposed to WET. When applied to an alcoholic, it means abstinent. The term is also used, particularly in ALCOHOLICS ANONYMOUS, to describe

Alcohol-Drug Interactions

Drug	Possible effects
AMPHETAMINES: Benzedrine, Dexadrine, Rialtin etc.	Excessive rise in blood pressure with alcoholic beverages containing the chemical tyramine, e.g., Chianti wine; possible antagonism of central nervous system (CNS) depressant effects of alcohol but no improvement of impaired motor coordination; may result in false sense of security; at high levels of both, possible gastrointestinal upset.
ANALGESICS, NARCOTIC: Darvon, Demerol, Dilaudid etc.	Reduction in function of the CNS; may lead to loss of effective breathing function (respiratory arrest); may be fatal.
ANALGESICS, NON-NARCOTIC: Aspirin, APC, Pabalate etc.	Increased stomach irritation and/or internal bleeding.
ANESTHETICS, General: ANTABUSE (disulfiram)	Additive CNS depressant effects in acute stage of intoxication; in alcoholics possible high tolerance, requiring large dosage. Blocks oxidation of alcohol at acetaldehyde stage; results in nausea, dizziness, flushing, vomiting. (See also ANTABUSE.)
ANTIALCOHOL PREPARATIONS (excluding Antabuse): Calcium Carbonate	Reaction resulting in nausea, vomiting, headache, increased blood pressure and possible erratic heartbeat; may be fatal.
ANTIANGINAL PREPARATIONS: Nitrates, Nitrites	Possible excessive lowering in blood pressure resulting in fainting, dizziness or lightheadedness.
ANTIBIOTICS	May reduce therapeutic effects; may produce acetaldehyde toxicity similar to that caused by Antabuse.
ANTICOAGULANTS: Coumadin, Dicumarol, Panwarfin, Sintrom etc.	Possible increased anticoagulant effects, which may lead to hemorrhage.
ANTICONVULSANTS: Dilantin, Diphenyl, EKKO etc.	Decrease of drug's ability to stop convulsions.
ANTIDEPRESSANTS: Elavil, Sinequan, Tofranil, Vivacti etc.	Increased CNS depression, reduced motor skills; high blood pressure crisis in combination with Chianti wine; reduced motor skills.
ANTIDIABETIC DRUGS: Chloronase, Diabinese, Insulin, Orinase etc.	With insulin, may induce severe hypoglycemia; with the others, may cause a reaction producing such symptoms as dizziness, flushing and nausea.
ANTIHISTAMINES: ChlorTrimeton, Dramamine, Norflex etc.; most cold remedies; Actified Coricidin	Increased sedative effects.
ANTIHYPERTENSIVE AGENTS; Aldomet, Esidrix, Serpasil etc.	Increase in blood pressure-lowering effects with possibility of dizziness. Some agents also cause increased CNS depressant effects.
ANTI-INFECTIVE AGENTS: Chloromycetin, Flagyl etc.	Possible Antabuse effects.
ASPIRIN SUBSTITUTES (containing acetaminophen): Datril, Tylenol	Alcohol appears to enhance the liver-damaging effects of aspirin substitutes.
BARBITURATES: Amytal, Butisol, Nembutal, Seconal etc.	Increased CNS depression with possible coma and respiratory arrest. Chronic alcohol consumption can produce a cross-tolerance to sedative effects but not to respiratory depressive effects. May be fatal.
BROMIDES	Confusion; delirium; increased intoxication
CAFFEINE	False sense of security; no improvement of impaired motor coordination
CANNABIS: Marijuana, hashish	Greater impairment of motor and mental skills than with either drug alone.
DIURETICS: Diuril, Lasix, Hydromox etc.	Increase in blood pressure-lowering effects; possible dizziness when standing.
MORPHINE AND OTHER OPIATE DERIVATIVES: heroin, methadone etc.	Possible potentiation of alcohol's depressant effect; frequently results in death. Chronic use of alcohol may sensitize an individual to the effects of opiates and vice versa. (A large proportion of heroin addicts and methadone maintenance patients are heavy users of alcohol.)
NARCOTICS: (See also ANALGESICS, NARCOTIC)	Excessive sedation.
PENICILLIN	Alcohol enhances the degradation of penicillin and large amounts of alcohol interfere with the amount of penicillin available for absorption.
SEDATIVE-HYPNOTICS: Doriden, Nembutal Quaalude etc.	Increased CNS depresssion with possible coma or respiratory arrest; may be fatal.
TRANQUILIZERS, MAJOR: Tindal, Mellaril, Thorazine etc.	Increased CNS depression; possible severe impairment of voluntary movements. Combination can cause loss of effective breathing function and may be fatal.
TRANQUILIZERS, MINOR	Increased CNS depression, especially during first few weeks of drug use; decreased alertness and judgment.
VITAMINS	Prevention of vitamins from entering blood stream, which is reversible once drinking is stopped.

(See also CAFFEINE, CODEINE WITH ALCOHOL, MARIJUANA WITH ALCOHOL, METHADONE WITH ALCOHOL, NICOTINE.)

someone who is marginally sober and abstinent but who may relapse at any time. Such a person is also called a "dry drunk." (See also SOBRIETY.)

dry drunk   One who has stopped drinking but who still craves alcohol. The term, particularly as used by ALCOHOLICS ANONYMOUS, refers to a person who has not achieved real SOBRIETY but exists in a sort of "white-knuckled sobriety," gritting his teeth and trying hard not to drink. Such sobriety is seen as a temporary condition, with an inevitable return to drinking unless help is accepted. The term "dry drunk" is also used to describe an experience in which the alcoholic participates, without consuming any alcohol, in a social and emotional occasion (usually in a drinking environment) that he or she associates with excessive drinking. If the psychological impact and aftermath of an experience have many of the aspects and symptoms of a drunken spree, it is called a dry drunk. The term is also used to describe a person who shows symptoms of intoxication although having had nothing to drink.

DUI   Driving under the influence. See DRIVING WHILE INTOXICATED.

Dutch gin   See GIN.

DWI   See DRIVING WHILE INTOXICATED.

dysphoria   A feeling of malaise or nonspecific illness or general discomfort that often accompanies a HANGOVER or WITHDRAWAL.

E

eau de vie   (French, "water of life.") Any spirit distilled from wine, especially BRANDY.

ebriate   (From Latin *ebriare* to intoxicate.) To intoxicate, inebriate.

ebriety   (From Latin *ebrius* intoxicated.) See INEBRIETY.

economic impact   The economic costs of alcohol abuse result both from a decrease in normal production levels and from increased spending for such items as health and social services and police and fire protection.

A Research Triangle Institute (RTI) report in 1985, "Social and Economic Costs of Alcohol Abuse and Alcoholism," put the figure at $116.9 billion during the year 1983. The report attributes $71 billion of this to lost employment and reduced productivity, and $15 billion to alcoholism treatment expenditures. Assuming that drinking patterns remain constant, the economic cost of alcohol abuse and dependence was projected to rise to $136.3 billion by 1990 and $150 billion by 1995.

Enoch Gordis, M.D., ed., *Seventh Special Report to the U.S. Congress on Alcohol and Health* (Rockville, Md.: National Institute on Alcohol Abuse and Alcoholism, 1990), chapter VII.

Henrick J. Harwood et al., *Social and Economic Costs of Alcohol Abuse and Alcoholism* (Research Triangle, N.C.: Research Triangle Institute, June 1985).

L. G. Schifrin, C. E. Hartsog and D. H. Brand, "Costs of Alcoholism and Alcohol Abuse and Their Reaction to Alcohol Research," in *Alcoholism and Related Problems: Opportunities for Research* (Washington, D.C.: Institute of Medicine of the National Academy of Sciences, 1980).

education campaigns and programs   There has been a noticeable increase in recent years of educational programs and MEDIA CAMPAIGNS designed to build awareness, improve knowledge, change attitudes and modify behavior of the general public, thereby reducing alcohol-related problems. These various, ongoing educational programs may be successful, especially in the long run, but the

National Institute on Alcohol Abuse and Alcoholism believes "significantly more research is needed in this area."

Moreover, research has shown that educational efforts for drunk drivers are less effective than license revocation. Controversy continues, too, over the role of ADVERTISING in alcohol consumption. Occupational alcoholism programs have reported highly positive results and are being expanded into EMPLOYEE ASSISTANCE PROGRAMS offering counseling and referral services for alcohol abuse, alcoholism and other problems detected in the workplace. PARENT EDUCATION is also being studied.

Encouraging progress has been made in making physicians more aware of the importance of early detection of alcohol problems, and federal and private initiatives have increased the emphasis on alcohol abuse education in the medical school curricula (see HEALTH CARE PROVIDERS).

Eighteenth Amendment   Under the Eighteenth Amendment, which banned the manufacture, transportation and sale of intoxicating beverages, PROHIBITION officially began on January 17, 1920. The VOLSTEAD ACT provided the mechanism for its enforcement. It was repealed in 1932 by the TWENTY-FIRST AMENDMENT.

elderly   Research has consistently indicated that alcohol consumption levels are lower and alcohol abuse is less prevalent among persons over 60 than among any younger age group. Nonetheless, in the United States and other countries alcohol abuse among the elderly is a serious and growing problem. The number of alcoholics age 65 and over in the United States is now estimated at 146,000 and by the year 2000, when the size of the elderly population will have greatly increased, it is estimated that 337,000 elderly people will have a major problem with alcoholism. Alcohol abuse is the foremost form of substance abuse among the elderly, but alcohol-related problems, including alcoholism,

are often ignored for a number of reasons. One is that DENIAL of an alcohol problem is greater in the elderly and is more likely to be encouraged by relatives and friends, for instance, who feel that alcohol is one of the few pleasures left in old age. Alcoholism and alcohol abuse are also difficult to diagnose in the elderly because their manifestations may be perceived as the result of frailty, senility or just the unsteadiness of old age. The symptoms exhibited by alcoholics are very similar to those of nonalcoholics suffering deterioration of cerebral function because of advanced age. Alcohol-related illness may be difficult to distinguish from other chronic illness and from adverse side effects of medicines.

As a result of more effective treatment, such as proper NUTRITION and antibiotics, more people with histories of alcoholism now survive into old age than in the past. Many elderly people, however, become addicted to alcohol after retirement as a result of loneliness, boredom and feelings of being unneeded. Stressful situations, such as bereavement, separation from children and physical deterioration, multiply in old age. The elderly who begin abusing alcohol late in life generally have fewer deep-seated psychological problems and are more amenable to counseling than those who become alcoholics at a younger age. Alcoholism is higher among elderly men than among elderly women and highest among widowers and the divorced.

According to the NIAAA's *Sixth Special Report*, one study found that around 5% of men over age 60 suffered alcohol problems as compared to about 1% in women over 60. About one-fourth of the people in this country over age 65 take prescribed medications, and the interactions of these drugs with alcohol may pose significant health risks.

Alcohol has a somewhat different effect on the elderly than on the rest of the adult population. Older people generally consume less alcohol, although they are more likely to drink every day, possibly because the slower metabolism associated with aging may induce WITHDRAWAL symptoms in those who have become dependent on alcohol, thus increasing the frequency of alcohol intake. Furthermore the ratio of body fat to body water increases with age, and as alcohol is almost completely soluble in water but not in fat, the same amount of alcohol intake per body weight consumed by older people results in higher concentrations in the blood and brain.

There are several problems related to treatment of alcoholism and alcohol abuse among the elderly. Social agencies for the aged are usually poorly equipped to treat alcohol problems and many alcohol treatment centers are geared to a younger patient population. In addition to staying in the body longer, alcohol as well as other drugs tend to have a more prolonged and toxic effect on elderly people. Alcohol can also mask pain and other warning signs of illness and disease and interfere with the therapeutic effects of prescription DRUGS, which older people frequently must take. The possible existence of cardiovascular difficulties in the aged person often restricts or prevents the use of such alcohol antagonist drugs as ANTABUSE and TEMPOSIL in the treatment of alcoholism.

A 1989 analysis of hospital discharge data since 1979 showed that the 65-and-older group led all other age groups with a 60% proportion of alcohol-related diagnoses that were not primary diagnoses. Findings like this underline the fact that considerable alcohol-related morbidity may go undetected and untreated, and that clinicians should be alert to alcohol consumption by the elderly.

electric shock   See AVERSION THERAPY. Electric shock is also sometimes used to treat depression associated with alcoholism.

emetine   A nausea-inducing drug used in AVERSION THERAPY.

employee assistance programs (EAPs)
Also known as occupational alcoholism programs, employee assistance programs were begun in the 1930s and 1940s, first by DuPont and Kodak and later by a small number of progressive companies. Between 1950 and 1973 the number of EAPs increased from about 50 to 500. And in 1989 some 10,000 firms and public agencies, including 70% of the Fortune 500 companies, had employee assistance programs.

According to Dr. Dale A. Masi, director of employee and counseling services for the U.S. Department of Health and Human Services, the highest rate of recovery from alcoholism is found in the office or factory rather than the clinic or hospital program. According to the U.S. National Council on Alcoholism the average alcoholic will allow his or her family ties to disintegrate five years before he or she loses a job. The rate of recovery for EAP referrals is between 50% and 85%. Critics say these success statistics are exaggerated and maintain best estimates are that only 12% to 25% of patients manage to stay on the wagon for three years.

The National Institute on Alcohol Abuse and Alcoholism has estimated that 50% of people with job performance problems suffer from alcoholism. Because it is a progressive disease, alcoholism frequently takes as long as 10 to 15 years to reach its middle stages. At this point the worker is often occupying a position of responsibility. Richard Bickerton, a spokesman for the Employee Assistance Professionals Association in Arlington, Virginia, notes that for every dollar spent on an EAP, employers can expect to recover $3 to $5 of loss.

Among the sources that provide programs for alcoholic employees are voluntary associations, labor unions and organizations for employees in both the public and private sectors. A variety of counseling services are offered but the basic orientation of most programs is alcoholism identification and intervention. The work place provides structures for effective early intervention and confrontation. Poor job performance is the best indicator of a possible drinking problem. The rationale underlying the modern approach to employee alcoholism is that any alcoholic, even one in the early stages of the disease, will tend to exhibit a pattern of deteriorating job performance that can be observed by an alert individual (Dunkin). A return to adequate job performance should be regarded as the criterion for judging whether or not treatment has been a success.

There are 120 million workers in the United States, 15% of the work force (excluding the military) is in the public sector. Few public sector programs existed before 1972, but gradually, partly because of legislation, they have been increasing. Today, 98% of all U.S. government installations report having alcoholism counseling services.

While many organizations are well served by EAPs, two-thirds of workers still do not have access to such programs according to Richard Bickerton. This is especially true for employees of small- and medium-sized businesses. There is also a strong need for programs to help women and minorities. In Canada, for example, women make up about one-third of the alcoholic population, but according to Louise Nadeau, director of the University of Montreal's training program in addiction, only about 5% of them are referred for treatment through assistance programs (Birenbaum). Women have a double problem on the job: drinking is part of the process of becoming accepted by male coworkers, but women also have to deal with men's ambivalence about competing with them (as well as their own identity conflicts).

Another group of hard-to-reach employees are those holding senior or high-income positions. Such employees often work in an isolated or insulated environment, frequently change job location, work with minimal supervision, or are responsible to multiple supervisors and have a flexible work schedule. Supervisors often cover up problems they see in senior personnel, and those in senior positions may feel that EAPs are only for lower-level employees. The key to reaching these individuals is to involve them in the development of the programs, in the advisory and policy-making processes and in educational awareness programs. When this is not possible, the best approach is through peers and colleagues.

Despite the gain in numbers of EAPs and increase in treatment facilities in the United States, only 15% to 20% of alcoholics get any treatment at all.

Rhonda Birenbaum, "EAPs Failing Female Alcoholics" (report of a speech given by Louise Nadeau, director of the University of Montreal's training program in addiction, to the 4th Biennial Canadian Conference on Alcohol and Addiction Problems in the Workplace, Ottawa), *The Journal* 10, no. 12 (Dec. 1, 1981): 3.

William Dunkin, "The EAP Movement, Past and Present," *Alcoholism* 1, no. 4 (March-April): 27-28.

"EAPs Neglect Execs, Shift Workers" (report of a speech given by John Harder, director of the Canadian Forces Addiction Rehabilitation Centre, Kingston Ontario, to the 4th Biennial Canadian Conference on Alcohol and Addiction Problems in the Workplace, Ottawa), *The Journal* 10, no. 12 (Dec. 1, 1981): 12.

Alan Massam, "EAPs Have Highest Alcoholism Recovery Rates" (report of a speech given by Dale A. Masi, director of employee and counseling services, for the U.S. Department of Health and Human Services, to the World Conference on Alcoholism, London), *The Journal* 11, no. 1 (Jan. 1, 1982): 12.

enabling   A term that refers to attempts to protect an alcoholic from the consequences of his or her drinking. Although these attempts are generally aimed at helping the alcoholic, they allow his or her alcoholism to continue unchecked. Any member of society can be an enabler—family members and friends can provide reassurance and sympathy; an employer may find ways of keeping an alcoholic on the job; doctors and counselors may be protective of the alcoholic or blind to his or her problem; law enforcement officials may choose not to penalize alcohol-related incidents. These methods "enable" an alcoholic to continue in an uncontrolled drinking pattern by shielding him or her from the consequences.

An awareness of the negative effects of enabling by the enabler could eventually help the alcoholic. If forced to suffer the negative consequences of his or her behavior, the alcoholic may eventually develop more motivation to change. (See also PARA-ALCOHOLIC.)

endocrine etiological theories   A physiological approach to the cause of alcoholism, endocrine etiological theories hypothesize that dysfunction of the endocrine system leads to the development of alcoholism. A pituitary-adrenocortical deficiency resulting in hypoglycemia is believed to cause symptoms that stimulate drinking. Alcohol temporarily relieves the hypoglycemia by elevating blood sugar, but ultimately it intensifies the hypoglycemic condition, causing dependence on increased amounts of alcohol. To date there has been no strong evidence to support this view. (See also PHYSIOLOGICAL ETIOLOGICAL MODELS.)

environment   See GENETICS.

epidemiology   (From the Greek *epidemos* among the people; *epi* in + *demos* people + *logy* discourse.) The medical study of the occurrence and prevalence of disease. The term "epidemiology" is often applied to the study of a disease that affects large numbers of people in a community.

Epsilon alcoholism   The fifth of five categories of alcoholism defined by JELLINEK, Epsilon alcoholism refers to periodic alcoholism. Less is known about the causes of Epsilon than about any of the other categories.

esophagus   Relative to the rest of the population, alcoholics and heavy drinkers show a high incidence of esophageal CANCER.

ethanol   The principal chemical in distilled spirits, wine and beer, ethanol is a highly soluble, colorless, inflammable liquid produced by the reaction of fermenting sugar with yeast spores. It can also be made in small amounts in the human intestines when dietary sugars are fermented, but it is then detoxified by a liver enzyme called alcohol dehydrogenase. (See also INTRODUCTION.)

ethyl alcohol   See ETHANOL.

etiological theories of alcoholism   Because of the complex nature of alcoholism, there are numerous theories on its cause. To date much is still unknown regarding the etiology of alcoholism, and no theory alone can completely explain the syndrome. The current theories generally can be divided into three main categories, each of which encompasses a number of different approaches to alcoholism. These are discussed in more detail under separate headings.

One main category is PHYSIOLOGICAL MODELS OF ETIOLOGY. Theories in this category postulate that individuals are predisposed to develop alcoholism because of some organic defect. They include GENETOTROPHIC ETIOLOGICAL THEORIES, ENDOCRINE ETIOLOGICAL THEORIES and genetic theories (see GENETICS).

A second main category is PSYCHOLOGICAL MODELS OF ETIOLOGY. Most psychological theories are based on the assumption that some flaw in the personality structure leads to the development of alcoholism. Among these is the theory, originally advanced by Freud, of ORAL FIXATION. BEHAVIORAL LEARNING THEORIES are another psychological model.

A third category of theories on the causes of alcoholism is SOCIOCULTURAL ETIOLOGICAL THEORIES, also known as CULTURAL ETIOLOGICAL THEORIES. These theories postulate relationships between various factors in society, such as ethnic and cultural differences, and the incidence of alcohol use. Also in this category are CULTURAL STRESS ETIOLOGICAL THEORIES.

In addition, there is a category known as MORAL ETIOLOGICAL THEORY, which holds that alcoholism is either a moral fault or a sin of the alcoholic. Once almost universally embraced in Western countries, this theory is now most commonly held by fundamentalist religious organizations.

etiology   (From the Greek *aitia* cause + *logos* discourse.) The science of causes, especially the investigation of the causes and origins of disease.

euphoria   After consuming alcoholic beverages, a drinker may feel elated and without worries or fears. For an alcoholic, however, the euphoric effect may be reduced because of his or her TOLERANCE for alcohol. While the desire to re-experience the euphoric effect may start a new drinker on the road to alcoholism, there is some debate as to whether alcoholics will continue to drink because they have not experienced the desired and expected euphoria they once did or because they have. It is agreed that the alcoholic expects this euphoria.

The effect of drinking alcohol on the human brain is almost identical to the effect of ether or most other surgical anesthetics. The first stage, usually corresponding to two or three drinks, is generally one of relaxation and euphoria, not unlike the first couple of whiffs of ether.

F

falls   Falls, a major cause of trauma, account for more accidental deaths than any other cause except automobile ACCIDENTS and for over 60% of all accidental injuries. A 1987 reveiw of the literature on falls indicated that alcohol played a role in 17% to 53% of fatal falls and from 21% to 77% of nonfatal falls (Hingson and Howland). A study of over 300 emergency room patients who had suffered accidental falls found that 60% had detectable levels of alcohol in their blood, and 53% of these fall victims had BLOOD ALCOHOL COUNTS (BACs) above 0.2% (Honkanen et al., 1983). Risk estimates in this study showed a steep rise in relative risk of accidental falls with increasing BAC. All fall injuries with BACs above 0.10% can be considered to have been caused by alcohol. Other studies have shown that alcoholics are more likely to suffer falls that result in death than the general population.

B. Honkanen et al., "The role of alcohol in accidental falls," *Journal of Studies on Alcohol* 44(1983):231-245.

R. Hingson and J. Howland. "Alcohol as a risk factor for injury and death resulting from accidental falls: A review of the literature," *Journal of Studies on Alcohol*, 48 (1987): 212-219.

familial etiological theories   A sociocultural approach to the etiology of alcoholism, these theories place emphasis on the role of the family in providing models and social learning experiences for children. Children will tend to follow the parental mode of coping with problems of depression, feelings of inadequacy and rejection. Studies of the family backgrounds of alcoholics have shown an unusually high incidence of familial alcoholism. While this finding may suggest a genetic interpretation, the pattern of drinking and the range of circumstances in which such drinking occurs is usually the same for both parents and offspring, giving weight to a social learning component.

The family plays an important role in the development of personality and behavior. In various studies it was found that the prevalence of alcoholism among parents of alcoholics was two to 10 times that among parents of nonalcoholics. Among siblings of alcoholics there was a prevalence of two to 14 times that among siblings of nonalcoholics. (See also

SOCIOCULTURAL ETIOLOGICAL THEORIES.)

David J. Amor, J. Michael Polich and Harriet B. Stambul, *Alcoholism and Treatment* (New York: John Wiley and Sons, 1978), pp. 25-26.

James G. Rankin, *Core Knowledge in the Drug Field (8 Etiology)* (Toronto: Addiction Research Foundation, 1978), p. 27.

family problems   See FAMILIAL ETIOLOGICAL THEORIES. See also SPOUSE ABUSE, CHILD ABUSE, CHILDREN OF ALCOHOLICS, ORAL FIXATION.

fatty liver   A type of liver damage characterized by an accumulation of fat in the liver. Alcohol upsets the normal METABOLISM of fat in the liver, resulting in an accumulation of fatty acids, and changes in the liver can occur after a few days of heavy drinking. The underlying cause of fatty liver is not well understood, but the primary cause may be damage to the liver MITOCHONDRIA, which break down chemical bonds in the complex molecules of nutrients during oxidation, causing an impairment of the oxidation of fatty acids and resulting in fatty acid accumulation. When alcohol is consumed with a high-fat diet, the fatty acids that accumulate are derived primarily from the diet; when alcohol is consumed with a low-fat diet, the fatty acids are synthesized within the liver. A low-fat diet is nevertheless preferable to a high-fat diet (see NUTRITION).

Fatty liver is a common occurrence among alcoholics: in one liver biopsy study of chronic alcoholics, 90% had fatty liver. In recent years the incidence of fatty liver has been increasing both in the United States and Europe. Patients with fatty liver may be quite asymptomatic, and an uncomplicated fatty liver is generally considered to be a relatively mild condition and fully reversible. However, in a number of autopsies performed on alcoholics, particularly younger alcoholics, the only finding was a massive fatty liver.

fetal alcohol syndrome (FAS)   The dangers of excessive drinking during pregnancy have been long recognized. The ancient Greeks noted that alcohol abuse by pregnant women often resulted in harmful effects to their unborn children. During the so-called gin epidemic in London during the 1700s the connection between alcohol abuse and birth defects was made again. However, it is only recently, in 1973, that an apparent clinical entity, the fetal alcohol syndrome, was identified by Kenneth L. Jones and David W. Smith of the University of Washington in Seattle, who utilized studies done a few years earlier by Christie Ulleland, also of the University of Washington. Alcohol-related birth defects are among the leading causes of congenital mental disorders, ranking with Down's Syndrome and Spina Bifida. (Some experts maintain it is *the* leading cause!) Of the three disorders only alcohol-related defects are preventable. Clearly, FAS is a major public health problem, with treatment costs for FAS in the United States estimated at nearly a third of a billion dollars per year as of 1988.

Children with fetal alcohol syndrome, born to mothers who have used alcohol excessively during pregnancy, exhibit a complex of characteristics, including growth deficiencies, physical malformations and mental retardation. FAS is not based on one single feature observable in all cases but on a constellation of abnormalities. It may be more appropriate to refer to fetal alcohol syndrome as fetal alcohol effects (FAS).

Certain features are commonly found in cases of FAS. Most victims fail to reach normal length, both before and after birth. At age one, children with FAS are, on the average, only 65% of normal length. They are also below normal weight, tend to remain thin and small as they get older and have unusually small head circumference. Most have elongated folds in their eyelids, causing eye slits. Other physical abnormalities that occur frequently include low nasal bridge, short nose, indistinct philtrum (the vertical groove between the nose and mouth), narrow upper lip, small chin and flat midface. About 30% of children with FAS have heart defects.

The effects of FAS on the central nervous system include retarded mental and motor development, tremulousness, hyperactivity and poor attention span. The average IQ of children with FAS is around 68. Varying degrees of mental deficiency are the most common signs of fetal damage among the children of maternal alcoholics. Such children show no improvement with time, even when placed in supportive atmospheres.

How Alcohol Affects the Fetus

When a pregnant woman drinks, alcohol passes freely across the placental barrier into the baby's bloodstream in concentrations at least as high as those in the mother (see BLOOD ALCOHOL CONCENTRATION). The system of the fetus, however, is not as equipped to handle the effects of alcohol as is the mother's system. The undeveloped liver of the unborn baby burns up alcohol at less than half the rate of the adult liver, so that alcohol remains in the fetal system longer than in the adult system. At low concentrations and for short durations, alcohol is a rapidly metabolized source of energy. At higher concentrations and for longer durations it is a toxic agent.

Deficiencies of MINERALS AND VITAMINS resulting from maternal drinking may also be harmful to the fetus. Alcoholic women commonly suffer from insufficient amounts of calcium, magnesium and zinc, all of which play an important role in fetal development. Low zinc content in certain infant diets has resulted in limited growth. Deficiencies of vitamins, such as folic acid and thiamine, also common in alcoholics, may play a role in fetal malformations and central nervous system lesions. Research in this area is still in its early stages.

Sudden WITHDRAWAL from alcohol by the mother during pregnancy may subject the fetus to major metabolic and physiologic disturbances. However, withdrawal under controlled conditions with progressively reduced doses of alcohol will probably be better for the fetus than continued drinking. Controlled withdrawal can result in rebound growth in the infant, compensating for an earlier disruption.

Heavy drinking is often associated with heavy SMOKING, which can also have harmful effects on the development of the fetus. Smoking mothers generally have a higher percentage of low-birth-weight infants. In 1976 French investigators reported stillbirth rates (also associated with maternal drinking) of 9.9 per 1,000 for light drinkers, 25.5 per 1,000 for heavy drinkers and 50.5 per 1,000 for women who both drank and smoked heavily.

Recent prospective and retrospective epidemiological studies on FAS frequency in 19 populations worldwide calculated incidence at 1.9 cases per 1,000 live births. Reported rates were higher in North America than in Europe (2.9 versus 1.1 per 1,000) (Abel & Sokol, 1987). A 1984 study reported that the incidence of FAS among only alcohol-dependent women may be as high as 25 cases per 1,000 births (Abel). With less restrictive criteria, the incidence of FAS could be approximately three times greater.

How Much Alcohol Is Safe?

Although most documented cases of FAS have been children of women whose drinking meets the criteria of alcoholism, it is not yet known exactly how much alcohol is harmful to the fetus. Many states and organizations, such as the National Institute on Alcohol Abuse and Alcoholism and the American Medical Association Panel on Alcoholism, recommend complete abstinence from alcohol during pregnancy. They warn that since the effects of even a small amount of alcohol are still unknown and safe levels of intake have not yet been established, the wisest course is to abstain completely. The March of Dimes, which once held that such a prohibition unnecessarily frightened women, now recommends complete abstinence as well.

Researchers currently believe that the harmful effects of prenatal exposure to alcohol exist on a continuum, ranging from extreme structural defects at one extreme to very subtle cognitive-behavioral dysfunctions at the other. The inability to test for a "threshold dose" above which FAS or FAE is a danger leads experts to prescribe extreme caution. Until more is known about exactly what level of alcohol intake is safe, most agencies and organizations continue to recommend abstinence.

E.L. Abel, *Fetal Alcohol Syndrome and Fetal Alcohol Effects* (New York: Plenum, 1984).

———— and R.J. Sokol, "Incidence of Fetal Alcohol Syndrome and Economic Impact of FAS-related Anomalies," *Drug Alcohol Dependence* 19(1987):51-70.

Judy Dobbie and Philippa Bell, *Fetal Alcohol Syndrome* (Addiction Research Foundation of Ontario, 1978).

Enoch Gordis, M.D., ed., *Seventh Special Report to the U.S. Congress on Alcohol and Health* (Rockville, Md.: National Institute on Alcohol Abuse and Alcoholism, 1990), chapter VI.

Henry L. Rosett, "Clinical Pharmacology of the Fetal Alcohol Syndrome," in *Biochemistry and Pharmacology of Ethanol*, vol. 2, ed. Edward Majchrowicz and Ernest P. Noble (Plenum Press: New York, 1979), pp. 485-509.

A. P. Streissguth, S. Landesman-Dwyer, D. C. Martin and D. W. Smith, "Teratogenic Effects of Alcohol in Humans and Laboratory Animals," *Science* 209 (July 18, 1980): 353-361.

K. Warren, "Alcohol-Related Birth Defects: Current Trends in Research," *Alcohol Health and Research World* (Fall 1985), p. 4.

Finland   The per capita consumption of alcohol in Finland seems in line with that of most other European nations, but for a variety of reasons specific to this country it has nevertheless been a cause for concern. This concern led in 1959 to the consolidation of studies on alcohol consumption issues, previously handled by various temperance societies, within a national Foundation for Alcohol Studies, a branch of the State Alcohol Monopoly, which regulates liquor sales throughout the country.

More than half of the alcoholic beverages consumed in Finland are strong liquors, usually a distilled vodka called *viina,* rather than beer or wine.

In liters of ABSOLUTE ALCOHOL based on total population, the apparent per capita consumption rate for 1987 was 7.1 liters, placing Finland 25th among 47 countries that reported consumption rates. Interestingly, Finland places fifth among survey countries for consumption of distilled spirits, with a total per capita rate of 3.22 liters for 1987. With a per capita rate of 5.12 liters for wine, the country ranks 34th for consumption of this beverage and ranks 18th in consumption of beer, with a per capita rate of 68.1 liters.

A tradition of illegal distilling for home use perseveres in most rural areas; estimates suggest that perhaps 10% of the alcohol consumed in Finland is distilled illegally. Since the country abolished its experiment with total prohibition following a referendum in 1931, legalized distribution has been controlled solely by the State Alcohol Monopoly, which maintains restricted distribution centers in cities but has eliminated them entirely in rural areas. To some extent these measures have unintentionally encouraged the national pattern of occasional but heavy drinking that prevails today.

Statistics on alcohol poisoning, recorded by the government since 1802, are particularly high because of the traditional acceptance of illegally distilled liquor. In 1981 (most recent available figures), the rate of death from alcohol poisoning was 5.7 per 100,000 population.

A special area of concern is the territory of Lapland, in the northern part of the country. Deprived of liquor stores by the State Alcohol Monopoly, the Lapps, heavy drinkers, travel great distances to purchase liquor legally or drink dangerous varieties of home-brewed alcohol. Many alcoholics among the Lapps are also known to drink industrial and medicinal alcohol products. One problem confronting those who travel to legal liquor stores is that the trip takes, on the average, a full day. These trips are themselves occasions for ritualistic and excessive drinking. Experiments have been conducted to test the effect of local liquor distribution on the Lapps' drinking habits. In these experiments legal alcohol replaced illegal brews in large proportions, but the overall problem of excessive drinking and drunkenness remained virtually unchanged.

Beginning in 1962 care of alcoholics in Finland has been regulated by a special "Act Governing the Treatment of Misusers of Intoxicants." However, the Finnish government has provided institutions for the care of alcoholics since 1937. In addition to hospitals these include outpatient clinics managed by the National Board of Social Welfare and, in eight large cities, voluntary admission A-clinics maintained since 1955 by an independent government foundation. There are also a variety of homes for skid row alcoholics, nursing homes for chronic abusers of alcohol and halfway houses for young alcoholics. The Finnish Temperance Movement privately funds several programs for the treatment of alcoholism.

Given the acknowledged failure of its experiment with total prohibition, the primary task facing this country of sporadic but excessive drinkers is to encourage moderation, perhaps by finding a way to shift consumption habits away from strong liquors toward beers and wines. At the same time, the country is aware of the danger of changing its citizens from occasional to habitual consumers of alcoholic beverages. Its emphasis at present is on increased governmental supervision of public drinking places, such as licensed restaurants, where drinking habits and cultural alcohol trends are most likely to be formed.

Hoeveel alcoholhoude dranken worden er in de wereld gedronken? (How many alcoholic beverages are being consumed throughout the world?) 27th ed. Schiedam, Netherlands: Produktschap Voor Gedistilleerde Dranken, 1987.

"International Trends in Alcohol Production, Trade, and Consumption, 1970 to 1977" prepared by the Statistical Information Section (Toronto), Table 97.

E. J. Immonen, "New Trends in the Alcohol Problem in Finland," *Social Psychiatry* 4, no. 4 (1969): 173-176.

Kari Poikolainen, "Increase in Alcohol-Related Hospitalizations in Finland 1969-1975," *British Journal of Addiction* 75 (1980): 281-291.

formaldehyde   Formaldehyde is a colorless pungent gas formed in the oxidation of methyl alcohol, which is produced naturally in the body in small amounts. Formaldehyde is even more toxic than the ACETALDEHYDE produced by the METABOLISM of ethyl alcohol, but normally the LIVER has ample capacity to break down both formaldehyde and acetaldehyde into nontoxic units. However, if the liver is flooded with ethyl alcohol, as occurs when someone has had a great deal to drink, the liver works first to metabolize the ethyl alcohol, at a rate 16 times faster than it breaks down the methyl alcohol. Therefore methyl alcohol builds up as the liver acts on the excess ethyl alcohol. When the methyl alcohol is finally metabolized, a considerable amount of formaldehyde is produced. This may be responsible for WITHDRAWAL symptoms and may also be at least partially responsible for the HANGOVER effect, which has been shown to begin as soon as all ethanol has been metabolized.

fortified wine   Wine to which another alcoholic substance, usually grape brandy, has been added during the vinification process. This addition not only increases the alcohol content of the wine—making it from 16% to 23% alcohol—but changes its flavor and character by interfering with the normal fermentation process. The principal fortified wines are PORT, SHERRY, MARSALA, MADEIRA and VERMOUTH.

Fox, Ruth, M.D. (1896-1989)   Noted psychoanalyst, who in 1959 became the first medical director of the National Council on Alcoholism. Dr. Fox performed pioneering research on the use of Antabuse, a chemical used widely in alcoholism treatment today. She was also founder and first president of the American Medical Society on Alcoholism and Other Drug Dependencies in 1954. Winner of numerous awards, including the American Medical Society on Alcoholism's annual award in 1973, Dr. Fox wrote, lectured and taught extensively on the subject of alcohol and drug abuse. She maintained a private practice as well and was one of the nation's first psychoanalysts willing to accept alcoholics as patients.

Dr. Fox was a fellow of several groups, including the American Psychiatric Association, the New York Academy of Medicine, the American Health Association and the Society of Clinical Hypnosis. She retired in 1979, 10 years before her death at age 93 in Washington D.C.

France   Throughout the history of France, alcohol, especially wine, has played a very important role culturally, socially and financially. The French have a liberal attitude toward the use of alcohol and abstinence is unusual. Any concern over consumption is more likely to focus upon a reduction of drinking moderate levels than upon complete abstinence. The French view alcohol as a natural part of their daily diet. Nonalcoholic drinks are often considered too sweet to be consumed with meals or to quench thirst, and in cafes wine is much cheaper than fruit juice or soft drinks. In 1980 (most recent available statistics), one Frenchmen in 10 derives his income directly or indirectly from the alcoholic beverage industry, and one in five French parliamentarians represents the industry.

France is a large-scale producer of alcoholic beverages, particularly wine. While there are controls on production, to date the amount of wine produced has far exceeded demand, even though exportation increased 500% from 1969 to 1979. There is some illicit brewing, principally of rums and aperitifs, both in homes and in larger operations.

According to a 1987 survey, the French have the highest rate of alcohol consumption in the world, although the rate has declined since the beginning of the century. Per capita consumption of ABSOLUTE ALCOHOL in 1987 for the total French population was 13.0 liters. As might be expected, wine is the most popular beverage, and although wine consumption is decreasing, France continues to have the highest level of any country after Italy. The 1987 consumption figure for wine totalled 75.1 liters per capita. The drop in wine drinking has been accompanied by an increase in the sales of beer and hard liquor. And although overall consumption of absolute alcohol is decreasing, alcoholic beverages still represented more than 80% of the total of all drinks consumed in the early 1980s; the French drink eight times as much alcohol as fruit juices. With the trend toward beer and hard liquor has come a change in drinking styles, as such beverages are usually drunk quickly and in public places while wine is traditionally drunk more slowly and primarily at home.

Alcohol consumption, after cardiovascular diseases and cancer, is the leading cause of death in France. In 1982 there were approximately 25.5. deaths per 100,000 people from cirrhosis and 6.2 deaths per 100,000 from alcoholism and alcoholic psychoses. Most cancers of the mouth and digestive tract are attributable to alcohol abuse.

Because of a growing awareness of the problem, the French government, under Valery Giscard d'Estaing, announced a drive against alcoholism in December 1980. The campaign represented a new political backing for a cause that has traditionally been unpopular. Politically alcohol abuse has never been a "noble subject," partly because of the enormous power of the wine and spirits industry. A committee was set up under Dr. Bernard to study the problem of alcoholism and determine what could be done to reduce it. Aiming to cut alcohol consumption by 20% in five years, the government passed 35 measures in the program to combat alcoholism, including higher taxes on alcohol, stricter application of breath tests for motorists, prohibition of store sales to minors and a publicity campaign.

Hoeveel alcoholhoude dranken worden er in de wereld gedronken? (How many alcoholic beverages are being consumed throughout the world?) 27th ed. Schiedam, Netherlands: Produktschap Voor Gedistilleerde Dranken, 1987.

Friends For Sobriety (FFS)

Friends For Sobriety (FFS)   A recovery support group, Friends For Sobriety was organized by five recovering alcoholics in March 1980 to help persons addicted to mood-altering chemicals, including alcohol. FFS offers an alternative, nontheistic recovery program in the belief that most people cannot endure a crisis of religious conscience and the crisis of confronting their alcoholism, for example, at the same time. Groups meet for one hour three times a week to hold open discussion structured around a Nine-Step Recovery Booklet. Emphasis is on both the emotional needs of the recovering individual and the necessity of assuming personal responsibility for one's behavior. FFS is not in competition with other recovery or support programs and encourages members to attend such programs as needed for maintaining their sobriety. The group's headquarters are located in Paradise Valley, Ariz.

fructose   A sugar that occurs naturally in fruits and honey, fructose may help to speed up the metabolic rate at which ethanol is metabolized, but the degree of acceleration of metabolism is thought to be relatively small. The mechanism by which the rate of elimination is increased is unknown. Although adding fructose to the diet may somewhat reduce the HANGOVER effect, it is not generally a practical sobering agent.

G

Gamma alcoholism   The third of five categories of alcoholism defined by JELLINEK. "*Gamma alcoholism* means that species of alcoholism in which (1) acquired increased tissue tolerance to alcohol, (2) adaptive cell metabolism, (3) withdrawal symptoms and 'craving,' i.e., physical dependence, and (4) loss of control are involved." There is a progression from psychological DEPENDENCE to physical ADDICTION. This type of alcoholism causes the most damage both to the interpersonal relationships of the individual and to his or her health. Gamma alcoholism is apparently the dominating form of alcoholism in the United States and is the type recognized by ALCOHOLICS ANONYMOUS. (See also LOSS OF CONTROL, METABOLISM, WITHDRAWAL.)

gastrointestinal tract   The organs from the mouth to the rectum associated with digestion (otherwise known as the GI tract). Alcohol passes through the mouth to the stomach, where about 20% of it is absorbed. The rest is absorbed in the upper small intestine. The presence of food in the stomach decreases the rate of alcohol absorption.

Alcohol is eliminated from the body chiefly through METABOLISM in the liver. Less than 10% of the amount consumed is lost through the kidneys, lungs and skin. Consumption of alcohol produces a number of deleterious effects on the gastrointestinal tract, depending on the quantity ingested and the susceptibility of the individual. (For the effects of alcohol on the various parts of the GI tract, see STOMACH, LIVER, PANCREAS.)

In addition to the damaging effects of chronic alcohol ingestion on the GI tract itself, alcohol impairs the absorption of certain VITAMINS AND MINERALS and interferes with the nutritional process, adversely affecting the well-being of the entire body (see NUTRITION).

gay alcoholics   See HOMOSEXUALS.

genetic models of etiology   See GE-
NETICS.

genetics   A familial link has long been
recognized in alcoholism, and research over
the last 30 years has begun to confirm that
much of this phenomenon is due to heredity,
rather than solely to environmental factors.
Currently, most scientists agree that alcoholism is based on a complex of genetic, cultural
and social factors. Much of the current evidence for a genetic contribution to alcoholism
is derived from Scandinavian studies of the
incidence and patterns of the disease among
children who were adopted away from their
biological parents, as well as of adopted twins
who were separated at birth. However, scientists continue to find evidence for a genetic
role in a number of studies along many different lines, including: selective breeding experiments of animals; analyses of similarities
between certain brain wave phenomena of
alcoholic fathers and their sons; examination
of hereditary psychological deficits; and studies of biochemical markers of a predisposition
to alcoholism.

In April 1990, it was reported in *The Journal of the American Medical Association* that
a research team headed by Dr. Ernest P. Noble
of the University of California at Los Angeles
and Dr. Kenneth Blum of the University of
Texas Health Science Center in San Antonio,
had identified a gene that is believed to be
linked to a higher risk of alcoholism. The
gene, located on chromosome 11, is the "D2"
receptor gene for dopamine, a chemical tied
to pleasure seeking behavior, and was found
in 77% of the brains of 35 people who had died
of alcoholism. The gene was present in only
28% of the brains of nonalcoholics. This statistical evidence is very strong, and bodes well
for future clinical testing of susceptibility for
alcoholism, but the finding will need to be
repeated on a larger number of alcoholics
before it can be considered certain. As a matter
of fact, a new National Institution on Alcohol
Abuse and Alcoholism (NIAAA) study in the
December 1990 issue of the same *Journal of*
the American Medical Association questioned
the theory of the proposed genetic predisposition to alcoholism.

Annabel M. Boles, M.D., Chief, Section on
Genetic Studies, NIAAA, stated the study
does not support a widespread or consistent
association between the (dopamine) receptor
gene and alcoholism. The study tested for
association in a large group of population
controls, in two families with multi-
generational alcoholism, and in a group of 40
living alcoholics who had been characterized
as to age of onset, severity, presence of ASP
(antisocial personality disorder) or family history.

In addition to the alcoholics, the authors
examined 127 racially mixed controls and two
white families with eight alcoholics and six
unaffected members. Two different tests were
used to detect the particular dopamine receptor gene. The authors wrote: "There was no
significant difference in the Al allele frequency between any alcoholic subpopulation
and the control group. Furthermore, there was
also no significant difference between the
fraction of alcoholics and controls positive for
the Al allele."

In the test results from the two families,
close linkage of the dopamine gene to alcoholism was ruled out. Furthermore, there was no
significant difference in the frequency of the
allele found in those alcoholics who were the
offspring of an alcoholic and those who were
not.

This study supports the derisive response to
the Blum-Noble study by geneticists when the
study was released in April.

The most frequently cited studies support-
ing a genetic role in alcoholism are the Scandinavian adoption studies, which consistently
show that the biological susceptibility for alcoholism is active even when children are
separated from their biological families.
These studies have become increasingly sophisticated since the landmark Swedish finding in 1960 that of identical twins separated at
birth, the chance that one twin would become
alcoholic if the other did as well, was on the

order of 74%. (In contrast, the concordance of alcoholism between fraternal twins was found to be 26%.) Given their number and variety, it is impossible to report on these studies in any but a cursory way here, and readers are referred to sources at the end of this entry for more information. Among the most compelling findings of these adoption studies, it was found that the biological sons of alcoholics, as well as the biological daughters of alcoholic mothers, were three times as likely as other adoptees to develop alcoholism. The most recent research in this area has focused on heritability of specific drinking behaviors, such as frequency, quantity and regularity of drinking at particular times. Interestingly, the heritability estimates for these behaviors have been found to range from 36% to 40%.

Among the most important adoption studies was the analysis of Swedish research that has revealed the existence of two types of genetic predisposition to alcoholism (see MILIEU-LIMITED TYPE I ALCOHOLISM). The more common type, called milieu-limited (or Type I) alcoholism, accounts for most cases. It occurs in both men and women, is usually not severe, and is associated with mild, adult-onset abuse in either biological parent. Its occurrence is thought to be heavily influenced by the postnatal environment. A more severe type of alcoholism, accounting for 25% of male alcoholics, is called male-limited (or Type II) alcoholism. This type of susceptibility was associated with severe alcoholism in the biological fathers of males only, and its transmission seems unaffected by environment, i.e., this type is thought to be completely caused by genetic makeup.

Another line of research has studied brain wave activity as a potential neurophysiological marker for a genetic predisposition. The most exciting studies have focused on two new electroencephalographic (EEG) techniques for examining deficits in the brain: event-related potential (ERP) and evoked potential (EP) techniques. One particular ERP feature, the P3 wave, was found to have a reduced amplitude in chronic alcoholics. A most startling discovery was that a group of young boys who were the sons of alcoholics, and who had yet to drink alcohol or use drugs, were found to have a similar flattening of the amplitude of the P3 wave (Porjesz and Begleiter).

Other research into the genetics of alcoholism have focused on animal breeding studies in which researchers have been able to breed genetic lines that differ in a number of alcohol-related traits. These include the breeding of alcohol-preferring and alcohol-non-preferring rats; the breeding of mouse lines that differ in sensitivity to alcohol's hypnotic effects; mouse lines that differ in susceptibility to alcohol withdrawal seizures; and lines that differ in sensitivity to animal models of alcohol euphoria. The evidence from such experiments offer additional evidence that drinking behavior is strongly influenced by genetic components.

Other important research has focused on biochemical markers of a susceptibility toward alcoholism. Numerous reports have been published on the enzyme oxidase (MAO), which has been found in lower levels in the blood platelets of alcoholics. Another platelet enzyme, adenylate cyclase (AC) has been found to react to stimulation differently among alcoholics.

Much genetic variation has been found in the characteristics of two enzymes that are crucial to alcohol metabolism in the liver—alcohol dehydrogenase (ADH), which converts ethanol to acetaldehyde, and aldehyde dehydrogenase (ALDH), which converts the acetaldehyde to acetate to facilitate elimination. Researchers have found that genetic variations in these enzymes can have a profound effect on the alcohol elimination rates among individuals, and have hypothesized that this can be an important factor in one's susceptibility to alcoholism. (See ACETALDEHYDE).

Although evidence continues to mount for a causal relationship between heredity and alcohol problems, researchers still agree that it is the interaction of genetic factors and the familial, social and cultural environment that truly determines the course of the disease. Thus, research is likely to focus less on proving a genetic contribution, than determining how exactly genetics and environment interact.

Lawrence K. Altman, "Scientists See a Link Between Alcoholism and a Specific Gene," *New York Times*, April 18, 1990, p. 1.

H. Begleiter and B. Porjesz, "Potential Biological Markers in Individuals at High Risk for Developing Alcoholism," *Alcoholism (NY)* 12 (1977): 488-493.

K.M. Fillmore, "The 1980s Dominant Theory of Alcohol Problems—Genetic Predisposition to Alcoholism: Where Is It leading us?" *Drugs and Society* 2 (1988): 69-87.

Kathleen Whalen FitzGerald, *Alcoholism: The Genetic Inheritance* (New York: Doubleday, 1988).

Enoch Gordis, M.D., ed., *Seventh Special Report to the U.S. Congress on Alcohol and Health* (Rockville, Md.: National Institute on Alcohol Abuse and Alcoholism, 1990), chapter III.

genetotropic etiological theory   A theory, first advanced by R. J. Williams, which suggests that alcoholism is related to a genetically determined biochemical defect—the desire to drink is an inner urge mediated by nervous structures, perhaps in the hypothalamus of the brain. These nervous structures, according to Williams' theory, are deranged by alcohol and malnutrition. Williams believes that satisfaction of all nutritional needs will end the desire for alcohol. Although his methods and studies have been criticized, it is acknowledged that NUTRITION may well play some role in the etiology of alcoholism.

Germany   In 1987, West Germany reported the seventh highest level of consumption of ABSOLUTE ALCOHOL in the world. This is not surprising in view of the fact that almost all meals and social occasions are complemented with beer, wine and other alcoholic beverages.

From 1975 until 1987 West Germany reported a decline in the consumption of pure alcohol from 12.4 liters to 10.6 liters, per capita. This drop was significant because until 1975 the level had been rising steadily.

A report by the Institut fur Demoskopie Allensbach attributed the drop in consumption to the public's increased awareness of the problem of alcohol abuse. This awareness has been brought about in part by the Anti-Alcohol Campaign of the Bundesfamilien- ministerium (the federal ministry for families) begun in 1975.

The problem of alcohol abuse in Germany is not limited to any particular age category, social group or sex. It is indicative of a general problem of the society that such large numbers of people are seeking their satisfaction through alcohol. Many of the factors contributing to alcohol abuse in Germany are the same as in numerous other countries: broken homes, unsuccessful marriages, lack of fulfillment in personal life and work and feelings of inability to cope with reality. Also, the effects of World War II should not be overlooked for the generation whose formative years coincided with the war period.

The following information concerning types of programs for alcoholics is based on reports from Frankfurt and Hamburg. Many of the programs, however, are available in towns and cities throughout the country. These programs fall into three general categories: self-help groups, advice bureaus (*Beratungsstellen*) and treatment centers.

Among the best known of the self-help groups is Anonymen Alkoholiker (ALCOHOLICS ANONYMOUS). Modeled after the American organization of the same name, Anonymen Alkoholiker has approximately 2,000 groups in Germany. In Frankfurt there are several programs for the families of alcoholics. Among these are the Al-Anon Familiengruppen and the Elternkreise des Jugenberatung und Jugendhilfe, a program for the parents of young alcoholics. In many towns an organization known as the Freundeskreise ("Circle of Friends") provides assistance to the families of alcoholics. None of the aforementioned programs are affiliated with any religious or political groups.

Self-help groups with a religious affiliation include the Protestant Blaue Kreuz ("Blue Cross"), the Catholic Kreuzbund ("League of the Cross") and the Jewish Guttempler ("Good Templar").

Advice bureaus are usually located in health services, churches, clubs and other organizations. Frankfurt lists among its advice bureaus the Sozialpadagogischen Dienst der Stadt ("Social-Educational Service of the City"), the Beratungsstellen von Evangelischen Regionalverband ("Advisory Board of the Protestant Regional Alliance") and, for young people, the Vereins Arbeits- und Erziehungshilfe ("Society for Work and Educational Assistance").

In Hamburg an organization known as Das Kreisgesundheitgesamt Hamburg ("The Collected Health Circle of Hamburg") has developed a program in which a doctor, a social worker and a self-help group work together with individual alcoholics.

In the mid-1970s the first centralized center for the intoxicated opened in Hamburg. The center was designed primarily to provide a place where individuals whom the police suspected of being drunk could sober up overnight. Such a center was felt to be necessary because of reported incidences of persons dying in police "coolers" because they were in need of medical attention. At the Hamburg center a doctor examines each person brought in by the police. Those in need of medical care are taken to a hospital and those who are merely drunk are kept in the center overnight at their own expense.

Among the other German cities considering opening such treatment centers are Stuttgart, Frankfurt, Dusseldorf and Cologne.

Hoeveel alcoholhoude dranken worden er in de wereld gedronken? (How many alcoholic beverages are being consumed throughout the world?) 27th ed. Schiedam, Netherlands: Produktschap Voor Gedistilleerde Dranken, 1987.

GI tract   See   GASTROINTESTINAL TRACT.

gin   An alcoholic beverage made from distilled fermented grains (chiefly rye but also corn, barley and oats) and flavored with juniper berries. Most gin is colorless and its proof usually falls between 80 and 94.

The name "gin" is an anglicized and abbreviated form of *jenever* (sometimes spelled *genever* or *geneva*), one of the terms that the Dutch used for gin. The Dutch term is an altered form of the French *genievre,* meaning juniper.

The word "gin" has been used in a number of popular expressions, particularly during the 20th century. Among the best known is the card game GIN RUMMY. At the turn of the century the expression "ginned up," meaning "drunk," came into use. Ginned up was shortened to "ginned" in the 1920s. During the same period cheap saloons, bars and nightclubs were sometimes referred to as "gin mills," an expression that is still used. Cirrhosis of the liver has sometimes been referred to as "gin drinker's liver."

Gin was first invented in the Netherlands during the 17th century by Dr. Franciscus Sylvius, also known as Franciscus de la Boe (1614-1672), a professor of medicine at Leyden University. Dr. Sylvius was attempting to find a prophylactic against certain tropical diseases by distilling spirits in the presence of juniper berries. His aim was to prepare a specific with known diuretic properties.

Since the origins of gin were medicinal, it was at first available only in apothecary shops. As its popularity increased, many apothecary shops set up their own distilleries. By the end of the 18th century, the Dutch were producing approximately 14 million gallons of gin each year, of which around 10 million were exported.

The taste for gin was brought to England in the 17th century by soldiers returning from wars on the Continent. It was officially introduced there by William of Orange, who reigned from 1686 to 1702. He thought that gin would be an acceptable substitute for French brandy, since at that time the English considered the French their enemies.

Gin rapidly acquired popularity in England. Within 40 years of its introduction there, annual production rose from a half million to 20 million gallons. Gin's popularity in the early years of the 18th century has been attributed in part to the fact that it was more refined than the spirits made by English distillers from beer and wine lees (dregs). Perhaps a more important reason was its low cost. Both William of Orange and his successor, Queen Anne, who reigned from 1702 until 1714, raised the duties and taxes on imported goods and lowered the excise on home products. In addition, during their reigns, anyone who applied to the excise bureau was allowed to set up a distillery, making it very easy to manufacture gin.

For many of the poor in England during the 18th century, there was almost no alternative alcoholic drink to gin. It was given the nickname "mother's ruin" because so many women could be seen lying in the streets drunk on gin. Gin was also sometimes referred to as "Dutch courage," a term still used for bravery (or perhaps foolhardiness) inspired by alcohol.

Today most countries that distill spirits produce gin. Its chief manufacturers are the Netherlands, Britain and the United States. Despite the many local variations, there are basically only two types of gin: Dutch gin, referred to variously as Geneva, Genever, Schiedam or Hollands; and London dry gin, which is distilled in both Britain and the United States. Another type of gin, so-called Plymouth gin, is manufactured only in Plymouth, England. Now Plymouth gin and London dry gin are about the same, but at one time the gin made in Plymouth was midway between London dry gin, which is only lightly flavored with juniper berries, and Dutch gin, which is more heavily flavored with juniper. In addition, Dutch gin and London dry gin are manufactured by different distillation processes using different ingredients.

Dutch gin is doubly distilled. First a low-proof spirit is distilled from a fermented mash consisting of approximately two-thirds rye meal. This low-proof spirit is then rectified and flavored with juniper berries, salt and other agents. The resultant spirits are then redistilled, producing a gin between 94 and 98 proof.

Dutch gins are not aged, which accounts for their lack of color, and have a strong, malty aroma, which makes them unsuitable for mixing in cocktails. Consequently they are usually chilled and drunk straight.

In contrast to Dutch gin, which is first distilled from a low-proof spirit, manufacturers of English and American gin begin by rectifying a high-proof (about 190) grain whiskey to a completely pure and flavor-free spirit. The spirit is then distilled off at approximately 160 proof, which is further decreased to around 114.2 by adding water. This product is placed in a pot still with various flavoring agents and redistilled. The resultant gin is reduced to either 80, 86 or 94 proof. Although gin is usually bottled immediately, some types produced in the United States are aged, giving them a pale golden color.

In addition to juniper berries, English and American gins usually contain other botanicals in varying proportions, including orris, angelica and licorice roots; bitter almonds, caraway, coriander, cardamom, anise and fennel seeds; and calamus, cassis bark, lemon peels, and sweet and bitter orange peels. The kinds and proportions of these flavorings account for the differences between the various brands of gin.

English and American gins have a dry, astringent taste, which makes them less likely to be drunk straight. In varying proportions they are combined with dry vermouth to make martinis. They are also mixed with tonic water, and with water and angostura bitters. Some ordinary gins are given a fruit flavor, such as orange, lemon or pineapple. Old Tom gin is slightly sweetened.

Sloe gin is not gin in the usual sense but a liqueur made by steeping sloe berries—small bluish-black plums with a sour, astringent taste—in gin.

grog   A mixture of rum and water. In 1740 a British admiral, Edward Vernon (1684-1757), concerned that his men were becoming habitually intoxicated on their daily RUM RATION, ordered the rum to be diluted with water. The resulting mixture was named for the admiral's sobriquet, "Old Grog," which he earned for his habit of braving inclement weather in a coat made of a wool-silk-mohair combination known as grogham. Vernon's practice was soon widely imitated, and some captains found a way to line their pockets by watering the grog further. Sailors, unhappy with "half and half grog," were incensed by the even weaker "seven-water grog." From the term "grog" are derived "groggy," "groggily," "grogginess," "grogged" and "grog-fight" (drinking party).

George Washington's brother, Lawrence, served under Adm. Vernon and the Washingtons' Virginia estate, Mount Vernon, was named after him.

grog blossom   (From GROG.) A pimple or reddishness of the nose often attributed to excessive drinking over a prolonged period (see RHINOPHYMA).

group therapy   Collective therapeutic treatment often led by a psychiatrist or psychologist. Groups are usually kept small, less than a dozen persons, to allow for the maximum amount of participation from each member. Under the direction of the leader, who acts as a moderator, individual members bring up recent or long-standing problems for discussion by the group. Ideally the individual benefits by opening his problems to the scrutiny of others and by being forced to analyze his behavior and come to grips with it. The group benefits from the communality of shared problems and by participating vicariously in the resolution of the problems of others that may be similar to their own. The communal and cathartic effect of group therapy differs

from that of "meetings" of such groups as ALCOHOLICS ANONYMOUS, which are larger, feature speakers and must consider topics of interest to a broader range of people. In such meetings there generally is no time for the same intimate, intensive exploration of problems as afforded by group therapy. (See also PSYCHODRAMA.)

H

habituation   Accommodation or adaptation to a stimulus or to an interfering response. The term is often used to refer to the process of forming a habit and as a synonym for TOLERANCE. Since it is frequently unclear which meaning is intended, it is preferable to use one of the other more specific terms, such as tolerance or ADDICTION.

halfway house   Also known as intermediate care facilities, these residences, developed mainly during the 1970s, are used as transition points for alcoholics moving from inpatient care to normal life. They were conceived as a result of the failure of larger, impersonal institutions to provide the needed support for this transition.

Halfway houses are primarily for the homeless alcoholic who does not need medical care but rather support and protection while he or she gradually finds a place in the community. They are generally staffed by nonprofessionals, although professionals are available for needed medical care. The setting provides residents with adequate food and shelter and a therapeutic environment that facilitates the maintenance of sobriety. Following discharge alcoholics may return to the house for evening meetings and social support. Halfway houses may be publicly or privately funded and the residents are usually expected to contribute what they can.

The halfway house movement developed with the belief that to be effective the houses should have only a small number of residents, impose few rules and maintain an informal "homelike" atmosphere. Today, however, many of these houses have grown to the size of large institutions, which, according to one study, limits their effectiveness (Rubington).

E. Rubington, "Halfway Houses and Treatment Outcomes: A Relationship between Institutional Atmosphere and Therapeutic Effectiveness," *Journal of Studies on Alcohol* 40, no. 5 (1979):419-427.

hangover   (In this sense "hang" means "linger," from the Gothic *hahan* via the Anglo-Saxon *hangian*.) Hangover is an Americanism introduced in the early 20th century. The use of the word "hang" to describe the unpleasant aftereffects of excessive drinking is similar to that in "just *hang*ing around," in the sense of aimlessly lingering.

A hangover generally follows intoxication by eight to 12 hours. Some common effects are a splitting headache and sensitivity to movement, bright light and loud sounds. Other symptoms may include nausea and vomiting, dizziness, sweating, loss of appetite and dry mouth. These are accompanied by general malaise or tiredness and, often, anxiety or depression or both.

The causes of hangover are not completely understood, but there are probably a number of factors involved. For most drinkers the stress of intoxication has been worsened by other contributing elements, such as heavy smoking, lack of sleep and feelings of guilt resulting from uninhibited behavior. The changes that are expected in the body following a stress reaction are seen in the signs of hangover. Another factor that may be at work is a state of lowered BLOOD SUGAR, or hypoglycemia. Blood glucose levels are at their lowest during the height of a hangover, and many symptoms of a hangover are similar to those of hypoglycemia.

When alcohol is consumed, its degradation in the liver causes an accumulation of organic acids and ketones in the blood, known as ketoacidosis (see METABOLISM). The degree of ketoacidosis corresponds fairly well to the intensity of the hangover and may be partially responsible for its onset. Water balance is also altered when alcohol is consumed. Increased urinary excretion, sweating, vomiting and diarrhea can lead to dehydration, which appears as dry mouth and thirst. On the other hand a drop in BLOOD ALCOHOL CONCENTRATION can stimulate an antidiuretic hormone, so that hyperhydration can also develop during a hangover. CONGENERS, the organic alcohols and salts other than ethanol that are formed when alcoholic beverages are manufactured, have been thought to play a role in the hangover effect, but it has been well demonstrated that pure ethanol can by itself produce a hangover. Therefore the role of congeners in causing hangovers is probably small. The irritation produced by alcohol on the STOMACH lining may be a cause of the nausea and vomiting that can occur during a hangover.

It has not been proved that the amount of alcohol consumed is related to the appearance and severity of a hangover, although this is generally thought to be the case. The hangover experience varies from individual to individual. Some consider the hangover syndrome a symptom of early WITHDRAWAL. According to this theory, a certain DEPENDENCY has been established by overdrinking, and the body is reacting because it has a need for more alcohol. The fact that resumption of drinking ("the hair of the dog that bit you,") will reverse or alleviate some hangover symptoms is evidence in support of this concept.

The traditional use of a small amount of alcohol to correct the metabolic rebound brought on by a hangover may be justified as long as it does not lead to another round of overindulgence. To correct acidosis, water balance disturbance and low blood sugar, fruit juice, such as orange juice, may be of help. Aspirin may be taken for a headache, but sedatives and tranquilizers are not indicated. Rest and time correct other unpleasant effects.

Sidney Cohen, "Hangover," *Drug Abuse and Alcoholism Newsletter* 9, no. 8 (October 1980).

Hawaiians, native

A recent survey of alcohol consumption by the four major ethnic groups in Hawaii found that native Hawaiians drank less alcohol than Caucasians but significantly more than Japanese or Filipinos. In all groups, men drink more than women. The proportion of heavier drinkers (defined by some as those who regularly consume two or more drinks per day) among native Hawaiians was 11%, compared with 14% for Caucasians, 7% for Filipinos and 5% for Japanese. More than half the Japanese and Filipinos were abstainers, compared with 41% of native Hawaiians and 31% of Caucasians.

One study showed that native Hawaiians are under-represented in treatment facilities in proportion to their estimated numbers of heavier drinkers. For example, in 1979, 41% of heavy drinkers in Hawaii were Caucasian, yet they represented 71% of treatment admissions. Native Hawaiians accounted for 19% of the state's alcohol abusers that year but only 10% of admissions.

Between 1975 and 1980, native Hawaiians were at less risk than Caucasians for liver CIRRHOSIS, with an estimated 6.8 deaths per 100,000 population versus 12.1 per 100,000 for Caucasians. During this period, native Hawaiians were at greater risk than the general state population for such causes of death related to alcohol as homicide (see CRIME), motor vehicle accidents (see DRIVING WHILE INTOXICATED) and SUICIDE.

F.M. Ahern, *Alcohol Use and Abuse among Four Ethnic Groups in Hawaii: Native Hawaiians, Japanese, Filipinos, and Caucasians,* in National Institute on Alcohol Abuse and Alcoholism's *Alcohol Use Among U.S. Ethnic Minorities,* Research Monograph No. 18, DHHS Pub. No. (ADM) 87-1435 (Washington, D.C.: U.S. Govt. printing Office, in press).

health care costs of alcohol abuse
See ECONOMIC IMPACT.

health care providers

Even though the primary care providers provide the initial intervention for most patients' health problems, this has not been the case with alcohol-related problems. Hingson found that only 45% of problem drinkers visiting a doctor were asked about their alcohol consumption, and only 25% of those who were asked were told to reduce their drinking or warned about alcohol-related health dangers. Only 3% of heavy drinkers were referred to a treatment program. These findings were corroborated by Clement, who found that misdiagnosis or oversight of alcohol-related problems is common among primary care physicians.

Inadequate medical school training in alcoholism, patient resistance and financial pressures of the health care system compound to obstruct appropriate treatment of alcohol dependence. Some physicians could have a negative attitude toward alcoholics. Alcohol abuse and alcoholism are, however, lately achieving new recognition in medical school curricula. The CAREER TEACHER PROGRAM, jointly sponsored by the NATIONAL INSTITUTE ON ALCOHOL ABUSE AND ALCOHOLISM (NIAAA) and the NATIONAL INSTITUTE ON DRUG ABUSE (NIDA), has been the impetus for many of the new courses or expanded substance abuse curricula at 60 medical education institutions (Holden, 1986).

All primary health care providers—physicians, nurses, nurse practitioners, physician assistants—have a responsibility to increase their knowledge and skills on substance abuse for the purpose of improving therapeutic care of alcoholic patients.

S. Clement, "The Identification of Alcohol Related Problems by General Practitioners," *British Journal of Addiction* 81 (1986): 257-264.

R. Hingson et al., "Seeking Help for Drinking Problems: A Study in the Boston Metropolitan Area," *Journal of Studies on Alcohol* 42 (1982): 273-288.

C. Holden, "Medical Schools Confront Another Taboo," *New Physician,* 40 (1986): 17-20.

Enoch Gordis, M.D., ed., *Sixth Special Report to the U.S. Congress on Alcohol and Health* (Rockville, Md.: National Institute on Alcohol Abuse and Alcoholism, 1987).

heart There are a number of alcohol-related diseases of the heart that can adversely affect blood pressure, heart muscle contractility and heart rhythm.

Hypertension (High Blood Pressure)

Numerous epidemiological studies around the world have reported a significant association between high alcohol consumption and high blood pressure. Estimates of the proportion of hypertension associated with alcohol vary from 5% to 24% (Klatsky). Klatsky has found that alcohol is associated most strongly with hypertension at drinking levels equivalent to three or more drinks daily and is strongest in men, Caucasians and people over 55. The risk of hypertension was increased by a factor of between two and three in frequent and/or heavy drinkers.

Alcohol use and hypertension may be linked through a common association with an unidentified third factor, such as stress, or other psychosocial factors. What seems more likely is that an average of three or more drinks per day may have a direct causal effect on the elevation of blood pressure. The proof has yet to be obtained and there is a need for further study to establish or refute a causal relationship between alcohol and hypertension.

Alcoholic Cardiomyopathy

Heavy alcohol consumption is the specific cause of alcoholic cardiomyopathy, a disease of the heart muscle associated with the development of coronary artery disease. In victims of alcoholic cardiomyopathy, which can occur in those who drink excessively over a long period of time regardless of the level of nutrition, the heart appears large and flabby, although the arteries and valves look normal. In such cases the tissue of the heart is remarkably similar to tissue seen in livers damaged by alcohol (see ALCOHOLIC LIVER DISEASE). Exactly how the heart muscle is affected is unknown. A study by A. I. Cederbaum and E. Rubin in 1975 and other more recent studies have shown that ACETALDEHYDE, the first metabolite of ethanol (see METABOLISM), damages the mitochondria of the heart muscle and may play a key role in the development of alcoholic cardiomyopathy.

While the evidence is not definite, it probably takes about 10 years of high alcohol intake to cause serious damage to the heart. If the damage is detected in time and if the patient stops drinking alcohol completely, there is a fairly good chance of recovery. If severe heart failure has occurred, however, the outlook is usually poor.

There appears to be great individual variation in susceptibility to alcoholic cardiomyopathy. It usually appears in men 25 to 50 years of age. Common early symptoms are difficult or labored breathing, swelling of feet and ankles, fatigue, and palpitations or chest pain. If excessive alcohol consumption continues, the disease often progresses to heart failure.

A very rare version of cardiomyopathy, known as beri-beri heart disease, is seen only in alcoholics who are extremely malnourished and is thought to be due to a thiamine deficiency (see NUTRITION).

Cardiac Arrhythmia

An irregularity in heartbeat, cardiac arrhythmia can occur both in patients with alcohol-related disease and in other individuals during alcoholic intoxication. The most common form in patients with a previous history of heart disease has come to be known as the "holiday heart syndrome." Cardiac arrhythmia is seen in individuals who show up in emergency rooms between Sunday and Tuesday or around holidays associated with high alcohol ingestion. They generally report palpitations, sharp left chest pain or "passing out" spells. Both the direct effects of alcohol on the heart muscle and the effects of either alcohol or acetaldehyde on the heart's conduction system are the likely causes of arrhythmia although recent studies suggest that mild alcohol withdrawal or some neurological factor may also be at fault. The best treatment generally is a few days abstinence.

Coronary Heart Disease

Coronary heart disease results from atherosclerosis, which is characterized by the localized accumulation of lipids on the inner lining of the large- and medium-sized arteries serving the heart. Several studies, including one by Charles Hennekens and associates in 1973-74, maintained that the consumption of alcohol in small amounts (up to 2 ounces of ABSOLUTE ALCOHOL per day) decreased the risk of coronary heart disease. More recently, studies that correlate moderate alcohol consumption with reduced risk of coronary heart disease have come under attack. Critics argue that moderate alcohol use is less a biological factor than a sign of a lifestyle that may also include balanced diet, exercise, and more relaxed attitudes. (Shaper et al.).

B.M. Altura, "Introduction to the Symposium and Overview," *Alcoholism (NY)* 10(6) (1986):557-559.

G. E. Burch, "Alcoholic Cardiomyopathy," *Comprehensive Therapy* 3, no. 8 (August 1977):10-15.

A. I. Cederbaum and E. Rubin, "Molecular Injury to Mitochondria Produced by Ethanol and Acetaldehyde," *Federation Proceedings* 34, no. 11 (1975):2045-2051.

"Drinkers and the 'Holiday Heart' Syndrome," *Medical World News,* Dec. 27, 1976, p. 19.

Charles Hennekens et al., "Effects of Beer, Wine, and Liquor in Coronary Deaths," *Journal of the American Medical Association* 242, no. 18 (Nov. 2, 1979):1973-1974.

A.L. Klatsky *The Cardiovascular Effects of Alcohol, Alcohol Alcohol* 22 (Suppl. 1) (1988): 117-124.

A.G. Shaper et al., *Alcohol and Ischaemic Heart Disease in Middle Aged British Men, British Medical Journal*, 1987.

heavy drinker   A person who drinks beyond the normal limits of moderation as defined by the society in which he or she lives. Often a heavy drinker is in danger of or well on his or her way to becoming an ALCOHOLIC. Many heavy drinkers, however, do not become alcoholic, although the figure is probably much higher than those revealed in the available studies since numerous alcoholic heavy drinkers have never been diagnosed as such. Some heavy drinkers escape most of the criteria for a PROBLEM DRINKER, but most cannot escape the cumulative effects of alcohol upon the human body, which are due to consumption at a given time or over a period of time rather than to addiction. For statistical purposes a heavy drinker has been defined (by Eagleville Hospital in Pennsylvania for the National Institute on Drug Abuse in 1979) as an individual with a consumption level "averaging above 3.82 ounces of 90-proof whiskey daily." This level amounts to an average daily consumption of 1.72 ounces of ABSOLUTE ALCOHOL. (See ANSTIE'S LAW.)

hemochromatosis   A little understood and relatively uncommon disorder that involves excessive deposition of iron within the body tissues and terminates after many years of widespread tissue damage. Victims often suffer from liver disease, diabetes and a bronze pigmentation of the skin.

The cause of hemochromatosis is not known, but one theory is that it may not be a single disease entity but rather a type of CIRRHOSIS in which two conditions occur simultaneously—an excess buildup of ingested iron and liver disease caused by alcohol consumption or malnutrition. At Boston City Hospital hemochromatosis was found to be most prevalent in patients who were heavy and chronic users of wine, which contains large amounts of iron.

hepatitis   See ALCOHOLIC HEPATITIS.

hepatoma   Also known as hepatocarcinoma, hepatoma is a cellular cancer of the liver, often associated with CIRRHOSIS (see CANCER).

heredity   See GENETICS.

high   *Slang* for being under the influence of alcohol or a drug, especially marijuana. The term "high" usually refers to a state of pleasurable intoxication, not to the point of unconsciousness. The "high" associated with alcohol, often expressed in uninhibited behavior bordering on or lapsing into the irresponsible, is an ironic effect of the SEDATIVE nature of the drug. The "high" phase of the effect is actually the result of the sedating of those areas of the brain that guard against abnormal behavior by producing inhibitions. The high from alcohol is thus the opposite of a high from such stimulants as amphetamines or cocaine.

high blood pressure   (hypertension) A number of studies have linked heavy alcohol consumption with high blood pressure (see HEART).

highway safety   See DRIVING WHILE INTOXICATED.

Hispanics   In the 1990s Hispanics are projected to surpass the black population as the nation's largest minority. The Hispanic population is not uniform but composed of many subgroups; Mexican Americans form the largest subgroup, followed by Puerto Ricans, Cubans, Central Americans, South Americans and those of Spanish ancestry.

A national sample of Hispanics in 1984 pointed to the vast differences in alcohol consumption between men and women (Caetano, 1989). More than 70% of Hispanic women drank either less than once a month or not at all; and yet the same percentage of men were drinkers. Like black men, Hispanic men showed heavier drinking rates in their thirties but declined thereafter. Mexican Americans had higher rates of abstention and heavy drinking than Puerto Ricans and Cubans.

Alcoholism is a leading public health problem among the Hispanic population in the United States. About 18% of Hispanic men and 6% of Hispanic women suffered at least one alcohol-related problem in 1983, with Mexican-Americans reporting a higher rate of drinking problems than Puerto Ricans or Cubans. In Los Angeles over half the deaths of Hispanic males between the ages of 30 and 60 are from disorders of the LIVER. Studies have reported that Hispanics have higher arrest rates for public drunkenness and drunk driving than the national average (although this may be due in part to overpolicing). Accidents while driving under the influence are reported to be higher among Hispanics than among the general population.

According to self-reported statistics, there is a lower percentage of drinkers and a higher percentage of abstainers among Hispanic youth than among Anglo youth; yet Hispanic adults have higher rates of alcohol use and abuse than their Anglo counterparts. Some of the major causes cited for this paradox are the poverty, inadequate health care and discrimination suffered by Hispanics. In addition there are problems of acculturation and language difficulties. Hispanics who try to meet Anglo economic goals and fail often feel deprived and alienated.

Hispanics are less likely to seek treatment voluntarily than are non-Hispanics. They may view alcoholism as a moral weakness, not as an illness, and are less familiar with treatment resources than the rest of the population. There are some Spanish-speaking AA groups, but more culturally specific treatment services staffed with bilingual personnel are needed. There is also a need for additional research on the Hispanic alcohol problem, which, like the drinking problem of many other minorities, has generally been overlooked.

R. Caetano, "Alcohol Use Among Hispanic Groups in the United States," *American Journal of Drug Alcohol Abuse* 14 (1988): 273-311.

H. Edmandson, "Mexican-American Alcoholism and Deaths at LAC-USC Medical Center," testimony before the Subcommittee on Alcoholism of the California Senate Health and Welfare Committee (Feb. 17, 1975).

Enoch Gordis, M.D., ed., *Seventh Special Report to the U.S. Congress on Alcohol and Health* (Rockville, Md.: National Institute on Alcohol Abuse and Alcoholism, 1990), pp. 52-52.

Antonio Melus, "Culture and Language in the Treatment of Alcoholism: The Hispanic Perspective," *Alcohol Health and Research World* 4, no. 4 (Summer 1980):19-20.

Richard Roth and David Fernandez, "Historic Accord between Hispanic Alcoholism Community and NIAAA," *Alcoholism* 1, no. 2 (November-December 1980):20-22.

holiday heart syndrome   An irregularity in the heartbeat that may occur after a period of high alcohol ingestion. (See *Cardiac Arrhythmia* under HEART).

homelessness   Best estimates by the U.S. Department of Housing and Urban Development are that roughly 250,000 to 350,000 persons in the United States are homeless at any given time—and their numbers are increasing. Although homeless people have usually been perceived as mostly alcoholics, drug addicts and transients, this group now includes increasing proportions of the elderly, women, children, minorities, the unemployed, displaced families and the mentally ill. A host of factors adds to the increasing number of homeless persons, but alcohol abuse remains high on the list.

Surveys in eight cities found that alcohol abuse among the homeless ranged from less than 20% to 45% (Mulkern and Spence, 1984). A recent review of health problems among 30,000 homeless clients of the national Health Care for the Homeless (HCH) program revealed that 45% of men and 15% of women seeking health care were alcohol abusers (Wright et al.). Two studies including significant numbers of women found overall problem drinking rates of 25% to 32%.

The co-existence of alcohol abuse, drug abuse and mental illness among the homeless is striking. In the HCH study, more than one-fourth of alcohol-abusing women and nearly one-fifth of men abused drugs in addition to alcohol. Mental illness was diagnosed in more than half of female abusers and in one-fourth of male abusers.

Homeless persons who drink heavily are especially susceptible to certain health problems—TRAUMA, thermoregulatory disorders, peripheral vascular disorders and general physical debilitation. The homeless exhibit active tuberculosis rates 100 to 200 times that of the general population. Heavy drinkers are considered at greater risk for tuberculosis because of their generally more debilitated condition, and sharing of bottles is a possible source of tubercular infection.

A study of 1,000 homeless persons in Ohio in 1984 found that those with alcohol problems were more likely than the total sample to be men (94% versus 78%), were older (median age 41 years versus 33 years), were more likely to be divorced (45% versus 20%), were less likely to be currently married (3% versus 11%), and were more likely to have been in jail (87% versus 51%). The group with alcohol problems had been homeless twice as long; 24% of the alcohol abusers had been homeless for two years or more, compared with 13% of the others in the study.

E.M. Corrigan, S.C. Anderson, "Homeless Alcoholic Women on Skid Row," *American Journal of Drug and Alcohol Abuse*, 10(1984):535-549.

V. Mulkern and R. Spence, *Alcohol Abuse/Alcoholism among Homeless Persons: A Review of the Literature* (Washington, D.C.: U.S. Govt. Printing Office, 1984).

D. Roth and J. Beau, *Alcohol and Homelessness: Findings from the Ohio Study (Summary),* in F.D. Wittman, ed., *The Homeless with Alcohol-Related Problems: Proceedings of a Meeting to Provide Research Recommendations to the NIAAA (1985)* (Rockville, Md.: NIAAA, 1985), pps. 5-11.

J.D. Wright, et al., "Ailments and Alcohol: Health Status among the Drinking Homeless," *Alcohol Health and Research World* 11 (2) 1987.

Health Problems Diagnosed Among Homeless Health Care Clients, by Sex, with Percentage of Alcohol Abusers and Nonabusers and Abuser/Nonabuser Ratio for Each Diagnosis

Diagnosis	Men			Women		
	Abusers (percent)	Nonabusers (percent)	Abuser/ nonabuser Ratio	Abusers (percent)	Nonabusers (percent)	Abuser/ nonabuser Ratio
Mental illness	27.7	21.3	1.3	52.8	35.2	1.5
Peripheral vascular disorder	15.5	13.2	1.2	14.1	10.7	1.3
Hypertension	21.9	12.3	1.8	14.1	10.3	1.4
Gastrointestinal disorder	17.1	11.2	1.5	20.0	14.9	1.3
Trauma						
Lacerations	13.5	8.8	1.5	8.5	3.7	2.3
Fractures	7.0	4.5	1.6	5.4	2.1	2.6
Contusions	8.0	4.4	1.8	10.6	4.5	2.4
Drug abuse	18.1	7.3	2.5	26.1	5.3	4.0
Eye disorder	18.1	7.3	2.5	9.6	6.9	1.4
Neurological disorder	9.7	6.7	1.4	11.7	9.6	1.2
Cardiac disease	8.5	6.1	1.4	6.3	5.6	1.1
Tuberculosis	6.9	5.5	1.3	3.1	2.7	1.1
Chronic obstructive pulmonary disease	6.0	4.2	1.4	8.9	3.7	2.4
Arterial disease	5.4	3.5	1.5	6.8	4.0	1.7
Diabetes mellitus	2.2	2.2	1.0	3.1	2.8	1.1
Seizures	6.8	2.2	3.1	5.6	2.5	2.2
Anemia	2.2	1.4	1.6	3.1	3.6	0.9
Nutritional disorder	2.4	1.3	1.8	4.5	2.1	2.1
Liver disease	3.0	0.7	4.3	4.2	0.6	7.0
Pregnancy				7.0	12.0	0.6

SOURCE: J. D. Wright, J. W. Knight, E. Weber-Burdin and J. Lam, "Ailments and Alcohol: Health Status among the Drinking Homeless," *Alcohol Health and Research World* 11 (3):22–27, 1987.

homicide   See CRIME.

homosexuals   It has been conservatively estimated that one out of every four homosexuals in the United States is an alcoholic (Stephens), compared with approximately one out of every 10 in the general population. A 1975 study found that approximately one-third of the total homosexual population of Los Angeles County abused alcohol on a regular basis.

Factors contributing to alcoholism stem from the stigma attached to homosexuality. Male and female homosexuals may perceive themselves as being outside of society and thus not required to follow certain societal norms. Some homosexuals who have difficulty dealing with their sexuality use alcohol to cope with this problem. The "coming out" process, whereby a person publicly acknowledges his or her homosexuality, often takes place in an environment where alcohol is prevalent and so a pattern of drinking develops as an important aspect of the homosexual identity. Ego defenses that homosexuals sometimes use to protect themselves against a hostile society may also block awareness of a growing dependency on alcohol. In the 1970s and early 1980s a large part of a homosexual person's social time was likely to be spent in bars, which undoubtedly encouraged excessive drinking. In the wake of the AIDS crisis, however, homosexual lifestyles have undergone significant transformations, and it is unclear whether this will impact on the perception of homosexuals as more prone to alcohol abuse.

Marian Sandmaier reports that lesbians are more likely to have a problem with alcohol than homosexual men. One study found that 35% of lesbians had problems with alcohol at some point in their lives compared with 28% of homosexual men and only 5% of heterosexual women. Lesbians suffer from the stigmas attached to homosexuals and to WOMEN who drink.

The majority of treatment centers are not geared to the specific problems of homosexual alcoholics. Many have a negative attitude toward homosexuals, and some centers may even refuse to treat them or try to cure their homosexuality rather than their alcoholism. Few staff members in treatment programs are homosexual themselves. As a result the success ratio for homosexual alcoholics in existing programs is much lower than that for the general population.

There is a need for recovery programs oriented toward homosexuals and for education on the problem in the various homosexual communities. Alcoholics Anonymous has a few homosexual groups in urban areas. In Boston the Homophile Alcohol Treatment Service (HATS), funded in part by the Massachusetts Division of Alcoholism, helps homosexuals with alcohol problems. The National Association of Lesbian and Gay Alcoholism Professionals publishes a newsletter and works to improve treatment for alcoholic clients.

Lilene Fifield, "Introductory Address to the National Council on Alcoholism Forum Session on Alcohol Abuse in the Gay Community," *National Institute on Alcohol Abuse and Alcoholism (NIAAA) Information and Feature Service,* no. 75 (Sept. 3, 1980).

Marian Sandmaier, *The Invisible Alcoholics* (New York: McGraw-Hill Book Company, 1980), pp. 179-183.

Bryan Stephens, "Alcoholism: The Dark Side of Gay," *The Magazine* 6, no. 3 (Fall 1980).

hooch   (Short form of *Hoochinoo,* a variation of *Hutsnuwu,* the name of an Alaskan Tlingit tribe. The name was applied to a liquor secretly produced by the tribe.) Slang for whiskey or liquor, especially inferior homemade or cheap whiskey or surreptitiously obtained whiskey. The term "hooch" became common during Prohibition, when it was used to refer to bootlegged whiskey of unknown origin. Today it is seldom used.

hops   Cones formed on the female *Humulus lupulus* vine. The cones are green with a surface of broad scales and a base that includes twin blossoms. When ripe, they are dried and used as an essential ingredient in the production of virtually all beers. It is the hop that produces the distinctively bitter, or "hoppy," flavor of beer, and the proportion of hops used in brewing is an important factor in creating distinct varieties of beer. First cultivated in Bavaria for use in beer, hops have been successfully transplanted to other areas for the same purpose. The shoots of the vine are also sometimes eaten as a vegetable and are especially popular in Belgium.

hormones, male sex Consumption of alcohol has been shown to have a dramatic effect on testosterone production in men. Many male alcoholics show signs of sexual impotence, loss of libido and symptoms of hypogonadism (diminished function of the sex glands), including breast enlargement, loss of facial hair and testicular atrophy, as a result of lower testosterone levels.

The lower levels may be due to either of two direct causes: increased breakdown of testosterone or reduced synthesis.

Breakdown of Testosterone

It appears that alcohol increases the synthesis of LIVER enzymes called 5-alpha-reductases, which are responsible for the degradation of testosterone by converting it to dehydrotestosterone. There is also evidence that administration of alcohol over a long period of time causes estrogen levels to rise, and this increase correlates with an increase in the level of a liver enzyme called hepatic aromatase, which is involved in the conversion of androgens (male sex hormones) to estrogens (female sex hormones). It has also been shown that there is an increased rate of conversion of testosterone to its respective estrogen. The signs of "feminization" in male chronic alcoholics are probably due to a simultaneous reduction in androgens and an increase in estrogens.

Reduced Testosterone Synthesis

In addition, there is evidence to indicate that alcohol administered acutely or chronically depresses testosterone synthesis in the testes. The levels of testosterone are lowest three to five hours after a high level of alcohol consumption and become normal or higher than normal six to eight hours later, when BLOOD ALCOHOL CONCENTRATION is very low. Apparently the effect of alcohol is biphasic—low doses increase testosterone levels and high doses depress them.

Most researchers have found that heavy use of alcohol over a long period of time has a strong toxic effect on the testes. Serum testosterone levels are low in chronic alcoholics and it appears that repeated and persistent alcohol use eventually causes irreversible damage to the structural and biochemical composition of the testes. Several recent studies have shown that the toxic agent may be ACETALDEHYDE, the metabolic product of ethanol, rather than ethanol. In one recent study, alcoholic men who were healthy in other respects experienced decreases in plasma testosterone levels after a 10-day administration of alcohol. It has long been known that chronic alcoholics experience impotence and this is probably due to inhibition of testosterone production.

Enoch Gordis, M.D., ed., *Seventh Special Report to the U.S. Congress on Alcohol and Health* (Rockville, Md.: National Institute on Alcohol Abuse and Alcoholism, 1990), pp. 66-67.

hyperglycemia Unusually high blood sugar level (see BLOOD SUGAR, DIABETES).

hypertension (high blood pressure). Heavy alcohol consumption has been linked with high blood pressure in a number of studies (see HEART).

hypoglycemia Low blood sugar; a condition sometimes seen in alcoholics (see BLOOD SUGAR).

I

imaging techniques   See BRAIN.

immune system   Chronic alcohol abuse can lead to increased susceptibility to several INFECTIOUS DISEASES and certain types of CANCER. Several immune deficiencies have been observed in alcoholics at the time of admission for treatment. For example, 4% to 8% of admitted patients have decreased circulating levels of white blood cells called neutrophils, indicating that the ability to engulf (phagocytize) bacteria is reduced.

Acute and chronic consumption of alcohol has been shown to suppress the immune defense system, though it is not yet proved that alcohol is involved in the progression of disease in persons who have been infected with the virus responsible for acquired immune deficiency syndrome (AIDS).

National Institute on Alcohol, *The Effects of alcohol on the immune system*, summary of a workshop to provide policy and research recommendations to the National Institute on Alcohol Abuse and Alcoholism, Alcohol Research Utilization System Working Document No. 85-02 (Rockville, Md.: National Institute on Alcohol Abuse and Alcoholism, 1986).

impairment   (From the Latin *in* intensive + *pejorare* to make worse.) Damage to an individual or impaired functioning as a result of the use of alcohol. Impairment must be measured on an individual basis, because there are people who drink large amounts of alcohol with few problems while others are strongly affected by small amounts. The term "impairment" is used to describe both short- and long-term effects. For a person on a drinking bout, for example, impairment may mean difficulty in walking and/or talking, confusion, and drowsiness or unconsciousness. Impairment is also used to determine whether or not a person is an alcoholic, since alcoholism can rarely be measured in terms of comsumption alone.

David J. Armor, J. Michael Polich and Harriet B. Stambul of the Rand Corporation list 12 signs of behavioral impairment that indicate a diagnosis of alcoholism:

1. Tremors (shakes)
2. Alcoholic blackouts (loss of memory)
3. Missing meals due to drinking
4. Drinking on awakening
5. Being drunk
6. Missing work days due to drinking
7. Difficulty in sleeping
8. Quarreling with others while drinking
9. Drinking on the job
10. Continuous drinking
11. Drinking alone
12. Time between drinking sessions

If alcohol is interfering with an individual's ability to function in society, then he or she is suffering from alcohol impairment.

David J. Armor, J. Michael Polich and Harriet B. Stambul, *Alcoholism and Treatment* (New York: John Wiley and Sons, 1978) p. 89.

inability to abstain   A term used to describe someone who is unable to abstain from drinking for even a day or two, although he or she can control the amount consumed on any given occasion. This inability is characteristic of DELTA ALCOHOLISM.

inebriate   An alcoholic.

inebriety   Excessive drinking or ALCOHOLISM.

infancy   In addition to the serious danger of being exposed to excessive amounts of alcohol (see FETAL ALCOHOL SYNDROME), an infant is also at risk if the mother drinks excessively after giving birth. Breast-fed infants may be exposed to alcohol in their mother's milk. Alcohol enters the breast milk at the same level it enters the mother's bloodstream. Ingesting breast milk that contains alcohol may cause an effect in the infant known as the pseudo-Cushing syndrome, which is characterized by high levels of the hormone cortisol and of glucose in the blood as well as obesity, purple striations on the abdomen, easy bruising and a "moon" face. The long-term effects are unknown. It has also been shown that alcohol inhibits the milk-ejection reflex and may cause a reduction in the milk supplied to the nursing infant. (See also CHILD ABUSE.)

infectious diseases Chronic alcohol abuse is associated with enhanced susceptibility to myriad infectious diseases, as well as certain types of cancer. Among these: tuberculosis, pneumonia, yellow fever, cholera, bacteremia, bacterial peritonitis, head and neck cancer, hepatitis. (See also IMMUNE SYSTEM.)

inpatient treatment Alcoholism treatment services have increased in recent years. More than 1.43 million persons were treated in 1987; with 15% in an inpatient setting, and 85% as active outpatients (see OUTPATIENT TREATMENT). State and local government control of in-hospital treatment units decreased by 17% from 1978 to 1984 while for-profit ownership of such units increased by 342%. Other drug abuse, alcohol or drugs, was recorded as a discharge diagnosis on 1.13 million (2.7%) of all discharges for short-term hospitals in 1983.

Continuing attention needs to be paid to the heterogeneity apparent among alcoholics, and attempts are being made to develop concepts and measurements appropriate to such heterogeneity. The alcohol dependence syndrome concept has been researched extensively. Possible applications of this concept involve approaches to individualized treatment planning.

Studies of inpatient and outpatient treatment indicate that some alcoholics do not require inpatient treatment. In fact, detoxification can be accomplished safely and effectively in both social settings and medical settings. Although inpatient treatment costs eight times as much as outpatient treatment, a recent study found that detoxification was completed by 95% of inpatients but only 72% of outpatients. Before advising against a medical detoxification, however, the patients complete medical and psychiatric condition must be evaluated.

Patient-treatment matching, with patients assigned to different treatments based on various characteristics noted above are correlated with outcome; this practice continues to be of considerable interest.

There have been no dramatic changes in PHARMACOTHERAPY for alcoholics. Interest continues in possible uses of disulfiram (Antabuse) as an adjunct to more comprehensive treatment. Lithium carbonate may constitute a useful therapy for some alcoholics, mainly those with coexisting affective disorders.

More studies are underway to better determine which treatment—inpatient or outpatient—is most suitable for which alcoholics.

Recovery rates for alcoholism and other drug dependencies vary considerably according to various studies. A study of 1,001 adults treated for chemical dependency in five Minneapolis-St. Paul clinics in 1983-1984 found that 58% of the patients maintained continuous abstinence for two years following treatment; only 28% relapsed to multiple or prolonged periods of substance abuse.

With regard to cost, all treatment expenditures, including a substantial portion for treatment of the medical consequences of alcoholism, are estimated at $15 billion a year. Alcoholism treatment is effective for many persons. Favorable cost-benefit ratios that show reduced general health care expenditures in treated alcoholics indicate that alcoholism treatment is an effective means of containing HEALTH CARE COSTS throughout the health care system.

Additional research is also needed to develop objective and reliable markers of treatment outcome. Continuing treatment goal studies indicate that abstention from alcohol (and other psychoactive drugs) is still the most reasonable treatment goal for diagnosed alcoholics in light of current scientific and clinical information.

Enoch Gordis, M.D., ed., *Sixth Special Report to the U.S. Congress on Alcohol and Health* (Rockville, Md.: National Institute on Alcohol Abuse and Alcoholism, 1987).

———, *Seventh Special Report to the U.S. Congress on Alcohol and Health* (Rockville, Md.: National Institute on Alcohol Abuse and Alcoholism, 1990), p. 408.

National Clearinghouse for Alcohol and Drug Information (NCADI), *Fact Sheet* (Rockville, Md.: NCADI, June 1987).

input-output model for treatment The input-output model is a method proposed by David J. Armor, T. Michael Polich and Harriet B. Stambul, authors of the RAND REPORTS, to help facilitate matching an alcoholic client with the proper treatment. Input is divided into client inputs and treatment inputs. Client inputs are the characteristics of the client at the onset of treatment that might be relevant in determining what treatment is best for him or her. Treatment inputs concern the type and amount of treatment available at a particular treatment center. A successful outcome depends on the appropriateness of the treatment selected for the type of client.

instability and crisis etiological theory
One of a number of SOCIOCULTURAL ETIOLOGICAL THEORIES, the instability and crisis etiological theory posits that social factors which produce heavy stress on the individual may bring about the onset of alcoholism. During crisis periods when significant changes have occurred in an individual's life, he or she may turn to alcohol to alleviate the stress. WOMEN are especially likely to become alcoholic as a result of a particular event, such as the death of a spouse, a divorce or the departure of children from home. Heavy consumption of alcohol, however, exacerbates the social picture, and a cyclical relationship develops in which a stressful event leads to heavy drinking that in turn causes more stress and more drinking.

An input-output model for treatment evaluation

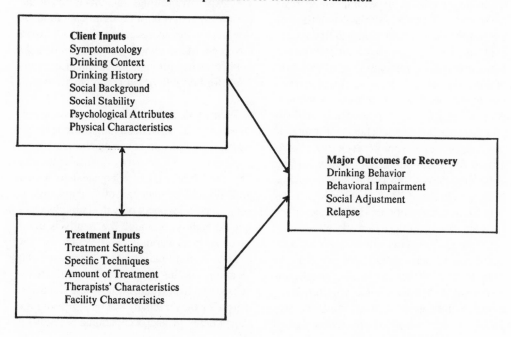

Client Inputs
Symptomatology
Drinking Context
Drinking History
Social Background
Social Stability
Psychological Attributes
Physical Characteristics

Treatment Inputs
Treatment Setting
Specific Techniques
Amount of Treatment
Therapists' Characteristics
Facility Characteristics

Major Outcomes for Recovery
Drinking Behavior
Behavioral Impairment
Social Adjustment
Relapse

insurance   The World Health Organization formally recognized alcoholism as a disease in 1951 and the American Medical Association followed suit in 1956. Before this time and for several years thereafter, large amounts of insurance money were spent to cover treatment for the complications and secondary manifestations of alcoholism, such as liver dysfunction or accidents involving alcohol abuse, but the primary disorder of alcoholism went undiagnosed and untreated. Gradually a few companies began to provide coverage for treatment of alcoholism. In 1964 Kemper Insurance Companies and Wausau became the first and they were followed by other companies, such as Capital Blue Cross in 1969. Today many companies provide some form of coverage for alcoholism, but a number of issues related to insurance coverage of alcoholism have yet to be solved, and policies are gradually changing as more is learned about the field.

Moreover, the insurance coverage matter is extremely difficult to summarize because state regulations, as well as individual employer plans, vary so greatly. Today, Blue Cross, most major medical plans, and even Medicare provide coverage for inpatient treatment. (Note: Call the Admissions Office of any hospital or treatment center to find immediate answers to your specific questions.) Medical insurance coverage in 1988 took care of about 70% of American workers in companies with more than 100 employees. Coincidentally, the logic of acting on the alcoholism problem sooner rather than later is still spreading throughout corporate America. Some 10,000 firms and public agencies, including 70% of the Fortune 500 companies, now have EMPLOYEE ASSISTANCE PROGRAMS to help alcohol/drug abuse victims pull their lives together and return to work.

One of the problems with insurance coverage for alcoholism is that systems for reimbursement tend to be related to traditional physician and hospital care. Alternative modes of treatment, such as outpatient services, residential programs and halfway houses, have generally not been included in basic health insurance coverage. Alternative programs are often less expensive and less disruptive to employed individuals and may be as effective as hospital treatment.

Insurance companies might well benefit from extending coverage to outpatient facilities, and some have started to do so. In 1973 Kemper began providing group health coverage for both outpatient and inpatient treatment in qualifying nonhospital alcoholism centers. Since then other companies have provided coverage for outpatient treatment.

Insurance companies must be able to determine what is appropriate, cost-effective treatment, and it is more difficult to evaluate nontraditional treatment modes. Some programs are now accredited by the Joint Commission on Accreditation of Hospitals and some are accredited by various states. Corporate occupational program directors can also evaluate local treatment programs.

Coverage for alcoholism treatment is not available to most disadvantaged members of minority groups in the country. Affluent people often pay for treatment of alcoholism without health insurance coverage, frequently in very expensive settings, and this is one of the reasons there has been no significant motivation to develop an insurance plan with broad coverage. Many minority group members do not belong to a group insurance plan and cannot afford an individual comprehensive policy.

Women alcoholics, many of whom have a DUAL ADDICTION, need longer for detoxification. The limit on coverage for detoxification services, however, is often a matter of days, which may not be adequate to treat dual addiction. More than half of all company insurance policies cover only the individual and not the family, although the family is often involved in an alcoholic's problem.

Data seem to indicate that treatment of an alcoholic and his or her family will decrease subsequent health care costs. There should be a growing movement by insurers to encourage their clients to use occupational alcoholism programs and other treatment so as to prevent the progression of the disease and its costly effects.

Donald M. Gallant, *Alcoholism: A Guide to Diagnosis, Intervention, and Treatment* (New York: W.W. Norton, 1987).

Gary Graham, "Occupational Programs and Their Relation to Health Insurance Coverage for Alcoholism," *Alcohol Health and Research World* 5, no. 4 (Summer 1981): 31-34.

Sandra S. Sternberger and Helen Drew, "Women, Health Insurance and Alcoholism," op. cit.:37-38.

Charles D. Watts, "Health Insurance Coverage for Underserved Populations," op. cit.:35-36.

William G. Williams, "Nature and Benefit Packages in Health Insurance Coverage for Alcoholism Treatment," op. cit.:5-11.

intellectual impairment   Findings of recent studies support the view that chronic alcohol ingestion leads to cell alterations and loss in the central nervous system. These are probably related to the functional impairment suffered by CHRONIC ALCOHOLICS.

Decreased brain size (cerebral or cortical atrophy)—demonstrated repeatedly by autopsy examination and computerized axial tomography (CT scan)—has been a major finding in studies of alcoholic patients. Autopsy examination has revealed widespread atrophy and cell loss in many brain regions, including at least areas of the diencephalon: (1) the mammillary bodies of the hypothalmus and (2) the middle and frontal area of the thalmus. Damage to these structures has been reported in various memory disorders, including Wernicke-Korsakoff syndrome (see WERNICKE'S ENCEPHALOPATHY).

Alcoholics are not the only people at risk for cognitive deficits. There is still controversy as to whether moderate alcohol consumption causes any permanent structural brain damage. The reversibility of alcohol-induced organic brain damage and neuropsychological impairment remains one of the most controversial yet important issues in

all of alcohol-related research. (See also IMPAIRMENT).

Enoch Gordis, M.D., ed., *Sixth Special Report to the U.S. Congress on Alcohol and Health* (Rockville, Md.: National Institute on Alcohol Abuse and Alcoholism, 1987).

intemperance   Habitual or excessive drinking or drunkenness.

International Classification of Diseases (ICD)   The World Health Organization (WHO) has played a major part in formalizing definitions of alcoholism. In the 1950s, WHO formulated criteria for a definition of alcoholism, which was later consistent with the definition of alcoholism under "Other Nonpsychotic Mental Disorders" in *International Classification of Diseases* (ICD-8) (WHO, 1974). In ICD-9 (WHO, 1978), the term "alcoholism" was eliminated and the concept of ALCOHOL DEPENDENCE SYNDROME (ADS) was introduced. ADS is described in terms of factors that characterize increasing dependence. ICD-10 will likely be in worldwide use in 1994. This edition will synthesize its system somewhat with the American Psychiatric Association system set forth in its *Diagnostic and Statistical Manual of Mental Disorders*. (See also CLASSIFICATION OF ALCOHOLICS.)

National Institute on Alcohol Abuse and Alcoholism, "Epidemiologic Bulletin No. 20," *Alcohol Health and Research World*, 13:1(1989), p.80-81.

World Health Organization, *Mental Disorders: Glossary and Guide to their Classification in Accordance with the Ninth Revision of the International Classification of Diseases* (Geneva: WHO, 1978).

intervention   A term used to describe the action taken by a person who confronts an alcoholic with his problem in order to interrupt the progress toward permanent disability or even death that may result if alcoholism is allowed to progress uninterrupted. Effective intervention can be achieved by someone who plays a significant role in the alcoholic's life, usually a member of the immediate family, a close friend or an employer. Even more effective is confrontation of the alcoholic by two or more persons genuinely concerned about his welfare. The subject must be sober and clearheaded and the best time is during a crisis, when his defenses are apt to be lowered. The alcoholic is then presented with factual data about his behavior and the costs of his addiction to himself and to those around him. It is important during a time of crisis to take advantage of the situation in a calm, rational manner. The alcoholic should be told that his behavior caused the crisis and the responsibility is his. When forced to face the consequences of his actions, he may become more depressed and seem to be regressing. Such a reaction, however, is a step toward his realization that he needs treatment. Those confronting the alcoholic should be prepared to help him find suitable treatment.

It is not enough for the alcoholic to make promises to do better; despite his good intentions the situation is generally not within his control. He must be made to accept professional help that will enable him to establish new patterns of behavior.

Donald M. Gallant, *Alcoholism: A Guide to Diagnosis, Intervention, and Treatment* (New York: W.W. Norton 1987).

intestine   Direct effects of alcohol on the small intestines can include changes in intestinal motility, metabolism, blood circulation and cellular structure. Studies by C.S. Lieber et al., indicate that injury to the intestinal tract may also take the form of varices (twisted and dilated veins or arteries) in the colon, which, though rare, may cause sudden massive rectal bleeding in patients with CIRRHOSIS. Alcohol may also have direct effects on colonic motility and morphology. An increased incidence of colon cancer has also been reported in alcoholics. Indeed, the range and complexity of alcohol's effects on the body are immense

and constitute a picture puzzle that still has many missing pieces.

C.S. Lieber, ed., *Medical Disorders of Alcoholism: Pathogenesis and Treatment, vol. 22 in Major Problems in Internal Medicine* (Philadelphia: Saunders, 1982a).

intoxication   (From Latin *in* + *toxicum* poison.) An abnormal state produced by ingesting alcohol (or another drug) that can range from exhilaration to stupor. Degree and experience of intoxication vary from individual to individual. Recent studies have indicated that intoxication may have as much or more to do with psychological processes as with physical processes. Psychologists G. Alan Marlatt and Damaris J. Rohsenow of the University of Wisconsin used a "balanced placebo" experiment to determine the physical effects of drinking alcohol as distinguished from the expected or imagined effects on someone who *thinks* he is drinking alcohol. Marlatt and Rohsenow divided subjects into four groups: one expecting alcohol and receiving alcohol, one expecting alcohol and receiving tonic, one expecting tonic and receiving alcohol, and one expecting tonic and receiving tonic. The groups were then observed with focus on social behavior, aggression and sexual arousal.

The study showed that men who mistakenly believed they had been drinking alcohol became less anxious in social situations. On the other hand, WOMEN in the same group became more anxious, possibly because their drinking experience and expectancies were different from those of the men.

Alcoholics were found to experience the same craving after taking one or two placebo drinks as they did after drinking real alcohol, but they reported little or no craving when they were given drinks containing alcohol that they believed were nonalcoholic.

Men became more aggressive when they drank tonic that they believed contained vodka and relatively less aggressive when they drank vodka believing they were getting only tonic. Men tended to become more sexually aroused when they believed they were drinking alcohol but actually were drinking only tonic. Women reported feeling more aroused when they believed they had been drinking alcohol, but a measure of vaginal blood flow showed that physically they were becoming less aroused.

The authors of this study reported that more than 25 other published experiments using the balanced placebo design had also found the "expectancy effect" in the use of alcohol. These studies suggest that people have strong beliefs about what alcohol does, and react accordingly. They indicate that women whose experiences with alcohol and expectancies about its effects differ from those of men will not react to alcohol in the same way as men. In most states a person with a BLOOD ALCOHOL CONCENTRATION of .10% is considered intoxicated. While the level of intoxication varies from individual to individual, depending on such factors as the amount of food in the stomach, body weight and individual tolerance, most people with a BAC of 0.15% are definitely intoxicated. Their voluntary motor action is affected, they are unable to walk properly and they have lost some control over their emotions. At a BAC of 0.20%, which can be achieved by drinking about 10 ounces of distilled spirits in a few hours, there is generally severe impairment, and behavior is loud and incoherent and emotionally confused. At 0.30% the deeper areas of the brain are affected and the drinker becomes stuporous, and at 0.40% he or she becomes unconscious. Death can occur between 0.40% and 0.70%, but this is rare because most drinkers have lapsed into unconsciousness at these levels.

John Langone, *Bombed, Buzzed, Smashed, or ... Sober.* (Boston: Little, Brown and Company, 1976), pp. 78-80.

Alan G. Marlatt and Damaris J. Rohsenow, "The Think-Drink Effect," *Psychology Today* 15, no. 12 (December 1981): 60-69, 93.

Ireland   It is a common belief that the Irish are prone to alcohol-related problems. The thought of Ireland is likely to conjure up images of beer drinking in public houses, Irish whiskey and boisterous celebrations. Surprisingly, however, by international standards alcohol consumption in Ireland (adjusted for total population) is quite low, beneath that in the United States. According to a 1987 study, apparent per capita consumption of ABSOLUTE ALCOHOL in that year was 5.4 liters, placing the Irish thirtieth among 47 reporting countries. In contrast, French per capita alcohol consumption was 13 liters during the same period. Interestingly, despite its reputation for beer consumption, the country ranked fifteenth for consumption of this beverage, with a per capita figure of 75 liters. By contrast, East Germans consumed 145 liters per capita; Americans consumed 90 liters.

Although consumption rose steadily from 1950 to 1979 (by a factor of 115%), alcohol consumption in Ireland is now declining slightly. In 1985, per capita consumption had fallen to 5.6 liters; by 1987, the consumption rate had fallen again by 3.6%.

Although drinking is relatively expensive in Ireland, cost does not seem to hinder those who drink. Evidence suggests that the expenditure on drink rises at least in proportion to income, and higher alcohol prices result in higher expenditures on drink rather than decreased consumption.

Most drinking in Ireland is done in public houses rather than at home, a contributing factor to the proportion of traffic accidents caused by alcohol, around 50%, which is close to the percentage in the United States. Premises where alcoholic beverages are sold must be licensed by the state and the number allowed is related to the population of an area and the existing distribution of already licensed premises.

The Irish are searching for effective ways to control alcohol abuse but have not yet found satisfactory solutions. The cost of alcohol is already extremely high and raising it does not seem to prevent people from purchasing alcohol. Restrictive social measures often impinge on the rights of drinkers who do not abuse alcohol, and resistance to these measures may result in increased abuse. One area that might warrant more attention is heavier penalization for drunk drivers and for those whose alcoholism causes absence from work. However, as Ireland has changed from a nation where drinking was polarized (e.g., heavy drinkers vs. abstainers) to one where there is increased social drinking, alcoholism problems have become more complex.

Hoeveel alcoholhoude dranken worden er in de wereld gedronken? (How many alcoholic beverages are being consumed throughout the world?) 27th ed. Schiedam, Netherlands: Produktschap Voor Gedistilleerde Dranken, 1987.

Brendan M. Walsh, *Drinking in Ireland* (Dublin: The Economic and Social Research Institute, 1980).

Irish Americans   Ethnic background and generational status are both important determinants of drinking patterns in the United States. It has been reported that Irish Americans have a rate of problem drinking two or three times as high as that of other ethnic groups. The Irish in general do not strongly disapprove of drunkenness, and a drunken man is frequently looked upon with amusement rather than pity or disgust. Intoxication is often deliberately sought. Drink is accepted as fulfilling a functional need of relieving stress, and it is not used in a ritualistic way, as with some ethnic groups. Irish Americans are likely to drink in public bars, to drink beer and to drink with members of their own sex. According to a recent study by the National Opinion Research Center, forty percent of Irish Americans reported there was a drinking problem in their homes when they were children.

Morris E. Chafetz and Harold W. Demone, Jr., *Alcoholism and Society* (New York: Oxford University Press, 1962), pp. 76-80.

Barry Glassner, "Differences in Ethnic Drinking Habits," *Alcoholism* 1, no. 4 (March/April 1981): 19-21.

John Langone, *Bombed, Buzzed, Smashed, or . . . Sober*. (Boston: Little, Brown and Company, 1976), pp. 47-49.

Irish whiskey   A distilled spirit made from mixed grains. The production of Irish whiskey differs from that of Scotch whisky in three ways: the grain mixture fermented contains a lower proportion of malted barley, the malted barley used is cured with charcoal rather than peat and the fermented mash is triple distilled. The result is a drier and more subtle spirit than most varieties of Scotch whisky.

The Irish were in all likelihood the first people of the British Isles to distill grain spirits, although the precise date is unknown. Some legends attribute the importation of distilling techniques to missionary monks from Europe who arrived after St. Patrick sometime between 500 A.D. and 600 A.D.. By about 1200 the Irish were known for their *uisce beathadh* ("water of life") more than anything except perhaps their Catholicism. The English word "whiskey" is an Anglicization of the Gaelic *uisce*.

Irish whiskey remained a notorious cottage industry through Elizabethan times despite English efforts to regulate and tax the trade. Even today, in response to high taxes on whiskey levied by the government of Ireland, home distilling remains a right insisted upon by the Irish in defiance of the authorities. The most common illegal distillate is *poteen,* a spirit that is colorless and raw to the taste because of a lack of aging. *Poteen* is currently available throughout the rural districts of Ireland, and it is often offered to visitors instead of licensed distillates as a gesture of greater ceremony.

In 1608, on the bank of the River Bush, Sir Thomas Phillips established the first distillery in Ireland chartered by the English crown. Bushmills, as the distillery was called, has remained the trade name of the leading whiskey of Northern Ireland. Despite this charter distilling continued to be largely a cottage industry, producing an erratic product heavy with congeners. In the 18th century efforts to evade British regulations took the form of a division of labor: "sugar bakers" assumed charge of fermenting the grain mash, an entirely legal activity at the time, and they then exchanged the mash with independent distillers for a quantity of the finished spirit. Realizing that measures to control the trade had failed, the British decided to charter a number of Irish distilleries. Between 1779 and 1829 virtually all the major Irish whiskey distillers other than Bushmills came into existence: John Jameson in 1780, John Power in 1791, Daly in 1807, Murphy Brothers in 1825 and Tullamore in 1829. The national industry underwent a major transformation during the 1960s, when most distillers merged to form the Irish Distillers Limited, a conglomerate that manufactures separate brand names and distinct distillates at a central location.

Irish whiskey is distilled from a grain mixture that is low in malted barley and peat-drying cured over charcoal to avoid giving it the heavy flavor of Scotch whisky produced by peat-drying the grains. Traditional Irish whiskeys are distilled in pot stills that are larger than those used to make Scotch. Most are triple distilled, a drawn-out process that reduces the quantity produced, strengthens it and brings it to an unusually high degree of rectification. Aging is generally done in casks that have previously held sherry or other whiskeys and continues for a minimum of three years. Most exported Irish whiskey is between 10 and 12 years old. As in the case of Scotch whisky, the product is usually blended with any number of whiskeys from other distillations to broaden its appeal in the marketplace and to ensure consistency of taste.

isopropyl alcohol   Also known as isopropanol and 2-propanol, isopropyl alcohol is a colorless liquid that can be mixed with water. Poisonous if taken internally, it is a major component of rubbing alcohol and has replaced ethanol for many uses because it is cheaper and has similar solvent properties.

Israel   Apparent per capita consumption of all alcoholic beverages in 1983-85 (in liters of ABSOLUTE ALCOHOL and based on total population) was only 1.0 liters. This is among the lowest known rates among countries who regularly report data. Israelis are known to have a relatively low incidence of alcoholism, but the Israeli government now recognizes that there is a problem of alcohol use within the country. Although by no means epidemiological, the incidence of alcoholism in Israel is high enough to have attracted the attention of the Ministry of Labour and Social Affairs and the Ministry of Social Welfare. Their investigations have isolated factors that tend to encourage alcoholism despite the cultural restraints inhibiting the disease among the Jewish people.

When Israel was established in 1948, only about 650,000 Jews lived within its borders. Today that figure is well over 3 million. The people who immigrated to Israel during these years came from about 80 different countries, and they brought with them as many different attitudes toward alcohol consumption as there were countries of origin. The traditional image of abstemious consumption of alcohol is for the most part derived from the habits of European Jews. This portion of the population brought with it virtually no habits of alcohol abuse, largely because drinking had been socially inhibited to avoid confrontations with the non-Jewish segments among which it had formerly lived.

Those Jews who immigrated from Asia and North Africa, however, brought with them a relatively casual attitude toward alcohol consumption because they had come from predominantly Islamic countries, which had prohibitions on the use of alcohol; in the past they therefore had less need to separate themselves from a non-Jewish population who drank and less fear of confrontations with antagonists as a result of alcohol abuse. Moreover once these Asian and North African immigrants entered Israel, they were forced to relinquish vestiges of their patriarchal culture, alter their traditional family structure and accept a lower position in the scale of classes than they had formerly enjoyed. The trauma of this integration into what was for these immigrants a secularized Israeli culture caused some of them to degenerate from moderate to excessive drinkers. By 1980 this group of Asian and North African immigrants accounted for more than half of the alcoholics in Israel.

Statistics on drunk driving offenses, drinking among youth and the incidence of alcoholism among women all suggest that alcohol abuse is worsening in Israel. In 1980 it was estimated that there were 6,000 alcoholics in the country. The figure represented the end result of years of neglect of the problem, an increasing acceptance of European social and dietary habits and a gradual loss of the special sense of mission associated with the early years of the state of Israel. Of the 6,000, 55.3% were immigrants from Asia and North Africa; 80% of the alcoholics born in Israel were descended from the same group of immigrants.

Italian Americans   Italian Americans have strong attitudes against drunkenness, apply little social pressure to participate in drinking and usually consume alcohol with meals. Wine is a staple in the diet of Italian Americans and most have their first drink between six and 10 years of age. First-generation Italian Americans drink frequently but have few alcohol-related problems; later generations have higher rates of heavy drinking, and they consume more distilled spirits than Italians in Italy and first-generation Italians. When there is drunkenness, it generally occurs at festive occasions where a group is present, including members of both sexes (as opposed to Irish-American drunkenness, which may be a regular occurrence and is not connected solely with festivity). As Italians become more Americanized, they may begin to lose the protective Italian drinking traditions and develop more drinking problems, but the rate of alcoholism among them is still significantly low compared with that of other groups, such as Irish Americans, Hispanics and blacks.

Morris E. Chafetz and Harold W. Demone, Jr., *Alcoholism and Society* (New York: Oxford University Press, 1962), pp. 80-84.

J

---

jackroller   SKID ROW slang for a thief, usually one who robs drunks.

Japan   There is a deeply ingrained acceptance of social consumption of alcoholic beverages in Japan that has led to a national pattern of infrequent but heavy drinking on special occasions. There is some actual encouragement of drunkenness during festive celebrations, and expensive distilled spirits are favored as gifts to hosts of social functions. One survey showed that 52% of the Japanese polled considered alcohol a part of their lives, and 35% of those polled considered abstinence harmful to social life. These patterns have a lengthy history, for although the majority of Japanese are nominally adherents to Buddhism or the native Shintoism, these religions have long been secularized in respect to prohibitions on alcohol consumption. Recent increases in the level of drinking, especially among women and youth, have resulted from wider advertisement of alcoholic beverages and a general trend toward westernization since World War II that has weakened the traditional hierarchical society.

Although Japan ranks 26th among 47 countries that reported their consumption rates, the country ranks first (together with the USSR) for average annual increase in consumption rate as measured from 1979 to 1984 (25 countries were included in this survey). The average annual increase worked out to be 3% (Horgan et al.). The magnitude of the increasing consumption rate is underlined by comparing the 1987 apparent per capita consumption rate—6.3 liters, based on total population with the rate in 1976—of 5.4 liters per capita, an increase of 17%.

Until quite recently, the preferred beverage in Japan was sake, a fermented rice wine usually sold in varieties that average 16% absolute alcohol. The popularity of sake has been gradually declining, and its market share stood at 31% of total alcohol consumed in 1984, about even with beer and slightly below spirits. The amount of illegal fermented or distilled beverages produced in the country is negligible. Most of the whiskey and beer in Japan is made by large corporations or imported, but sake is produced by smaller, more local companies. The manufacture and sale of alcoholic beverages in Japan employed 5% of the work force and account for 4% of the country's total revenues in 1982.

The Liaison Conference for Alcoholic Problems, an organization funded by the Ministry of Health and Welfare, coordinates alcoholism prevention and treatment programs, including the efforts of the Japanese Medical Society on Alcohol Studies and the All Nippon Sobriety Society, Japan's version of Alcoholics Anonymous. Significant contributions are also made by the Christian Women's Temperance Association and the Salvation Army.

Hoeveel alcoholhoude dranken worden er in de wereld gedronken? (How many alcoholic beverages are being consumed throughout the world?) 27th ed. Schiedam, Netherlands: Produktschap Voor Gedistilleerde Dranken, 1987.

Jellinek, E. M. (1890-1963)   Jellinek was the author of *The Disease Concept of Alcoholism,* an influential study of alcoholism, and founder of the Center of Alcohol Studies and Summer School of Alcohol Studies, formerly at Yale University and now at Rutgers University. He was also a cofounder of the National Council on Alcoholism and was the World Health Organization Consultant on Alcoholism.

In *The Disease Concept of Alcoholism* Jellinek distinguished between five categories of alcoholism, which he referred to as ALPHA ALCOHOLISM, BETA ALCOHOLISM, DELTA ALCOHOLISM, EPSILON ALCOHOLISM and GAMMA ALCOHOLISM.

Jews   Research has indicated that Jews have lower rates of alcoholism than other ethnic groups; a study by the National Opinion Research Center found that only 4% of Jews reported a drinking problem in their homes. Although Jews have largely avoided alcoholism for over 2,500 years, it is false to believe that they are somehow immune to alcoholism.

The vast majority of Jews drink on a fairly regular basis; only 5% are abstainers. Drinking is first introduced to children in a family context, which has been shown to be a strong force in determining later drinking habits. Alcoholic beverages are used in positive settings, including religious rituals and mixed social gatherings, rather than as a means of coping with stress. When a baby is circumcised, he is given a few drops of wine and wine is drunk at bar mitzvahs and weddings. Consumption of wine is a part of the Sabbath ceremony and all family members partake. Sobriety is a factor in Jewish identity and intoxication is generally not tolerated.

One study revealed that of all Jewish men, the most orthodox drank most frequently but also had the lowest incidences of intoxication (Snyder). Furthermore the study showed that in general the more orthodox the participant, the lower the incidence of intoxication. However, there are orthodox Jewish rabbis who are alcoholics, and religious disaffiliation is not necessarily an indication of a drinking problem. Rates of alcoholism are low among Reform Jews as well as Orthodox Jews, but there appears to be a correlation between a move away from orthodoxy and an increase in the incidence of alcoholism. Identification with Judaism generally seems to act as a protective factor against alcoholism and an aid in recovery from alcoholism when it develops.

In a 1975 study researchers W. Schmidt and R. E. Popham found four types of coping mechanism used by Jews to deal with their alcoholism: (1) denial—"Since I'm a Jew I can't be an alcoholic"; (2) disaffiliation—"Since I'm an alcoholic I can't be much of a Jew"; (3) rationalization—"I drink to excess but so do most Jews"; and (4) acceptance—"I drink excessively and I am Jewish."

Difficulties in treating Jews who are alcoholic stem from a generalized DENIAL of the problem by the Jewish community and a lack of tolerance, which make subjects feel isolated from their community and may worsen their situation. In addition ALCOHOLICS ANONYMOUS meetings are often held in churches, where Jews may feel uncomfortable. Increased awareness by the Jewish community of the problem of alcoholism is needed to eliminate denial. More AA meetings in synagogues might also help treatment.

Sheila Blume, Dee Dropkin and Lloyd Sokolow, "The Jewish Alcoholic: A Descriptive Study," *Alcohol Health and Research World* 4, no. 4 (Summer 1980):21-26.

Morris Chafetz and Harold W. Demone, Jr., *Alcoholism and Society* (New York: Oxford University Press, 1962), pp. 84-88.

Barry Glassner, "Irish Bars and Jewish Living Rooms: Differences in Ethnic Drinking Habits," *Alcoholism* 1, no. 4 (March-April 1981):19-21.

W. Schmidt and R. E. Popham, "Impressions of Jewish Alcoholics," *Quarterly Journal of Studies on Alcohol* 37 (1976):931-934.

C. R. Snyder, *Alcohol and the Jews: A Cultural Study of Drinking and Sobriety,* Yale Center of Alcohol Studies monograph no. 1 (New Haven, 1958).

job safety   See   ACCIDENTS, EMPLOYEE ASSISTANCE PROGRAMS.

Joint Commission on Accreditation of Hospitals (JCAH)   Specific alcoholism program accreditation was initiated in

1975 by JCAH under contract with the NATIONAL INSTITUTE ON ALCOHOL ABUSE AND ALCOHOLISM (NIAAA). In the years since, however, some authorities complain that alcoholism program identity has become increasingly diffused, first subsumed under psychiatric standards and now in danger of being absorbed under JCAH's general hospital standards, according to J. Lewis's *The Alcoholism Report.* A competitive agency, an ad hoc COMMISSION ON ACCREDITATION OF REHABILITATION FACILITIES (CARF), is planning standards for treatment programs as an alternative to the JCAH standards, ostensibly to give more emphasis to nonhospital care. CARF points out in its newsletter that the uncertainty about standards has worked a special hardship on nonhospital programs. Don Cahalan, in his book *Understanding America's Drinking Problem,* writes: "Since the issue of certification is vital to determining which treatment organizations get funded for what kinds of treatment, the controversy over turf (between such interests as the hospital-based programs and free-standing programs, and among various groups of professionals caught in the middle) is likely to delay the settlement of the certification-of-facilities issue for a while longer."

D. Cahalan, *Understanding America's Drinking Problem: How to Combat the Hazards of Alcohol* (San Francisco: Jossey-Bass, 1987), p. 169.

J. Lewis, *The Alcoholism Report* (a subscription newsletter), vol. 10 (1982) through 14 (1986).

Judaism   See RELIGION, JEWS.

K

katzenjammers   Slang for DELIRIUM TREMENS.

Keller, Mark   Alcohologist, a colleague of JELLINEK at Yale University and founding editor of the *Journal of Studies on Alcohol*. The first issue of the publication, then called the *Quarterly Journal of Alcohol Studies*, was June 1940. One of the country's foremost authorities in the field of alcoholism, Mark Keller was for many years associated with RUTGERS CENTER OF ALCOHOLIC STUDIES.

Kenya   The drinking patterns in Kenya, an independent member of the British Commonwealth since 1963, parallel those of other equatorial African nations. Approximately 90% of the population is composed of African ethnic groups living in rural areas, where alcoholic beverages are often home brews and drinking occasions are related to cultural activities among the various tribal societies. Imported liquors and bottled beers are sold through licensed retail stores, but there is widespread and unregulated consumption of busaa, a fermented beverage made from maize flour and sugar honey, and chang'aa, a beverage similar to gin distilled from a variety of fermented brews. Consumption of such alcoholic beverages is an integral part of social celebrations, settlements of disputes, agrarian festivals and hunting expeditions. Assistance from distant neighbors in construction and repair of rural farms and homes is usually rewarded with alcoholic beverages, and in certain places consumption of alcohol has become a part of sacrificial rites within communities.

In Nairobi and Mombasa there is a greater availability of imported wines and liquors, such as brandy, whiskey and gin, and the number of public bars has risen in recent years. Drinking of imported alcoholic beverages, as in other developing nations, is most common among educated people and is considered a mark of high social status. As Kenyan society becomes more modernized, licensed drinking premises have tended to replace the communal gatherings to which drinking was once limited and cultural restraints on drinking have been relaxed.

There is growing concern in Kenya about the spread of alcoholism resulting from this process of modernization. Figures on consumption are unreliable because of the amount of noncommercial alcoholic beverage production, and it is difficult to collect statistics because of increased migration within the country, which has further loosened social inhibitions on drinking as a result of the loss of traditional environments. Heavy costs to the country in lowered productivity have been attributed to the susceptibility of economically depressed peoples to drunkenness and the availability of inexpensive home-brewed alcoholic beverages.

Korsakoff's psychosis (syndrome, disease)   Named after Sergei Korsakoff (1854-1900), a Russian psychiatrist who founded the Moscow school of psychiatry and was the first to identify this form of psychosis in 1897. (The disease was officially named Korsakoff's psychosis at the 12th International Medical Congress in Moscow in 1897.)

Korsakoff's psychosis is primarily a mental disorder characterized by confusion, memory failure and a tendency to recite imaginary occurrences. Other symptoms include disorientation in time, emotional apathy and loss of insight, which prevents the patient from becoming aware of the disability. Patients are often moderately cheerful and noncomprehending. The disease usually affects only those who have been drinking steadily for years, although it has been known to appear in nonalcoholics suffering from severe nutritional deficiencies. Thiamine deficiency is suspected to be partly responsible. Treatment consists of nutritional supplements (see VITAMINS AND MINERALS), but Korsakoff's psychosis is usually irreversible. It is often preceded by WERNICKE'S ENCEPHALOPATHY and given the single designation Wernicke-Korsakoff syndrome.

L

lager   A light, foamy BEER brewed by means of BOTTOM FERMENTATION. The procedure utilizes a yeast that sinks to the bottom of the brewing vat and bubbles up through the liquid. The name "lager" is derived from the German *Lagern,* meaning "to rest," in reference to the yeast. Lager beer is usually aged several months in a cool place to clear it of sediment.

Lager beer was first brewed in Bavaria, and the process has remained the principal brewing method for German beers. Since that time it has also become the dominant process used by the American brewing industry. The first known lager brewery was started in Philadelphia some time prior to 1840. It initially served the German-American population of that city, but lager beers quickly became popular across the country and were the basis of the major American brewing industries established in Milwaukee and St. Louis. In the United States the influence of German lager beer has completely eclipsed that of English ALE.

labor   See EMPLOYEE ASSISTANCE PROGRAMS.

laudanum   Formerly any of various preparations of opium, laudanum is now a TINCTURE, or alcoholic solution, of opium. Before it was known to be addictive, it was used to treat a variety of disorders. Laudanum was first compounded by Paracelsus in the 16th century and used medicinally through the 19th century.

L-Dopa   Currently used in treating the crippling effects of Parkinson's disease, L-Dopa is under investigation as a possible counteractant to the effects of alcoholism. Researchers interested in developing AMETHYSTIC, or sobering, agents have been studying drugs that might reverse the acute effects of alcohol intoxication and thus stop or relieve the depression of CENTRAL NERVOUS SYSTEM function caused by consumption of alcohol. A study of nonalcoholic volunteers by Ronald L. Alkana and Ernest P. Noble investigated the potential of L-Dopa for

reversing the effects of moderate doses of alcohol (0.8 grams of alcohol per kilogram of body weight). Treatment with L-Dopa significantly reduced alcohol's effects on coordination, maintenance of attention and brain functions as recorded on electroencephalograms. Use of the drug for treating alcohol-related problems is still very much in the experimental stage.

Ronald L. Alkana and Ernest P. Noble, "Amethystic Agents: Reversal of Acute Ethanol Intoxication in Humans," in *Biochemistry and Pharmacology of Ethanol,* vol. 2, ed. Edward Majchrowicz and Ernest P. Noble (New York: Plenum Press, 1979).

Ernest P. Noble, ed., *Third Special Report to the U.S. Congress on Alcohol and Health.* (Rockville, Md.: National Institute on Alcohol Abuse and Alcoholism, 1978), p. 100.

legal aspects of alcohol abuse   Until recently the approach to alcohol abusers was to consider them or their behavior a criminal justice matter and to imprison them for PUBLIC DRUNKENNESS. This approach was not very successful; abusers often were repeatedly arrested with no improvement in their condition. Prior to 1971 the alcoholic population was estimated to account for one-third of all arrests excluding traffic violations.

In the last 20 years the criminal justice philosophy has been replaced by an approach that defines the problem as a public health issue and calls for treatment and rehabilitation rather than incarceration. In 1971 the Uniform Alcoholism and Intoxication Treatment Act was adopted by the National Conference of Commissioners on Uniform State Laws. This act declares that alcoholics and intoxicated persons may not be subjected to criminal prosecution because of their consumption of alcoholic beverages but should instead be provided with appropriate treatment.

The major piece of social legislation dealing with problems of alcohol abuse and alcoholism is the Comprehensive Alcohol Abuse and Alcoholism Prevention, Treatment, and

Rehabilitation Act of 1970, also known as the Hughes Act. This act created the NATIONAL INSTITUTE ON ALCOHOL ABUSE AND AL-COHOLISM (NIAAA) and was amended in 1973 to establish the Alcohol, Drug Abuse, and Mental Health Administration, of which NIAAA became a part.

Each state has its own particular set of laws concerning the legal drinking age, purchase and sale of alcoholic beverages, business hours for establishments that sell liquor etc. (See ALCOHOLIC BEVERAGE CONTROL LAWS.) States also determine their own regulations regarding DRIVING WHILE INTOXICATED.

1988 has seen a new wave of product-liability suits in federal courts in Pennsylvania and Washington State, charging that alcohol caused serious birth defects or fatal illnesses. These new cases are based on plaintiffs' arguments that "moderate drinking" caused harm and that companies should have warned them of the danger. Several are scheduled for trial in the spring of 1989. In early 1989, Congress passed a bill requiring "health-warning labels" on beer, wine and liquor containers (not unlike the surgeon general's warning on cigarette packages) that "pregnant women should not drink" alcohol because of risks of birth defects, and that alcohol "may cause other health problems." It is now a Federal law.

National Institute on Alcohol Abuse and Alcoholism, *Federal Activities on Alcohol Abuse and Alcoholism: FY 1977 Final Report,* (Silver Spring, Md.: Marco Systems, 1978), pp. 4-6.

Stuart Taylor Jr., "V.A.'s Denial of Benefits to Alcoholics Upheld," *The New York Times,* April 21, 1988.

lesbians   See WOMEN.

lethal dose   It is difficult to die from an overdose of alcohol, as people usually lose consciousness before they are able to drink themselves to death. For death to result, more than a quart of whiskey or its equivalent must be drunk in a short time. Cases of death have occurred during drinking contests.

At a BLOOD ALCOHOL CONCENTRATION of 0.4% a drinker usually becomes unconscious. Deep coma sets in at 0.5% and at 0.6% death may result from suppression of the nerve centers that control the heartbeat and breathing (see CENTRAL NERVOUS SYSTEM).

liqueur   An alcoholic beverage, usually from 35 to 60 proof, produced by combining a distilled spirit with strong flavorings and, in most cases, a sweetener. In the United States liqueurs are sometimes known as cordials, and in the United States and elsewhere they are often referred to as fruit brandies.

Today's liqueurs have in all likelihood evolved from the flavored wines popular in earlier times when fermentation processes were erratic and vintages sometimes scarcely potable. Liqueurs that were based on distilled spirits rather than on wines probably originated in Italy during the 15th century, and their present name derives from the Italian *liquori,* corrupted by later French usage. Benedictine, a liqueur that is still produced today, may have been made as early as 1510 in a monastery in Fecamp, France. Early liqueurs were produced exclusively by monasteries for their reputed medicinal powers. Monks in the Middle Ages were experienced herbalists, and it is likely that they switched from a wine base to a distilled spirit base in the hope of increasing the potency of their remedies.

The distilled spirit base of a liqueur and the flavoring additive are combined by one of two methods. The first is percolation, in which alcohol vapors are circulated through flavoring herbs, spices or fruit and then recondensed by cooling. The second is infusion, in which the flavoring additives are simply soaked in a distilled spirit and filtered out once the flavor has been absorbed. In either case the flavored distillate is generally rectified for greater strength, sweetened, artificially colored and aged before being bottled for distribution.

Liqueurs are produced from virtually every combination of spirit and flavoring imaginable, and the precise ingredients and proportions in any given liqueur are usually a matter of long tradition and professional secrecy. The spirit bases vary according to country of origin, with France and Italy being known for grape brandy liqueurs, Scotland and Ireland for whiskey liqueurs, and many other countries for a variety of grain and potato spirit liqueurs. The flavorings used are even more varied, although the majority are natural produce, such as fruit and fruit rinds, herbs, spices, roots and even flowers used in combination with each other. The most common liqueurs are those flavored principally with oranges, strawberries, almonds or honey, all marketed under a number of different brand names.

liquor   The Latin term for liquidity in general. In its earliest English usages, the term "liquor" was used to refer to any mixed liquid, such as "meat liquor," or to any measured solution of a solid in liquid. It was only in the 17th century that the term came to be closely associated with specifically alcoholic beverages. Its most common usage today is in reference to those alcoholic beverages created by diluting a distilled spirit with water.

liver   The largest and most metabolically complex organ, the liver has among its functions circulation, excretion, immunology and detoxification. Seventy-five percent of the blood carried to the liver comes from the intestinal tract through the portal circulatory system. The liver is therefore the first recipient of digested material, including alcohol, absorbed from this tract. It also receives blood from the hepatic artery that carries alcohol and other substances from the general circulatory system.

Unlike fats and carbohydrates, alcohol is not effectively oxidized in the tissues. Ninety percent of the alcohol in the system is rapidly absorbed from the gastrointestinal tract and must be oxidized in the liver. As a result the liver, more than any other organ, bears the brunt of alcohol's deleterious effects. While alcohol is detoxified in the liver by oxidation (see METABOLISM), both alcohol and its metabolic products, especially ACETALDEHYDE, can scar the liver and break down liver tissue. Because the liver has many functions, such as conversion of vitamins and foods into usable forms needed by other organs and tissues, production of enzymes and antibodies, and storage and release of sugar, damage to it adversely affects other parts of the body. (For diseases of the liver, see ALCOHOLIC LIVER DISEASE, ALCOHOLIC HEPATITIS, CIRRHOSIS, FATTY LIVER.)

London Dry Gin   See GIN.

loss of control   A major symptom of alcoholism, loss of control is an inability on the part of an alcoholic to choose consistently between drinking and not drinking. There are two types of loss of control: an inability to stop drinking once drinking has begun and an inability to refrain from starting to drink. Loss of control does not mean that every time an alcoholic takes a drink he or she will be unable to stop before getting drunk. The symptom appears only sporadically. However, at certain times, the alcoholic, compelled by some unknown stimulus, is powerless to decide not to drink. The stimulus may be outside of the alcoholic's conscious awareness, and after a while alcohol itself may become the stimulus.

The unpredictable nature of this symptom has been used to bolster the concept of absolute ABSTINENCE for alcoholics, since there can be no loss of control if an alcoholic refrains from alcohol completely. There have been studies examining the possibility of CONTROLLED DRINKING for some alcoholics under certain conditions.

lithium carbonate therapy   Research shows mixed results on the initial reports of the effectiveness of lithium carbonate in alcoholism treatment. More research is called for in this particular area of PHARMACOTHER-APY.

low birth weight   Recent studies show that both drinking and smoking are related to low birth weight. Effects of prenatal alcohol exposure on infants are measurable over a broad range of maternal drinking levels, including even "social" drinking. The best advice for pregnant women continues to be to abstain from alcohol.

For more information regarding associations between alcohol and adverse pregnancy outcome, see BIRTH DEFECTS and FETAL ALCOHOL SYNDROME (FAS).

M

macronodular cirrhosis   A contemporary classification of a type of cirrhosis that is similar to postnecrotic cirrhosis (see CIRRHOSIS).

Madeira   The name given to any of several fortified wines made on Madeira, a Portuguese-owned island located in the Atlantic Ocean about 400 miles off the northwestern coast of Africa.

There are four basic types of Madeira: Malmsey, a very sweet dark brown wine that is usually drunk as a dessert wine; Bual (or Boal), a golden-brown wine that is only slightly less sweet than Malmsey and also drunk as a dessert wine; Verdelho, a golden wine that is less sweet than either Malmsey or Bual and drunk either with dessert or as an aperitif; and Sercial, a pale gold wine that is the driest of the four and is generally drunk as an aperitif. In addition to these four types there is a blend of different Sercial wines called Rainwater Madeira. The alcohol content of Madeira wines usually falls between approximately 18.5% and 19.5% by volume.

The wines made on Madeira are fortified with brandy, which is added during the fer-mentation process. The brandy serves to slow down and gradually halt fermentation. The longer the wine is allowed to ferment before the brandy is added, the drier it will be.

After fermentation is completed, the wine is subjected to a special heating process unique to the production of the Madeira wines. The fermented wine is placed in a heated chamber called an *estufa*, where its temperature is gradually raised to 140°F. It is held at this temperature for six weeks and then gradually reduced to normal. The process is intended to simulate the effects of a slow sea voyage through the tropics. Madeira wine has been subjected to this procedure since the 18th century, when it was discovered that such a voyage had actually improved the flavor of the wine.

male-limited (Type II) alcoholism   See MILIEU-LIMITED (TYPE I) ALCOHOLISM.

Mallory-Weiss syndrome   A condition caused by frequent vomiting that results in laceration of the gastroesophageal junction and, in turn, massive hemorrhage. Many victims of the syndrome are alcoholics, as the local toxic and irritating effects of alcohol may result in frequent morning nausea and vomiting. The syndrome, however, is not restricted to alcoholics, and the bleeding may accompany any condition associated with frequent vomiting. Prognosis is excellent once the bleeding has been stopped, although surgery is usually necessary to stop the bleeding.

malt   A grain, almost invariably barley, steeped in water until it germinates, or "malts," and produces the soluble sugar maltose. It is then spread and dried to produce pure malt. Pure malt is a highly nutritive ingredient of certain nonalcoholic beverages and many cereal foods, but it has traditionally been used in brewing or distilling processes. In fact it is one of the oldest ingredients of alcoholic beverages, dating back to the ancient Egyptians, who used it to produce beer. Malted barley is found in nearly all lager, ale, stout, porter and bock beers. It is also mixed with other ingredients to make most types of whiskey. Some nearly 100% malt whiskey is produced in Scotland, but it is rarely consumed in this form.

The drying process for malt is especially important, and several different methods of turning the malt during drying have been developed. In the traditional method drying is accomplished on a malting floor large enough to scatter the grain, which is turned with hand shovels to disperse the heat generated by germination and to speed the drying process. In the more modern Saladin technique the grain is strewn along troughs and turned by mechanical blades. Some malters employ a procedure known as the drum method, in which the grain is poured into barrels that can be rotated and ventilated with cool air.

Whatever method is used, malting is a very delicate process that continues for up to two weeks until the germinated sprout has reached the desired length.

malt beverage   A beerlike beverage made from MALT. Most malt beverages are about the same as NEAR BEER. Popular during Prohibition, they began to reappear in the 1970s as a refreshment for those who enjoyed the taste of beer but who did not want the effects of the alcohol in beer. For this reason malt beverages have enjoyed some popularity among alcoholics who no longer consume alcohol. (see also DE-ALCOHOLIZED BEVERAGE.)

malt liquor   An alcoholic beverage similar to BEER but with a higher alcohol content (6.5% to 7.0%).

Marchiafava-Bignami disease   This disease was first detected in Italy in 1903 by two pathologists, Ettore Marchiafava (1847-1935) and Amico Bignami (1862-1929), among heavy drinkers of wine. It mainly afflicts middle-aged alcoholic males, although only a few cases have been reported. The disease can take several months to develop. Symptoms include agitation, confusion, hallucinations, memory disturbances and disorientation. The exact causes of this disease are unknown, but it has been seen in conjunction with WERNICKE'S ENCEPHALOPATHY and ALCOHOL AMBLYOPIA and may be due to malnutrition.

marijuana with alcohol   A pattern of multiple drug use is common among those who use marijuana and other cannabinoids. The National Commission on Marijuana and Drug Abuse found that alcohol and tobacco were the two other substances most commonly used by regular marijuana smokers. Today alcohol seems to be replacing marijuana as the drug of choice among the young (under 21). (See also DRUGS.)

Massachusetts Society for the Suppression of Intemperance   One of the earliest temperance societies in America, founded in Andover in 1813. It was organized by a number of Calvinist ministers and included other prominent community members. They published a number of antialcohol tracts and spread their message around the country.

mead   A beverage made of fermented honey, water and spices. Although it is often incorrectly identified as a kind of beer, mead is essentially a honey wine. It is considered to have been among the earliest alcoholic beverages developed by man, along with fermented fruit juice (wine) and fermented grains (beer). Little is known about the history of mead, but it has been especially associated with Anglo-Saxon and Teutonic cultures of the early Middle Ages. The name "mead" has also been used to refer to numerous other beverages, some not in any way related to honey and some nonalcoholic.

medical education   See   HEALTH CARE PROVIDERS.

medication   Alcohol is a basic ingredient in many liquid medications (see COUGH MEDICINE). Historically alcohol alone was used as a medicine; before the introduction of antibiotics, physicians prescribed small doses of whiskey for infants suffering from pneumonia. Today it is dispensed in some chronic disease wards as a sedative.

memory   Alcoholics and nonalcoholics alike commonly report an experience of impaired memory function after consumption of a large quantity of alcohol. While the effects of alcohol on memory have been studied, they are difficult to measure objectively because of such factors as the uniqueness of each person's memory and the difficulty of obtaining controls in studies; for example, there is no way to determine if a recovered alcoholic would have a better memory if he or she had never had a drink or how much better that memory would be.

Investigation of the relationship between alcohol and memory has centered on two areas. The first concern is to determine the impact on memory produced by the state of intoxication: how does the memory function during intoxication? The second aspect is to ascertain the long-term effects of chronic alcohol use on memory: are there different degrees of impairment for different levels of consumption? what aspects of memory are affected? is any of the damage reversible?

Among the factors that must be assessed when investigating the effects of intoxication are the dose size; the kind of memory impaired—recent or remote or both; the impact of rising or falling BLOOD ALCOHOL CONCENTRATION, if any; the effect on storage of information or the ability to recall information previously stored (retrieval); and the sex of the participant. When studying the impact of alcohol on memory over a long period of time, the duration of alcoholism as well as the age and sex of the subject must be considered.

Effects of Alcohol on Memory During a Period of Intoxication

Dose Size

For some kinds of memory function it appears that a greater amount of alcohol consumed in a sitting causes a corresponding impairment of memory. Researchers Ben Morgan Jones and Marilyn K. Jones tested two groups, one of which was given a high dose of alcohol and the other a low dose, for immediate and short-term memory. To test immediate memory, subjects were given six lists of 12 words each and tested for immediate memory after each list. To test short-term memory the subjects were given five minutes to recall words from all six lists in any order. It was found that on the short-term memory test a high dose of alcohol (1.04 grams of ethanol per kilogram of body weight) caused a significantly greater level of impairment than a low dose (0.52 grams per kilogram). On the test of immediate memory, however, there were no significant differences in the amount of impairment caused by high and low doses.

Rising or Falling Blood Alcohol Concentration

When someone has a drink, his or her blood alcohol concentration rises to a peak and then gradually falls off. Acute alcohol doses can seriously disrupt memory according to the resultant blood alcohol concentration (BAC). A BAC as low as .04 g. per 100 ml. of blood depresses memory functions, and the disruption increases as the BAC rises, causing increasing levels of amnesia (Parker, 1984).

Storage and Retrieval

When the mind receives information, it must first construct an internal representation of the data (encoding). The translation of encodings into a permanent form (consolidation) must take place before data can be stored in the memory. Later, in order to use such information, the representation that has been stored must be searched for and found, a process known as retrieval. (Parker, 1984) It is possible to have information stored in the memory that is not available for immediate retrieval; this is demonstrated by the "tip of the tongue" phenomenon—someone is sure he or she knows a fact but, at the moment, is unable to recall it. When an individual is able to remember something learned previously, it is assumed that first the information was consolidated in the storage process and that later it was searched for and retrieved. In the case of an individual who cannot recall information previously learned, researchers studying the affects of alcohol on memory must determine whether the encoding storage or the retrieval phase of memory has been affected. Most researchers today agree that alcohol impairs the encoding of information and not its consolidation or retrieval. This conclusion is supported by the work of Isabel M. Birnbaum and Elizabeth S. Parker, who found that information previously learned in the sober state could be retrieved equally well under sober and intoxicated conditions (1977). Parker's more recent research with Weingartner has analyzed amnesia after acute doses of alcohol, and has suggested that alcohol has its primary effect on encoding activities, rather than other memory processes (1984). In fact, it has been found that alcohol facilitates memory consolidation once an event has been encoded (Esposito et al.).

Sex Difference

Jones and Jones report that males and females given equal doses of alcohol adjusted for body weight perform equally well on immediate memory tests, but that females experienced greater impairment than males on memory tests which required a delayed response. The researchers are continuing their study of this area.

Long-Term Effects of Alcohol Use

Many alcoholics, when they finally submit to treatment, complain of memory disturbances. In studies of those who submitted to neuropsychological tests, it was reported that 45% to 75% of alcoholics show specific deficits in cognitive functions such as memory (*Seventh Special Report*). It is known that prolonged overuse of alcohol affects the BRAIN. If alcoholism has reached the stage of diagnosable organic brain syndrome, memory disturbance is typically present; it is often one of the primary symptoms leading to such a diagnosis. The most notable example of such a state is KORSAKOFF'S PSYCHOSIS, characterized by loss of recall of recent events, and the inability to learn new data or tasks. Recent research of this syndrome has also focused on victims' difficulty in retrieving information from long-term memory that was stored before the onset of illness (Butters). In some alcoholics with this condition immediate memory of information is relatively unimpaired, but the same information appears to be inaccessible after even short periods of delay. Alcoholics with a history of 10 or more years of heavy drinking perform significantly worse on abstracting tasks than those with a history of less than 10 years of such drinking. Age appears to exacerbate the loss of memory by alcoholics—those around age 50 perform considerably worse than those around 40 even when the duration of alcoholism is the same. Both age and alcoholism can result in failure of the cognitive system to process information in sufficient depth or with sufficient elaboration.

Jones and Jones found that drinking habits and age have an additive effect in female social drinkers. Alcohol had a significantly greater impact on the short-term memory scores of middle-aged women than on those of young women and on the scores of female moderate drinkers than on those of female light drinkers. These findings suggest that social drinking may lead to certain types of cognitive impairment which increase as a woman ages and as she drinks more alcohol.

For the alcoholic without severe brain damage there is often marked improvement of memory function after three or more weeks of abstinence, although this improvement does not generally reach the extent of non-drinking controls. Research is proceeding to ascertain the reversibility of cognitive impairments in alcoholics who abstain (Goldman). However, alcohol withdrawal symptoms often obscure the interpretation of findings concerning such reversibility.

Blackout

Perhaps the most dramatic disturbance in memory function associated with alcoholism is BLACKOUT, a loss of memory by an individual for events during a period when he or she was completely conscious. About two-thirds of chronic alcoholics frequently experience blackouts while drinking; these generally occur midway or late in the course of alcoholism and rarely after the ingestion of moderate amounts of alcohol.

State Dependency

In some cases it has been reported that information learned in one state—either sober or intoxicated—is recalled better in that state than in the other state. This phenomenon is known as state dependency. State-dependent retrieval is demonstrated most readily using moderate doses of alcohol—high doses often produce severe retention deficits and low doses are not sufficient either to greatly inhibit or facilitate the memory process. State dependency has been under investigation only since the mid-1960s. There have been several reports of alcohol-related state dependency, but to date the findings are not consistent.

Isabel M. Birnbaum and Elizabeth S. Parker, "Acute Effects of Alcohol on Storage and Retrieval," in *Alcohol and Human Memory,* edited by Isabel M. Birnbaum and Elizabeth S. Parker (New Jersey: Lawrence Erlbaum Associates, 1977), pp. 99-108.

N. Butters, "Alcoholic Korsakoff's Syndrome: Some Unresolved Issues...," *Journal of Clinical and Experimental Neuropsychology* 7 (1983): 181-210.

R.V. Esposito et al., "Enkelphalinegic-dopaminergic 'reward pathways,'" *Substance and Alcohol Actions and Misuse* 5 (1984): 111-119.

M.S. Goldman et al., "Neuropsychological Recovery in Alcoholics: Endogenous and Exogenous Processes," *Alcoholism (NY)* 10 (2) (1986): 136-144.

Enoch Gordis, M.D., ed., *Seventh Special Report to the U.S. Congress on Alcohol and Health* (Rockville, Md.: National Institute on Alcohol Abuse and Alcoholism, 1990).

Ben Morgan Jones and Marilyn K. Jones, "Alcohol and Memory Impairment in Male and Female Social Drinkers," in *Alcohol and Human Memory*, edited by Isabel M. Birnbaum and Elizabeth S. Parker (New Jersey: Lawrence Erlbaum Associates, 1977), pp. 127-138.

Elizabeth S. Parker, "Alcohol and Cognition," *Psychopharmacology Bulletin* 20 (1984): 494-496.

menstrual cycle   See REPRODUCTIVE FUNCTIONS.

metabolism   Once ingested, alcohol is absorbed into the bloodstream from the stomach, duodenum and gastrointestinal tract by a process of passive diffusion. It is then carried in the blood through the circulatory system from the digestive organs to the LIVER. The rest is excreted through sweat, saliva and breath. Unlike fat and most carbohydrates, which can be metabolized by almost all tissues, more than 90% of the alcohol absorbed into the body is metabolized in the liver, a process that accounts for many of the damaging effects alcohol can have on that organ.

The primary pathway of metabolism of ethyl alcohol (C_2H_5OH) consists of a series of reactions. The first reaction is catalyzed by the enzyme alcohol dehydrogenase, which removes two hydrogen atoms from each molecule of ethyl alcohol to form ACETALDEHYDE (CH_3CHO). Acetaldehyde is even more toxic to the body than ethyl alcohol before the enzyme catalysis, but it is quickly oxidized to form acetic acid (CH_3COOH), which is eventually converted to carbon dioxide (CO_2) and water (H_2O). (See formula below.)

METABOLISM OF ETHANOL

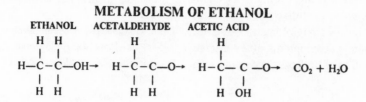

A number of the metabolic effects of alcohol on the body are linked to the products of oxidation. One consequence of heavy alcohol consumption is a metabolic derangement called alcoholic ketoacidosis—the production of excess blood acidity. The excessive breakdown of fatty acids causes a buildup of the intermediate acidic products of the breakdown, which normally would be burned to carbon dioxide. These intermediate compounds back up into the bloodstream, increase blood acidity and produce toxic effects. Susceptibility to alcoholic ketoacidosis varies from individual to individual. It appears to be more prevalent in women than in men.

Another effect of alcohol is that the excess hydrogen given off in the first reaction upsets the liver cell's chemical balance. The cell must get rid of the excess hydrogen, and one way in which it does this involves the formation of lipids (fats). The hydrogen is used in the synthesis of the precursors of the lipids that accumulate and result in alcoholic FATTY LIVER. In addition the liver uses the excess hydrogen from the alcohol as a fuel instead of fat that would normally be metabolized, again causing an accumulation of lipids leading to fatty liver.

The excess acetaldehyde produced in the reactions may have direct toxic effects on the liver. Acetaldehyde also affects the heart and other muscles and, possibly, the brain. Some researchers suggest that acetaldehyde may play a part in the development of DEPENDENCY.

A secondary metabolic pathway occurs at high levels of alcohol consumption. This pathway utilizes the microsomal system of structures within the cells, which also works to metabolize certain drugs. As a result alcohol competes with other drugs normally metabolized by this system, thereby delaying their metabolism and increasing their effect (see SYNERGY).

A figure frequently cited for the rate at which alcohol can be metabolized is 7 grams, or about 3/4 of an ounce, of alcohol per hour for a man weighing 70 kilograms or 150 pounds (see BLOOD ALCOHOL CONCENTRATION). However, this rate can vary as much as +/-50%. There is a widespread belief (if little hard evidence) that heavy drinkers can develop an increased metabolic rate and that in time the rate of metabolism for an alcoholic without liver disease may become double the average (see TOLERANCE). Nevertheless the rate of alcohol metabolism is decreased in those with liver disease (see LIVER, ALCOHOLIC LIVER DISEASE).

Lucinda Franks, "A New Attack on Alcoholism," *New York Times Magazine*, October 20, 1985.

Charles S. Lieber, "The Metabolism of Alcohol," *Scientific American* 234, no. 3 (March 1976):25-33.

methadone with alcohol   It is a common but false belief that there is an absence of alcoholism among heroin addicts. People who consume large quantities of either alcohol or heroin have a tendency to use other drugs, and investigators have found a considerable amount of crossover between the use of these agents. Increasing evidence suggests a relationship between alcohol and opiate dependency and there may be a specific interaction between the two drugs. Studies reported by Dr. Barry Stimmel of the Mount Sinai School of Medicine in New York suggest that alcohol is the drug initially and most frequently abused before heroin is first used and before addiction occurs. In addition, when heroin or other opiates are not available, alcohol is the drug most often sought as a substitute to relieve symptoms of anxiety and discomfort brought on by withdrawal.

Methadone is an opium derivative that blocks the euphoric effects of heroin. In maintenance programs it is administered in controlled doses that allow the addict to function normally. Such programs are thought to help prevent the criminal activity through which addicts get money to buy heroin.

Figures on the prevalence of alcoholism among methadone-maintained addicts vary. For example, it has been estimated that 40% of such patients consume excessive amounts of alcohol and 5% are severe alcoholics (Bihari), but other estimates of the proportion of methadone patients who drink excessively have ranged from 12% to 40%. These rates, however, are no greater and may be even less than those for similar socioeconomic populations of nonaddicts. Alcoholism does not develop as a result of methadone maintenance. However, for persons on methadone maintenance the medical consequences of consuming large quantities of alcohol are considerable. The majority of heroin addicts have had an episode of viral hepatitis, and if such a pre-existing liver condition is aggravated by alcohol abuse, a rapid progression to FATTY LIVER or CIRRHOSIS may occur. In addition there is the danger of a significant increase in the depressant effects of alcohol when combined with methadone (see SYNERGY). Mortality rates are much higher for methadone patients who are also alcoholics than for those patients who are not alcoholic.

Alcoholism interferes with the rehabilitative process and may be responsible for the termination of methadone therapy. A methadone client suffering from alcoholism is likely to become aggressive and refuse to follow clinic rules. This refusal, and the complexities of his CROSS-ADDICTION, may lead to improper detoxification and premature discharge from the program.

Withdrawal from methadone does not necessarily alleviate alcoholism and, in fact, may have the opposite effect, especially if rehabilitation has not progressed to a sufficient degree. After completion of detoxification, alcoholism appears to be the single most important obstacle preventing an individual from functioning well in society.

It is difficult, if not impossible, to refer alcoholic methadone patients for treatment because most alcoholism programs will not accept methadone-maintained patients. Therefore methadone programs must be geared toward recognizing alcoholism and treating it. Both psychological and biological tests can help identify the problem drinker as well as the potential problem drinker. Treatment should be geared to the individual's needs and the highest success has been achieved with patients who were offered a number of different treatment modes.

B. Bihari, "Alcoholism and Methadone Maintenance," *American Journal of Drug and Alcohol Abuse* 1 (1974): 79-89.

Barry Stimmel, "Methadone Maintenance and Alcohol Use," in *Drug and Alcohol Abuse: Implications for Treatment* (Rockville, Md.: National Institute on Drug Abuse, 1981).

methanol   Also known as methyl alcohol or wood alcohol, methanol is a colorless flammable liquid that can be mixed with water in all proportions. It is a fatal poison and, in small doses, may cause blindness. Because it is poisonous, it is sometimes used as a denaturant (see DENATURED ALCOHOL) for ethanol, making the latter unfit to drink. Methanol is often called wood alcohol because it was once produced chiefly as a by-product of the distillation of wood; today it is produced synthetically.

Many people have died from unknowingly drinking wood alcohol in bootleg whiskey or moonshine; others have died after knowingly consuming it because it is an alcohol and may initially have intoxicating effects.

methyl alcohol   See METHANOL.

Michigan Alcoholism Screening Test (MAST)   A formal questionnaire that allows for scoring or measuring a history of alcoholism problems, including self-reported daily alcohol intake during the preceding two weeks, nutrition, other drug use, and medical and obstetric information. MAST may be used as part of a routine health maintenance visit. The MAST has a high sensitivity to drinking problems (95%), so it will usually point to problem drinking, even by those alcoholics displaying strong DENIAL.

micronodular cirrhosis   A contemporary classification of a type of cirrhosis that is similar to portal cirrhosis (see CIRRHOSIS).

milieu-limited (Type I) alcoholism
Adoption studies have traditionally been viewed as offering the most promise for proving a genetic component in alcoholism, because these studies can clearly differentiate between the hereditary and environmental factors in a given subject's drinking. In 1981, researchers made a breakthrough in their analysis of Swedish adoption studies by revealing the existence of two types of genetic predispositions toward alcoholism (Cloninger et al., 1981) Type I, or milieu-limited alcoholism fit most closely into existing etiological paradigms for alcoholism. This type was found to occur in both sexes (i.e., it could be transmitted by either biological parent, and could be passed to children of either sex) and was implicated in most cases of alcoholism. It was associated with low-level, late-onset drinking behavior in either biological parent, and little parental criminal behavior (a further indicator of a lower severity of drinking behavior). Adoptees with this type of predisposition were reported to be heavily influenced in their drinking behavior by factors in their postnatal environment—or milieu—rather than exclusively by the genes they inherited from their biological parents.

Type II alcoholism was said to be male-limited, as it was transmitted exclusively from father to son, and accounted for approximately 25% of male alcoholics. This type of susceptibility was found to be unaffected by environment. In cases of severe alcoholism in the biological father, for example, as evidenced by early-onset drinking as well as increased criminal behavior and extensive treatment, adopted sons, regardless of their postnatal environment, were nine times more likely than controls to abuse alcohol. Despite the strong heritability of this type of alcoholism, some environmental influence was suspected in the severity of alcohol abuse, as the sons tended to be less alcoholic than their fathers.

Recently, Cloninger has suggested other traits that can be associated with these types of alcohol heritability—novelty seeking, harm avoidance and reward dependence. Type I behaviors will tend to represent low levels of novelty seeking and exhibit traits of a "passive dependent personality," as well as high harm avoidance and concern for others' feelings (high reward dependence). type II behaviors, in contrast, are more strongly antisocial, and exhibit high levels of novelty seeking and impulsivity, uninhibited behavior (low harm avoidance) and little reward dependence, i.e., weak development of social relations (Cloninger, 1987). (See also GENETICS.)

C. Robert Cloninger, "Neurogenetic Adaptive Mechanisms in Alcoholism," *Science* 236 (1987): 410-416.

C.R. Cloninger, M. Bohman and S. Sigvardsson, "Inheritance of Alcohol Abuse," *Archives of General Psychiatry* 38 (1981): 861-868.

minimum drinking age   In the 1970s, many states lowered their legal minimum drinking ages, usually to 18. Notable increases in alcohol-related accidents among drivers 18 to 20 resulted. By 1984, legislation was passed

to withhold federal highway funds from states that did not raise their drinking ages to 21; by 1988, all 50 states and the District of Columbia had raised the minimum drinking age to 21. Data from the Fatal Accident Reporting System of the National Traffic Safety Administration indicates that this measure has reduced fatal car crashes among drivers 16 to 20 by 30%. (Data was extrapolated from states that had raised their drinking ages by 1986.)

National Highway Traffic Safety Administration, *Alcohol Involvement in Fatal Traffic Crashes, 1986.* Technical Report DOT HS 807 268, Springfield, Va.: NTIS, 1988.

minerals   See VITAMINS AND MINERALS.

Minnesota Multiphasic Personality Inventory (MMPI)   A test used in many studies to help define the alcoholic personality. It is scored on scales arranged in diagnostic categories—e.g., hysteria, depression, etc. In general, studies indicate that alcoholics score high on the "psychopathic deviant" scale. This trait, however, is also found among other groups, such as criminals and heroin addicts, and does not appear to be unique to alcoholics. There is some question about how useful this test is for distinguishing a separate alcoholic personality.

The McAndrew Alcoholism Scale, derived from the MMPI, has been used as a detection instrument to assess early symptoms of alcoholism as well as the psychological and social functioning of the alcoholic patient.

Donald M. Gallant, *Alcoholism: A Guide to Diagnosis, Intervention, and Treatment* (New York: W.W. Norton, 1987).

mitochondria   The part of the cell that supplies the organism with energy by breaking down the chemical bonds in the molecules of complex nutrients. Mitosis is cell division in which the chromosomes split, with one half of each chromosome going to the daughter cell.

mixed cirrhosis   Any combination of MICRONODULAR and MACRONODULAR CIRRHOSIS (see CIRRHOSIS).

mixing drinks   Contrary to popular belief, mixing, or changing, alcoholic beverages in the course of a drinking session does not in itself cause a HANGOVER. It is rather the alcohol content and concentration of the drinks consumed that are to blame. In addition the CONGENERS in the various beverages may intensify the hangover.

In some cases the order in which drinks are mixed produces a different effect. If beer, for instance, is taken before whiskey, the first alcohol entering the bloodstream (in the form of beer) has already been diluted and is therefore less potent. Beer takes up volume in the stomach, which slows the absorption of whiskey, diluting it and delaying its effects.

If whiskey is followed by beer, the effect is a concentrated rush of alcohol to the bloodstream, with the alcohol in the whiskey reinforced by the alcohol in the beer. This combination, known as a boilermaker, is more dangerous to the drinker and results in more rapid intoxication.

moderate drinking   Occasional drinking or a regular habit of drinking small amounts of alcohol, perhaps a drink or two; a level and frequency of drinking consistent with the pattern in the community and resulting in no pathological behavior or consequences. According to statistics published in the *Second Report to the U.S. Congress on Alcohol and Health* (1974), moderate drinkers, as a group, live longer than ex-drinkers, heavy drinkers or abstainers. (See ANSTIE'S LAW.) Although studies in the 1970s suggested that moderate drinking, even on a daily basis, could protect drinkers from heart disease and could result in a longer life, these studies have recently come under attack for not having adequately controlled for other lifestyle factors such as exercise. To date, the question is not settled and controversy still surrounds the issue (See HEART).

moderation   See MODERATE DRINK-
ING.

mono amine oxidase (MAO)   An enzyme involved in brain neurotransmitter metabolism but also found in blood platelets.
MAO has been reported in several studies to
be abnormally low in alcoholics and their
offspring. Research continues into MAO's appropriateness as a biochemical marker of genetic susceptibility to male-limited
alcoholism, a severe form of the disease.

moonshine   Moonshine is the name
given to corn whiskey that is not aged to any
extent. It has the clear color and raw taste of
pure alcohol, and its other name, "white light-
ning," is well merited. Moonshine dates back
to the days when the government first started
imposing taxes on whiskey — 1791. Distillers
and private whiskey makers sought to avoid
paying government taxes by producing whiskey secretly. They set up stills in out-of-the-
way places and usually worked at night by
moonlight. This illegal production became
known as moonshining and the product was
called moonshine.

Moonshining is still common in Tennessee,
Kentucky, North Carolina and other parts of
the rural South. Moonshine is said to be the
preferred drink of some Americans and is now
legally available in some areas. However, illegal manufacture continues. A major incen-
tive for moonshining is the opportunity to
make an extra profit by not paying customs
and/or excise taxes. If the government increases taxes on legally produced liquor substantially to recoup the lost tax revenues, the
public may rebel and encourage moonshiners.

John A. Ewing, and Beatrice A. Rouse, "Drinks,
    Drinkers, and Drinking" in *Drinking,* ed. Rouse
    and Ewing (Chicago: Nelson-Hall, 1978), pp.
    12-13.

morning drinking   A warning sign indicating the possibility of alcoholism.

mortality   Clinical research has shown
that alcoholics and people admitted for treatment of alcohol problems have a higher mortality rate than that of the general population.
The mortality rate for men with alcohol problems is two to six times higher than average
for men.

There are two major causes of alcohol-related mortality. Alcohol is directly responsible for a number of DISEASES resulting in
death; it is indirectly involved in deaths from
ACCIDENTS and from aberrant behavior, such
as SUICIDE and CRIME.

An increase in the CONSUMPTION level
usually results in an increase in the number of
individuals with diseases related to alcohol
abuse and, consequently, an increase in mortality. This conclusion has been demonstrated
by dramatic drops in deaths from cirrhosis
during times of war or prohibition, when alcohol was not available. More recent statistics
concerning alcohol-related death rates are to
be found in Appendix 1.

Ernest P. Noble, ed., *Third Special Report to the
    U.S. Congress on Alcohol and Health,* (Rock-
    ville, Md.: National Institute on Alcohol Abuse
    and Alcoholism, 1978), pp. 17-20.

**Mothers Against Drunk Driving
(MADD)**   A community action group
organized to fight drunken driving, the organization was begun by Candy Lightner in
1979 after her daughter was killed by a
drunk driver who had had five drunk driving
arrests since 1976. MADD seeks to change
the climate of acceptance and tolerance of
the drunk driver and to change the response
of the legal system toward drunk driving. It
also serves as an advocate for those who
have been victimized by drunk drivers. Primarily through its 400 local chapters,
MADD mobilizes victims and their allies to
establish the public conviction that drunk
driving is unacceptable and criminal in
order to promote public policies, programs
and personal accountability.

Estimated Number of Deaths Attributable to Alcohol: United States, 1980

Cause of Death	Number of Deaths	Estimated Number Attributable to Alcohol	Percentage Attributable to Alcohol
Alcohol as the main cause			
Alcoholic psychoses	454	454	100
Alcohol dependence syndrome	4,350	4,350	100
Nondependent use of alcohol	889	889	100
Alcoholic polyneuropathy	4	4	100
Alcoholic cardiomyopathy	650	650	100
Alcoholic gastritis	84	84	100
Alcoholic fatty liver	1,166	1,166	100
Acute alcoholic hepatitis	794	794	100
Alcoholic cirrhosis of the liver	9,166	9,166	100
Alcoholic liver damage unspecified	1,812	1,812	100
Accidental poisoning by alcohol	218	218	100
Subtotal		19,587	
Alcohol as a contributing cause			
Cancer of directly exposed tissues			
Malignant neoplasm of lip, oral cavity, pharynx	8,553	2,138	25
Malignant neoplasm of larynx	3,412	853	25
Malignant neoplasm of stomach	14,372	2,874	20
Malignant neoplasm of liver	5,618	1,404	25
Subtotal		7,269	
Other diseases			
Diabetes mellitus	35,649	1,782	5
Hypertensive diseases	32,633	1,632	5
Pneumonia and influenza	54,619	2,731	5
Diseases of esophagus, stomach, duodenum	8,734	873	10
Chronic liver disease and cirrhosis not specified as alcoholic	18,645	4,661	25
Subtotal		11,679	
Accidents			
Railway accidents	632	63	10
Motor vehicle traffic accidents	51,930	25,965	50
Other road vehicle accidents	232	46	20
Water transport accidents	1,429	286	20
Air and space accidents	1,494	149	10
Accidental falls	13,294	3,324	25
Accidents caused by fire and flames	5,822	1,455	25
Accidents due to natural and environmental factors	3,194	799	25
Accidents caused by submersion, suffocation, and foreign bodies	10,216	3,576	35
Other accidents	8,744	2,186	25
Subtotal		37,849	

Estimated Number of Deaths Attributable to Alcohol: United States, 1980

Cause of Death	Number of Deaths	Estimated Number Attributable to Alcohol	Percentage Attributable to Alcohol
Violence			
Suicide	26,869	8,061	30
Homicide	23,967	11,984	50
Undetermined whether accidental or purposely inflicted	3,663	1,099	30
Subtotal		21,144	
All causes		97,528	

SOURCE: R. T. Ravenholt, "Addiction Mortality in the United States, 1980: Tobacco, Alcohol and Other Substances." *Population and Development Review* 10:697–724 (1984).

motorcycle accidents   Of the total deaths from motor vehicle accidents, more than 60% involve passenger cars; motorcycles and motor scooters account for 8%. In 1986, alcohol was involved in nearly 54% of fatal motorcycle accidents compared with 35% of drivers of passenger cars. One trauma center study of victims of motorcycle crashes over an 18-month period found a 25% incidence of intoxication. Intoxicated motorcyclists were responsible for the crash 50% more often than those who were not intoxicated, and their mortality rate was four times higher. Although intoxicated motorcyclists constituted only 25% of the crash victims, they sustained 39% of the severe head injuries and 57% of the mortalities. Furthermore, intoxicated motorcyclists wore helmets one-third as often and sustained head injuries twice as frequently.

National Highway Traffic Safety Administration, *Alcohol Involvement in Fatal Crashes, 1986,* (Washington, D.C.: National Highway Safety Administration, 1988).

Mouthwashes with High Alcohol Content

Brand	% of alcohol
Cepacol	14.0
Listerine	26.9
Scope	18.5
Signal	15.5

mouthwash   Many mouthwashes contain a high percentage of alcohol, as high as 26.9% (Listerine); most hard liquor—gin, vodka, whiskey—is about 40% alcohol, and wine generally contains about 12% alcohol.

While mouthwash containing alcohol has potential for abuse, the main danger posed by such products is that an alcoholic using one of them legitimately may develop a CRAVING for more. Also those who are taking ANTABUSE may have a reaction to the alcohol.

muscle, noncardiac
See ALCOHOLIC MUSCLE DISEASE.

N

National Center for Health Statistics (NCHS)   One of several key organizations that provides a broad data base for analysis of patterns and trends in consumption, morbidity, and mortality in the area of alcohol abuse and alcoholism. The Center provides information to assist in the development of health measures for health researchers, administrators and planners in the field of alcoholism. The NCHS is located in Hyattsville, Maryland.

National Council on Alcoholism (NCA)

Started by Marty Mann in 1944 as the National Committee for Education on Alcoholism. Mann, an energetic doer and captivating speaker, had joined Alcoholics Anonymous (AA) in 1939. At her death in 1980, she held the record for continuous sobriety of any woman in Alcoholics Anonymous. Mann had enriched her knowledge in 1943 at the newly founded Yale School of Alcohol Studies, the country's first such education program.

The National Council on Alcoholism was the first nation-wide volunteer agency in the field of alcoholism. Today NCA works for prevention and control of alcoholism through programs of public and professional education, medical and scientific information, and public policy advocacy.

National Highway Traffic Safety Administration (NHTSA)

Staffed by experts who investigate consumer complaints and provide assistance to resolve problems, the NHTSA provides information and referral on the effectiveness of occupant protection, such as safety belt use and child safety seats, and auto recalls. NHTSA also provides information and analysis of patterns and trends relating to driving and drinking, minimum drinking age/driving, traffic accidents and fatalities, and alcohol-related data dealing with traffic/safety for driving, passengers, pedestrians and bicyclists, and gives referrals to other government agencies for consumer questions on warranties, service, and auto safety regulations. NHTSA is located in Washington, D.C.

National Institute on Alcohol Abuse and Alcoholism (NIAAA)

The NIAAA (established in 1971) predates the Alcohol, Drug Abuse, and Mental Health Administration (ADAMHA), of which it is a component institute. It is charged with providing

leadership, policies, and goals for the Federal effort in the prevention, control, and treatment of alcohol abuse and alcoholism and the rehabilitation of affected individuals. In carrying out these responsibilities the Institute conducts and supports research on the biological, psychological, sociological, and epidemiological aspects of alcohol abuse and alcoholism; supports the training of professional and paraprofessional personnel in prevention, treatment, and control of alcoholism; conducts and supports research on the development and improvement of alcoholism services delivery, administration, and financing, and supports alcoholism services programs and projects, including facilities construction as appropriate; collaborates with and provides technical assistance to State authorities and Regional offices, and supports State and community efforts in planning, establishing, maintaining, coordinating and evaluating more effective alcohol abuse and alcoholism programs; collaborates with, provides assistance to, and encourages other Federal agencies, national, foreign, State, and local organizations, hospitals, and voluntary groups to facilitate and expand programs for the prevention of alcohol abuse and alcoholism, and for the care, treatment, and rehabilitation of alcoholic persons; develops, implements, and administers an alcoholism detection, referral, and treatment program for Federal civilian employees within the Public Health Service; carries out administrative and financial management, policy development, planning and evaluation, and public information functions which are required to implement such programs.

(United States Government Manual, 1979–1980.)

As part of its information program, the NIAAA has published seven special reports to the U.S. Congress on alcohol and health since 1971.

The NIAAA has also funded various research projects in the field. Perhaps the best known, and most controversial, is an ongoing study, conducted by the Rand Corporation, designed "to assess the nature of treatment outcomes." The findings of this study have been published in the RAND REPORT and RAND REPORT II.

National Institute on Drug Abuse (NIDA)

NIDA is a component institute (established in 1972) of the Alcohol, Drug Abuse, and Mental Health Administration (ADAMHA), which is charged with providing "leadership, policies, and goals for the Federal effort in the prevention, control, and treatment of narcotic addiction and drug abuse, and the rehabilitation of affected individuals." *(United States Government Manual, 1979-1980.)* Its mandate is much the same as that of the NATIONAL INSTITUTE ON ALCOHOL ABUSE AND ALCOHOLISM.

National Institute of Mental Health (NIMH)

One of several major organizations that provides data for analysis of patterns and trends in consumption, morbidity and mortality relating to alcohol use and abuse. The NIMH also has an in-progress Epidemiologic Catchment Area (ECA) program that is assessing the prevalence and incidence of psychiatric disorders among adults in specific geographic locations, several of which indicate that alcohol abuse and dependence is one of the most common factors found. NIMH is located in Rockville, Maryland.

National Prohibition Act   See VOLSTEAD ACT.

National Temperance League   A British TEMPERANCE organization.

near beer   Beer with an alcoholic content of less than 0.5%. Near beer is not considered an alcoholic beverage either for purposes of taxation or for the regulation of sale or consumption. During PROHIBITION much near beer was manufactured and sold, but because of its weakness or poor quality or both, it was generally ridiculed even by those who drank it. When Prohibition ended, near beer all but disappeared until the 1970s, when it surfaced under a new and less objectionable

name: MALT BEVERAGE. (See also DE-ALCOHOLIZED BEVERAGE.)

Netherlands, The   Alcohol has an important place in the life style of most Dutch citizens. Proportionately, drinkers in the country made up 93% of the male population and 82% of the female population in 1976 (most recent statistics available). Even more striking is the fact that only 3% of the population recommended abstinence from alcoholic beverages and that an overwhelming majority approve of drinking by adolescents when they reach the legal age of 16 years. One reason why alcohol use is so widely accepted is because there is little obvious evidence of alcohol abuse in the Netherlands. More than two-thirds of the nation's total consumption takes place in the home, where familial restrictions are an effective control. Although some consumption of alcohol is widespread, less than one-quarter of the population drinks daily.

There is no appreciable production of illegal alcoholic beverages in the Netherlands. Of commercial alcoholic beverages beer is preferred by a vast majority of the country's drinkers. Computed as ABSOLUTE ALCOHOL, the per capita amount of alcoholic beverages consumption for the entire population in 1987 was 8.3 liters, placing the country 17th among 47 countries that reported such data. The Dutch apparent per capita rate for consumption of beer was 84.3 liters; for wine, 14.61 liters; and 2.07 liters of distilled spirits. The rate of mortality from liver cirrhosis in 1986 was 6.7 males and 4.2 females per 100,000 population; this is a marked drop from 1976, when the rates were respectively, 18.4 and 7.6 deaths per 100,000. A problem of greater national concern is abuse of other drugs aggravated by alcohol.

New Zealand   Alcoholism is recognized as one of New Zealand's major public health problems. The pattern of drinking in New Zealand is one of excessive consumption, usually of beer, in homes and clubs. Fully

Total Estimated Consumption of Alcohol in New Zealand (million liters)

	Beer [a]	Wine [b]		Spirits [a][c]
1955	211.5	3.6		8.6
1956	218.7	3.1		8.8
1957	231.2	3.4		7.9
1958	219.1	4.2		6.7
1959	209.5	4.3		4.9
1960	237.4	5.0		5.8
1961	242.7	5.0		6.2
1962	256.6	5.3		5.6
1963	256.8	5.9		6.5
1964	264.0	6.6		7.2
1965	274.0	7.2		7.7
1966	288.2	8.6		7.7
1967	300.4	10.0		7.2
1968	304.5	11.5		6.4
1969	309.4	13.6		6.8
1970	329.2	15.9		7.3
1971	347.4	19.6		7.9
1972	353.2	22.1		8.5
1973	372.9	25.6		10.4
1974	374.3	27.5		12.2
1975	389.8	26.3		13.1
1976	373.4	30.1		14.8
1977	383.3	29.4		14.9
1978	398.7	36.1		15.0
1979	370.1	35.2		15.8
1980	378.7	41.4		14.6
1981	376.0	45.5		13.7
1982	381.4	41.8		15.7
		T	F	
1983	365.2 [d]	30.8	10.3	12.8
1984	378.0	35.8	9.7	13.4
1985	374.9	38.3	8.8	13.3
1986	392.2	46.6	8.1	10.9
1987	399.1	41.6	8.1	12.3

NOTES:
(a) Prior to 1981, for year ended December. From 1981 onwards, for year ended June.
(b) Prior to 1971, for year ended December. From 1971 onwards, for year ended June.
(c) From 1981 to June 1987 figures for New Zealand-produced whiskey were excluded by the Department of Statistics.
(d) 1983 and later data is not directly comparable with earlier data because from 1983 the Department of Statistics changed from using "production for sale" data to using "excise paid" data for estimating beer consumption.
T Table Wine
F Fortified Wine
SOURCE: New Zealand Department of Statistics.

supervision. New Zealand's Alcohol Liquor Advisory Council, created in 1976, cites ignorance of the dangers of excessive consumption among the important factors contributing to the country's drinking problems.

In the mid-1980s, problem drinkers were estimated to number 270,000, of which 100,000 were women. In the period between 1976 and 1985, per capita ABSOLUTE CONSUMPTION, based on total population, rose 27% to 8.2 liters. In 1987, consumption was 8.3 liters, placing New Zealand 18th among 47 countries. In the same survey, New Zealanders placed among leading countries in beer consumption, in the number four spot, with a yearly rate of 121.7 liters per

Estimated Consumption of Absolute Alcohol Per Head of Mean Population Aged 15 Years and Over in New Zealand (liters)

Year	Beer [a]	Wine		Spirits [b]	Total	% Change
1975	7.2	1.8		2.5	11.5	+0.4
1976	6.8	2.0		2.8	11.6	+0.4
1977	6.9	1.9		2.8	11.5	−0.2
1978	7.1	2.2		2.8	12.1	+4.7
1979	6.5	2.1		2.9	11.6	−4.0
1980	6.6	2.5		2.7	11.8	+1.6
1981	6.5	2.7		2.5	11.7	−0.7 [d]
1982	6.5	2.3		2.8	11.7	0.0
		T	F			
1983	6.2 [c]	1.4	0.8	2.3	10.6	−9.1 [e]
1984	6.3	1.6	0.7	2.3	11.0	+3.6
1985	6.2	1.7	0.6	2.3	10.8	−1.7
1986	6.4	2.1	0.6	1.8	10.9	+0.3
1987	6.4	1.8	0.6	2.1	10.9	+0.2

NOTES:
(a) Prior to 1981, for year ended December. From 1981 onwards, for year ended June.
(b) From 1981 to June 1987 figures for New Zealand-produced whiskey were excluded by the Department of Statistics.
(c) 1983 and later data is not directly comparable with earlier data because from 1983 the Department of Statistics changed from using "production for sale" data to using "excise paid" data for estimating beer consumption.
(d) Change over a full year for wine, but only over half a year for beer and spirits.
(e) The real decrease from 1982 to 1983 was 5.9% because 3.2 of the percentage change was attributable to the changed method of estimating beer consumption.
T Table Wine
F Fortified Wine
SOURCE: New Zealand Department of Statistics.

half the country's alcohol consumption takes place in such private residences and facilities, which are not liable to normal legislative restrictions. A problem related to this high proportion of alcohol consumption in private places is that of adolescent access to alcohol, which is facilitated by a lack of necessary person. In the same year, wine consumption was 15.3 liters, and spirits consumption was 1.6 liters.

Hoeveel alcoholhoude dranken worden er in de wereld gedronken? (How many alcoholic beverages are being consumed throughout the world?) 27th ed. Schiedam, Netherlands: Produktschap Voor Gedistilleerde Dranken, 1987.

NIAAA   See NATIONAL INSTITUTE ON ALCOHOL ABUSE AND ALCOHOLISM.

nicotine   See SMOKING.

NIDA   See NATIONAL INSTITUTE ON DRUG ABUSE.

Nigeria   The most populous country in Africa, Nigeria has lately experienced a period of relative economic well-being, based on oil and natural gas production, that brought with it an increase in the manufacture and consumption of alcoholic beverages, particularly beer. An already well-established permissive attitude toward consumption of alcoholic beverages has resulted in greater alcohol abuse. Drinking and even drunkenness are generally tolerated, and both social and familial gatherings are now considered incomplete without alcohol. Representatives of the older tribal society, such as traditional "healers," now commonly incorporate alcohol into their functions. The general pattern is one of heavy consumption, with the unusual feature of virtually indistinguishable drinking habits among both adolescents and adults. Consumption is high during both traditional festivals and nontraditional holidays; the heaviest consumption of all is commonly on nontraditional occasions among skilled laborers, such as factory workers. This rising consumption of alcoholic beverages has completely outpaced any governmental efforts or mechanisms to control alcohol-related problems.

The preferred alcoholic beverage in Nigeria is beer, including various kinds of stout. There are no prohibitions on home brewing and distilling in Nigeria, and enormous quantities of palm wine are fermented from local trees across the country. This beverage is also distilled into native gin in large quantities. Thus availability of alcoholic beverages is so widespread that it is difficult to measure precisely.

The Nigerian government has acknowledged alcoholism as a major medical problem, but the country has no mechanism for documenting the extent of it. Limited hospital facilities and a general reluctance to contact those that exist render statistics on alcohol-related clinical admissions completely inadequate. Similarly the country maintains poor police records on traffic fatalities and incidents of public disorders related to alcohol. Most sources, however, completely agree on the widespread and increasing prevalence of alcoholic psychosis, delirium tremens, and gastric and malnutrition problems related to alcohol.

Despite its acknowledgment as a medical problem in Nigeria, alcoholism has been given a low priority because of the country's other problems.

nonaddictive alcoholic   See NONADDICTIVE PATHOLOGICAL DRINKER.

nonaddictive pathological drinker Someone who drinks excessively as a way of handling unconscious problems and who is in some way impaired by this drinking but who does not have the same overwhelming need or compulsion or LOSS OF CONTROL characteristic of alcohol ADDICTION.

Norway   As reported by Norway's Central Bureau of Statistics, the country's per capita consumption of ABSOLUTE ALCOHOL in 1987, based on total population, was 4.4 liters, placing the country 34th among the 47 countries who reported such data. Beer consumption, by far, accounted for most of alcohol consumption, with a per capita rate of 51.44 liters for the same year. Norway ranks near the bottom among reporting countries for consumption of wine and spirits.

Norway has recently experienced a reversal in consumption trends. According to a 1979 report in *News of Norway*, the consumption level rose by approximately 156% between 1955 and 1979. In the next six-year period, however, consumption declined, at an average annual rate of 2% per year.

Norway has one of the most stringent approaches to drunk driving in the world. Police conduct spot tests on motorists regularly, and drivers have come to expect them about once a month. Any driver found with a BLOOD ALCOHOL CONCENTRATION of 0.05% or more is required to serve a minimum prison sentence of three weeks. In addition a judge may extend the sentence and impose a fine at his discretion, in certain cases the judge may substitute a fine for the prison term. Any person convicted of drunk driving will also have his license suspended for at least a year and sometimes permanently. About 7,000 Norwegians serve time in prison each year for drunk driving.

Insurance regulations in Norway penalize drunk driving too. If a person causes an accident while drunk, he receives no compensation. Furthermore no insurance is paid to his estate if the accident is fatal.

Norway's severe penalties for drunk driving have been effective in curtailing accidents and discouraging people from driving under the influence of alcohol. However, arrests for drunk driving began to rise gradually in the first half of the 1980s, perhaps reflecting the increase in the number of cars in operation.

One way in which the Norwegian government has attempted to control the rise in alcohol consumption is through advertising. In 1975 the *Storting* (Parliament) passed a bill banning the advertising of alcoholic beverages in the print media, which became effective immediately.

In 1980 the Norwegian government proposed over 30 measures to reduce the consumption of alcohol by providing information, altering licensing and pricing

policies and creating a greater awareness of the alcohol problem. The measures proposed included a ban on wine making in the home, a complete ban on strong beers (5.5% alcohol content), a lowering of the alcohol content in mild beers (from 4.7% to 3.5%), and stricter control of all these areas by police, customs officers and licensing authorities.

According to available information, it seems that almost all cases involving alcohol abuse are handled by Temperance Committees. Under the Act concerning Temperance Committees and the Treatment of Alcohol Addicts passed in 1932, a Temperance Committee was set up in almost every municipality. In municipalities where there is no temperance committee, a Social Welfare Board serves the same purpose.

The Temperance Committees have four main functions: to take care of persons who abuse alcohol, where necessary making decisions about their possible committal to hospitals or sanatoria; to give advice and assistance to the families of alcohol abusers; to promote education and information concerning the use and abuse of alcohol in schools and other areas of life; and to submit proposals and recommendations to municipal authorities for implementing committee programs.

With respect to the individual alcohol abuser, a Temperance Committee may act either at the request of someone functioning on behalf of the abuser or on its own initiative. According to a 1978 report compiled by the Central Bureau of Statistics, the possible courses of action open to Temperance Committees are counseling, ANTABUSE treatment, selection of a person to support a discharged alcoholic patient, suggestion that an alcoholic join a temperance society and imposition of restrictions on the way an alcoholic spends his wages.

The bureau's statistical report lists the following types of institutions where treatment may be obtained.

1. detoxification stations
2. sections for medical treatment

3. A-clinics
4. sanatoria
5. supervision homes
6. protection homes
7. psychiatric clinics and hospitals

These institutions may be owned either by the central government or by private concerns licensed by the government.

Norwegian hospitals admit about 100,000 patients each year for alcohol-related injuries and accidents.

A-clinics are generally run by private organizations. Patients are admitted on the same basis as in ordinary hospitals. These A-clinics are financed according to the regulations of the Hospital Act.

Many patients discharged from sanatoria and A-clinics are placed in supervision homes. In such homes patients live and receive treatment while working. Supervision homes that are connected with A-clinics are also financed under the Hospital Act. Those that are not attached to A-clinics are financed in part by the National Insurance Fund and in part by either a municipality, if it referred the patient, or by the patient himself.

Protection homes are for those patients who have been judged not capable of being rehabilitated to working life. The financing of these homes is somewhat similar to that of the supervision homes which are not attached to A-clinics.

Hoeveel alcoholhoude dranken worden er in de wereld gedronken? (How many alcoholic beverages are being consumed throughout the world?) 27th ed. Schiedam, Netherlands: Produktschap Voor Gedistilleerde Dranken, 1987.

novelty-seeking   See MILIEU-LIMITED (TYPE I) ALCOHOLISM.

nursing mothers   According to findings reported in August 1989 by Harold Kaminetzky, of the American College of Obstetricians and Gynecologists, nursing mothers who regularly drink moderate amounts of alcohol (one drink a day) may put their babies at a slight risk for delayed development of motor skills. The finding, reported in *New England Journal of Medicine*, is based on a study of 400 infants that correlated alcohol use during breast feeding with scores on a psychomotor test and a mental developmental test when infants were about one year old.

The University of Michigan team of researchers found infants exposed to at least one drink a day scored five points lower on the motor test than infants exposed to less alcohol. There were no differences in mental development. The team concluded that larger tests are needed to see if a consistent pattern related to alcohol exists. Dr. Kaminetzky noted that moderate drinking appears to be more significant than an occasional "binge" with four or five drinks.

nutrition   Unlike other drugs, alcohol has a high caloric value. A gram of alcohol provides 7.1 calories, compared with 4 calories provided by a gram of carbohydrates and 9 calories provided by a gram of fat. Twenty ounces, slightly more than one pint, of an 86-proof beverage contains about 1,500 calories, or from one-half to two-thirds of a person's normal daily caloric requirement. While a small dose of alcohol may stimulate the appetite, a larger intake often diminishes appetite. Alcoholics are likely to devote more time and energy to drinking than eating, and since alcohol contains no proteins, vitamins or minerals, an individual who consumes large quantities of it in place of other food is likely to receive insufficient amounts of the essential nutrients. The calories in alcohol may provide energy but cannot be stored for future use. They also do not aid in building body tissue, as do carbohydrates, fats and proteins. As a result alcoholics often suffer from primary malnutrition in addition to the directly damaging effects of alcohol itself.

Heavy consumption of alcohol causes inflammation of the stomach, pancreas and intestine, which can impair the digestion of food and the absorption of nutrients into the blood, resulting in secondary malnutrition. Alcohol inhibits the transport of nutrients to the GASTROINTESTINAL TRACT and adversely affects nutrient absorption even when a balanced diet is maintained. Alcoholics exhibit poor absorption of a number of essential nutrients, including vitamins B_{11} and B_{12}. Malnutrition can in turn cause a sluggish intestine.

Alcohol may also interfere with the activation of vitamins by the liver cells (see VITAMINS AND MINERALS), often resulting in deficiency diseases. Vitamin deficiencies, such as zinc or thiamine deficiency, common in alcoholics, may contribute to a decreased desire for food. Malnutrition can play a role in the LIVER damage associated with alcoholism, although a heavy drinker who is well nourished can also develop liver disease. A low fat diet, however, may have some effect in the prevention of a FATTY LIVER. A study conducted by Charles S. Leiber and N. Spritz showed that for a given alcohol intake there was more abnormal fat formation on the liver with a diet of normal fat content than with a diet low in fat (see ALCOHOLIC LIVER DISEASE). There is some evidence that the development of CANCER may also be influenced by the direct consequences of alcoholism resulting from malnutrition. Deficiencies of various vitamins and minerals associated with alcoholism may play a role in carcinogenesis.

Some researchers have theorized that vitamin deficiencies play a role in the initial development of alcoholism. So far, however, there is little proof of this theory, and most nutritional deficiencies in alcoholics appear to be a result of the disease rather than the cause.

Nutrition also plays an important role in the rate that alcohol is absorbed into the body tissues and blood (see BLOOD ALCOHOL CONCENTRATION). Two factors are involved: the quantity and the type of food in the stomach. Alcohol is absorbed rapidly from an empty stomach and more slowly from a full stomach. A high-carbohydrate meal has been shown to reduce alcohol absorption more than a high-fat or high-protein meal. In addition different alcoholic beverages are absorbed at different rates, perhaps because of ingredients other than alcohol.

In the treatment of alcoholism, nutrition plays an important role. For treatment of cirrhosis and other liver diseases, a high-protein diet and massive amounts of B vitamins are prescribed. Regularly scheduled meals, especially breakfast, are important for an alcoholic because the lowering of blood sugar at any time of day increases the desire for alcohol. An alcoholic who is properly nourished may find it easier to abstain from alcohol, although good nutrition in itself is not a cure for alcoholism.

Beer and wine contain some carbohydrates and vitamins, but distilled spirits have none. (See Table 43, Appendix 1.) Drinkers often fail to account for the high caloric value of all alcoholic beverages.

Daphne A. Roe, *Alcohol and the Diet* (Westport, Conn.: AVI Publishing Company, 1979), passim.

C.S. Lieber, "Alcohol-Nutrition Interaction—An Update," *Alcohol* 1 (1984): 151-157.

O

oral fixation   A psychoanalytic theory on the cause of alcoholism. According to this theory, trauma affects the infant in the earliest stage of psychosexual development, a time when his sole means of achieving security and release from tension is through stimulation of the oral cavity. During this stage the child feels ominpotent and through his mouth he is given sustenance and expresses there his love and hate. However, as a result of an absent or uncaring mother, the infant is deprived of a warm relationship with a mother figure and subsequently continues to seek gratification of his primary emotional hunger. There is fixation at this oral stage of development and an unconscious desire for warmth and nurturance that cannot be satisfied in normal inter personal relationships. As the infant seeks through ingestion to fill his emptiness so does the alcoholic. Alcohol is a liquid nourishment that generates a sensation of warmth and satisfaction. The alcoholic's feelings of anger and rage at his parents, who failed him, coupled with an intense fear of losing them and a need to obtain some sort of gratification cause him to redirect his rage from his parents (or later other people who cannot meet his excessive needs) to himself, and so he consumes his rage in alcohol.

David J. Armor, J. Michael Polich and Harriet B. Stambul, *Alcoholism and Treatment* (New York: John Wiley and Sons, 1978), p. 17.

Morris E. Chafetz and Harold W. Demone, Jr., *Alcoholism and Society* (New York: Oxford University Press, 1962), pp. 21-25, 220-223.

Order of Good Templars   The first international TEMPERANCE organization, the Order of Good Templars, began in 1851 in Utica, N.Y. Started by a society of abstainers, it spread throughout the United States and Canada, and in 1868 it was introduced into Britain. Some years later the organization emerged in Scandinavia and other countries. The first international conference was held in 1885 in Antwerp, Belgium.

Orientals   See ASIANS.

outpatient treatment   In recent years medical centers and alcoholic treatment programs have proliferated across the United States. There are now nearly 6,000 treatment programs nationwide. More than 1.43 million persons were reported to be treated in the 12-month period ending October 30, 1989, with 15% of those in INPATIENT treatment or in a residential setting and 85% as active outpatients.

Just as alcoholics do not always need formal treatment to recover, those treated for alcoholism do not always require intensive or longer-term inpatient treatment. Indeed, studies of inpatient-outpatient treatment indicate that some alcoholics do not require inpatient

treatment. Severity of alcohol dependence and withdrawal symptoms, general medical condition, psychiatric features and other factors determine which setting for DETOXIFICATION is most appropriate. Patient-treatment matching is an ongoing area of research and interest to professionals in the field of alcohol abuse and alcoholism.

As a rule, patients who are married, stably employed, free of severe psychological impairments, and of higher socioeconomic status respond most favorably to treatment. However, many patients in outpatient facilities for the treatment of alcoholism drop out of such programs soon after admission. E. J. Larkin reviewed the literature on treatment termination, including literature not specifically related to alcoholism, and compiled a summary of terminator characteristics. He found that patients who terminated treatment were more restless, nomadic, impulsive and rigid in their attitudes and less dependable and less inhibited by anxiety than patients who remained in treatment. They were also less willing to reveal personal feelings or express ideas spontaneously. Aside from personality characteristics, lower economic class patients were more likely to terminate psychotherapy prematurely than patients from higher economic classes.

The cost of treatment varies. A four-week drying out regimen can cost anywhere from $4,000 to $20,000 for inpatient care and given that most studies have been unable to uncover significant differences in outcome among inpatient and outpatient programs, for most patients it is likely that outpatient programs will continue to serve the majority of alcoholics receiving treatment.

E.J. Larkin, *The Treatment of Alcoholism* (Toronto: Addiction Research Foundation, 1974), pp. 31-36.

W.R. Miller and R.K. Hester, "Treating the Problem Drinker: Modern Approaches," in W.R. Miller, ed., *The Addictive Behaviors: Treatment of Alcoholism, Drug Abuse, Smoking and Obesity* (Oxford: Pergamon Press, 1980), pp. 11-141.

Oxford Group Originally called The First Century Christian Fellowship, the Oxford Group was founded in 1908 by Frank Buchman. Its popularity under the name the "Oxford Group"—from Buchman's preaching among the students at Oxford—peaked in the late 1920s and early 1930s. It was a non-denominational, theologically conservative, evangelical attempt to recapture the spirit of what its members understood to be primitive Christianity.

Bill Wilson, founder of ALCOHOLICS ANONYMOUS, became familiar with the Oxford Group while he was still drinking. He included a number of its principles, such as self-survey, confession, restitution and giving of oneself in service to others, in the philosophy of AA.

P

pancreas A flat glandular organ situated below and behind the stomach and connected to the small intestine at the duodenum (where the stomach ends and the small intestine begins). The pancreas secretes a clear fluid, called pancreatic juice, that contains three important digestive enzymes which complete the digestion of proteins, carbohydrates and fats. It also secretes two hormones—insulin and glucagon—that regulate the level of glucose in the blood. Failure of the insulin-secreting cells to function properly results in DIABETES.

The association between alcoholism and pancreatic disease is well established. Alcoholics often experience acute pancreatitis after heavy drinking bouts, and the incidence of alcoholism in patients with pancreatitis is high. In alcoholics pancreatitis is usually preceded by episodes of abdominal pain following heavy drinking, although in some cases no preceding pain occurs.

Pancreatitis may be caused by a dual effect produced by consumption of alcohol, which simultaneously stimulates pancreatic secretion and obstructs pancreatic outflow. The increased pressure on the ducts of the pancreas results in pancreatic tissue swelling, and, in severe cases, cell death. The exact mechanism behind these effects is still unknown.

Pancreatitis is classified as either chronic or acute. In patients with acute pancreatitis, pancreatic functioning returns to normal and symptoms disappear when the causes are removed. In those with chronic pancreatitis, or chronic relapsing, functional and anatomic changes remain even if the causes are removed. Protein plugs obstruct the smaller ducts of the pancreas and result in distal dilation of the ducts. Scarring occurs initially at the site of the plug and then spreads. Chronic pancreatitis is associated with a number of symptoms, including abdominal pain, nausea, vomiting, diabetes mellitus and digestive disturbances. In milder cases abstinence from alcohol and a low-fat diet may be all the treatment required. Malnutrition may also play a role in the development of pancreatitis (see NUTRITION).

pancreatitis Inflammation of the PANCREAS.

para-alcoholic Often referred to as a co-alcoholic, a para-alcoholic is anyone who has an ongoing close relationship with an alcoholic, such as a spouse, a parent, a brother or sister or even an employer.

It is recognized today that the persons directly involved with an alcoholic can be victims of the disease and its damaging effects. When the relationship is examined, the para-alcoholic will often find that his or her needs are being served in some way by being involved in such a potentially destructive relationship.

DENIAL of a drinking problem plays a large role in alcoholism, and the para-alcoholic is almost as likely to deny the problem as the alcoholic. Rev. Joseph Kellerman, former director of the Charlotte (N.C.) Council on Alcoholism, reports that on an average the family of an alcoholic does not admit that he or she is an alcoholic until the illness has been critical for seven years. Once this fact has been admitted, the family generally waits another two years before seeking help. Such denial is usually to the detriment of the alcoholic, who is best served by receiving treatment as soon as possible.

Frequently the para-alcoholic will attempt to assign blame. Wives often feel at fault if their husbands drink too much. They blame themselves and feel they have failed as wives. Husbands of alcoholics may also blame themselves, but more often they tend to blame their drinking wives and the wives accept this blame. (Men are also more likely to desert their alcoholic spouses than are women.) Casting blame obscures the fact that alcoholism is a disease. The para-alcoholic may also attempt to protect the alcoholic from the consequences of his or her drinking, but this generally encourages the alcoholic to continue drinking.

Both the alcoholic and the para-alcoholic need treatment. The para-alcoholic must learn his or her own role in the perpetuation of the alcoholism and the ways in which it has served him or her. Geraldine Youcha points out that the woman who marries an alcoholic often may show striking similarities to women who drink too much. Both tend to have had a parent who was an alcoholic and both generally think very little of themselves.

Should the alcoholic become sober, the para-alcoholic may continue to have problems. Sometimes the para-alcoholic has an investment in keeping the alcoholic in a dependent role and finds it hard to change a familiar pattern. When the alcoholic changes, the para-alcoholic may lose some control over the household and may feel replaced and unappreciated. The outside world will forget what a rough time he or she has had keeping the family together, and there will no longer be a scapegoat for all family problems. In addition the alcoholic's time is often taken up by treatment.

Organizations such as AL-ANON are equipped to deal with the problems of the para-alcoholic. (See also ENABLING.)

Joseph Kellerman, "The Souse's Spouse: Victim or Villain?" *Alcoholism* 1, no. 3 (January/February 1981):26-29.

Geraldine Youcha, *A Dangerous Pleasure* (New York: Hawthorn Books, 1978), passim.

paregoric   A solution, first prepared in the 18th century, of opium, camphor and alcohol. Paregoric has been commonly used as a constituent of many cough medicines and also, because of its constipating effects, as an antidiarrhetic.

Like any substance containing substantial amounts of alcohol, paregoric is subject to abuse orally. In addition it is sometimes taken by injection for the effects of the opium, which, because of the blood-clotting potential of the camphor, may result in death.

parent education   Recent research has shown that involving parents in alcohol prevention is an effective strategy. A review of 127 evaluations of drug abuse prevention programs suggested that programs built upon peers and parents are more effective than those using only teachers (Schaps et al.). Prevention programs seek to train parents to help shape positive health behaviors in their children. Given research into child-rearing methods among different ethnic groups, it does appear necessary to tailor such programs to respond to cultural differences. Such EDUCATIONAL CAMPAIGNS AND PROGRAMS may prove successful, especially in the long run, but considerably more research is needed in this area.

E. Schaps et al., "Primary Prevention Evaluation Research: A Review of 127 Impact Studies," *Journal of Drug Issues* 11 (1980): 14-17.

pathological drinker   Someone who drinks excessively as a means of handling unconscious problems; an alcoholic or problem drinker.

pathological intoxication   Also known as alcohol idiosyncratic intoxication, pathological intoxication is an infrequent condition that has as a primary characteristic a strong behavioral change, usually in the form of explosive rage or aggressiveness, following the ingestion of a small amount of alcohol. The amount may be as little as one drink or it may be more, but it is not a quantity sufficient to produce intoxication. The resultant behavior is a radical change from the person's normal behavior. Confusion and disorganization of thought are evident, and speech can be incoherent or delusional. The episode ends in deep sleep, with no memory of the event upon awakening.

Pathological intoxication appears to be due to the hypersensitivity of a few people to small, nonintoxicating amounts of alcohol. It may occur in brain-damaged individuals or those with tissue or behavioral intolerance. Although difficult to diagnose, the condition represents a distinct diagnostic entity.

Sidney Cohen, "Pathological Intoxication," *Drug Abuse and Alcoholism Newsletter,* Vista Hill Foundation, 10, no. 5 (June 1981).

pathological reaction to alcohol   See PATHOLOGICAL INTOXICATION.

pedestrian accidents   Alcohol plays a significant role in pedestrian traffic fatalities, as shown by results of blood alcohol test findings obtained from 41% of victims (NHTSA, 1985). In about 42% of these tests, the blood alcohol level (see BLOOD-ALCOHOL CONCENTRATION) exceeded the intoxication level of 0.10%, and in 23% of the tests, the BAC was 0.20% or higher. In 1980, the mean BAC from such tests was 19%. The NATIONAL HIGHWAY TRAFFIC SAFETY ADMINISTRATION estimates that 50% to 55% of all fatal CAR ACCIDENTS involve either a driver or a pedestrian who is drunk.

Cerelle, E.C., *Alcohol in Fatal Accidents: National Estimates—U.S.A. Executive Summary,* NHTSA Tech. Note DOTHS 806 746 (Spring-field, Va.: National Technical Information Service, 1985).

periodic alcoholism   A form of alcoholism characterized by bouts of excessive drinking with intervals of abstinence or moderate drinking. Periodic alcoholism is also known as EPSILON ALCOHOLISM.

periodic drinking   See PERIODIC ALCOHOLISM

peripheral neuritis   See ALCOHOLIC POLYNEUROPATHY.

Pernod   An anise-flavored aperitif named after Henri-Louis Pernod, the first manufacturer of ABSINTHE. Pernod was initially produced as a substitute for absinthe when the latter was banned for health reasons because it contained wormwood.

When diluted with water, Pernod takes on a cloudy appearance. In comparison with absinthe, it is lower in alcoholic content (45% compared with 60% to 80%) and contains no wormwood.

personality trait theories   One category in a group of PSYCHOLOGICAL MODELS OF ETIOLOGY used to explain alcoholism. Personality trait theories have concentrated on finding a specific set of characteristics that would be associated with the development of alcoholism. However, most studies have generally failed to identify any set of personality traits that clearly distinguish alcoholics from other deviant groups or from persons judged to be normal.

Studies done on alcoholics have revealed a certain grouping of personality traits, including low-stress tolerance, dependency, negative self-image, and feelings of isolation and depression. A 1987 analysis of Swedish adoption studies has suggested that particular subtypes of alcoholism may be associated with the intensity of traits like novelty seeking, harm avoidance and reward dependence. (See also MILIEU-LIMITED (TYPE I) ALCOHOL-ISM.)

pharmacotherapy   Pharmacotherapeutic agents continue to be used as adjuncts for limited purposes in the treatment of alcohol dependence. Various agents have been tested over the years, but no pharmacotherapy has emerged as being effective in ameliorating long-term drinking behavior. Because it seems useful only in the short term, AN-TABUSE (Disulfiram) is no longer recommended for use alone in treating alcoholism. Antabuse seems to be effective in solidifying abstinent behavior until the patient seeks to establish an initial program of recovery.

Although Lithium carbonate therapy seemed to be a promising alternative when first researched in the 1970s, subsequent research has been ambivalent. Research continues into the usefulness of lithium medication for alcoholics with coexistent affective disorders.

Enoch Gordis, M.D., ed., *Sixth Special Report to the U.S. Congress on Alcohol and Health* (Rockville, Md.: NIAAA, 1987), pp. 125-126.

physicians   See HEALTH CARE PROVIDERS.

physiological models of etiology   Theories in this category postulate that some individuals are predisposed to develop alcoholism because of an organic defect: an underlying biological malfunction results in a craving for alcohol that in turn leads to alcoholism. Models in this group include GENETOTROPHIC ETIOLOGICAL THEORIES, ENDOCRINE ETIOLOGICAL THEORIES and genetic theories (See GENETICS).

It is difficult to measure physiological differences between alcoholics and nonalcoholics because researchers must use those who are already alcoholic for their studies. The results of testing may therefore be due to the consequences of alcohol abuse rather than to physiological differences antecedent to this abuse. To date there is no clear evidence about what role physiological variables play in alcoholism. (See also PSYCHOLOGICAL MODELS OF ETIOLOGY, SOCIOCULTURAL MODELS OF ETIOLOGY.)

pilsner beer   Now generally used as a generic name for any light lager beer, the term originally was applied only to a product brewed in Pilsen (Plzen), in what is now Czechoslovakia.

Pilsner beer originated during the Middle Ages, when Slavic peoples developed an especially light beer because of a lack of barley, which forced them to combine a high proportion of wheat with the malted barley in the cereal mash from which they brewed their beer. At the time private brewing rights were an especially sensitive issue in Bohemia, which is today western Czechoslovakia. Attempts to restrict private trade in beer resulted in the brief Parsons War of the 14th century, a struggle by monasteries to protect their brewing rights.

Modern pilsner beer dates from the 19th century, when, in response to similar restrictions, families in Pilsen joined together to form a cooperative brewery. That venture lasted until World War II ended its ability to export and brought about its collapse. Today the only true pilsner beer is brewed under the brand name "Pilsner Urquell," but because of its long and distinguished reputation other brewers have adopted the label "pilsner" to describe their finest beers.

Plymouth gin   See GIN.

Poland   In 1987, per capita consumption of ABSOLUTE ALCOHOL, based on total population, ranked Poland 24th among 47 countries with a rate of 7.2 liters per person. Due to the cultural preference for vodka and other liquors, the country ranked third in the same survey for consumption of spirits. In consumption of wine and beer, Poland ranked below most of the same countries: 30th and 36th, respectively.

Very little information is available concerning alcohol abuse in Poland. According to a 1981 report in the *New York Times*, the consumption of alcohol in Poland had been increasing for the last several decades. At the time of the report, the Polish people consumed seven times as much alcohol as they did a decade before. In 1987, the rate of cirrhosis was 13.4 per 100,000 for men and 6.8 for women, slightly lower than the U.S. rate.

Until recently, Poland had no comprehensive program designed to combat alcoholism. However, stemming in part from attacks by leaders of the independent labor movement, the communist government began a campaign against alcohol abuse. Information is not yet available as to similar programs by the new non-communist government.

port   A fortified wine (18% to 20% alcohol) traditionally associated with the town of Oporto on the upper Douro river in Portugal. It is now produced in the United States, Australia and South Africa as a varietal wine.

Fermentation of port wine grapes begins when they are pressed and the grape sugars and juice combine. The process is then halted at an early stage, and brandy is added to the mixture of grape juice and wine. The mixture is then aged by one of two methods: in bottles or in casks.

When the quality of the grape harvest is exceptional, the grapes are reserved for a vintage port. In this case the mixture of grape juice, wine and brandy is kept for one year and then refortified and bottled. Vintage port is aged in bottles for 15 to 20 years in order to produce the desired strength and flavor. Further aging is considered a mark of distinction, and vintage ports survive in the bottle for more than 40 years before separating and deteriorating.

When the quality of the harvest is less exceptional, the grapes are used to make tawny port, the only variety produced outside of Portugal. Tawny port is the product of a blend of grapes from several years aged in wooden casks for periods shorter than those for vintage port. After 12 years of aging the wine is considered tawny port, but it is commonly bottled earlier and sold as ruby port. These wines usually survive less than five years in the bottle.

Port from Oporto is usually bottled and sold in Britain, where a taste for it developed when wars with France halted importation of French wines. There are a number of different blends and types, including a white port. It is often drunk like wine, but because of its alcoholic strength it is also commonly mixed with lemon or tonic water and poured over ice.

portal cirrhosis   Also known as Laennec's, nutritional or alcoholic CIRRHOSIS, portal cirrhosis is the most common form of cirrhosis among alcoholics.

porter   A dark and sweet ALE that is in effect a combination of ale and stout, although more carbonated than stout. Porter is supposed to have originated in response to the demands of 18th century market porters in London for a "half and half" potion of ale and stout. Now generally referred to as "dark ale," "porter" remains the designation of stouts in Ireland that are more carbonated than those intended for bottling and exportation.

postintoxicated state   A term with no specific meaning that is used to refer to the agitated state immediately following a drinking bout, to a HANGOVER or to the symptoms attributed to WITHDRAWAL.

postnecrotic cirrhosis   A form of CIRRHOSIS that follows hepatitis or other inflammations of the liver. It may occur in alcoholics.

pot still   A primitive form of still used especially in the DISTILLATION of Irish grain whiskey and Scotch malt whisky. The heat of the fire is applied directly to the pot containing the wash.

potentiation   A condition that occurs when the net effect of two drugs in combination is greater than the effect of each drug added together (see SYNERGY).

predisposition   See GENETICS.

pregnancy   See FETAL ALCOHOL SYNDROME (FAS).

pricing (of alcohol)   See ALCOHOL BEVERAGE CONTROL LAWS.

problem drinker   A person who experiences personal, social and/or professional problems whenever he or she drinks. The problems may take various forms, such as frequent excessive drinking or infrequent excessive drinking usually resulting in extreme drunkenness, accidents, bizarre or antisocial behavior etc. Often the distinction between problem drinking and ALCOHOLISM is a matter of degree or depends on the number of symptoms exhibited. Problem drinkers are almost always heavy drinkers (see HEAVY DRINKER), but there are exceptions.

problem drinking   See PROBLEM DRINKER.

progression   While the disease of alcoholism follows no single course in every individual affected, a number of the same symptoms are often observed. Alcoholism progresses through several stages of varying length, depending on the individual.

During the onset of alcoholism it may be difficult to distinguish the alcoholic from the heavy drinker. However, the alcoholic has a stronger emotional response to alcohol and often, from the very first drink, attaches an unusual amount of significance to it. One sign of alcoholism may be that alcohol has become a requirement for pleasure or enjoyment rather than an accompaniment to it. Alcohol becomes the highlight of social activities and is soon used for other reasons, such as to cope with stress or anxiety. In time the alcoholic

becomes severely intoxicated with increasing frequency and usually is annoyed with those commenting on his intake or behavior.

In the second stage the alcoholic begins to hide his drinking; to drink faster; and to start drinking earlier in the day. Along with a growing preoccupation with alcohol comes a strong feeling of guilt, leading him to become defensive about his drinking and hostile when it is alluded to by others. The alcoholic may try to gain control of the problem by rationing intake, changing brands or trying to prove he can "take it or leave it." He may use other drugs as a substitute for alcohol in an attempt to attain abstinence.

As the illness progresses, BLACKOUT becomes common. Irresponsible behavior and excessive emotion are often observed at this time and the alcoholic may make great plans for the future in an attempt to restore his image in the eyes of others.

Next the alcoholic experiences LOSS OF CONTROL over drinking. He plans his life around alcohol in order to maintain a high intake, commonly leaving work and dropping old friends who show concern about his behavior. Supplementation of alcohol with other drugs frequently increases. Social, mental and occupational disintegration commonly occur as the alcoholic seeks more and more isolation. Eventually physical complications of the disease often begin to dominate the psychological and social aspects. Finally the alcoholic "reaches bottom," at which point he may either seek help or drop out of normal life entirely. Ultimately the alcoholic may drink himself to death.

American Medical Association, *Manual on Alcoholism* (1977), pp. 34-36.

proof   A measure of the amount of ABSOLUTE ALCOHOL in a distilled spirit. As early as the 15th century, drinkers demanded "proof" that a liquor was fit (i.e., had a high enough alcohol content) for human consumption. To this end various tests were devised. Oil was floated on liquor; if it sank, that was

A Comparison of Common British and American Proofs

British Proof	American Proof	Absolute Alcohol (Percent)
100.0	114.2	57.1
87.6	100.0	50.0
76.0	86.8	43.4
70.0	80.0	40.0

"proof" of the spirit's strength. If a liquor-soaked cloth could be easily and satisfactorily ignited, that was "proof." If a mixture of liquor and gunpowder burned smoothly with a blue flame, it was exactly on the mark; if it blew up, it was over "proof."

John Clarke in 1725 and Bartholomew Sikes in 1803 pioneered modern measurements of proof in Britain with the use of hydrometers. The height at which the hydrometer floated in the liquor determined the proof.

The British and the Americans use different systems for measuring proof. The British system is based upon a comparison of equal volumes of water and liquor at 51°F. If the liquor weighs 12/13th as much as the water, it is 100° proof. In Britain liquor bottled for home consumption has a lower proof and a slightly lower alcohol content than that intended for export. For example, Scotch whisky meant for the domestic market is bottled at 70 proof (40% alcohol), but that exported to the United States is 86.8 proof (43.4% alcohol) under the American system. British proof is lower than American proof for spirits of equal strength.

The American system is based upon the percentage of absolute alcohol in the liquor at 60°F. The proof measurement is double the percentage of alcohol: 100 proof = 50% alcohol.

psychodrama A form of GROUP THERAPY in which individuals act out their problems before a group under the direction of a therapist. Usually a member with a problem portrays himself while a different member takes the role (father, wife, boss) of another person associated with the member and his problem. The two (or more) "performers" then act out their roles. Sometimes roles will be reversed, with the member acting out a role other than his own. The purpose of psychodrama is to heighten the member's awareness of his problem through performance, giving it an immediacy that simple discussion lacks.

psychological models of etiology A category of theories, with sociocultural theories and physiological theories, on the etiology of alcoholism. Most psychological theories are based on the assumption that some element in the personality structure leads to the development of alcoholism. There has been a search for an "alcoholic personality" that would have a built-in vulnerability to the development of alcoholism. However, most studies have failed to find any specific personality traits that clearly differentiate alcoholics from either normal people or those with problems. There is evidence that once drinking patterns have been established, alcoholics display certain common traits. These include low stress tolerance, dependency, negative self-image, and feelings of insecurity and depression. Since most studies have been made on populations of alcoholics, however, it is not clear whether these traits precede alcoholism or are a result of it.

There are several different psychological models of etiology. Under the psychodynamic model alcoholism results from unconscious tendencies that are expressed in excessive consumption of alcohol. A major theory, developed by Freud, posits that alcoholism is related to a traumatic experience in early childhood caused by a poor parent-child relationship. The loss or absence of the object of love, usually the mother, in the oral stage creates demands in the alcoholic that are insatiable. As a result his interpersonal relations eventually fail and are interpreted by him as rejection. A consequent loss of self-esteem develops and there is an enormous rage stemming from the original rejection by the parent figure. He turns a desire to destroy that figure upon himself and consumes his rage in alcohol (see ORAL FIXATION). Another theory holds that alcoholics suffer from strong feelings of inferiority and powerlessness but are inhibited from expressing their hostility or aggression. Alcohol, which provides improved feelings of self-esteem and confidence, allows them to feel competent and to express their impulses.

It has also been postulated that alcoholics experience unusually strong conflicts between dependency needs and a desire for autonomy. Drinking allows dependency through sociability and dependence on alcohol, and at the same time it gives rise to feelings of independence and strength.

Behavioral models propose that alcoholism is a conditioned behavioral response which can be helped through modification of stimuli and reinforcement in the environment (see BEHAVIORAL LEARNING THEORY).

David J. Armor, J. Michael Polich and Harriet B. Stambul, *Alcoholism and Treatment* (New York: John Wiley and Sons, 1978), pp. 17-29.

Morris E. Chafetz and Harold W. Demone, Jr., *Alcoholism and Society* (New York: Oxford University Press, 1962), pp. 19-29, 39-56.

public drunkenness   The public inebriate is the most visible alcoholic and therefore has symbolic importance for all alcoholics. Public intoxication has been regarded as a legal matter ever since the English Parliament prescribed punishment in 1606 for that "loathesome and odious sin of drunkenness" that is "the root and foundation of many other sins" (Kurtz and Regier). This approach was brought to America and remained the general rule for three centuries. Around 1910 the merit of treating alcoholics as criminals was questioned, and attempts were made to develop alternative facilities. These attempts failed and local police departments continued to be responsible for public inebriates. Several other attempts were made through the years to provide treatment for public inebriates but without success. By 1965 arrests for public drunkenness numbered more than 1.5 million annually, accounting for approximately 40% of all nontraffic arrests (FBI). In the 1960s alcoholism gradually came to be regarded as a disease and in the early 1970s the Uniform Alcoholism and Intoxication Act was established, which provided the states with "a legal framework within which to approach alcoholism and public intoxication from a health standpoint." The Declaration Policy of the Uniform Act states, "It is the policy of this State that alcoholics and intoxicated persons may not be subjected to criminal prosecution because of their consumption of alcoholic beverages but rather should be afforded a continuum of treatment in order that they may lead normal lives as productive members of society" (National Conference of Commissioners on Uniform State Laws). To date this act, which decriminalizes public drunkenness, has been adopted by a majority of states (Finn, 1985) and the District of Columbia.

While the Uniform Act has worked to reduce the number of alcoholics incarcerated for drunkenness, it has not been sufficient to eliminate the public inebriate problem. The act has helped to destigmatize alcoholism and to increase access to treatment, but it has not brought chronic public inebriates into treatment voluntarily or kept them in treatment. One reason is that not enough funds have been appropriated to develop the needed resources for treatment. Skid row programs in particular are often given low priority, and public inebriates are frequently written off by treatment programs as unlikely to recover.

John R. DeLuca, ed., *Fourth Special Report to the U.S. Congress on Alcohol and Health* (Rockville, Md.: National Institute on Alcohol Abuse and Alcoholism, 1981), pp. 155-156.

P. Finn, "Decriminalization of Public Drunkenness: Response of the Health Care System," *Journal of Studies on Alcohol*, 46:(1985), 7-23.

N. R. Kurtz and M. Regier, "The Uniform Alcoholism and Intoxication Treatment Act: The Compromising Process of Social Policy

Formulation," *Journal of Studies on Alcohol* 36, no. 11 (1975):1421-1441.

National Conference of Commissioners on Uniform State Laws, *Uniform Alcoholism and Intoxication Treatment Act* (Washington, D.C.: U.S. Government Printing Office, 1973).

National Institute on Alcohol Abuse and Alcoholism (NIAAA) Information and Feature Service, *Client Funds Contribute to Public Inebriate Program* (July 18, 1980).

————. *Public Inebriate Conference Addresses Range of Issues,* August 28, 1981, p. 3.

Ernest P. Noble, ed., *Third Special Report to the U.S. Congress on Alcohol and Health* (Rockville, Md.: National Institute on Alcohol Abuse and Alcoholism, 1978), pp. 329-330.

U.S. Federal Bureau of Investigation, *Uniform Crime Reports for the United States, 1965* (Washington, D.C.: U.S. Government Printing Office, 1965).

Puerto Rico   The U.S. island commonwealth now has the world's highest per capita consumption of ethanol in the form of distilled spirits, and consumption of distilled spirits continues to rise while that of beer and wine has been falling. The Puerto Rican Department of Addiction Services has attributed this trend to several factors, including a deeply ingrained tradition of drinking in Puerto Rico and a general tolerance of drunkenness as well as the dramatic change affecting all spheres of life since Puerto Rico became a U.S. territory following the Spanish-American War in 1898. Various kinds of alienation associated with drinking have been traced to the Spanish-speaking population's constitutional link with the English-speaking U.S. authorities. The social problems affecting most of the population are also considered a contributing factor. About 53% of the population lives in densely populated urban areas (1980 census), and unemployment is high—15% of the work force in 1988. The per capita income in 1988 was $5,287, and 62% of the population was below the official U.S. poverty level in 1980.

Finally, the most popular alcoholic beverage in Puerto Rico is rum. The national preference for this strong and highly intoxicating drink over all other alcoholic beverages is perhaps the most important factor in Puerto Rico's widespread alcohol abuse problem.

The largest consumers of alcohol in Puerto Rico are classified as "heavy drinkers," rather than alcoholics, by the Department of Addiction Services. Three out of every 10 drinkers fall into the heavy drinker category, defined as an individual who consumes 4 drinks or more at least one or two times a week. Statistics show that these heavy drinkers tend to be males between the ages of 20 and 49. The age at which this group begins to drink has been constantly declining.

The Assistant Secretariate for Alcoholism Treatment in Puerto Rico served 18,471 clients in 1988–89, 46% of whom had been referred to it after being apprehended for drunken driving.

To help deal with the toll of these alcohol-related problems, the Department of Addiction Services was established in 1973 to coordinate efforts aimed at treatment, rehabilitation and prevention of alcohol and drug abuse.

R

railroad accidents   A 1979 study of drinking practices among 234,000 railroad employees suggested that 44,000 (19%) of the workers were problem drinkers. Between 1975 and 1984, alcohol or drug impaired employees were implicated in 48 train accidents/incidents that resulted in 37 deaths, 80 nonfatal injuries and $34.2 million in damage (*Federal Register*, 1985). The NATIONAL INSTITUTE ON ALCOHOL ABUSE AND ALCOHOLISM believes that "because of the existing latitude in the current reporting system, alcohol and drug involvement in railroad accidents and injuries is very likely to go undetected or unreported in a significant number of cases." The *Federal Register* (1985) concedes that their figures probably understate alcohol and drug use among railroad workers.

In November 1988, the U.S. Department of Transportation announced regulations imposing in 1989 random drug tests for the nation's four million private transportation workers, including airline pilots and navigators, interstate truckers, bus drivers, and railroad engineers and conductors. Opponents have promised to challenge the regulation in the courts.

Rand Report   In June 1976 the Rand Corporation of Santa Monica, Calif. issued a highly controversial report on alcoholism. The report was sponsored and subsidized by the National Institute on Alcohol Abuse and Alcoholism (NIAAA), which contracted with the Rand Corporation, an independent, nonprofit research organization, to participate in an analysis of its comprehensive alcoholism treatment program begun in 1971, to codify and examine the results and to release the findings. The Rand Corporation published its report under the title *Alcoholism and Treatment.* [1]

While many aspects of the report were attacked, two conclusions in particular drew outraged response. The first was that after treatment some alcoholics were able to resume "normal" drinking. The second was that the rate of relapse for alcoholics who resumed normal drinking was no higher than the rate for alcoholics who adopted a program of complete abstinence.

Challenges came from all quarters. Dr. Marvin A. Block, former head of the Committee on Alcoholism of the American Medical Association, stated that "an addict trying to use the drug alcohol again runs the risk of becoming addicted again." The National Council on Alcoholism and the American Medical Association's Committee on Alcoholism jointly stated, "Abstinence from alcohol is necessary to recovery from the disease of alcoholism." Alcoholics Anonymous declined comment but quoted from its own "Big Book": "We have seen the truth demonstrated again and again; 'Once an alcoholic; always an alcoholic.' Commencing to drink after a period of sobriety, we are in a short time as bad as ever." Other adverse comments from professionals in the field ranged from "almost criminal" to "death on the installment plan" to "haphazard study."

Dr. Ernest P. Noble, who was the director of the NIAAA at the time the findings were released (but not when the study was funded), expressed his concern over "the manner in which the results of this report have been isolated and construed to suggest that recovered alcoholic people can return to moderate drinking with limited risk." He added that "until further definite scientific evidence exists to the contrary. ... I feel that abstinence must continue as the appropriate goal in the treatment of alcoholism. Furthermore, it would be extremely unwise for a recovered alcoholic to even try to experiment with controlled drinking."

Supporters of the report emphasized the scientific professionalism of its approach and findings, hailing the fact that some long accepted dogma was receiving much needed scrutiny. They saw this challenge as an opportunity, a new, unemotional step toward more productive research and a continuing dialogue between those who held opposing points of view. Yet in a generally favorable review of the report, Drs. Samuel B. Guze and Spencer T. Olin of Washington University, St. Louis pointed out that "its [the report's] initial distribution to the news media and its tone of exaggerated optimism ... raise misgivings which the authors could easily have avoided."

---

[1] The Rand Report, *Alcoholism and Treatment,* was republished in 1978 by John Wiley and Sons, Inc. The reissue included an important new section: "Appendix B. Reaction to the Rand Report on 'Alcoholism and Treatment,'" which contained documents and analyses by supporters and detractors of the original report. The appendix was prepared by the authors of the original report.

Conclusions and Considerations of the Rand Report

The major conclusions and considerations of the Rand Report were as follows:

Treatment

Clients who underwent treatment had a slightly higher rate of remission than those who had a single contact with a treatment center, with some slight additional advantage as the amount of treatment increased. ("Single contact" and "untreated" are used synonymously throughout the report.)

Remission rates

1. Untreated clients; "natural" remission: 50%
2. Untreated clients with AA attendance: almost 70%
3. Treated clients: 70%

The remission results for treated clients varied little from one treatment program to another.

The report contained a new "definition of remission that includes both abstention and 'normal' drinking. Normal drinking means consumption in moderate quantities commonly found in the general nonalcoholic population, provided no serious signs of impairment are present."

Relapse analysis

1. " ... relapse rates for normal drinkers are no higher than those for long-term abstainers. ..."
2. " ... [the study] suggests the possibility that for some alcoholics moderate drinking is not necessarily a prelude to full relapse. ..."

Other Conclusions

1. The study was unable to find a pattern upon which to conclude that one program was best for one type of client and another was best for another client.
2. It was found that "recovery from alcohol dependency may depend upon mechanisms quite unrelated to the factors that led to excessive drinking in the first place."

Future Considerations

1. Total abstinence is not the only goal of treatment *if* future research confirms the initial conclusions of the survey.
2. If the survey's initial conclusions are confirmed, research is needed to determine which alcoholics can return to normal drinking.
3. If the theory that the results of most programs are uniform is true, not only as applied to an individual's drinking but other behavior patterns as well, less expensive methods of treatment can be used.

Throughout the report, the authors pointed out the limitations of their sample: that the size of the sample was small and the time frame of the study was limited; that the conclusions about behavior were based on observation and not on controlled, experimental data; and that future behavior would not necessarily conform to the data in the survey.

Critics' Conclusions

Critics of the report seized upon the limitations noted by the authors. What the authors viewed as a careful delineation of the limitations of their survey was seen by its detractors as factors that made the report not merely worthless but actively harmful. They claimed the facts did not support the conclusions and that the result was a "legitimized" report which deluded alcoholics into believing that they could resume drinking, with disastrous results. A summary of some of their objections follows:

Size of Sample

Critics of the report challenged its use of "on the basis of over 1000 subjects ..." and countered that the Rand sample was "(actually a subsample of only 161 former patients, not randomly selected and from only 8 out of 45 government alcoholism treatment centers) with about 74% of all interviews at 4 sites (a large proportion over the phone by opinion interviewers who had 2-weeks training)."

Time Period

Noting "the time period for the Rand study *was 18 months after entering treatment*" [emphasis theirs], critics pointed out that Drs. D. L. Davies and John A. Ewing had examined the possibilities of alcoholics resuming social drinking in independent studies over substantially longer periods and had rejected them.

Makeup of Sample

Critics have questioned whether all the clients in the Rand sample were in fact alcoholics.

The Ongoing Controversy

In January 1980 a second Rand Report, *The Course of Alcoholism: Four Years After Treatment,* was published. In this new study (actually a continuation of the previous one) many of the conclusions of the original report were modified, although it was not, as some of the original report's critics claimed, a "retraction." The authors suggested a greater complexity of the issues involved than originally reported and characterized the report as another phase of a continuing program of study by the Rand Corporation. (See also RAND REPORT II.)

Rand Report II   Critics of the first RAND REPORT pointed out two major defects: the study's follow-up period of six months was too short (a substantial number of clients were still in treatment) and only about one-quarter of all clients in the study responded to the six-month follow-up interviews. As a result the National Institute on Alcohol Abuse and Alcoholism (NIAAA) drew up a series of contracts for follow-up studies of sample clients involved in the first Rand study. The subjects were to be interviewed at 18 months and then again four years after entry into treatment. The second report

was completed by the same three doctors who worked on the first report: J. Michael Polich, David J. Armor and Harriet B. Stambul. The four-year study of alcoholism, which cost about $500,000, was the most extensive and comprehensive of its kind to date.

The findings of the study were published in January 1980 in a 361-page report entitled *The Course of Alcoholism: Four Years After Treatment.* This second report received much less criticism and press coverage than the first Rand Report, and the picture that emerged from it was less optimistic than that of the earlier report. While the first report concluded "clients of NIAAA treatment centers show substantial improvement on a number of outcome indices," the second stated that "although there is a frequent improvement there is also frequent relapse and much instability."

The second Rand Report nevertheless confirmed the earlier finding that some alcoholics are able to return to social drinking. But for most, the study showed, total abstinence seemed to be the surest method of maintaining remission. The second report substantiated the need for a more flexible definition of "recovering from alcoholism," but it significantly refined the earlier report's conclusions.

Rand Report II found that there were at least two different types of alcoholics and that what worked best for one type might not work as well for the other. In general the second report showed that alcoholics who were under 40 years old and who had shown relatively few symptoms of alcohol dependence within the month previous to treatment were less likely to relapse into alcoholism if they resumed social drinking. Those under 40 who attempted total abstinence were more likely to relapse. For alcoholics over 40 with strong symptoms of alcohol dependence, total abstinence offered the best prognosis. (Dependence symptoms included tremors and shakes, morning drinking, blackouts, missed meals because of drinking, loss of control while drinking, and continuous drinking for 12 hours or more.)

In other words, for younger unmarried alcoholics who are often under social pressures to drink, the attempts to maintain abstinence may be more stressful than nonproblem, social drinking; older married alcoholics are more likely to be encouraged by their spouses to remain abstinent and less likely to relapse than if they attempted controlled drinking.

Remission Rates

Four years after entering treatment at one of eight centers around the country, 46% of the approximately 900 men studied were found to be "in remission" from the symptoms of alcoholism, with 28% abstaining and 18% drinking socially. Among those engaged in social drinking, half consumed more than 4 drinks a day and half drank less than that.

The study showed that alcoholics who entered treatment programs were highly unstable in their ability to refrain indefinitely from problem drinking. Many relapsed several times during the four years, and most entered other treatment programs from time to time. Only 28% of the respondents were free of alcoholism problems both at 18 months and at four years after they first entered treatment and only 15% were in continuous remission for the entire four years. (Of the latter 7.5% maintained abstinence for the entire four-year study period and 7% maintained low amounts of consumption or a mixture of abstinence and low consumption without adverse consequences or symptoms.) Fifty-four percent were having drinking problems four years after they first started treatment. Nevertheless there was some improvement, since upon admission to treatment at least 90% were drinking with serious problems.

Alcoholic men who regularly attended AA meetings had the highest rate of long-term abstinence: 57%. However, while regular attendance at AA sessions offered the best chance for recovery from alcoholism, those who attended the sessions were just as likely to have relapsed as those who had not attended. Alcoholics who regularly went to AA

were not more likely than others to be free of serious alcohol problems later. (Permanent abstinence is fairly infrequent, even for regular AA members.) Those who attended AA irregularly or sometime in the past were even more likely to have relapsed at four years than those who had never been to the organization's meetings.

Alcoholics who abstained for less than six months had the worst prognosis; these "short-term" abstainers had a much higher rate of relapse and many more alcohol-related deaths than either long-term abstainers or social drinkers.

The authors of the second Rand Report emphasized again that the study "does not recommend a particular treatment approach and does not recommend that any alcoholic resume drinking." It does, however, raise questions about the nature and treatment of alcoholism.

rational emotive therapy (RET) Sometimes used to treat alcoholics undergoing REHABILITATION, rational emotive therapy (RET) is an educational, rather than psychodynamic or medical, model of psychotherapy. RET, developed by Albert Ellis and Robert A. Harper, asserts that people have choice in their lives, that most of their conditioning consists of self-conditioning and that the therapist serves to help them see a range of alternatives to their behavior. RET stresses a semantic approach to understanding; change in semantic usage is stressed so as to concomitantly change thinking, emotions and behavior. The therapy shows people how they behave self-defeatingly and how they can get themselves to change. Both individual and small-group therapy as well as large workshops and lectures are used.

reality therapy   Developed by a psychiatrist, Dr. William Glasser, who has worked extensively in corrections and education, reality therapy is based on the theory that behavior is generated by what happens in the mind rather than what happens in the real world. Individuals attempt to control the world outside through use of a control system made up of millions of perceptions, including perceptions of what is ideal. A gap between the perceived world and the ideal world is called a "perceptual error" and is sensed through comparison. Actions are adjusted so that the perception from the real world eventually corresponds with the mind's idealization. Alcohol, according to Glasser, blots out perceptual error and destroys the comparing system that shows the difference between what a person wants and what he or she gets. In reality therapy alcoholics are taught alternative solutions to drinking and learn to fulfill their needs through ALCOHOLICS ANONYMOUS or other forms of REHABILITATION.

Anita Diamant, "Reality Therapy," *U.S. Journal of Drug and Alcohol Dependence* 5, no. 9 (November 1981): 13.

recovery   Defining recovery from alcoholism is not a simple matter, since there is no clear-cut definition of alcoholism. It is difficult to say that an alcoholic who no longer drinks has recovered because at some future date he quite possibly may resume alcoholic drinking or he may be suffering from some other alcohol-related impairment. Some definition of recovery, however, is desirable in order to distinguish alcoholics who are still drinking excessively from those who are managing to deal with their problem.

Recovery is defined differently by different groups; for those who espouse the philosophy of ALCOHOLICS ANONYMOUS or who are strong believers in the ADDICTION model of alcoholism, only complete abstinence for a long period constitutes recovery. AA, in fact, prefers to use the term "recovering alcoholic," indicating a process that leads to a change of attitudes and behavior that makes it possible to begin a new and positive way of life, one day at a time. Other schools of thought, however, hold that once the psychological causes of alcoholism are removed and reconditioning

has been achieved, the alcoholic can return to nonalcoholic, social drinking.

The best definition of recovery appears to be a stable REMISSION of symptoms over a period of time. This means that for a relatively long period the patient has exhibited no alcoholic drinking behavior; emphasis is on the drinking rather than on the social condition of the patient, although there are those who use social criteria to judge whether or not an alcoholic has recovered.

Recovery seems to be a distinct stage in the course of alcoholism and is not strongly related to the social and psychological factors that may cause alcoholism in the first place. A great deal of the recovery process appears to depend on the individual, who must recognize the costs of his alcoholism, allow a breakdown of the defenses that prolong his alcoholism (see DENIAL) and commit himself to change.

David J. Armor, J. Michael Polich and Harriet B. Stambul, *Alcoholism and Treatment* (New York: John Wiley and Sons, 1978).

red wine   Red wine is produced by fermenting grape juice with the grape skins and a certain quantity of grape stems. It is the presence of the skins, in particular, that gives red wines their color, for the juice of virtually all grapes is colorless. Unlike red wines, white wines are produced by fermenting grape juice without the grape skins, and rose wines are usually produced by fermenting grape juice that has had limited contact with grape skins. The alcohol content of red wines ranges from 10% to 14%.

Once grapes intended for red wines have been gathered, they are crushed and loaded into fermenting tanks with the skins and, according to the tannin content desired, some amount of stems from the vine. This wine "must" is then mixed with less than one part per thousand of an antiseptic, usually sulfur dioxide, to eliminate all but the alcohol-tolerant natural yeasts in the grapes. Other active yeast cultures are sometimes added at this stage to assist fermentation.

In the fermentation process the sugars in the grapes are converted into alcohol and carbonic gas by the yeasts. The skins and the stems are forced to the surface of the fermenting must by the gas (some red wine vinters use a grill to keep this "cap" submerged in the fermenting vat for greater flavor and color). Fermentation of red wines lasts anywhere from two days to two weeks, with wines that are intended for long aging being fermented the longest. When the grape juice has attained the desired level of alcohol content and has extracted the desired level of tannin from the skins and stems, the solids are separated and the process follows the same steps used in the production of white and rose wines (see WINE).

Most experts agree that the finest red wines in the world are those bottled in the Bordeaux district of France. Located in the southeastern part of the country, this area is officially about 90 miles from north to south and about 60 miles from east to west. The soil is an especially favorable one for growing grapes, consisting of a sandy topsoil and a clay subsoil, and it is drained by the Garonne and Dordogne rivers that meet to form the Gironde, a term sometimes considered synonymous with Bordeaux. The principal subdivisions of the region include Medoc, Saint-Emilion and Pomerol, which produce red wines exclusively, and Graves, which produces both red and white wines. Second only to Bordeaux is Burgundy, located in eastern France, which holds the distinction of being the oldest wine-producing region in the country. It is hillier than Bordeaux, and the finest vineyards in Burgundy are those located midway up the slopes of the hills. The most famous vineyards in the region are those of the Cote d'Or, a range of low hills to the southwest of Dijon. Among the notable Cote d'Or red wines is Beaujolais, a fruity red wine usually drunk young. It is sometimes sold after incomplete fermentation as a seasonal wine known as *beaujolais nouveau*. The other principal red wine regions of France are the Rhone Valley,

in the southeast, and the Loire Valley, in the southwest.

Besides French wines the famous European red wines are mostly Italian. These include the northern Piedmont wines, such as Barbaresco, Barbera and Barolo; the Tuscany wines from central Italy known as Chianti; and wines from the Lago di Garda region, such as Bardolino and Valpolicella. Other leading European red wines include the Riojas from Spain, the Dao red wines from Portugal and the Tokay wines from Hungary. Numerous red wines are also produced in places as far apart as Rumania and South America, and the wine regions of the United States have for many years produced red wines from grape vines imported from Europe.

rehabilitation   After   DETOXIFICATION a patient is physically free of alcohol dependence, but his or her behavior patterns and needs have not been changed. Therefore some sort of follow-up treatment is usually necessary to enable the patient to function soberly in society without relapsing into alcoholism. Patients may be encouraged to go to ALCOHOLICS ANONYMOUS meetings, to individual or group therapy or to both. Some enter special rehabilitation centers for a certain length of time in order to establish ways of living without alcohol.

The same facilities may provide detoxification and rehabilitation services, but generally these services are offered in different places. Detoxification usually takes place in a hospital setting and lasts about a week. Rehabilitation is normally accomplished in a special environment, where patients dress in their everyday clothes (as opposed to hospital clothing) and keep regular hours. The duration of rehabilitation in private treatment centers varies, but usually the stay is longer than for detoxification, often up to four weeks. Many private treatment centers are located in non-hospital settings, often in rural areas or other pleasant surroundings. Some, however, are in general hospitals.

Modes of treatment also vary, but almost all emphasize the value of Alcoholics Anonymous and AL-ANON. Alcoholism is treated as a disease, patient responsibility is stressed and abstinence is a primary aim. During rehabilitation patients receive a good deal of instruction about alcoholism and living without alcohol. Most programs encourage family involvement and aftercare following the inpatient stay, either through therapy, AA or both.

In a private rehabilitation treatment center the patient is surrounded by an enormous support system. He is also removed from the pressures of daily life and the presence of alcohol and is surrounded by people who understand the problem. This environment may help him to restructure his life, but because it is so sheltered a return to normal living may be difficult. There, with the availability of liquor stores and bars and daily pressures of work and social life, he may soon return to drinking. Or the opposite may occur: the alcoholic may feel that he is cured and free of alcohol problems and therefore can return to drinking normally, the so-called "flight into health," which generally leads to a relapse. This is one reason why aftercare is stressed and why it is important to involve the family.

relapse   A return to uncontrolled drinking by an alcoholic in a stage of recovery. Recovery may mean complete abstinence or the ability of an alcoholic to drink moderately without LOSS OF CONTROL. Alcoholism is a disorder characterized by a tendency to relapse.

Relapse seems related to a number of factors, including personality, environmental influences, physiology, social attitudes and the availability of alcohol. Social pressures during treatment that tempt the alcoholic to break abstinence are particularly important. Individual problems or even positive achievement may lead to relapse. An alcoholic may begin to feel confident after he has made progress in treatment, and attempt to tackle a difficult situation that he is not ready to handle, causing him to return to drinking. Or he may relapse because of depression or frustration. But an alcoholic generally is not considered to be completely recovered until he is able to maintain continued sobriety without relapse.

religion   The attitudes of different religious groups toward the use of alcoholic beverages vary widely. A number of religious groups regard drinking alcohol as immoral or sinful; total abstinence is the accepted norm in these groups. Other religions permit members to use alcohol socially, as well as in such ceremonies as Holy Communion, which may involve the drinking of wine. All the major religions frown on drunkenness. The views on alcoholism of most of the major religions in the United States follow:

Roman Catholics

The Roman Catholic Church permits the use of alcoholic beverages by all except those who are diagnosed as alcoholic. Use is considered to be appropriate on holidays and during celebrations. Alcoholism is considered a disease involving the physical, mental and spiritual qualities of man. The church recommends INTERVENTION and treatment followed by membership in ALCOHOLICS ANONYMOUS.

A national study of American drinking practices conducted in 1969 by the Rutgers Center for Alcohol Studies found relatively high proportions of drinkers and heavy drinkers among Catholics. Those who attended church more often were more likely to report infrequent drinking and consumed less per occasion. The incidence of alcoholism among Catholics appears to be determined by ethnic background; both Irish Americans and Italian Americans are primarily Catholic but Irish Americans have a higher rate of drinking problems while Italian Americans have a lower rate.

Greek Orthodox

The Greek Orthodox Archdiocese permits the use of alcoholic beverages and finds them traditionally appropriate following a wedding or baptism. Occasional overindulgence of alcoholic beverages is tolerated but not condoned. Alcoholism is considered an illness to be understood and treated.

Jews

Judaism permits the use of any alcoholic beverage that conforms to the laws of kashruth. The only prohibition against drinking is during fast days, when consumption of food is not allowed. There are several religious ceremonies that require the use of wine, including the Passover seder and certain rites of passage. People who do not consume alcoholic beverages may substitute grape juice on occasions when wine is required. There is one holiday during the year when excessive intake of alcohol is sanctioned: Purim.

Jews have the lowest percentage of abstainers of any of the major American religions. They also have a very high proportion of light drinkers and the lowest proportion of heavy drinkers. The rate of alcoholism among Jews is very low.

Protestants

The Protestant position on the use of alcohol varies from sect to sect. Many sects that preached abstinence at one time have switched to an emphasis on moderation. In the aforementioned survey liberal Protestants demonstrated a drinking pattern somewhat similar to that of Catholics, although there were fewer heavy drinkers. Conservative Protestants had a large proportion of abstainers and a low proportion of heavy drinkers.

Methodists

The Methodist Church is the largest American church proscribing the use of alcohol. In a 1980 position paper, the United Methodist Church stated: "We affirm our long-standing support of abstinence from alcohol as a faithful witness to God's liberating and redeeming love for persons. ... The drug dependent person is an individual of infinite human worth in need of treatment and rehabilitation and misuse should

be viewed as a symptom of underlying disorders for which remedies should be sought." An increasing number of younger Methodists, however, are using alcohol, sometimes in an extreme manner, possibly indicating that the ideal of abstinence implies conversely that any drinking is equivalent to drunkenness.

Baptists

The American Baptist Association forbids the use of alcoholic beverages and considers alcoholism a sin rather than a disease, a "violation of God's will and word toward man." The Christian Life Commission of the Southern Baptist Convention also holds that use of alcohol is immoral but it advocates the demonstration of "love, patience, and forgiveness of God in dealing with alcoholics."

Presbyterians

In 1970 the General Assembly of the Presbyterian Church noted the obligation of persons to make responsible decisions regarding the use of alcoholic beverages, the danger of excessive drinking and the responsibility to seek constructive solutions for social problems related to the use of alcoholic beverages.

Mormons

The Mormons recommend strongly against the use of alcohol. Only 21% of Mormon males who attend church weekly consume alcohol.

Jehovah's Witnesses

Jehovah's Witnesses allow the use of alcohol, since according to their teachings, God's word does not require total abstinence. Wine is a symbol of happiness in the Bible; therefore it is not forbidden to mankind. However, the Witnesses caution strongly against alcohol dependence and abuse.

Friends United Meeting (Quakers)

The position of the Friends toward the use of alcohol is based on the belief that the human body is the temple of the Lord and that to mar it is to dishonor Him. Any pleasurable or exhilarating effects produced by intoxicants are temporary and tend to react injuriously on both mind and body. Total abstinence is advocated and the entire liquor traffic is considered detrimental to human welfare.

Seventh-Day Adventists

Seventh-Day Adventists forbid the use of alcohol. Temperance is considered to be a way of life and is equated with self-control through Jesus Christ.

Morris E. Chafetz and Harold W. Demone, Jr., *Alcoholism and Society* (New York: Oxford University Press, 1962), pp. 84-99.
John Langone, *Bombed, Buzzed, Smashed, or … Sober* (Boston: Little, Brown and Company, 1976), pp. 48-49.
Unpublished correspondence with spokesmen of various denominations (1982).

remission   Remission is defined as "a relatively prolonged lessening or disappearance of the symptoms of a disease," according to *Webster's New World Dictionary* (Second College Edition, 1984). In the field of alcoholism the term "remission" is often used instead of "recovery," since it is extremely difficult to say when someone is completely recovered from alcoholism (see RECOVERY). Remission is generally measured in terms of drinking behavior rather than social behavior.

There are two conflicting schools of thought on what constitutes remission. One school, including ALCOHOLICS ANONYMOUS, believes that remission exists only when an alcoholic is in a state of complete abstinence. Another school, which includes the authors of the RAND REPORT, expands the definition of remission to cover an alcoholic who is able to maintain a course of "normal drinking," defined as a daily consumption of less than 3 ounces of ABSOLUTE ALCOHOL, no tremors and no serious symptoms related to drinking, such as frequent episodes of blackouts, absences from work or drunken-

ness. Both abstainers and those who drink at normal levels without showing signs of alcoholism are considered to be in remission.

Reproductive Functions   Alcohol use takes a toll on the entire endocrine system, including reproductive functioning. Disturbances in the menstrual cycle, infertility and loss of secondary sex characteristics are often witnessed in alcoholic women. A study of a national sample of women revealed that heavy menstrual flow, dysmenorrhea (painful menstruation) and premenstrual discomfort increase with drinking (Wilsnack et al.). It is known that chronic intoxication can lead to amenorrhea (absence of menstruation) and can also result in pathologic changes in the ovaries and ovulation. A history of miscarriage or still-birth, premature birth, birth defects and infertility was found to be associated with high levels of alcohol consumption. Drinking during pregnancy can also lead to mental retardation in children (see also FETAL ALCOHOL SYNDROME).

Alcoholism can also lead to marked reproductive dysfunction in men, including impotence, low testosterone production and sperm counts, and testicular atrophy (Cicero). Alcohol-related changes in hormone levels has also been associated with enlargement of breasts in male alcoholics. Even acute or periodic heavy drinking may result in impotence and reduced levels of testosterone. (See also HORMONES, MALE SEX.)

T.J. Cicero, "Alcohol-induced Deficits in the Hypothalmic-Pituitary-Luteinizing Hormone Axis in the Male," *Alcoholism (NY)* 6 (1982): 207-215.
R.W. Wilsnack, S.C. Wilsnack and A.D. Klassav, "Drinking and Reproductive Dysfunction among Women in a 1981 National Survey," *Alcoholism Clinical and Experimental Research* 8 (1984): 451-458.

rhinophyma   (New Latin, from Greek *rhinos* nose + *phyma* swelling.) A skin condition of the nose characterized by swelling, redness and, often, broken capillaries. It is sometimes, but not always, caused by heavy drinking over a prolonged period. W. C. Fields was a well-known victim of rhinophyma; in his case it was called by its popular name—"whiskey nose."

RNA Ribonucleic acid. One of the two main types of nucleic acid (the other is DNA), RNA is an organic substance found in the chromosomes of all living cells. RNA plays an important part in the storage and replication of hereditary information and in protein synthesis.

rose wine Having an alcohol content from 12% to 15%, rose wine is produced by fermenting grape juice that has had limited contact with grape skins. Since the juice of virtually all grapes is colorless, the difference in color between red and white wines stems from the fact that the former is fermented in a "must" that includes grape skins and the latter is fermented in a "must" of pure grape juice.

Once grapes intended for rose wines have been gathered, they are crushed to extract their juice, which is allowed to mix with the grape skins for a period of 12 to 36 hours. Then the solids are separated and the process continues through steps similar to those used to produce red or white wines (see WINE). Today some inexpensive rose wines are produced in bulk by simply adding a tasteless red coloring, called cochineal, to finished white wines. The product is a wine that resembles true rose in color but lacks the flavoring tannins extracted from the grape skins in the traditional process.

The most prized rose wines come from the Anjou, Bordeaux and Tavel wine districts of France. The south Tyrol region of Italy is also noted for its rose wines, and both Portugal and Spain produce roses in virtually all of their wine districts. A number of rose wines made in California are considered comparable to the European varieties. Inexpensive rose wines are produced in nearly all wine-producing countries, often by means of artificial coloring, as a way to dispose of marginal wines.

rubbing alcohol A nondrinkable solution made with isopropyl alcohol rather than ethyl alcohol, or ethanol. Rubbing alcohol is used externally for medicinal purposes. It has a bad taste and is poisonous.

rum An alcoholic beverage made from the distillation of fermented products of sugar cane. Most frequently rum is produced by distilling molasses, but it is also sometimes made from the juice of sugar cane.

It is thought that the term "rum" has its origins in the British word "rumbullion" (meaning tumult or uproar), or possibly "rumbustion" (meaning rum). When rum was first manufactured in the West Indies during the early 17th century, it was referred to as "kill devil" and, later, "rumbullion." By 1667 "rumbullion" had been abbreviated to "rum."

Rum is often thought of as the drink of romantics and adventurers. In the 18th century, British sailors used rum as the base of their daily GROG, which consisted of rum, water and lemon juice. Rum was also the alcoholic beverage consumed in the largest quantities by the American colonists just before the Revolutionary War. It has been estimated that at that time the colonists, women and children included, drank 3 3/4 gallons of rum per person per year (Tannahill).

Throughout the 17th and 18th centuries until the time of the Revolution, rum was the key item of trade in what was dubbed the New England Rum Triangle, a trade route between New England, Africa and the West Indies. In this trade route rum manufactured in New England was shipped to Africa, where it was exchanged for slaves. The slaves in turn were taken to the West Indies, where they were traded for the molasses needed to make rum. This trade route was a major source of revenue for New England shipowners. Their business as well as that of the rum manufacturers thus suffered greatly during the Revolutionary War, when molasses supplies were cut off from Cuba and the West Indies. At the time that the American rum business began to suffer, the newly emerging American WHISKEY business began to flourish, since it did not depend upon foreign trade for its essential ingredients. The rum business never fully recovered, and whiskey gradually replaced rum as the most popular alcoholic beverage in the United States (see RYE, BOURBON).

In the 19th century, rum acquired a rather low reputation in the United States. Its name became a synonym for intoxicating beverages in general, and a hard drinker was referred to as a "rum sucker" (in the 1850s) and a "rummy" or "rummie" (in the 1860s). In addition cheap saloons were sometimes called "rum holes" (1830s). During the 20th century, "rumdum" (1920s) and "rumbag" (1940s) became slang expressions for a drunkard. The popular card game GIN RUMMY made references to both gin and rum.

Although rum is produced in most countries where sugar cane is grown, the chief producers on an international scale are the islands in the West Indies, of which the more important sources are Barbados, Jamaica, Trinidad, Cuba, Puerto Rico, Haiti and the Virgin Islands. Other important producers of rum are Indonesia, Australia, South Africa, Germany and the United States.

Basically there are two kinds of rum: white rum, which is usually dry and light-bodied; and dark rum, a richer, more full-bodied product that ranges in color from amber to mahogany. The best known white rums are made in Puerto Rico, Cuba and the Virgin Islands, and the best known dark or heavier rums are made in Jamaica, Barbados and Guyana (formerly British Guiana). In the United States, white rum is preferred, but in other northern countries, such as Britain and Germany, heavier rums are favored.

The many variations within the two basic types of rum are the result of differences in the quality of the ingredients used and in the methods of fermentation, distillation and aging. The two most common fermentation techniques are the Demerara (the name of a river and an early name for Georgetown in Guyana) method and the Jamaican method. In the Demerara method, which takes approxi-

mately 48 hours, the molasses or sugar cane is prepared into a liquid known as wash, to which sulfuric acid and ammonium sulfate are added to encourage fermentation of the alcohol yeasts. In the Jamaican method, neither sulfuric acid nor ammonium sulfate are added to the alcohol yeasts in the wash to hasten fermentation. As a result fermentation by this method takes 10 to 12 days.

Distillation may take place in either a pot still or a continuous still. If a pot still is used, two distillations are required, as the product of the first distillation is too weak for consumption. Distillation in a continuous still is more economical and the product can be brought to any strength with only one distillation.

All rum is colorless when first distilled. Many rums, especially those sold in the United States, are not aged or aged for only a year. These rums are often colored by the addition of artificial caramel coloring. The better rums are aged in oak casks for three to 20 years, during which time they acquire some of their color, but even these more expensive rums are subjected to artificial coloring. The proof of rum ranges from 80 to 150.

In the United States, rum is most often used in mixed drinks, especially those made with fruit juices, although it is occasionally drunk straight. It is also employed as a flavoring agent in meat marinade, dessert sauces and ice cream.

Reay Tannahill, *Food in History* (New York: Stein and Day, 1973).

rum fits   Convulsive seizures associated with WITHDRAWAL from alcohol, rum fits appear to develop in a minority of alcoholics (13%, according to two studies). The seizures are of the grand mal type, in which the patient loses consciousness. They often occur in clusters, although the number can vary from one to several repeated attacks. The seizures may start as early as 12 hours after abstinence but usually develop during the second or third day. Once the period of seizure activity has passed, the patient is free of convulsions until another cycle of drinking occurs. Rum fits may be followed by the last stage of withdrawal: DELIRIUM TREMENS.

Rush, Dr. Benjamin   One of the signers of the Declaration of Independence, Rush was a Philadelphian and arguably the most respected American physician of his time. He was the first American to call chronic drunkenness a distinct, progressive disease. His powerful tract, "An Inquiry into the Effects of Ardent Spirits on the Human Mind and Body," published in 1784, identified alcohol as addictive and claimed that once an "appetite" or "craving" for it became fixed, the victim lost all control over his drinking. His argument that drunkenness was the fault of the drinker only in the early stages of the disease, before alcohol took command, was a radical departure from previous thinking. It became a classic in temperance literature.

Rutgers Center of Alcoholic Studies One of the nation's formost centers for the study of alcohol abuse and alcoholism and a central source of research information, the Rutgers Center of Alcohol Studies is located in Piscataway, New Jersey (See also Appendix 2).

rye whiskey   A spirit distilled from a grain mash that contains at least 51% rye. The production of rye, along with that of bourbon and corn whiskeys, is an American adaptation of European distilling practices. Today most Canadian whiskey is also produced from a grain mixture like that used to make American rye.

Rye was probably the first grain whiskey distilled in America. Its beginnings date from the arrival of Irish and Scottish immigrants in colonial Pennsylvania. Because of the difficulty involved in transporting grain to market, distillation of grain into whiskey became economically advantageous. Nevertheless during colonial times rye was slow to challenge rum in popularity. During the American Revolu-

tion rum distillers were forced to shut down for lack of foreign sugar cane supplies, and rye distillers, who required only domestic products, came into prominence.

As a result of abundant grain supplies the popularity of rye whiskey rose steadily during the 1790s and quickly attracted the interest of the new government as a source of revenue. In 1791 the first whiskey tax was levied. A segment of the population, however, firmly believed that having won independence from Britain, they had a right to distill whiskey. The result of this conflict was the Whiskey Rebellion of 1794, in which distillers based in western Pennsylvania refused to pay the new tax. President George Washington was forced to dispatch a military contingent to confront the distillers in Pittsburgh, but the distillers dispersed and their leader, David Bradford, fled the state. Thus rye whiskey was the provocation of one of the first domestic political crises in American history and the means by which the new government demonstrated its federal authority.

Rye remained the leading spirit in the United States through the Civil War years. Its principal domestic competitor, after the decline of rum, was corn whiskey, a raw tasting, colorless spirit that was sold without aging. Rye's appeal was advanced during the early 19th century, when distillers began to age the product in charred barrels. This process moderated the alcoholic taste of rye and gave it an amber color. After the Civil War bourbon began to rise in popularity. Distilled like rye but from a greater proportion of corn grains, bourbon was originally a compromise between harsh corn whiskey and smoother but more expensive rye.

Rye distillers usually buy malted barley from specialized manufacturers rather than malt their own, as in Scotland and Ireland. The grain mixture, predominantly rye filled out with barleys, corns and oats, is cooked into a mash called "slurry," either by atmospheric cooking in an open vat, pressure cooking or a continuous cooking method that utilizes steam. Once cooked, the slurry is cooled and poured into fermentation tanks, which traditionally have been made of wood but today are usually stainless steel. Yeast is then added, and fermentation produces the "distiller's beer" from which the spirit can be distilled, generally in large patent stills. The rectified spirit is then barreled in charred white oak. Rye is almost always blended, a process that involves combining the products of several distillations, for consistency of flavor and appeal to a broad market.

S

safety belts and alcohol use
Alcohol use is correlated with a lower rate of safety belt use. Although only 7.2% of sober drivers involved in fatal accidents in 1984 were wearing safety belts, a significantly smaller proportion of the drivers who had been drinking (2.2%) wore such restraints, according to the National Highway Transportation Safety Administration. (See also DWI)

sake
A "rice wine" fermented from a mixture of rice and malted barley. Sake is not a true wine because a raw material other than grapes is used, but since the fermented beverage is colorless or amber in color and slightly sweet, it resembles a wine in both appearance and taste.

Sake, which has an alcohol content of about 17%, is the traditional alcoholic beverage of Japan and probably originated as an outgrowth of the brewery fermentation of beers there. It is generally served in ceramic cups and often heated.

saloon
(From French *salon* drawing room, lounge; Italian *salone* room.) Generally speaking, a saloon is a place to which the public may go for any specified purpose, such as billiards, boxing or other recreation. In the United States the term "saloon" is used generally to refer to a shop where intoxicating beverages are sold and drunk, usually without meals. In this usage, saloon and BAR are synonymous.

In Britain the expression "saloon bar" is used to refer to the best of the bars in an ordinary public house. Bar in this sense simply means the counter over which drinks are sold.

schnapps
(German *Schnaps* spirits, brandy, gin, liquor.) A broad term that may refer to any distilled alcoholic beverage. Often the beverages called schnapps resemble Holland GIN. They are usually a colorless grain distillate and have a fiery taste. Schnapps is particularly associated with Sweden, Norway, Denmark, the Netherlands and northern Germany, each of which produces its own variety. In Scandinavia the term "schnapps" is sometimes used to mean AQUAVIT.

Alternate spellings of schnapps include *schnaps* (Denmark) and *snaps* (Sweden).

Scotch whisky
A spirit distilled in Scotland from a fermented mash of cereal grains. Scotch whisky is considered by many to be the finest in the world. Unlike American, Canadian or Irish whiskeys, true Scotch whisky is usually identified by the region where it is produced. There are four principal regional varieties: Highland malts, Lowland malts, Campbeltowns and Islays. They all differ subtly because of their various water sources, grain contents, methods of malting and distillation processes.

Although the precise origins are obscure, methods of distilling grain whiskies probably came to Scotland directly from Europe, rather than from Europe through Ireland, as many believe. This must have taken place during the early Middle Ages, although there is no written record of whisky in Scotland until the Scottish Exchequer Rolls of 1494. By that time the liquor was already accepted as a legal unit for business transactions.

The Scottish Parliament, then independent of England, first attempted to tax whisky as a source of public revenue in 1644. The trade proved impossible to control, and illicit distillation became a matter of fierce local pride. Increasing English intervention in Scotland brought further attempts to tax the whisky trade, which eventually led to riots in Edinburgh in 1713. England's control over Scotland became complete with its victory at the Battle of Culloden in 1746, giving the English control over the Scottish Highlands and the especially prized malt whiskies produced there. In 1823 the Duke of Gordon proposed legalization of local distillation and taxation of the trade at a new lower rate. Once in effect, this program slowly eroded the illegal whisky trade. In 1860 the first organized exportation of Scotch whisky to England began, and since that time whisky has become one of Scotland's most valuable exports.

There are two principal types of Scotch whisky: POT STILL and PATENT STILL, distinguished by the methods used to produce them. Pot-still malt whiskies are the most traditional sort. The only grain employed in their manufacture is barley that has been malted over peat, making them smokier in taste than the Irish malt whiskeys, which are cured over charcoal. Pot-still Scotch whiskies are nevertheless extremely heavy in taste and usually blended with the lighter, patent-still types. Only a small amount of pot-still Scotch whisky, intended for a limited but affluent market of aficionados, is bottled. Most commercial Scotch whiskies are produced by patent stills and employ a mixture of grains that includes only a portion of malted barley. The different grain content and distillation process of patent-still Scotch yields a lighter and clearer product, which for a time was challenged by some as not deserving of the designation "Scotch" or "Scotch whisky." Both pot-still and patent-still distillates are matured in casks made of either new wood or woods previously used to age sherry or whisky. Virtually all Scotch whiskies commercially available are blends of several types and distillations; only those called "self-whiskies" are the yield of a single distillation.

sedative   Any of a number of substances, including alcohol, that acts as an irregular depressant of the central nervous system (CNS). A depressant is a substance that diminishes or stops normal body function. Sedatives are irregular because they do not depress all parts of the CNS at once but work first on the cerebrum and cerebellum, second on the spinal cord and finally on the vital centers. Sedatives (or soporifics) include liquid substances, such as alcohol; solid drugs, such as barbiturates; and gases, such as ether and chloroform. All these belong to a group of compounds that produces similar pharmacological behavior. All sedatives are potentially addicting compounds with associated severe withdrawal syndromes. However, for physical dependence to develop, the daily intake of each drug must exceed a certain threshold level. Sedatives are probably the most widely abused drugs in Western nations.

When alcohol or other sedatives enter the system, they first work on the brain to depress psychomotor-activity, thereby relieving anxiety and tension. For approximately two to three hours the blood alcohol (or sedative) level rises and a sedative, or calming, effect is produced. Then, however, the level of alcohol or sedative in the blood begins to fall and the psychomotor activity level increases. This second effect usually lasts for about 12 hours after consumption of a large drink. Thus the sedative effect is always followed by an agitating effect, which often leaves the subject more tense than before he or she began drinking. This is one reason why people who have been drinking often crave another drink and also why a drink can relieve some of the agitating effects of a hangover. The agitation is multiplied with each pill or drink, and at high levels of consumption the individual may become tremulous, have hallucinations or—at severer levels, when unable to get another drink— experience DELIRIUM TREMENS (WITHDRAWAL).

Aside from alcohol the most commonly used (and abused) sedatives are barbiturates and the so-called minor tranquilizers, such as

Librium and Valium, which were at first believed to be safer than barbiturates but subsequently found to produce similar patterns of addiction and withdrawal.

The most commonly abused barbiturates are short acting agents, such as pentobarbital (Nembutal), secobarbital (Seconal) and amobarbital (Amytal). The first barbiturate (barbital) was made available for medical use in 1903, followed by a second (phenobarbital) in 1912. By 1914 German medical literature already contained a description of barbiturate withdrawal syndrome.

Valium is one of the most widely prescribed drugs in North America. Dependence on Valium can develop even at prescribed doses. After 10 to 14 weeks larger doses may be required to maintain a patient's feeling of well being. After four to six months abrupt cessation may result in physical withdrawal symptoms. Discomforts, such as tremors, agitation, stomach cramps and sweating, can occur for two to four weeks.

Perhaps the most dangerous effect of barbiturates and other sedatives occurs when they are used in combination with alcohol, which multiplies the potency and dangers of each drug (see SYNERGY). In humans a level of 100 milligrams of ethanol per 100 milliliters of blood combined with a level of 0.5 milligrams of barbiturate per 500 milliliters of blood has proved fatal. This compares to lethal blood levels of alcohol alone of 100 to 800 milligrams per 100 milliliters and of phenobarbital alone of 10 to 29 milligrams per 100 milliliters.

Alcoholics with a high tolerance to alcohol have a similar tolerance to other sedatives (see CROSS-TOLERANCE). It takes a large amount of ether to induce surgical anesthesia in an alcoholic. In addition CROSS-ADDICTION occurs in alcoholics, for one sedative drug can be replaced with another that produces approximately the same effects. The rate increase in the number of people, especially young women, addicted to both Valium and alcohol is alarming, especially in view of the low threshold level for fatalities when these substances are combined. Nevertheless some

Minimal (or Threshold) Doses of Some Generalized Depressant Drugs Required for Establishment of Physical Dependence

Drug	Threshold Dose (mg/day)
pentobarbital (Nembutal)	400
secobarbital (Seconal)	400
ethchlorvynol (Placidyl)	2,000*
ethinamate (Valmid)	13,000*
glutethimide (Doriden)	2,500*
methyprylon (Noludar)	2,400*
chlordiazepoxide (Librium)	300
diazepam (Valium)	100
meprobamate (Miltown, Equanil)	1,600–2,400

*The true threshold dose may be lower; the value given is merely the lowest thus far reported to have produced physical dependence.

doctors continue to prescribe sedatives to patients with emotional problems, often without bothering to inquire about their drinking habits. Complaints of anxiety, nervousness and insomnia may in fact reflect the early stages of alcoholism, and treatment with sedatives only exacerbates the problems of an alcoholic.

As late as 1978 the October issue of the Federal Drug Administration's *Consumer* said that such minor tranquilizers as Valium "are of value in treating such conditions as alcoholism and epilepsy. . . ." (See also DRUGS; PHARMACOTHERAPY.)

P. M. Broughton, G. Higgins, and J. R. P. O'Brien, "Acute Barbiturate Poisoning," *The Lancet* 270 (1956):180-184.

Stanley E. Gitlow, "A Pharmacological Approach to Alcoholism," *A. A. Grapevine,* October 1968.

R. C. Gupta and J. Kofold, "Toxicological Statistics for Barbiturates, Other Sedatives and Tranquilizers in Ontario: a 10-year Survey," Canadian Medical Association Journal 94 (1966):863-865.

Frederick G. Hofmann, *A Handbook on Drug and Alcohol Abuse: The Biomedical Aspects* (New York: Oxford University Press, 1975).

Frank A. Seixas "Alcohol and Its Drug Interactions," *Annals of Internal Medicine* 83, no. 1 (July 1975):86-92.

sedativism   Addiction to one of the sedatives, which includes alcohol. The term "sedativism" is also used to describe dual or multiple addiction to sedatives. (See also SEDATIVE, CROSS-ADDICTION.)

self-esteem   See PSYCHOLOGICAL MODELS OF ETIOLOGY.

sensitivity   The term sensitivity is sometimes used to explain why an individual may be prone to alcoholism. However, it is generally used without being well defined and may refer to TOLERANCE or to an inability to abstain from drinking. There is usually a more precise alternate term. J.P. Chaplin, Ph.D., in his Dictionary of Psychology, defines sensitivity: "The condition or ability involved in being receptive to stimuli."

James P. Chaplin, *Dictionary of Psychology* 3rd rev. ed. (New York: Dell, 1985), p. 418.

Serenity Prayer   A prayer used by members of ALCOHOLICS ANONYMOUS in times of stress or anxiety. It is used to open AA meetings and is often analyzed in group discussions. The full text is as follows: "God grant me the serenity to accept the things I cannot change, the courage to change the things I can, and the wisdom to know the difference."

The prayer is based on one delivered by the Protestant theologian Reinhold Neibuhr (1892-1971) at a church near Heath, Mass. in the summer of 1934. Since then it has been widely quoted. It reads: "O God, give us serenity to accept what cannot be changed, courage to change what should be changed, and the wisdom to distinguish the one from the other."

server training   See TIPS.

sex   Small doses of alcohol may relax people and help remove inhibitions, thereby allowing freer expression of sexual inclina-

TYPICAL EFFECTS OF ALCOHOL ON SEXUAL FUNCTIONING

ACUTE

1. May increase sexual desire, if taken in small quantities.
2. In larger quantities, sedates the cerebral cortex, reducing inhibitions, but also impeding translation of external sexual information for the hypothalamus.
3. Interferes with transfer of sexual functioning messages from the brain to other parts of the central nervous system and sex organs.
4. Relaxes necessary muscle tension.
5. In males, may impede or prevent erection; in females, may interfere with or prevent lubrication.
6. Reduces serum testosterone level.
7. Prevents orgasm.
8. Reduces sexual desire.
9. Produces sedation to the point of sleep.
10. In males, can aid in development of psychological impotence.

CHRONIC

1. Any of the above, occurring on a repeated basis, can become chronic and permanent.
2. Liver damage—reduces serum sex hormone levels.
3. Brain damage—prevents sexual messages from being transmitted and/or interpreted.
4. In males, may produce testicular atrophy.
5. In males, may produce permanent impotence.

SOURCE: "Sexual Dysfunction and the Alcoholic," *Focus on Alcohol and Drug Issues,* July–August 1981.

tions. In this respect alcohol can be considered an indirect aphrodisiac, anesthetizing the control centers of the brain. Alcohol is also used as an excuse by some individuals for engaging in normally forbidden sexual activity without taking responsibility for their actions.

While small doses of alcohol may enhance sexual relations, after a number of drinks men may be unable to complete the sex act. Shakespeare noted the subject of alcohol *vis a vis* sexual activity in *MacBeth* (II, iii):

Macduff: What three things does drink especially provoke?

Porter: Marry, sir, nose-painting, sleep and urine. Lechery, sir, it provokes and unprovokes; it provokes the desire, but it takes away the performance.

It is a tribute to Shakespeare's acute observation that after almost four centuries of further scientific endeavor, not much can be added to his description of the effects of alcohol on sexual activity. (See also HORMONES, MALE SEX; REPRODUCTIVE FUNCTIONS; WOMEN.)

sherry   A fortified wine varying in color from amber to dark brown, sherry is the product of fermented palomino grapes to which spirits distilled from other wines have been added. Historically Spanish sherry has been extremely popular in Britain since the 15th century, and the present name is an Anglicization of Jerez, or Jerez de La Frontera, a town in southern Spain where the wine was first produced. The name is now a generic designation, applied to specific wines made around the world, but purists insist that true sherry is still produced only in Jerez, Sanlucar de Barrameda and Puerto de Santa Maria, all just west of Gibraltar.

Palomino grapes for sherry production are allowed to stand for one day after harvesting to increase their acidity before crushing. After pressing, gypsum is added to the grape juice to increase acidity, and because of the technique it takes longer to ferment sherry than to

ferment most other wines—about three months. After "racking" (when the clear liquid is siphoned off from the dregs), the fermented grape juice secretes a sediment known as *flor*, a fungus that is considered essential to the character of sherry wines.

Once filtered, sherries are fortified by the addition of Spanish brandies, or the distilled spirits of other wines, to give them an alcohol content between 15% and 20%. They are then aged in wood for up to two years. After this initial aging period all sherries are blended in a *bodega* containing casks of different local varieties and vintages. Blended sherry is often shipped from Spain to Britain for final processing and bottling.

Sherry comes in two varieties, dry (*fino*) and sweet (*oloroso*). The first sort, dry in taste and light in color, includes the varieties called Manzanilla and amontillado. The second sort, artificially sweetened and darker in color, includes the varieties called amorosa and "cream" sherry. Dry sherry is usually drunk as an aperitif, and *oloroso* is generally consumed as a dessert wine or a substitute for port. Marginal sherries are commonly used as cooking wines.

shot   A single drink of liquor usually consumed in one gulp. A shot glass or jigger generally holds 1 1/2 ounces of liquor. When used as an adjective, shot can mean drunk or afflicted with a hangover.

skid row   The term "skid row" originated in Seattle, Wash. The city's first sawmill was built in 1852 in the Pioneer Square district near Puget Sound. The logs were dragged into the mill over a set of tracks, or skids, and the road along which they were dragged became known as Skid Road (which later was shortened to Skid Row). As Seattle grew, the Pioneer Square area became dilapidated and the term took on the meaning it has today: a hangout for alcoholics and vagrants.

One false stereotype of alcoholics is that they are mostly skid row bums, sleeping in doorways without a home or job. In reality only about 3% to 5% of alcoholics are true skid row types and many skid row bums are not alcoholics.

sleep   While a small amount of alcohol taken before going to bed may help relieve tension and thus induce sleep, a large quantity is likely to have the opposite effect. Alcohol blocks REM (rapid eye movement) sleep, or dreaming sleep, which is necessary for complete rest. Alcohol anesthetizes the control centers that regulate sleep and dreaming.

A team of investigators at the University of Florida College of Medicine found that drinking results in lower levels of oxygen in the blood and periods when breathing is arrested for 10 seconds or more. This condition is called sleep apnea, and while it is usually harmless in healthy people, it could prove fatal for those with serious pulmonary or cardiac conditions. Sleep disturbances are a common feature of alcohol dependency, particularly insomnia and fatigue during the day. Use can also result in increased incidence of bed wetting, nightmares, sleep terrors and snoring.

"Drinkers' Sleep Disturbed, Not helped, by Nightcap," *The Journal* 11, no. 1 (Toronto, Jan. 1, 1982): 7.

slip   An ALCOHOLICS ANONYMOUS (AA) term used to describe a member's taking a drink (which almost always leads to several drinks) after a period of sobriety through total abstinence.

sloe gin   See GIN.

small intestine   See GASTROINTESTINAL TRACT.

Smith, Dr. Robert (1899-1970)   Cofounder with BILL WILSON of ALCOHOLICS ANONYMOUS. A native of Vermont, Robert Holbrook Smith (known to grateful AA members simply as Dr. Bob) was an Ohio surgeon. He had become a desperately ill drunk, with-

out hope, until he met a stockbroker from New York, Bill W., who urgently needed a fellow alcoholic to help him maintain his own sobriety. They met in Akron, Ohio, in the spring of 1935, and out of that chance meeting there gradually developed the rough outlines of a concept that, through trial-and-error, was eventually to become AA. Through it all, Dr. Bob was a steadying central figure. Thirty-five years later, on November 16, 1970, Robert H. Smith, M.D., died. But his influence on the worldwide AA program is permanent and profound.

smoking   People who drink heavily also tend to smoke heavily, and most alcoholics are heavy smokers. One study showed that more than 90% of male and female alcoholics were smokers. Another study found that 60% of all alcoholics smoked more than one pack of cigarettes a day and 30% smoked more than two packs (Bates).

There is a high incidence of pulmonary disease among alcoholics. It has been noted that in patients with severe alcoholism, chronic lung disorders, such as lung abscess, bronchitis and emphysema, are the most common problems other than liver disease (Pollard). Numerous studies have established the strong association between alcohol and tobacco consumption and cancers of the head and neck (see CANCER). It has been suggested that alcohol acts as a solvent and dissolves the tars in tobacco smoke, making them more available to the body tissues, particularly those in the head, neck and esophagus. Alcohol may alter the intracellular metabolism of the epithelial cells at cancer sites, resulting in an enhanced metabolic activation of tobacco-associated carcinogens. There is an apparent SYNERGY between alcohol and tobacco consumption that increases the risk of developing cancers of the upper alimentary tract and upper respiratory tract. According to some researchers, the risk of developing cancer of the mouth and throat among those who both smoke and drink is 15 times greater than the risk among those who neither smoke nor drink.

Heavy drinking appears to increase the urge to smoke, and therefore a high level of cigarette smoking may in some ways be attributable to the use of alcohol. Cigarette burns between the fingers are frequently exhibited by drunks who "nod off" while smoking.

According to the Surgeon General's 1989 report on smoking and health, the prevalence of smoking among adults decreased from 40% in 1965 to 29% in 1987. Surgeon General C. Everett Koop, has zealously campaigned in recent years for a "smoke-free society."

R. C. Bates, "Pathologies Associated with Alcoholism," *Quarterly Journal of Studies on Alcohol,* 27 (1966): 110.

C. S. Lieber, et al., "Alcohol-Related Diseases and Carcinogenesis," *Cancer Research* 39, no. 7 (July 1979): 2863-2885.

A. B. Lowenfels, M. Mohman and K. Shibutani, "Surgical Consequences of Alcoholism." *Surgery, Gynecology and Obstetrics* 131 (July 1970): 129-138.

G. D. McCoy and E. L. Wynder, "Etiological and Preventive Implications in Alcohol Carcinogenesis," *Cancer Research* 39 (July 1979): 2844-2850.

H. M. Pollard, W. A. Gracie, and J. C. Sisson, "Extrahepatic Complications Associated with Cirrhosis of the Liver," *Journal of the American Medical Association* 169 (1959): 318.

sober   Not under the influence of alcohol. The term is also used to describe an alcoholic who is no longer drinking. A person with a BLOOD ALCOHOL CONCENTRATION (BAC) of 0.05% or less is considered legally sober. However, someone with a BAC of 0.05% is not necessarily as sober as someone who has had nothing to drink.

sobering pill   See L-DOPA, AMETHYSTIC.

sobering up   Detoxification after drinking. To date no way of speeding up the detoxification process (other than by kidney dialysis) has been found. Coffee or a cold shower may wake up someone who is drunk, but he or she will still be drunk. It usually takes an hour for a 150-lb person to metabolize three-quarters of an ounce of absolute alcohol (see METABOLISM).

sobriety   Among alcoholics, and particularly among members of ALCOHOLICS ANONYMOUS, sobriety has a precise meaning. It refers to a state of abstinence in which the alcoholic is comfortable and secure, either free of a desire to drink or able to cope with such urges. The patient usually accepts outside help and support, including formal rehabilitation and therapy programs. AA insists upon the support systems of group fellowship and regular attendence at meetings as necessary to continuing sobriety.

The words SOBER and sobriety have been part of all languages as long as drunk and drunkenness, but in the view of AA and others, the definition has been narrowed and made more precise. In this context sobriety does not mean a state characterized by moderation in drinking or one short of intoxication—it means total abstinence. AA, among others, is firm in its belief that an alcoholic can attain sobriety only through total abstinence and that he can never resume "normal" drinking or CONTROLLED DRINKING. If he resumes drinking, in AA's view, that first drink will trigger a chain of events which will lead, perhaps not immediately but certainly eventually, to a return to active alcoholic behavior.

In this belief they have followed the lead of the TEMPERANCE societies, without embracing the moral and religious tenets of that earlier movement. However, just as the temperance movement changed the meaning of the word "temperance" from moderation to prohibition, AA has changed the meaning of the word "sober" from unaffected by liquor to absolutely free of liquor.

In AA sobriety begins after the alcoholic has taken his last drink, admitted that he is "powerless over alcohol" and begun to live a sober life. Length of sobriety, as counted in years, months and even days, looms large as a measure of the alcoholic's success in coping with his enemy—alcohol. Alcoholics joining the AA program are often urged to make "ninety meetings in ninety days," which translates into one meeting a day every day for three months. Thereafter the number of meetings to attend is up to the individual, although the recommended number continues to be high indefinitely. Many AA groups call special attention to attendance achievements at their regular meetings and award "ninety day" pins. Anniversaries—a year's sobriety, two years' and so on—are faithfully remembered and celebrated. Length of sobriety is thus a major concern in the lives of AA members, and while the groups are informally democratic, longtime sobriety confers a measure of seniority. Thus a woman of 40 with 20 years of sobriety has more of the authority of an "elder" than a man of 60 with only two years of sobriety.

While length of sobriety is used as a major reinforcement factor in AA, fears over the "interminability" of sobriety are an ever present danger. The prospect of "never having another drink as long as I live" can be depressing, even terrifying, and can lead to disaster. To counter this danger, AA focuses on short-term sobriety. "One day at a time" is the slogan used to help face down immediate desires to drink. The idea is to concentrate on remaining sober today without worrying about tomorrow. The same procedure is followed tomorrow and so on. Fears, doubts and anxieties must not be projected into the future. On the other hand, grandiose dreams and expectations of remaining sober are also considered dangerous. Sobriety is grounded in today and in a realistic assessment of today's pitfalls and opportunities.

One measure of sobriety is quality. There is "good" sobriety and "poor" sobriety. Good sobriety consists of staying sober, attending meetings and functions and participating in the activities of the group, and enjoying your sobriety and the fellowship of those like you. If you do these things, particularly if you make

an effort to do them properly and systematically, you are said to be "following your program" and the prognosis is good.

Poor sobriety is ignoring or fighting some, if not all, of the aspects of the program. This attitude may stem from a basic subconscious DENIAL of alcoholism, an inability to accept help or face up to reality of the situation. These are seen as symptoms of conflict and turmoil that may lead the alcoholic back to drinking. Another form of poor sobriety is "white-knuckled" sobriety, which means that the alcoholic stays sober through grim determination. He lives in constant fear of a relapse and thinks incessantly of drinking, often with the feared result.

The term "dry drunk" is often applied to those with poor sobriety. The dry drunk has "dried out" and is no longer drinking but that is the only step he has taken. The implication is that the "dry" drunk will soon be "wet," or active, again.

social class   In the United States different social classes have different attitudes toward drinking. It has been found that as education and income rise there is a rise in the number of drinkers and the frequency of drinking (with the exception of young males). Those in the upper socioeconomic groups do not regard drinking as a moral problem, as is often the case with members of the lower socioeconomic groups, and upper-class groups generally have more permissive attitudes toward drinking. There are more abstainers in the lower class; according to statistics in the first RAND REPORT *(Alcoholism and Treatment)* 52% of the population in the lower social class were abstainers, compared with 34% in the middle class, and 21% in the upper class. However, poor males under 25 are perhaps the most likely to encounter trouble with the police or society because of drinking.

As education and income rise, there is less difference between the drinking patterns of men and WOMEN. Drinking settings also differ according to class, with upper-class groups doing more drinking in cocktail party settings and lower-class groups engaging in more pub drinking. Alcoholics in the upper socioeconomic class appear less in official statistics because their style of drinking is less visible and is covered up by the stability of their jobs, marriages and residences. They are more likely to be protected by others close to them, who help to hide their alcoholism from their peers. (see PARA-ALCOHOLIC).

Social class also may play a role in treatment. The authors of the first Rand Report found that lower-class patients drop out of therapy more quickly than patients from the middle and upper class.

David J. Armor, J. Michael Polich and Harriet B. Stambul, *Alcoholism and Treatment* (New York: John Wiley and Sons, 1978), pp. 61-77.

social drinking   Social drinking usually refers to moderate drinking on social occasions. Alcohol stimulates sociability and relaxes inhibitions among people in groups. The term "social drinking" is also used to refer to drinking in a way accepted by a certain cultural group. Sometimes an individual participates in social drinking as a result of social pressures, at a cocktail party, for example, where one is urged to have a drink or to have another.

sociocultural models of etiology   The many theories about what causes alcoholism can generally be divided into three major groups: physiological, psychological and sociocultural. Sociocultural etiological theories postulate relationships between various factors in society and the incidence of alcohol use. For example, ethnic and cultural differences in the use of alcohol suggest that society plays an important role in the development of alcoholism. Different cultures have different attitudes toward alcohol, set different standards for what constitutes appropriate use of intoxicants, and provide greater or lesser environmental support for drinking. Jews, Mormons and Moslems have very low rates of

alcoholism, and the French have a very high rate. This disparity may be due to cultural proscriptions against alcohol in the case of the first three groups, and cultural support for high consumption of alcohol in the case of the last group.

Stress factors in a culture may also contribute to alcoholism. Individuals may react to a crisis situation generated by external events with an increase in consumption of alcohol. WOMEN in particular are likely to begin heavy drinking in response to a traumatic event. There is a cyclical relationship between social instability and alcoholism: heavy consumption in reaction to social stress in turn increases the deterioration of the social environment.

Family patterns are another social factor that plays a role in alcoholism. An unusually high incidence of familial alcoholism has been found in the backgrounds of alcoholics. While the part played by GENETICS cannot be ignored, there no doubt is also a strong social learning factor involved in the development of alcoholism.

Sociocultural etiological theories of alcoholism receive wide support among experts in the field today. However, they are generally considered in conjunction with physiological and psychological theories, since none of these alone can completely explain the causes of alcoholism.

solitary drinking   Drinking alone is generally considered to be a sign of a drinking problem. Those who often take a drink alone after work or before bed or who drink a beer or two while mowing the lawn are not usually classified as solitary drinkers. Drinking to excess is characteristic of solitary problem drinkers, since there are no social activities to divert them from almost continuous drinking. Then, too, many solitary drinkers choose to be alone as a way of escaping from other problems. These problems lead the solitary drinker into a cycle in which the seclusion, the drinking and the initial problems all feed on each other and contribute to a worsening of the original situation.

Often solitary drinking is distinguished from BAR DRINKING, and the activities of many alcoholics tend to fall largely within one of these two categories. While individual behavior may vary from time to time, distinctions have been made between those who seek out public places to do their drinking and those who drink at home. It has been suggested, although more documentation is needed, that those who are more outwardly gregarious in their drinking habits are more likely to seek out and be more comfortable in highly supportive and organized groups, such as ALCOHOLICS ANONYMOUS, when attempting to resolve their drinking problems.

sour mash   A particular grain mixture used to prepare the mash, or "wash," from which bourbon is distilled. The grain content of bourbon is at least 51% corn (Indian maize), with the remainder being made up of rye and malted barley. In sour mash bourbon this grain content is mixed with a residue from a previous distillation in order to encourage fermentation. The residue, called "slop," is acidic in taste and smell, and these characteristics, rather than the taste of the finished bourbon, give sour mash whiskey its name. The chief alternative to sour mash as an aid to fermentation is SWEET MASH, in which a high proportion of malted barley is blended with the corn and rye grains.

Spanish Americans   See HISPANICS.

sparkling wine   Wine that has been subjected to a second fermentation to make it effervescent and heavily carbonated. Champagne is the best known sparkling wine. It is now produced in all wine-growing countries and not just in the Champagne region of France. While Champagne is a white sparkling wine, there are also many red sparkling wines and rose, or "pink," sparkling wines. The alcohol content of sparkling wines is about 12% to 12.5%.

Wine has been produced in the Champagne district since the third century A.D., but sparkling wine is a relatively recent invention of the region. By most accounts, it originated in the 1690s and, according to tradition, was the work of Dom Perignon, a monk in the Haut Villers Abbey. He is also credited with the first use of cork stoppers, without which carbonation of effervescent wines in bottles would not be possible.

The discovery of sparkling wine most likely happened when a wine in the later stages of fermentation was bottled and stoppered with a cork. The effect of the carbonic gas produced by the continuing fermentation and retained in the bottle by a close-fitting cork would then have been obvious once the wine was opened. After it became desirable to produce such effervescent wines, the precise technique became a closely guarded secret. Sparkling wines did not gain popularity until the end of the 18th century. Since that time they have often been imitated in various fashions, which have included simply pumping a STILL WINE full of gas.

The traditional method of producing sparkling wines is to subject a chosen wine to a second fermentation in the bottle. In this case the chosen wine, called the cuvee, is bottled in especially thick glass, combined with controlled amounts of yeast and sugar and stoppered with a cork that is held in place by a wire wrapping. The wine is then aged for a period between one and three years. With a minimum loss of pressure the sediment produced by fermentation must be removed before shipment to market. For this reason the bottles are temporarily stored upside down, allowing the sediment to collect on the cork. The pressure in the bottle is reduced for a time by chilling it to about 25g F. Then, in a step called *degorgement,* the cork is pulled, the frozen yeast sediment is removed, the bottle is topped off with a clarified wine and sugar solution and a new cork is inserted.

Because of the costs involved in bottle fermentation, many sparkling wines today are produced by subjecting the cuvee to a second fermentation in large closed stainless steel tanks. Once fermentation has reached the desired level, the wine can be filtered in bulk, mixed with the clarified wine and sugar solution and then bottled. This method, called *cuve close,* is considered inferior to bottle fermentation because of the different contact of the wine with the yeast in the second fermentation.

The finest sparkling wine is of course French Champagne, a term that refers to a region recently broken into titular districts called Marne, Heute-Marne, Aube and Ardennes. Spain, however, produces a greater quantity of sparkling wines than France, many of which are red or rose. The Panades district in northeastern Spain is especially noted for its sparkling wines, and some argue that the sparkling wines produced at Cordorniu by the *cuve close* method of second fermentation actually predate all French sparkling wines. Portugal is also known for sparkling wines bottled in the southern Dao district, and in Germany such wines are bottled under the Perlwein and Sekt designations. Sparkling wines are also produced in most of the wine-producing areas of the United States, with New York state being the leader.

spirit still   The second and smaller of the two stills employed in some double-distillation processes. The first and larger still, known as a WASH STILL, produces a weak and impure distillate, called "low wine," that is usually strengthened and purified by further rectification in the spirit still. Passed once or repeatedly through the spirit still, the distillate is then collected in a final receiver vessel.

spirits   Originally the term "spirit" or "spirits" meant the essence of any substances. Now it is commonly used to refer to the alcoholic essence of a fermented substance from which it has been extracted. In a more general sense the term "spirits" is also a synonym for alcoholic beverages, as distinguished from the many varieties of chemical alcohols and denatured ethanols, which are nonpotable.

The alcohol content of all potable spirits is ethanol, a clear and colorless distillate. The variations in potable spirits are produced by impurities retained from the fermented mash, by flavorings added after distillation and by containers used for aging. The purest are the so-called natural spirits, which are flavorless and high in ethanol content.

The distinguishing feature of most common spirits is provided by the content of the fermented mash from which they are distilled. Gin and whiskey are spirits distilled from grains, brandy is a spirit distilled from wine, rum is a spirit distilled from sugar cane or molasses and vodka is a spirit traditionally distilled from potatoes. A variety of other fermented substances, such as agave or dates, are distilled throughout the world to produce less well-known potable spirits.

sports, alcohol use in   The American College of Sports Medicine (ACSM), a leading organization in sports medicine located in Indianapolis, Indiana, recently studied research that showed the effects of alcohol on physical performance. Its position stand report stated that:

Although athletes may consume alcohol to improve psychological function, it is psychomotor performance that deteriorates most. Information processing is consistently impaired. Small to moderate amounts of alcohol impair reaction time, hand-eye coordination, accuracy, balance and complex coordination or gross motor skills. Performance will be most adversely affected in sports that require rapid reactions to changing stimuli, such as basketball, football, tennis, golf and auto racing. Thus, while some people believe alcohol may improve self-confidence, the available research reveals a deterioration in psychomotor performance.

ACSM, in its publication *Alcohol in Sports: Position Stand* (1988), states that acute ingestion of alcohol will not substantially influence metabolic or physiological functions essential to physical performance; alcohol appears to have no beneficial effects on the metabolic and physiological responses to exercise.

American College of Sports Medicine, *Alcohol in Sports: Position Stand* (Indianapolis, Ind.: ACSM, 1988).

spouse abuse   Family violence in the United States is a significant and often ignored problem. American society tolerates a high level of violence in general and is usually unwilling to interfere in people's private lives. Spouse abuse consists of physical and mental injury of a wife or husband by a marital partner. The overwhelming majority of such abuse involves the battering of wives by husbands. Estimates in 1985 of all spouse abuse determined that one severe assault occurred among 58 of every 1,000 couples. A survey of studies using various methods and examining diverse samples revealed that a significant number of battered wives consider their husbands to have alcohol problems (Leonard and Jacob, 1988). Both men and women may be the aggressors, although wives are more often seriously injured, because of their physical disadvantage. Women, however, are just as likely to kill their spouses as are men, often citing as motivation the abuse they received from their husbands.

Spouse abuse is also related to CHILD ABUSE. A man who beats his wife may also beat his children; the abused wife may take out her anger and resentment on the children. A chain reaction may start with each member in turn and in his or her own way provoking or imposing violence. Quarrels arise when one partner complains about the other's behavior, leading to violence by the second partner, leading to more complaints. M. A. Stuart and C. S. de Blois in 1978 found that at one psychiatric clinic 65% of mothers who had abused their sons had been abused by their husbands.

A clear connection has been shown between alcoholism and all kinds of family violence. According to one estimate, up to 80% of all cases of family violence involve drinking, either before, during or after the incident (Flanzer). Moderate and problem drinkers are more frequently involved in such incidents than light drinkers.

Alcohol breaks down inhibitions, often resulting in violent behavior between husbands and wives. However, most research supports the conclusion that alcohol abuse does not itself cause family violence, but rather that the use of alcohol may provide an excuse to be violent. Intoxication may be perceived by the abuser as a time when normal rules for behavior do not apply.

Alcoholism and family abuse have many characteristics in common. Some consider family violence to be a disease, just as alcoholism is considered a disease. Both allow the subject to gain temporarily some form of mastery over his or her world, both resolve conflicts and both temporarily mask depression. Similarities have been found in the characters of spouse abusers and alcoholics, members of each group often are dependent, impulsive, frustrated and depressed and have low self-esteem (Sanchez-Dirks). Both violence and alcoholism seem to provide coping mechanisms for abusers and alcoholics. More research is needed to uncover the particular circumstances leading to these traits. Children of alcoholics also show many of the same character patterns.

Violence and drinking may be connected in several different ways. Perhaps the most common pattern is an eruption of violence that happens only when alcohol is consumed—either the abuser drinks and then hits, or the victim drinks until he or she becomes a target for abuse. The drinker, however, may drink to avoid hitting someone or, in some instances, hit someone instead of taking a drink. Violence occurs in a more subtle form when a heavy drinker neglects or disturbs his or her family to such an extent that it causes severe damage. Such neglect may also cause so much pressure in the family that it eventually erupts into violence. In addition quarrels that begin over a spouse's drinking can result in physical abuse.

Because there is a high acceptance of violence in American society and victims often hide the fact that they have been abused because of fear of reprisal or lack of understanding by the community, treatment of the dual problem of alcoholism and spouse abuse can be difficult. Women often do not report the beatings they receive because of their own sense of helplessness and despair. They may believe that they have failed their marriage and are incompetent as wives and mothers. Instead of seeing alcoholism or their husbands' violence as the problem, they feel that they have gotten what they deserved and are powerless to change things. Both alcoholism and family violence are often part of a repetitive cycle from generation to generation. Abusers and alcoholics have learned to hit and drink in order to resolve their problems and reassert control. Children from abusive families learn these coping patterns from the same individuals who teach them to love. Thus loving and hitting become linked in their minds. It is therefore important to involve the whole family in treatment.

A problem in treatment of alcohol-related abuse is that the programs designed to deal with battered victims frequently are not capable of addressing alcohol problems, and often alcoholic counselors do not know much about the mechanics of family violence. The two problems tend to be treated separately, although in reality they are closely linked. It is important to look for alcohol problems when dealing with family violence, for while treating an alcoholism problem will not necessarily stop the violence, it will make it easier to work on.

Robert J. Ackerman, Ph.D. *Let Go and Grow: Recovery for Adult Children* (Pompano Beach, Florida: Health Communications, Inc., 1987).

Jerry Flanzer, "The Vicious Circle of Alcoholism and Family Violence," *Alcoholism* 1, no. 3 (January/February 1981): 30-32.

Margaret H. Hindman, "Family Violence," *Alcohol Health and Research World* 4, no. 1 (Fall 1979).

K. Leonard and T. Jacob, "Alcoholism and Family Violence," in *Handbook of Family Violence* (New York: Plenium, 1988) pp. 383-406.

Judy Seixas & Geraldine Youcha, *Children of Alcoholics* (New York: Crown, 1985).

M. A. Stewart and C. S. de Blois, "Is Alcoholism Related to Physical Abuse of Wives and Children?" (paper presented at the National Council on Alcoholism Annual Meeting, St. Louis, 1978).

Ruth Sanchez-Dirks, "Reflections on Family Violence," *Alcohol Health and Research World* 4, no. 1 (Fall 1979).

M. A. Straus, "A Sociological Perspective in the Prevention and Treatment of Wifebeating," *Battered Women,* ed. M. Roy (New York: Van Nostrand Reinhold, 1977).

spree   A drinking bout; an episode of prolonged excessive drinking.

spree drinking   Drinking characterized by periods of sobriety lasting weeks or months and drinking binges that continue for days or weeks. This type of periodic drinking is more common in the United States than in a country like FRANCE, where there is a higher percentage of steady drinkers.

While a spree drinker may not consume more alcohol over the space of a year than a steady moderate drinker, he or she is at more of a health risk. For expectant mothers particularly, a drinking spree presents a grave danger to the fetus (see FETAL ALCOHOL SYNDROME). JELLINEK categorized this type of drinking as EPSILON ALCOHOLISM.

Sri Lanka   Some medical authorities in Sri Lanka, formerly known as Ceylon, argue that alcoholism is the single most important health and social problem facing the country. Heavy drinking is concentrated among a small segment of the population, but a pattern of excessive consumption appears to be spreading as the country becomes more urban and less rigorous in the observance of Buddhist and Hindu strictures on drinking.

Of legal liquors, the preferred beverages were arrack, a spirit made from rice or coconut milk with an alcohol content of 35%, and toddy, a beverage made from molasses and various beers with an alcohol content of 6% to 8%. In addition various wines, brandies, whiskeys and gins are imported. However, illegally produced alcoholic beverages are estimated to equal half the amount of legal alcohol available, and production of these home brews, which have an alcohol content ranging from 20% to 60%, has doubled in recent years. As is true throughout the world, illegal liquor in Sri Lanka is often based on methylated spirits, contains hazardous amounts of distillation by-products and has gained wide acceptance because it sells at a cheaper price than licensed, taxed liquors.

Statistics on per capita consumption indicate the presence of a large proportion of abstainers and, consequently, a small proportion of heavy drinkers. These figures, however, do not take into account illegal alcoholic beverages, and there is ample evidence to suggest a greater alcoholism problem than official estimates acknowledge. Consumption of home-brewed alcohol is especially high among the lower classes, whose members are unlikely ever to seek professional help. Alcohol has had no traditional place in the country's social or ceremonial occasions, but in recent times drinking has become common at such events. Weekend drinking in urban areas and drinking at agrarian celebrations in rural areas are also rising.

There has been an increase in physical complications, sometimes resulting in coma or death, associated with drinking illegal alcoholic beverages. Because of the lack of special hospital facilities for the treatment of alcoholism in Sri Lanka, statistics on the incidence of alcoholism are unavailable, but it is known that the incidence is higher in the capital city of Colombo than in other areas of the country.

The sole authority charged with alcoholism prevention policies in Sri Lanka is the Department of Excise. This agency, assisted by the police, concentrates entirely on licensing of public drinking places and taxation of legally produced liquors. Neither of these efforts have much impact because of the number of private drinking clubs in the country and the easy availability of illegal alcoholic beverages. There are at present no public education programs regarding the dangers of alcohol abuse, and the Department of Health has no alcoholism-related activities.

steam beer   A bottom-fermented lager beer distinguished by a bitter, "hoppy" flavor similar to that of ales. Steam beer is fermented at lower than normal temperatures and naturally carbonated. It is named for the fact that during its unique fermentation process the fermentation vat builds up pressure like a steam engine.

Steam beer is the only kind of beer entirely indigenous to the United States. It originated in San Francisco in the mid-19th century, when the Gold Rush brought a sudden population explosion to the area. Lacking ice for the chilling required in normal fermentation, California brew masters were forced to experiment with fermentation at higher temperatures, and in the process they discovered a beer especially prized for its flavor by the working class in San Francisco. Steam beers were hurt by the shift in American taste to lighter, paler lager beers and the status that was attached to them around the turn of the century. The final blow to the industry came from Prohibition, and today steam beer is brewed and bottled by only one company, Anchor, in San Francisco.

Steam beer is brewed exclusively from barley malt, unlike most lager beers, which use other cereal grains. It also has a far higher hop content, about four times the average of other beers. After a bottom-fermentation yeast is added to the hop wort, fermentation of steam beer takes place at temperatures between 65° and 75° F, as opposed to the 40° to 60° F range for most lagers, and the fermentation tank is usually an exceptionally shallow one. Carbonation is entirely accomplished by "krausening"—the introduction of carbolic acid from a newly fermented and active wort—rather than by injection of artificially produced carbon dioxide. The result is a distinctive but rather fragile beer, one subject to clouding when excessively chilled and often drunk at warmer than usual temperatures for that reason.

still   An apparatus used to distill alcohol from a fermented mash. In its simplest form a still consists of a vessel in which to heat the fermented mash, a collector in which to catch the alcohol vapor then given off, an exterior tube in which to cool and, thus, recondense the alcohol vapor and a receiving vessel in which to collect the liquid distillate.

The pot still is the oldest, the most traditional and the simplest type currently in use. It produces intermittent batches of distillate according to the process described above. In the years before legalization of private distilling, the pot still was prized because it was small and easily dismantled for hiding and was extremely portable. The product of the pot still, however, was and remains erratic—subject to unintentional variations in temperatures—and relatively impure. This "low wine" distillate is weak in strength and heavy in taste unless further rectified by costly secondary distillations. However, the pot still remains the favorite of those who want the strong character and variable qualities of a single distiller's product. Most pot-still products, especially Scotch whiskies, enter the commercial marketplace only after being blended with other, lighter distillates.

The patent still, or continuous still, is the type most used today. It was invented in 1831 by Aeneas Coffey, an Irish exciseman, and has remained essential to commercially efficient distillation. The key advantage offered by the patent still is the fact that it combines twin distillation columns for semi-independent double distillations that can operate without halt. Although the product lacks the strong character of pot-still distillates, it can be mass produced. Patent-still spirits are generally blended with small amounts of pot-still spirits

to create a product that is distinctive and yet light enough to appeal to a broad market.

still wine   A noncarbonated wine. Still wine refers to any wine except SPARKLING WINE, which is heavily carbonated and not "still" when poured in a glass.

stomach   The ingestion of alcohol has been widely associated with inflammation of the stomach, especially its mucous membrane. The actual mechanism of damage has not been conclusively established, but it is generally accepted that alcohol stimulates secretion of stomach acid. Solutions of less than 10% ethanol stimulate the gastric glands to produce acid and ingestion of higher concentrations of alcohol produces gastric irritation and reduces appetite. In addition alcohol delays the emptying time of the stomach. These factors in combination may cause a hyperacidic condition that in time could lead to stomach disorder. The most frequent are nausea, vomiting and diarrhea.

Irritation of the mucous membrane is common after a period of prolonged drinking. In most cases this subsides after alcohol consumption ceases, but prolonged and excessive use of alcohol may result in more serious erosion of the stomach membrane, ranging from inflammation to ulceration and hemmorrhage. Excessive drinking is frequently associated with heavy smoking and together these abuses may have an additive or synergistic effect causing chronic inflammation of the stomach (see SYNERGY).

stout   A very dark and especially sweet variety of ale that was traditionally common in England but is now almost exclusively associated with Ireland. The grain content of stout has a far higher proportion of malted barley than that of other ales, and the maltose, a soluble sugar produced by malting, gives stout its distinctive taste and color. Stout is top fermented and processed in ways that are otherwise indistinguishable from those used in making ale.

Students Against Drunk Driving (S.A.D.D.)   A program that encourages students to not drink and drive, but, if they find that they have taken alcohol, to feel free to call their parents for a ride home. The program built itself around a signed contract between students and their parents. Similar to most alcohol advocacy groups, S.A.D.D. now incorporates a focus on drugs. S.A.D.D. is headquartered in Marlboro, Massachusetts.

substance abuse   A general term used to describe ABUSE of alcohol and other drugs, including tobacco and caffeine.

Sudan   The largest country in Africa, Sudan has a population of about 17 million. The Moslem religion, embraced by 85% of the population, is the single greatest restraint on drinking in the country, for the Koran prohibits consumption of alcoholic beverages and no Moslem in Sudan is permitted to hold a license for a drinking establishment or liquor store. As a result of the Koran's prohibition, there is virtually no drinking among the female Moslem population, but among the male Moslem population drinking may be rising lately, indicating this religious ban may be losing its effect. Fifteen percent of the Sudanese population consists of Christians and persons belonging to no recognized sect, on whom the religious law against drinking has no effect.

The predominant legally produced liquors in Sudan are beer and sherry, and demand for both exceeds supply. Because of limited production and distribution problems restricting the availability of these beverages, there is widespread unregulated production—and consumption—of two illegal alcoholic beverages: *marisa,* a fermented sorghum, and *aragi,* a liquor distilled from either date or sorghum mashes. *Marisa,* which has alcohol content ranging from 1.8% to 5.1%, is common throughout the country. The date variety of *aragi,* with an alcohol content as high as 49%, is especially common in the northern districts of the country; the *aragi* distilled from sorghum has a lower alcohol content.

Consumption of illegally produced aragi is an especially serious health problem in Sudan because this beverage often contains toxic by-products resulting from crude distillation processes.

Studies of drinking patterns in Sudan suggest that the drinking population is small and that excessive drinking is occasional. One survey of Khartoum province found that the rate of alcoholism among the male population was 1.8%, that less than half the male population drank and that of these drinkers only about 13% drank to excess. (Drinking to excess in this context meant taking a drink daily, for most drinkers surveyed drank only once or twice each month.) These statistics are thought to be above the national average because they included the country's largest urban population. Consequently the rate of alcoholism for the entire country is estimated to be somewhere below 1.8%.

Even this limited drinking, however, has a significant effect on the nation. Most excessive drinkers in Sudan suffer from symptoms of liver cirrhosis aggravated by endemic diseases, a high percentage of social drinkers suffer physical complications from illegally distilled alcohols, and as a result one-quarter of the hospital admissions in the entire country are either directly or indirectly related to alcohol abuse.

The only efforts to combat alcohol abuse in Sudan are nongovernmental, and it is generally agreed that what legal penalties exist for alcohol-related crimes are rarely enforced. The nation's general policy toward alcohol abuse is to encourage abstinence on religious rather than social grounds. Religious groups have begun to contribute to antialcohol campaigns, particularly in the country's most heavily populated areas to the north. These organizations, however, remain the sole source of preventative measures.

sugar   See BLOOD SUGAR, FRUCTOSE.

suicide   Alcoholics are at a particularly high risk of committing suicide. Although estimates of the level of risk vary, at least one study reported it to be 30 times greater than the risk of suicide among the general population (Medhus). According to Gallant (1987), "The suicide risk in known alcoholics is indeed frightening." In a valuable 30-year prospective study of 1,312 alcoholics, 88 (16%) of the 537 deaths were found to be definite suicides (Berglund, 1984).

Alcoholics who commit suicide have attempted to kill themselves more often than nonalcoholics who commit suicide, and alcoholic suicide attempters more closely resemble actual suicides than do nonalcoholic attempters. These findings suggest that alcoholics who try to kill themselves form a significant part of the population that eventually succeeds in committing suicide. Studies have shown that between 15% and 64% of suicide attempters and up to 80% of suicides were drinking at the time of the event. Other studies cited in the *Seventh Special Report* (1990) indicate that 20% to 36% of suicide victims have a history of alcohol abuse or were drinking shortly before their suicides. Use of other DRUGS with alcohol is probably responsible for a substantial proportion of accidental deaths as well as suicides.

In the general population women have a higher attempted suicide rate than men but men have a higher completed suicide rate than women. Among alcoholic women the number of suicide attempts clearly exceeds that among the female population as a whole, and recent data indicate that the rate of completed suicides among female alcoholics is 23 times the general population rate (Adelstein).

A. Adelstein, "Alcoholism and Mortality," *Population Trends* 7 (1977).

M. Berglund, "Suicide in Alcoholism," *Archives of General Psychiatry*, 41(1984), 888-891.

Glen Evans & Norman L. Farberow, Ph.D., *The Encyclopedia of Suicide* (New York: Facts On File, 1988), pps. 95-98.

D.M. Gallant, *Alcoholism: A Guide to Diagnosis, Intervention, and Treatment* (New York: W.W. Norton, 1987).

Enoch Gordis, M.D., ed., *Seventh Special Report to the U.S. Congress on Alcohol and Health* (Rockville, Md.: National Institute on Alcohol Abuse and Alcoholism, 1990), chapter VII.

A. Medhus, "Mortality among Female Alcoholics," *Scandinavian Journal of Social Medicine* 3 (1975):111-115.

supra-additive effect　　See SYNERGY.

surgery　　When operating on alcoholics, surgeons must be aware of a number of factors. The depressive effects of general anesthesia and those of alcohol on acutely intoxicated patients are synergistic (see SYNERGY). Chronic alcoholics may have a CROSS-TOLERANCE to general anesthesia, requiring greater amounts to induce sleep. They may also undergo a prolonged second stage of anesthesia after the administration of inhalation anesthetics. In addition there is the possibility of myocardial depression and altered blood volume in alcoholics, which increases the risk of anesthesia.

Often alcoholics who are apparently healthy have damaged liver function, which may seriously affect the postoperative course. Even in the absence of severe liver damage, increased bleeding frequently complicates operations on alcoholic patients, who have been found to have a decreased number of platelets, which aid in clotting of the blood.

Delirium tremens is another serious potential complication for the alcoholic patient. Patients who drink the equivalent of 1 or more pints of whiskey per day or who have a previous history of delirium tremens are likely to develop this condition after the operation. Delirium tremens usually starts within 48 to 72 hours after cessation of drinking, a period when it is wise to avoid operating on known heavy drinkers.

Albert B. Lowenfels, Michael Rohman and Kinichi Shibutani, "Surgical Consequences of Alcoholism," *Surgery, Gynecology, and Obstetrics* 131 (July 1970):129-138.

susceptibility   Certain individuals may show a strong readiness to turn to alcohol in times of stress, and such people who cannot cope in any other way are said to be more "susceptible" to alcohol. "Susceptibility," however, is a vague term that does little to clarify or explain alcoholism and is generally best avoided. (See GENETICS.)

Sweden   In 1987, apparent Swedish per capita consumption of ABSOLUTE ALCOHOL, based on the total population, was measured at 5.4 liters. This rate ranked Sweden 29th among 47 countries that reported such data. In the same year Swedes consumed 51.5 liters of beer, 11.83 liters of wine and 1.96 liters of distilled spirits. In the six-year period from 1979 to 1984, Sweden reported an average annual decline in the consumption rate of 3% per year.

Sweden's well-known adoption studies have made this country recognized as a leader in alcohol research (see GENETICS). Also Sweden, together with Norway, has served as an effective model for drinking and driving laws.

Hoeveel alcoholhoude dranken worden er in de wereld gedronken? (How many alcoholic beverages are being consumed throughout the world?) 27th ed. Schiedam, Netherlands: Produktschap Voor Gedistilleerde Dranken, 1987.

sweet mash   A grain mixture used in preparation of the mash, or "wash," from which bourbon is distilled. The grain content of bourbon is at least 51% corn (Indian maize), with the remainder made up of rye and malted barley. In sweet mash bourbon there is an unusually high proportion of malted barley, which is rich in maltose, a soluble sugar that enhances fermentation by combining with yeast to produce alcohol. The chief alternative to sweet mash is SOUR MASH, in which a residue from a previous distillation is added as an aid to fermentation in the grain wash of bourbon.

Switzerland   A 1987 report showed Switzerland's per capita consumption of ABSOLUTE ALCOHOL, based on total population, to be 11.0 liters, placing it among the world leaders in consumption. Of 47 reporting countries, Switzerland ranked fourth for overall consumption. The Swiss consumed most of their alcohol in the form of wine, with a per capita rate of 49.5 liters per person; beer consumption averaged 69.3 liters per capita, and spirits were consumed at a per capita rate of 2.04 liters. Long known for its progressive attitude toward alcoholism and alcohol-related problems, Switzerland opened its first treatment center for alcoholics in Zurich before 1900. The Swiss temperance movement is one of the oldest in Europe.

In the early 19th century the most prevalent drinking pattern was consumption of potato schnapps, a distilled alcohol that was produced in abundance because of surplus potato crops. When the Swiss Federal State was established in 1848, an indirect effect of its new constitution was increased availability of cheap potato schnapps because of liberalized trade controls. To change that situation the government in 1885 introduced a constitutional amendment that imposed heavy taxes on potato schnapps, restricted sales of the liquor and created a state monopoly on its production. The result was a shift in agricultural production to fruit and a consequent rise in distillation of various cider and fruit schnapps. In 1930 these products were also brought under the state alcohol monopoly and made subject to similar sales taxes and restrictions.

Today the revenues of the state alcohol monopoly are distributed equally among the federal and canton, or provincial, authorities. The cantons are required to devote 10% of their share to programs aimed at combating alcoholism.

Treatment of alcoholism in Switzerland is difficult to describe because the government stresses a broad-based scientific, educational and economic initiative to reduce alcohol consumption over the more traditional public health model. This program has to some extent been inhibited by the structure of the federal constitution, which grants some autonomy to individual cantons.

There are three agencies addressing the problem of alcoholism: the Federal Commission Against Alcoholism formed in 1947; the Swiss National Science Foundation, created in 1952, which has devoted a significant proportion of its energies to the country's alcohol abuse problem; and the Swiss Institute for the Prevention of Alcoholism. Now working in cooperation to emphasize the social causes of alcoholism, these agencies have the avowed purpose of creating "an intact alcohol legislation which is above all always aimed at the greatest possible efficiency on behalf of public welfare."

Cases of Liver Cirrhosis Caused by Alcoholism

Years	Men	Women	Total	Number per 100,000 Population
1951–55	409	79	488	10.0
1956–60	467	79	546	10.5
1961–65	583	92	675	11.7
1966–70	638	105	743	12.1
1971–75	614	139	753	11.8
1987	520	222	742	11.4

SOURCE: Swiss Institute for the Prevention of Alcoholism.

Hoeveel alcoholhoude dranken worden er in de wereld gedronken? (How many alcoholic beverages are being consumed throughout the world?) 27th ed. Schiedam, Netherlands: Produktschap Voor Gedistilleerde Dranken, 1987.

symptomatic alcoholism   Alcoholism that is secondary to another medical problem, such as psychoneurosis, psychosis or mental deficiency.

symptomatic drinking   E x c e s s i v e drinking that is used as a way of handling

tensions or unconscious problems or drinking that is a symptom of some mental disorder other than alcoholism.

synergistic effect   See SYNERGY.

synergy   Also known as potentiation. When two or more drugs are taken together, the joint action increases the normal effect of each. A classic case involves the use of alcohol in combination with barbiturates. A small amount of alcohol combined with a very small dose of barbiturates produces a synergistic effect, or an effect that is much greater than the individual effects of alcohol and barbiturates added together.

The synergistic process begins in the liver, which metabolizes ingested materials. When two drugs are taken together, the enzyme system that processes them is overwhelmed. The two drugs, alcohol and barbiturates, for example, compete for the same enzymes, which do not have the capacity to metabolize both drugs at the same time. Alcohol is always processed first, allowing the second drug, barbiturates in this case, to accumulate in the blood. While the second drug is not being metabolized, it has an exaggerated effect on the body and mind. The delayed metabolization of the second drug can result in a tripling or quadrupling of its potency when it enters the central nervous system. Because of this phenomenon, an amount of a drug that might normally be safe can have devastating effects if taken with a drug that acts synergistically with it. (See also DRUGS.)

T

tank   (From "drunk tank.") Slang for a cell or jail where drunks are kept to sober up. The term is also used to refer to a drunk.

teetotal   (From "tee-total", a local British intensive for "total.") Total abstinence.

teetotaler   One who teetotals (see TEE-TOTAL).

temperance   While the word "temperance" has usually been synonymous with moderation, in the 1800s it took on the narrower meaning of abstinence. Although as early as 1785 Dr. Benjamin Rush presented a strong scientific argument on the dangers of alcohol and the need for temperance, Americans were more receptive to moral pleas. The first temperance organization in the United States was founded in 1789 by some residents of Litchfield, Conn. who pledged never to drink. Similar groups began to operate on a local scale. The first national organization, the American Temperance Society, was formed in 1826. The movement was supported by Presbyterian and Methodist churches and drew its largest following in rural areas. By 1830 there were more than 1,000 temperance societies in existence and these organizations gained strength in rural communities between 1830 and 1860.

Temperance leaders used two techniques to persuade people to abstain: they advocated religious faith as a means for people to ease the anxieties that might lead them to drink and they portrayed liquor as the agent of the devil and, therefore, a source of these anxieties. During this time a number of states adopted antialcohol measures ranging from licensing to complete prohibition. These measures lacked the support of the general nonrural populations and many were rapidly repealed. The earlier temperance groups (1825-40) were concerned with the plight of drunkards and many tried to help them to sobriety. After 1830, however, the societies began to stress that the drunk was a moral sinner who could stop drinking if he so desired. The goal of the groups changed from helping the drunkard to removing the cause of his problem—alcohol. The idea of universal prohibition became prominent and all who drank were attacked as moral degenerates. The early temperance movement was very powerful among rural populations and those with strong religious backgrounds.

The Civil War divided the early and late temperance movements. After the war the notion of temperance grew increasingly popular. More churches became directly involved in the movement. Catholics formed the Total Abstention Union in 1872, and the WOMAN'S CHRISTIAN TEMPERANCE UNION was founded in 1874. Eventually the movement shifted from moral attacks toward legislative measures, particularly PROHIBITION. On December 18, 1917 Congress submitted the Eighteenth Amendment to the states for ratification and on January 16, 1920 Prohibition went into effect.

Richard W. Howland and Joe W. Howland, "200 Years of Drinking in the United States: Evolution of the Disease Concept," in *Drinking,* ed. John A. Ewing and Beatrice A. Rouse (Chicago: Nelson-Hall, 1979), pp. 39-60.

W. J. Rorabaugh, *The Alcoholic Republic* (New York: Oxford University Press, 1979), pp. 187-222.

Temposil   The compound calcium carbamide, Temposil is used to produce an ANTABUSE effect in alcoholics participating in recovery programs. It differs fron Antabuse in that its effect lasts only 12 to 24 hours whereas that of Antabuse can extend four to five days before the danger of a reaction passes. Temposil is administered in alcohol treatment programs in Canada and Japan but has not been approved for use in the United States.

tequila   A spirit distilled from a pulque, or fermented mash, of some species of agave plant, usually maguey. Its name derives from the district in the Mexican state of Jalisco where it originated. Tequila is sometimes referred to as mescal.

The national alcoholic beverage of Mexico, tequila dates from the Spanish exploration of that country in the 15th and 16th centuries. Its production undoubtedly began when the Spanish, who already possessed knowledge of distillation, adapted distillation processes to the local vegetation most suitable for fermentation because of its natural sugar content. The maguey agave they employed is also known as blue agave. Now, because its principal use is distillation, it is sometimes called the tequilana plant.

Tequila is a strong spirit, ranging from 86 to 100 proof, traditionally drunk straight, preceded by a taste of salt and followed by a taste of lemon or lime. Since being mass marketed in recent times, it is now also used in cocktails.

testosterone-lowering effects of alcohol
See HORMONES, MALE SEX.

Thailand   Thailand, like many other countries in Southeast Asia, has been subjected to severe military conflicts and a general undermining of cultural stability by foreign influences. The effects of these factors are especially apparent in the rise in alcohol consumption among the Thai people. The population is 90% Buddhist, 4% Islamic and 2% Confucian. Although these religions have traditional strictures against alcohol consumption, alcohol-related job absenteeism produces daily expressions of concern from the business community. While in the past the country had little need for strict licensing of drinking places, the current situation appears to justify some control of drinking environments. One-third of the alcoholism cases in urban areas, such as Bangkok, where such establishments have proliferated, are estimated to be female employees of the various pubs, clubs and cafes that serve a clientele of national military officers. Importation of beer and whiskey remains relatively low, but there is an increasing daily use of such bootleg products as "Mekong whiskey" in both rural and urban areas.

The Thais have a tradition of limited alcohol consumption with evening meals. Authorities have noted, however, a recent general trend toward consumption of alcohol with other meals, including, in rural areas, breakfast, and a new pattern of continued drinking

into the night in public places. Illegally distilled liquors comprise the primary alcoholic drinks for most of the population; during a typical drinking occasion various alcoholic beverages are mixed. The increasing acceptance of alcohol as a social beverage has reached all levels of Thai society, from the military officers' clubs, stocked with imported brandy, to the rural villages, where rice whiskey is distilled.

The cost of alcoholism to Thailand is difficult to estimate due to a lack of data. The government's overriding concern at present is control of narcotic drugs.

Prevention of alcohol-related problems in Thailand is delegated to the Department of Treasury, with responsibility for educational programs left to the Ministry of Public Health. In February 1975 the International Congress on Alcohol and Drug Dependency met in Bangkok, and one year later the country established a Drug Education and Prevention Office. Each of the 72 provinces has its own Provincial Health Authority and mobile teams to treat health problems of all sorts in rural areas. There are 30 centers specifically designed for the treatment of alcohol and drug problems in Thailand.

tight   A slang term used to describe someone who is intoxicated, more so than someone who is HIGH.

TIPS (Training for Intervention Procedures by Servers of Alcohol)   National efforts to prevent alcohol abuse lack a coherent conceptual structure. Although many public service messages and pamphlets create awareness of the problem and inform the drinkers of the consequences of becoming drunk (and especially driving), the problems continue to mount.

A recent prevention approach of great potential is server training. Server training bridges the gap between messages designed to admonish and advise people and techniques designed to give people skills to act. The skills of identification and intervention that servers acquire are designed to interrupt the patterns of alcohol abuse in order to prevent drunkenness and, failing that, to prevent a drunken person from driving.

The conceptual framework of the program is based on the knowledge that alcohol taken in heavy doses undermines cognitive skills, interferes with recently learned information, sabotages plans to limit drinking, and confounds the ability to keep track of the number of drinks. Public service announcements, slogans and pamphlets are directed, in other words, at the people least likely to retain what they have learned.

The conceptual framework is further based on the thesis that behavioral change takes place in society where social values and limits of behavior are determined by the approval or disapproval of small groups of people in the social networks of the individual.

The most used and best known program has the acronym TIPS—Training for Intervention Procedures by Servers of Alcohol—a program developed by the Health Education Foundation under the guidance of the founding director of the National Institute on Alcohol Abuse and Alcoholism, Morris E. Chafetz, M.D.

Although the program was initially designed to educate servers of alcohol in the skills needed to reduce the incidence of drunkenness and thereby reduce the incidence of alcohol-related accidents or injury by patrons who consume alcohol in commercial settings, including concessions, off-premise establishments and the like. The program's success in these areas permitted the development of three prevention programs for the noncommercial arena: TIPS for Universities, TIPS for the Workplace and TIPS for Parents.

TIPS is the only proven effective server training program. Independent university researchers proved that not a single patron served by a TIPS-trained server was able to achieve a blood alcohol level of intoxication whereas almost 50 percent of patrons served by non-TIPS-trained servers were legally drunk.

TIPS is a unique and valuable tool that people can use to help curb the abuse of alcohol and thereby promote the health and general well-being of the public.

M.E. Chafetz, "Training in Intervention Procedures: A Prevention Program," *Abstracts and Reviews in Alcohol and Driving*, 5(4):17-19, October-December 1984.

W. Nason and E.S. Geller, "Training Bar Personnel to Prevent Drunk Driving: A Field Evaluation," *American Journal of Public Health* 77(8), August 1987.

E.S. Geller et al, "Does Server Training Make a Difference? An Empirical Field Evaluation," *Alcohol Health and Research World* 11(4), Summer 1987.

Enoch Gordis, ed., *Seventh Special Report to the U.S. Congress on Alcohol and Health*, January 1990.

tobacco   See SMOKING.

Tokay   (In Hungarian, Tokaji.) A famous Hungarian wine named after Tokay, a village in northeast Hungary near the Carpathian mountains.

There are three basic types of Tokay wine: Tokay Essencia, Tokay Aszu and Tokay Szamorodini. With the exception of some types of Tokay Szamorodini, Tokay wines are very sweet and thus generally used as dessert wines. The distinctive flavor of Tokay wines comes from *aszu* berries, which are grapes that have been allowed to remain on the vine until late autumn, when they have shriveled and their juice has become very concentrated with sugar. The particular type of Tokay is determined by the amount of *aszu* berries used in making the wine.

Tokay Essencia is made entirely from *aszu* berries and is so rare that it is not marketed but used as private stock. Tokay Aszu is made from a carefully measured blend of normally ripened grapes and *aszu* berries. *Aszu* berries are added in amounts that vary from 1 to 6 *puttonys,* a *puttony* holding approximately 30 pounds of grapes. Tokay Aszu varies in taste from rather dry to extremely sweet, depending on the number of *puttonys* added. It is golden or amber in color and around 7 or 8 proof.

The term "Szamorodini" means "as it is grown," and it indicates that in making Tokay Szamorodini no special attention is given to the *aszu* berries. Whatever *aszu* berries get into the vats are pressed with the other grapes. If the result is a very dry wine, it is drunk as an aperitif rather than as a dessert wine.

tolerance The variation in the effect on different individuals of a specific amount of alcohol. After a few drinks an inexperienced drinker may become intoxicated rapidly, while an experienced drinker can consume the same amount with little visible effect. The degree of intoxication exhibited at a given BLOOD ALCOHOL CONCENTRATION varies widely among individuals.

The most significant factor in tolerance to alcohol is related to the adaptation of the CENTRAL NERVOUS SYSTEM to alcohol. Long-term alcoholics display higher than average adaptation of the CNS to alcohol, which enables them to tolerate larger doses of all sedatives. They also have an increased ability to metabolize alcohol, but this is rapidly lost when drinking stops. One study showed that metabolic tolerance could be lost after three weeks of abstinence even in those who had been severe alcoholics for five years or more.

Some alcoholics have reported losing their high tolerance to alcohol suddenly; in such cases a relatively small amount of alcohol would have an unexpectedly strong effect. This effect may be due to impaired METABOLISM or to the increased sensitivity of an organically damaged brain to alcohol.

While alcoholics may have a higher tolerance for alcohol than social drinkers or abstainers, the size of a lethal dose is probably not much greater than for others.

top fermentation Fermentation of a hop wort with a yeast that rises to the surface of the liquid in the course of brewing beer. Top fermentation is the process used in brewing ales, whereas BOTTOM FERMENTATION is used to brew lager beers. Beer yeasts are selected strains of bacterial enzymes that flocculate, or separate themselves from the brewing beer, so that they may be drawn off at the end of the process. Top fermentation, in conjunction with the blend of different cereal grains employed, accounts for the heavier flavor of ales in comparison with that of lagers. Typically top fermentation is carried out at temperatures between 50° and 70° F, and it ordinarily takes between five and six days to produce the desired level of alcohol content.

tranquilizer See SEDATIVE.

trauma See ACCIDENTS.

Traynor v. Turnage In a landmark decision handed down on April 20, 1988, the Supreme Court ruled 4-3 that the Veterans Administration can continue to deny disability and other benefits to most veterans disabled by alcoholism because their condition is caused by "willful misconduct."

The decision, which directly concerns only veterans, stressed the majority's view of what Congress intended in two ambiguously worded statutes (in 1977 and 1978) that define who is entitled to veterans' benefits and that prohibit discrimination against handicapped people.

Both the majority and the dissent stressed the view expressed by Associate Justice Byron R. White (who wrote for the majority) that "this litigation does not require the Court to decide whether alcoholism is a disease whose course its victims cannot control."

Writing for the majority in the case *Traynor v. Turnage*, No. 86-622 and 86-737, Justice White noted that the Veterans Administration policy with regard to alcoholism as a disability had been consistent since at least 1964.

Many specialists worry that the flow of money into treatment programs—from employers, insurance companies and governments—may slow considerably as a result of the Supreme Court's decision, despite Justice

White's remarks about this litigation not requiring the Court to rule on the disease concept of alcoholism. Some lawyers doubt the decision is cause for worry in this particular regard. Marcus A. Rothschild, M.D., editor of *Alcoholism: Clinical and Experimental Research*, the journal of the American Medical Society on Alcoholism, says the Supreme Court decision is discouraging. "The ruling," he told *The New York Times* (April 22, 1988), "will lend itself to misinterpretation. To consider this genetic-inherited trait as willful misconduct is to deny all our more recent knowledge and advances."

Stuart Taylor Jr., "V.A.'s Denial of Alcoholic Benefits to Alcoholics Upheld," *New York Times*, April 21, 1988.

treatment   Treatment of alcoholism may begin with INTERVENTION, when a concerned party steps in to alert the alcoholic about his or her problem. The next step for the alcoholic is DETOXIFICATION, where he or she is sobered up and treated for any alcohol-related DISEASES. After detoxification some type of REHABILITATION is usually required for successful treatment. This may take place in an INPATIENT TREATMENT program or an OUTPATIENT TREATMENT program. The alcoholic may enter ALCOHOLICS ANONYMOUS or GROUP THERAPY or undergo BEHAVIOR MODIFICATION. In addition he or she may be taught proper NUTRITION.

According to a 1987 National Drug and Alcoholism Treatment Unit Survey (NDATUS), 4.1% of the 263,510 alcohol and drug abuse clients were in a hospital-inpatient environment, 10.4% in a residential environment and 85.6% in an outpatient environment. Considered by modality, 4.1% of all clients were in detoxification, 31.4% in maintenance and 64.5% in drug-free treatment. All were being instructed about the vital importance of proper nutrition.

Treatment facilities reported $3.2 billion in total financial support for drug and alcohol services for their fiscal years including October 1987. For alcohol treatment, the total was $1.71 billion, and for drug treatment it was $1.31 billion.

More than 1.43 million Americans were treated for alcoholism in fiscal year 1987.

National Institute on Drug Abuse and National Institute on Alcohol Abuse and Alcoholism, *1987 National Drug and Alcoholism Treatment Unit Survey* (Rockville, Maryland: NIDA/NIAAA, February 1989), p. 6.

Twenty-First Amendment   This amendment repealed the EIGHTEENTH AMENDMENT and returned to the states the right to make their own liquor laws. Michigan was the first state to ratify the Twenty-First Amendment and Utah was the 36th, completing the ratification process. On December 5, 1933 it became part of the Constitution and ended Prohibition.

U

Ulster Temperance Society   One of the earliest temperance organizations in Europe, it was founded in Northern Ireland in 1829. Thereafter, the organized temperance movement began to make effective progress.

uncontrolled drinking   A rather vague term generally used to refer to behavior that deliberately transgresses the social rules related to drinking. (JELLINEK suggested the use of the term "undisciplined drinking" to describe such behavior.) This behavior is not the same as LOSS OF CONTROL, which deprives the drinker of free choice.

under the influence of alcohol   When used in the general sense, this term refers to a mild disturbance of function caused by alcohol consumption. In many parts of the United States the condition is defined by the law in terms of specific concentrations of alcohol in the blood. The BLOOD ALCOHOL CONCEN-TRATION of someone who is considered to be "under the influence of alcohol" is generally lower than that of someone classified as legally intoxicated. (See also DRIVING WHILE INTOXICATED.)

undisciplined drinking   See UNCON-TROLLED DRINKING.

Union of Soviet Socialist Republics (USSR)   In 1987, apparent Soviet per capita consumption of ABSOLUTE ALCOHOL, based on the total population, was measured at 3.2 liters. This rate ranked the USSR 37th among 47 countries who reported such data. In the same year Soviet inhabitants consumed 18.2 liters of beer, 5.7 liters of wine and 1.6 liters of distilled spirits. In the six-year period from 1979 to 1984, the USSR reported an average annual decline in consumption rate of 3% per year.

Due to the widespread consumption of illegal alcohol in the USSR, these numbers can be considered to be highly understated, although beer and wine figures are probably accurate. In fact, the problem of illegal alcohol production was deemed severe enough in 1987 to result in a nationwide rationing program of refined sugar, which can be used in the distillation process. Some researchers maintain that the USSR could have the highest per capita consumption of distilled alcohol in the world.

According to Soviet watchers, 25% of the nation's alcohol supply comes from illegal sources. Primary among these is *samogon,* a moonshine vodka that is often distilled to more than 100 proof. One interesting aspect of this moonshine industry is that it apparently has no long tradition in the rural areas in which it is most common. There is little mention of illegal home brews in Russian literature prior to 1914. In that year, however, Czar Nicholas II instituted a national prohibition of alcoholic beverages in preparation for World War I. Although this prohibition was repealed by the Bolshevik government in 1923, the black-

market trade in moonshine had become firmly established. Since that time *samogon* has consistently sold at half the price of legal alcohol, and a 1972 limit of 90 proof on legally distilled alcohols has since given the home brew the additional attraction of greater potency. It has been estimated that over 250,000 Soviets are full-time moonshiners, a trade that pays them up to six times the national average income.

The problems associated with this high rate of alcohol consumption are difficult to assess because of the previous old guard's reluctance to acknowledge it, but programs have been initiated in the Soviet Union to cope with the social costs of alcohol abuse. Studies have established links between alcoholism and infant mortality, heart disease, industrial accidents and automobile fatalities. By the late 1960s the average Soviet family spent an estimated 13% of its income on alcohol, and feminist documents from the USSR have charged the male population with a pattern of widespread drunkenness that forces women to endure food queues and other hardships of daily life. Reports suggest that 90% of Soviet alcoholics are male. Isolated studies have also begun to suggest the social costs of widespread alcoholism in the USSR. For example, 39% of the suicides in Leningrad in one year were alcoholics, and of those, 36% committed suicide while drunk. It has been estimated that 75% of all murders and rapes and 80% of robberies in the Soviet Union are alcohol related. One study estimated that half the hospital beds in the Soviet Union were occupied by people with alcohol problems.

In 1987, Premier and General Secretary Mikhail Gorbachev, in an attempt to cope with the growing problem of alcoholism, ordered a nationwide cutback in the production of vodka and instituted a system of rationing throughout the U.S.S.R. No data has been forthcoming as yet on just what the full impact has been for the premier's program of control, but it appears his program is not working too well. What is known is that the annual death rate for alcohol poisoning is around 20 deaths per 100,000 population, 10 times higher than the average for other countries. (Many of these deaths are attributed to home-made brews, which often contained impurities or alcohol levels in excess of state-produced commercial brands.) It appears that Gorbachev is in the process of revising—and somewhat liberalizing—his 1987 program.

United Kingdom   In 1987, apparent British per capita consumption of ABSOLUTE ALCOHOL, based on the total population, was measured at 7.3 liters. This rate ranked the United Kingdom slightly behind the United States, and placed the country 23rd among 47 countries who reported such data. By far, the British consumed most of their alcohol in the form of beer, with a per capita rate of 110.5 liters per person—placing the British 9th in consumption of this beverage; wine consumption averaged 11.3 liters per capita, and spirits were consumed at a per capita rate of 1.73 liters.

In the six-year period from 1979 to 1984, the United Kingdom reported an average annual decline in consumption rate of 1% per year.

Lately there has been a great deal of concern expressed about alcoholism in the United Kingdom, a country where the government actively intervened to shift drinking patterns away from gin toward beer in the late 19th century. In this century, however, a pub society has evolved and drinking in public places has become the primary form of entertainment outside the home. While beer has remained the most popular alcoholic beverage in the United Kingdom, consumption of this relatively diluted alcohol had reached dangerous proportions in the past. In 1980, Secretary of Health and Social Services Patrick Jenkins described alcohol abuse as a national "epidemic." Perhaps due to increased government attention and public education, per capita beer consumption declined 6% from 1977 to 1987.

Drinking patterns within the United Kingdom vary considerably, with a far higher incidence of alcohol abuse in Scotland and Northern Ireland than in England and Wales.

Deaths from Liver Cirrhosis in the United Kingdom

Year	Male	Female	Total
1970	741	651	1,392
1971	806	764	1,570
1972	858	804	1,662
1973	943	861	1,804
1974	901	853	1,754
1975	920	915	1,835
1976	1,038	852	1,,990
1977	991	829	1,820
1978	1,023	903	1,926
1979	1,198	988	2,186
1980	1,163	1,055	2,218
1981	1,159	1,063	2,212
1987	1,753	1,415	*3,168

Source: Office of Population Censuses and Surveys.
*Source: World Health Organization.

Not only is average consumption higher in Scotland and Northern Ireland, but there are more heavy drinking days and concentrated drinking occasions. Two reasons cited for the greater rate of alcohol abuse in these lands are the poorer economy of each and a lack of public education about the dangers of alcoholism. Surveys have shown that a mythical association between drinking and health survives in the harsh climate of Scotland, in particular, but not in southern England. Deaths from cirrhosis of the liver per capita are twice as high in Scotland as in England.

The British government has estimated that 700,000 citizens personally suffer from alcohol-related problems. According to the Department of Health and Social Services, taking into account the impact of alcoholism on family and friends, one in 25 persons in England and Wales are affected by alcohol abuse. In Scotland and Northern Ireland the figure is one in 10.

Within the United Kingdom both legislative controls on alcohol and treatment for alcohol-related problems are handled by the individual divisions. In Scotland alcohol problems fall under the authority of the Scottish Health Education Unit and the Scottish Council on Alcoholism. In Northern Ireland the sole autonomous agency handling alcohol problems is the Council on Alcohol-Related Problems. In England and Wales the Department of Health acts in cooperation with the national Council on Alcoholism, which is primarily concerned with preventative education, and with the Advisory Committee on Alcoholism, which deals mainly with clinical facilities. These agencies attempt to reverse or, at least, to slow drinking trends in the United Kingdom by means of public education, promotion of stricter laws governing alcohol-related legal offenses, and revision of licensing and taxing laws affecting alcohol consumption. Legislative efforts along these lines, however, have met opposition from the public, the liquor industry and the British Exchequer.

Treatment of alcohol-related problems is handled mostly by volunteer organizations, assisted by the Department of Health and by substantial grants from the liquor industry.

The government's recent concern that the country's alcohol problems have indeed reached epidemic proportions is reflected in several white papers. Current reassessment of its responsibility to control alcohol problems among its citizens promises to result in a significant reorganization of governmental efforts to control alcohol abuse in the future.

United States   There is in the United States an unusually acute awareness of the dangers of alcohol abuse. Many believe this awareness is a direct result of the country's role in developing early theories about the "disease concept" of alcoholism and its experience with the most sweeping prohibition of alcoholic beverages among western countries. Most states have operated antialcohol programs since the 1950s, and the federal government has been involved in similar efforts to reduce abuse of alcohol since the 1960s. Many surveys have found that an overwhelming ma-

jority of Americans consider alcohol a harmful influence on their lives and alcoholism as a social and medical problem of major proportions.

At the same time, however, availability and consumption of alcohol in the United States rose during the 1950s and 1960s at a rate surpassing that of population growth. Americans have deeply ingrained associations between alcohol and release from familial and occupational pressures and a heavy use of alcohol is seen as an "escape" from these and other tensions. Thus, among many American adults there is an apparent divergence between avowed beliefs about alcohol and actual use of alcohol. Some observers have theorized that overt public campaigns against teenage drinking and drug use are in part a manifestation of adult Americans' position in regard to alcohol; such campaigns are, in this view, an oblique response to addiction problems that leave the habits of most adult drinkers untouched. However, adults may be taking more of their own advice in recent years, as increases in alcohol CONSUMPTION moderated in the 1970s, and then began a gradual decrease during the 1980s, dropping 8% from 1980 to 1987.

Domestic production accounts for an unusually high proportion of the alcoholic beverages available in the United States. Domestic products comprise 95% of the beer, 85% of the wine and 68% of the distilled spirits consumed in the United States. In 1980

Annual Per Capita Consumption of Liters of Absolute Alcohol in the United States

Year	Total Population	Population Over 15 Yrs.
1950	5.60	7.72
1960	5.29	7.83
1970	6.85	9.88
1984	7.6	9.61*

*Population over 14 yrs.

Per Capita Consumption of Liters of Absolute Alcohol in the United States, by Beverage (1987)

Beverage	Population Over 14 Yrs.
Beer	5.07
Wine	1.44
Spirits	3.14
Total	9.65

the number of retail liquor stores in the United States totaled 16,556, which was 1,000 more than the previous year's total and more than double the number of such retail outlets as hardware stores or shoe stores.

In 1988, nearly 18 million adults in the United States were problem drinkers, according to the government's latest report on alcoholism and alcohol abuse. More than 10 million of these drinkers suffer from alcoholism. Alcohol is now a factor in nearly half of America's murders, suicides and accidental deaths, such as drownings (see ACCIDENTS; CRIME; and SUICIDE). In all, it claims an estimated 100,000 lives per year, 25 times as many as all legal drugs combined. Drunk drivers were responsible for roughly half the 44,000 driving fatalities in 1988 (see DRIVING WHILE INTOXICATED). The economic costs to society of alcoholism and alcohol abuse was projected to reach $136 billion in 1990 (see ECONOMIC IMPACT). Gallons of alcohol consumed per year per person was down slightly in the 1980s, from 2.64 in 1977 to 2.54 in 1987 (Note: These figures represent the alcohol one would obtain from roughly 50 gallons of beer or 20 gallons of wine or four gallons of whiskey, gin or vodka, according to the National Institute on Alcohol Abuse and Alcoholism). (See CONSUMPTION.) Nevertheless, alcohol is used by more Americans than any other drug, including cigarette tobacco.

Drinking habits of the sexes in the United States show that among men with full-time jobs, 14% are considered "heavier drinkers" (i.e., 14 or more drinks per week), 36% are "moderate drinkers" (4-13 drinks per week), 28% are "light drinkers" (3 drinks per week), and 22% are "abstainers." Among women, 7% are heavier drinkers, 21% are moderate drinkers, 40% are light drinkers, and 32% are abstainers. Among part-time workers, 35% of men and 4% of women are heavy drinkers.

The health costs of alcohol consumption in the United States as tabulated in 1986, included over 26,000 deaths attributed to liver cirrhosis. Statistics indicated that in fiscal year 1987, more than 1.4 million persons were treated for alcohol abuse and dependence. In 1985, out of approximately 27.4 million short-stay hospital discharges (excluding those related to pregnancy) among Americans age 14 and older, about 1.1 million (4%) involved an alcohol diagnosis.

Whatever the cause, excessive drinking continues to take a heavy toll on American life. A 1988 Gallup Poll showed one in four families troubled by alcohol—the highest incidence of problem drinking in almost four decades. No ethnic group is spared, though some are affected more than others. National Black Alcoholism Council Chairperson Maxine Woman reports that "in the black community, the fire tends to spread much, much faster and burn a whole lot longer" (See BLACKS). It remains a common problem for American Indians and people of Irish descent. It's also showing up more among groups in which it was previously rare—among JEWS, and among ASIAN-AMERICANS, even though many feel uncomfortable and develop a skin flush on drinking alcohol. In addition, as many as 45% of the country's more than 250,000 homeless are alcoholics (see HOMELESSNESS). Alcohol is also the culprit in 40% of family-court cases and accounts for between 25% and 50% of violence between spouses (see CHILD ABUSE; SPOUSE ABUSE). Also, nearly 5 million ADOLESCENTS, or three in every ten, have drinking problems."

Between 1978 and 1988 arrests for alcohol-related abuses declined in some categories.

Drunkenness arrests fell from 11% of total arrests in 1978 to 6% of total arrests in 1988, and disorderly conduct arrests dropped from 7% of total arrests to 5% of total arrests during the same period. These figures reflect a general trend toward decriminalization of such offenses, however, rather than a decline in excessive drinking. In the same decade arrests for driving under the influence of alcohol (or narcotics) fell from 12% of total arrests to 9% of total arrests.

Prevention of alcohol abuse in the United States is the goal of various federal programs that generally operate in conjunction with similar efforts by state and local governments. The principal federal body charged with combating alcohol-related problems is the National Institute on Alcohol Abuse and Alcoholism (NIAAA) which was established in 1970. In addition to its own programs, this body operates the National Clearinghouse for Alcohol Information. The U.S. Department of Transportation has actively worked to reduce alcohol-related driving fatalities since the 1960s, and the Department of Education is responsible for school antialcohol programs.

user   Anyone who drinks alcoholic beverages, as opposed to ABSTAINER.

V

---

valium   A trade name for diazepam, a tranquilizer and sedative hypnotic. Diazepam, a benzodiazepine derivative, is used in the treatment of tension and anxiety, and for alcohol withdrawal. Users can develop tolerance along with a potential for physical and psychological dependence. Valium, or diazepam, is one of the mostly widely prescribed drugs in the United States, and has a significant potential for abuse when taken with alcohol or other CENTRAL NERVOUS SYSTEM (CNS) depressants.

vascular system   Several studies have shown associations between drinking alcohol and elevated blood pressure. One such study indicated a cause-and-effect relationship between alcohol consumption and hypertension was suggested, and was a genetic factor that independently predisposes a person both to drinking and to hypertension (see HEART).

Diseases associated with blood clots that obstruct blood vessels are thought to be more common in alcoholics. Depressed platelet counts, a higher hematocrit (number of red blood cells) and decreased dissolution of fibrin, the basic element of blood clots have been noted in the blood of alcoholics (Hillbom et al.).

The *Seventh Special Report* notes that "the question whether moderate drinking protects against coronary heart disease . . . continues to generate controversy." (See HEART.)

P.D. Arkwright, L.J. Beilin, J. Rouse, B.K. Armstrong and R. Vandogen, "Effects of Alcohol Use and Other Aspects of Lifestyle on Blood Pressure Levels and Prevalence of Hypertension in a Working Population," *Circulation* 66(1982): 60-66.

P.D. Arkwright, L.J. Beilin, R. Vandogen, B.K Armstrong and J.R.I. Masarei, "Alcohol and Hypertension," *Australian and New Zealand Journal of Medicine*, 14(1984): 463-469.

Enoch Gordis, M.D., ed., *Seventh Special Report to the U.S. Congress on Alcohol and Health* (Rockville, Md.: National Institute on Alcohol Abuse and Alcoholism, 1990).

Venezuela   Thanks to its vast oil resources, Venezuela experienced enormous economic growth during the 1970s, which resulted in a major increase in the availability of alcoholic beverages. Wine and beer production doubled in that decade, and the production of distilled spirits rose 500% between 1970 and 1976. Substantial increases were also reported in the importation of spirits, most of them entering the country through the duty-free port of Margarita. Available information suggests that the illegal production of alcoholic beverages also grew despite this glut of regulated alcoholic beverages. The primary illegal drinks are *cocuy,* a distillate of cactus agave similar to Mexican tequila, and *guarapo fuerte,* a meadlike drink fermented from molasses. Almost 2,000 illegal stills were seized in 1975 alone.

In 1987, apparent Venezuelan per capita consumption of ABSOLUTE ALCOHOL, based on the total population, was measured at 3.7 liters. This figure is probably highly understated, however, as it does not include consumption of illegal alcoholic beverages that is known to occur. In the same year, consumption of beer was measured at 72.4 liters per annum, and wine was consumed at a nearly negligible rate of .7 liters per person.

Hoeveel alcoholhoude dranken worden er in de wereld gedronken? (How many alcoholic beverages are being consumed throughout the world?) 27th ed. Schiedam, Netherlands: Produktschap Voor Gedistilleerde Dranken, 1987.

vermouth   A popular aperitif with a base of either red or white wine. During its manufacture vermouth is flavored with as many as 40 aromatic herbs, fortified with spirits, pasteurized, refrigerated and thoroughly filtered. In the United States and many other places, it is used mainly as an ingredient in cocktails. The lighter dry vermouth, known as French vermouth, frequently is combined with gin to make a martini. Italian vermouth, which is sweeter, is often served on the rocks. Vermouth contains up to 19% alcohol (38 proof).

violence   See CRIME.

vision problems   Among the many physical problems evident in very young children of severely alcoholic mothers who drank during pregnancy are vision problems. Two reports by K.L. Jones and D.W. Smith (1973) and colleagues (K.L. Jones et al., 1973) described, among other gross physical deformities in these children, short palpebral fissures (small eye openings), ptosis (drooping eyelids), microphthalmia (small eyes) and epicanthal folds (skin folds across the inner corners of the eyes, which are abnormal in Caucasians). A 1985 Swedish study confirmed that children of alcholic mothers are likely to have severe distortions in visual perception. While there is much to be learned in this area, it is evident that FETAL ALCOHOL SYNDROME (FAS) is a major known cause of birth defects.

K.L. Jones and D.W. Smith, "Recognition of the Fetal Alcohol Syndrome in Early Infancy," *Lancet II*: (1973), 999-1001.

K.L. Jones, D.W. Smith, C.N. Ulleland and A.P. Steissguth, "Pattern of Malformation in Offspring of Chronic Alcoholic Mothers," *Lancet I*: (1973), 1267-1271.

vitamins and minerals   Vitamin and mineral deficiencies may occur in alcoholics with or without an adequate food supply. According to an expert in the field, Dr. Esteban Mezey, "Alcoholism is probably the principal cause of vitamin and protein deficiencies among civilized people with adequate food supplies."

Nutritional deficiencies found in alcoholics can be attributed to a number of factors. One is malnutrition, commonly found in alcoholics with poor eating habits (see NUTRITION). A second factor is impairment of the absorption and storage of ingested vitamins caused by consumption of ethanol. Most vitamins are stored in the liver, but alcoholics with liver damage frequently lack the capacity to store them. Third is a diminished ability to convert vitamins into metabolically active cofactors, preventing the body from using vitamins properly. Fourth is an increased need for some minerals required by the enzymes that are used to metabolize excessive amounts of ingested ethanol and to repair tissue damaged by ethanol. Zinc, for example, is needed for a number of enzymes. Excessive amounts of alcohol also affect mineral metabolism and cause excessive excretion of minerals in the urine.

Chronic alcoholism is most frequently associated with deficiencies of thiamine, vitamin B_{12} and folic acid. The minerals most commonly affected by excessive use of alcohol are magnesium, calcium and zinc.

Vitamins

Thiamine

There is a direct connection between thiamine deficiency and alcoholism. Thiamine deficiency results from impaired absorption (from 40% to 60% of the body's ability to absorb thiamine is impaired by alcohol), decreased dietary intake and acute liver injury. Because a damaged liver lowers the body's response to administered thiamine, alcoholic patients need increasing amounts of thiamine in order to make certain enzymes react properly. Thiamine deficiency can cause beriberi, a condition associated with disease of the HEART muscle. It also appears to play a major role in WERNICKE'S ENCEPHALOPATHY.

Vitamin B_{12}

Vitamin B_{12} is necessary for cell replication. High alcohol consumption causes impairment of vitamin B_{12} absorption, even with adequate intake of nutrients. Increased amounts of this vitamin are needed for metabolism of a high quantity of alcohol and for repair of tissue damage.

Folic Acid

Deficiencies of folic acid have been found in alcoholics, especially those with liver disease. Lack of folic acid, which is used in cell replication, may lead to impairment of DNA and protein synthesis.

Minerals

Magnesium

An element involved in energy production of cells, magnesium plays an important role in the work of the central nervous system (CNS) and in the action of many body enzymes. During periods of alcohol ingestion there is a depletion of magnesium through urinary excretion. Because of magnesium's influence on the CNS this diminution may account in part for the irritability experienced after a period of drinking. Symptoms of WITHDRAWAL are similar to those of magnesium deficiency. Deficiencies of magnesium may play a role in cardiac arrhythmia (see HEART) and interfere with the body's response to thiamine.

Calcium

Acute ethanol consumption increases urinary excretion of calcium, particularly during withdrawal. Lack of calcium may be involved in alcoholic cardiomyopathy (see HEART). Osteoprosis, a degeneration of bone tissue associated with calcium deficiency, is frequently found in alcoholics.

Zinc

Many enzymes associated with DNA synthesis and RNA metabolism require zinc. Zinc is important to the growth and repair of the liver. Alcoholics are often deficient in zinc, generally because of poor dietary habits. Zinc deficiency has been related to anorexia, which leads to further malnutrition.

C.S. Lieber, "Alcohol-Nutrition Interactions: 1984 Update," *Alcohol* 1 (1984): 151-152.

Esteban Mezey "Effects of Alcohol on the Gastrointestinal System," in *Practice of Medicine*, 10 vols. (Hagerstown, Md.: Harper and Row, Harper Medical, 1970) 7:1-9.

Gary and Steve Null, *Alcohol and Nutrition* (New York: Pyramid Publications, 1977).

vodka   (Russian, a little water, diminutive of *voda* water.) Vodka is the traditional alcoholic beverage of Russia, Poland and the Baltic states. In Russian the term is sometimes used to refer to any kind of distilled alcoholic beverage, which is not incompatible with the fact that vodka may be distilled from a wide variety of agricultural products. The substances from which vodka is most often distilled are rye, corn, barley, wheat, potatoes, and less frequently, sugar beets. In its history, however, vodka has been produced from whatever material was abundant and cheap at any given time. The base from which vodka is made is not especially important because it is first distilled at or above 190 proof, which is almost pure alcohol.

Vodka was first produced in Russia during the 14th century, and up until World War II, its production and consumption were limited almost exclusively to Russia, Poland and the Baltic states. After the war the production and consumption of vodka spread to other countries, particularly the United States but also Austria, Britain, the Netherlands, Finland, Denmark and Israel, where a kosher vodka has been produced.

The basic method currently used to make vodka was first developed in Russia and Poland; producers of vodka in other countries follow this basic method but have added their own variations. Today the distilling operation is usually dispensed with. Producers begin by buying distilled spirits that have already been highly rectified, or purified. These spirits are further rectified by filtration through beds of vegetable charcoal. The resultant liquid is at least 190 proof, which is reduced to a marketable strength by the addition of distilled water. Unlike other distilled alcoholic beverages, such as brandy or whiskey, vodka is not aged. Russian vodka is usually bottled at about 80 proof, and Polish vodka at around 90 proof. According to U.S. government regulations, vodka must be bottled at not less than 80 proof and not more than 110 proof.

In the United States federal regulations describe vodka as "neutral spirits … without distinctive character, aroma or taste." However, although vodka is usually colorless, contrary to popular opinion, it is not without odor or taste. Like any alcoholic beverage, it has both a taste and a smell. The absolute alcohol in vodka gives a mild burning sensation, or "sting," accompanied by an astringent taste. The CONGENERS present, depending on the particular type of vodka, can also contribute to the taste. The smell of vodka on the breath (or through the pores), while not so pro-

nounced as that of whiskey, rum or, to a lesser extent, gin, is still detectable in close quarters, even when the vodka has been diluted by the addition of fruit juice, tonic or other mixers. While it does not change the basic taste of orange juice or tomato juice, for example, vodka's presence is clearly detectable in cocktails made with fruit juice or other mixers. Some varieties of vodka have additional coloring or flavoring added to them. One Polish vodka, for instance, is flavored with buffalo grass, which gives it a yellowish color and a somewhat bitter taste. Certain other foreign vodkas are colored brown (from walnut shells), blue and even lavender.

In the Soviet Union vodka is popular as an aperitif. It is gulped from a small glass and followed by hors d'oeuvres, such as caviar, herring and anchovies. In the United States vodka is often added to orange juice and tomato juice to make the drinks known respectively as a screwdriver and a Bloody Mary. It is also sometimes used as a substitute for gin in mixed drinks. For example, it may be substituted for gin with tonic water or mixed with vermouth, in place of gin, to make a vodka martini.

Volstead Act   The National Prohibition Act, popularly known as the Volstead Act, provided for the enforcement of wartime PROHIBITION and constitutional prohibition as established by the EIGHTEENTH AMENDMENT to the U.S. constitution.

The bill, introduced in the House of Representatives on May 17, 1919, was quickly adopted by both the House and Senate but was vetoed by President Woodrow Wilson on the ground that since the emergency of war had long since passed, the section authorizing wartime prohibition was unnecessary. Wilson's veto was overruled by the House on October 27 and by the Senate on the next day.

The Volstead Act consisted of three titles: Title I provided for the enforcement of wartime prohibition; Title II banned intoxicating beverages; and Title III contained technical provisions for users of industrial alcohol.

Title II comprised the general provisions for the enforcement of constitutional prohibition. The text of this title follows:

Title II. Prohibition of Intoxicating Beverages.

Sec. I . . . (1) the word "liquor" or the phrase "intoxicating liquor" shall be construed to include alcohol, brandy, whiskey, rum, gin, beer, ale, porter, and wine, and in addition thereto any spirituous, vinous, malt, or fermented liquor, liquids, and compounds, whether medicated, proprietary, patented, or not, and by whatever name called, containing one-half of 1 per centum or more of alcohol by volume which are fit for use for beverage purposes. . . .

Sec. 2. The Commissioner of Internal Revenue, his assistants, agents, and inspectors shall investigate and report violations of this act to the United States Attorney for the district in which committed. . . .

Sec. 3. No person shall on or after the date when the Eighteenth Amendment to the Constitution of the United States goes into effect, manufacture, sell, barter, transport, import, export, deliver, furnish or possess any intoxicating liquor except as authorized in this act, and all the provisions of this act shall be liberally construed to the end that the use of intoxicating liquor as a beverage may be prevented.

Liquor for non-beverage purposes and wine for sacramental purposes may be manufactured, purchased, sold, bartered, transported, imported, exported, delivered, furnished, and possessed, but only herein provided. . . .

Sec. 4. The articles enumerated in this section shall not, after having been manufactured and prepared for the market, be subject to the provisions of this act if they correspond with the following descriptions and limitations, namely: (a) Denatured alcohol or denatured rum produced and used as provided by laws and regulations now or hereafter in force. (b) Medicinal prepara-

tions manufactured in accordance with formulas prescribed by the United States Pharmacopoeia, National Formulary, or the American Institute of Homeopathy that are unfit for use for beverage purposes. (c) Patented, patent, and proprietary medicines that are unfit for use for beverage purposes. (d) Toilet, medicinal, and antiseptic preparations and solutions that are unfit for use for beverage purposes. (e) Flavoring extracts and syrups that are unfit for use as a beverage, or for intoxicating purposes. (f) Vinegar and preserved sweet cider. A person who manufactures any of the articles mentioned in this section may purchase and possess liquor for that purpose, but he shall secure permits to manufacture such articles and to purchase such liquor, give the bonds, keep the records, and make the reports specified in this act and as directed by the Commissioner. No such manufacturer shall sell, use, or dispose of any liquor otherwise than as an ingredient of the articles authorized to be manufactured therefrom. No more alcohol shall be used in the manufacture of any extract, syrup, or the articles named in paragraph b, c, and d of this section, which may be used for beverage purposes, than the quantity necessary for extraction or solution of the elements contained therein and for the preservation of the article.

Sec. 6. No one shall manufacture, sell, purchase, transport, or prescribe any liquor without first obtaining a permit from the Commissioner so to do, except that a person may, without a permit, purchase and use liquor for medicinal purposes when prescribed by a physician as herein provided, and except that any person who in the opinion of the Commissioner is conducting a bona fide hospital or sanatorium engaged in the treatment of persons suffering from alcoholism, may, under such rules, regulations, and conditions as the Commissioner shall prescribe, purchase, and use, in accordance with the methods in use in such institution, liquor, to be administered to the patients of such institution under the direction of a duly qualified physician employed by such institution. . . . Nothing in this title shall be held to apply to the manufacture, sale, transportation, importation, possession, or distribution of wine for sacramental purposes, or like religious rites. . . .

Sec. 7. No one but a physician holding a permit to prescribe liquor shall issue any prescription for liquor. . . .

Sec. 11. All manufacturers and wholesale or retail druggists shall keep as a part of the records required of them a copy of all permits to purchase on which a sale of any liquor is made. . . .

Sec. 17. It shall be unlawful to advertise anywhere, or by any means or method, liquor, or the manufacture, sale, keeping for sale, or furnishing of the same, or where, how, from whom, or at what price the same may be obtained. No one shall permit any sign or billboard containing such advertisement to remain upon one's premises. But nothing herein shall prohibit manufacturers and wholesale druggists holding permits to sell liquor from furnishing price lists, with description of liquor for sale, to persons permitted to purchase liquor, or from advertising alcohol in business publications, or trade journals circulating generally among manufacturers of lawful alcoholic perfumes, toilet preparations, flavoring extracts, medicinal preparations, and like articles. . . .

Sec. 20. Any person who shall be injured in person, property, means of support, or otherwise by any intoxicated person, or by reason of the intoxication of any person, whether resulting in his death or not, shall have a right of action against any person who shall, by unlawfully selling to or unlawfully assisting in procuring liquor for such intoxicated person, have caused or contributed to such intoxication, and in any such action such person shall have a right to recover actual and exemplary damages. In case of the death of either party, the action or the right of action

given by this section shall survive to or against his or her executor or administrator, and the amount so recovered by either wife or child shall be his or her sole and separate property. Such action may be brought in any court of competent jurisdiction. In any case where parents shall be entitled to such damages, either the father or the mother may sue alone therefor, but recovery by one of the parties shall be a bar to suit brought by the other.

Sec. 21. Any room, house, building, boat, vehicle, structure, or place where intoxicating liquor is manufactured, sold, kept, or bartered in violation of this title, and all intoxicating liquor and property kept and used in maintaining the same, is hereby declared to be a common nuisance, and any person who maintains such a common nuisance shall be guilty of a misdemeanor and upon conviction thereof shall be fined not more than $1,000, or be imprisoned for not more than one year, or both. . . .

Sec. 26. When the Commissioner, his assistants, inspectors, or any officer of the law shall discover any person in the act of transporting in violation of the law, intoxicating liquors in any wagon, buggy, automobile, water or air craft, or other vehicle, it shall be his duty to seize any and all intoxicating liquors found therein being transported contrary to law. . . .

Sec. 29. Any person who manufactures or sells liquor in violation of this title shall for a first offense be fined not more than $1,000, or imprisoned not exceeding six months, and for a second or subsequent offense shall be fined not less than $200 nor more than $2,000, and be imprisoned not less than one month nor more than five years. . . .

Sec. 33. After February 1, 1920, the possession of liquors by any person not legally permitted under this title to possess liquor shall be prima facie evidence that such liquor is kept for the purpose of being sold, bartered, exchanged, given away, furnished, or otherwise disposed of in violation of the provision of this title. . . .

W

wagon, on the   A phrase meaning temporary abstinence from alcoholic beverages. The term was probably first used by the American Army during the 19th century to refer to the water wagon taken by soldiers on extended trips, on which, presumably, they had no access to liquor.

wash still   The first and largest of the two stills employed in some double-distillation processes. The wash still produces a weak and impure distillate, known as "low wine," that is usually strengthened and purified by further rectification in a small and secondary SPIRIT STILL.

Washingtonian movement   A 19th-century group that ALCOHOLICS ANONYMOUS (AA) came most to resemble. The temperance group swelled from six drunks meeting in Baltimore in 1840 to 150,000 before the end of the decade. The Washingtonians, alone among such groups of that time, did not involve themselves with organized religion, politics or social reform. (Their later involvement in the abolitionist movement *did* lead to factions that split the group apart.) Nan Robertson, writing in her bestseller *Getting Better: Inside Alcoholics Anonymous*, wrote: "Their purpose was remarkably single-minded, just like A.A.—sobered-up alcoholics saving other alcoholics who still drank, while teaching them to avoid the temptations that led them to drink in the first place." Abraham Lincoln said of the Washingtonians in 1842: "Those whom they desire to convince and persuade are their old friends and companions. They know they are not demons, not even the worst of men." Although short-lived, the Washingtonian movement had an impact and inspired other similar efforts in Boston, San Francisco and Chicago. By the late 1860s, the Washingtonians had, for the most part, passed from the American scene to be succeeded by a variety of new, secret temperance societies and fraternities.

Nan Robertson, *Getting Better: Inside Alcoholics Anonymous* (New York: William Morrow, 1988).

water of life   Any of several distilled spirits, the term "water of life" originally was used to refer to an elixir, probably not alcoholic, that would confer immortality or even perpetual youth on the drinker. The obsessive quest of mankind for such an elixir was probably best exemplified by Ponce de Leon's search for the Fountain of Youth. As early as Roman times, the term was associated with particularly strong forms of drink that would produce in the user a temporary feeling of blissful immortality. There was the added implication that life without this water was not worth living.

   The Latin term was aqua vitae ("water of life"), which was translated into the Irish Gaelic *uisce beathadh* and the Scotch Gaelic *uisge beatha* and later anglicized to WHISKEY. It also became the Scandinavian AQUAVIT and the French EAU DE VIE.

Webb-Kenyon Law   Adopted by Congress in 1913, this law was designed to allow the dry states to exercise sovereignty over alcohol-related affairs within their borders. The law gave each state the right to make its own laws concerning mail-order shipments of liquor. It was approved by a large majority in both houses, vetoed by President William Howard Taft, and passed over his veto.

Wernicke's encephalopathy (syndrome, disease)   Named after Carl Wernicke (1848-1905), a German neurologist who first described this condition, Wernicke's syndrome is a central nervous system disorder characterized by an acute confusional state, loss of balance and disorders of the eye nerves and is often accompanied by ALCOHOLIC POLYNEUROPATHY and a high risk of congestive heart failure.

Wernicke's encephalopathy is caused by the combination of a thiamine deficiency (see VITAMINS AND MINERALS) and chronic heavy drinking for years. Although victims of the disease require hospitalization, and with the administration of thiamine, treatment is often successful if the condition is caught in its early stages. If not, it may progress into KORSAKOFF'S PSYCHOSIS, which has a much lower rate of cure. The signs of Wernicke's encephalopathy may coexist with those of Korsakoff's psychosis, and the two are sometimes linked together under the single designation Wernicke-Korsakoff syndrome.

Wernicke-Korsakoff syndrome   See KORSAKOFF'S PSYCHOSIS and WERNICKE'S ENCEPHALOPATHY.

whiskey (or whisky)   A potable alcoholic beverage distilled from the mash of fermented grains, such as rye, wheat, corn, oats and barley, in various combinations. The name is derived from the Irish Gaelic *uisce beathadh* and the Scottish Gaelic *uisge beatha,* meaning "water of life," shortened to *uisce* and then to the current pronunciation and spelling. "Whiskey" (plural "whiskeys") is the preferred spelling in Ireland and the United States, and "whisky" (plural "whiskies") is the preferred spelling in Scotland and Canada. None of these countries produce a whiskey or whisky that remotely resembles the original beverage, a raw alcohol flavored with saffron, nutmeg and other spices to make it palatable. However, the whiskeys or whiskies they make are distinct, although the Canadian and American varieties may be considered together.

There are two types of Scotch whisky: pot still and patent still. Pot-still whiskies are made from malted barley only, and patent-still whiskies are made from a variety of cereal gains, including malted barley. Pot-still whiskies are the heaviest "malt" whiskies and are traditionally distinguished by their place of origin: the Highlands, the Lowlands, the Cambeltowns and the Islays. The distinct flavor created in each region is the result of the type of barley used, the method of curing, or "malting," the distillation process and the aging technique. Patent-still products are the lighter "grain" whiskies, which are generally less expensive and have a wider appeal than the pot-still types. In the production of patent-still whiskies the grain mixture is varied and the barley is cured without the traditional peat-drying, or turf-drying, process. These whiskies have lower levels of congeners because the rectification process used to make them takes longer than that employed to produce pot-still whiskies. Traditionalists sometimes object to the classification of these patent-still beverages as true Scotch whisky.

For the past 100 years most Scotch whiskies have been blended for greater market appeal. This process has led to a more consistent and generally more palatable beverage at the cost of the local distinctions favored by traditionalists. All Scotch whisky is aged for a minimum of three years, although a period of at least 12 years is favored. Aging for the most part takes place in wood casks of two sorts: "plain wood," seasoned oak that has never come in contact with another liquor; or "sherry wood," oak seasoned with that liquor and, in some cases, brandy or Madeira.

Irish whiskeys are also produced by the pot-still and patent-still techniques. However, unmalted grain and a different distilling process are used in their production. Irish pot-still whiskeys are made from a mash of less than 50% malted barley supplemented by such grains as rye, wheat and oats. Irish patent-still whiskeys are made the same way as the Scotch varieties until the distillation stage: all Irish whiskeys are distilled three times whereas Scotch whiskies are distilled twice. The result is a lower level of congeners and, therefore, a "cleaner" and "sweeter" beverage. Irish whiskeys are aged at least seven years, but longer aging periods are preferred.

The American and Canadian varieties of whiskey are bourbon, produced principally in the United States, and rye, generally associated with Canada. The primary difference is that rye is blended from a mash in which rye predominates and bourbon is blended from a mash in which corn predominates. Both the distinctions in mash content and the aging of rye and bourbon in charred wood casks give the liquors a heavier body and a stronger taste than either Scotch whiskies or Irish whiskeys. The American and Canadian varieties are considered to have roughly twice the quantity of congeners and by-products as the Scotch and Irish varieties.

Many more countries than these four produce flavored neutral grain spirits that can be considered whiskey, but the products inevitably derive from and fall within one of the four principal categories discussed.

whiskey nose   See RHINOPHYMA.

Whiskey Rebellion   In 1794, western Pennsylvania farmers rose up against imposition of a federal excise tax on liquor, which threatened the marketing of their grain in transportable liquid form. During the presidential terms of Thomas Jefferson and Andrew Jackson (1800-1808 and 1829-1837), personal freedom was popularized and rough frontier manners prevailed. Saloons were everywhere, and heavy drinking was commonplace. In reaction, temperance and prohibition sentiments grew and a vociferous minority had concluded that distilled spirits were a "demon" and "destroyer." But it was the first internal revenue statute passed by Congress—the Revenue Act of 1791—calling for taxes on tobacco and distilled spirits that prompted the embattled farmers of Pennsylvania to armed struggle. They fought to preserve local "rights" to sell their untaxed whiskey but the uprising was quelled after President Washington called out the militia. Jefferson repealed excises in 1802, referring to the "infernal" excise system, "hostile to the genius of a free people." Federal taxes on alcohol and tobacco were not invoked again until 60 years later, in 1862.

Don Cahalan, *Understanding America's Drinking Problem: How to Combat the Hazards of Alcohol* (San Francisco: Jossey-Bass, 1988).

white wine   An almost colorless wine produced by fermenting grape juice without the grape skins or stems, which give red and rose wines their color. Red wines are produced by fermenting grape juice with grape skins and stems, and rose wines are made by fermenting grape juice that has usually been allowed to soak for a period in grape skins. The alcohol content of white wines is about the same as that of red wines, ranging from 10% to 14%.

Once grapes intended for white wines have been gathered, they are crushed in an extractor or wine press to drain off their juice. The juice is then allowed to settle for a period of up to two days and decanted to ensure a product that is as clear as possible. The making of white wines differs from that of red wines in two other ways: a slightly higher proportion of antiseptic, usually sulfur dioxide, is used to eliminate all but the alcohol-tolerant natural yeasts, and additional active yeast cultures are added to assist fermentation.

White wines are usually fermented at low temperatures, ranging from 50° to 60°F. Fermentation is usually allowed to proceed until virtually all of the soluble sugars in the grape juice have been converted into alcohol and carbonic gas by the yeasts. The yeasts and sediments created by fermentation are then removed from the alcoholic grape juice, and the process continues through the same steps used in making red or rose wines (see WINE).

The most valued white wines currently produced are those from the French wine-growing regions. The white wines of the Bordeaux region are produced in Graves, south of the city of Bordeaux, and Sauterne, known for its sweeter, dessert wines. The most renowned white wine of the Burgundy region is Montrachet, produced in the southern areas of the Cote d'Or, but the most commonly known is Chablis, which has become a generic name for white wines made outside of France.

Other notable white wines include the Or-
vieto, Frascati and Soave varieties produced in
Italy, and the Rhine and Moselle wines of Germany, where far more white than red wines are
made. Portugal's Dao wine district is known for
white wines produced from the grapes of its
mountain vineyards, and Hungary, which makes
twice as much white wine as red wine, is known
for Riesling grape white wines produced near
Balaton Lake. Austria, Switzerland, Czechoslovakia and Yugoslavia also produce significant
quantities of white wine, as does the United
States, where far more white wine than red wine
is consumed.

Wilson, Bill (1876-1971)   Cofounder
with surgeon ROBERT H. SMITH of ALCO-
HOLICS ANONYMOUS (AA) in May 1935, in
Akron, Ohio. Wilson, a New York stock bro-
ker was the idea man of AA, a talker and
writer, impulsive, compassionate and a
dreamer with intellectual pretensions who
was never able to complete his formal education. Nan Robertson writes of the two men that
Dr. Bob "was the steady hand that held the
cord of Bill Wilson's high-flying, erratic
kite." Wilson married LOIS BURNHAM (WIL-
SON), cofounder of the AL-ANON movement
for families of alcoholics, in 1918. The marriage lasted to Bill W.'s death at age 95 in
1971. Upon his death, Bill Wilson's obituary
ran with a full-face photograph across three
columns of the front page of *The New York
Times*, continuing inside for three columns.
AA had almost a half-million membership in
the United States and 88 other countries at the
time of Wilson's death. William Griffith Wilson, the man who shaped what has been called
the greatest, most influential self-help group
in the world, was born in East Dorset, Vermont, son of a marble quarry foreman. Says
Nan Robertson, "The only world in which
Wilson succeeded was the world of Alcoholics Anonymous."

Nan Robertson, *Getting Better: Inside Alcoholics
   Anonymous* (New York: William Morrow,
   1988).

Wilson, Lois Burnham (1892-1988)
Cofounder of AL-ANON, the self-help movement for families of alcoholics, and wife of
ALCOHOLICS ANONYMOUS cofounder BILL
WILSON. Lois, eldest of six children, was a
graduate of the Packer Collegiate Institute in
Brooklyn. From the time of their marriage in
1918, through Bill's catastrophic drinking
years in the late 1920s and early 1930s and
beyond into sobriety, Lois was both confi-
dante and nurse to her husband, his
decisionmaker and financial support. Al-
Anon, which today numbers roughly a half
million members, was started in 1951. The
organization uses AA's famed 12-step program for recovery, but is completely independent of AA. It was with the help of the late
Anne B., who was a close friend and the wife
of an alcoholic and a Westchester (New York)
neighbor, that Lois founded Al-Anon (eventually Anne moved away from the New York
area and became less active in the movement).
Anne B. died in 1984 at the age of 84. Lois
Wilson died in 1988 at the age of 96.

Nan Robertson, *Getting Better: Inside Alcoholics
   Anonymous* (New York: William Morrow,
   1988).

wine   (From the Latin *vinum* wine.) The
fermented juice of grapes. The fermented
juices of other fruits are only designated as
wines when qualified by their basic raw material: i.e., "rice wine," "apple wine," "plum
wine," etc. In addition to this etymological
distinction grape juice is chemically distinct
from other fruit juices by the presence of
tartar, or potassium bitartrate, and natural
yeasts that will produce fermentation without
addition of active cultures.

The history of wine making, or viticulture,
began before the first Egyptian dynasty,
around 4000 B.C., according to the first
known hieroglyphic records on the subject,
which were found in funereal carvings. Most
historians agree that wine making postdates
fermentation of grains for beer and honey for
mead, both in Egypt and elsewhere. The dis-

covery of the fermentative properties of grape juice in all likelihood occurred accidently. The length of time required for grape vines to mature would have restricted their cultivation to settled rather than nomadic societies, suggesting that viticulture was probably a development of the later stages of early agrarian civilizations.

Because climate and soil conditions limited the yield of vineyards, wine was less a staple of Egyptian life than beer. Before 1000 B.C. viticulture was introduced in Greece, where the combination of better conditions for grape cultivation and a relatively advanced knowledge of botany brought wine, or *oinos,* a new prominence. Greek literature contains many tracts on the art of wine making, and Greek society was the first to ritualize and institutionalize wine drinking. Other Greek contributions to practical viticulture were the introduction of efficient pressing devices, flavoring methods and aging vessels. The Greeks invariably drank their wine mixed with water, suggesting that these beverages were somewhat lacking in palatability, but wine making was nevertheless an important part of their culture spread during the Greek age of exploration and conquest.

The Romans further advanced viticulture after it was introduced in Rome immediately prior to the advent of Christianity. They were the first to coat the insides of the *amphorae,* ("aging vessels") to prevent evaporation, and because of this superior aging technique they were the first to develop an appreciation of individual vintages. One of the earliest vintages to be stored for its special value was Opimian wine, fermented in individual seasons during the late second century B.C. and named for the reigning first consul. Like the Greeks before them, the Romans spread viticulture during their own period of conquest and expansion. Their introduction of wine grape vineyards in Spain was so successful that by the first century A.D. the Roman republic introduced trade controls on Spanish wine to protect the domestic wine industry. Wine making became common in the Rhone

and Moselle valleys following the Gallic Wars, and the beginnings of the French and German wine industries also date from the Roman occupation.

In the Dark Ages, following the collapse of the Roman Empire, viticulture declined, but in medieval times a slow rediscovery of wine making re-emerged because of the demand for sacramental wines that accompanied the spread of Christianity. Fermentation practices during this time were often based on incomplete classical texts, with the result that important improvisations were introduced in France and Germany. Lacking ceramic vessels, for example, wine makers substituted wooden casks which are now considered essential for controlled aging of wines. Presented with other problems, they devised fortified wines, dwarf grape vines, "plastering" (a method of producing good wine from thin grape juice) and a number of other variations that have become essential steps in modernized wine making.

Production of wine begins with the cultivation of grapes, generally varieties of *Vinum vinifera.* Since fermentation processes are relatively uniform, the particular character of any distinct wine or vintage depends primarily on the choice of the grape variety, the composition of the soil and the weather during the growing season. The goal is to harvest a grape with a particular sugar content, generally between 18% and 24%, before the crop begins to deteriorate in early fall. Once harvested, grapes are crushed to release their juice, a step now accomplished by means of either roller crushers or rotary paddle crushers. In the production of WHITE WINE the skins are then separated from the juice; in the making of ROSE WINE the skins are generally allowed to soak in the juice for a day or two before separation; and in the manufacture of RED WINE the skins are allowed to remain in the juice. After an antiseptic, usually sulfur dioxide, has been introduced to kill all but the alcohol-tolerant natural yeasts in the grape juice, fermentation begins naturally, although it is sometimes assisted by the introduction of active yeast cultures. After fermentation, which can last anywhere from two days to two weeks, the alcoholic juice is subjected to "racking," a process that removes suspended yeasts and various sedimentary deposits. Further purification is achieved by filtration and "fining," in which substances are added to assist the separation of wine from deposits. All wines are then aged in wood for at least one year and often far longer before being bottled, and aging continues in the bottle. The amount of aging that will produce the wine's finest quality depends on both its variety and the character of its vintage.

withdrawal   A syndrome that develops in some physically dependent users of alcohol after abstinence or a sharp reduction of intake. The effects of withdrawal from alcohol closely resemble the effects of abstinence from other generalized depressant drugs. Both the nature and the intensity of the withdrawal syndrome usually depend on the length and degree of chronic intoxication before abstinence. The abruptness of the cessation of drinking and individual susceptibility also play a role. There are different degrees of withdrawal, from the kind associated with a severe hangover to the terrifying hallucinations (alcoholic hallucinosis) accompanying DELIRIUM TREMENS.

The first symptoms of withdrawal appear within a few hours after the discontinuation of drinking. The BLOOD ALCOHOL CONCENTRATION may still be as high as 100 milligrams of ethanol per 100 milliliters of blood or even higher. Usually the first signs to develop are weakness and tremulousness, possibly accompanied by anxiety, headache, nausea and abdominal cramps. The patient is restless and agitated and has a craving for alcohol or a sedative drug. In time the tremors become more marked and the patient may begin to "see" or "hear" things.

For an alcoholic with only a mild degree of physical dependence, the withdrawal syndrome may not extend beyond the duration of these symptoms, which disappear within a few days. However, some alcoholics experience a second stage, marked by convulsive seizures known as RUM FITS. These seizures may begin as early as 12 hours after abstinence, but more often they appear during the second or third day. The number of seizures varies depending on the individual.

The third stage of withdrawal involves alcoholic hallucinosis and delirium tremens, in which auditory, visual and tactile hallucinations occur, commonly with loss of insight. This period often lasts three to four days, during which the patient is in a severe state of agitation, is often completely disoriented and sleeps little, if at all. The delusions are almost always terrifying to patients and may produce violent behavior in them. Yet it is difficult to prescribe a safe dose of a depressant drug to calm the patient sufficiently. There is a 10% mortality rate associated with the third stage of withdrawal. After the patient passes through this stage, recovery is usually complete, although a small percentage of alcoholics remain chronically incapacitated in a psychotic state. The entire withdrawal process usually lasts from five to seven days.

One explanation of alcohol withdrawal symptoms focuses on the manufacture and detoxification of small amounts of various alcohols in the body. These alcohols include ethanol, which is the kind used in alcoholic beverages, and methanol, which is the main component in wood alcohol. Usually both are detoxified in the liver (see METABOLISM), with acetaldehyde produced from ethanol and formaldehyde produced from methanol. Because the liver enzymes involved in oxidation have a preference for ethanol, they break it down 16 times more rapidly than methanol. When ethanol is consumed, the liver, which has the capacity to handle all the alcohols that the body produces, becomes occupied with detoxifying it and consequently the amount of methanol builds up. After all the ethanol has been disposed of, the liver enzymes begin to work on the methanol, producing a large amount of formaldehyde, which is very toxic to the body. This greatly increased production of formaldehyde may be responsible for withdrawal symptoms.

Proper treatment can eliminate some of the worst aspects of withdrawal. A gradual tapering off of the use of alcohol is known to be safer than abrupt deprivation. It has been found that convulsions can often be avoided by the substitution of a drug that is cross-dependent with alcohol (see CROSS-DEPENDENCY); the minimal dosage that will alleviate the symptoms should be given. It is unlikely that dependence on a substitute drug will develop, since the drug is administered on a short-term basis and in small, decreasing dosages.

Samuel Kaim, "The Acute Withdrawal Syndrome," *Alcoholism* 1, no. 5 (May-June, 1981): 43.

"Wo (sic) to Drunkards"   A treatise written in 1673 by Increase Mather, the Puritan preacher and scholar, depicting the idea of drunkenness as sinful and a disgrace. Said Mather: "Drink is in itself a good creature of God – but the abuse of drink is from Satan – and the Drunkard is from the Devil."

Woman's Christian Temperance Union (WCTU)   Founded in Cleveland in 1874, this union grew out of a women's crusade to shut down saloons and promote morality, and gradually developed into a national organization. In 1883 the organization was carried to other countries, increasing its total membership to a half million. By 1907 the WCTU had branches in every state in the nation, with an aggregate national membership of 350,000.

The WCTU was a strong voice during the Prohibition era, and it gradually became concerned with other problems of society, particularly when Frances Willard became its president. The members spoke out on women's rights, civil reform and the general morals of society.

Although the WCTU lost members and influence during the Depression and thereafter,

it still exists today, claiming a national membership of 250,000 as of 1972.

women   Although statistics from the 1970s showed that nearly one-third of all alcoholics in the United States were women (Sandmaier) and more recent estimates indicate that the figure is approaching 50%, alcoholism has traditionally been considered a male problem. Women's drinking, especially excessive drinking, has been and still is less acceptable than men's. The consumption of large amounts of alcohol can be interpreted as a sign of masculinity for a man; for a woman it is inappropriate, nonfeminine behavior. The same person who laughs at a drunk man may find a drunk woman disgusting. Women have been expected to maintain social and moral values that men have not been held to, and it is assumed that the morals of a woman who drinks heavily are questionable. While female drinking has grown to be more publicly acceptable, a woman drinking alone in public is still regarded in quite different terms than a man drinking alone. As a result women have hidden their drinking more than men have and women with drinking problems have received little attention. Dr. Marc Shuckit noted that between 1929 and 1970 there were only 29 English-language studies on women alcoholics. The additional fact that women *do* have lower rates of heavy drinking than men, and that a smaller percentage of women than men drink at all—56% of women versus 77% of men, in 1988—adds to the stigma of women who do have drinking problems.

Although many believed that consumption rates for women were increasing in the 1970s and early 1980s, a series of surveys reported in the *Sixth Special Report* has uncovered no evidence of a major increase in consumption of alcohol by women in this period. One national survey in particular focused on women who drank moderately or heavily, and did identify specific demographic groups of women who did display higher rates of heavy drinking (R. Wilsnack et al. 1984, 1986). Among the women at greater risk for alcohol abuse were: 1) women who were unemployed; 2) women who were employed part-time outside the home; 3) divorced or separated women; 4) women who had never married; and 5) unmarried women who lived with a partner. Women in the fourth category had the highest incidence of drinking problems. Women in their twenties or thirties, and women with heavy-drinking husbands also exhibited higher drinking rates. Interestingly, a study of the demographic data pertaining to women arrested for drunken driving in one city, showed that most women fit into the above categories (Shore et al.). Seventy-two percent of the arrested women were single, divorced or living with a partner. Fifty-seven percent were under 30, and 31% were unemployed at the time of their arrest.

Recent figures from ALCOHOLICS ANONYMOUS indicate that women alcoholics are becoming more willing to seek help. The percentage of female members in AA has steadily risen, from 22% in 1968, to 29% in 1977, to 34% in 1986.

Women are known to begin drinking alcohol at an earlier age now than they did in the past, and there has been a dramatic increase in alcohol consumption by adolescent girls. Studies conducted in San Mateo County, California in 1968 showed that 15% of girls reported some alcohol use. Figures released by the National Institute on Drug Abuse in 1990 indicate that among high school girls in the class of 1989, 81.4% had used alcohol in the past year, compared with 83.9% of senior boys.

History

Women throughout history have been consumers as well as, at times, producers of alcohol. Babylonian women around 5000 B.C. brewed beer and ran wine shops. To honor Bacchus, the god of wine and fertility, the ancient Greeks held drunken rites for women only. Nevertheless the double standard toward men's drinking and women's drinking began early. In ancient Rome a man could kill his wife if he smelled wine on her breath, because drinking was thought to lead women to adultery. In the literature of the Middle Ages women's drinking is rarely discussed, but it is known that alcohol was given to women for medicinal purposes. And during the Renaissance women were allowed to drink fairly openly. In London's gin epidemic, between 1700 and 1750, women's drinking was impossible to ignore (see GIN). Women were blamed for their drinking and especially for its effects on their children (see FETAL ALCOHOL SYNDROME). In colonial America women often ran taverns and were allowed to enjoy alcohol at parties. Drunkenness, however, was not accepted and offenders were subject to punishment by being whipped publicly or forced to wear the letter "D". During the 1800s some women began to oppose the use of alcohol and out of this grew the TEMPERANCE movement, which included such groups as the WOMAN'S CHRISTIAN TEMPERANCE UNION. The movement eventually led to PROHIBITION in the early 20th century. (Most historians feel that without women's involvement this social movement would never have gotten underway.) Women in this movement felt that liquor led men to financial ruin, disruption of family life and physical harm, which they inflicted both on themselves and their wives and children. In addition Victorian culture promoted the idea that women should be morally above reproach, and the use of alcohol did not fit in with this concept.

One ironic aspect of the temperance movement was that many of the women who campaigned vehemently against the use of alcohol were at the same time consuming large amounts of patent medicines, which often contained up to 50% opiates or alcohol.

In the 1920s women began drinking more openly, and during Prohibition some made money from bootlegging. Today women's drinking is taken for granted, but female drunkenness is still frowned upon. The stigma attached to female alcoholism continues to prevent many women from seeking help.

Female Alcoholic Population

Poor women are more likely to have alcohol problems than affluent women (the same holds true for men) and rural women are more likely to have them than those living in cities (the opposite is true for men). Alcoholism makes women vulnerable to extreme economic deprivation and to forced separation from their families, because men are often unwilling to support women who can no longer care for them and their children.

Housewives

Some women are not happy being housewives but feel guilty about wanting a life beyond the home. Others have enjoyed being at home, but when their children leave or their spouse dies or a divorce occurs, they may be left with few economic resources—no job— and few interests outside the family. They are often overwhelmed by feelings of insecurity and loneliness, which can create an emotional crisis that leads to drinking.

Women have been expected to derive their sense of self-worth primarily through their relationships with men rather than through achievements and activities of their own. If something happens to this relationship, they may have little to fall back on.

Working Women

The stress faced by women on the job is greater than that confronting working men, as indicated by the fact that employed women are almost as likely to have drinking problems as unemployed women, whereas employed men are only about half as likely to have problems as unemployed men (Sandmaier). The reason the rate is so high among working women may not be because women's liberation is causing an increase in alcoholism, but because women are not really liberated yet. Women must work harder than their male counterparts to prove that they are competent, and there is pressure to act like a man and, hence, to drink like a man. A job can also produce additional conflicts about moving away from the traditional roles of wife and mother. On the other hand employed women who are also wives and mothers are overburdened because they must both work and take care of the home. And, of course, an unsatisfactory job situation can contribute to drinking problems. Divorced or separated women often have financial difficulties and the responsibilities of child care, and loneliness is frequently a problem for them.

Minority Women

Minority women with drinking problems have not received much attention. In 1980 there existed not a single study devoted entirely to the alcohol problems of nonwhite women (Sandmaier). Nevertheless a study conducted by Metropolitan Life which compared mortality rates for white and minority women showed that between 1964 and 1974 alcohol-related deaths among white women rose 36% and among nonwhite women 71%. More recent statistics, however, reveal that 46% of black women were abstainers in 1984, compared with 34% of white women.

Minority women face oppression both because of their race and their sex. They have higher unemployment rates than either white women or minority men and are far more likely to head families subsisting below the official poverty level. Because of strong cultural taboos against drinking or, alternately, because of a more compassionate view of drinking by the community, the minority woman is less likely to seek or receive treatment.

Lesbians

Alcoholism is a particularly severe problem for both male and female homosexuals and the percentage of homosexuals with alcohol problems is much higher than found in the general population. According to a variety of estimates, one out of four homosexuals is an alcoholic as opposed to one out of 10 in the general population.

Lesbians are even more likely to have alcohol problems than homosexual men. A study in 1970 found that 35% of all lesbians had severe drinking problems, compared with 28% of homosexual men and only 5% of heterosexual women (Sandmaier). This high rate has been attributed to the effects of an environment that is openly hostile to lesbians and forces isolation upon them. One of the few places where lesbians are socially accepted is the gay bar, which reinforces their isolation in an atmosphere of alcohol. Outside of the homosexual environment, their sexual preference must usually be kept secret for fear of being fired from their jobs or, in some cases, losing custody of their children. Lesbian alcoholics have even experienced discrimination in applying for treatment.

Women on Skid Row

Because SKID ROW women have been isolated and generally ignored by society until recently, their problems are only now being studied. It is known that they are usually poorer than their male counterparts and end up on skid row at an earlier age. Many of these "shopping bag ladies" wandering the streets of major cities are alcoholics. About two-thirds of them drink alone, as opposed to one-quarter of the male derelicts. Little in the way of shelter or treatment has been offered to these women, and even when such services are provided, most of these women have no place to return to other than the streets.

Causes

The causes and consequences of alcoholism are now acknowledged to be different for women than for men; in earlier studies women were considered to be a subgroup of men.

There is no single cause of alcoholism for either men or women. Alcoholics of both sexes often suffer an unusual amount of stress and deprivation in their lives. It has been theorized that men drink because of dependency needs or to create an illusion of power over others. Neither of these seem to be true for women. Studies show women drink primarily to relieve loneliness, inferiority feelings and

conflicts about their sex role regardless of their life style. Nearly all alcoholic women express doubts about their adequacy as women. Those who subscribe to the traditionally "feminine" modes of behavior are forced to deny any supposedly "masculine" traits, and the women who consciously reject the feminine role may be punished by society and feel they are not proper women. Drinking helps them to forget the conflicts imposed by the narrow social role assigned to them.

Edith Gomberg of the University of Michigan has described a number of ways in which women's drinking differs from men's. Women begin to drink and experience their first intoxication later than do men. Female drinking bouts are shorter than male drinking bouts. Women more often use alcohol to reduce stress on the job, but men lose their jobs more frequently because of drinking. Women are more inclined to perceive their alcoholism as getting worse.

Women are very likely to have had an alcoholic father or other important male relative who was an alcoholic (Gomberg). Unlike men, whose alcoholism generally progresses slowly, the symptoms of alcoholism appear rapidly in women. A period of 15 years or more leading up to severe alcoholism in men is telescoped into a few years in women. Women are more prone to begin drinking after experiencing a severe crisis, such as divorce, death or separation. Periods of depression prior to the onset of problem drinking occur far more frequently in women than in men (this is not surprising since in the United States twice as many women as men suffer from depression). Such depression may be the result of the restricted and self-denying roles women must often play.

Women drink alone more often than men, probably in large part because society frowns on women going to bars alone. Male alcoholics are publicly more visible and, as a result, are sent to treatment more often than women. A woman must deal with the consequences of her drinking within a circle of family and friends who are likely to try to hide or ignore the problem because it is so shameful, and therefore their "protection" actually interferes with proper treatment. When drinking becomes out of control, however, men are much more likely to leave their alcoholic spouses than are women. The alcoholic woman is considered a failure as a wife and mother as well as an "unnatural" woman. Excessive use of alcohol is seen as overstepping the bounds of the feminine role. Although excessive drinking among women has always been linked to promiscuity and neglect of the home, evidence to support these assumptions is limited and contradictory. Furthermore women alcoholics generally show more concern for their children than do male alcoholics.

Women with alcohol problems are much more likely to use prescribed drugs, particularly tranquilizers, than are men. The alcoholic woman often does not want her doctor to know about her drinking and thus exhibits the symptoms for which tranquilizers are normally prescribed: anxiety, tension, depression and so on. Use of tranquilizers, however, can lead to dual addiction (see SEDATIVE, CROSS-ADDICTION) and it can be harder to break a dual addiction than an addiction to alcohol alone. A 1986 survey of more than 15,000 AA members showed that 46% of the women but only 37% of the men were addicted to drugs other than alcohol. Taking alcohol with certain psychoactive drugs is also dangerous because of the synergistic effect of the combination (see SYNERGY). A drug and alcohol taken together have a much more powerful effect than would be expected from either alone and the chances of an overdose are greatly increased. The availability of drugs also increases the temptation to commit suicide, a real concern since alcoholic women are more suicidal than alcoholic men.

Physical Effects

Physically alcohol has different effects on women than on men. Women show higher BLOOD ALCOHOL CONCENTRATION lev-els, adjusted for weight, than men for equivalent doses of alcohol. This disparity stems from the fact that women have more fatty tissue and men have more muscle tissue. Muscle tissue contains more water than fatty tissue, and as alcohol is distributed through the body in proportion to the water content of the body tissue, the alcohol tends to be more diluted in men's bodies than in women's. This process is ignored by many researchers who base their definition of alcoholism on the quantity of alcohol consumed and use the same figure for both sexes, also ignoring the fact that women weigh much less than men. In addition since sex hormone levels are apparently related to blood alcohol concentrations, and to consequent behavioral effects—the same amount of alcohol will produce higher blood alcohol concentrations during premenstrual phases than at other times.

Gynecological and obstetrical problems are relatively high among alcoholic women. They have a comparatively larger number of infertility problems, miscarriages and hysterectomies (see REPRODUCTIVE FUNCTIONS). However, these problems may sometimes precipitate the onset of alcoholism rather than be the result of it. Because of the high incidence of alcoholism in the families of alcoholic women, it is thought that a genetic component may be a contributing factor. Although it has been documented that excessive use of alcohol can damage a fetus (see FETAL ALCOHOL SYNDROME), it must be remembered that many alcoholic women are also heavy smokers and are on inadequate diets during pregnancy.

Women appear to be more susceptible than men to alcoholic CIRRHOSIS, and it has been hypothesized that there is an interaction between menopausal hormonal status and the susceptibility of the liver to the toxic effects of alcohol. Studies have shown that women die of cirrhosis earlier than men, even though they consume less alcohol, says Judith Gavaler, an epidemiologist at the University of Pittsburgh Medical School.

Treatment

Programs that admit women may respond to them in exactly the way they do to men, despite the fact that women have different reasons for drinking. And child care is rarely provided by alcoholism programs.

Follow-up support may be more important for alcoholic women than for alcoholic men, since women are less likely to receive support from their families (if they have not already lost them). Yet few alcohol treatment programs provide any sustained follow-up service, and as a result a large percentage of the women who complete treatment do not recover. Another problem is the stigma attached to female alcoholics, which may make it difficult for these women to find jobs.

More attention is now being paid to women alcoholics and some therapy and support groups are designed specifically for them. These groups may make it easier for women to talk freely about issues such as sexuality and family relationships. There are now several hundred all-women's AA groups across the country. A new network designed specifically for alcoholic women, Women for Sobriety (WFS), now has approximately 200 to 300 groups in the 50 states. Founded in 1975 by Jean Kirkpatrick, a sociologist who had been an alcoholic for 28 years, WFS is geared toward dealing with the different emotional needs of women which are often neglected by AA. The WFS program is secular and offers 13 steps as guidelines in the affirmation of the value of each woman. Anonymity is left up to the individual. Many women are members of both WFS and AA.

Holly Atkinson, M.D., "Women & Alcohol: The New Problem Drinkers," *New Woman*, September, 1988.

Sheila B. Blume, "Diagnosis, Casefinding, and Treatment of Alcohol Problems in Women," *Alcohol Health and Research World 2,* no. 3 (Fall 1978): 10-22.

Ed Vasanti Burtle, *Women Who Drink* (Springfield, Ill.: Charles C. Thomas, 1979).

Health Communications, *An Emerging Issue: The Female Alcoholic* (Hollywood, Fla.: 1977).

Edith Lynn Hornik, *The Drinking Woman* (New York: Association Press, 1977).

E.R. Shore et al., "Arrests of Women for Driving Under the Influence," *Quarterly Journal of Studies on Alcohol* 49 (1988): 7-10.

R. W. Wilsnack et al., "Women's Drinking and Drinking Problems: Patterns from a 1981 National Survey," *American Journal of Public Health* 74 (1984): 1231-1238.

Marian Sandmaier, *The Invisible Alcoholics: Women and Alcohol Abuse in America* (New York: McGraw-Hill, 1980).

Geraline Youcha, *A Dangerous Pleasure* (New York: Hawthorn Books, 1978), passim.

wood alcohol   See METHANOL.

World Health Organization   See INTERNATIONAL CLASSIFICATION OF DISEASES.

Y

Yale University Center of Alcohol Studies   Established in 1943 as the School of Alcohol Studies in New Haven, Connecticut, it was the nation's first such formal educational program and almost immediately conferred a new respectability on the subject of alcoholism. E.M. JELLINEK, long the guru of those who assert that alcoholism is a disease, was one of the Center's founders and its first director. The NATIONAL COUNCIL ON ALCOHOLISM (NCA) started as an offshoot of the National Committee for Education on Alcoholism (NCEA), which was founded in 1944 at the Yale Center of Alcohol Studies. Yale sponsored the *Quarterly Journal of Studies on Alcohol*, the Yale Summer School of Alcohol Studies (of which Professor Jellinek was director), and the Yale Plan Clinics (with its well-known research division). E.M. Jellinek was not a physician but a physiologist and biostatistician. At Yale he managed to pull together the most advanced knowledge of his time and became one of the world's foremost if not *the* foremost, authorities on alcoholism.

Don Cahalan, *Understanding America's Drinking Problem: How to Combat the Hazards of Alcohol* (San Francisco: Jossey-Bass, 1988).

Nan Robertson, *Getting Better: Inside Alcoholics Anonymous* (New York: William Morrow, 1988).

youths   If an individual is ever going to be a drinker, he or she usually starts before graduating from high school. While state laws prohibit the sale or serving of alcoholic beverages to minors, surveys show that most teenagers drink, generally beginning at age 13 or 14. Alcohol is the most widely used drug among American teenagers. According to a nationwide survey of the high school class of 1989 funded by the National Institute on Drug Abuse, 90.7% of seniors reported that they had tried alcohol at least once; 60% reported drinking in the past 30 days and 33% reported drinking five or more drinks in a row during the past two weeks.

Adolescent drinking cannot be judged by the same standards as adult drinking. Alcohol-related diseases, classical symptoms of alcohol dependence and many other adverse consequences of drinking that develop in adult alcoholics show up infrequently in adolescent drinkers. However, problem drinking affects a substantial proportion of adolescents. Adolescents have only recently developed many adult skills and these skills can be easily disrupted by lower quantities of alcohol than those necessary to produce similar effects in adults. For example, it has been established that adolescents become involved in fatal automobile crashes at significantly lower blood alcohol concentrations than those found in adults involved in such accidents (see BLOOD ALCOHOL CONCENTRATIONS).

Many teenagers look upon drinking as a mature, adult form of behavior. They wish to be admitted to the adult world and their drinking reflects this desire. While drinking can be a form of rebelliousness for some teenagers, for many it is a normal adaptive behavior. Most adolescents who drink during their high school years do not later become delinquent or drunkards. Sensible, moderate drinking may help prepare adolescents for their role in adult society, where social drinking is the norm.

Both parental attitudes and peer pressure influence youthful drinking. Most studies of the effects of parental drinking on youths indicate that children of parents who drink usually drink too and children of parents who abstain are likely to abstain. Peers may pressure adolescents to drink at a stage when their sense of individual identity is still weak and the need to be accepted by a group is very strong. Adolescents may drink with peers in order to relax and be comfortable as much as from the pressure to conform to the dictates of the group.

Consumption

A nationwide survey that has been conducted since 1975 provides a highly accurate picture of adolescent drinking. The University of Michigan Institute for Social Research measures the alcohol and drug use of approximately 17,000 high school seniors every year (Johnston et al. 1990). This survey has shown consistently decreasing consumption of alcohol since 1980, and the most recent results show continuing decreases of most alcohol-related indicators. Although the percentage of the 1989 senior class who had tried alcohol had decreased only slightly from 92% in 1988 to just under 91% in 1989, the proportion of seniors who were current drinkers had declined significantly for the first time in many years in 1988, from 66% in 1987 to 64% in 1988, down from a high of 72% in 1978. The number of seniors who indicated heavy drinking, i.e., consumption of five or more drinks at one time during the preceding two weeks, had dropped to 33% in 1989, from a high of 41% in 1981. Slightly more than 4% of respondents drank every day in 1989, down from a rate of 7% in 1979. Attitudes toward drinking had also changed. More than 20% of seniors disapproved of trying alcohol, three-fourths disapproved of drinking every day, and 92% frowned upon daily heavy drinking (1988).

Drinking-and-Driving

In 1988, the National Highway Traffic Safety Administration (NHTSA) reported that approximately 40% of all teenage deaths (ages 15 to 19) occurred in motor vehicle accidents (NHTSA 1988). However, the decreasing adolescent alcohol consumption rates were reflected in the number of fatal crashes involving teenage drunk drivers, which fell from 28% of teenage crashes in 1982, to 18% in 1987. This decrease occurred despite an overall increase in the number of fatal accidents involving teenagers.

Donald M. Gallant, M.D., director of medical student education in psychiatry, Tulane University of Medicine, notes that "well-documented reports reveal and confirm the consistent correlation between minimum legal drinking ages and traffic morbidity and mortality rates in young people with high blood alcohol concentrations at the time of the accident (Gallant, 1987)." In 1972, Michigan reduced the minimum legal driving age from 21 to 18 years. In a five-year follow-up report by the University of Michigan's Highway Safety Institute, the study showed an increase of 32% in the 18-20-year-old drinking drivers involved in fatal accidents and a 21% increase in that age group who were involved in nonfatal personal injury accidents. During this same five-year follow-up period, the number of 18-to-20-year-old licensed drivers increased by only 9% (Wagenaar & Douglas, 1980). Similar data are available from Massachusetts and in Ontario, Canada (see also MINIMUM DRINKING AGE).

Treatment

Treatment of youthful alcoholics and problem drinkers is a relatively new area, as is research on its effectiveness. It appears that the rate of successful treatment for adolescents is the same or higher than that for older alcoholics and problem drinkers. A number of different methods are being put into practice today to reduce the incidence of alcohol problems among teenagers. These range from alcohol education programs to more general health promotion projects. Most seek to help adolescents understand the risks associated with drinking rather than reduce the supply of alcoholic beverages. Parents can help by educating themselves about the signs of alcohol problems so that they can recognize them in their children. Many states have developed programs that focus on prevention of both drug and alcohol problems.

D.M. Gallant, *Alcoholism: A Guide to Diagnosis, and Treatment* (New York: W.W. Norton, 1987).

Enoch Gordis, M.D., ed., *Sixth Special Report to the U.S. Congress on Alcohol and Health* (Rockville, Md.: NIAAA, 1987), passim.

———. *Seventh Special Report to the U.S. Congress on Alcohol and Health* (Rockville, Md.: National Institute on Alcohol Abuse and Alcoholism, 1990), passim.

Lloyd Johnston et al., *Drug Use, Drinking, and Smoking: National Survey Results from High School, College and Young Adult Populations, 1975–1988*, DHHS Pub. No. (ADM) 89-01638 (Rockville, Md.: ADAMHA, 1989).

National Highway Traffic Safety Administration, *Alcohol Involvement in Fatal Crashes, 1986*, Report No. DOT HS 807 268 (Washington, D.C.: NHTSA, 1988).

National Institute on Drug Abuse and University of Michigan Institute for Social Research, "Monitoring the Future: A Continuing Study of the Lifestyles of Youth" (Rockville, Md.: NIDA, 1990, in press).

J. V. Rachal et al., "Alcohol Use Among Adolescents," *Alcohol Consumption and Related Problems*, National Institute on Alcohol Abuse and Alcoholism, Alcohol and Health Monograph no. 1 (Rockville, Md.: in press).

A.C. Wagenaar and R.K. Douglass, "An Evaluation of Changing the Legal Drinking Age," *The Bottom Line*, 4(1980), 16-17.

Millree Williams and Jill Vejnoska, "Alcohol and Youth: State Prevention Approaches," *Alcohol Health and Research World* 6, no. 1 (Fall 1981): 2-13.

Z

zinc supplements   There are no controlled studies to substantiate improvement for alcohol-related diseases by taking vitamin supplements such as vitamin B. However, because of occasional episodes of night blindness and reports of ALCOHOL AMBLYOPIA (characterized by vision blurring due to central scotomas), vitamin A therapy and zinc supplements have been occasionally recommended by some clinicians. Though results are uncertain in this area of vitamin therapy, vitamin and mineral supplements on a short-term basis will seldom be harmful to alcoholic patients who are still undergoing the withdrawal syndrome. (See also VITAMINS AND MINERALS.)

Donald M. Gallant, *Alcoholism: A Guide to Diagnosis, Intervention, and Treatment* (New York: W.W. Norton, 1987), p. 184.

APPENDIXES

Appendix 1
Tables and Figures

Appendix 2
Sources of Information

APPENDIX 1

Tables and Figures

Tables and figures have been grouped in this appendix so that they can be consulted conveniently without disrupting the main text.

The following abbreviations are used in several tables and figures:

1. NDATUS—National Drug and Alcoholism Treatment Utilization Survey
2. NIAAA—National Institute on Alcohol Abuse and Alcoholism
3. SAPIS—State Alcoholism Profile System

CONTENTS

Alcohol and Treatment Funding Information

Table 1   Total Financial Support for Alcoholism and Drug Abuse Treatment Services, by Funding Source, and Number of Units Reporting Receiving Funds from Each Source: Fiscal Year Including October 1987

Table 2   Funding for Alcoholism and Drug Abuse Treatment (in thousands of dollars), by State and Funding Source, and Number of Units Reporting Funding: Fiscal Year Including October 30, 1987

Table 3   Funding for Alcoholism Treatment (in thousands of dollars), by State and Funding Source, and Number of Units Reporting Funding: Fiscal Year Including October 30, 1987

Alcoholism Treatment Units

Table 4   Total Number of Reporting Units by State and Unit Function: October 30, 1987

Table 5   Total Number of Reporting Units and Clients in Treatment, by Unit Function and Orientation: October 30, 1987

Table 6   Number of Alcoholism and Combined Treatment Units, Alcoholism Clients in Treatment, Budgeted Capacity and Utilization Rate, by State: October 30, 1987

Table 7   Number of Alcoholism Treatment Units, Alcoholism Clients in Treatment, Budgeted Capacity, and Utilization Rate According to Unit Orientation and Ownership: October 30, 1987

Table 8   Number of Alcoholism and Combined Units, Alcoholism Clients in Treatment, Budgeted Capacity, and Utilization Rate, by Unit Location and Type of Care: October 30, 1987

Table 9   Number of Alcoholism Only and Combined Units, Alcoholism Clients in Treatment, Budgeted Capacity, and Utilization Rate, by Unit Location and Facility Location: October 30, 1987

Table 10   Number and Percent Distribution of Alcoholism Clients by Age, Sex, and Race/Ethnicity According to Inpatient-Outpatient Setting: October 30, 1987

Table 11   Alcoholism Clients in Alcohol Only and Combined Units by State and Age: October 30, 1987

Table 12   Alcoholism Clients in Alcohol Only and Combined Units by State and Sex: October 30, 1987

Table 13   Alcoholism Clients in Alcohol Only and Combined Units by State and Race/Ethnicity: October 30, 1987

Table 14   Number and Percent Distribution of Alcoholism Clients by Age, Sex, and Race/Ethnicity According to Type of Care in Single Type of Care Alcoholism Only and Combined Units: October 30, 1987

Table 15   Number and Percent Distribution of Alcoholism Clients by Age, Sex, and Race/Ethnicity According to Unit Location in Single Location Alcoholism Only and Combined Units: October 30, 1987

Table 16   Annual Unduplicated Count of Alcoholism Clients Served in the 12-Month Period Ending October 30, 1987, by Type of Care in Alcoholism Only and Combined Units

Table 17   Average Number of Inpatient and Outpatient Alcoholism Clients per Counselor and Units Reporting Clients per Counselor in Alcoholism Only Units According to Unit Location and Type of Care Provided by Unit

International Alcohol Consumption Rate

Table 18   International Apparent Per Capita Consumption of Wine, 1985–1987 (in liters of wine, based on total population)

Table 19   International Apparent Per Capita Consumption of Beer, 1985–1987 (in liters of beer, based on total population)

Table 20   International Apparent Per Capita Consumption of Distilled Spirits 1983–1985 (in liters of absolute ethanol, based on total population)

Figure 1   Average Annual Rate of Change (percent) in Per Capita Alcohol Consumption for 25 countries, 1979–1984

United States Consumption Rates

Map 1   Total Per Capita Consumption in Gallons of Ethanol by State, 1987

Map 2   Percent Change in Total Per Capita Ethanol Consumption by State, 1977–1987

Table 21   Apparent Alcohol Consumption for States, Census Regions, and United States, 1987 (volume and ethanol in thousands of gallons, per capita consumption in gallons, based on population age 14 and older)

Figure 2   Apparent U.S. Per Capita Consumption of Pure Alcohol, 1977–1987

Figure 3   Percent Change in Total Per Capita Consumption of Ethanol, 1977–1987

Figure 4   Total Per Capita Ethanol Consumption by Region, 1977–1987

Figure 5   Beer Per Capita Ethanol Consumption by Region, 1977– 1987

Figure 6   Wine Per Capita Ethanol Consumption by Region, 1977– 1987

Figure 7   Apparent Per Capita Ethanol Consumption by Region, 1977–1987

Adverse Medical Consequences

Figure 8   Age-Adjusted Death Rates of Liver Cirrhosis (all 571): Death Registration Rates, 1910–1932, and the United States, 1933–1986 (death rates per 100,000 population)

Figure 9   Age-Adjusted Death Rates of Liver Cirrhosis by Race and Sex: United States, 1945–1986 (death rates per 100,000 population)

Table 22   Most Consistent Features of the Fetal Alcohol Syndrome

Adverse Social Consequences

Figure 10   Alcohol-Related Traffic Fatalities, 1977–1987

Table 23   Traffic Crashes, Traffic Crash Fatalities, and Alcohol-Related Traffic Crash Fatalities: 1977–1987

Table 24   Mean Blood Alcohol Content of Drivers, Pedestrians, and Pedacyclists Involved in Fatal Traffic Crashes with Positive Blood Alcohol Test Results: 1977–1987

Table 25   Alcohol-Related Traffic Crash Fatalities Associated with Drivers Aged 16 to 24 Years, According to Person's Role: 1977–1987

Table 26   Alcohol-Related Traffic Fatalities, According to Age: 1977–1987

Table 27   Alcohol Involvement in Aviation Accidents, United States, 1975–1981

Table 28   Economic Costs to Society of Alcohol Abuse and Alcoholism, United States, 1983

Drinking Patterns

Table 29   Drinking Levels by Marital and Employment Status for Women and Men (weighted percent)
Figure 11   Percentage of High School Seniors Who Are Current Drinkers (used alcohol in the past 30 days) and Percentage Who Were Occasional Heavy Drinkers (took five or more drinks at a sitting during the past two weeks), 1975–1988
Figure 12   Percentage of Drinkers by Age Group and Sex, United States, 1984
Table 30   Percentage of Population Who Are Moderate or Heavier Drinkers, by Year of Survey

Miscellaneous

Figure 13   A Chart of Alcohol Addiction and Recovery
Figure 14   The Three Phases of Alcoholism (Alberta Red Line Chart)
Figure 15   Factors That Can Lead to Alcoholism in Women
Table 31   Calories and Carbohydrates in Selected Alcoholic Beverages
Figure 16   Perceived Harmfulness of Drugs as Reported by High School Seniors, United States, 1985

NOTE: Tables 1 through 17 are excerpted from the NIDA/NIAAA NATIONAL DRUG AND ALCOHOLISM TREATMENT UNIT SURVEY (NDATUS), 1987 FINAL REPORT. This report was published by the U.S. Department of Health and Human Services in 1989.

The survey was conducted by mailing over 14,000 pre-printed forms to state administrators for distribution to treatment programs or units. Altogether, 11,701 forms were accounted for in the final results. It is not known how many of the nonresponding units were treatment units. It must be recognized that units which did not respond to the survey are not reflected in the data presented.

Table 1
Total Financial Support for Alcoholism and Drug Abuse Treatment Services, by Funding Source, and Number of Units Reporting Receiving Funds from Each Source: Fiscal Year Including October 1987

Funding Source	Drug Funds		Alcohol Funds		Total Funds	
	Amount ($1,000's)	Units Reporting	Amount ($1,000's)	Units Reporting	Amount ($1,000's)	Units Reporting
Federal						
ADAMHA Program Support (other than Block Grants)	11,160	183	9,440	179	20,600	240
Other Federal Funds	36,268	460	76,957	530	113,225	647
Subtotal	47,429	621	86,397	686	133,825	852
State/Local Government						
State (includes ADAMHA Block Grants)	355,402	2,533	345,023	2,588	700,425	3,506
Local (e.g., city, county)	64,184	1,565	107,660	1,852	171,844	2,398
Government Fees for Service	73,834	706	78,830	805	152,664	954
Subtotal	493,420	3,180	531,513	3,386	1,024,933	4,355
Other Public						
Public Welfare (e.g. Title XX, Food Stamps)	55,800	704	27,778	887	83,578	1,106
Public Third-Party (e.g. CHAMPUS, Medicaid)	139,224	1,284	145,746	1,368	284,970	1,694
Subtotal	195,024	1,822	173,524	2,088	368,548	2,574
Private						
Donations	27,576	1,128	26,906	1,274	54,482	1,605
Private Third-Party (e.g., Blue Cross/Blue Shield, HMO)	346,963	1,804	592,447	2,209	939,409	2,455
Client Fees	157,185	3,158	236,531	3,727	393,716	4,510
Subtotal	531,724	3,551	855,884	4,114	1,387,607	4,965
Other	40,411	763	64,752	927	105,163	1,134
Total	1,308,008	4,403	1,712,069	4,949	3,020,077	6,001

NOTE: As funding amounts have been rounded to the nearest thousand, values may not sum to totals. The number of units reporting does not equal the total of units reporting separate funding sources because of units receiving funding from multiple sources. In addition, the number of units reporting in the total funds column does not equal the sum of the number reporting alcoholism and drug abuse funds because units may receive funds for both types of treatment.

SOURCE: NIDA and NIAAA, 1987 National Drug and Alcoholism Treatment Unit Survey.

Table 2
Funding for Alcoholism and Drug Abuse Treatment (in thousands of dollars),
by State and Funding Source, and Number of Units Reporting Funding:
Fiscal Year Including October 30, 1987

State	State Government	Local Government	ADAMHA	Other Federal	State/Local Fees	Private Donations
Alabama	4,785	184	134	28	89	358
Alaska	7,941	1,410	45	1,413	398	345
Arizona	8,656	1,938	748	2,377	4,652	907
Arkansas	2,442	24	70	81	78	238
California	73,494	24,053	126	25,528	25,651	7,590
Colorado	7,719	3,125	0	84	1,721	210
Connecticut	20,699	919	0	1,009	3,149	1,008
Delaware	2,586	10	0	14	630	33
District of Columbia	564	7,578	0	300	0	40
Florida	37,713	7,900	7,670	1,907	1,821	3,995
Georgia	27,011	1,571	181	1,597	499	10
Hawaii	1,939	51	19	469	597	517
Idaho	1,917	30	170	13	1	55
Illinois	36,426	4,041	68	4,051	4,813	2,782
Indiana	6,739	559	230	5,047	641	371
Iowa	15,036	979	8	3,829	593	529
Kansas	3,347	1,348	4	176	320	228
Kentucky	5,420	466	379	380	2,783	457
Louisiana	10,961	108	0	342	249	552
Maine	4,014	209	28	1,731	538	141
Maryland	25,033	4,558	592	2,224	2,292	615
Massachusetts	20,051	1,057	1,221	1,205	10,188	847
Michigan	10,871	5,819	0	2,568	8,151	1,985
Minnesota	4,081	6,524	0	5,133	9,370	976
Mississippi	3,336	257	274	746	165	19
Missouri	10,519	191	629	3,210	5,097	1,683
Montana	3,301	1,488	0	459	50	25
Nebraska	4,987	842	614	1,583	924	257
Nevada	2,810	270	27	598	270	325
New Hampshire	1,839	86	0	376	2,909	147
New Jersey	19,157	8,233	470	5,131	1,801	2,408
New Mexico	8,912	914	366	2,275	1,092	34
New York	149,881	32,895	369	4,376	18,152	3,088
North Carolina	15,750	5,799	647	917	1,742	1,904
North Dakota	6,881	42	0	78	575	314
Ohio	17,266	7,897	842	2,951	4,965	2,959
Oklahoma	3,669	6	521	1,945	2,518	559
Oregon	8,496	4,680	147	2,272	524	1,021
Pennsylvania	9,756	12,179	313	1,561	14,556	4,306
Rhode Island	6,696	180	229	273	488	39
South Carolina	10,662	2,053	0	2,172	34	289
South Dakota	866	851	0	1,182	233	77
Tennessee	6,243	168	1,086	4,188	354	825
Texas	19,363	2,002	1,318	3,495	3,511	3,959
Utah	5,617	1,708	30	1,308	222	225
Vermont	1,878	16	0	25	141	104
Virginia	11,866	5,609	737	5,828	1,845	500
Washington	6,203	1,630	212	1,711	3,454	1,261
West Virginia	3,355	104	0	24	1,884	736
Wisconsin	8,283	6,653	42	2,829	5,693	472
Wyoming	2,113	185	36	70	229	12
Puerto Rico	11,275	446	0	140	15	2,148
Total	700,425	171,844	20,600	113,225	152,664	54,483

Continued on the next page. See footnotes at end of table.

Table 2 (continued)
Funding for Alcoholism and Drug Abuse Treatment (in thousands of dollars), by State and Funding Source, and Number of Units Reporting Funding: Fiscal Year Including October 30, 1987

State	Public Welfare	Public Third Party	Private Third Party	Client Fees	Other	Total	Number of Units
Alabama	163	1,365	6,350	1,796	800	16,052	40
Alaska	40	32	1,364	802	741	14,532	31
Arizona	498	1,725	23,698	7,010	4,094	56,300	73
Arkansas	1,414	710	2,191	444	1,586	9,277	50
California	9,519	38,193	352,168	132,759	2,899	691,978	1,108
Colorado	29	5,821	16,456	8,543	1,483	45,189	133
Connecticut	1,753	3,558	5,465	6,824	1,424	45,808	116
Delaware	0	6	0	1,368	136	4,783	18
District of Columbia	139	17	271	336	0	9,244	18
Florida	505	5,978	26,363	16,045	2,855	112,752	206
Georgia	4	2,098	12,836	16,556	31	62,394	50
Hawaii	442	26	82	1,816	2,462	8,417	25
Idaho	9	19	558	1,013	23	3,808	15
Illinois	883	2,972	22,414	10,008	1,962	90,419	204
Indiana	1,886	2,793	14,626	4,805	4,813	42,510	86
Iowa	716	3,048	8,459	1,192	834	35,223	87
Kansas	170	1,225	5,568	2,358	437	15,181	62
Kentucky	21	2,956	5,042	1,895	970	20,768	114
Louisiana	37	3,250	3,344	7,297	206	26,345	63
Maine	61	644	1,094	1,319	610	10,391	32
Maryland	305	9,614	5,077	9,124	2,881	62,315	163
Massachusetts	507	3,280	10,550	6,011	3,629	58,545	160
Michigan	2,451	5,121	31,862	6,916	5,846	81,590	183
Minnesota	2,928	5,533	20,649	9,998	2,117	67,309	104
Mississippi	455	364	890	986	223	7,714	67
Missouri	153	1,189	8,013	2,420	662	33,764	91
Montana	0	226	6,333	2,377	656	14,915	36
Nebraska	89	347	3,497	6,542	769	20,452	109
Nevada	276	29	158	1,114	115	5,993	35
New Hampshire	122	650	7,241	561	123	14,053	36
New Jersey	695	1,247	20,692	11,013	3,584	74,432	170
New Mexico	21	1,221	2,524	3,251	563	21,172	44
New York	43,996	104,498	50,757	29,806	15,406	453,223	625
North Carolina	503	2,140	8,962	6,279	1,873	46,516	102
North Dakota	76	2,121	7,284	3,625	495	21,491	28
Ohio	4,301	14,041	62,206	9,290	3,992	130,710	247
Oklahoma	70	1,167	2,481	2,404	516	15,854	46
Oregon	289	647	6,701	6,625	889	32,293	132
Pennsylvania	3,926	25,940	51,797	7,968	1,601	133,904	297
Rhode Island	365	1,463	15,573	2,622	255	28,185	48
South Carolina	161	1,229	4,487	3,970	794	25,852	47
South Dakota	24	13	987	467	27	4,726	26
Tennessee	227	2,398	4,442	1,945	262	22,138	49
Texas	359	10,564	47,920	14,244	18,794	125,531	176
Utah	353	401	1,967	3,318	771	15,921	37
Vermont	26	274	487	375	53	3,378	19
Virginia	1,117	3,006	21,585	5,886	5,136	63,115	78
Washington	1,261	2,881	9,647	5,944	1,642	35,846	101
West Virginia	12	736	915	553	0	8,318	17
Wisconsin	117	6,094	14,638	3,464	2,811	51,095	124
Wyoming	20	101	741	386	107	3,998	19
Puerto Rico	84	0	3	47	205	14,364	54
Total	83,578	284,970	939,409	393,716	105,163	3,020,077	6,001

NOTE: As funding amounts are rounded to the nearest thousand, values shown may not sum to totals vertically (across States) or horizontally (across funding categories).
SOURCE: NIDA and NIAAA, 1987 National Drug and Alcoholism Treatment Unit Survey.

Table 3
Funding for Alcoholism Treatment (in thousands of dollars), by State and Funding Source, and Number of Units Reporting Funding: Fiscal Year Including October 30, 1987

State	State Government	Local Government	ADAMHA	Other Federal	State/Local Fees	Private Donations
Alabama	2,255	166	103	26	49	106
Alaska	5,953	1,329	0	1,045	230	296
Arizona	5,536	1,851	450	1,929	2,058	526
Arkansas	1,712	17	36	60	64	187
California	34,345	15,254	51	18,273	1,743	4,335
Colorado	6,290	2,948	0	36	1,361	167
Connecticut	10,619	142	0	364	1,365	329
Delaware	1,327	7	0	4	620	30
District of Columbia	0	1,782	0	100	0	0
Florida	18,238	4,142	3,792	809	564	1,068
Georgia	14,804	790	139	884	354	5
Hawaii	1,032	23	17	351	245	253
Idaho	1,318	26	88	12	1	45
Illinois	21,913	2,340	54	1,915	1,874	1,687
Indiana	4,122	423	168	3,013	454	246
Iowa	9,815	725	6	3,741	373	383
Kansas	1,896	813	4	71	205	138
Kentucky	3,984	345	140	205	2,183	162
Louisiana	5,158	40	0	283	97	261
Maine	3,074	59	14	909	422	102
Maryland	13,175	3,133	296	1,338	667	274
Massachusetts	13,532	342	479	1,152	7,517	492
Michigan	5,989	3,166	0	1,807	5,261	1,234
Minnesota	2,593	3,681	0	3,695	7,480	657
Mississippi	2,493	188	186	738	120	19
Missouri	5,200	125	444	1,763	3,165	999
Montana	2,458	1,423	0	459	50	23
Nebraska	3,155	495	456	1,424	640	150
Nevada	1,523	183	14	317	157	164
New Hampshire	1,158	53	0	365	1,453	89
New Jersey	2,909	7,033	185	2,624	1,416	1,181
New Mexico	7,048	447	30	2,201	842	29
New York	42,465	22,201	25	2,469	14,412	701
North Carolina	10,928	4,178	448	521	1,062	745
North Dakota	6,313	26	0	41	288	158
Ohio	9,395	4,193	295	1,795	1,548	1,769
Oklahoma	1,755	2	285	1,069	1,207	246
Oregon	5,428	3,517	59	2,084	491	814
Pennsylvania	5,307	5,987	231	1,245	6,689	2,175
Rhode Island	3,335	122	22	152	483	11
South Carolina	7,667	1,635	0	1,733	20	192
South Dakota	630	668	0	1,082	216	61
Tennessee	3,876	114	216	2,209	160	357
Texas	7,014	883	389	2,401	1,352	1,361
Utah	3,466	1,064	30	788	152	68
Vermont	1,379	11	0	22	109	69
Virginia	6,613	3,115	126	4,108	472	237
Washington	4,220	1,016	90	1,063	2,499	654
West Virginia	2,478	68	0	21	973	368
Wisconsin	4,324	4,769	42	2,169	3,516	283
Wyoming	1,068	155	32	63	151	3
Puerto Rico	2,738	445	0	8	2	1,002
Total	345,023	107,660	9,440	76,957	78,830	26,906

Continued on the next page. See footnotes at end of table.

Table 3 (continued)
Funding for Alcoholism Treatment (in thousands of dollars), by State and Funding Source, and Number of Units Reporting Funding: Fiscal Year Including October 30, 1987

State	Public Welfare	Public Third Party	Private Third Party	Client Fees	Other	Total	Number of Units
Alabama	85	722	3,993	816	747	9,065	37
Alaska	34	16	1,100	534	629	11,166	29
Arizona	214	777	13,552	3,820	1,259	31,972	69
Arkansas	1,338	357	1,287	270	1,308	6,635	45
California	4,967	20,414	252,014	82,302	1,750	435,448	856
Colorado	29	2,067	6,953	6,082	796	26,731	127
Connecticut	1,148	1,761	3,883	4,603	763	24,976	90
Delaware	0	1	0	1,306	136	3,430	16
District of Columbia	0	0	30	26	0	1,938	7
Florida	221	3,532	11,511	6,137	1,009	51,023	156
Georgia	0	1,620	5,645	13,839	26	38,106	43
Hawaii	275	3	67	613	808	3,688	23
Idaho	8	14	286	563	20	2,380	15
Illinois	229	1,745	12,622	4,950	605	49,935	153
Indiana	1,391	1,701	8,531	2,685	2,385	25,119	84
Iowa	428	1,930	5,014	783	471	23,669	87
Kansas	93	728	3,412	1,216	162	8,738	60
Kentucky	7	1,795	2,621	990	593	13,023	111
Louisiana	21	1,370	1,642	3,454	53	12,378	61
Maine	49	399	686	848	371	6,932	32
Maryland	50	6,583	2,842	5,313	806	34,478	116
Massachusetts	290	2,637	5,068	3,967	2,769	38,245	140
Michigan	1,456	3,508	15,022	4,373	3,366	45,182	178
Minnesota	2,038	3,196	11,904	5,229	1,067	41,537	103
Mississippi	452	249	676	620	205	5,945	67
Missouri	107	689	4,433	1,346	389	18,661	82
Montana	0	216	5,566	2,289	645	13,129	34
Nebraska	40	201	2,759	5,726	680	15,728	105
Nevada	101	8	75	409	71	3,021	32
New Hampshire	67	454	4,374	384	18	8,416	35
New Jersey	192	460	17,988	4,967	2,681	41,635	121
New Mexico	15	610	1,288	1,755	544	14,809	42
New York	5,657	45,725	39,952	18,712	10,523	202,841	324
North Carolina	333	804	2,704	4,171	1,774	27,668	91
North Dakota	38	1,397	4,505	1,989	251	15,005	28
Ohio	2,713	7,832	32,989	6,119	2,939	71,587	214
Oklahoma	37	640	1,240	878	270	7,628	40
Oregon	231	425	3,462	4,210	655	21,375	123
Pennsylvania	826	11,750	25,094	3,863	893	64,059	279
Rhode Island	257	1,435	15,569	1,510	176	23,070	37
South Carolina	120	799	2,908	2,851	666	18,589	46
South Dakota	22	13	814	421	23	3,949	26
Tennessee	103	1,382	3,035	1,251	156	12,859	49
Texas	94	5,709	23,576	6,606	11,804	61,189	150
Utah	168	181	918	1,755	503	9,093	34
Vermont	25	202	331	281	32	2,461	19
Virginia	787	1,475	10,548	3,167	3,813	34,461	66
Washington	912	1,606	6,935	3,865	1,510	24,372	85
West Virginia	6	487	599	377	0	5,378	17
Wisconsin	66	4,071	10,033	2,055	1,547	32,875	123
Wyoming	15	52	390	232	75	2,237	18
Puerto Rico	25	0	0	5	12	4,237	24
Total	27,778	145,746	592,447	236,531	64,752	1,712,069	4,949

NOTE: As funding amounts are rounded to the nearest thousand, values shown may not sum to totals vertically (across States) or horizontally (across funding categories).
SOURCE: NIDA and NIAAA, 1987 National Drug and Alcoholism Treatment Unit Survey.

Table 4
Total Number of Reporting Units by State and Unit Function:
October 30, 1987

State	Treatment Units	Prevention/ Education Units	Central Intake and Other Units	Total Units[1]
Alabama	47	21	18	54
Alaska	32	34	14	45
Arizona	79	51	37	93
Arkansas	51	37	32	53
California	1,133	879	824	1,403
Colorado	169	152	98	227
Connecticut	141	64	62	179
Delaware	19	18	9	25
District of Columbia	24	17	9	31
Florida	248	210	162	343
Georgia	60	54	39	67
Hawaii	32	27	16	41
Idaho	29	24	13	31
Illinois	251	176	146	312
Indiana	100	92	63	140
Iowa	94	71	64	119
Kansas	76	52	41	89
Kentucky	132	92	80	148
Louisiana	79	72	42	99
Maine	41	26	12	46
Maryland	197	156	81	232
Massachusetts	185	122	81	224
Michigan	214	159	96	271
Minnesota	140	72	65	155
Mississippi	84	54	39	88
Missouri	103	64	58	130
Montana	36	29	13	36
Nebraska	111	70	52	126
Nevada	43	28	13	49
New Hampshire	54	58	32	82
New Jersey	203	128	86	222
New Mexico	49	40	22	58
New York	705	525	279	915
North Carolina	109	100	93	160
North Dakota	30	26	25	31
Ohio	273	307	208	434
Oklahoma	61	51	29	61
Oregon	139	86	38	154
Pennsylvania	346	180	171	448
Rhode Island	52	42	26	65
South Carolina	52	44	32	53
South Dakota	29	28	16	40
Tennessee	55	32	31	62
Texas	262	268	172	418
Utah	42	41	27	67
Vermont	19	16	11	22
Virginia	92	73	59	126
Washington	113	83	69	130
West Virginia	22	21	19	23
Wisconsin	131	102	95	170
Wyoming	24	19	10	26
Puerto Rico	54	18	15	67
Total	6,866	5,211	3,844	8,690

1 Total is not equal to the sum across columns because units may report more than one function.
SOURCE: NIDA and NIAAA, 1987 National Drug and Alcoholism Treatment Unit Survey.

Table 5
Total Number of Reporting Units and Clients in Treatment, by Unit Function and Orientation: October 30, 1987

Unit Function	Unit Orientation			Total
	Alcohol Only	Drug Only	Combined Alcohol and Drug	
Treatment Units	1,708	1,075	4,083	6,866
Clients in Treatment				
Drug Abuse Clients	N/A	144,446	119,064	263,510
Alcoholism Clients	136,917	N/A	213,696	350,613
Total Clients	136,917	144,446	332,760	614,123
Prevention/Education Units	1,132	603	3,476	5,211
Other Units	946	406	2,492	3,844
Total Number of Units[1]	2,132	1,198	5,360	8,690

[1] Total is not equal to the sum of units shown above because units may report more than one function.

N/A Not applicable.

SOURCE: NIDA and NIAAA, 1987 National Drug and Alcoholism Treatment Unit Survey.

Table 6
Number of Alcoholism and Combined Treatment Units, Alcoholism Clients in Treatment, Budgeted Capacity, and Utilization Rate, by State: October 30, 1987

State	Treatment Units	Clients in Treatment	Budgeted Capacity	Utilization Rate
Alabama	41	1,339	1,671	80.1
Alaska	30	1,293	1,934	66.9
Arizona	72	3,796	4,865	78.0
Arkansas	45	1,946	2,325	83.7
California	880	63,177	73,600	85.8
Colorado	160	8,678	11,826	73.4
Connecticut	106	3,279	3,781	86.7
Delaware	16	1,323	1,509	87.7
District of Columbia	12	646	1,229	52.6
Florida	187	11,416	12,797	89.2
Georgia	51	5,927	6,589	90.0
Hawaii	29	598	808	74.0
Idaho	28	1,332	1,669	79.8
Illinois	175	10,989	12,785	86.0
Indiana	93	5,367	6,959	77.1
Iowa	94	3,398	4,433	76.7
Kansas	74	2,596	3,301	78.6
Kentucky	116	4,617	5,681	81.3
Louisiana	76	5,146	4,756	108.2
Maine	39	2,308	3,694	62.5
Maryland	141	9,647	11,742	82.2
Massachusetts	164	12,025	14,106	85.2
Michigan	206	11,976	17,259	69.4
Minnesota	137	2,475	3,802	65.1
Mississippi	71	3,266	5,196	62.9
Missouri	93	3,976	5,436	73.1
Montana	33	1,400	1,548	90.4
Nebraska	107	4,435	4,973	89.2
Nevada	40	777	916	84.8
New Hampshire	51	2,344	2,089	112.2
New Jersey	154	8,852	11,887	74.5
New Mexico	47	4,015	4,090	98.2
New York	367	31,946	38,888	82.1
North Carolina	98	6,331	7,196	88.0
North Dakota	30	1,671	2,269	73.6
Ohio	238	12,793	15,736	81.3
Oklahoma	52	2,431	3,271	74.3
Oregon	130	7,376	8,359	88.2
Pennsylvania	325	14,680	22,894	64.1
Rhode Island	41	2,760	3,404	81.1
South Carolina	51	10,299	11,156	92.3
South Dakota	29	1,469	1,863	78.9
Tennessee	55	3,116	3,552	87.7
Texas	221	5,235	9,115	57.4
Utah	39	4,254	4,209	101.1
Vermont	19	1,082	1,246	86.8
Virginia	77	7,307	8,044	90.8
Washington	99	9,550	11,793	81.0
West Virginia	16	530	652	81.3
Wisconsin	125	6,553	7,756	84.5
Wyoming	23	956	1,289	74.2
Puerto Rico	24	3,230	4,389	73.6
Total	5,627	337,928	416,337	81.2

NOTE: Excludes units which did not report budgeted capacity for alcoholism clients. See table 5 for all clients and table 30 for drug abuse clients.
SOURCE: NIDA and NIAAA, 1987 National Drug and Alcoholism Treatment Unit Survey

Table 7
**Number of Alcoholism Treatment Units, Alcoholism Clients in Treatment,
Budgeted Capacity, and Utilization Rate According to Unit Orientation and
Ownership: October 30, 1987**

Unit Orientation	Unit Ownership				Total
	Private		Public		
	For-Profit	Non-Profit	State/Local	Federal	
Alcohol Only					
Number of Units	236	1,086	286	56	1,664
Clients	23,990	68,484	31,366	7,401	131,241
Capacity	32,046	81,067	35,132	9,036	157,281
Utilization Rate	74.9	84.5	89.3	81.9	83.4
Combined					
Number of Units	643	2,607	609	104	3,963
Clients	18,338	125,870	51,757	10,722	206,687
Capacity	31,984	159,490	56,408	11,174	259,056
Utilization Rate	57.3	78.9	91.8	96.0	79.8
Total					
Number of Units	879	3,693	895	160	5,627
Clients	42,328	194,354	83,123	18,123	337,928
Capacity	64,030	240,557	91,540	20,210	416,337
Utilization Rate	66.1	80.8	90.8	89.7	81.2

NOTE: See table 6 for all clients and table 18 for drug abuse clients.
SOURCE: NIDA and NIAAA, 1987 National Drug and Alcoholism Treatment Unit Survey.

Table 8
Number of Alcoholism and Combined Units, Alcoholism Clients in Treatment, Budgeted Capacity, and Utilization Rate, by Unit Location and Type of Care: October 30, 1987

Type of Care	Community Mental Health Center	Hospital[1]	Correctional Facility	Halfway House	Other Residential Facility	Outpatient Facility	Other	Total[2]
Inpatient/Residential								
Medical Detoxification								
Number of Units	65	707	3	14	89	15	46	939
Clients	302	4,467	214	90	686	169	463	6,391
Capacity	497	7,518	264	123	1,065	185	701	10,353
Utilization Rate	60.8	59.4	81.1	73.2	64.4	91.4	66.1	61.7
Social Detoxification								
Number of Units	57	65	3	51	144	8	61	390
Clients	532	477	30	292	1,533	105	1,032	4,015
Capacity	652	680	30	382	2,064	53	2,272	6,154
Utilization Rate	81.6	70.1	100.0	76.4	74.3	198.1	45.4	65.2
Rehabilitation/Recovery								
Number of Units	87	779	17	624	551	30	96	2,185
Clients	997	13,094	892	9,613	10,620	264	2,011	37,501
Capacity	1,285	18,760	1,014	11,601	14,209	369	3,369	50,615
Utilization Rate	77.6	69.8	88.0	82.9	74.7	71.5	59.7	74.1
Custodial/Domiciliary								
Number of Units	10	22	8	62	56	5	19	182
Clients	187	312	124	774	857	119	315	2,688
Capacity	196	564	168	920	1,148	125	701	3,822
Utilization Rate	95.4	55.3	73.8	84.1	74.7	95.2	44.9	70.3
Inpatient Total								
Number of Units[3]	148	1024	27	691	672	46	161	2,770
Clients	2,018	18,350	1,260	10,769	13,696	657	3,821	50,595
Capacity	2,630	27,522	1,476	13,026	18,486	732	7,043	70,944
Utilization Rate	76.7	66.7	85.4	82.7	74.1	89.8	54.3	71.3
Outpatient								
Number of Units	735	527	35	78	183	1,932	211	3,701
Clients	53,562	36,379	1,685	2,069	7,932	166,874	18,832	287,333
Capacity	60,152	42,789	2,928	2,721	9,296	205,623	21,884	345,393
Utilization Rate	89.0	85.0	57.6	76.0	85.3	81.2	86.1	83.2

[1] Hospital category includes general hospitals, alcoholism hospitals, mental/psychiatric hospitals and other specialized hospitals.

[2] Total includes data from one unit that did not report unit location.

[3] Total number of units may not equal the sum of the numbers of units across types of care as units may provide more than one type of care.

NOTE: Excludes data from units that did not report budgeted capacity. Sum of units reporting in type of care does not equal total units reporting because units may offer more than one type of care. Some outpatient units reported providing services to residential/inpatients.

SOURCE: NIDA and NIAAA, 1987 National Drug and Alcoholism Treatment Unit Survey.

Table 9
Number of Alcoholism Only and Combined Units, Alcoholism Clients in Treatment, Budgeted Capacity, and Utilization Rate, by Unit Location and Facility Location: October 30, 1987

Facility Location	Community Mental Health Center	Hospital[1]	Correctional Facility	Halfway House	Other Residential Facility	Outpatient Facility	Other	Total[2]
Inpatient/Residential								
Hospital								
Number of Units	59	965	3	31	64	15	36	1,173
Clients	560	16,304	59	455	1,190	36	1,027	19,631
Capacity	690	24,465	59	554	1,796	92	2,042	29,698
Utilization Rate	81.2	66.6	100.0	82.1	66.3	39.1	50.3	66.1
Nonhospital								
Number of Units	106	86	24	660	620	32	127	1,656
Clients	1,458	2,046	1,201	10,314	12,506	621	2,794	30,964
Capacity	1,940	3,058	1,417	12,472	16,690	640	5,001	41,247
Utilization Rate	75.2	66.9	84.8	82.7	74.9	97.0	55.9	75.1
Total								
Number of Units[3]	148	1,024	27	691	672	46	161	2,770
Clients	2,018	18,350	1,260	10,769	13,696	657	3,821	50,595
Capacity	2,630	27,522	1,476	13,026	18,486	732	7,043	70,944
Utilization Rate	76.7	66.7	85.4	82.7	74.1	89.8	54.3	71.3
Outpatient/Nonresidential								
Hospital								
Number of Units	16	224	0	1	10	33	5	289
Clients	888	14,613	0	8	99	2,789	77	18,474
Capacity	1,063	17,678	0	10	211	3,387	101	22,450
Utilization Rate	83.5	82.7	N/A	80.0	46.9	82.3	76.2	82.3
Nonhospital								
Number of Units	721	308	35	77	173	1901	208	3,423
Clients	52,674	21,766	1,685	2,061	7,833	164,085	18,755	268,859
Capacity	59,089	25,111	2,928	2,711	9,085	202,236	21,783	322,943
Utilization Rate	89.1	86.7	57.6	76.0	86.2	81.1	86.1	83.3
Total								
Number of Units[3]	735	527	35	78	183	1932	211	3,701
Clients	53,562	36,379	1,685	2,069	7,932	166,874	18,832	287,333
Capacity	60,152	42,789	2,928	2,721	9,296	205,623	21,884	345,393
Utilization Rate	89.0	85.0	57.6	76.0	85.3	81.2	86.1	83.2

[1] Hospital category includes general hospitals, alcoholism hospitals, mental/psychiatric hospitals and other specialized hospitals.

[2] Total includes data from one unit that did not report unit location.

[3] Total number of units may not equal the sum of the numbers of units across facility locations as units may provide treatment in more than one location.

N/A Not applicable.

NOTE: Excludes data from units that did not report budgeted capacity. Sum of units reporting in type of care does not equal total units reporting because units may offer more than one type of care. Some outpatient units reported providing services to residential/inpatients.

SOURCE: NIDA and NIAAA, 1987 National Drug and Alcoholism Treatment Unit Survey.

Table 10
Number and Percent Distribution of Alcoholism Clients by Age, Sex, and Race/Ethnicity According to Inpatient-Outpatient Setting: October 30, 1987

Demographic Characteristics	Inpatients		Outpatients		Total	
	Number	Percent	Number	Percent	Number	Percent
Age[1]						
Under 18	3,535	7.2	17,474	6.3	21,009	6.4
18-20	2,562	5.2	18,287	6.6	20,849	6.4
21-24	6,166	12.5	38,755	13.9	44,921	13.7
25-34	15,113	30.7	86,433	31.0	101,546	31.0
35-44	11,858	24.1	66,849	24.0	78,707	24.0
45-54	6,036	12.3	32,316	11.6	38,352	11.7
55-64	2,919	5.9	13,986	5.0	16,905	5.2
65 and over	1,046	2.1	4,363	1.6	5,409	1.7
Subtotal	49,235	100.0	278,463	100.0	327,698	100.0
Unknown	2,444		20,097		22,541	
Total	51,679		298,560		350,239	
Units Reporting	2,715		3,781		5,674	
Sex[2]						
Male	38,916	78.5	218,088	75.9	257,004	76.3
Female	10,641	21.5	69,232	24.1	79,873	23.7
Subtotal	49,557	100.0	287,320	100.0	336,877	100.0
Unknown	1,262		12,065		13,327	
Total	50,819		299,385		350,204	
Units Reporting	2,714		3,782		5,674	
Race/Ethnicity[3]						
White	34,566	71.6	201,347	71.5	235,913	71.5
Black	8,379	17.4	42,584	15.1	50,963	15.4
Hispanic	3,195	6.6	29,422	10.4	32,617	9.9
Asian/Pacific Islander	188	0.4	1,503	0.5	1,691	0.5
American Indian/ Alaskan Native	1,837	3.8	5,746	2.0	7,583	2.3
Other	88	0.2	1,137	0.4	1,225	0.4
Subtotal	48,253	100.0	281,739	100.0	329,992	100.0
Unknown	2,532		17,247		19,779	
Total	50,785		298,986		349,771	
Units Reporting	2,712		3,778		5,671	

[1] Excludes data from units that did not report clients by age.
[2] Excludes data from units that did not report clients by sex.
[3] Excludes data from units that did not report clients by race/ethnicity.
NOTE: Sum of units reporting inpatients and outpatients does not equal total units reporting because units may offer both types of services. Column percentages are based on subtotal, excluding unknowns for age, race and sex. Percentages may not sum to 100 because of rounding. See table 8 for all clients and table 21 for drug abuse clients.
SOURCE: NIDA and NIAAA, 1987 National Drug and Alcoholism Treatment Unit Survey.

Table 11
Alcoholism Clients in Alcohol Only and Combined Units by State and Age:
October 30, 1987

State	Under 18	18-20	21-24	25-34	35-44	45-54	55-64	65 and over	Unknown	Total	Units Reporting
Alabama	30	64	159	420	357	212	139	11	99	1,491	41
Alaska	78	100	200	461	273	134	37	8	2	1,293	29
Arizona	298	219	438	966	1,024	385	208	37	239	3,814	72
Arkansas	128	166	306	488	368	278	180	34	2	1,950	45
California	3,255	3,134	8,396	19,728	16,356	6,861	2,910	909	1,628	63,177	879
Colorado	394	503	1,223	2,855	1,663	726	267	131	764	8,526	157
Connecticut	67	207	284	702	382	236	108	50	1,435	3,471	102
Delaware	12	52	187	555	341	131	83	30	2	1,393	17
District of Columbia	14	15	58	279	346	154	58	12	308	1,244	12
Florida	320	598	1,685	3,389	3,115	1,477	682	308	209	11,783	193
Georgia	160	181	549	1,750	1,648	867	354	103	320	5,932	51
Hawaii	90	22	90	201	79	32	14	5	205	738	30
Idaho	146	113	216	398	285	91	51	22	10	1,332	27
Illinois	829	914	1,561	3,898	3,031	1,107	556	146	480	12,522	194
Indiana	355	463	842	1,236	944	532	220	58	730	5,380	98
Iowa	374	292	486	1,024	570	265	122	50	215	3,398	94
Kansas	151	191	467	569	356	145	79	29	609	2,596	71
Kentucky	290	574	568	1,311	800	412	127	46	978	5,106	126
Louisiana	438	334	654	1,779	1,103	530	214	67	27	5,146	75
Maine	101	130	367	600	615	210	73	32	191	2,319	40
Maryland	528	621	1,458	3,242	2,322	1,285	594	197	80	10,327	142
Massachusetts	375	581	1,745	3,507	2,613	1,210	533	174	1,270	12,008	165
Michigan	741	689	1,565	3,348	2,588	1,318	521	152	1,109	12,031	205
Minnesota	249	151	352	722	447	263	141	86	70	2,481	137
Mississippi	117	254	438	823	489	281	201	41	1,291	3,935	84
Missouri	262	226	511	1,109	824	339	170	36	499	3,976	90
Montana	148	135	182	414	320	156	67	19	0	1,441	34
Nebraska	521	472	857	1,235	745	345	181	67	7	4,430	105
Nevada	85	28	100	235	177	101	38	10	3	777	37
New Hampshire	212	128	194	516	350	140	58	14	789	2,401	51
New Jersey	955	575	1,116	2,516	1,822	1,119	460	142	137	8,842	154
New Mexico	265	282	601	1,297	884	322	200	67	97	4,015	47
New York	1,369	1,382	3,987	9,399	8,258	5,317	1,979	471	3,964	36,126	398
North Carolina	151	258	605	1,778	1,579	870	345	120	625	6,331	98
North Dakota	149	138	201	499	378	147	81	33	45	1,671	30
Ohio	1,250	767	1,641	3,913	2,649	1,239	551	214	540	12,764	239
Oklahoma	141	352	305	636	491	236	110	46	114	2,431	52
Oregon	608	382	923	2,469	1,556	805	342	94	197	7,376	130
Pennsylvania	1,765	1,170	2,137	3,868	3,348	1,434	596	170	196	14,684	313
Rhode Island	114	108	257	912	696	321	192	60	100	2,760	41
South Carolina	584	627	1,126	3,252	2,669	1,114	586	223	118	10,299	51
South Dakota	72	181	152	294	177	106	39	15	433	1,469	29
Tennessee	167	127	349	779	681	436	163	61	353	3,116	54
Texas	626	323	673	1,319	1,183	561	293	165	271	5,414	216
Utah	154	303	596	1,641	919	367	166	69	39	4,254	38
Vermont	111	160	199	315	169	71	27	16	14	1,082	18
Virginia	631	495	988	2,199	1,361	594	294	80	859	7,501	79
Washington	370	710	1,301	2,608	2,352	1,276	598	230	105	9,550	98
West Virginia	239	203	428	1,018	659	387	190	62	0	3,186	22
Wisconsin	462	668	940	2,191	1,126	609	321	102	345	6,764	117
Wyoming	56	63	72	140	121	59	23	4	418	956	23
Puerto Rico	2	18	186	743	1,098	739	363	81	0	3,230	24
Total	21,009	20,849	44,921	101,546	78,707	38,352	16,905	5,409	22,541	350,239	5,674

NOTE: See table 9 for all clients and table 22 for drug abuse clients.
SOURCE: NIDA and NIAAA, 1987 National Drug and Alcoholism Treatment Unit Survey.

Table 12
Alcoholism Clients in Alcohol Only and Combined Units by State and Sex:
October 30, 1987

State	Sex				Units Reporting
	Male	Female	Unknown	Total	
Alabama	1,148	343	0	1,491	41
Alaska	917	361	15	1,293	29
Arizona	2,698	1,010	106	3,814	72
Arkansas	1,648	302	0	1,950	45
California	47,853	14,095	1,229	63,177	879
Colorado	6,549	1,654	328	8,531	158
Connecticut	2,322	633	516	3,471	102
Delaware	1,144	249	0	1,393	17
District of Columbia	860	269	115	1,244	12
Florida	8,786	2,965	32	11,783	193
Georgia	4,246	1,331	355	5,932	51
Hawaii	594	144	0	738	30
Idaho	885	447	0	1,332	27
Illinois	9,195	3,222	106	12,523	194
Indiana	4,214	1,104	62	5,380	98
Iowa	2,572	811	15	3,398	94
Kansas	1,560	391	645	2,596	71
Kentucky	3,107	1,061	894	5,062	125
Louisiana	3,788	1,356	2	5,146	75
Maine	1,592	548	179	2,319	40
Maryland	8,554	1,766	13	10,333	142
Massachusetts	8,606	2,961	441	12,008	165
Michigan	8,140	3,132	759	12,031	205
Minnesota	1,826	599	56	2,481	137
Mississippi	2,267	401	1,267	3,935	84
Missouri	3,097	853	26	3,976	90
Montana	1,000	441	0	1,441	34
Nebraska	2,944	1,482	4	4,430	105
Nevada	547	228	2	777	37
New Hampshire	1,131	563	707	2,401	51
New Jersey	6,453	2,316	73	8,842	154
New Mexico	3,072	900	43	4,015	47
New York	26,500	8,467	1,159	36,126	398
North Carolina	4,402	1,340	589	6,331	98
North Dakota	1,082	524	65	1,671	30
Ohio	9,015	3,338	411	12,764	239
Oklahoma	1,781	631	19	2,431	52
Oregon	5,569	1,797	10	7,376	130
Pennsylvania	10,706	3,696	282	14,684	313
Rhode Island	1,961	799	0	2,760	41
South Carolina	8,470	1,829	0	10,299	51
South Dakota	1,184	247	38	1,469	29
Tennessee	2,276	824	16	3,116	54
Texas	4,156	1,092	166	5,414	216
Utah	3,439	765	50	4,254	38
Vermont	720	362	0	1,082	18
Virginia	4,920	1,853	728	7,501	79
Washington	7,730	1,819	1	9,550	98
West Virginia	1,542	384	1,260	3,186	22
Wisconsin	4,745	1,896	120	6,761	117
Wyoming	361	172	423	956	23
Puerto Rico	3,130	100	0	3,230	24
Total	257,004	79,873	13,327	350,204	5,674

NOTE: See table 10 for all clients and table 23 for drug abuse clients.
SOURCE: NIDA and NIAAA, 1987 National Drug and Alcoholism Treatment Unit Survey.

Table 13
Alcoholism Clients in Alcohol Only and Combined Units by State and Race/Ethnicity: October 30, 1987

State	White Not Hispanic	Black Not Hispanic	Hispanic	Other	Unknown	Total	Units Reporting
Alabama	1,054	376	2	3	56	1,491	41
Alaska	615	17	9	647	5	1,293	29
Arizona	2,217	154	692	424	297	3,784	72
Arkansas	1,416	457	30	34	13	1,950	45
California	38,583	6,958	14,110	2,121	1,405	63,177	879
Colorado	5,178	306	1,802	208	1,023	8,517	157
Connecticut	1,424	294	246	10	1,497	3,471	102
Delaware	446	116	18	9	804	1,393	17
District of Columbia	131	960	8	28	117	1,244	12
Florida	8,927	1,672	862	50	330	11,841	193
Georgia	3,385	2,155	18	18	356	5,932	51
Hawaii	240	15	32	233	218	738	30
Idaho	1,156	7	122	47	0	1,332	27
Illinois	9,308	1,958	626	250	381	12,523	194
Indiana	3,809	718	75	36	721	5,359	97
Iowa	3,013	120	27	34	204	3,398	94
Kansas	1,698	110	89	53	646	2,596	71
Kentucky	3,728	404	17	24	889	5,062	125
Louisiana	3,307	1,731	69	26	13	5,146	75
Maine	2,202	13	4	53	47	2,319	40
Maryland	6,907	3,231	134	40	21	10,333	142
Massachusetts	9,860	1,055	439	267	388	12,009	165
Michigan	8,325	2,055	290	259	845	11,774	205
Minnesota	2,039	100	28	248	66	2,481	137
Mississippi	1,347	955	5	4	1,624	3,935	84
Missouri	2,715	663	25	21	552	3,976	90
Montana	1,107	5	19	310	0	1,441	34
Nebraska	3,814	167	168	251	30	4,430	105
Nevada	627	71	26	48	5	777	37
New Hampshire	1,979	25	12	8	377	2,401	51
New Jersey	5,979	2,014	677	30	142	8,842	154
New Mexico	917	73	1,770	1,207	48	4,015	47
New York	23,420	7,488	3,171	399	1,475	35,953	397
North Carolina	3,711	1,892	21	76	631	6,331	98
North Dakota	1,380	3	10	181	97	1,671	30
Ohio	9,715	2,081	474	72	422	12,764	239
Oklahoma	1,754	220	42	393	22	2,431	52
Oregon	6,099	223	484	546	24	7,376	130
Pennsylvania	11,503	2,474	383	39	285	14,684	313
Rhode Island	1,936	125	39	28	632	2,760	41
South Carolina	7,097	3,029	14	43	116	10,299	51
South Dakota	791	4	6	253	415	1,469	29
Tennessee	2,246	500	6	2	362	3,116	54
Texas	3,115	659	1,085	108	447	5,414	216
Utah	3,330	94	479	276	75	4,254	38
Vermont	1,003	9	5	0	65	1,082	18
Virginia	4,813	1,742	144	43	759	7,501	79
Washington	7,794	844	387	459	66	9,550	98
West Virginia	2,919	263	1	3	0	3,186	22
Wisconsin	5,363	350	159	542	350	6,764	117
Wyoming	471	8	26	35	416	956	23
Puerto Rico	0	0	3,230	0	0	3,230	24
Total	235,913	50,963	32,617	10,499	19,779	349,771	5,671

NOTE: See table 11 for all clients and table 24 for drug abuse clients.
SOURCE: NIDA and NIAAA, 1987 National Drug and Alcoholism Treatment Unit Survey.

Table 14
Number and Percent Distribution of Alcoholism Clients by Age, Sex, and Race/Ethnicity According to Type of Care in Single Type of Care Alcoholism Only and Combined Units: October 30, 1987

Demographic Characteristics	Medical Detoxification		Social Detoxification		Rehabilitation/Recovery	
	Number	Percent	Number	Percent	Number	Percent
Age[1]						
Under 18	85	3.0	40	2.0	1,513	7.9
18-20	145	5.0	74	3.7	1,126	5.9
21-24	301	10.4	240	11.9	2,785	14.6
25-34	793	27.5	600	29.7	6,351	33.2
35-44	770	26.7	544	26.9	4,211	22.0
45-54	419	14.5	320	15.8	2,087	10.9
55-64	257	8.9	161	8.0	833	4.4
65 and over	111	3.9	44	2.2	229	1.2
Subtotal	2,881	100.0	2,023	100.0	19,135	100.0
Unknown	252		76		571	
Total	3,133		2,099		19,706	
Units Reporting	201		100		1,066	
Sex[2]						
Male	2,387	77.4	1,753	83.8	15,256	78.8
Female	695	22.6	339	16.2	4,104	21.2
Subtotal	3,082	100.0	2,092	100.0	19,360	100.0
Unknown	51		7		302	
Total	3,133		2,099		19,662	
Units Reporting	201		100		1,065	
Race/Ethnicity[3]						
White	1,937	67.8	1,381	67.5	13,471	70.3
Black	589	20.6	446	21.8	3,398	17.7
Hispanic	277	9.7	112	5.5	1,408	7.4
Asian/Pacific Islander	5	0.2	5	0.2	102	0.5
American Indian/ Alaskan Native	46	1.6	99	4.8	722	3.8
Other	5	0.2	4	0.2	49	0.3
Subtotal	2,859	100.0	2,047	100.0	19,150	100.0
Unknown	274		52		512	
Total	3,133		2,099		19,662	
Units Reporting	201		100		1,065	

Continued on the next page. See footnotes at end of table.

Table 14 (continued)
Number and Percent Distribution of Alcoholism Clients by Age, Sex, and Race/Ethnicity According to Type of Care in Single Type of Care Alcoholism Only and Combined Units: October 30, 1987

Demographic Characteristics	Custodial/Domiciliary		Total Inpatient		Outpatient Rehabilitation	
	Number	Percent	Number	Percent	Number	Percent
Age[1]						
Under 18	63	4.3	1,701	6.7	14,735	6.6
18-20	68	4.7	1,413	5.5	15,178	6.8
21-24	124	8.5	3,450	13.5	31,763	14.2
25-34	391	26.9	8,135	31.9	69,400	31.1
35-44	363	25.0	5,888	23.1	53,225	23.8
45-54	230	15.9	3,056	12.0	25,395	11.4
55-64	163	11.2	1,414	5.5	10,395	4.7
65 and over	49	3.4	433	1.7	3,219	1.4
Subtotal	1,451	100.0	25,490	100.0	223,310	100.0
Unknown	9		908		11,686	
Total	1,460		26,398		235,003	
Units Reporting	100		1,467		2,945	
Sex[2]						
Male	1,260	86.3	20,656	79.5	172,834	75.5
Female	200	13.7	5,338	20.5	56,085	24.5
Subtotal	1,460	100.0	25,994	100.0	228,919	100.0
Unknown	0		360		6,089	
Total	1,460		26,354		235,008	
Units Reporting	100		1,466		2,946	
Race/Ethnicity[3]						
White	1,076	73.7	17,865	70.0	161,903	71.5
Black	241	16.5	4,674	18.3	32,433	14.3
Hispanic	105	7.2	1,902	7.5	25,454	11.2
Asian/Pacific Islander	1	0.1	113	0.4	1,277	0.6
American Indian/ Alaskan Native	35	2.4	902	3.5	4,391	1.9
Other	1	0.1	59	0.2	1,034	0.5
Subtotal	1,459	100.0	25,515	100.0	226,492	100.0
Unknown	1		839		8,343	
Total	1,460		26,354		234,900	
Units Reporting	100		1,466		2,945	

[1] Excludes data from units that did not report clients by age.
[2] Excludes data from units that did not report clients by sex.
[3] Excludes data from units that did not report clients by race/ethnicity.
NOTE: Excludes data from facilities that provided multiple types of care. Column percentages are based on subtotal, excluding unknowns for age, race and sex. Percentages may not sum to 100 because of rounding.
SOURCE: NIDA and NIAAA, 1987 National Drug and Alcoholism Treatment Unit Survey.

Table 15
Number and Percent Distribution of Alcoholism Clients by Age, Sex, and Race/Ethnicity According to Unit Location in Single Location Alcoholism Only and Combined Units: October 30, 1987

Demographic Characteristics	Hospital		Nonhospital		Total	
	Number	Percent	Number	Percent	Number	Percent
Age[1]						
Under 18	2,454	6.2	18,197	6.4	20,651	6.4
18-20	1,686	4.3	18,824	6.7	20,510	6.4
21-24	4,050	10.2	39,957	14.1	44,007	13.7
25-34	11,155	28.2	88,571	31.3	99,726	31.0
35-44	10,138	25.7	67,434	23.9	77,572	24.1
45-54	5,560	14.1	32,138	11.4	37,698	11.7
55-64	3,271	8.3	13,364	4.7	16,635	5.2
65 and over	1,208	3.1	4,121	1.5	5,329	1.7
Subtotal	39,522	100.0	282,606	100.0	322,128	100.0
Unknown	7,572		14,262		21,834	
Total	47,094		296,875		343,969	
Units Reporting	1,082		4,542		5,624	
Sex[2]						
Male	34,698	80.0	218,018	75.8	252,716	76.3
Female	8,651	20.0	69,677	24.2	78,328	23.7
Subtotal	43,349	100.0	287,695	100.0	331,044	100.0
Unknown	3,742		9,141		12,883	
Total	47,091		296,836		343,927	
Units Reporting	1,082		4,542		5,624	
Race/Ethnicity[3]						
White	27,773	71.8	204,065	71.4	231,838	71.4
Black	7,059	18.2	42,814	15.0	49,873	15.4
Hispanic	2,924	7.6	29,561	10.3	32,485	10.0
Asian/Pacific Islander	139	0.4	1,543	0.5	1,682	0.5
American Indian/ Alaskan Native	722	1.9	6,697	2.3	7,419	2.3
Other	69	0.2	1,150	0.4	1,219	0.4
Subtotal	38,686	100.0	285,830	100.0	324,516	100.0
Unknown	8,130		10,847		18,977	
Total	46,816		296,742		343,558	
Units Reporting	1,081		4,540		5,621	

[1] Excludes data from units that did not report clients by age.
[2] Excludes data from units that did not report clients by sex.
[3] Excludes data from units that did not report clients by race/ethnicity.
NOTE: Excludes data from units that provided both hospital and nonhospital care. Column percentages are based on subtotal, excluding unknowns for age, race and sex. Percentages may not sum to 100 because of rounding.
SOURCE: NIDA and NIAAA, 1987 National Drug and Alcoholism Treatment Unit Survey.

Table 16
Annual Unduplicated Count of Alcoholism Clients Served in the
12-Month Period Ending October 30, 1987, by Type of Care in
Alcoholism Only and Combined Units

Type of Care	Annual Alcoholism Clients		Number of Units
	Number	Percent	
Alcohol Only Units			
Medical Detoxification	49,589	10.8	66
Social Detoxification	60,719	13.2	63
Inpatient Rehabilitation	72,878	15.8	451
Custodial/Domiciliary	3,670	0.8	48
Outpatient Rehabilitation	273,922	59.4	806
Subtotal	460,778	100.0	1,434
Multiple Types	128,275		248
Total	589,053		1,682
Combined Units			
Medical Detoxification	49,750	9.7	146
Social Detoxification	13,088	2.5	36
Inpatient Rehabilitation	63,378	12.3	610
Custodial/Domiciliary	2,620	0.5	54
Outpatient Rehabilitation	384,472	74.9	2,070
Subtotal	513,308	100.0	2,916
Multiple Types	327,673		988
Total	840,981		3,904
Total			
Medical Detoxification	99,339	10.2	212
Social Detoxification	73,807	7.6	99
Inpatient Rehabilitation	136,256	14.0	1,061
Custodial/Domiciliary	6,290	0.6	102
Outpatient Rehabilitation	658,394	67.6	2,876
Subtotal	974,086	100.0	4,350
Multiple Types	455,948		1,236
Total	1,430,034		5,586

NOTE: Percentages based on subtotal for single type of care only.
Percentages may not sum to 100 because of rounding. As clients could
have been treated at more than one unit, this table may include some
multiple counting of clients.
SOURCE: NIDA and NIAAA, 1987 National Drug and Alcoholism Treatment Unit Survey.

Table 17
Average Number of Inpatient and Outpatient Alcoholism Clients per Counselor and Units Reporting Clients per Counselor in Alcoholism Only Units According to Unit Location and Type of Care Provided by Unit

Type of Care Provided	Community Mental Health Center	Hospital[1]	Correctional Facility	Halfway House	Other Residential Facility	Outpatient Facility	Other	Total
Inpatient								
Medical Detoxification Only Units								
Clients Per Counselor	5.0	5.9	N/A	4.0	6.3	N/A	8.8	6.1
Units Reporting	3	49	0	1	7	0	6	66
Social Detoxification Only Units								
Clients Per Counselor	5.8	8.7	N/A	5.7	8.5	N/A	8.4	8.2
Units Reporting	4	6	0	3	30	0	19	62
Rehabilitation/Recovery Only Units								
Clients Per Counselor	5.0	6.0	16.3	7.6	7.8	10.0	6.8	7.5
Units Reporting	3	51	4	285	96	1	12	452
Custodial/Domiciliary Only Units								
Clients Per Counselor	13.0	5.0	30.0	9.4	11.5	N/A	6.7	10.2
Units Reporting	1	1	1	29	13	0	3	48
Multiple Type of Care Units								
Clients Per Counselor	11.1	6.7	16.0	7.5	7.1	5.4	8.6	7.3
Units Reporting	10	103	1	46	69	5	17	251
Total								
Clients Per Counselor	8.4	6.4	18.5	7.7	7.8	6.2	8.1	7.5
Units Reporting	21	210	6	364	215	6	57	879
Outpatient								
Total								
Clients Per Counselor	32.8	27.6	21.3	18.4	19.8	31.8	37.6	30.8
Units Reporting	105	135	4	21	48	597	65	975

[1]Hospital category includes general hospitals, alcoholism hospitals, mental/psychiatric hospitals and other specialized hospitals.
N/A Not applicable.
NOTE: Excludes data for units which did not report inpatient or outpatient clients per counselor and those to which these items did not apply. Data on clients per counselor are unweighted averages across units.
SOURCE: NIDA and NIAAA, 1987 National Drug and Alcoholism Treatment Unit Survey.

Table 18
International Apparent Per Capita Consumption of Wine, 1985–1987
(in liters of wine based on total population)

Country	1985	1986	1987
Italy	84.8	73.3	79.0
France	79.7	76.4	75.1
Portugal	87.0	70.8	64.3
Luxembourg	57.3	55.4	58.5
Argentina	60.1	59.2	58.1
Spain	48	47	54
Switzerland	49.6	48.6	49.5
Chile	40	35	35
Austria	34.3	32.8	32.1
Greece	37.3	23.7	31.8
Rumania	ca. 28	ca. 28	ca. 28
West Germany	25.6	23.3	25.8
Uruguay	24.3	22.0	25.7
Yugoslavia	17.4	27.5	ca. 25
Belgium	22.7	21.7	23.0
Bulgaria	20.2	22.1	22.5
Hungary	24.8	23.2	21.5
Australia	21.6	20.6	21.5
Denmark	20.71	19.82	20.63
New Zealand	14.3	16.2	15.3
Netherlands	14.96	14.9	14.61
Czechoslovakia	16.0	12.3	13.7
Cyprus	11.9	11.8	13.2
Sweden	11.7	11.96	11.83
United Kingdom	9.96	10.40	11.03
East Germany	10.3	10.9	ca. 10
Canada	10.01	9.85	na
U.S.A.	9.15	9.16	9.05
South Africa	9.7	9.3	9.0
Poland	7.9	8.2	8.4
Iceland	7.25	6.77	6.8
Ireland	6.1	6.1	ca. 6
Norway	5.12	5.17	5.93
U.S.S.R.	11.6	5.6	5.7
Finland	4.49	4.92	5.12
Tunisia	3.18	3.18	3.18
Paraguay	1.9	1.9	1.9
Morocco	1.3	1.6	1.6
Brazil	2.5	2.4	1.5
Algeria	1.2	1.2	1.2

Table 18 (continued)
International Apparent Per Capita Consumption of Wine, 1985–1987
(in liters of wine based on total population)

Country	1985	1986	1987
Japan	0.7	0.71	0.80
Venezuela	0.7	0.7	0.7
Peru	0.6	0.6	0.6
Turkey	1.0	0.4	0.4
Mexico	ca. 0.2	ca. 0.2	ca. 0.2

na: Data not available
NOTE: Sales data were lacking for a number of consumption figures, which were then calculated from production figures for wine.
SOURCE: *Hoeveel alcoholhoude dranken worden er in de wereld gedronken?* (How many alcoholic beverages are being consumed throughout the world?) 27th ed. (Schiedam, Netherlands: Produktschap voor gedistilleerde dranken, 1987).

Table 19
International Apparent Per Capita Consumption of Beer, 1985–1987
(in liters of beer based on total population)

Country	1985	1986	1987
East Germany	141.6	142.1	ca. 145.0
West Germany	145.5	146.4	144.2
Czechoslovakia	130.8	133.4	130.0
New Zealand	115.2	120.8	121.7
Belgium	121.0	119.8	121.1
Austria	111.6	118.5	118.3
Denmark	121.26	125.78	118.05
Luxembourg	120.4	119.3	116.5
United Kingdom	108.9	108.1	110.5
Australia	115.5	111.3	108.2
Hungary	92.4	99.4	100.2
U.S.A.	90.3	90.8	90.1
Netherlands	84.5	86.0	84.3
Canada	81.6	81.1	n/a
Ireland	77.0	77.3	ca. 75
Venezuela	59.5	60.7	72.4
Switzerland	69.2	69.4	69.3
Finland	61.7	65.4	68.1
Bulgaria	63.3	64.3	66.4
Spain	61.0	62.0	64.5
Colombia	52.3	54.7	56.3
Sweden	46.8	50.0	51.5
Norway	47.52	50.78	51.44
Yugoslavia	45.9	50.1	51.0
Cyprus	42.0	44.1	46.6
South Africa	38.8	41.8	46.4
Rumania	50	48	44
Peru	30.0	36.7	43.3
Japan	38	40.38	43.16
Portugal	38.1	38.8	40
France	40.1	40.4	38.9
Mexico	32.7	35	36.4
Paraguay	34	25.7	34.2
Brazil	22.3	31.6	33.6
Greece	33.9	34.4	32.3
Poland	29.5	29.7	30.4
Cuba	25.6	28.7	29.0
Italy	21.6	19.5	25.6
Uruguay	17.7	20.3	20.8
Chile	16.2	16.6	20.7

Table 19 (continued)
International Apparent Per Capita Consumption of Beer, 1985–1987
(in liters of beer based on total population)

Country	1985	1986	1987
Argentina	13.02	17.57	18.54
U.S.S.R.	24	17.8	18.2
Iceland	17.0	15.8	16.0
Turkey	4.0	3.8	4.0
Tunisia	5.8	4.6	3.6
Algeria	3.4	2.7	3.2
Morocco	1.6	1.8	2.1

na: Data not available

NOTE: Sales data were lacking for a number of consumption figures, which were then calculated from production figures for beer.

SOURCE: *Hoeveel alcoholhoude dranken worden er in de wereld gedronken?* (How many alcoholic beverages are being consumed throughout the world?) 27th ed. (Schiedam, Netherlands: Produktschap voor gedistilleerde dranken, 1987).

Table 20
International Per Capita Consumption of Distilled Spirits, 1983–85
(in liters of absolute ethanol, based on total population)

Country	1985	1986	1987
East Germany	4.8	4.9	ca. 5
Hungary	5.4	5.3	4.7
Poland	4.6	4.7	4.7
Czechoslovakia	3.52	3.40	3.32
Finland	3.01	3.17	3.22
Spain	ca. 3	ca. 3	ca. 3
Bulgaria	3.21	3.41	2.83
Canada	2.61	ca. 2.55	na
Luxembourg	ca. 2.5	ca. 2.5	ca. 2.5
U.S.A.	2.72	2.45	2.41
Iceland	2.26	2.44	2.40
Cyprus	2.1	2.3	2.4
Japan	2.4	2.38	2.30
France	2.33	2.34	2.30
West Germany	2.37	2.29	2.24
Belgium	2.12	1.98	2.15
Netherlands	2.24	2.21	2.07
Switzerland	2.18	2.08	2.04
Rumania	ca. 2	ca. 2	ca. 2
Yugoslavia	1.9	ca. 2	ca. 2
Sweden	2.06	2.12	1.96
United Kingdom	1.72	1.71	1.73
Ireland	1.8	1.7	ca. 1.7
U.S.S.R.	3.1	1.9	1.6
Uruguay	1.5	1.5	1.6
New Zealand	1.72	1.4	1.6
Denmark	1.61	1.58	1.50
Austria	1.46	ca. 1.45	ca. 1.45
Norway	1.41	1.28	1.32
Australia	1.22	1.20	1.3
South Africa	1.07	1.27	1.02
Italy	ca. 1.2	ca. 1.2	ca. 1.0

na: Data not available
SOURCE: *Hoeveel alcoholhoude dranken worden er in de wereld gedronken?* (How many alcoholic beverages are being consumed throughout the world?) 27th ed. (Schiedam, Netherlands: Produktschap voor gedistilleerde dranken, 1987).

Figure 1
**Average Annual Rate of Change (percent) in Per Capita Alcohol Consumption
for 25 Countries, 1979–1984**

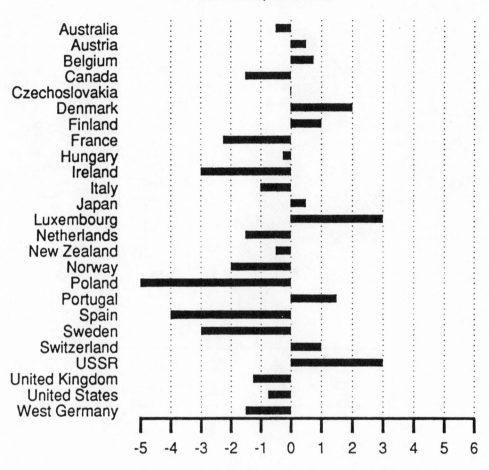

Average annual rate of change (percent)

SOURCE: M. M. Horgan, M.D. Sparrow and R. Brazcau, *Alcoholic Beverage Taxation and Control Policies*, 6th ed., Ottawa: Brewers Association of Canada, 1986.

Map 1
Total Per Capita Consumption in Gallons of Ethanol by State, 1987

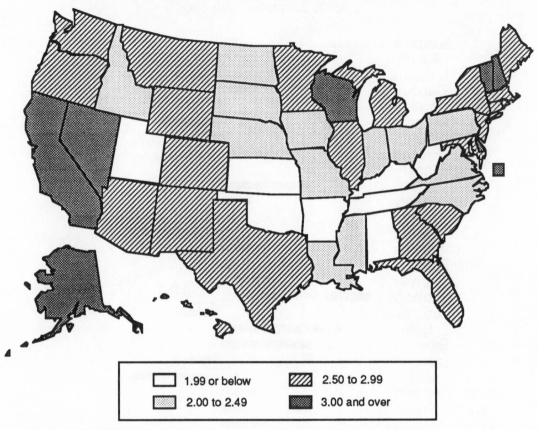

☐ 1.99 or below	▨ 2.50 to 2.99
▧ 2.00 to 2.49	■ 3.00 and over

SOURCE: NIAAA, 1989.

Map 2
Percent Change in Total Per Capita Ethanol Consumption by State, 1977–1987

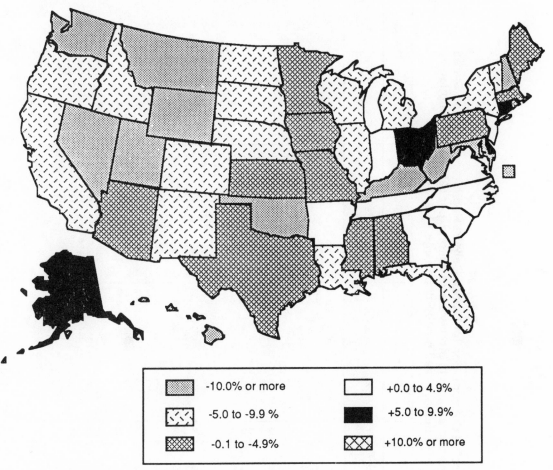

	-10.0% or more		+0.0 to 4.9%
	-5.0 to -9.9 %		+5.0 to 9.9%
	-0.1 to -4.9%		+10.0% or more

SOURCE: NIAAA, 1989.

Table 21
Apparent Alcohol Consumption for States, Census Regions, and United States, 1987 (volume and ethanol in thousands of gallons, per capita consumption in gallons, based on population age 14 and older)

State or Other Geographic Area	BEER			WINE			SPIRITS			ALL BEVERAGES		
	Volume	Ethanol	Per Capita	Volume	Ethanol	Per Capita	Volume	Ethanol	Per Capita	Ethanol	Per Capita	U.S. Decile
AL.........	78,730	3,543	1.10	4,571	590	0.18	4,803	1,988	0.61	6,121	1.89	9
AK.........	14,041	632	1.64	1,605	207	0.54	1,208	500	1.30	1,339	3.48	1
AZ.........	98,739	4,443	1.67	9,557	1,233	0.46	5,546	2,296	0.86	7,972	2.99	2
AR.........	45,262	2,037	1.08	1,548	200	0.11	2,420	1,002	0.53	3,238	1.72	10
CA.........	662,484	29,812	1.36	125,764	16,224	0.74	49,516	20,500	0.94	66,535	3.04	2
CO.........	83,022	3,736	1.43	8,941	1,153	0.44	5,875	2,432	0.93	7,322	2.80	3
CT.........	67,603	3,042	1.15	10,596	1,367	0.52	7,183	2,974	1.13	7,383	2.80	3
DE.........	16,691	751	1.44	1,711	221	0.42	1,537	636	1.22	1,608	3.08	2
DC.........	16,926	762	1.48	3,987	514	1.00	2,971	1,230	2.39	2,506	4.87	1
FL.........	332,631	14,968	1.51	32,128	4,145	0.42	24,895	10,306	1.04	29,419	2.96	2
GA.........	132,740	5,973	1.22	10,166	1,311	0.27	11,971	4,956	1.01	12,241	2.50	6
HI.........	29,852	1,343	1.57	2,661	343	0.40	1,587	657	0.77	2,344	2.74	3
ID.........	21,972	989	1.31	2,219	286	0.38	1,061	439	0.58	1,714	2.27	7
IL.........	288,792	12,996	1.41	27,637	3,565	0.39	19,489	8,068	0.87	24,629	2.67	4
IN.........	121,685	5,476	1.24	7,624	983	0.22	7,150	2,960	0.67	9,419	2.13	8
IA.........	65,507	2,948	1.30	3,699	477	0.21	3,171	1,313	0.58	4,738	2.09	9
KS.........	48,926	2,202	1.12	2,481	320	0.16	2,671	1,106	0.56	3,628	1.84	9
KY.........	67,736	3,048	1.03	3,155	407	0.14	4,297	1,779	0.60	5,234	1.77	10
LA.........	103,346	4,651	1.36	6,348	819	0.24	6,218	2,574	0.75	8,044	2.35	7
ME.........	26,872	1,209	1.26	2,783	359	0.38	2,113	875	0.91	2,443	2.55	5
MD.........	105,649	4,754	1.29	10,791	1,392	0.38	9,534	3,947	1.07	10,093	2.74	3
MA.........	138,965	6,253	1.29	19,189	2,475	0.51	13,255	5,488	1.13	14,216	2.93	2
MI.........	215,038	9,677	1.32	18,944	2,444	0.33	15,204	6,294	0.86	18,415	2.51	6
MN.........	98,593	4,437	1.31	8,256	1,065	0.32	7,689	3,183	0.94	8,685	2.57	5
MS.........	56,609	2,547	1.26	1,455	188	0.09	3,217	1,332	0.66	4,067	2.01	9

MO	123,762	5,569	1.36	8,682	1,120	0.27	7,164	2,966	0.72	9,655	2.35	7
MT	22,017	991	1.57	1,624	209	0.33	1,178	488	0.77	1,688	2.67	4
NE	39,155	1,762	1.40	2,162	279	0.22	2,011	832	0.66	2,873	2.28	7
NV	36,850	1,658	2.05	5,292	683	0.84	4,118	1,705	2.11	4,046	5.00	1
NH	36,631	1,648	1.93	3,302	426	0.50	4,118	1,705	1.99	3,779	4.42	1
NJ	164,728	7,413	1.18	26,171	3,376	0.54	15,388	6,371	1.01	17,159	2.73	4
NM	41,494	1,867	1.63	3,128	404	0.35	1,863	771	0.67	3,042	2.64	4
NY	370,987	16,694	1.15	53,585	6,912	0.48	31,814	13,171	0.91	36,778	2.54	5
NC	127,989	5,760	1.11	11,174	1,441	0.28	8,965	3,712	0.72	10,913	2.11	8
ND	15,635	704	1.34	817	105	0.20	1,110	460	0.88	1,269	2.42	6
OH	258,237	11,621	1.35	15,795	2,038	0.24	12,292	5,089	0.59	18,747	2.18	8
OK	59,591	2,682	1.04	2,975	384	0.15	3,539	1,465	0.57	4,531	1.76	10
OR	61,539	2,769	1.26	8,925	1,151	0.53	3,814	1,579	0.72	5,500	2.51	6
PA	299,912	13,496	1.38	15,352	1,980	0.20	14,607	6,047	0.62	21,524	2.20	8
RI	25,221	1,135	1.40	3,242	418	0.51	1,858	769	0.95	2,322	2.86	3
SC	80,644	3,629	1.34	5,699	735	0.27	5,791	2,397	0.89	6,762	2.50	6
SD	15,215	685	1.24	829	107	0.19	1,063	440	0.79	1,232	2.22	8
TN	101,866	4,584	1.17	4,600	593	0.15	5,876	2,432	0.62	7,610	1.94	9
TX	461,986	20,789	1.61	28,992	3,740	0.29	19,066	7,893	0.61	32,423	2.52	5
UT	21,850	983	0.84	1,366	176	0.15	1,407	582	0.50	1,742	1.49	10
VT	15,229	685	1.56	1,970	254	0.58	1,055	437	0.99	1,376	3.13	1
VA	148,506	6,683	1.40	9,497	1,225	0.26	8,233	3,408	0.71	11,316	2.37	7
WA	99,376	4,472	1.23	15,647	2,018	0.56	6,978	2,889	0.80	9,379	2.59	4
WV	37,683	1,696	1.11	1,525	197	0.13	1,508	624	0.41	2,517	1.65	10
WI	151,475	6,816	1.78	10,516	1,357	0.36	9,066	3,753	0.98	11,926	3.12	1
WY	12,020	541	1.46	698	90	0.24	780	323	0.87	954	2.57	5
Regions											
Northeast	1,146,148	51,577	1.25	136,190	17,569	0.43	91,391	37,836	0.92	106,980	2.60	•
Midwest	1,442,020	64,891	1.37	107,442	13,860	0.29	88,080	36,465	0.77	115,216	2.43	•
South	1,974,585	88,856	1.33	140,322	18,102	0.27	124,841	51,684	0.78	158,643	2.38	•
West	1,205,256	54,237	1.39	187,427	24,178	0.62	84,931	35,161	0.90	113,577	2.91	•
U.S. Total	5,768,009	259,560	1.34	571,381	73,708	0.38	389,243	161,147	0.83	494,416	2.54	•

Decile values apply only to state-level data. Numbers may not add due to rounding.
SOURCE: NIAAA, 1989.

Figure 2
Apparent U.S. Per Capita Consumption of Ethanol, 1977–1987

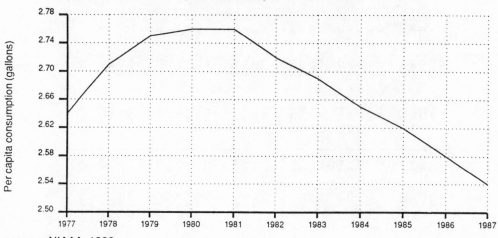

SOURCE: NIAAA, 1989.

Figure 3
Percent Change in Total Per Capita Consumption of Ethanol, 1977–1987

SOURCE: NIAAA, 1989.

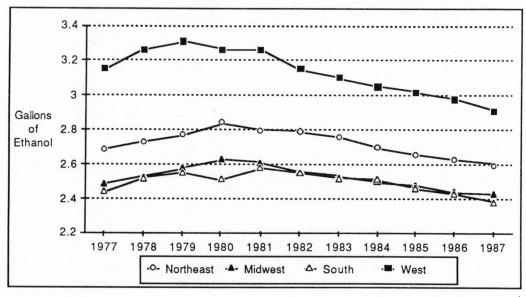

Figure 4
Total Per Capita Ethanol Consumption by Region, 1977–1987

SOURCE: NIAAA, 1989.

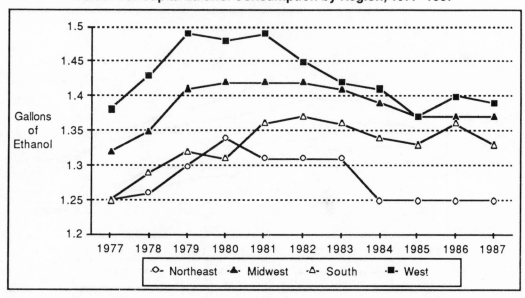

Figure 5
Beer Per Capita Ethanol Consumption by Region, 1977–1987

SOURCE: NIAAA, 1989.

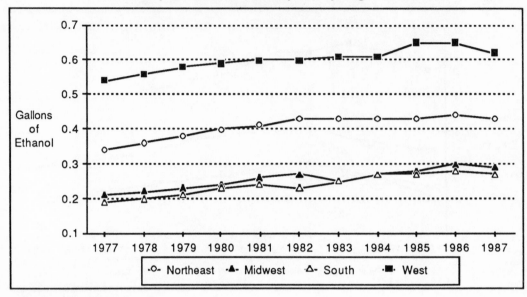

Figure 6
Wine Per Capita Ethanol Consumption by Region, 1977–1987

SOURCE: NIAAA, 1989.

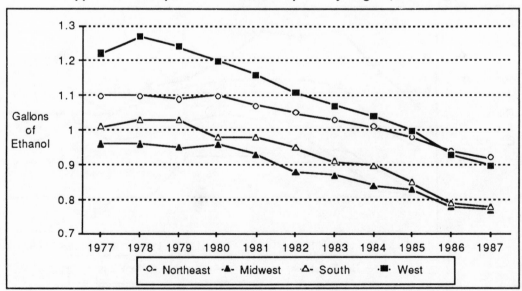

Figure 7
Apparent Per Capita Ethanol Consumption by Region, 1977–1987

SOURCE: NIAAA, 1989.

Figure 8
Age-Adjusted Death Rates of Liver Cirrhosis (all 571): Death Registration Rates, 1910–1932, and the United States, 1933–1986 (death rates per 100,000 population)

REVISIONS OF THE INTERNATIONAL CLASSIFICATION OF DISEASES

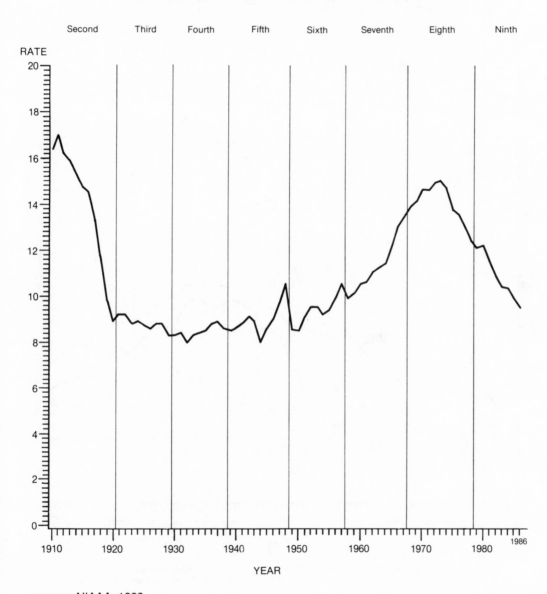

SOURCE: NIAAA, 1989.

Figure 9
Age-Adjusted Death Rates of Liver Cirrhosis by Race and Sex: United States, 1945–1986 (death rates per 100,000 population)

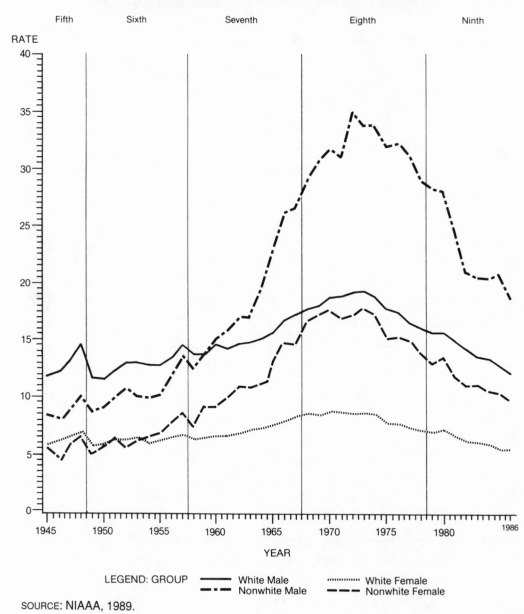

SOURCE: NIAAA, 1989.

Table 22
Most Consistent Features of the Fetal Alcohol Syndrome

Growth and Performance

- Prenatal onset growth deficiency, more pronounced in length than in weight
- Concomitant microcephaly (small head circumference) even when corrected for small body weight and length
- Postnatal growth deficiency in weight and length, usually below 3rd percentile
- Delay of intellectual development and/or mental deficiency (mean IQ from Seattle study = 64, range 16–92)
- Fine motor dysfunction (poor coordination)

Head and Face

- Microcephaly
- Short palpebral fissures (narrow eye slits)
- Midfacial (maxillary) hypoplasia (underdevelopment of midfacial region)
- Flattened, elongated philtrum (middle of upper lip) associated with thin, narrow vermilion lip borders (highly specific to FAS)
- Minor ear anomalies including low set ears

Limbs

- Abnormal creases in the palm of the hand
- Minor joint anomalies
  —syndactyly (fingers or toes joined together)
  —clinodactyly (abnormal bending of fingers or toes)
  —camptodactyly (one or more fingers constantly flexed at one or more phalangeal joints)

Heart

- Ventricular atrial septal defect (valve defects)

Brain

- Absence of corpus callosum
- Hydrocephalus (excess fluid in cranium)
- Brain cell migratory abnormalities

Other

- Minor genital anomalies
- Hemangiomas (benign tumors made up of blood vessels) in infancy

SOURCE: Data from Kenneth L. Jones and David W. Smith, "The Fetal Alcohol Syndrome," *Teratology* 12, no. 1 (1975):1–10, reprinted in Ernest P. Noble, ed., *Third Special Report*, p. 172.

Figure 10
Alcohol-Related Traffic Fatalities: 1977–1987

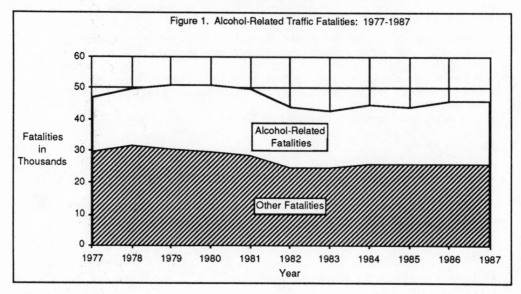

Figure 1. Alcohol-Related Traffic Fatalities: 1977-1987

SOURCE: NIAAA, 1989.

Table 23
Traffic Crashes, Traffic Crash Fatalities, and Alcohol-Related Traffic Crash Fatalities: 1977–1987

Year	Event			
	Traffic Crashes	Traffic Crash Fatalities (a)	Alcohol-Related Traffic Crash Fatalities (b)	Percent of All Traffic Crash Fatalities (b/a)
1987	41,435	46,386	19,918	42.9
1986	41,090	46,082	20,038	43.5
1985	39,196	43,825	18,040	41.2
1984	39,622	44,241	18,523	41.9
1983	37,971	42,584	17,847	41.9
1982	38,899	43,721	18,622	42.6
1981	43,979	49,268	20,662	41.9
1980	45,271	51,077	21,114	41.3
1979	45,212	51,084	20,245	39.6
1978	44,433	50,327	18,362	36.5
1977	42,064	47,715	17,414	36.5

SOURCE: NIAAA, 1989.

Table 24
Mean Blood Alcohol Content of Drivers, Pedestrians, and Pedacyclists Involved in Fatal Traffic Crashes with Positive Blood Alcohol Test Results: 1981–1987

Year/Person's Role	Blood Alcohol Content		
	N	Mean	Standard Deviation
1987			
Driver	14,344	0.16	0.08
Pedestrian	1,958	0.20	0.10
Pedacyclist	117	0.14	0.10
Total	16,419	0.17	0.09
1986			
Driver	14,530	0.16	0.08
Pedestrian	2,013	0.19	0.10
Pedacyclist	87	0.13	0.09
Total	16,630	0.16	0.08
1985			
Driver	12,771	0.16	0.08
Pedestrian	1,932	0.19	0.10
Pedacyclist	76	0.15	0.09
Total	14,779	0.16	0.08
1984			
Driver	12,578	0.16	0.08
Pedestrian	1,852	0.19	0.10
Pedacyclist	63	0.14	0.10
Total	14,587	0.17	0.08
1983			
Driver	11,273	0.17	0.08
Pedestrian	1,571	0.20	0.10
Pedacyclist	51	0.13	0.09
Total	12,895	0.17	0.08
1982			
Driver	11,479	0.17	0.08
Pedestrian	1,697	0.20	0.10
Pedacyclist	54	0.13	0.08
Total	13,230	0.17	0.08
1981			
Driver	12,191	0.17	0.08
Pedestrian	1,598	0.19	0.10
Pedacyclist	41	0.15	0.12
Total	13,830	0.17	0.08

SOURCE: NIAAA, 1989.

Table 25
Alcohol-Related Traffic Crash Fatalities Associated with Drivers Aged 16 to 24 Years, According to Person's Role: 1977–1987

| | Person's Role[1] | | | | | | | |
| | Driver | | Passenger | | Nonoccupant | | All | |
Year	N	Percent	N	Percent	N	Percent	N	Percent
1987	4,832	61.7	2,600	33.2	392	5.0	7,827	100.0
1986	5,273	62.2	2,802	33.0	403	4.7	8,483	100.0
1985	4,706	63.1	2,360	31.6	396	5.3	7,462	100.0
1984	5,075	62.4	2,636	32.4	418	5.1	8,132	100.0
1983	4,724	60.7	2,608	33.5	452	5.8	7,784	100.0
1982	5,088	60.5	2,787	33.1	531	6.3	8,409	100.0
1981	5,652	61.1	3,046	32.9	545	5.9	9,246	100.0
1980	6,047	61.0	3,319	33.5	545	5.5	9,918	100.0
1979	5,741	59.3	3,373	34.8	563	5.8	9,683	100.0
1978	5,156	59.2	3,058	35.1	490	5.7	8,704	100.0
1977	4,911	58.4	3,041	36.2	449	5.3	8,403	100.0

SOURCE: NIAAA, 1989.

[1]There were 2, 6, 7, 3, 3, 3, 5 and 3 cases of unknown person's role for the years 1977, 1979, 1980, 1981, 1982, 1984, 1986 and 1987, respectively.

Table 26
Alcohol-Related Traffic Fatalities, According to Age: 1977–1987

Year	Under 16		16-24		Age 25-44		45-64		Over 64		Unknown		All Ages	
	N	Percent	N	Percent	N	Percent	N	Percent	N	Percent	N	Percent	N	Percent
1987	829	4.2	7,027	35.3	8,766	44.0	2,313	11.6	940	4.7	43	0.2	19,918	100.0
1986	842	4.2	7,685	38.4	8,372	41.8	2,202	11.0	864	4.3	73	0.4	20,038	100.0
1985	742	4.1	6,823	37.8	7,431	41.2	2,141	11.9	824	4.6	79	0.4	18,040	100.0
1984	727	3.9	7,359	39.6	7,427	40.0	2,176	11.7	831	4.5	64	0.3	18,584	100.0
1983	731	4.1	7,064	39.6	7,139	40.0	2,138	12.0	751	4.2	38	0.2	17,861	100.0
1982	794	4.3	7,629	41.0	7,123	38.3	2,244	12.1	768	4.1	64	0.3	18,622	100.0
1981	844	4.1	8,294	40.1	7,923	38.4	2,667	12.9	880	4.3	54	0.3	20,662	100.0
1980	955	4.5	8,941	42.4	7,637	36.2	2,676	12.7	834	4.0	71	0.3	21,114	100.0
1979	972	4.8	8,624	42.6	7,159	35.4	2,597	12.8	819	4.1	70	0.4	20,241	100.0
1978	926	5.0	7,884	42.9	6,290	34.3	2,416	13.2	773	4.2	73	0.4	18,362	100.0
1977	963	5.5	7,528	43.2	5,642	32.4	2,470	14.2	742	4.3	69	0.4	17,414	100.0

SOURCE: NIAAA, 1989.

Table 27
Alcohol Involvement in Aviation Accidents, United States, 1975–1981

	General aviation							Total general aviation	Total all aviation
	1975	1976	1977	1978	1979	1980	1981		
All accidents	4,006	4,023	4,083	4,218	3,825	3,597	3,502	27,249	28,849
Fatal accidents	636	662	663	721	638	622	654	4,596	4,947
Conclusive toxicological tests[a]	443	462	469	502	455	438	487	3,256	3,536
Positive alcohol tests	48	52	45	52	36	57	53	343	358
Percentage positive	10.9	11.3	9.6	10.4	7.9	13.0	10.9	10.5	10.1
Other known alcohol-related accidents[b]	19	19	24	16	6	4	9	97	102
Total alcohol-related accidents	67	71	69	68	42	61	62	440	460

SOURCE: NTSB, 1984.

[a]Toxicological tests are not always possible.

[b]Accidents in which alcohol involvement was determined from witness statements.

Table 28
Economic Costs to Society of Alcohol and Alcoholism, United States, 1983

Types of costs	Costs ($ millions)
Core costs	
Direct	
Treatment[a]	$13,457
Health support services	1,549
Indirect	
Mortality[b]	18,151
Reduced productivity	65,582
Lost employment	5,323
Other related costs	
Direct	
Motor vehicle crashes	2,697
Crime	2,631
Social welfare administration	49
Other	3,673
Indirect	
Victims of crime	194
Incarceration	2,979
Motor vehicle crashes	590
Total	$116,875

SOURCE: H. J. Harwood, P. Kristiansen and J. V. Rachal, "Social and Economic Costs of Alcohol Abuse and Alcoholism. Issue Report No. 2. Research Triangle Park, NC: Research Triangle Institute, 1985.

[a]For alcohol abuse and alcoholism, liver cirrhosis, other illnesses, motor vehicle crashes, and other injuries.

[b]At 6 percent discount rate.

Table 29
Drinking Levels by Marital and Employment Status for Women and Men (weighted percent)

	All women		Married women			All men	
Drinking level	Employed full time (N = 361)	Employed part time (N = 135)	Employed full time (N = 189)	Employed part time (N = 97)	Full-time homemaker (N = 177)	Employed full time (N = 265)	Employed part time (N = 28)
Abstainers	32	31	41	34	43	22	33
Light drinkers	40	38	40	37	42	28	14
Moderate drinkers	21	26	14	24	9	36	17
Heavier drinkers	7	4	4	4	6	14	35

SOURCE: Data from Wilsnack, Wilsnack and Klassen, "Drinking and Drinking Problems Among Women in U.S. National Survey," *Alcohol Research World* 9:3–13, 1985.

Figure 11
Percentage of High School Seniors Who Are Currently Drinkers (used alcohol in the past 30 days) and Percentage Who Were Occasional Heavy Drinkers (took five or more drinks at a sitting during the past two weeks), 1975–1988

Current drinkers

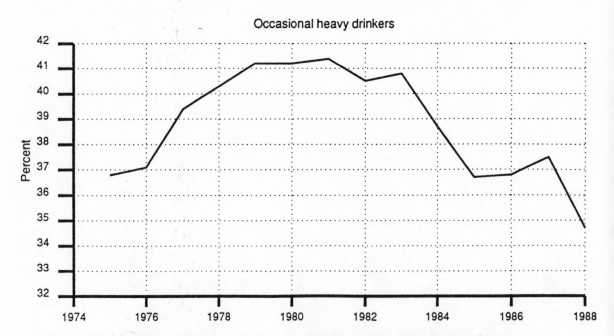

Occasional heavy drinkers

SOURCE: Chart by NIAAA, 1989. Data from *Drug Use, Drinking and Smoking: National Survey Results from High School, College and Young Adult Populations, 1975–1988*, DHHS Pub. No. (ADM) 89–1638, 1989.

Figure 12
Percentage of Drinkers by Age Group and Sex, United States, 1984

SOURCE: Chart by NIAAA, 1987. Data from M. E. Hilton, "Drinking Patterns and Drinking Problems in 1984: Results from a general population survey," *Alcoholism: Clinical and Experimental Research*, in press.

Table 30
Percentage of Population Who Are
Moderate or Heavier Drinkers,
by Year of Survey

Drinking level	1979	1983	1985
Males			
Moderate[a]	31	28	29
Heavier[b]	14	16	14
Females			
Moderate	18	15	15
Heavier	4	4	3
Total			
Moderate	24	21	21
Heavier	9	10	8

SOURCES: Chart by NIAAA, 1987; data from Clark and Midanik, 1982, Malin et al., 1986; Thornberry et al., 1986.

[a]Moderate drinkers are defined as those who consume an average of 0.22 to 0.99 ounce of pure alcohol per day.

[b]Heavier drinkers are defined as those who consume an average of 1.0 ounce or more of pure alcohol per day.

Figure 13
A Chart of Alcohol Addiction and Recovery (to be read from left to right)

SOURCE: M.M. Giatt, "Group Therapy in Alcoholism." *The British Journal of Addiction*, 54, no. 2, reprinted in R. Gordon Bell, "Classifications and Symptomatology." *Core Knowledge in the Drug Field*. Vol. 7 (Ottawa: National Planning Committee on Training of the Federal Provincial Working Group on Alcohol Problems, 1978). p. 17.

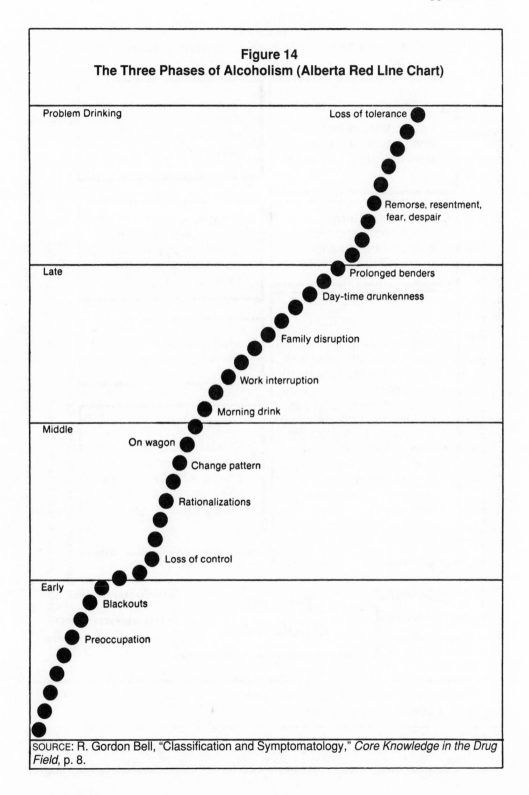

Figure 14
The Three Phases of Alcoholism (Alberta Red LIne Chart)

Problem Drinking   Loss of tolerance

                                        Remorse, resentment,
                                        fear, despair

Late   Prolonged benders
                                        Day-time drunkenness

                        Family disruption

                Work interruption

                Morning drink

Middle
        On wagon
                Change pattern

        Rationalizations

                Loss of control

Early
        Blackouts

        Preoccupation

SOURCE: R. Gordon Bell, "Classification and Symptomatology," *Core Knowledge in the Drug Field*, p. 8.

Figure 15
Factors That Can Lead to Alcoholism in Women

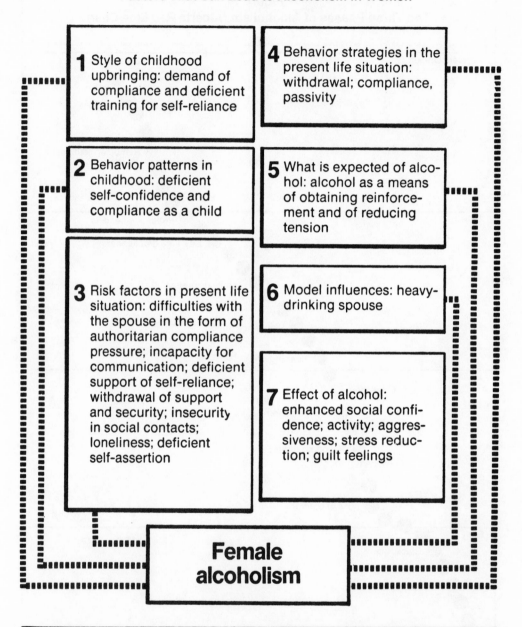

1 Style of childhood upbringing: demand of compliance and deficient training for self-reliance

2 Behavior patterns in childhood: deficient self-confidence and compliance as a child

3 Risk factors in present life situation: difficulties with the spouse in the form of authoritarian compliance pressure; incapacity for communication; deficient support of self-reliance; withdrawal of support and security; insecurity in social contacts; loneliness; deficient self-assertion

4 Behavior strategies in the present life situation: withdrawal; compliance, passivity

5 What is expected of alcohol: alcohol as a means of obtaining reinforcement and of reducing tension

6 Model influences: heavy-drinking spouse

7 Effect of alcohol: enhanced social confidence; activity; aggressiveness; stress reduction; guilt feelings

Female alcoholism

The more these risk factors are present, the greater becomes the danger of female alcoholism.

SOURCE: Marijke Mantek, "Alkoholismus Bei Frauen," *Psychologie Heute*, pp. 39-46.

Table 31
Calories and Carbohydrates in Selected Alcoholic Beverages

Beverage	% Alcohol or Proof (pr)	Quantity (oz)	Calories	Carbohydrates (grams)
ale	5%	12	162	13.8
Anisette	42–60 pr	1	64–111	7.5–13.9
beer	4.6–4.9%	12	144–165	11.0–14.1
beer, 3.2 low gravity	3.8%	12	142	13.6
beer, low carbohydrate	4.6%	12	96–145	0.2–4.2
beer, near	0.4%	12	62–73	13.7–15.0
Bordeaux	11.5–12.5%	3	63–96	trace–7.5
brandy, flavored	70 pr	1	72–100	1.0–8.9
burgundy	12–14%	3	12–82	trace–1.8
Chianti	12–13%	3	59–90	0.1–6.3
distilled spirits*				
	80 pr	1	65	trace
	86 pr	1	70	trace
	90 pr	1	74	trace
	94 pr	1	77	trace
	100 pr	1	83	trace
Drambuie	80 pr	1	110	11.0
Madeira	19%	3	120	6.3
port	16–20%	3	94–165	2.0–11.8
sherry	16–20%	3	76–158	1.2–11.6

Cocktails**

Beverage	% Alcohol or Proof (pr)	Quantity (oz)	Calories	Carbohydrates (grams)
daiquiri	52.5 pr	3	177	12.0
Manhattan	55 pr	3	147	3.0
martini, gin	67.5 pr	3	168	0.6
martini, vodka	65 pr	3	147	0
Old Fashioned	62 pr	3	165	3.0
whiskey sour	12.5%	8	256	17.6

*Distilled spirits include all hard liquors, such as whiskey, gin, rum, unflavored brandies, etc.
**Figures are for premixed cocktails (with alcohol). The potency and the amount of calories and carbohydrates in cocktails mixed in bars and at home vary.

Figure 16
Perceived Harmfulness of Drugs as Reported by High School Seniors,
United States, 1985

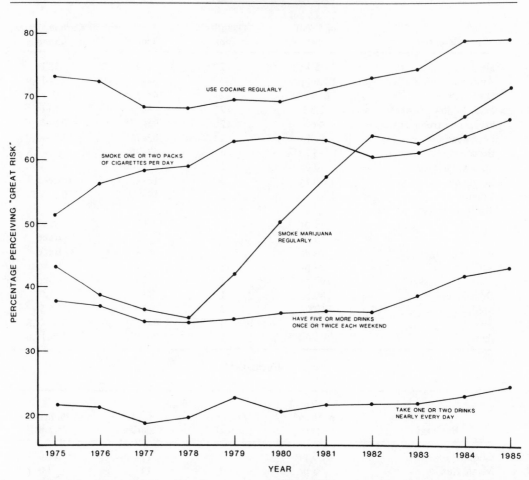

SOURCE: L. Johnston, P. M. O'Malley and J.G. Bachman, *Drug Use Among American High School Students, College Students, and Other Young Adults: National Trends Through 1985.* DHHS Pub. No. (ADM) 86–1450.

APPENDIX 2

Sources of Information

This section contains selected major sources of information on alcohol abuse and alcoholism. The sources do *not* include listings of treatment centers. Detailed lists of these are generally available from national or local governments. In addition it was not possible to provide information sources for every foreign country, since many countries failed to or chose not to supply such information despite repeated requests.

CONTENTS

UNITED STATES

National Organizations
State and Territorial Clearinghouses and Agencies for Alcohol and Other
    Drug Information
Self-Help Groups for Professional and Special Populations (see attached)

CANADA

Provincial and Territorial Agencies

FOREIGN SOURCES

National
International

SELECTED ENGLISH-LANGUAGE JOURNALS AND PERIODICALS

UNITED STATES

NATIONAL ASSOCIATIONS, INSTITUTES, ORGANIZATIONS AND GOVERNMENT AGENCIES

A.A. World Services, Inc.
P.O. Box 459
Grand Central Station
New York, New York 10163-1100

ACTION
Drug Prevention Program
806 Connecticut Avenue, N.W.
Washington, D.C. 20525

AFL-CIO, Building & Trades Department
Drug-Alcohol and Safety and Health Policies Programs
815 Sixteenth Street, N.W., Suite 603
Washington, D.C. 20006-4189

Al-Anon Family Group Headquarters
P. O. Box 862
Midtown Station
New York, New York 10018-0862

Alcohol and Drug Problems Association of
  North America
1101 Fifteenth Street, N. W. #204
Washington, D. C. 20005

Alcohol Epidemiologic Data System (AEDS)
c/o CSR, Incorporated
1400 Eye Street, N.W., Suite 600
Washington, D.C. 20005

Alcoholics Anonymous
General Service Office
468 Park Avenue South
New York, New York 10016

Alcohol, Drug Abuse and Mental Health
  Administration
Department of Health and Human Services
5600 Fishers Lane, Room 6C15
Rockville, Maryland 20857
Tel: (301) 443-4797

Almaca (Association of Labor-Management
  Administrators and Consultants on
  Alcoholism)
1800 North Kent Street, Suite 907
Arlington, Virginia 22209

Alcohol-Narcotics Education Council, Inc.,
  of Virginia Churches
3202 West Cary Street
Richmond, Virginia 23221

Adult Children of Alcoholics
Central Service Board
P.O. Box 3216
Torrance, California 90505
Tel: (213) 534-1815

American Association Against Addiction
1668 Bush Street
San Francisco, California 94019
Tel: (415) 775-0165

American Correction Association
4321 Hartwick Road
College Park, Maryland 20740

American Council on Alcohol Problems
119 Constitution Avenue, N.E.
Washington, D.C. 20002

American Association of Critical Care
  Nurses
One Civic Plaza
Newport Beach, California 92660

American Council for Drug Education
  (ACDE)
204 Monroe Street, Suite 110
Rockville, Maryland 20850
Tel: (301) 294-0600

American Institute of Family Relations
5287 Sunset Boulevard
Los Angeles, California 90027

American Medical Association
Department of Health Education
535 N. Dearborn Street
Chicago, Illinois 60610

American Medical Society on Alcoholism
and Other Drug Dependencies, Inc.
(AMSAODD)
12 West 21st Street
New York, New York 10010

American Medical Students Association
(AMSA)
1890 Preston White Drive
Reston, Virginia 22091

American Nurses Association
2420 Pershing Avenue
Kansas City, Missouri 64108
Tel: (816) 474-5720

American Public Health Association
(APHA)
Alcohol & Drug Section
University of Michigan
2501 Baxter Road
Ann Arbor, Michigan 48901-2150

Americans for Democratic Action
Consumer Affairs Committee
3005 Audubon Terrace, N.W.
Washington, D.C. 20008

Association for Advancement of Health
Education
1201 16th Street, N.W.
Washington, D.C. 20036

Association of Halfway House Alcoholism
Programs of North America
786 East 7th Street
St. Paul, Minnesota 55106

Association for Medical Education and
Research in Substance Abuse
(AMERSA)
Center for Alcohol and Addiction Studies
Box G, Brown University
Providence, Rhode Island 02912

B'nai B'rith C.V.S.
1640 Rhode Island Avenue, N.W.
Washington, D.C. 20036

Center of Alcohol Studies
Rutgers, The State University of New Jersey
P.O. Box 965
Piscataway, New Jersey 08454

Center for Multicultural Awareness
2924 Columbia Pike
Arlington, Virginia 22204

Center for the Study of Drug Policy
530 Eighth Street, S.E.
Washington, D.C. 20003
Tel: (202) 547-3708

Center for the Study of Responsive Law
P.O. Box 19367
Washington, D.C. 20036

Chemical People Institute
Duquesne University
Pittsburgh, Pennsylvania 15282

Children Are People, Inc.
493 Selby Avenue
St. Paul, Minnesota 55102

Children of Alcoholics Foundation
200 Park Avenue, 31st Floor
New York, New York 10166

COSSMHO
1030 15th Street, N.W., Suite 1053
Washington, D.C. 20005

Commission for the Advancement of Public
  Interest Organization
1875 Connecticut Avenue, N.W.
Washington, D.C. 20009

Committee on Problems of Drug Dependence
4105 Dunnel Lane
Kensington, Maryland 20795

Comp Care Publications
2415 Annapolis Lane
Minneapolis, Minnesota 55441

Consumer Federation of America
1314 14th Street, N.W.
Washington, D.C. 20005

Daytop
54 West 40th Street
New York, New York 10018
Tel: (212) 324-6000

Do it Now Foundation
P.O. Box 5115
Phoenix, Arizona 85010
Tel: (602) 257-0797

ETOH, Alcohol & Alcohol Problems
  Science Database
c/o BRS Information Technologies
Latham, New York
Tel: 1-800-468-0908 or 1-800-345-4277

Families in Action
3845 North Druid Hills Road, Suite 300
Decatur, Georgia 30333
Tel: (404) 325-5799

Families Anonymous, Inc.
P.O. Box 528
Van Nuys, California 91408
Tel: (818) 989-7841

Family Life Publications
Box 427
Saluda, North Carolina 28773

Federal Trade Commission
Bureau of Consumer Protection
Division of Professional Service
6th Street & Pennsylvania Avenue, N.W.
Washington, D.C. 20580

Food and Drug Administration (FDA)
Consumer Inquiries HF1-10
5600 Fishers Lane
Rockville, Maryland 20857

Hazelden Foundation, Inc.
Pleasant Valley Road
Box 176
Center City, Minnesota 55012-1076

Health Communications, Inc.
1721 Blount Road
Pompano Beach, Florida 33069

Health Communications, Inc.
c/o TIPS
600 New Hampshire Ave., N.W.
Suite 100
Washington, D.C. 20037

Health Education Foundation
600 New Hampshire Ave., N.W.
Suite 452
Washington, D.C. 20037

House Select Committee on Narcotics
  Abuse & Control
3287 House Office Building-Annex 2
2nd and D Streets, S.W.
Washington, D.C. 20515

Independent Community Consultants, Inc.
Design and Planning Assistance Center
120 Yale, S.E.
Albuquerque, New Mexico 87109

Indian Alcoholism Counseling and
  Recovery House Program
375 South 300 West
Salt Lake City, Utah 84101
Tel: (801) 328-8515

Indian Health Service (IHS)
Alcohol and Substance Program
5600 Fishers Lane, Rm. 64-63
Rockville, Maryland 20857
Tel: (301) 443-4297

Institute on Pluralism and Group Identity
165 East 56th Street
New York, New York 10022

Institute on Black Chemical Abuse
2614 N. Nicollet Avenue South
Minneapolis, Minnesota 55408
Tel: (612) 871-7878

Johnson Institute
7151 Metro Boulevard
Minneapolis, Minnesota 55435

Mental Health Material Center
30 East 29th Street
New York, New York 10016

The Myrin Institute
521 Park Avenue
New York, New York 10021

Narcotic Educational Foundation of
    America
5055 Sunset Boulevard
Los Angeles, California 90027
Tel: (213) 663-5171

Narcotics Anonymous
P.O. Box 9999
Van Nuys, California 41409
Tel: (818) 780-3951

Narcotics Educational Foundation of
    America
5055 Sunset Boulevard
Los Angeles, California 90027

National Asian Pacific American Families
    Against Substance Abuse
6303 Friendship Court
Bethesda, Maryland 20857
Tel: (301) 530-0945

National Association of Addiction
    Treatment Providers
22082 Michaelson Drive, Suite 304
Irvine, California 92715
(Information source on intensive alcoholism
    rehab centers)

National Association for Children of
    Alcoholics
31706 Coast Highway, Suite 201
South Laguna, California 92677

National Association for City Drug and
    Alcohol Coordination
House Officers Building, Suite 711
818 Harrison Avenue
Boston, Massachusetts 02118
Tel: (617) 424-4757

National Association on Drug Abuse
    Problems
355 Lexington Avenue
New York, New York 10017
Tel: (212) 986-1170

National Association of Lesbian and Gay
    Alcoholism Professionals (NAL-GAP)
1208 E. State Boulevard
Fort Wayne, Indiana 46805

National Association of Social Workers
    (NASW)
7981 Eastern Avenue
Silver Spring, Maryland 20910
Tel: (301) 565-0333

National Association of State Alcohol and
    Drug Abuse Directors
918 F Street, N.W., Suite 400
Washington, D.C. 20004
Tel: (202) 783-6868

National Center for Health Statistics
3700 East-West Highway, Room 157
Hyattsville, Maryland 20782

National Center for Voluntary Action
1785 Massachusetts, N.W.
Washington, D.C. 209036

National Clearinghouse for Drug Abuse
    Information
Department of Health and Human Services
5600 Fishers Lane, Room 10A53,
P.O. Box 2345
Rockville, Maryland 20857
Tel: (301) 443-6500

National Clergy Council on Alcoholism and
    Related Drug Problems (NCCA)
1200 Varnum Street, N.E.
Washington, D.C. 20017

National Committee for the Prevention of
    Alcoholism and Drug Dependency
6830 Laurel Street, N.W.
Washington, D.C. 20012

National Coucil on Alcoholism
12 West 21st Street, 7th Floor
New York, New York 10010

National Council on Alcoholism, Inc.
1424 16th Street, N.W.
Washington, D.C. 20036

National Council on Crime and Delinquency
Continental Plaza
422 Hackensack Avenue
Hackensack, New Jersey 07601

National Crime Prevention Council (NCPC)
733 15th Street, N.W., Suite 540
Washington, D.C. 20005
Tel: (202) 393-7141

National Family Council Against Drug
    Abuse
40 Westminister Drive
Pearl River, New York 10965
Tel: (914) 735-9250

National Federation of Parents for
    Drug-Free Youth
9805 Dameron Drive
Silver Spring, Maryland 20902
Tel: (301) 593-9256

National Foundation—March of Dimes
Public Health Education Department
Box 2000
White Plains, New York 10602

National Institute on Alcohol Abuse and
    Alcoholism
Department of Health and Human Services
P.O. Box 2345
5600 Fishers Lane
Rockville, Maryland 20857
Tel: (301) 468-2600

National Institute on Drug Abuse
Division of Research
Department of Health and Human Services
5600 Fishers Lane
Rockville, Maryland 20857

National Nurses Society on Addictions
    (NNSA)
2506 Grosse Point Road
Evanston, Illinois 60201
Tel: (312) 475-7300

National Self-Help Clearinghouse
Graduate School and University Center—
    CUNY
33 West 42nd Street Room 620-N
New York, New York 10036

Navy Drug and Alcohol Abuse
    Treatment Program
Navy Drug & Alcohol Drug Abuse
    Prevention and Control Division
Naval Military Personnel Command
    (NMPC-63)
Washington, D.C. 20370
Tel: (202) 694-8008

New York City Affiliate, Inc.
National Council on Alcoholism
133 East 62nd Street
New York, New York 10021

North Conway Institute
14 Beacon Street
Boston, Massachusetts 02108

Odyssey Institute
656 Avenue of the Americas
New York, New York 10010
Tel: (212) 691-8510

Office of National Drug Control Policy
Executive Office of the President
Washington, D.C. 20500

Office for Substance Abuse Prevention
P.O. Box 2345
Rockville, Maryland 20852
Tel: (301) 468-2600

Nurses Society on Addictions,
    Committee on Impaired Nurses
1020 Sunset Drive
Lawrence, Kansas 66044
Tel: (816) 254-3652

Parent Resources and Information
    on Drug Education
Georgia State University
University Plaza
Atlanta, Georgia 30303
Tel: (404) 658-2548

Pharmaceutical Manufacturers Association
Consumer Services
115 15th Street, N.W.
Washington, D.C. 20005

Phoenix House Foundation
164 West 74th Street
New York, New York 10023
Tel: (212) 595-5810

Pills Anonymous
P.O. Box 473
Ansonia Station
New York, New York 10023
Tel: (212) 375-8872

The Proprietary Association
1700 Pennsylvania Avenue. N.W.
Washington, D.C. 20006

Public Affairs Pamphlets
381 Park Avenue South
New York, New York 10016

Public Citizen, Inc.
Health Research Group
2000 P Street, N.W.
Washington, D.C. 20036

RID, Remove Intoxicated Drivers
P.O. Box 520
Schenectady, New York 12301

Rutgers Center of Alcohol Studies
P.O. Box 969
Piscataway, New Jersey 08854

SADD, Students Against Drunk Driving
P.O. Box 800
272 Main Street
Marlboro, Massachusetts 01752

Substance Abuse Treatment Programs
    and National Cocaine Hotline
1-800-COCAINE
Fair Oaks Hospital
1 Prospect Street
Summit, New Jersey 07901

Synanon Church
P.O. Box 786
6055 Marshall-Petaluma Road
Marshall, California 94940
Tel: (415) 663-8111

Toughlove
P.O. Box 1069
Doylestown, Pennsylvania 18901
Tel: (215) 348-7090

U.S. Department of Health and Human
    Services
Office of Education
Alcohol and Drug Education Program
400 Maryland Avenue, S.W.
Washington, D.C. 20202

U.S. Department of Education
    Drug-Free Schools and Communities
400 Maryland Avenue, S.W.
Washington, D.C. 20202-4101

Women for Sobriety
P.O. Box 618
Quakertown, Pennsylvania 18951
Tel: (215) 536-8026

For further information contact:
National Clearinghouse for Alcohol
    and Drug Information (NCADI)
P.O. Box 2345
Rockville, Maryland 20852
Tel: (301) 468-2600

STATE AND TERRITORIAL CLEARINGHOUSES AND AGENCIES FOR ALCOHOL AND OTHER DRUG INFORMATION

Alabama
Division of Mental Illness and Substance
    Abuse Community Programs
Department of Mental Health
200 Interstate Park Drive
P.O. Box 3710
Montgomery, Alabama 36193
Tel: (205) 271-9253

Alaska
Office of Alcoholism and Drug Abuse
Department of Health & Social Services
Pouch H-05-F
Juneau, Alaska 99811
Tel: (907) 586-6201

Arizona
Office of Community Behavioral Health
Arizona Department of Health Services
701 East Jefferson, Suite 400A
Phoenix, Arizona 85034
Tel: (602) 220-6478

Office of Community Behavioral Health
Arizona Department of Health Services
701 East Jefferson, Suite 400A
Phoenix, Arizona 85034
Tel: (602) 255-1152

Arkansas
Office on Alcohol and Drug Abuse
    Prevention
Donaghey Plaza, North, Suite 400
P.O. Box 1437
Little Rock, Arkansas 72203-1437
Tel: (501) 682-6650

California
Department of Alcohol and Drug Programs
111 Capitol Mall, Suite 450
Sacramento, California 95814
Tel: (916) 445-0834

Colorado
Alcohol and Drug Abuse Division
Department of Health
4210 East 11th Avenue
Denver, Colorado 80220
Tel: (303) 331-8201

Connecticut
Connecticut Alcohol and Drug Abuse
    Commission
999 Asylum Avenue, 3rd Floor
Hartford, Connecticut 06105
Tel: (203) 566-4145

Delaware

Delaware Divison of Alcoholism,
    Drug Abuse and Mental Health
1901 North Dupont Highway
Newcastle, Delaware 19720
Tel: (302) 421-6101

District of Columbia

Health Planning and Development
1875 Connecticut Avenue, N.W.
Suite 836
Washington, D.C. 20009
Tel: (202) 673-7481

Florida

Alcoholic Rehabilitation Program
Department of Health & Rehabilitation
    Services
1323 Winewood Boulevard
Tallahassee, Florida 32301
Tel: (904) 488-0900

Georgia

Alcohol and Drug Abuse Section
Division of Mental Health & Mental
    Retardation
Georgia Department of Human Resources
618 Ponce De Leon Avenue, N.E.
Atlanta, Georgia 30308
Tel: (404) 894-4785

Hawaii

Department of Health
State Substance Abuse Agency
Alcohol and Drug Abuse Branch
1270 Queen Emma Street, Room 505
Honolulu, Hawaii 96813
Tel: (808) 548-7655

Idaho

Bureau of Substance Abuse
Department of Health & Welfare
450 West State Street, 4th Floor
Boise, Idaho 83720
Tel: (208) 334-4368

Illinois

Alcohol Division
Illinois Department of Mental Health
    & Developmental Disabilities
160 North Lasalle Street, Room 1500
Chicago, Illinois 60601
Tel: (312) 793-2907

Indiana

Division of Addiction Services
Department of Mental Health
5 Indiana Square
Indianapolis, Indiana 46204
Tel: (317) 232-7818

Iowa

Department of Substance Abuse
Insurance Exchange Building, Suite 202
505 5th Avenue
Des Moines, Iowa 50319
Tel: (515) 281-3641

Kansas

Alcoholism and Drug Abuse Section
Department of Social Rehabilitation Service
2700 West Sixth Street
Biddle Building
Topeka, Kansas 66606
Tel: (913) 296-3925

Kentucky

Alcohol and Drug Branch
Bureau of Health Services
Department of Human Resources
275 East Main Street
Frankfort, Kentucky 40621
Tel: (502) 564-7450

Louisiana

Office of Mental Health & Substance Abuse
Department of Health & Human Resources
655 North 5th Street
Baton Rouge, Louisiana 70829
Tel: (504) 342-2590

Maine

Office of Alcoholism and Drug Abuse
    Prevention
Department of Human Services
32 Winthrop Street
Augusta, Maine 04330
Tel: (207) 289-2781

Maryland

Alcoholism Control Administration
201 West Preston Street
4th Floor
Baltimore, Maryland 21201
Tel: (301) 383-2781, 2782, 2783

Massachusetts

Massachusetts Division of Alcoholism
 755 Boylston Street
Boston, Massachusetts
Tel: (617) 727-1960

Michigan

Office of Substance Abuse Services
Department of Public Health
3500 North Logan Street
Lansing, Michigan 48909
Tel: (517) 373-8600

Minnesota

Chemical Dependency Program Division
Department of Public Welfare
4th Floor Centennial Building
658 Cedar Street
St. Paul, Minnesota 55155
Tel: (612) 296-4610

Mississippi

Division of Alcohol and Drug Abuse
Department of Mental Health
619 Robert E. Lee State Office Building
Jackson, Mississippi 32901
Tel: (601) 354-7031

Missouri

Division of Alcoholism and Drug Abuse
Department of Mental Health
2002 Missouri Boulevard
Jefferson City, Missouri 65102
Tel: (314) 751-4942

Montana

Alcohol and Drug Abuse Division
Department of Institutions
1539 11th Avenue
Helena, Montana 59601
Tel: (406) 449-2827

Nebraska

Division of Alcoholism and Drug Abuse
Department of Public Institutions
P.O. Box 94728
Lincoln, Nebraska 68509
Tel: (402) 471-2851, Ext. 5583

Nevada

Bureau of Alcohol and Drug Abuse
Department of Human Resources
505 East King Street
Carson City, Nevada 89710
Tel: (702) 885-4790

New Hampshire

Office of Alcohol and Drug Abuse
    Prevention
Health and Welfare Building
Hazen Drive
Concord, New Hampshire 03301
Tel: (603) 271-4627

New Jersey

New Jersey Division of Alcoholism
129 East Hanover Street
Trenton, New Jersey 08625
Tel: (609) 292-8947

Division of Narcotic and Drug
    Abuse Control
129 East Hanover Street
Trenton, New Jersey 08625
Tel: (609) 292-5760

New Mexico

Substance Abuse Bureau
Behavioral Health Service Division
P. O. Box 968
Santa Fe, New Mexico 87504-0968
Tel: (505) 827-0117

New York
New York Division of Alcoholism and
    Alcohol Abuse
194 Washington Avenue
Albany, New York 12210
Tel: (518) 474-5417

Division of Substance Abuse Services
Executive Park South, Box 8200
Albany, New York 12203
Tel: (518) 457-7629

North Carolina
Alcohol and Drug Abuse Section
Division of Mental Health and Mental
    Retardation Services
325 North Salisbury Street
Raleigh, North Carolina 27611
Tel: (919) 733-4670

North Dakota
Division of Alcoholism and Drug Abuse
North Dakota Department of Human
    Services
State Capitol/Judicial Wing
Bismarck, North Dakota 58505
Tel: (701) 224-2769

Ohio
Bureau on Alcohol Abuse and Recovery
Ohio Department of Health
170 North High Street, 3rd Floor
Columbus, Ohio 43266-0586
Tel: (614) 466-3445

Bureau on Drug Abuse
Ohio Department of Health
170 North High Street, 3rd Floor
Columbus, Ohio 43266-0586
Tel: (614) 466-7893

Oklahoma
Alcohol and Drug Programs
Oklahoma Department of Mental Health
P.O. Box 53277, Capitol Station
Oklahoma City, Oklahoma 73152
Tel: (405) 271-7474

Oregon
Office of Alcohol and Drug Abuse Problems
301 Public Service Building
Salem, Oregon 97310
Tel: (503) 378-2163

Pennsylvania
Deputy Secretary for Drug and Alcohol
    Abuse Programs
Pennsylvania Department of Health
P.O. Box 90
Harrisburg, Pennsylvania 17108
Tel: (717) 787-9857

Rhode Island
Rhode Island Division of Substance Abuse
Substance Abuse Administration Building
Cranston, Rhode Island 02920
Tel: (401) 464-2091

South Carolina
South Carolina Commission on Alcohol and
    Drug Abuse
3700 Forest Drive
Columbia, South Carolina 29204
Tel: (803) 734-9520

South Dakota
Division of Alcohol and Drug Abuse
Joe Foss Building
523 East Capitol
Pierre, South Dakota 57501
Tel: (605) 773-3123

Tennessee
Alcohol and Drug Abuse Services
Tennessee Department of Mental Health
    and Mental Retardation
706 Church Street, 4th Floor
Nashville, Tennessee 37219
Tel: (615) 741-1921

Texas
Texas Commission on Alcohol and
    Drug Abuse
1705 Guadalupe Street
Austin, Texas 78701
Tel: (512) 463-5510

Utah
Division of Substance Abuse
120 N. 200 West, 4th Floor
P. O. Box 45500
Salt Lake City, Utah 84145-0500
Tel: (801) 538-3939

Vermont
Office of Alcohol and Drug Abuse Programs
Department of Social and Rehabilitation
   Services
103 South Maine Street
Waterbury, Vermont 05676
Tel: (802) 241-2170/241-1000

Virginia
Office of Substance Abuse Services
State Department of Mental Health and
   Mental Retardation
P. O. Box 1797
109 Governor Street
Richmond, Virginia 23214
Tel: (804) 786-3906

Washington
Bureau of Alcoholism and Substance Abuse
Washington Department of Social and
   Health Services
Mail Stop OB-44W
Olympia, Washington 98504
Tel: (206) 753-5866

West Virginia
Department of Health
Division of Alcoholism and Drug Abuse
State Capitol
1800 Washington Street, East, Room 451
Charleston, West Virginia 25305
Tel: (304) 348-2276

Wisconsin
Office of Alcohol and Other Drug Abuse
1 West Wilson Street
P.O. Box 7851
Madison, Wisconsin 53707
Tel: (608) 266-3442

Wyoming
Alcohol and Drug Abuse Programs
Hathaway Building
Cheyenne, Wyoming 82002
Tel: (307) 777-7115, Ext. 7118

Guam
Department of Mental Health and Substance
   Abuse
P.O. Box 9400
Tamuning, Guam 96911
Tel: (671) 646-9262-69

Puerto Rico
Department of Anti-Addiction Services
Box B-Y, Rio Piedras Station
Rio Piedras, Puerto Rico 00928
Tel: (809) 764-3795

Virgin Islands
Division of Mental Health Alcoholism and
   Drug Dependencey
P.O. Box 520
St. Croix, Virgin Islands 00820
Tel: (809) 773-1992

American Samoa
Social Services Division
Alcohol and Drug Program
Government of American Samoa
Pago Pago, American Samoa 96799

Trust Territories
Health Services
Offices of the High Commissioner
Saipan, Trust Territories 96950
Tel: (615) 741-1921

SELF-HELP GROUPS FOR PROFESSIONALS AND SPECIAL POPULATIONS

Adult Children of Alcoholics
Central Service Board
P.O. Box 3216
Torrance, California 90505

Alcoholics Anonymous
P.O. Box 459
Grand Central Station
New York, New York 10163

Al-Anon Family Groups
P.O. Box 862
Midtown Station
New York, New York 10016

American Atheist Addiction Recovery
    Groups (AARG!)
Box 6120
Denver, Colorado 80206

Anesthetists in Recovery (AIR)
5626 Preston Oaks Road, Unit 40D
Dallas, Texas 75240

Birds of a Feather
213 Glenridge Lane
Shaumburg, Illinois 60194
    (Endorsed by the GSO of A.A.,
comprised of active and retired members of
military and civilian aircraft cockpit crews)

Black Women of Alcoholic Parents
    (B-WAP)
139 D. LaBonnevie Drive West
East Patchogue, New York 11772

Calix Society
7601 Wayzata Boulevard
Minneapolis, Minnesota 55426
(Primarily for Catholic members of A.A.)

Dentists Concerned For Dentists (DCD)
450 North Syndicate Street, Suite 117
St. Paul, Minnesota 55104

The Emerging Women, Inc.
R.D. 1, Box 266
Thomasville, Pennsylvania 17364

Families Anonymous
P.O. Box 528
Van Nuys, California 91408

Families in Action Drug Information Center
3845 N. David Hills Road
Suite 300
Decatur, Georgia 30033

International Advisory Council For
    Homosexual Men and Women in A.A.
    (IAC)
P.O. Box 492
Village Station
New York, New York 10014

International Doctors in A.A. (IDAA)
1950 Volney Road
Youngstown, Ohio 44511

International Lawyers in A.A. (ILAA)
39 Smith Neck Road
Old Lyme, Connecticut 06371

Lawyers Concerned for Lawyers (LCL)
450 North Syndicate Street—Suite 117
St. Paul, Minnesota 55104

Mothers Against Drunk Driving (MADD)
National Office
669 Airport Freeway, Suite 310
Hurst, Texas 76053-3944

National Nurses Society on Addiction
2506 Gross Point Road
Evanston, Illinois 60201

Psychologists Helping Psychologists (PHP)
23439 Michigan Avenue
Dearborn, Michigan 48124

Recovered Alcoholic Clergy Association
    (RACA)
5615 Midnight Pass Road
Sarasota, Florida 34242

RID - Remove Intoxicated Drivers
P.O. Box 520
Schenectady, New York 12301

Social Workers Helping Social Workers
84 Wadsworth Street
Hartford, Connecticut 06106
c/o Dr. John Fitzgerald

Students Against Drunk Driving (
    S.A.D.D.)
P.O. Box 800, 277 Main Street
Marlboro, Massachusetts 01752

Toughlove
P.O. Box 1069
Doylestown, Pennsylvania 18901

Women For Sobriety, Inc.
P.O. Box 618
Quakertown, Pennsylvania 18952

Youth Who Care
Box 4074
Grand Junction, Colorado 81502

CANADA

PROVINCIAL AND TERRITORIAL AGENCIES

Alberta
Alberta Alcoholism & Drug Abuse
    Commission
10909 Jasper Avenue
Edmonton, Alberta T5J 3M9
Tel: (403) 427-4275

British Columbia
The Alcohol & Drug Commission of
    British Columbia
805 West Broadway, 8th Floor
Vancouver, British Columbia V5Y 1P9
Tel: (604) 731-9121

Manitoba
Alcoholism Foundation of Manitoba
1580 Dublin Avenue
Winnipeg, Manitoba R3E 0L4
Tel: (204) 775-8601

New Brunswick
Alcoholism & Drug Dependency
    Commission
103 Church Street
P. O. Box 6000
Fredericton, New Brunswick E3B 5H1
Tel: (506) 453-2136

Newfoundland
Department of Health
 Confederation Building
St. John's, Newfoundland A1C 5T7
Tel: (709) 737-2300

Alcohol & Drug Addiction Foundation
    of Newfoundland
3 Blackmarsh Road
St. John's, Newfoundland A1E 1S2
Tel: (709) 579-4041

Nova Scotia
Nova Scotia Commission on Drug
    Dependency
5668 South Street
Halifax, Nova Scotia B3J 1A6
Tel: (902) 424-4270

Ontario
Ministry of Health
9th Floor, Hepburn Block
Queen's Park
Toronto, Ontario M7A 1S2
Tel: (416) 965-5167

Alcoholism & Drug Addiction Foundation
33 Russell Street
Toronto, Ontario M5S 2S1
Tel: (416) 595-6000

Prince Edward Island
Addiction Foundation of Prince Edward
    Island
Box 37
Charlottetown, Prince Edward Island
C1A 7K2
 Tel: (902) 892-4265

Quebec
Department of Social Affairs
Information Centre on Alcoholism and
    Other Addictions
1075. Chemin ste-Foy
Quebec, P. Q. G1S 2M1
Tel: (418) 643-9621

Saskatchewan
Alcoholism Commission of Saskatchewan
3475 Albert Street
Regina, Saskatchewan S4S 6X6
Tel: (306) 565-4085

Northwest Territories
Alcohol & Drug Program
Department of Social Services
Government of the Northwest Territories
Yellowknife, N.W.T. X1A 2L9
Tel: (403) 873-7155

Alcohol & Drug Coordinating Council
Box 1769
Yellowknife, N.W.T. X0E 1H0
Tel: (403) 873-7155

Yukon Territory
Alcohol & Drug Services
Box 2703
Whitehorse, Y. T. Y1A 2C6
Tel: (403) 667-5777

FOREIGN SOURCES

INTERNATIONAL

World Health Organization
1121 Geneva 27,
Switzerland

NATIONAL

Argentina
Ministerio de Salud Publica
Defensa 120
Buenos Aires
Argentina

Australia
Australian Council of Social Services, Inc.
149 Castelereagn Street
Sydney, New South Wales 2000
Australia

Australian Foundation on Alcoholism
    & Drug Dependence
2nd Floor
T and G Building
London Circuit
Canberra City, A. C. T. 2601
Australia

New South Wales
Health Commission
9-13 Young Street
Sydney, New South Wales 2000
Australia

Queensland
Department of Health
Alcohol and Drug Dependence Service
"BIALA"
270 Roma Street
Brisbane, Queensland 4000
Australia

South Australia
Alcohol & Drug Addicts Treatment Board
1st Floor
3/161 Greenhill Road
Parkside, South Australia 5063
Australia

Tasmania
Department of Health Services
Public Buildings
Davey Street
Hobart, Tasmania 7000
Australia

Victoria
Alcohol and Drug Services
Mental Health Division
Health Commission of Victoria
Enterprise House
555 Collins Street
Melbourne, Victoria 3000
Australia

Western Australia
Western Australia Alcohol and Drug
    Authority
Greenchurch House
25 Richardson Street
West Perth
Western Australia, 6005
Australia

Austria
Republik Oesterreich
Bundeministerium fuer Gesundheit und
    Umweltschutz
Stubenring 1
1010 Wein
Austria

Belgium
Comite National pour l'Etude et
    la Prevention de l'Alcoolisme et des
    Autres Toxicomanies
Ministry of Public Health
Ministere de Sante Publique
Cabinet du Ministre
Rue Joseph II 30
Brussels 1040
Belgium

Colombia
Corporacion Colombiana contra
    Alcoholismo
Carrera 50C # 60-13
Bogota,
Colombia

Ministerio de Salud
Calle 16 No. 7-39
Bogota,
Colombia

Denmark
Ministry of Education
Frederiksholms Kanal 21
1220 Copenhagen K
Denmark

National Board of Health
1, St. Kongensgade
DK-1264 Copenhagen K
Denmark

Egypt
Ministry of Health
People's Assembly Street
Lazogli
Cairo,
Egypt

Finland
State Alcohol Monopoly
Social Research Institute of Alcohol Studies
Kalevankatu 12
00100 Helsinki 10
Finland

France

Haut Comite d'Etude et d'Information
    sur l'Alcoolisme
27, Rue Oudinot
75700 Paris
France

Germany

Hygiene Museum
8010 Dresden
Julius—Fucik—Allee
Germany

Deutsche Hauptstelle gegen
    die Suchtoefahren
Westring 2 4700
Hamm
Germany

Hungary

Alkolizmus Elleni Orszagos Bizottsag
Budapest, V.,
Arany Janos v. 31
1051
Hungary

Egeszsegugyi Miniszterium
Budapest, V.,
Akademia v. 10
1055
Hungary

Iceland

Liquor Prevention Council
Eiriksgata 5
101 Reykjavik
Iceland

India

Indian Council on Medical Research
Ansari Nagar,
Post Box 4508
New Delhi—110029
India

Ireland

The Economic and Social Research Institute
4 Burlington Road
Dublin 4,
Republic of Ireland

Department of Health
Customs House
Dublin 1,
Republic of Ireland

Israel

Department of Alcoholism Treatment
    Services
Ministry of Labour and Social Affairs
10 Yad Harutzim Street, Talpiot
P. O. Box 1260
Jerusalem 91000
Israel

Italy

Ministero della Sanita'
D. G. Servizi Medicina Sociale
Viale della Civilta' Romana (EUR)
00144 Roma, Italy

Jamaica

The Permanent Secretary
Ministry of Health
10 Caledonia Avenue
Kingston 5, Jamaica WI

Japan

Mental Health Division
Public Health Bureau
Ministry of Health and Welfare
1—2—2 Kasumigaseki
Chiyoda-ku, Tokyo, Japan

Mexico

Instituto Mexicano de Psiquiatria
Antiguo Camino a Xochimilco 101
Mexico City 22, D. F.
Mexico

Secretaria de Salubridad y Asistencia
Direccion General de Control de Alimentos
     Bebidas y Medicamentos
Mexico City 6, D. F.
Mexico

New Zealand
National Society on Alcoholism and Drug
     Dependence New Zealand (Inc.)
Box 1642
Wellington
New Zealand

Alcoholic Liquor Advisory Council
P. O. Box 5023
Wellington
New Zealand

Poland
Spoteczny Komitet Przeciwalkoholowy
     (Committee to Fight Alcoholism)
UL. Kopernika 36/40
00—328 Warszawa
Poland

South Africa
The Department of Health, Welfare &
     Pensions
Private Bag X88
Pretoria 0001
Republic of South Africa

Sweden
Centralforbundet for Alkohol
Karlavagen 117
Box 27302
10254 Stockholm, Sweden

Switzerland
Schweizerische Fachstelle
fuer Alkoholprobleme
avenue Ruchonnet 14
CH—1003 Lausanne/Switzerland

L'Institut suisse de prophylaxie
     de l'alcoolisme
ISPA, Case postale 203
1000 Lausanne 13
Switzerland

United Kingdom
Alcoholics Anonymous
11 Redcliffe Gardens
London SW 10
United Kingdom

Government Advisory Committee on
     Alcoholism
Dept. of Health and Social Security
Alexander Fleming House
Elephantine and Castle
London SE1
United Kingdom

Institute of Psychiatry
Addiction Research Unit
DeCrespigny Park
London SE5
United Kingdom

Medical Council on Alcoholism
3 Grosvenor Crescent
London SW1
United Kingdom

Venezuela
Division de Higiene Mental
Ministerio de Sanidad
Edificio Sur, Picso 8,
Centro Simon Bolivar
Caracas 1010,
Venezuela

SELECTED ENGLISH-LANGUAGE JOURNALS AND PERIODICALS

Alcohol Awareness Service
(Publication of the National Clearinghouse
    for Alcohol Information—NCALI)
P.O. Box 2345
Rockville, Maryland 20852
Bimonthly

Alcohol Health and Research World
(Publication of the National Institute on
    Alcohol Abuse and Alcoholism)
P.O. Box 2345
Rockville, Maryland 20852
Quarterly

Alcoholism & Addiction Magazine
P.O. Box 31329
Seattle, Washington 98103
Monthly

Alcohol: An International Biomedical
    Journal
Center for Alcohol Studies,
University of North Carolina
School of Medicine
Chapel Hill, North Carolina 27514
Bimonthly

Alcohol and Alcoholism: International
    Journal of the Medical Council
    on Alcoholism
University of Nebraska Medical Center
4101 Woolworth Avenue
Omaha, Nebraska 68105
Quarterly

Alcohol and Drug Research: An
    International Journal for Rapid
    Communications in Clinical Science
University of Colorado Health Science Center
4200 East Ninth Avenue
Denver, Colorado 80262
Bimonthly

Alcohol, Drugs and Traffic Safety
Box 5815
S-102 48 Stockholm, Sweden
Quarterly

Alcoholism
Center for Study and Control on Alcohol
    and Addictions
University Hospital
Zagreb, Yugoslavia
Semiannual

Alcoholism & Drug Abuse Week
3 Governor Street
P.O. Box 3357 - Wayland Square
Providence, Rhode Island 02906-0357

Alcoholism: Clinical and Experimental
    Research
Nuclear Medical Service, 115 VA Hospital
408 First Avenue
New York, New York 10010
Bimonthly

Alcoholism Treatment Quarterly
Arkansas Counseling Associates
P.O. Box 5011
Hillcrest Station
Little Rock, Arkansas 72225
Quarterly

American Journal of Drug and Alcohol Abuse
University of California,
Irvine Medical Center
101 City Drive South
Orange, California 92668
Quarterly

Australian Alcohol/Drug Review
Royal Prince Alfred Hospital
Missenden Road
Camperdown, N.S.W. 2050
Australia
Quarterly

British Journal of Addiction
Addiction Research Unit
Institute of Psychiatry
DeCrespigny Park
London SE5 8AF
England
Bimonthly

British Journal on Alcohol and Alcoholism
3 Grosvenor Crescent
London SW1X 7EE
United Kingdom
Quarterly
(Publication of the Medical Council on
Alcoholism)

Drug and Alcohol Dependence
Elsevier Science Publishers,
Journal Information Center
52 Vanderbilt Avenue
New York, New York 10017
Eight times yearly

International Journal of Addictions
Marcel Dekker Journals
P.O. Box 11305
Church Street Station
New York, New York 10249
Monthly

Journal on Alcohol and Drug Education
Alcohol and Drug Problems Association
400 N. Capitol Street
Washington, D.C. 20001
No determined frequency

Journal of Studies on Alcohol
Alcohol and Drug Abuse Research Center
McLean Hospital—Harvard Medical School
115 Mill Street
Belmont, Massachusetts 02178
Bimonthly

The Counselor
c/o NAADAC
951 S. George Mason Drive
Arlington, Virginia 22204
Bimonthly
(Published by the National Association of
Alcoholism and Drug Abuse Counselors)

Digest of Alcoholism Theory and
   Application (DATA)
10700 Olson Memorial Highway
Minneapolis, Minnesota 55441-6199
Quarterly
(Published by the Johnson Institute)

DISCUS Newsletter
c/o Communications Division, DISCUS
1250 Eye Street, N.W.
Washington, D.C. 20005
Periodically
(Published by the Distilled Spirits Council
of the U.S., Inc.)

Dram Shop and Alcohol Reporter
P.O. Box 590
Falmouth, Massachusetts 02541
Monthly

Drug and Alcohol Dependence
Elsevier Sequoia, S.A., P.O. Box 851
1001 Lausanne 1
Switzerland
Monthly
(Published under the auspices of the Interna-
tional Council on Alcohol and Alcoholism)

Fetal Alcohol Syndrome & Other Drugs
   Update
AHTDS-Prevention Resource Center
901 South Second Street
Springfield, Illinois 62703
Quarterly

The Forum
Al-Anon Family Group Headquarters, Inc.
P.O. Box 862, Midtown Station
New York, New York 10018-0862
(International monthly journal of Al-Anon)

The Grapevine
The A.A. Grapevine, Inc.
P.O. Box 459
Grand Central Station
New York, New York 10163-1100
(International monthly journal of Alcoholics
Anonymous)

The Journal
33 Russell Street
Toronto, Ontario M5S 2S1
Canada
Monthly newspaper published by Addiction
Research Foundation

The NACoA Network
c/o National Association for Children of
Alcoholics
31706 Coast Highway—Suite 201
South Laguna, California 92677
Quarterly

NASADAD Alcohol and Drug Use Report
444 North Capitol Street N.W.—Suite 530
Washington, D.C. 20001
Semimonthly
(Published by the National Association of
State Alcohol and Drug Abuse Directors)

SALIS News
c/o Alcohol Research Group
1816 Scenic Avenue
Berkeley, California 94709
Quarterly
(Published by Substance Abuse Librarians
and Information Specialists)

SPAB Bulletin
University Medical School
Indianapolis, Indiana 42223
Quarterly
(Published by the Society of Psychologists
in Addictive Behaviors - SPAB)

Traffic Safety
444 N. Michigan Avenue
Chicago, Illinois 60611
Bimonthly
(Published by the National Safety Council)

BIBLIOGRAPHY

Ackerman, Robert J. *Children of Alcoholics.* Hollywood, Fla.: Health Communications, 1978.

———. *Let Go and Grow: Recovery for Adult Children.* Pompano Beach, Fla.: Health Communications, Inc., 1967.

Ackoff, R. L.; Gupta, S.; and Minas, J. S. *Scientific Method: Optimizing Applied Research Decisions.* New York: John Wiley and Sons, 1969.

Addeo, Edmund G., and Addeo, Jovita R. *Why Our Children Drink.* Englewood Cliffs, N.J.: Prentice-Hall, 1975.

Addiction Research Foundation. *Alcohol, Drugs and Traffic Safety.* Toronto, 1976.

———. *Alcohol—Public Education and Social Policy.* Toronto, 1981.

———. *The Forgotten Children.* Toronto, 1969.

———. *Halfway Houses for Alcoholics.* Toronto, 1978.

———. *Proposal for a Comprehensive Health-Oriented Alcohol Control Policy in Ontario.* Toronto, 1973.

———. *R.I.D.E.— A Driving-While-Impaired Countermeasure Program.* Toronto, 1979.

———. *Statistical Supplement to the ARF Annual Report.* Toronto, 1982.

———. *The Treatment of Alcoholics: An Ontario Perspective.* Toronto, 1978.

Ahlstrom, Salme. *Trends in Drinking Habits among Finnish Youth from the Beginnings of the 1960s to the Late 1970s.* Helsinki: Social Research Institute of Alcohol Studies, 1979.

Aitken, P. P. *Ten-to-Fourteen-Year-Olds and Alcohol: A Development Study in the Central Region of Scotland.* Edinburgh: Scottish Health Education Unit, 1978.

Akins, Carl, and Beschner, George. *Ethnography: A Research Tool for Policymakers in the Drug and Alcohol Fields.* Rockville, Md.: National Institute on Drug Abuse, 1980.

Al-Anon Family Group Headquarters. *Al-Anon Faces Alcoholism.* New York, 1973.

———. *Alateen—Hope for Children of Alcoholics.* New York, 1973.

———. *The Dilemma of the Alcoholic Marriage.* New York, 1967.

———. *Living with an Alcoholic.* New York, 1978.

———. *Youth and the Alcoholic Parent.* New York, 1960.

Alcoholics Anonymous World Services. *The Alcoholic Husband.* New York, 1954.

————. *The Alcoholic Wife.* New York, 1954.

————. *Alcoholics Anonymous.* New York, 1955.

————. *Alcoholics Anonymous Comes of Age: A Brief History of A.A.* New York, 1957.

————. *Alcoholism—The Illness.* New York, 1959.

————. *As Bill Sees It.* New York, 1967.

————. *Dr. Bob and the Good Oldtimers: A Biography with Recollections of Early A.A. in the Midwest.* New York, 1980.

————. *Sedatives, Stimulants, and the Alcoholic.* New York, 1964.

————. *The Story of How Many Thousands of Men and Women Have Recovered from Alcoholism.* New York, 1955.

————. *Twelve Steps and Twelve Traditions.* New York, 1952.

Allen, H. W. *A History of Wine.* London: Faber and Faber, 1961.

American Medical Association. *Manual on Alcoholism.* Chicago, 1977.

Anastasi, Anne. *Psychological Testing.* New York: Macmillan Co., 1961.

Anderson, D. S., and Gadaleto, A. F. *That Happy Feeling: An Innovative Model for a Campus Alcohol Education Program.* Atlanta: Southern Area Alcohol Education and Training Program, 1979.

Anderson, J. R., and Bower, G. H. *Human Associative Memory.* Washington, D.C.: Winston and Sons, 1973.

Angmann and Associates. *Health Insurance Coverage of Alcoholism Benefits: Results of a National Survey and Implications for California.* San Francisco: California State Senate Committee on Health and Welfare, n.d.

Ansbacher, H., and Ansbacher, R. *The Individual Psychology of Alfred Adler.* New York: Basic Books, 1946.

Archard, Peter. *Vagrancy, Alcoholism and Social Control.* London: Macmillan and Co., 1979.

Armor, David J.; Polich, J. Michael; and Stambul, Harriet B. *Alcoholism and Treatment.* New York: John Wiley and Sons, 1978.

Asbury, Herbert. *The Great Illusion, an Informal History of Prohibition.* Garden City, N.Y.: Doubleday and Co., 1950.

Asimi, A. A. D. *Teenage Drinking Behavior: Report of a Survey in Northwestern Ontario.* Thunder Bay, Ont.: Lakehead University, 1971.

Australian Foundation on Alcoholism and Drug Dependence. *National Alcohol and Drug Dependence Multidisciplinary Institute, August 27 to September 1, 1978.* Canberra, 1978.

Ausubel, David P. *Drug Addiction: Physiological, Psychological and Sociological Aspects.* New York: Random House, 1958.

Avogaro, P.; Sirtori, C. R.; and Tremoli, E. *Metabolic Effects of Alcohol.* New York: Elsevier, 1979.

Ayars, Albert L., and Milgram, Gail G. *The Teenager and Alcohol.* New York: Richards Rosen Press, 1970.

Bacon, Margaret, and Jones, Mary Brush. *Teen-Age Drinking.* New York: Thomas Y. Crowell, 1968.

Bacon, Selden D. *Alcoholism: Nature of the Problem.* New York: National Council on Alcoholism, 1964.

————. *Understanding Alcoholism.* Philadelphia: American Academy of Political and Social Science, 1958.

Bahr, Howard M. *Skid Row: An Introduction to Disaffiliation.* New York: Oxford University Press, 1973.

Bailey, C. B.; Ginter, D. J.; and Woodlock, B. K. *Handbook for Alcoholism Counselors.* Cleveland: Alcoholism Services of Cleveland, 1978.

Bain, D.; Taylor, L.; Bohm, P. E.; Boudreau, R. J.; Chaudron, D. C.; and Sharma, N. *Counseling Skills for Alcoholism Treatment Services: A Literature Review and Experience Survey.* Ottawa: Health Promotion Directorate, Health and Welfare Canada, 1980.

Bandura, Albert. *Principles of Behavior Modification.* New York: Holt, Rinehart and Winston, 1969.

Barnard, Charles P. *Families, Alcoholism and Therapy.* Springfield, Ill.: Charles C. Thomas, 1981.

Barnes, G. M.; Abel, E. L.; and Ernst, C. A. S. *Alcohol and the Elderly: A Comprehensive Bibliography.* Westport, Conn.: Greenwood Press, 1980.

Barnes, T., and Price, S. *Interaction of Alcohol and Other Drugs—Supplement.* Toronto: Addiction Research Foundation, 1973.

Barr, H. L., and Cohen, A. *The Problem-Drinking Drug Addict.* Washington, D.C.: National Institute on Drug Abuse, 1979.

Bartimole, Carmella R., and Bartimole, John E. *Teenage Alcoholism & Substance Abuse: Causes Consequences and Cures.* Hollywood, Fla.: Frederick Fell, 1987.

Bean, Margaret H., and Zinberg, Norman E. *Dynamic Approaches to the Understanding and Treatment of Alcoholism.* New York: Free Press, 1981.

Beauchamp, Dan E. *Beyond Alcoholism: Alcohol and Public Health Policy.* Philadelphia: Temple University Press, 1980.

Begleiter, H. *Biological Effects of Alcohol.* New York: Plenum Press, 1980.

Bell, Judith, and Billington, D. Rex. *Annotated Bibliography of Health Education Research Completed in Britain from 1948-1978.* Edinburgh: Scottish Health Education Unit, 1980.

Bemko, Jane. *Substance Abuse Book Review Index 1980.* Toronto: Addiction Research Foundation, 1981.

Benjamin, F. B. *Alcohol, Drugs and Traffic Safety: Where Do We Go from Here?* Springfield, Ill.: Charles C. Thomas, 1980.

Berger, Gilda. *Addiction: Its Causes, Problems, and Treatments*. New York: Franklin Watts, 1982.

Bergin, A. E., and Strupp, H. H. *Changing Frontiers in the Science of Psychotherapy*. Chicago: Aldine Atherton, 1972.

Billings, J. S. *The Liquor Problem*. Boston: Houghton Mifflin and Co., 1905.

Birnbaum, Isabel M., and Parker, Elizabeth S. *Alcohol and Human Memory*. Hillsdale, N.J.: Lawrence Erlbaum Associates, 1977; dist. John Wiley and Sons.

Black, Claudia. *My Dad Loves Me, My Dad Has a Disease*. Newport Beach, Calif.: ACT, 1980.

Blakeslee, Alton, and Sullivan, Brian. *Alcohol: The New Teen-Age Turn-On*. New York: Associated Press, 1975.

Blane, H. T. *The Personality of the Alcoholic: Guises of Dependency*. New York: Harper and Row, 1968.

————. *The Role of the Nurse in the Care of the Alcoholic Patient in the General Hospital*. Boston: Division of Alcoholism, Massachusetts Department of Public Health, 1960.

————, and Chafetz, M. E. *Youth, Alcohol, and Social Policy*. New York: Plenum Press, 1979.

Bloch, Sidney. *An Introduction to the Psychotherapies*. Oxford: Oxford University Press, 1979.

Block, Jean Libman. *Alcohol and the Adolescent*. New York: National Council on Alcoholism, n.d.

Block, Marvin, A. *Alcohol and Alcoholism: Drinking and Dependence*. Belmont, Calif.: Wadsworth, 1970.

————. *Could Your Child Become an Alcoholic?* New York: National Council on Alcoholism, 1960.

————. *Guide Lines for Admission of Alcoholics to Hospitals*. New York: Smithers, Christopher D., Foundation, 1968.

Blocker, Jack S., Jr. *Alcohol, Reform and Society: The Liquor Issue in Social Context*. Westport, Conn.: Greenwood Press, 1979.

Blomberg, R. D.; Preusser, D. F.; Hale, A.; and Ulmer, R. G. *A Comparison of Alcohol Involvement in Pedestrians and Pedestrian Casualties*. Springfield, Va.: National Technical Information Service, 1979.

Blum, Eva M., and Blum, Richard H. *Alcoholism, Modern Psychological Approaches to Treatment*. San Francisco: Jossey-Bass, 1967.

Blumberg, Leonard; Shipley, T. E.; and Shandler, I. W. *Skid Row and Its Alternatives*. Philadelphia: Temple University Press, 1973.

————, and Barsky, Stephen F. *Liquor and Poverty: Skid Row as a Human Condition*. monograph no. 13. New Brunswick, N.J.: Rutgers Center of Alcohol Studies, 1978.

Blume, Sheila B. *Fetal Alcohol Syndrome: Task Force Report to the Governor*. Albany: New York State Division of Alcoholism and Alcohol Abuse, 1979.

Bogue, Donald. *Skid Row in American Cities*. Chicago: University of Chicago Press, 1963.

Bolger, J. *A Study of the Legal Drinking Age Policy in Ontario.* Toronto: Centre for Urban and Community Studies and The Child in the City Programme, University of Toronto, 1979.

Bortenstein, R. F.; Crowther, R. F.; Shumate, R. P.; Ziel, W. B.; and Zylman, R. *The Role of the Drinking Driver in Traffic Accidents.* Bloomington: Department of Police Administration, Indiana University, 1964.

Brandsma, Jeffrey M.; Maultsby, M. C.; and Welsh, R. J. *Outpatient Treatment of Alcoholism: A Review and Comparative Study.* Baltimore: University Park Press, 1980.

Brasch, R. *How Did It Begin?* New York: David McKay Co., 1965.

Brill, Leon, and Winick, Charles. *The Yearbook of Substance Use and Abuse.* Vol. II. New York: Human Sciences Press, 1980.

Brisolara, Ashton. *The Alcoholic Employee: A Handbook of Useful Guidelines.* New York: Human Sciences Press, 1979.

British Royal College of Psychiatrists. *Alcohol and Alcoholism.* Report of a Special Committee of the Royal College of Psychiatrists. London: Tavistock Publications, 1979.

Bronetto, J. *Alcohol Price, Alcohol Consumption and Death by Liver Cirrhosis.* Toronto: Addiction Research Foundation, 1960-63.

Brooks, Cathleen. *The Secret Everyone Knows.* San Diego: Operation Cork, 1981.

Bruun, Kettil, and Hauge, Kagnar. *Drinking Habits among Northern Youth.* Helsinki: Finnish Foundation for Alcohol Studies, 1963.

————; Koura, E.; Popham, R. E.; and Seeley, J. R. *Liver Cirrhosis Mortality as a Means to Measure the Prevalence of Alcoholism.* Helsinki: Finnish Foundation for Alcohol Studies, 1960.

Bureau of National Affairs. *Alcoholism and Employee Relations: A BNA Special Report.* Washington, D.C., 1978.

Bush, Patricia J. *Drugs, Alcohol & Sex.* New York: Richard Marek, 1980.

Busse, S.; Mulloy, C. T.; Weise, C. E.; Chamberlain, C. M.; and Tetera, D. R. *Disulfiram in the Treatment of Alcoholism: An Annotated Bibliography.* Toronto: Addiction Research Foundation, 1978.

Butters, Nelson, and Cermak, Laird S. *Alcoholic Korsakoff's Syndrome: An Information-Processing Approach to Amnesia.* New York: Academic Press, 1980.

Cahalan, Donald. *Implications of American Drinking Practices and Attitudes for Prevention and Treatment of Alcoholism.* Berkeley: Social Research Group, School of Public Health, University of California, n.d.

————. *Problem Drinkers.* San Francisco: Jossey-Bass, 1970.

————, and Room, Robin. *Problem Drinking among American Men.* New Brunswick, N.J.: Rutgers Center of Alcohol Studies, 1974.

————; Cisin, I. H.; and Crossley, H. M. *American Drinking Practices.* New Haven: College and University Press, 1969.

———. *American Drinking Practices: A National Survey of Behavior and Attitudes*. monograph no. 6. New Brunswick, N.J.: Rutgers Center of Alcohol Studies, 1969.

———. *Understanding America's Drinking Problem: How to Combat the Hazards of Alcohol*. San Francisco: Jossey-Bass, 1987.

California Department of Public Health. *Alcoholism and California: Follow-up Studies of Treated Alcoholics; Description of Studies*. Berkeley, 1961.

Callaway, E.; Jones, R. T.; Stone, G. C.; Peeke, S. C.; and Doyle, J. *Neuropsychological Studies of Alcohol: Final Report*. Springfield, Va.: National Technical Information Service, 1978.

Camberwell Council on Alcoholism. *Women and Alcohol*. New York: Methuen, 1980.

Carroll, Charles R. *Alcohol: Use, Non-Use, and Abuse*. Dubuque: William C. Brown, 1970.

Carroll, R. S. *What Price Alcohol?* New York: Macmillan Co., 1941.

Catanzaro, Ronald J. *Alcoholism*. Springfield, Ill.: Charles C. Thomas, 1968.

Catlin, C. E. G. *Liquor Control*. New York: Henry Holt and Co., 1931.

Cavan, S. *Liquor License: An Ethnography of Bar Behavior*. Chicago: Aldine Publishing Co., 1966.

Chafetz, Morris E., *Liquor: The Servant of Man*. Boston: Little, Brown and Co., 1965.

———. *Why Drinking Can Be Good for You*. New York: Stein and Day, 1976.

———, and Demone, Harold W., Jr. *Alcoholism and Society*. New York: Oxford University Press, 1962.

———; Blane, Howard T.; and Hill, Marjorie J. *Frontiers of Alcoholism*. New York: Science House, 1970.

———. *The Alcoholic Patient: Diagnosis & Management*. Medical Economics Books, 1983.

Chalfant, H. Paul; Roper, B. S.; and Rivera-Worley, C. *Social and Behavioral Aspects of Female Alcoholism: An Annotated Bibliography*. Westport, Conn.: Greenwood Press, 1980.

Cherrington, Ernest H. *The Evolution of Prohibition in the United States of America*. Westerville, Ohio: American Issue Press, 1920.

Cicchinelli, L.; Potter, A.; and Halpern, J. *The Relationship between Yearly Earnings and Client Characteristics for Persons Receiving Alcoholism Treatment*. Springfield, Va.: National Technical Information Service, 1978.

Clark, P. M. S., and Kricka, L. J. *Medical Consequences of Alcohol Abuse*. New York: Halsted Press, and John Wiley and Sons, 1980.

Claypool, Jane. *Alcohol and You*. New York: Franklin Watts, 1981.

Clinebell, Howard J. *Understanding and Counseling the Alcoholic*. New York: Abingdon Press, 1968.

Cohen, Sidney. *The Substance Abuse Problems*. New York: Haworth Press, 1981.

Coleman, James S. *The Adolescent Society*. New York: Free Press, 1961.

Collier, D. F., and Somfay, S. A. *Ascent from Skid Row: the Bon Accord Community 1967-1973.* Toronto: Addiction Research Foundation, 1974.

Collins, James J., Jr. *Drinking and Crime: Perspectives on the Relationships between Alcohol Consumption and Criminal Behavior.* New York: Guilford Publications, 1981.

Colvin, D. L. *Prohibition in the United States.* New York: George H. Doran Co., 1926.

Connecticut State Department of Mental Health, Alcoholism Division. *Teaching about Alcohol in Connecticut Schools.* Hartford, 1966.

Conrad, Barnaby. *Time Is All We Have: Four Weeks at the Betty Ford Center.* New York: Arbor House, 1986.

Cook, Jim, and Lewington, Mike. *Images of Alcoholism.* London: British Film Institute, 1979; New York: New York Zoetrope, 1980.

Cooper, M. L. *Private Health Insurance Benefits for Alcoholism, Drug Abuse and Mental Illness.* Washington, D.C.: Intergovernmental Health Policy Project, 1979.

Cooper, W. E.; Schwar, T. G.; and Smith, L. S. *Alcohol, Drugs and Road Traffic.* Cape Town: Juta and Co., 1979.

Corrigan, Eileen M. *Alcoholic Women in Treatment.* New York: Oxford University Press, 1980.

Corsini, Raymond J. *Current Psychotherapies,* 2nd ed. Itasca, Ill.: F. E. Peacock Publishers, 1979.

Costales, Clare, and Berry, Jo. *Alcoholism: The Way Back to Reality.* Glendale, Calif.: Regal Books Division, G/L Publications, 1980.

Cox, Ann E. *Training Guidelines and Workbook for the Behavioral Management of Intoxicated and Disruptive Clients.* Toronto: Addiction Research Foundation, 1981.

Cronbach, Lee J. *Essentials of Psychological Testing.* New York: Harper and Row, 1960.

Cross, Wilbur. *Kids & Booze: What You Must Know to Help Them.* New York: Dutton and Co., 1979.

Crowder, R. G. *Principles of Learning and Memory.* Hillsdale, N.J.: Lawrence Erlbaum Associates, 1976.

Crumbaugh, James C.; Wood, William M.; and Wood, W. Chadwick. *Logotherapy: New Help for Problem Drinkers.* Chicago: Nelson-Hall, 1980.

Curlee-Salisbury, Joan. *When the Woman You Love Is an Alcoholic.* St. Meinrad, Ind.: Abbey Press, 1978.

Cutler, R., and Storm, T. *Drinking Practices in Three British Columbia Cities. II. Student Survey.* Vancouver: Alcoholism Foundation of British Columbia, 1973.

Czechowicz, D. *Detoxification Treatment Manual.* Washington, D.C.: U.S. Government Printing Office, 1979.

Dahlstrom, W. G., and Welsch, G. S. *An MMPI Handbook: A Guide to Use in Clinical Practice and Research.* Minneapolis: University of Minnesota Press, 1965.

David, Kenneth, and Cowley, James. *Pastoral Care in Schools and Colleges.* London: Edward Arnold, n.d.

Dawkins, Marvin P. *Alcohol and the Black Community: Exploratory Studies of Selected Issues.* Saratoga, Calif.: Century Twenty-One, 1980.

DeLuca, John R., ed. *Fourth Special Report to the U.S. Congress on Alcohol and Health.* Rockville, Md.: National Institute on Alcohol Abuse and Alcoholism, 1981.

Demone, Harold W. *Alcohol Education: What Does a Teacher Need to Know to Teach?* Montpelier, Vt.: Vermont State Department of Education, 1960.

Dennison, Darwin; Prevet, T.; and Affleck, M. *Alcohol and Behavior: An Activated Education Approach.* St. Louis: Mosby, 1980.

Diehm, A. P.; Seaborn, R. F.; and Wilson, G. C. *Alcohol in Australia: Problems and Programmes.* New York: McGraw-Hill Book Co., 1978.

Dimas, George C. *Alcohol Education in Oregon Schools.* Portland: Alcohol Studies and Rehabilitation Section, Oregon State Mental Health Division, 1964.

Distilled Spirits Council of the United States. *DISCUS Facts Book 1979. The Beverage Alcohol Industry: Public Attitudes and Economic Patterns.* Washington, D.C., 1980.

———. *Distilled Spirits Industry Annual Statistical Review 1979.* Washington, D.C., 1980.

Dollard, John, and Miller, Neal E. *Personality and Psychotherapy.* New York: McGraw-Hill Book Co., 1950.

Dorchester, Daniel. *The Liquor Problem in All Ages.* New York: Phillips and Hunt, 1884.

Dorris, Michael. *The Broken Chord.* New York: Harper & Row, 1989.

Douglass, R. L.; Wagenarr, A. C.; and Barkey, P. M. *Alcohol Availability, Consumption and the Incidence of Alcohol-Related Social and Health Problems in Michigan.* Ann Arbor: Highway Safety Research Institute, University of Michigan, 1979.

Downard, William L. *Dictionary of the History of the American Brewing and Distilling Industries.* Westport, Conn.: Greenwood Press, 1980.

Drews, Toby R. *Getting Them Sober.* Plainfield, N.J.: Haven Books, 1980.

Durfee, C. H. *To Drink or Not to Drink.* New York: Longmans and Green, 1937.

Durkheim, Emile. *Suicide.* New York: Free Press, 1962.

Du-Torr, B. M. *Drugs, Rituals, and Altered States of Consciousness.* Rotterdam: A. A. Balkema, 1977.

Eddy, Cristen C., and Ford, John L. *Alcoholism in Women.* Dubuque: Kendall/Hunt, 1980.

Edwards, Griffith, and Grant, Marcus. *Alcohol Treatment in Transition.* Baltimore: University Park Press, 1980.

———. *Alcoholism: New Knowledge and New Responses.* London: Crown Helm, 1977.

Efron, Daniel E., ed. *Psychopharmacology: A Review of Progress.* Public Health Service Publication, no. 1836. Washington, D.C.: Public Health Service, 1968.

Emerson, Edward Randolph. *Beverages, Past and Present.* New York: G. P. Putnam's Sons, 1908.

Emerson, Haven. *Alcohol: Its Effects on Man.* New York: Appleton-Century-Crofts, 1934.

Emerson, Vivian J.; Holleyhead, R.; Isaacs, M. D. J.; Fuller, N. A.; and Hunt, D. J. *The Measurement of Breath Alcohol: The Laboratory Evaluation of Substantive Breath Test Equipment and the Report of an Operational Police Trial.* Harrogate, England: Forensic Society; Edinburgh, Scotland; Scottish Academic Press, 1980.

Engelmann, Larry. *Intemperance: The Lost War against Liquor.* New York: Free Press, 1979.

Englebardt, Stanley L. *Kids and Alcohol—the Deadliest Drug.* New York: Lothrop, Lee and Shepard Co., 1975.

Engs, Ruth C. *Responsible Drug and Alcohol Use.* New York: Macmillan Co., 1979.

Entine, A. D. *The Relationship between the Number of Sales Outlets and the Consumption of Alcoholic Beverages in New York and Other States.* Albany: New York State Moreland Commission of the Alcoholic Beverage Control Law, 1963.

Erdoes, Richard. *Saloons of the Old West.* New York: Alfred A. Knopf, 1979.

Eriksson, K.; Sinclair, J. D.; and Kiianmaa, K. *Animal Models of Alcohol Research.* New York: Academic Press, 1980.

Estes, Nada J.; Smith-DiJulio, K.; and Heinemann, M. E. *Nursing Diagnosis of the Alcoholic Person.* St. Louis: Mosby, 1980.

Everest, Allan S. *Rum across the Border: The Prohibition Era in Northern New York.* Syracuse: Syracuse University Press, 1978.

Ewing, John A. *Drinking to Your Health.* n.p. Reston, Va., 1981.

———, and Rouse, Beatrice A. *Drinking. Alcohol in American Society—Issues and Current Research.* Chicago: Nelson-Hall, 1978.

Fann, William E.; Karacan, I.; Pokorny, A. D.; and Williams, R. L. *Phenomenology and Treatment of Alcoholism.* New York: SP Medical and Scientific Books, 1980.

Faris, Robert E. L., and Dunham, H. Warren. *Mental Disorders in Urban Areas.* New York: Hofner, 1939.

Feit, Marvin D. *Management and Administration of Drug and Alcohol Programs.* Springfield, Ill.: Charles C. Thomas, 1979.

Fenichel, Otto. *The Psychoanalytic Theory of Neurosis.* New York: W. W. Norton and Co., 1945.

Fields, W. C. *Never Trust a Man Who Doesn't Drink.* Compiled by Paul Mason. New York: Stonyan Books, 1971.

Fillmore, K. M.; Bacon, S. D.; and Hyman, M. *The 27-Year Longitudinal Panel Study of Drinking by Students in College, 1949-1976. Final Report.* Springfield, Va.: National Technical Information Service, 1979.

Fitzgerald, Kathleen Whalen. *Alcoholism: The Genetic Inheritance.* New York: Doubleday, 1988.

Fitzgibbon, Constantine. *Drink.* New York: Doubleday and Co., 1979.

Fleit, L. *Alcohol and Sexuality: A Handbook for the Counselor/Therapist.* Arlington, Va.: H/P Publishing Co., 1979.

Fleming, Alice. *Alcohol, the Delightful Poison.* New York: Dell Publishing Co., 1975.

Follmann, Joseph F., Jr. *Helping the Troubled Employee.* New York: Amacom, 1978.

Forbes, Thomas Rogers. *Crowner's Quest.* The American Philosophical Society, *Transactions,* vol. 68, part I. Philadelphia, 1978.

Ford, J. C. *Depth Psychology, Morality and Alcoholism.* Weston, Mass.: Weston College Press, 1951.

Fort, Joel. *Alcohol: Our Biggest Drug Problem.* New York: McGraw-Hill Book Co., 1973.

Fowler, R. D., Sr. *Studies in Alcoholism.* Montgomery: Alabama Commission on Alcoholism, 1960.

Fox, Ruth. *The Alcoholic Spouse.* New York: National Council on Alcoholism, 1956.

———. *Alcoholism: Behavioral Research and Therapeutic Approaches.* New York: Springer Publishing Co., 1967.

———, and Lyon, Peter. *Alcoholism: Its Scope, Cause and Treatment.* New York: Random House, 1955.

Freed, Earl X. *An Alcoholic Personality?* Thorofare, N.J.: Charles B. Slack, 1979.

Freedman, M., and Kaplan, H. I. *Comprehensive Textbook of Psychiatry.* Baltimore: Williams and Wilkins, 1967.

Freeman, K. M., and Koegler, R. R. *From Skid Row to the Olympics.* Castaic, Calif.: Institute of Creative Leisure, 1978.

Freudenberger, Herbert J., and Richelson, Geraldine. *The High Cost of High Achievement.* Garden City, N.Y.: Anchor Press, 1980.

Furnas, J. C. *The Life and Times of the Late Demon Rum.* New York: G. P. Putnam's Sons, 1965.

Galanter, Marc. *Alcohol and Drug Abuse in Medical Education.* Rockville, Md.: National Institute on Drug Abuse, 1980.

———. *Currents in Alcoholism. Vol. VI: Treatment and Rehabilitation and Epidemiology.* Ontario: Academic Press, 1979.

———. *Currents in Alcoholism. Vol. VII: Recent Advances in Research and Treatment.* Ontario: Academic Press, 1980.

Gallant, Donald M. *Alcoholism: A Guide to Diagnosis, Intervention, and Treatment.* New York: W.W. Norton, 1987.

Gastineau, Clifford F.; Darby, W. J.; and Turner, T. B. *Fermented Food Beverages in Nutrition.* New York: Academic Press, 1979.

Gerard, D. L., and Saenger, G. *Out-Patient Treatment of Alcoholism: A Study of Outcome and Its Determinants.* Toronto: University of Toronto Press, 1966.

Gerstel, E. K.; Mason, R. E.; Piserchia, P. V.; and Kristiansen, P. L. *A Pilot Study of the Social Contexts of Drinking and Correlates.* Research Triangle Park, N.C.: Research Triangle Institute, 1975.

Gibbins, R. I. *Chronic Alcoholism.* Brookside Monograph, no. I. Ontario: Alcoholism Research Foundation, 1953.

Gibbins, Robert J; Israel, Yedy; Kalant, Harold; Popham, Robert E.; Schmidt, Wolfgang; and Smart, Reginald G. *Research Advances in Alcohol and Drug Problems, Vol. 1.* New York: John Wiley and Sons, 1974.

————. *Research Advances in Alcohol and Drug Problems, Vol. 2.* New York: John Wiley and Sons, 1975.

————. *Research Advances in Alcohol and Drug Problems, Vol. 3.* New York: John Wiley and Sons, 1976.

Gilmore, Thomas B. *Equivocal Spirits.* Chapel Hill: University of North Carolina Press, 1987.

Gitlow, Stanley E., and Peyser, Herbert S. *Alcoholism: A Practical Treatment Guide.* New York: Grune and Stratton, 1980.

Glaser, Frederick B.; Greenberg, Stephanie W.; and Barrett, Morris. *A Systems Approach to Alcohol Treatment.* Toronto: Addiction Research Foundation, 1978.

Gonzalez, Gerardo M. *Procedures and Resource Materials for Developing a Campus Alcohol Abuse Prevention Program: A Tested Model.* Gainesville: University of Florida, 1978.

Goodman, Donald. *Is Alcoholism Hereditary?* Oxford, New York and London: Oxford University Press, 1976.

Goodman, L., and Gilman, A. *The Pharmacological Basis of Therapeutics.* 2nd ed. New York: Macmillan Co., 1955.

Goodwin, Donald W., and Erickson, Carlton K. *Alcoholism and Affective Disorders: Clinical, Genetic, and Biochemical Studies.* New York: SP Medical and Scientific Books, 1979.

Gordis, Enoch, M.D., ed. *Sixth Special Report to the U.S. Congress on Alcohol and Health.* Rockville, Md.: National Institute on Alcohol Abuse and Alcoholism, 1987.

Gottheil, Edward; McLellan, A. Thomas; and Druley, Keith A. *Substance Abuse and Psychiatric Illness: Proceedings of the Second Annual Coatsville-Jefferson Conference on Addiction, 1978.* New York: Pergamon Press, 1980.

————, and Alterman, Arthur I. *Addiction Research and Treatment: Converging Trends.* London: Pergamon Publishing Co., 1979.

Grant, Marcus; Plant, Martin; and Saunders, W. *Drinking and Alcohol Problems in Scotland.* Edinburgh: Scottish Health Education Unit, 1980.

Greeley, Andrew M.; McCready, William C.; and Theisen, G. *Ethnic Drinking Subcultures.* New York: Bergin Publishers, 1980.

Griffin, Tom, and Svendsen, Roger. *The Student Assistance Program: How It Works.* Center City, Minn.: Hazelden, 1980.

Grimm, Anne C., and Huber, Kristina R. *Alcohol/Safety Public Information Materials Catalog, No. 5*. Ann Arbor: University of Michigan, 1981.

Gross, Milton M., ed. *Alcohol Intoxication and Withdrawal, Experimental Studies*. New York: Plenum Press, 1973.

———. *Alcohol Intoxication and Withdrawal, Experimental Studies II*. New York: Plenum Press, 1975.

———. *Alcohol Intoxication and Withdrawal—IIIA. Biological Aspects of Ethanol*. New York: Plenum Press, 1976.

———. *Alcohol Intoxication and Withdrawal—IIIB. Studies in Alcohol Dependence*. New York: Plenum Press, 1976.

Group Health Association of America. *Alcoholism Services Handbook for Prepaid Group Plans*. Springfield, Va.: National Technical Information Service, 1979.

Groupe, Vincent. *Alcoholism Rehabilitation: Methods and Experiences of Private Rehabilitation Centers*. New Brunswick, N.J.: Rutgers Center of Alcohol Studies, 1978.

Groves, W. E.; Rossi, P. H.; and Grafstein, D. *Study of Life Styles and Campus Communities: Preliminary Report*. Baltimore: Johns Hopkins University, 1970.

Gusfield, Joseph R. *The Culture of Public Problems: Drinking-Driving and the Symbolic Order*. Chicago: University of Chicago Press, 1981.

———. *Symbolic Crusade: Status Politics and the American Temperance Movement*. Urbana: University of Illinois Press, 1963.

Guthrie, D. *A History of Medicine*. London: Nelson and Sons, 1945.

Gwinner, Paul, and Grant, Marcus. *What's Your Poison*. London: British Broadcasting Corp., n.d.

Hackwood, Frederick W. *Inns, Ales and Drinking Customs of Old England*. New York: Sturgiss and Walton Co., 1909.

Hamer, John, and Steinbring, Jack. *Alcohol and Native Peoples of the North*. Lanham, Md.: University Press of America, 1980.

Hammond, R. L. *Almost All You Ever Wanted to Know about Alcohol but Didn't Know Who to Ask*. Lansing: American Business Men's Research Foundation, 1978.

Harper, Frederick D. *Alcoholism Treatment and Black Americans*. Rockville, Md.: National Clearinghouse for Alcohol Information, 1979.

———. *Jogotherapy: Jogging as a Therapeutic Strategy*. Alexandria, Va.: Douglass Publishers, 1979.

Harris, D. H., and Howlett, J. B. *Visual Detection of Driving While Intoxicated*. Springfield, Va.: National Technical Information Service, 1979.

Hartford, T. C.; Parker, D. A.; and Light, L. *Normative Approaches to the Prevention of Alcohol Abuse and Alcoholism*. Rockville, Md.: National Institute on Alcohol Abuse and Alcoholism, 1980.

Haskins, James. *Teen-age Alcoholism.* New York: Hawthorn Books, 1976.

Heath, Dwight B., and Cooper, A. M. *Alcohol Use and World Cultures: A Comprehensive Bibliography of Anthropological Sources.* Toronto: Addiction Research Foundation, 1981.

Hill, Art, "The Alcoholic on Alcoholism," *Canadian Literature*, Autumn 1974.

Himwich, H. E. *Alcoholism: Basic Aspects and Treatment.* Washington, D.C.: American Association for the Advancement of Science, 1951.

Hofmann, Frederick G. *A Handbook on Drug and Alcohol Abuse: The Biomedical Aspects.* New York: Oxford University Press, 1975.

Hollingshead, A. B., and Redlich, F. C. *Social Class and Mental Illness.* New York: John Wiley and Sons, 1958.

Hollis, S. *Casework: a Psychosocial Therapy.* New York: Random House, 1965.

Hooton, C. *What Shall We Say about Alcohol?* New York: Abingdon Press, 1960.

Hore, Brian D., and Plant, Martin A. *Alcohol Problems in Employment.* London: Croom Helm, 1981.

Hornik, Edith Lynn. *You and Your Alcoholic Parent.* New York: Association Press, 1974.

Houthakker, H. S., and Taylor, Lester D. *Consumer Demand in the United States: Analyses and Projections.* Cambridge, Mass.: Harvard University Press, 1970.

Howard, Marion. *Did I Have a Good Time? Teenage Drinking.* New York: Continuum, 1980.

Huelke, D. F., and Davis, R. A. *Pedestrian Fatalities.* Ann Arbor: Highway Safety Research Institute, University of Michigan, 1969.

Hughes, H. E., and Schneider, D. *The Man from Ida Grove: A Senator's Personal Story.* Lincoln, Va.: Chosen Books, 1979.

Hugunin, M. B. *Helping the Impaired Physician. Proceedings of the AMA Conference on "The Impaired Physician: Answering the Challenge," February 4-6, 1977: Atlanta, Georgia.* Chicago: American Medical Association, 1979.

Hyde, Margaret O. *Alcohol: Drink or Drug?* New York: McGraw-Hill Book Co., 1974.

Idestrom, Carl-Magnus, ed. *Alcohol and Brain Research.* Copenhagen: Munksgaard, 1980.

Institute of Medicine, Division of Health Promotion and Disease Prevention. *Alcoholism, Alcohol Abuse and Related Problems: Opportunities for Research.* Washington, D.C.: Academy Press, 1980.

Israel, Yedy, and Mardones, Jorge, eds. *Biological Basis of Alcoholism.* New York: John Wiley and Sons, 1971.

Jackson, Michael. *The World Guide to Beer.* New York: Ballantine Books, 1978.

Jacobs, Michael R. *Problems Presented by Alcoholic Clients.* Toronto: Addiction Research Foundation, 1981.

Jacobson, Michael, Atkins, Robert, and Hacker, George. *The Booze Merchants: The Inebriating of America*, a report from the Center For Science in the Public Interest, foreword by Nicholas Johnson, Washington, D.C.: CSPS Books, 1984.

Jaffe, Jerome H.; Peterson, Robert; and Hodgson, Ray. *Addictions: Issues and Answers.* London: Harper and Row, 1980.

Jellinek, E. M. *The Alcoholism Complex.* New York: Smithers, Christopher D., Foundation, 1960.

———. *The Disease Concept of Alcoholism.* New Haven: Hillhouse Press, 1960.

———. *Government Programs on Alcoholism: A Review of the Activities in Some Foreign Countries.* Ottawa: Department of National Health and Welfare, 1963.

Jessor, Richard; Graves, T. D.; Hanson, R. C.; and Jessor, S. L. *Society, Personality, and Deviant Behavior.* New York: Holt, Rinehart and Winston, 1968.

Johns, T. R., and Pascarella, E. A. *An Assessment of the Limited Driving License Amendment to the North Carolina Statutes Relating to Drunk Driving.* Chapel Hill, N.C.: Highway Safety Research Center, University of North Carolina, 1971.

Johnson, Vernon E. *I'll Quit Tomorrow.* New York: Harper & Row, 1973.

Johnston, Lloyd. *Drugs and American Youth.* Ann Arbor: Institute for Social Research, 1973.

Joint Commission on Accreditation of Hospitals. *Consolidated Standards for Child, Adolescent, and Adult Psychiatric Alcoholism and Drug Abuse Programs.* Chicago, 1979.

Jones, D. C.; Schlenger, W. E.; and Zelon, H. S. *Alcoholism Manpower Information System. Final Report.* Research Triangle Park, N.C.: Center for Health Studies, Research Triangle Institute, 1979.

Jones, R. K., and Joscelyn, K. B. *Alcohol and Highway Safety 1978: A Review of the State of Knowledge. (Summary Volume).* Springfield, Va.: National Technical Information Service, 1978.

Jordan, Donald K. *Alcohol Abuse Prevention: A Comprehensive Guide for Youth Organizations.* Boys' Club of America Project TEAM, 1978.

Josephson, E. *An Assessment of Statistics on Alcohol-Related Problems.* Washington, D.C.: Distilled Spirits Council of the United States, 1980.

Kalant, Oriana Josseau. *Alcohol and Drug Problems in Women.* Vol. 5. New York: Plenum Publishing Corp., 1980.

———, and Kalant, H. *Drugs, Society and Personal Choice.* Toronto: General Publishing, 1971.

Kane, Geoffrey P. *Inner-City Alcoholism: An Ecological Analysis and Cross-Cultural Study.* New York: Human Sciences Press, 1981.

Kant, F. *The Treatment of the Alcoholic.* Springfield, Ill.: Charles C. Thomas, 1954.

Kaufman, Edward, and Kaufmann, Pauline N. *Family Therapy of Drug and Alcohol Abuse.* New York: Gardner Press, 1979.

Keithahn, C. F. *The Brewing Industry: Staff Report of the Bureau of Economics, Federal Trade Commission.* Springfield, Va.: National Technical Information Service, 1978.

Keller, Mark, and McCormick, M. *A Dictionary of Words about Alcohol.* New Brunswick, N.J.: Rutgers Center of Alcohol Studies, 1968.

———, and Seeley, John R. *The Alcohol Language: With a Selected Vocabulary.* Toronto: University of Toronto Press, 1958.

Kellermann, Joseph L. *A Guide for the Family of the Alcoholic.* New York: National Council on Alcoholism, 1960.

Kemper Insurance Co. *A Neglected Area of Loss Reduction: What to Do about the Employee with a Drinking Problem.* Chicago, 1966.

Keniston, Kenneth. *Youth and Dissent: The Rise of a New Opposition.* New York: Harcourt Brace Jovanovich, 1971.

Kent, Patricia. *An American Woman and Alcohol.* New York: Holt, Rinehart and Winston, 1967.

Kerlinger, Frederick N. *Foundations of Behavioral Research.* New York: Holt, Rinehart and Winston, 1964.

———, and Pedhazur, E. J. *Multiple Regression in Behavioral Research.* New York: Holt, Rinehart and Winston, 1973.

King, F. A. *Beer Has a History.* New York: Hutchinson's Scientific and Technical Publications, 1947.

Kinney, Jean, and Leaton, Gwen. *Loosening the Grip: A Handbook of Alcohol Information.* Center City, Minn.: Hazelden, 1978.

Kinsey, Barry A. *The Female Alcoholic: A Social Psychological Study.* Springfield, Ill.: Charles C. Thomas, 1966.

Kirkpatrick, Jean. *Goodbye Hangovers Hello Life.* New York: Atheneum, 1986.

Kissin, Benjamin, and Begleiter, Henri, eds. *The Biology of Alcoholism, Vol. I, Biochemistry.* New York: Plenum Press, 1972.

———. *The Biology of Alcoholism, Vol. 2, Physiology and Behavior.* New York: Plenum Press, 1972.

———. *The Biology of Alcoholism, Vol. 3, Clinical Pathology.* New York: Plenum Press, 1974.

———. *The Biology of Alcoholism, Vol. 4, Social Aspects of Alcoholism.* New York: Plenum Press, 1976.

———. *The Biology of Alcoholism, Vol. 5, Treatment and Rehabilitation of the Chronic Alcoholic.* New York: Plenum Press, 1977.

Klausner, S. Z.; Foulks, E. F.; and Moore, M. H. *The Inupiat: Economics and Alcohol on the Alaskan North Slope.* Philadelphia: Center for Research on the Acts of Man, 1979.

———. *Social Change and the Alcohol Problem on the Alaskan North Slope.* Philadelphia: Center for Research on the Acts of Man, 1980.

Krasnegor, N. A. *Behavioral Analysis and Treatment of Substance Abuse.* Washington, D.C.: National Institute on Drug Abuse, 1979.

Kricka, L. J., and Clark, P. M. S. *Biochemistry of Alcohol and Alcoholism.* New York: Halsted Press, 1979.

Krout, J. A. *The Origins of Prohibition.* New York: Alfred A. Knopf, 1924.

Kruse, H. D., and Grob, Gerald N. *Alcoholism as a Medical Problem.* New York: Hoeber-Harper, 1956.

Kurtz, Ernest. *Not-God: A History of Alcoholics Anonymous.* Center City, Minn.: Hazelden, 1979.

Kuusi, P. *Alcohol Sales Experiment in Rural Finland.* Helsinki: Finnish Foundation for Alcohol Studies, 1957.

Kyvig, David E. *Repealing National Prohibition.* Chicago: University of Chicago Press, 1979.

Langone, John, and Langone, Dolores deN. *Women Who Drink.* Reading, Mass.: Addison-Wesley, 1980.

Lanu, K. E. *Control of Deviating Drinking Behavior: An Experimental Study of Formal Control over Drinking Behavior.* Helsinki: Finnish Foundation for Alcohol Studies, 1956.

Larkin, E. J. *The Treatment of Alcoholism: Theory, Practice, and Evaluation.* Ontario: Addiction Research Foundation, 1974.

Lee, Essie E. *Alcohol—Proof of What?* New York: Julian Messner, 1976.

Lee, John Parks. *What Shall We Tell Our Children about Drinking?* New York: National Council on Alcoholism, 1960.

Leiberman, M. A., and Borman, L. D. *Self-Help Groups for Coping with Crises: Origins, Members, Processes, and Impact.* San Francisco: Jossey-Bass, 1979.

Leigh, C. D. *Prohibition in the United States: A History of the Prohibition Party and of the Prohibition Movement.* New York: George H. Doran, Co., 1926.

Leite, Evelyn. *To Be Somebody.* Center City, Minn.: Hazelden, 1979.

Lemert, E. W. *Alcohol and the Northwest Coast Indians.* Berkeley: University of California Press, 1954.

Lennard, Henry, and Bernstein, A. *The Anatomy of Psychotherapy: Systems of Communication and Expectation.* New York: Columbia University Press, 1960.

Levy, H. *Drink: An Economic and Social Study.* London: Routledge and Kegan Paul, 1951.

Levy, J. E., and Kunitz, S. J. *Indian Drinking: Navajo Practices and Anglo-American Theories.* New York: John Wiley and Sons, 1974.

Li, T. K.; Schenker, S.; and Lumeng, L. *Alcohol and Nutrition: Proceedings of a Workshop, September 26-27, 1977, Indianapolis, Indiana.* Washington, D.C.: U.S. Government Printing Office, 1979.

Liban, Carolyn B., and Smart, Reginald G. *The Value of the Informant Method for Studying Drinking Habits.* Toronto: Addiction Research Foundation, 1980.

Lichine, Alexis. *Encyclopedia of Wines and Spirits.* New York: Alfred A. Knopf, 1968.

Lingeman, Richard R. *Drugs from A to Z.* New York: McGraw-Hill Book Co., 1974.

Linn, R. *You Can Drink and Stay Healthy: A Guide for the Social Drinker.* New York: Franklin Watts, 1979.

Little, J. W., and Hartman, B. S. *Review of Legal Literature Published between July 1974 and July 1978 Pertaining to Alcohol and Drug Involvement in Highway Safety.* Springfield, Va.: National Technical Information Service, 1978.

Lockhard, Sir R. B. *Scotch: The Whisky of Scotland in Fact and Story.* London: Putnam and Co., 1971.

Lockhart, D. L. *The Swinging Door: An Evaluation of Services to and Needs of Street People in Downtown Salinas.* Salinas: Sun Street Centers, Community Alcoholism Programs, 1979.

Lolli, Giorgio. *Social Drinking, the Effects of Alcohol.* New York: Collier Books, 1961.

————; Serianni, E.; Golder, G.; and Luzzatto-Fegiz, P. *Alcohol in Italian Culture: Food and Wine in Relation to Sobriety among Italians and Italian Americans.* New Haven: Yale Center of Alcohol Studies, 1958.

Lord, Luther, and Lord, Eileen. *Here's How to Sobriety.* Center City, Minn.: Hazelden, 1977.

Lotter, J. M. *Social Problems in the RSA.* Pretoria: Institute for Sociological, Demographic and Criminological Research, South African Human Sciences Research Council, 1979.

Louria, D. B. *The Drug Scene.* New York: McGraw-Hill Book Co., 1968.

Lovell, H. W. *Hope and Help for the Alcoholic.* Garden City, N.Y.: Doubleday and Co., 1951.

Lowinson, Joyce H., and Ruiz, Pedro. *Substance Abuse: Clinical Problems and Perspectives.* Easton, Md.: Williams and Wilkins Co., 1981.

Lucia, Salvatore P. *Alcohol and Civilization.* New York: McGraw-Hill Book Co., 1960.

————. *A History of Wine as Therapy.* Philadelphia: J. B. Lippincott Co., 1963.

Ludwig, Arnold M. *Understanding the Alcoholic's Mind: The Nature of Craving and How to Control It.* New York: Oxford University Press, 1988.

Luks, Alan. *Having Been There.* New York: Charles Scribner's Sons, 1979.

MacAndrew, Craig, and Edgerton, Robert B. *Drunken Comportment: A Social Explanation.* Chicago: Aldine Publishing Co., 1969.

MacLennan, Anne. *Women: Their Use of Alcohol and Other Legal Drugs.* Toronto: Addiction Research Foundation, 1976.

Macurdy, E. A., and Hollander, M. J. *A Survey of Drinking Practices and Attitudes to Alcohol Use in B.C.* Vancouver: Alcohol and Drug Commission, Ministry of Health, 1978.

Madden, J. S. *Guide to Alcohol and Drug Dependence.* Bristol, England: J. Wright and Sons, 1979.

————; Walker, Robin; and Kenyon, W. H. *Aspects of Alcohol and Drug Dependence.* Kent, England: Pitman Medical Limited, 1980.

Maddox, George L. *The Domesticated Drug: Drinking among Collegians.* New Haven: College and University Press, 1970.

————, and McCall, Bevode C. *Drinking among Teen-Agers.* New Brunswick, N.J.: Rutgers Center of Alcohol Studies, 1964.

Madsen, William. *The American Alcoholic: The Nature-Nurture Controversy in Alcoholic Research and Therapy.* Springfield, Ill.: Charles C. Thomas, 1974.

Majchrowicz, Edward, and Noble, Ernest P. *Biochemistry and Pharmacology of Ethanol.* 2 vols. New York and London: Plenum Publishing Corp., 1979.

Makela, Klaus. *Prices of Alcoholic Beverages in Finland, 1950-1975.* Helsinki: Social Research Institute of Alcohol Studies, 1980.

————. *Unrecorded Consumption of Alcohol in Finland, 1950-1975.* Helsinki: Social Research Institute of Alcohol Studies, 1979.

————; Room, Robin; Single, Eric; Sulkunen, Pekka; and Walsh, Brendan. *Alcohol, Society and the State. Vol. 1: A Comparative Study of Alcohol Control.* Toronto: Addiction Research Foundation, 1982.

Malzberg, Benjamin. *The Alcoholic Psychosis.* New Haven: Yale Center of Alcohol Studies, 1960.

Mandell, W. *Youthful Drinking.* New York: Wakoff Research Center, 1962.

Manello, Timothy A.; Paddock, J. A.; Wick, W.; and Seaman, F. J. *Problem Drinking among Railroad Workers: Extent, Impact and Solutions.* Washington, D.C.: University Research Corp., 1979.

Mann, George A. *Recovery of Reality: Overcoming Chemical Dependency.* New York: Harper and Row, 1979.

Mann, Marty. *New Primer on Alcoholism.* New York: Holt, Rinehart and Winston, 1963.

————. *Primer on Alcoholism.* New York: Holt, Rinehart and Winston, 1958.

Manning, William O., and Vinton, Jean. *Harmfully Involved.* Center City, Minn.: Hazelden, 1978.

Marden, P. G., and Kolodner, K. *Alcohol Abuse among Women: Gender Differences and Their Implications for the Delivery of Services.* Springfield, Va.: National Technical Information Service, 1979.

Marr, D. *From Liquor and Loneliness to Love and Laughter.* Kansas City, Kan.: Sheed Andrews and McMeel, 1978.

Marshall, Mac. *Beliefs, Behaviors, and Alcoholic Beverages: A Cross-Cultural Survey.* Ann Arbor: University of Michigan Press, 1979.

————. *Weekend Warriors: Alcohol in a Micronesian Culture.* Palo Alto: Mayfield Publishing Co., 1979.

Martin, J. P. *Violence and the Family.* New York: John Wiley and Sons, 1978.

Marvin, D. *World's Original Social Drinker's Almanac.* Oceanside, Calif.: Marvin, 1979.

Mass Observation. *The Pub and the People*. London: Gollancz, 1943.

Maultsby, Maxie C., Jr. *A Million Dollars for Your Hangover*. Lexington, Ky.: Rational Self-Help Books, 1978.

———, and Welsh, Richard J. *Outpatient Treatment of Alcoholism*. Baltimore: University Park Press, 1979.

Maxwell, Ruth. *Beyond the Booze Battle*. New York: Ballantine, 1986.

Mayer, John E., and Filstead, William J. *Adolescence and Alcohol*. Cambridge, Mass.: Ballinger Publishing Co., 1980.

McCarthy, Raymond G. *Alcohol Education for Classroom and Community: A Source Book for Educators*. New York: McGraw-Hill Book Co., 1964.

———. *Discussion Guides for Questions about Alcohol*. New York: National Council on Alcoholism, 1956.

———. *Drinking and Intoxication*. New Haven: Yale Center of Alcohol Studies, 1959.

———. *Exploring Alcohol Questions*. New York: National Council on Alcoholism, 1962.

———. *What Shall Our Schools Teach about Alcohol?* New York: National Council on Alcoholism, 1964.

McClelland, David C.; Davis, W. N.; Kalin, R.; and Wanner, E. *The Drinking Man*. New York: Free Press, 1972.

McCord, William, and McCord, Joan. *Origins of Alcoholism*. Stanford, Calif.: Stanford University Press, 1960.

Mecca, A. M. *Alcoholism in America: A Modern Perspective*. San Rafael: California Health Research Foundation, 1980.

Mello, Nancy K. *Advances in Substance Abuse: Behavioral and Biological Research*. Greenwich, Conn.: JAI Press, 1980.

———, and Mendelson, Jack H., eds. *Recent Advances in Studies of Alcoholism*. publication no. (HSM) 71-9045. Washington, D.C.: U.S. Government Printing Office, 1971.

Meltzoff, Julian, and Kornreich, Melvin. *Research in Psychotherapy*. New York: Atherton Press, 1970.

Mendelson, Jack H., and Mello, Nancy K. *The Diagnosis and Treatment of Alcoholism*. New York: McGraw-Hill Book Co., 1979.

Mendlewicz, J., and Van Praag, H. M. *Alcoholism: A Multidisciplinary Approach*. Basel: Karger, 1979.

Menninger, Karl A. *Man against Himself*. New York: Harcourt, Brace and Co., 1938.

Meryman, Richard. *Broken Promises, Mended Dreams*. Boston: Little, Brown, 1984.

Metropolitan Life Insurance Co. *Alcoholism*. New York, 1967.

Michigan Department of Education. *A Curriculum Guide on Alcohol Education*. Lansing, 1970.

Milam, James R., and Ketshaw, Katherine. *Under the Influence: A Guide to the Myths and Realities of Alcoholism.* New York: Bantam, 1987.

Milgram, Gail Gleason. *Alcohol Education Materials 1973-1978: An Annotated Bibliography.* New Brunswick, N.J.: Rutgers Center of Alcohol Studies, 1980.

————. *Coping with Alcohol.* New York: Richards Rosen Press, 1980.

————. *What Is Alcohol? And Why Do People Drink?* New Brunswick, N.J.: Rutgers Center of Alcohol Studies, 1975.

Miller, Merlene; Gorski, Terence T.; and Miller, David K. *Learning to Live Again: A Guide for Recovery from Alcoholism.* Hazel Crest, Ill.: Human Ecology Systems, 1980.

Miller, P. M. *Behavioral Treatment of Alcoholism.* Toronto: Pergamon Press, 1976.

————. *Personal Habit Control.* New York: Simon and Schuster, 1978.

Miller, William R. *The Addictive Behaviors: Treatment of Alcoholism, Drug Abuse, Smoking and Obesity.* Elmsford, N.Y.: Pergamon Press, 1980.

Mishara, Brian L., and Kastenbaum, Robert. *Alcohol and Old Age.* New York: Grune and Stratton, 1980.

Mississippi State Department of Education. *Alcohol Education Handbook.* Mississippi School Bulletin, no. 141. Jackson, n.d.

Morewood, Samuel. *Inebriating Liquors.* Dublin: W. Curry, Jun. and Company, and W. Carson, 1838.

Morrison, L. W. *Wines and Spirits.* Baltimore: Penguin Books, 1968.

Moser, Joy. *Prevention of Alcohol-Related Problems.* Toronto: Alcoholism and Drug Addiction Research Foundation for World Health Organization, 1980.

————. *Problems and Programmes Related to Alcohol and Drug Dependence in 33 Countries.* Geneva: World Health Organization, 1974.

Mueller, L. Ann, and Ketcham, Katherine. *Recovering: How to Get and Stay Sober.* New York: Bantam, 1987.

Mulford, H. A. *Meeting the Problems of Alcohol Abuse: A Testable Action Plan for Iowa.* Cedar Rapids: Iowa Alcoholism Foundation, 1970.

Mullan, Hugh, and Sangiuliano, Iris. *Alcoholism: Group Psychotherapy and Rehabilitation.* Springfield, Ill.: Charles C. Thomas, 1966.

Mumey, Jack. *Loving an Alcoholic.* New York: Bantam, 1988.

Nathan, Peter E.; Marlatt, G. Alan; and Loberg, Tor. *Alcoholism: New Directions in Behavioral Research and Treatment.* New York: Plenum Press, 1978.

National Center for Alcohol Education. *Services for Alcoholic Women: Foundations for Change. Trainer Manual.* Washington, D.C.: U.S. Government Printing Office, 1979.

National Clergy Conference on Alcoholism. *The Blue Book, Vol. XXXI. Proceedings of the 31st National Clergy Conference on Alcoholism, Omaha, Nebraska, May 22-26, 1979.* n.d.

The National Council of Women Working Party on Alcohol Problems. *Alcohol and the Unborn Child—The Fetal Alcohol Syndrome*. London: National Council of Women, 1980.

National Council on Alcoholism. *Do's and Don'ts for the Wives of Alcoholics*. New York, 1960.

————. *Facts on Alcoholism*. New York, 1966.

————. *The Rights of Alcoholics and Their Families*. New York, 1976.

National DWI Conference. *Proceedings of the Second National DWI Conference, Rochester, Minnesota, May 30-June 1, 1979*. Falls Church, Va.: AAA Foundation for Traffic Safety, 1980.

National Industrial Conference Board. *The Alcoholic Worker*. New York, 1958.

National Institute on Alcohol Abuse and Alcoholism. *Alcohol and Health*. First Special Report to the U.S. Congress from the Secretary of Health, Education and Welfare. Washington, D.C.: U.S. Government Printing Office, 1971.

————. *Alcohol and Health: New Knowledge*. Second Special Report to the U.S. Congress from the Secretary of Health, Education and Welfare. Washington, D.C.: U.S. Government Printing Office, 1974.

————. *Alcohol and Health*. Third Special Report to the U.S. Congress from the Secretary of Health, Education and Welfare. Washington, D.C.: U.S. Government Printing Office, 1978.

(For Fourth, Fifth and Sixth "Special Reports," see under editors DeLuca, Gordis and Niven.)

————. *Alcoholism and Alcohol Abuse among Women: Research Issues*. Washington, D.C.: U.S. Government Printing Office, 1980.

————. *Alcoholism Prevention: Guide to Resources and References*. Rockville, Md., 1979.

————. *The Public Health Approach to Problems Associated with Alcohol Consumption*. Rockville, Md., 1980.

————. *Recent Advances in Studies of Alcoholism*. Washington, D.C., 1970.

Navin, R. B. *Analysis of a Slum Area*. Washington, D.C.: Catholic University Press, 1934.

Newlove, Donald. *Those Drinking Days: Myself and Other Writers*. New York: Horizon Press, 1981.

Newman, Henry W. *Acute Alcoholic Intoxication: A Critical Review*. Stanford, Calif.: Stanford University Press, 1979.

Newman, I. M. *Dissemination and Utilization of Alcohol Information*. Lincoln: Nebraska Alcohol Information Clearinghouse and Health Education Department, University of Nebraska, 1980.

Newman, J. *Time for Change in Alcoholism Treatment? Traditional and Emerging Concepts*. Pittsburgh: University of Pittsburgh, 1979.

Nicholi, Armand M., Jr. *The Harvard Guide to Modern Psychiatry*. Cambridge, Mass.: Harvard University Press, 1979.

Niven, Robert G. ed. *Fifth Special Report to the U.S. Congress on Alcohol and Health*. Rockville, Md.: National Institute on Alcohol Abuse and Alcoholism, 1983.

Norback, Judith. *The Alcohol and Drug Abuse Yearbook/Directory 1979-80*. New York: Van Nostrand Reinhold Co., 1979.

North, Robert, and Orange, Richard, Jr. *Teenage Drinking*. New York: Macmillan Co., 1980.

O'Gorman, P. A., and Lacks, H. *Aspects of Youthful Drinking*. New York: National Council on Alcoholism, 1979.

Olive, G. *Drug-Action Modifications—Comparative Pharmacology*. Oxford: Pergamon Publishing Corp., 1979.

Ontario Department of Health. *Report on the Activities of the Ontario Council of Health*. 1969.

Opperman, D. J. *Spirit of the Vine*. Cape Town: Human and Rousseau, 1968.

Orford, Jim, and Edwards, Griffith. *Alcoholism*. Oxford: Oxford University Press, 1977.

Osterberg, E. *Alcohol Policy Measures and the Consumption of Alcoholic Beverages in Finland, 1950-1975*. Helsinki: Social Research Institute of Alcohol Studies, 1980.

Ottenberg, J. F. X. Carroll, and Bolognese, C. *Treating Mixed Psychiatric-Drug Addicted and Alcoholic Patients*. Eagleville, Pa.: Eagleville Hospital and Rehabilitation Center, 1979.

Palmer, Charles E. *Inebriety: Its Source, Prevention and Cure*. Philadelphia: Union Press, 1912.

Paolino, Thomas J., and McGrady, Barbara S. *The Alcoholic Marriage: Alternative Perspectives*. New York: Grune and Stratton, 1977.

Paredes, Alfonso, ed. *The Alcoholism Services Delivery System*. San Francisco: Jossey-Bass, 1981.

Partanen, J. *Our National Commodity Consumption Patterns and the Use of Alcohol*. Helsinki: Social Research Institute of Alcohol Studies, 1979.

————; Bruun, K.; and Markkanen, T. *Inheritance of Drinking Behavior: A Study of Intelligence, Personality, and Use of Alcohol of Adult Twins*. Helsinki: Finnish Foundation for Alcohol Studies, 1966.

Pasciutti, J. *Mental Health Aspects of Alcohol Education*. Boston: Massachusetts Office of the Commissioner of Alcoholism, 1958.

Patrick, Clarence H. *Alcohol, Culture and Society*. Durham: Duke University Press, 1952.

Pattison, E. Mansell; Sobell, Mark B.; and Sobell, Linda Carter. *Emerging Concepts of Alcohol Dependence*. New York: Springer, 1977.

Pearl, Raymond. *Alcohol and Longevity*. New York: Alfred A. Knopf, 1926.

Pearson, Charles C., and Hendricks, James Edwin. *Liquor and Anti-Liquor in Virginia 1619-1919*. Durham: Duke University Press, 1967.

Peele, Stanton. *How Much Is Too Much*. Englewood Cliffs, N.J.: Prentice-Hall, 1981.

Pekkanen, L. *Nutritional Factors in the Regulation of Voluntary Ethanol Drinking in the Laboratory Rat*. Helsinki: Research Laboratories of the State Alcohol Monopoly (Alko), 1980.

Perrine, M. W.; Waller, J. A.; and Harris, L. S. *Alcohol and Highway Safety: Behavioral and Medical Aspects.* U.S. Department of Transportation NHTSA Technical Report. Washington, D.C., 1971.

Petrie, Asenath. *Individuality in Pain and Suffering.* Chicago: University of Chicago Press, 1967.

Pfeffer, Arnold Z. *Alcoholism.* Modern Monographs in Industrial Medicine, no. 2. New York: Grune and Stratton, 1958.

Pickett, D. *Alcohol and the New Age.* New York: Methodist Book Concern, 1926.

Pinkham, Mary Ellen. *How to Stop the One You Love From Drinking.* New York: Putnam, 1986.

Pittman, David Joshua. *Primary Prevention of Alcohol Abuse and Alcoholism: An Evaluation of the Control Consumption Policy.* St. Louis: Social Science Institute, Washington University, 1980.

————. *Society, Culture, and Drinking Patterns.* New York: John Wiley and Sons, 1962.

————. *World Health Organization Committee of Experts in Alcoholism.* New York: Harper and Row, 1967.

————, and Gordon, C. W. *Revolving Door: A Study of the Chronic Police Case Inebriate.* Glencoe, Ill.: Free Press, 1958.

Plant, Martin A. *Drinking Careers—Occupations, Drinking Habits and Drinking Problems.* London: Tavistock Publications, 1979.

Plaut, Thomas F. *Alcohol Problems: A Report to the Nation by the Cooperative Commission on the Study of Alcoholism.* New York: Oxford University Press, 1967.

Polacsek, E.; Barnes, T.; Turner, N.; Hall, R.; and Weise, C. *Interaction of Alcohol and Other Drugs.* Toronto: Addiction Research Foundation, 1972.

Poley, Wayne; Lea, Gary; and Vibe, Gail. *Alcoholism: A Treatment Manual.* New York: Gardner Press, 1979.

Polich, J. Michael, and Armor, David J. *The Course of Alcoholism: Four Years after Treatment.* Santa Monica: Rand Corp., 1980.

————, and Orvis, B. R. *Alcohol Problems: Patterns and Prevalence in the U.S. Air Force.* Santa Monica: Rand Corp., 1979.

Polk, K. *Drinking and the Adolescent Culture.* Eugene, Ore.: Lane County Youth Project, 1964.

Pollack, S.; Didenko, O. R.; McEachern, A. W.; and Berger, R. M. *Drinking Driver and Traffic Safety Project.* U.S. Department of Transportation NHTSA Technical Report. Washington, D.C., 1972.

Popham, R. E. *Alcohol and Alcoholism.* Toronto: University of Toronto Press, 1970.

Powell, David J. *Clinical Supervision, Skills for Substance Abuse Counselors: Manual.* New York: Human Sciences Press, 1980.

————. *Clinical Supervision, Skills for Substance Abuse Counselors: Trainees Workbook.* New York: Human Sciences Press, 1980.

Pratt, Arthur. *How To Help and Understand the Alcoholic or Drug Addict.* Louisville: Love Street Books, 1980.

Presnall, Lewis F. *The Modern Approach to Alcoholism.* New York: National Council on Alcoholism, 1965.

Province of Ontario. *Effective Management through P.P.B.S.* Treasury Board of Ontario, 1969.

Purich, D. J. *Drinking and Driving: What to Do If You're Caught.* Vancouver: International Self-Counsel Press, 1978.

Rachman, S., and Teasdale, J. *Aversion Therapy and Behavior Disorders.* London: Routledge and Kegan Paul, 1969.

Rankin, J. G., ed. *Alcohol, Drugs and Brain Damage.* Toronto: Alcoholism and Drug Addiction Research Foundation of Ontario, 1975.

Rathod, N. H.; Caldwell, D.; and Glatt, M. M. *Abuse of Alcohol amongst Medical Practitioners: Proceedings of a Symposium Organized Jointly by the Medical Council on Alcoholism and the Society for the Study of Addiction, 26th January, 1977.* London: Society for the Study of Addiction, 1979.

Rea, F. B. *Alcoholism: Its Psychology and Cure.* London: Epworth Press, 1956.

Regier, Marilyn. *Social Policy in Action: Perspectives on the Implementation of Alcoholism Reforms.* Lexington, Mass.: Lexington Books, 1979.

Regional Council on Alcoholism of Cuyahoga, Geauga, Lake and Lorain Counties. *Guidelines for the Establishment of a Residential Program for the Treatment of Alcoholism.* Cleveland, 1978.

Reid, J. *A Social and Legal Profile of Saskatchewan Impaired Drivers: Final Report.* Regina: Saskatchewan Alcoholism Commission, 1978.

Reuss, C. *History of Beer Consumption in Belgium 1900-1957.* Louvain: Universitaire de Louvain, 1959.

Richter, Derek. *Addiction and Brain Damage.* Baltimore: University Park Press, 1980.

Rigter, H., and Crabbe, J. C., Jr. *Alcohol Tolerance and Dependence.* New York: Elsevier/North-Holland Biomedical Press, 1980.

Rittenhouse, J. D. *Consequences of Alcohol and Marijuana Use: Survey Items for Perceived Assessment.* Rockville, Md.: National Institute on Drug Abuse, 1979.

Rix, Keith J. B. *Alcohol: Questions and Answers.* Edinburgh: Scottish Council on Alcoholism, 1977.

Robe, Lucy Barry. *Haunted Inheritance.* Minneapolis: CompCare Publications, 1980.

Robertson, J. J. *The Impaired Physician: Proceedings of the Third AMA Conference on the Impaired Physician, September 29-October 1, 1978, Minneapolis, Minnesota.* Chicago: American Medical Association, 1980.

Robertson, Nan. *Getting Better: Inside Alcoholics Anonymous.* New York: William Morrow, 1988.

Robinson, David. *Alcohol Problems: Reviews, Research and Recommendations.* New York: Holmes and Meier, 1979.

———. *From Drinking to Alcoholism: A Sociological Commentary.* New York: John Wiley and Sons, 1976.

———. *Talking Out of Alcoholism: The Self-Help Process of Alcoholics Anonymous.* London: Croom Helm, 1979.

Robinson, Robert R. *On the Rocks.* Ontario: Scholastic-TAB Publications, 1979.

Roe, Daphne. *Alcohol and the Diet.* Westport, Conn.: AVI Press, 1981.

Room, Robin. *Governing Images and Prevention of Alcohol Problems.* Berkeley: University of California, n.d.

———. *Minimizing Alcohol Problems.* Berkeley: University of California, n.d.

———. *Prevention—Of What?* Berkeley: University of California, n.d.

Rorabaugh, W. J. *The Alcoholic Republic: An American Tradition.* New York: Oxford University Press, 1979.

Rossi, Peter H.; Freeman, Howard E.; and Wright, Sonia R. *Evaluation: A Systematic Approach.* Beverly Hills: Sage Publications, 1979.

Roueche, Berton. *The Neutral Spirit.* Boston: Little, Brown and Co., 1960.

Royce, James E. *Alcohol Problems and Alcoholism.* New York: Free Press, 1981.

Ruggels, W. L. et al. *A Follow-up Study of Clients at Selected Alcoholism Treatment Centers Funded by NIAAA.* Stanford, Calif.: Stanford Research Institute, May 1975.

Rutledge, B., and Kaye, Fulton E. *International Collaboration: Problems and Opportunities.* Toronto: Addiction Research Foundation, 1977.

Ryan, L. C., and Mohler, S. R. *Current Role of Alcohol as a Factor in Civil Aircraft Accidents.* Springfield, Va.: National Technical Information Service, 1980.

Saltman, J. *The New Alcoholics: Teenagers.* New York: Public Affairs Pamphlet, 1973.

Sandler, Merton. *Psychopharmacology of Alcohol.* New York: Raven Press, 1980.

Sandmaier, Marian. *The Invisible Alcoholics: Women and Alcohol Abuse in America.* New York: McGraw-Hill Book Co., 1980.

Sargent, Margaret. *Drinking and Alcoholism in Australia: A Power Relations Theory.* Melbourne: Longman Cheshire, 1979.

Schecter, Arnold J., ed. *Drug Dependence and Alcoholism, Vol. 1, Biomedical Issues.* New York: Plenum Press, 1980.

———. *Drug Dependence and Alcoholism, Vol. 2, Social and Behavioral Issues.* New York: Plenum Press, 1980.

Schmidt, W., and Kornaczewski, A. *A Note on the Effect of Lowering the Legal Drinking Age on Alcohol Related Motor Vehicle Accidents.* Toronto: Addiction Research Foundation, 1973.

Schuckit, M. A. *Drug and Alcohol Abuse: A Clinical Guide to Diagnosis and Treatment.* New York: Plenum Medical Book Co., 1979.

Schulberg, A.; Sheldon, A.; and Baker, F. *Program Evaluation in the Health Fields.* New York: Behavioral Publications, 1969.

Scoles, P., and Fine, E. W. *Alcohol and Traffic Safety: Proceedings of the First Conference on Alcohol-Highway Safety Programs in the Commonwealth of Pennsylvania, Lancaster, Pennsylvania, October 5, 6, 7, 1977.* Philadelphia: Michael C. Prestegord and Co., 1978.

Scrimgeour, G. J.; Palmer, J. A.; Edwards, L.; Goldspiel, S.; and Logan, A. B. *Comparative Analysis of Alcohol Highway Safety Judicial Standards and Existing Professional Standards. Vol. I: Technical Report.* Springfield, Va.: National Technical Information Service, 1978.

Seeger, Francis M. D. *Until My Last Breath.* Hollywood, Fla.: Health Communications, 1980.

Seixas, Judith A., and Youcha, Geraldine. *Children of Alcoholism: A Survivor's Manual.* New York: Crown, 1985.

Seixas, Judith A. *Living With a Parent Who Drinks Too Much.* New York: William Morrow, Greenwillow Books, 1979.

Seltman, C. *Wine in the Ancient World.* London: Routledge and Kegan Paul, 1957.

Shadwell, A. *Drink in 1914-1922: A Lesson in Control.* London: Longsman, Green and Co., 1923.

Shain, Martin, and Groeneveld, Judith. *Employee Assistance Programs: Philosophy, Theory and Practice.* Toronto: Lexington, 1980.

————; Suurvali, Helen; and Kilty, H. L. *The Parent Communication Project.* Toronto: Addiction Research Foundation, 1980.

Shapiro, L., and Mortimer, R. G. *Literature Review and Bibliography of Research and Practice in Pedestrian Safety.* Ann Arbor: Highway Safety Research Institute, University of Michigan, 1969.

Silverstein, Alvin, and Silverstein, Virginia B. *Alcoholism.* Philadelphia: J. B. Lippincott Co., 1975.

Silverstein, Lee M.; Edelwich, Jerry; and Flanagan, Donald. *High on Life.* Hollywood, Fla.: Health Communications, 1981.

Sinclair, Andrew. *Prohibition: The Era of Excess.* Boston: Atlantic Monthly Press Book; Little, Brown and Co., 1962.

Single, Eric, and Giesbrecht, Norman. *Rates of Alcohol Consumption and Patterns of Drinking in Ontario 1950-1975.* Toronto: Addiction Research Foundation, 1979.

————; Morgan, Patricia; and de Lint, Jan. *Alcohol, Society, and the State. Vol. 2: The Social History of Control in Seven Countries.* Toronto: Addiction Research Foundation, 1982.

Small, Jacquelyn. *Transformers.* Hollywood, Fla.: Health Communications, 1982.

Smart, Reginald G. *The New Drinkers: Teenage Use and Abuse of Alcohol.* 2nd ed. Toronto: Addiction Research Foundation, 1980.

————; Storm, T.; Baker, E. F. W.; and Solursh, L. *Lysergic Acid Diethylamide (LSD) in the Treatment of Alcoholism: An Investigation of Its Effects on Drinking Behavior, Personality Structure and Social Functioning.* Toronto: University of Toronto Press, 1967.

Smith, Cedric M. *Alcoholism, Treatment.* Vol. 2. Edinburgh: Churchill Livingstone, 1977.

Smith, W. H., and Helwig, F. C. *Liquor, the Servant of Man.* Boston: Little, Brown and Co., 1939.

Smithers, Christopher D., Foundation. *Alcohol and Alcoholism: A Police Handbook.* New York, 1966.

————. *Alcoholism—A Family Illness.* New York, 1967.

————. *Arresting Alcoholism.* New York, 1962.

————. *Biochemical and Nutritional Aspects of Alcoholism.* New York, 1964.

————. *A Company Program on Alcoholism—Basic Outline.* New York, 1959.

————. *Experimentation.* New York, 1965.

————. *Pioneers We Have Known in the Field of Alcoholism.* Mill Neck, N.Y.: 1979.

————. *Understanding Alcoholism: For the Patient, the Family, and the Employer.* New York, 1968.

Snyder, Charles R. *Alcohol and the Jews.* New Brunswick, N.J.: Rutgers Center of Alcoholic Studies, 1958.

Sobell, Linda Carter; Sobell, Mark B.; and Ward, Elliott. *Evaluating Alcohol and Drug Abuse Treatment Effectiveness.* New York: Pergamon Press, 1980.

Sobell, Mark B., and Sobell, Linda Carter. *Behavioral Treatment of Alcohol Problems.* New York: Plenum Press, 1978.

Solomon, Joel. *Alcoholism and Clinical Psychiatry.* New York: Downstate Medical Center, 1982.

Southerby, Norm, and Southerby, Alexandra. *Twelve Young Women.* Long Beach, Calif.: Southerby and Associates, 1975.

Spahr, John Howard. *Sober Life.* Ardmore, England: Dorrance and Co., 1979.

Spicer, Jerry. *Program Management. Outcome Evaluation: How to Do It.* Center City, Minn.: Hazelden, 1980.

Stanton, Alfred H., and Schwartz, Morris S. *The Mental Hospital.* New York: Basic Books, 1954.

Steiner, Claude. *Games Alcoholics Play.* New York: Grove Press, 1974.

————. *Healing Alcoholism.* New York: Grove Press, 1979.

Stepney, Rob. *Alcohol.* New York: Franklin Watts, 1987.

Stewart, Ernest I., and Malfetti, James L. *Rehabilitation of the Drunken Driver.* New York: Teachers College Press, 1970.

Stewart, George R. *American Ways of Life.* New York: Doubleday and Co., 1954.

Straus, R. *Escape from Custody: A Study of Alcoholism and Institutional Dependency as Reflected in the Life Record of a Homeless Man.* New York: Harper and Row, 1974.

Straus, Robert, and Bacon, Selden D. *Drinking in College.* New Haven: Yale University Press, 1953.

Stroh, Carl M. *Addiction, Society and Self.* Vancouver: Alcohol and Drug Commission, 1980.

Sulkunen, P. *Abstainers in Finland 1946-1976: A Study in Social and Cultural Transition.* Helsinki: Social Research Institute of Alcohol Studies, 1979.

Sunshine, Linda, and Wright, John. *The 100 Best Treatment Centers for Alcoholism and Drug Abuse.* New York: Avon, 1988.

Tahka, V. *The Alcoholic Personality.* Helsinki: Finnish Foundation for Alcohol Studies, 1966.

Talland, George A. *Deranged Memory.* New York: Academic Press, 1965.

———, and Waugh, N. C., eds. *The Pathology of Memory.* New York: Academic Press, 1969.

Tarter, Ralph E., and Sugerman, A. Arthur. *Alcoholism.* Reading, Mass.: Addison-Wesley, 1976.

Taylor, William B. *Drinking, Homicide and Rebellion in Colonial Mexican Villages.* Stanford, Calif.: Stanford University Press, 1979.

Terhune, William B. *The Safe Way to Drink: How to Prevent Alcohol Problems Before They Start.* New York: Pocketbooks, 1969.

Tessler, Diane Jane. *Drugs, Kids, and Schools: Practical Strategies for Educators and Other Concerned Adults.* Rockville, Md.: National Institute on Drug Abuse, 1980.

Thompson, J. *Alcohol and Drug Research in Saskatchewan, 1970-1978: Subject, Index and Abstracts.* Regina: Saskatchewan Alcoholism Commission, 1978.

Thomsen, Robert. *Bill W.* New York: Harper and Row, 1975.

Thurman, Ronald G. *Alcohol and Aldehyde Metabolizing Systems—IV.* New York: Plenum Publishing Corp., 1980.

Todd, J. E. *Drunkenness a Vice, Not a Disease.* Hartford: Case, Lockwood and Brainard, 1882.

Towery, O. B.; Seidenberg, G. R.; and Santoro, V. *Quality Assurance for Alcohol, Drug Abuse, and Mental Health Services: An Annotated Bibliography.* Rockville, Md.: U.S. Alcohol, Drug Abuse, and Mental Health Administration, 1979.

Towle, L. H. et al. *Alcoholism Program Monitoring System Development: Evaluation of the ATC Program.* Stanford, Calif.: Stanford Research Institute, 1973.

Trice, Harrison M. *Alcoholism in America.* New York: McGraw-Hill Book Co., 1966.

———. *Alcoholism in Industry—Modern Procedures.* New York: Smithers, Christopher D., Foundation, 1962.

Truax, Lyle H. *Judge's Guide for Alcohol Offenders.* New York: National Council on Alcoholism, 1972.

Twerski, Abraham J. *Caution: "Kindness" Can Be Dangerous to the Alcoholic.* Englewood Cliffs, N.J.: Prentice-Hall, 1981.

Tyrrell, Ian R. *Sobering Up: From Temperance to Prohibition in Antebellum America, 1800-1860.* Westport, Conn.: Greenwood Press, 1979.

Ullman, A. D. *To Know the Difference.* New York: St. Martin's Press, 1960.

U.K., Home Office. *Habitual Drunken Offenders.* Report of the Working Party. London: Her Majesty's Stationary Office, 1971.

U.S., Congress, Senate, Committee on Labor and Human Resources. *Comprehensive Alcohol Abuse and Alcoholism Prevention, Treatment, and Rehabilitation Act Amendments of 1979.* Washington, D.C.: U.S. Government Printing Office, 1979.

————. *Report on Consumer Health Warnings for Alcoholic Beverages and Related Issues, 96th Congress.* Washington, D.C.: U.S. Government Printing Office, 1979.

U.S., Department of Health, Education and Welfare. *Alcohol and Health.* Washington, D.C.: U.S. Government Printing Office, 1971.

————. *Alcohol and Health: New Knowledge.* Washington, D.C.: U.S. Government Printing Office, 1974.

U.S., Department of Transportation. *The 1968 Alcohol and Highway Safety Report.* Washington, D.C.: U.S. Government Printing Office, 1968.

U.S., General Accounting Office. *The Drinking-Driver Problem—What Can Be Done about It?* Springfield, Va.: National Technical Information Service, 1979.

U.S., National Center for Alcohol Education. *Services for Alcoholic Women: Foundations for Change: Resource Book.* Rockville, Md.: U.S. Government Printing Office, n.d.

U.S., National Clearinghouse for Alcohol Information and Division of Special Treatment and Rehabilitation. *Classification of Alcoholism Treatment Settings.* Rockville, Md., 1978.

Vaillant, George E. *The Natural History of Alcoholism.* Cambridge, Mass.: Harvard University Press, 1983.

Valle, Stephen K. *Alcoholism Counseling: Issues for an Emerging Profession.* Springfield, Ill.: Charles C. Thomas, 1979.

Vischi, T. R.; Jones, K. R.; Shank, E. L.; and Lima, L. H. *The Alcohol, Drug Abuse, and Mental Health National Data Book.* Washington D.C.: U.S. Alcohol, Drug Abuse and Mental Health Administration, 1980.

Vogler, Roger E., and Bartz, Wayne R., Dr. *The Better Way to Drink.* New York: Simon and Schuster, 1982.

Vuylsteek, K. *Health Education: Smoking, Alcoholism, Drugs.* Albany: WHO Publications Centre, 1979.

Waddell, Jack O., and Everett, Michael W. *Drinking Behavior among Southwestern Indians: An Anthropological Perspective.* Tucson: University of Arizona Press, 1980.

————, and Watson, O. Michael. *The American Indian in Urban Society.* Boston: Little, Brown and Co, 1971.

Wagner, Robin S. *Sarah T: Portrait of a Teen-age Alcoholic.* New York: Ballantine Books, 1976.

Walker, Lenore E. *The Battered Woman.* New York: Harper and Row, 1979.

Wallerstein, R. S. *Hospital Treatment of Alcoholism: A Comparative Experimental Study.* Menninger Clinic Monograph Series, no. 11. New York: Basic Books, 1957.

Wallgren, H. *On the Relationship of the Consumption of Alcoholic Beverages to the Genesis of Alcoholic Disorders.* Helsinki: Alkon Keskuslaboratorio, 1970.

————, and Barry, H. *Actions of Alcohol.* Vol. II. Amsterdam: Elsevier, 1970.

Warburton, Clark. *The Economic Results of Prohibition.* New York: Columbia University, 1932.

Ward, David A. *Alcoholism: Introduction to Theory and Treatment.* Dubuque: Kendall/Hunt, 1980.

Washburne, Chandler. *Primitive Drinking.* New Haven: College and University Press, 1961.

Waterbury, J. *Your Thoughts and Feelings.* Knoxville: St. Mary's Medical Center, 1979.

Wechsler, Henry. *Minimum-Drinking-Age Laws.* Lexington, Mass.: Lexington Books, 1980.

Weiner, Jack B. *Drinking.* New York: W. W. Norton and Co., 1976.

Weise, C. E. *Behavior Modification for the Treatment of Alcoholism.* Toronto: Addiction Research Foundation, 1975.

Weiss, Mildred H. *What We Know about Alcohol.* Cleveland: Cleveland Health Museum, 1957.

Weiss, Richard M. *Dealing with Alcoholism in the Workplace.* Ottawa: Conference Board in Canada, 1980.

West, Elliot. *The Saloon on the Rocky Mountain Mining Frontier.* Lincoln: University of Nebraska Press, 1979.

West, L. H. T., and Hore, T. *An Analysis of Drink Driving Research.* Clayton, Victoria, Australia: Higher Education Advisory and Research Unit, Monash University, 1980.

Western Electric. *Policy and Program—Employees with Drinking Problems (A Guide for Supervisors).* New York, 1962.

White House Conference for A Drug Free America. *Final Report*, Lois Haight Herrington, Chairman. Washington, D.C.: U.S. Government Printing Office, 1988.

Whitney, Elizabeth D. *The Lonely Sickness.* Boston: Beacon Press, 1965.

Wiener, Carolyn. *The Politics of Alcoholism: Building an Arena around a Social Problem.* New Brunswick, N.J.: Transaction Books, Rutgers University, 1981.

Wilerson, D. *Sipping Saints.* Old Tappan, N.J.: Fleming H. Revell Co., 1978.

Wilkinson, Rupert. *The Prevention of Drinking Problems: Alcohol Control and Cultural Influences.* New York: Oxford University Press, 1970.

Williams, Roger J. *Alcoholism: The Nutritional Approach.* Austin: University of Texas Press, 1959.

Williams, T. K. *The Ethanol-Induced Loss of Control Concept in Alcoholism.* Kalamazoo: Western Michigan University, 1970.

Willoughby, Alan. *The Alcohol-Troubled Person: Known & Unknown.* Chicago: Nelson-Hall, 1979.

W[ilson], Bill. *The AA Way of Life.* New York: Alcoholics Anonymous World Services, 1967.

Wilson, Lois. *Lois Remembers: Memoirs of the Co-Founder of Al-Anon and Wife of the Co-Founder of Alcoholics Anonymous.* New York: Al-Anon Family Group Headquarters, 1979.

Wisconsin Department of Health and Social Services. *Youth, Alcohol, and the Law: Final Report. Wisconsin 1933-1978.* Madison, 1978.

Wiseman, Jacqueline P. *Stations of the Lost: The Treatment of Skid Row Alcoholics.* Chicago: University of Chicago Press, 1979.

Woititz, Janet Geringer. *Adult Children of Alcoholics.* Pompano Beach, Florida: Health Communications, Inc., 1983.

———. *Marriage on the Rocks: Learning to Live with Yourself and an Alcoholic.* New York: Delacorte, 1979.

Wolpe, Joseph. *Psychotherapy of Reciprocal Inhibition.* Stanford, Calif.: Stanford University Press, 1958.

World Health Organization. *Alcohol-Related Disabilities.* Geneva, 1977.

———. *Expert Committee on Mental Health, Alcoholism Subcommittee, Second Report.* World Health Organization Technical Report Series, no. 48. Geneva, 1952.

———. *Problems Related to Alcohol Consumption.* Albany: WHO Publications Centre, 1980.

———. *Public Health Aspects of Alcohol and Drug Dependence: Report of a WHO Conference, Dubrovnik, 21-25 August 1978.* Copenhagen: WHO Regional Office for Europe, 1979.

Youcha, Geraldine. *A Dangerous Pleasure.* New York: Hawthorn Books, 1978.

Young, M. E. *Drinking Drivers (A Bibliography with Abstracts).* Springfield, Va.: National Technical Information Service, 1979.

Zador, P. *Statistical Evaluation of the Effectiveness of "Alcohol Safety Action Programs."* Washington, D.C.: Insurance Institute for Highway Safety, 1974.

Zimberg, Sheldon; Wallace, John; and Blume, Sheila B. *Practical Approaches to Alcoholism Psychotherapy.* New York and London: Plenum Press, 1978.

INDEX

Boldface numbers indicate main headings.

A

Absenteeism, 1
Absinthe, 1
  aperitif, 36
  Pernod, 163
Absolute alcohol, 1
  Argentina, 37
  Belgium, 44
  calories, 59
  Canada, 59–60
  cononary heart disease, 119
  consumption—See Consumption
  Denmark, 84
  Finland, 106
  France, 108
  Germany, 112
  heavy drinker, 119
  Ireland, 131
  Israel, 133
  Netherlands, 154
  New Zealand, 155–156
  Norway, 156–157
  Poland, 164
  proof, 166–167
  remission, 178
  Sweden, 199
  Switzerland, 199
  United Kingdom, 207
  USSR, 206
  Venezuela, 211
Abstainer, 1–2
Abstinence, 2
  Alcoholics Anonymous, 173
  convulsions, 78
  loss of control, 140
Abuse, 2
  alcohol pathology, 14
Accidents, 2–3
  aviation, 277
  bicycling, 45
  boating, 50
  drowning, 3, 95
  falls, 103
  mortality, 150
  traffic fatalities, 272–276
Acetaldehyde, 3–4, 124
  Antabuse, 35
  Asian skinflush reaction, 39
  brain, 56
  formaldehyde vs., 107
  liver, 140
  metabolism, 145–146
Acetate, 3
Ackoff's model, 4
Acne rosacea, 4
Acquired immune deficiency syndrome—See AIDS
Act for Encouraging the Distillation of Brandy and Spirits from Corn, xv
Acute, 5, 67
Acute alcoholic myopathy, 18
Acute alcoholic state, 5
Acute alcohol intoxication, 5
Acute alcoholism, 5

Adaptive cell metabolism, 5
  addiction, 6
Addiction, 5–6
  acetaldehyde, 4
  alcohol discharge rate, 13
  behavioral learning theory, 44
  chart, 280
  Gamma alcoholism, 109
  habituation, 115
  recovery, 174
Addiction Research Foundation, 17, 70
Adenylate cyclase (AC), 111
Advertising, 6–8
  education campaigns and programs, 99
Advisory Technical Committee on Alcoholism (COTESAL) (Argentina), 38
Age
  alcoholism clients by, 247–248, 251–253
  traffic fatalities by, 276
AIDS (acquired immune deficiency syndrome), 8, 123
  immune system, 125
Al-Anon, 8–9, 219
  Alateen, 10
  Alcoholics Anonymous, 8–9
  Argentina, 38
  children of alcoholics, 66
  para-alcoholic, 162
Alaskan natives, 9–10
  death rates, 28–31
Alateen, 10
  Al-Anon and, 9
  Argentina, 38
Alateen: Hope for Children of Alcoholics (newsletter), 10
Alberta Red Line Chart, 281
Alcohol addict, 10
Alcohol amblyopia, 11
  central nervous system, 64
  Marchiafava-Bignami disease, 142
  zinc, 230
Alcohol and Drug Addicts Treatment Act of 1961 (Australia), 39
Alcohol and Health, Special Reports to the U.S. Congress on—See Special Reports to the U.S. Congress on Alcohol and Health
Alcohol concentration, 11
Alcohol dehydrogenase (ADH), 111
Alcohol Dependence Scale, 11
  alcohol dependence syndrome, 11
Alcohol Dependence Syndrome (ADS), 11, 71
Alcohol discharge rate (ADR), 12–14
  American Indians, 30
Alcohol Epidemiologic Data System (AEDS), 14
Alcoholic
  heavy drinker vs., 119
Alcoholic beverage, 14
Alcoholic beverage control laws (ABC laws), 14–16
Alcoholic cardiomyopathy, 118
Alcoholic disease, 16

Alcoholic hepatitis, 16–17
  alcoholic liver disease, 17
  cirrhosis, 68
Alcoholic hyaline, 17
Alcoholic liver disease, 17–18
Alcoholic myopathy (alcoholic muscle disease), 18
Alcoholic poisoning, 18
Alcoholic polyneuropathy (peripheral neuritis), 18–19
  beta alcoholism, 45
  central nervous system, 64
  Wernicke's encephalopathy, 216
Alcoholic psychosis, 19
Alcoholics Anonymous (AA), 19–25, 187, 223
  abstainer, 2
  abstinence rates, 173
  Alateen, 10
  allergy, 27
  American Indians, 33
  Argentina, 38
  bar drinkers, 41
  blacks, 47
  Canada, 60
  Catholic Church, 176
  drug survey, 96
  group therapy, 115
  Jews, 136
  Oxford Group, 161
  recovery model, 174
  rehabilitation, 175–176
  remission, 178
  Serenity Prayer, 185
  sobriety, 188–189
  solitary drinking, 191
  Washingtonian movement, 216
  Bill Wilson and, 219
  women, 227
Alcoholics Anonymous (book), 23
Alcoholic Treatment Center (ATC), 19
Alcohol in Sports: Position Sound (publication), 192–193
Alcoholism, 25–26
  abuse vs., 2
  alcohol discharge rate, 12–13
  chronic alcohol intoxication vs., 67
  problem drinker, 166
Alcoholism: Clinical and Experimental Research (journal), 205
Alcoholism and Treatment (report), 170
Alcoholism Report, The (J. Lewis), 136
Alcoholismus Chronicus (Magnus Huss), xvi
Alcoholist, 26
Alcohol pathology, 14
Alcohol Use Inventory (Horn and Wanberg), 11
Alcoolisation, 26
Alcoolist, 26
Aldehyde dehydrogenase (ALDH), 111
Ale, 26–27
  porter, 165
Alexandre le Grand, 45
Alkana, Ronald L., 34, 138

Allergy, 27
Alpha alcoholism, 27
AMA—See American Medical Association
American Bar Association, 26
American College of Sports Medicine, 192
American Indians, 28–33
  cirrhosis, 68
American Medical Association, 26, 128, 170
  allergy, 27
  disease concept, 89
  drinking during pregnancy, 105
American Temperance Society, xvii
Amethystic, 33–34
  L-Dopa, 138
Amnesia, 34
Amobarbital (Amytal), 184
Amphetamines with alcohol, 34
Amyl alcohol, 34
Amytal—See Amobarbital
Animal models of alcoholism, 34–35
Anisette, 35
Anne, Queen, 114
Anstie, Sir Francis, 35
Anstie's Law, 35
Antabuse, 35
  acetaldehyde, 4
  elderly, 100
  Ruth Fox and, 108
  mouthwash, 152
  Norway, 157
  pharmacotherapy, 164
  Temposil, 201
Anti-Saloon League, 35–36
Anton, R. F., 39
Anxiety, 36
Aperitif, 36
Apomorphine, 36
  aversion therapy, 40
Applejack, 37, 56
Aquavit, 37
  schnapps, 182
Aragi, 197
Argentina, 37–38
Armagnac, 38, 57
Armor, David J., 19, 125, 127, 172
Arnaldus de Villanova, xiv
Arnold, Robert D., 94–95
Arrack, 195
Arthur, T. S., xvii
Asian-Americans, 38–39, 209
Asian skinflush reaction, 39
Aspirin and alcohol, 39
Australia, 39–40
Aversion therapy, 40
  apomorphine, 36
  behavior modification, 42
Aviation accidents, 277

B

Babylonians, ancient, xii, 42, 223
Bacchus, xiii, 40–41
Bacteremia, 126
Bales, R. F., 82
Bandura, Albert, 44
Baptists, 177
Bar, 41
Barbiturate, 41, 183–184
Bar drinker, 41
Bar drinking
  solitary drinking vs., 191
Bates, R. C., 187

B & B, 41
Beaujolais, 41, 175
Beer, 41–42
  ancient Egypt, xii
  Belgium, 44
  brewing, 57–58
  international per capita consumption, 258–259
  mixing drinks, 149
Behavioral learning theory, 43–44, 102–103
Behavior modification, 42–43
Behling, Daniel W., 65
Belgium, 44–45
Bender, 45
Benedictine, 41, 45, 139
Berglund, M., 198
Beriberi, 212
Beta alcoholism, 45
Bible, xi, xii–xiii
Bickerton, Richard, 100–101
Big Book—See Alcoholics Anonymous (book)
Bignami, Amico, 142
Birnbaum, Isabel M., 144
Black, Claudia, 66
Black, Rebecca, 66
Black Americans, 45–47
Blackout, 47–48
  brain, 56
  memory, 145
  progression, 166
Block, Marvin A., 170
Blois, C. S. de, 193
Blood alcohol concentration (BAC), 48–50, 124
  acetaldehyde, 4
  alcoholic poisoning, 18
  bicycle accidents, 45
  boating accidents, 50
  calculation of, 49
  central nervous system, 63
  driving while intoxicated, 92–93
  falls, 103
  hangover, 116
  under the influence of alcohol, 205–206
  intoxication, 131
  lethal dose, 139
  memory, 143
  metabolism, 146
  nutrition, 159
  sober, 188
  tolerance, 204
  withdrawal, 221
  women, 226
Blood alcohol discrimination training, 42–43
Blood sugar, 50
  hangover, 116
Blum, Kenneth, 110
Boating accidents, 50–52
Boating laws by state, 51–52
Bock beer, 52
Boe, Franciscus de la—See Sylvius, Franciscus
Boles, Annabel M., 110
Bonne chauffe, 71
Boom towns, 52–53
  depressed communities vs., 85
Bootlegging, 53–54
Booze, 53
Booze, E. G., 53

Booze fighter, 53
Booze hound, 53
Bordeaux wine, 175
Bottom fermentation, 54
  ale, 27
  beer, 58
  top fermentation vs., 204
Bourbon, 54–55, 217–218
Bowery, 55
Bradford, David, 181
Brain, 55–56
  animal models of alcoholism, 34
  memory, 144
Brainstem abnormalities, 55
Brain wave activity, 111
Brandy, xiv–xv, 56–57
Breathalyzer, 93
Brewing, 57–58
British Road Safety Act of 1967, 58
Brunschwig, Hieronymus, xiv
Bual, 141
Buddhism, 134
Burgundy wine, 175
Burnham, Lois—See Wilson, Lois Burnham
Burns, 3, 58
Bushmills, 132–133
Butters, N., 144
Butyl alcohol (butanol), xix–xx, 58–59
Byrrh, 36

C

Caetano, R., 120
Caffeine, 59
Cahalan, Don, 43, 136
Calcium, 212
Calorie, 59, 87–88
  chart, 283
  nutrition, 158
Calvados, 56, 59
  applejack, 37
Campari, 59
Canada, 59–61
  organizations, 298–299
Canadian whisky, 61
Cancer, 61–63
  blacks, 46
  congeners, 72
  esophagus, 102
  immune system, 125
  nutrition, 159
Canon of History, xii
Capital Blue Cross, 128
Carbohydrate, 63
  chart, 283
Cardiac arrhythmia, 118–119
Career Teacher Program (CTP), 63, 117
Cederbaum, A. I., 118
Central nervous system (CNS), 63–64
  amethystic, 34
  behavioral learning theory, 44
  cross-tolerance, 82
  L-Dopa, 138
  magnesium, 212
  sedative, 183
  tolerance, 204
Central pontine myelinolysis, 64
Cerebral atrophy, 64–65
Ceylon—See Sri Lanka
Chafetz, Morris E., 203
Champagne, 191–192
Chaplin, J. P., 185

Chaser, 65
Chaucer, Geoffrey, 26
"Cheshire Blitz," 58
Chianti wine, 34
Chilcote, Sam D., 8
Child abuse, **65–66**
  spouse abuse and, 193
Children of alcoholics, **66–67**
China, xii
Chlordiazepoxide (Librium), 82, 184
  detoxification, 87
Cholera, 126
Chronic, **67**
  acute vs., 5
Chronic alcoholic myopathy, 18
Chronic alcohol intoxication, 67
Chronic alcoholism, 67
  intellectual impairment, 129
Chronische Alkohols-Krankheit (Magnus Huss), 25–26
Chug-a-lug, 67
Chung K'iang, Emperor, xii
Church of England Temperance Society, 68
Cicero, Theodore J., 34, 178
Cirrhosis, **68–70**
  alcohol discharge rate, 12
  alcoholic beverage control laws, 15
  alcoholic hepatitis, 16
  alcoholic liver disease, 17
  American Indians, 28, 30
  beta alcoholism, 45
  blacks, 46
  death rates, 269–270
  hemochromatosis, 119
  intestine, 130
  Laennec's—*See Cirrhosis—portal*
  liver cancer, 62
  macronodular, 70, **141**
  methadone with alcohol, 147
  micronodular, 69, **148**
  mixed, **149**
  native Hawaiians, 117
  portal (Laennec's), 68–69, **165**
  postnecrotic, 70, **165**
  women, 226
City Brewing Company (London), 27
Clarke, John, 167
Classification of alcoholics, **70–71**
Clement, S., 117
Cloniger, C. Robert, 148
Closed meetings, 23
Coast Guard, U.S., 50
  bootlegging, 53
Codeine with alcohol, **71**
Coffey, Aeneas, xvi
Cognac, 57, **71**
Cognitive function, 71
Cold turkey, 71
Coleridge, Samuel Taylor, xviii
Commission on Accreditation of Rehabilitation Facilities, 136
Comprehensive Alcohol Abuse and Alcoholism Prevention, Treatment, and Rehabilitation Act (Hughes Act), 138–139
Compulsion, 71
Computerized tomography (CT) scan, 55, 129
Congeners, **71–72**
  brandy, 57
  Canadian whisky, 61
  cancer, 62
  hangover, 116

mixing drinks, 149
  vodka, 213
Congress, U.S.—*See Special Reports to the U.S. Congress on Alcohol and Health*
Consumption, **72–77**
  international, 257–261
  mortality, 150
  United States, 208, 262–268
  youths, 228–229
Controlled drinking, **77–78**
  behavior modification, 43
  loss of control, 140
  sobriety, 188
Controlled substance, 78
Control system, 15
Convulsions, 78
Cordial, 78
Corn whiskey, 78–79
Coronary heart disease, 119
Costa Rica, 79
Cough medicine, 79–80
Counseling, 80
Counteradvertising, 7–8
Course of Alcoholism, The: Four Years After Treatment (report), 172
Craig, Elijah, 54
Craving, 80
  adaptive cell metabolism, 5
  addiction, 6
  blackout, 48
  cough medicine, 79
  dipsomania, 88
  mouthwash, 152
Creatine phosphokinase (CPK), 18
Crime, **80–81**
Cross-addiction, **81–82**
  methadone with alcohol, 147
  sedatives, 184
  women, 226
Cross-dependence, 82
Cross-tolerance, 82
  barbiturates, 41
  surgery, 198
CT scan—*See Computerized tomography scan*
Culloden, Battle of, 183
Cultural etiological theories, 82
Cultural stress etiological theories, **82**, 103

D

Davies, D. L., 172
De-alcoholized beverage, **83**
Debauch, **83**
Delirium tremens, **83**
  alcohol discharge rate, 12
  dentistry, 85
  surgery, 198
  withdrawal, 221
Delta alcoholism, 83
  inability to abstain, 125
Dementia, **83–84**
Denial, **84**
  blacks, 47
  elderly, 99
  Jews, 136
  para-alcoholic, 161–162
  sobriety, 189
Denmark, 84
Dentistry, **85**
Dependency, **85**
  acetaldehyde, 4

alcoholic liver disease, 17
  animal models of alcoholism, 34
  brain, 56
  central nervous system, 64
  Gamma alcoholism, 109
  hangover, 116
  metabolism, 146
Depressed communities, **85–86**
Depression, **86**
Deprivation, **86**
Detoxification, **86–87**
  addiction, 6
  rehabilitation, 175
  treatment, 205
    at ATC, 19
    inpatient, 126
    outpatient, 160
Diabetes, **87–88**
  pancreas, 161
Diagnostic and Statistical Manual of Mental Disorders (DSM), 70–71, 129
Dickens, Charles, xvi
Digestion, 88
Dionysus, xiii, 41
Dipsomania, **88**
Disease concept, **88–89**
  alcoholic beverage control laws , 15
Disease Concept of Alcoholism, The (E. M. Jellinek), 135
Diseases, **89–90**
  alcoholism, 26
  mortality, 150
Distillation, **90**
  origin, xiv
  rum, 180
Distilled spirits, international per capita consumption of, 260
Distilled Spirits Council of the United States (DISCUS), 7–8, **90**
Disulfiram—*See Antabuse*
DNA, **90–91**
Doctor, **91**
Dole, Vincent P., 6
Domitian, Emperor, xiv
Douglass, Richard L., 16
Dram, **91**
Drambuie, xv
Dram shop law, **91**
Drinker, **91**
Driving while intoxicated (DWI), **91–95**
  American Indians, 28, 30
  blood alcohol concentration (BAC), 48
  boom towns, 53
  depressed communities, 86
  Norway, 157
  United States, 209
  youths, 229
Drowning, 3, **95**
Drug addiction
  Alcoholics Anonymous (AA), 20
Drugs, **96**
  elderly, 100
  interactions with alcohol (table), **97**
Drunk, **96**
Dry, **96**
  advertising, 7
Dry drunk, **98**
DSM—*See Diagnostic and Statistical Manual of Mental Disorders*
Dual addiction
  insurance, 128
Dubonnet, 36

Duke of Gordon, 183
DuPont Company, 100
Dutch gin, 114
Dysphoria, **98**

E

Eau de vie, 57, **98**
Ebriate, **98**
Economic impact, **98**
  United States, 277
Edgar, King, 27
Education campaigns and programs, 98–99
EEG—*See Electroencephalograph*
Egyptians, ancient, xii, 42, 57, 141
  wine, 220
Eighteenth Amendment, xvii, **99**, 205
  temperance movement and, 201
Einbecker Bier, 52
Elderly, **99–100**
Electric shock, **100**
Electroencephalograph (EEG), 111
  children of alcoholics, 66
Ellis, Albert, 173
Emetine, 40, **100**
Employee assistance programs (EAPs), 99, **100–101**
  insurance, 128
Employment status, 277
Enabling, **101–102**
Endocrine etiological theories, **102**
England, xv, xv–xvi—*See also United Kingdom*
  ale, 26–27
  public drunkenness, 168
Epicanthal folds, 211
Epidemiologic Catchment Area, 154
Epidemiology, **102**
Epsilon alcoholism, **102**
  spree drinking, 194
Esophagus, **102**
  cancer of, 62
Ethanol, xix, **102**
  blood sugar, 50
Etiological theories, **102–103**
Etiology, **103**
Euphoria, **103**
  depression and, 86
Event-related potential (ERP), 111
Evoked potential (EP), 111
Ewing, John A., 172
Expert Committee on Addiction-Producing Drugs, 5

F

Falls, **103**
Familial etiological theories, **103–104**
Fatal Accident Reporting Service, U.S. (FARS), vii
Fatty liver, **104**
  alcoholic liver disease, 17
  cirrhosis, 68–69
  metabolism, 146
  methadone with alcohol, 147
  nutrition, 159
Fecamp, Abbey, 45
Federal Commission Against Alcoholism (Switzerland), 200
Federal Trade Commission, 7

Fetal Alcohol Syndrome (FAS), vii–viii, 90, **104–106**
  central nervous system, 64
  features of, 271
  vision problems, 211
Fibrosis
  alcoholic hepatitis, 16
Fields, W. C., 179
Finland, **106–107**
Finnish Temperance Movement, 107
First Century Christian Fellowship—*See Oxford Group*
Flanzer, Jerry, 193
Folic acid, 212
Foreign organizations, 299–302
Formaldehyde, **107**
  withdrawal, 222
Fortified wine, **107**
Forum, The (newsletter), 8
Fountain of Youth, 216
Fox, Ruth, **107–108**
France, **108–109**
  absinthe, 1
  Delta alcoholism, 83
Franks, Lucinda, 63
Freud, Sigmund, 102
Friends For Sobriety (FFS), **109**
Friends United Meeting (Quakers), 177–178
Fructose, **109**

G

Gallant, Donald M., 198, 229
Gamma alcoholism, **109**
  adaptive cell metabolism, 5
  Alpha alcoholism and, 27
  Delta alcoholism and, 83
Gamma amino-butyric acid (GABA), 56
Gastrointestinal tract, **109**
  nutrition, 159
Gavaler, Judith, 226
Genetics, **110–112**
  sociocultural models of etiology, 190
Genetotropic etiological theory, 102, **112**
Germany, xv, **112–113**
Getting Better: Inside Alcoholics Anonymous (Nan Robertson), 216
Gilgamesh, xi
Gin, xv, **113–115**
Gin epidemic, 104
Gin rummy, 113, 180
Giscard d'Estaing, Valery, 108
Glasser, William, 173–174
Glucose—*See Blood sugar*
Goldman, M. S., 145
Gomberg, Edith, 225
Gorbachev, Mikhail, 206
Grain alcohol—*See Ethanol*
Grant, Ulysses S., 54
Grapevine, The (newsletter), 21
Grappa, 57
Greek Orthodoxy, 176–177
Greeks, ancient, xiii
  beer, 42
  brewing, 57
  distillation, 90
  wine, 220
  women, 223
Grog, **115**
  rum, 179
Grog blossom, **115**

Group therapy, **115**
  Al-Anon, 9
  psychodrama, 167
Guze, Samuel B., 170

H

Habituation, **115**
  addiction vs., 5
Half-life (of drugs), 96
Halfway house, 19, **115–116**
Hammurabi, Code of, xii, 14
  beer, 42
Hangover, **116–117**
  blood sugar, 50
  congeners, 72
  dysphoria, 98
  formaldehyde, 107
  fructose, 109
  mixing drinks, 149
Harper, Frederick O., 46
Harper, Robert A., 173
Haut Villers Abbey, 191
Hawaiians, native, **117**
Health care costs
  inpatient treatment, 126
Health Care for the Homeless (HCH) program, 121
Health care providers, **117–118**
Health Education Foundation, 203
Heart, **118–119**
  acetaldehyde, 4
Heavy drinker, **119**
  advertising, 7
Hemochromatosis, **119**
Hennekens, Charles, 119
Henry II, King, 27
Henry VIII, King, 27
Hepatitis
  alcoholic—*See Alcoholic hepatitis*
  infectious, 126
Hepatoma, **119–120**
Herd, D., 46
High, **120**
High blood pressure, **120**
  heart, 118
High school seniors, 278, 284
Hindman, Margaret, 65–66
Hispanics, **120–121**
Historia Naturalis (Pliny the Elder), xiv
Hodgson, R., 11
Hogarth, William, xvi
Holden, C., 117
Holiday heart syndrome, **121**
Holy Communion, 176
Homelessness, **121–122**
Homosexuals, **123**
  lesbians, 224–225
Hongson, R., 50
Hooch, **123**
Hops, **123–124**
Hormones, male sex, **124**
Horton, D., 82
Hospital treatment, 19
Housewives, 224
Howland, J., 50
Hughes Act—*See Comprehensive Alcohol Abuse and Alcoholism Prevention, Treatment, and Rehabilitation Act*
Huss, Magnus, xvi, 25
Hyaline, 17
Hydroxyl group, xviii

Hyperglycemia, **124**
Hypertension, **124**
  blacks, 46
  heart, 118
Hypertriglyceridemia, 88
Hypoglycemia, 88, **124**
  carbohydrate, 63
  endocrine etiological theories, 102
  hangover, 116
Hysterectomy, 226

I

Imaging techniques
  brain, 55–56
Immune system, **125**
Impact (trade publication), 73
Impairment, **125**
Inability to abstain, **125**
  adaptive cell metabolism, 5
  addiction, 6
  Delta alcoholism, 83
India, 2
Indian Health Service (IHS), 33
Individualized behavior therapy, 43
Infancy, **125–126**
Infectious diseases, **126**
  immune system, 125
Infertility, 226
Infusion, 139
Inpatient treatment, **126–127**
Input-output model for treatment, 127
"Inquiry into the Effects of Ardent Spirits
  on the Human Mind and Body, An"
  (Benjamin Rush), 181
Instability and crisis etiological theory, **127**
Insurance, **128–129**
  disease concept and, 89
Intellectual impairment, **128–129**
Intemperance, **129**
Intermediate treatment, 19
International Classification of Diseases
  (ICD), 70, **129**
Inter-Tribal Alcoholism Center (Sheri-
  dan, Wyo.), 33
Intervention, **129–130**
  Roman Catholic Church, 176
  treatment, 205
Intestine, **130**
Intoxication, **130–131**
  alcoholic poisoning, 18
Ireland, **131–132**
Irish Americans, **132**
Irish whiskey, **132–133**, 217
Isopropyl alcohol, **133**
Israel, **133–134**
Israel, Yedy, 17, 70
Italian Americans, **134**

J

Jackroller, **134**
Jackson, Andrew, 218
Jameson, John, 133
Jamshid, King, xi, xii
Japan, **134–135**
Jefferson, Thomas, 218
Jehovah's Witnesses, 177
Jellinek, E. M., **135**
  addiction, 6, 89
  alpha alcoholism, 27
  anxiety, 36

Belgium, 44
Beta alcoholism, 45
  Delta alcoholism, 83
  Epsilon alcoholism, 102
  Gamma alcoholism, 109
  uncontrolled drinking, 205
  Yale University Center of Alcohol
    Studies, 227–228
Jews, **135–136**, 190
  cirrhosis, 68
  cultural etiological theories, 82
  Israel, 133–134
  religious aspects, 177
  United States, 209
Johnson, Samuel, xvi
Joint Commission on Accreditation of
  Hospitals (JCAH), **136**
Jones, Ben Morgan, 143–144
Jones, Kenneth L., 104, 211
Jones, Marilyn K., 143–144
Journal of Studies on Alcohol, 137
*Journal of the American Medical Associa-
  tion, The*, 110
Journals (list), 303–305
Justice, U.S. Department of, 80–81

K

Kaminetzky, Harold, 158
Kansas, 53
Katzenjammers, **136**
Keller, Mark, 18, 88, **136–137**
Kellerman, Joseph, 161–162
Kemper Insurance Companies, 128
Kentucky bourbon, 54
Kenya, 137
Ketoacidosis, 116
Khayyam, Omar, xii
Kirkpatrick, Jean, 227
Klatsky, A. L., 118
Kodak, 100
Koop, C. Everett, 188
Koran, 197
Korsakoff, Sergei, 137
Korsakoff's psychosis, **137**
  alcohol discharge rate, 12
  brain, 55
  central nervous system, 64
  cerebral atrophy, 65
  memory, 144
  Wernicke's encephalopathy, 217
Krausening (beer carbonation method),
  58, 195–196

L

Lager, **137–138**
Lapps, 106–107
Larkin, E. J., 160
Laudanum, **138**
L-Dopa, **138**
Legal aspects of alcohol abuse, **138–139**
Leiber, Charles S., 159
Lesbians, 224–225
Lethal dose, **139**
Lewis, J., 136
Librium—*See Chlordiazepoxide*
Lieber, Charles S., 4, 130
Lightner, Candy, 150
Lillet, 36
Lincoln, Abraham, 216
Liqueur, **139–140**

Liquor, **140**
Listerine, 152
Lithium carbonate therapy, **140–141**, 164
Liver, **140**
  acetaldehyde, 4
  animal models of alcoholism, 34
  blood sugar, 50
  cancer, 62–63
  diseases, 89
  formaldehyde, 107
  Hispanics, 120
  metabolism, 145
  nutrition, 159
  synergy, 200
London dry gin, 114
Loss of control, **140**
  adaptive cell metabolism, 5
  addiction, 6
  alpha alcoholism, 27
  anxiety, 36
  behavior modification, 43
  controlled drinking, 78
  progression, 166
  relapse, 176
  uncontrolled drinking vs., 205
Low birth weight, **141**
Lully, Raymond, xiv

M

Macbeth (William Shakespeare), 186
Madeira, 37, **141**
Magnesium, 212
Mallory-Weiss syndrome, **141**
Malmsey, 141
Malt, **141–142**
Malt beverage, **142**
Malt liquor, **142**
Mann, Marty, 153
Mannello, T. A., 3
Marc, 56–57
Marchiafava, Ettore, 142
Marchiafava-Bignami disease, **142**
March of Dimes, 105
Marijuana with alcohol, **142**
  blackout, 47
Marisa, 197
Marital status, 277
Marlatt, G. Alan, 43, 130
Masi, Dale A., 100
Massachusetts Society for the Suppres-
  sion of Intemperance, **142**
Mather, Increase, 222
Mayer, Joseph, 66
McAndrew Alcoholism Scale, 149
Mead, xi, **142**
Medhus, A., 198
Media campaigns, 98–99
Medication, **143**
Memory, **143–145**
Merck Manual, The, 17
Mesopotamia, xi–xii, 57
Metabolism, **145–146**
  acetaldehyde, 3
  amethystic, 34
  Antabuse, 35
  fatty liver, 104
  gastrointestinal tract, 109
  tolerance, 204
Metamorphoses (Ovid), xiii
Methadone with alcohol, **146–147**
Methanol, xix, **147–148**

Methodists, 177
Methyl alcohol—*See Methanol*
Mexican-Americans, 120
Mezey, Esteban, 211
Michigan, 16
Michigan Alcoholism Screening Test (MAST), **148**
Microphthalmia, 211
Microtubules, 17
Milieu-limited (Type I) alcoholism, **148**
Minimum drinking age, **148–149**
Minnesota Multiphasic Personality Inventory (MMPI), **149**
Miscarriage, 226
Mitochondria, 62, **149**
  acetate, 3
  fatty liver, 104
Mitosis, 149
Mixing drinks, **149**
Moderate drinking, **149**
Mono amine oxidase (MAO), 111, **150**
Monopoly system, 15
Moonshine, **150**
Moral etiological theory, 103
Mormons, 177, 190
Morning drinking, **150**
Mortality, **150–152**
  Indians and Alaska natives, 28–31
Moslems, 190
  cultural etiological theories, 82
  distillation, 90
  Sudan, 197
Mothers Against Drunk Driving (MADD), **150**
Motorcycle accidents, **152**
Mouthwash, **152**
Murphy Brothers, 133

N

Nadeau, Louise, 101
National Board of Social Welfare (Finland), 107
National Center for Health Statistics (NCHS), **152–153**
  alcohol discharge rate, 12
  Alcohol Epidemiologic Data System, 14
National Commission on Alcohol and Narcotics (Denmark), 84
National Committee for Prevention of Child Abuse, 65
National Committee for Study and Prevention of Alcoholism and Other Drug Addiction (Belgium), 44–45
National Committee on Alcohol and Other Drugs (Belgium), 45
National Council on Alcoholism (NCA), 7, **153**, 227
National Drug and Alcoholism Treatment Unit Survey (NDATUS), 205
National Federation of Consulting Bureaux and Institutions for the Care of Alcoholics and Other Drug Addicts (Belgium), 45
National Highway Traffic Safety Administration (NHTSA), 45, 92–94, **153**, 229
  Alcohol Epidemiologic Data System, 14
National Institute of Mental Health (NIMH), **154**
National Institute on Alcohol Abuse and Alcoholism (NIAAA), vii, 19, 63, 117, **153–154**, 210

Alcohol Epidemiologic Data System, 14
  aspirin and alcohol, 39
  drinking during pregnancy, 105
  elderly, 99
  employee assistance programs, 100
  Joint Commission on Accreditation of Hospitals, 136
  railroad accidents, 169
National Institute on Alcoholism (Costa Rica), 79
National Institute on Drug Abuse (NIDA), 63, 117, **154**, 223, 228
National Prohibition Act—See Volstead Act
National Safety Council, 7
National Study on Child Neglect and Abuse Reporting, 65
National Temperance League, **154**
NDATUS—*See National Drug and Alcoholism Treatment Unit Survey*
Near beer, **154**
Neibuhr, Reinhold, 185
Nembutal—*See Pentobarbital*
Netherlands, The, **154**
New Brunswick, 60
New England Journal of Medicine, 158
New England Rum Triangle, 179
New York Times, The, 219
New Zealand, **154–156**
NIAAA—*See National Institute on Alcohol Abuse and Alcoholism*
Nicholas II, Czar, 206
NIDA—*See National Institute on Drug Abuse*
Nigeria, 156
Nine-Step Recovery Booklet, 109
Noble, Ernest P., 34, 56, 110, 138, 170
Nonaddictive pathological drinker, **156**
North American Indian Women's Council on Chemical Dependencies, 33
Northwest Territories, 59
Norway, xv, **156–158**
Nursing mothers, **158**
Nutrition, **158–159**
  alcohol amblyopia, 11
  central nervous system, 64
  cirrhosis, 68
  elderly, 99
  genetotropic etiological theory, 112
  vitamins and minerals, 211–212

O

Olin, Spencer T., 170
Open meetings, 23
Oral fixation, 102, **159–160**
  deprivation and, 86
Order of Good Templars, 160
Outpatient treatment, 19, **160**
Ovid, xiii
Oxford Group, 22–23, **161**

P

Pace, Nicholas, 63
Pancreas, 161
Pancreatitis, **161**
Para-alcoholic, **161–162**
Paregoric, **162**
Parent education, 99, **162**
Parker, Elizabeth S., 144
Parsons, O. A., 55

Passamaquoddy Indian language, 32
Patent still, 196
  Scotch whisky, 183
Pathological drinker, **162**
Pathological intoxication, **163**
  crime, 80
Pavlov, Ivan, 40
Pedestrian accidents, **163**
Pentobarbital (Nembutal), 41, 184
Percolation, 139
Perignon, Dom, 191
Periodic alcoholism, **163**
Periodicals (list), 303–305
Peritonitis, bacterial, 126
Pernod, **163**
Pernod, Henri-Louis, 1, 163
Perrine, M. W., 92
Persia, xi, xii
Personality trait theories, **163–164**
PET scan—*See Positive emission tomography scan*
Pharmacotherapy, **164**
  inpatient treatment, 126
Phillips, Sir Thomas, 132
Physiological models of etiology, 102, 164
Pilsner beer, **164**
Plato, xiii
Pliny the Ender, xiv
Plymouth gin, 114
Pneumonia, 126
Poland, **164–165**
Polich, J. Michael, 19, 78, 125, 127, 172
Ponce de Leon, 216
Popham, R. E., 136
Porche Sr., Melvin, 47
Port, **165**
Porter, **165**
Positron emission tomography (PET) scan, 55–56
Postintoxicated state, **165**
Poteen, 132
Potentiation, **166**
Pot still, **165**, 196
  Scotch whisky, 183
Power, John, 133
Presbyterians, 177
Prince Edward Island, 60
Problem drinker, **166**
  driving while intoxicated, 92
  heavy drinker vs., 119
Progression, **166**
Prohibition
  alcoholic beverage control laws, 14
  bootlegging, 53
  Canada and, 61
  Eighteenth Amendment, 99
  near beer, 154
  temperance movement, 201
Proof, **166–167**
Propanol, xix
Property crime, 80–81
Protestants, 177
Pseudo-Cushing syndrome, 126
Psychodrama, **167**
Psychological models of etiology, 102, **167–168**
  personality trait theories, 163
P3 wave, 111
Ptosis, 211
Public drunkenness, 138, **168–169**
Puerto Rico, **169**

Q

Quakers, 177–178
Quarterly Journal of Studies on Alcohol, 227
Quarterway house, 19
Quass, 42

R

Race
  alcoholism clients by, 250–253
Railroad accidents, **169–170**
Rainwater Madeira, 141
Randall, C. L., 39
Rand Corporation, 153–154
Rand Report, **170–172**
  controlled drinking, 78
  remission, 178
  social class, 189
Rand Report II, **172–173**
Rational emotive therapy (RET), **173**
Reality therapy, **173–174**
Recovery, **174**
Reduced testosterone synthesis, 124
Red wine, **174–175**
Rehabilitation, **175–176**
  detoxification, 87
  treatment, 205
Relapse, **176**
Religion, **176–178**
Remission, **178**
  recovery, 174
REM (rapid-eye movement), 187
Reproductive functions, **178**
Research Triangle Institute (RTI), 98
Revenue Act of 1791, 218
Rhinophyma, **178–179**
Rice wine, 182
Richard II, King, 27
RNA, 56, **179**
Robertson, Nan, 216, 219
Rohsenow, Damaris J., 130
Roizen, R., 43
Roman Catholic Church, 176
Romans, ancient, xiii–xiv
  beer, 42
  brewing, 57
  Britain, 26–27
  distillation, 90
  wine, 220
  women, 223
Rose wine, **179**
Rothschild, Marcus A., 205
Rubbing alcohol, **179**
Rubin, E., 118
Rum, **179–180**
  colonial America, xvi–xvii
  Puerto Rico, 169
Rum fits, **180–181**, 221
Rum ration, 115
Rush, Benjamin, xvii, 26, 88–89, **181**, 201
Rutgers Center of Alcohol Studies, 18, **181**
Rye whiskey, xvii, **181–182**, 217–218
  bourbon, 54

S

Safety belts and alcohol use, **182**
St. Christopher, Order of, xv
St. Raphael, 36
Sake, 42, **182**
Saladin technique, 141

Saloon, **182**
Salvation Army, 60
Samogon, 206
Samshu, 42
Sanchez-Dirks, Ruth, 193
Sandmaier, Marian, 123
San Francisco, 195
Scandinavia, 93
Schaps, E., 162
Schmidt, W., 136
Schnapps, **182**
Scotch whisky, **182–183**, 217
Scotland, xv
Seaman, F. J., 3
Seattle Indian Health Board, 32
Secobarbital (Seconal), 41, 184
Sedative, **183–184**
  cross-addiction, 82
Sedativism, **185**
Seneca, 26, 88
Sensitivity, **185**
Sercial, 141
Serenity Prayer, **185**
Seventh-Day Adventists, 178
Sex, **185–186**
  alcohol discharge rate by, 12
  alcoholism clients by, 247, 249, 251–253
  blood alcohol concentration by, 48
Shakespeare, William, 186
Shaper, A. G., 119
Sherry, **186**
Shintoism, 134
Shoemaker, Samuel, 22
Shot, **186**
Shuckit, Marc, 222
Sikes, Bartholomew, 167
Silkworth, Robert, 22
Silkworth, William D., 27
Skid row, **186–187**
  Bowery, 55
  women, 225
Skinner, H. A., 11
Sleep, **187**
Slip, **187**
Sloe gin, 114–115
"Slop," 191
Smith, David W., 104, 211
Smith, Robert Holbrook, 22–23, **187**, 219
Smoking, **187–188**
  fetal alcohol syndrome, 105
Sobel, L. C., 43
Sobell, M. B., 43
Sober, **188**
Sobering up, **188**
Sobriety, **188–189**
  Alcoholics Anonymous (AA), 20
"Social and Economic Costs of Alcohol Abuse and Alcoholism" (report), 98
Social class, **189–190**
Social drinking, **190**
Sociocultural models of etiology, **190**
Solitary drinking, **190–191**
Sour mash, **191**
  bourbon, 54–55
  sweet mash vs., 199
Sparkling wine, **191–192**
Special Reports to the U.S. Congress on Alcohol and Health
  Second, 149
  Third, 96
  Fourth, 65, 80

  Sixth, 62, 222
  Seventh, 65, 70, 88, 144, 198, 210
Spirits, **192**
Spirit still, **192**, 216
Sports, alcohol use in, **192–193**
Spouse abuse, **193–194**
Spree, **194**
Spree drinking, **194**
Spritz, N., 159
Sri Lanka, **194–195**
Stambul, Harriet B., 19, 78, 125, 127, 172
Steam beer, **195–196**
Still, xvi, **196**
Still wine, **196**
  sparking wine, 191
Stimmel, Barry, 146–147
Stomach, **196**
  hangover, 116
Stout, **196**
Stuart, M. A., 193
Students Against Drunk Driving (SADD), **197**
Subclinical myopathy, 18
Substance abuse, **197**
Sudan, **197**
Suicide, **197–198**
  American Indians, 28
Supra-addictive effect, 96
Supreme Court, U.S., 204–205
Surgery, **198**
Susceptibility, **199**
Sweden, **199**
  advertising, 6
Sweet mash, **199**
  sour mash vs., 191
Swiss National Science Foundation, 200
Swiss Office for the Prevention of Alcoholism, 200
Switzerland, xv, **199–200**
  absinthe, 1
Sylvius, Franciscus (Franciscus de la Boe), xv, 113
Symptomatic alcoholism, **200**
Symptomatic drinking, **200**
Synergy, **200**
  cancer, 62
  driving while intoxicated, 92
  smoking, 187–188
  women, 226

T

Tacitus, 42
Taft, William Howard, 216
Tank, **200**
Taxation
  United States, 16
Taylor, R., 58
Teetotal, **200**
Teetotaler, **201**
Tei-Tsung, Emperor, xii
Temperance, **201**
  Europe, xv
  sobriety, 188
  women, 223
Temperance Committees (Norway), 157
Temposil, **201**
  elderly, 100
Ten Nights in a Bar-Room (T. S. Arthur), xvii
Tequila, **201–202**
Testosterone, 124

Tewari, Sujata, 56
Thailand, 202
Thiamine, 212, 217
Tight, 202
Tincture, 138
TIPS (Training for Intervention Procedures by Servers of Alcohol), 202–203
Toddy, 195
Tokay, 203–204
Tolerance, 204
    adaptive cell metabolism, 5
    addiction, 6
    animal models of alcoholism, 34–35
    blackout, 48
    central nervous system, 64
    euphoria, 103
    habituation, 115
    sensitivity, 185
Top fermentation, 204
    ale, 26
    beer, 58
    bottom fermentation vs., 54
Total Abstention Union, 201
Total Community Action Alcoholism Program (New Orleans), 47
Traffic fatalities, 272–276
Trauma
    homelessness, 121
Traynor v. Turnage, 204–205
Treatment, 205
    funding (tables), 236–240
    units (tables), 241–255
Tuberculosis, 126
Twelve Concepts of Service, 8
Twelve Steps, 24
Twelve Traditions, 24–25
Twenty-First Amendment, 205
Tyramine, 34

U

Ulleland, Christie, 104
Ulster Temperance Society, 205
Uncontrolled drinking, 205
Understanding America's Drinking Problem (Don Cahalan), 136
Under the influence of alcohol, 205–206
Uniform Alcoholism and Intoxication Treatment Act, 138
    public drunkenness, 168
Union of Soviet Socialist Republics (USSR), 206–207
    driving while intoxicated, 93
    vodka, 213
United Kingdom, 207–208
    alcoholic liver disease, 17
United States, 208–210
    absinthe, 1
    accidents, 2
    alcoholic beverage control laws, 15
    consumption, 73–75, 77, 262–268
    economic costs, 277
    organizations, 286–298
    rum, 179–180
    rye whiskey, 181
    taxation, 16
    vodka, 213
United States Brewers Association, 7

User, 210
USSR—See Union of Soviet Socialist Republics

V

Valium, 96, 184, 210
Valle, S. R., 80
Vascular system, 210
Venezuela, 210–211
Verdelho, 141
Vermouth, 211
Vernon, Edward, 115
Veterans Administration, U.S., 204
Vincelli, Dom Bernardo, 45
Vision problems, 211
Vitamin B12, 212
Vitamin deficiencies
    nutrition, 159
Vitamins and minerals, 211–212
    alcohol amblyopia, 11
    cancer, 62
    fetal alcohol syndrome, 105
    gastrointestinal tract, 109
Vodka, xv, 212–213
    bootlegging, 54
Volksbond (Belgium), 45
Volstead Act, xvii, 213–215
    Canada and, 61
    Eighteenth Amendment and, 99
Voughtsberger, K., 58

W

Wagon, on the, 216
Waller, A., 92
Wallerstein, Robert S., 40
Washington, George, 115, 181, 218
Washingtonian movement, 216
Wash still, 192, 216
Water of life, 216
Webb-Kenyon Law, 216
Wernicke, Carl, 216
Wernicke-Korsakoff syndrome, 129
Wernicke's encephalopathy, 216–217
    brain, 55
    central nervous system, 64
    cerebral atrophy, 65
    Korsakoff's psychosis, 137
    Marchiafava-Bignami disease, 142
    thiamine deficiency, 212
Wet, 7
Whiskey, xiv–xv, 217–218—See also Canadian whisky; Corn whiskey; Irish whiskey; Rye whiskey; Scotch whisky
    mixing drinks, 149
    rum and, 179–180
Whiskey Rebellion, xvii, 181, 218
White, Byron R., 204–205
White wine, 218–219
WHO—See World Health Organization
William of Orange, 113–114
Williams, R. J., 112
Wilsnack, R. W., 178, 222
Wilson, Bill, 22–23, 187, 219
    Oxford Group and, 161
Wilson, Lois Burnham, 219
    Al-Anon, 8

Wilson, Woodrow, 213
Wine, 219–221
    international per capita consumption, 256–257
Wine Institute, 7
Wisdom of Ani, xii
Withdrawal, 221–222
    adaptive cell metabolism, 5
    addiction, 5–6
    alpha alcoholism, 27
    animal models of alcoholism, 34
    barbiturates, 41
    behavioral learning theory, 44
    beta alcoholism, 45
    cancer, 63
    compulsion, 71
    convulsions, 78
    craving, 80
    delirium tremens, 83
    dependency, 85
    detoxification, 86–87
    dysphoria, 98
    elderly, 99–100
    fetal alcohol syndrome, 105
    formaldehyde, 107
    hangover, 116
    magnesium, 212
    rum fits, 180–181
Woman, Maxine, 209
Woman's Christian Temperance Union (WCTU), 222
Women, 222–227
    American Indians, 33
    blacks, 46–47
    instability and crisis etiological theory, 127
    intoxication, 130
    memory, 144
    risk factors (chart), 282
    social class, 189
    sociocultural models of etiology, 190
Women for Sobriety (WFS), 227
Wood alcohol—See Methanol
World Health Organization (WHO), 128
    addiction, 5–6
    alcohol dependence syndrome, 11
    disease concept, 89
    International Classification of Diseases, 129
World Service Conference, 8
World Service Office (WSO), 9
Wormwood, 163
"Wo to Drunkards" (Increase Mather), 222

Y

Yale University Center of Alcohol Studies, 227–228
Yellow fever, 126
Youcha, Geraldine, 65–66, 162
Youths, 228–230
Yukon, 59

Z

Zinc, 212
Zinc supplements, 230